34th Conference on Computational Linguistics and Speech Processing (ROCLING 2022)

Taipei, Taiwan
21-22 November 2022

Editors:

Yung-Chun Chang
Yi-Chin Huang
Jheng-Long Wu
Ming-Hsiang Su
Hen-Hsen Huang
Yi-Fen Liu
Lung-Hao Lee
Chin-Hung Chou
Yuan-Fu Liao

ISBN: 978-1-7138-6764-7

Printed from e-media with permission by:

Curran Associates, Inc.
57 Morehouse Lane
Red Hook, NY 12571

Some format issues inherent in the e-media version may also appear in this print version.

Printed with permission by Curran Associates, Inc. (2023)

For permission requests, please contact the Association for Computational Linguistics at the address below.

Association for Computational Linguistics
209 N. Eighth Street
Stroudsburg, Pennsylvania 18360

Phone: 1-570-476-8006
Fax: 1-570-476-0860

acl@aclweb.org

Additional copies of this publication are available from:

Curran Associates, Inc.
57 Morehouse Lane
Red Hook, NY 12571 USA
Phone: 845-758-0400
Fax: 845-758-2633
Email: curran@proceedings.com
Web: www.proceedings.com

Table of Contents

The 34th

ROCLING 2022

第三十四屆自然語言與語音處理研討會

November 21-22, 2022, Taipei, Taiwan, R.O.C.

Proceedings of the Thirty-fourth Conference on Computational Linguistics and Speech Processing

ROCLING 2022: The 34th Conference on Computational Linguistics and Speech Processing

第三十四屆自然語言與語音處理研討會

November 21-22, 2022

Taipei Medical University, Taipei, Taiwan, R.O.C.

主辦單位：

臺北醫學大學、國立屏東大學、中華民國計算語言學學會

協辦單位：

國家科學技術委員會、教育部、東吳大學巨量資料管理學院

贊助單位：

玉山金控、賽微科技股份有限公司、中華電信研究院、台達電子工業股份有限公司、華亨科技股份有限公司、台灣連線股份有限公司、意藍資訊股份有限公司、財團法人人工智慧科技基金會、國家實驗研究院高速網路與計算中心、中央研究院資訊科學研究所、中央研究院資訊科技創新研究

First Published in November 2022
By The Association for Computational Linguistics and Chinese Language Processing (ACLCLP)

Yung-Chun Chang, Yi-Chin Huang, Jheng-Long Wu, Ming-Hsiang Su, Hen-Hsen Huang, Yi-Fen Liu, Lung-Hao Lee, Chin-Hung Chou, Yuan-Fu Liao (eds.)

Proceedings of the 34th Conference on Computational Linguistics and Speech Processing (ROCLING XXXIV)
2022-11-21—2022-11-22

ACLCLP
November 2022

Organizing Committee

Honorary Chair

Chien-Huang Lin, Taipei Medical University

Conference Chairs

Yung-Chun Chang, Taipei Medical University

Yi-Chin Huang, National Pingtung University

Program Chairs

Jheng-Long Wu, Soochow University

Ming-Hsiang Su, Soochow University

Demo Chair

Hen-Hsen Huang, Academia Sinica

Publication Chair

Yi-Fen Liu, Feng Chia University

Special Session Chairs

Chin-Hung Chou, National Central University

Yuan-Fu Liao, National Yang Ming Chiao Tung University

Shared Task Chair

Lung-Hao Lee, National Central University

Program Committee

Jia-Wei Chang (張家瑋), National Taichung University of Science

Yung-Chun Chang (張詠淳), Taipei Medical University

Ru-Yng Chang (張如瑩), AI clerk international co., ltd.

Chung-Chi Chen (陳重吉), National Taiwan University

Kuan-Yu Chen (陳冠宇), National Taiwan University of Science and Technology

Yun-Nung Chen (陳縕儂), National Taiwan University

Yu-Tai Chien (簡宇泰), National Taipei University of Business

Hong-Jie Dai (戴鴻傑), National Kaohsiung University of Science and Technology

Min-Yuh Day (戴敏育), National Taipei University

Yu-Lun Hsieh (謝育倫), CloudMile

Wen-Lian Hsu (許聞廉), Academia Sinica

Hen-Hsen Huang (黃瀚萱), Academia Sinica

Yi-Chin Huang (黃奕欽), National Pingtung University

Jeih-Weih Hung (洪志偉), National Chi Nan University

Chih-Hao Ku (顧值豪), Cleveland State University

Wen-Hsing Lai (賴玟杏), National Kaohsiung First University of Science and Technology

Ying-Hui Lai (賴穎暉), National Yang Ming Chiao Tung University

Lung-Hao Lee (李龍豪), National Central University

Cheng-Te Li (李政德), National Cheng Kung University

Chun-Yen Lin (林君彥), Taipei Medical University

Jen-Chun Lin (林仁俊), Academia Sinica

Szu-Yin Lin (林斯寅), National Ilan University

Shih-Hung Liu (劉士弘), Digiwin

Chao-Lin Liu (劉昭麟), National Chengchi University

Jenn-Long Liu (劉振隆), I-Shou University

Yi-Fen Liu (劉怡芬), Feng Chia University

Wen-Hsiang Lu (盧文祥), National Cheng Kung University

Shang-Pin Ma (馬尚彬), National Taiwan Ocean University

Emily Chia-Yu Su (蘇家玉), Taipei Medical University

Ming-Hsiang Su (蘇明祥), Soochow University

Richard Tzong-Han Tsai (蔡宗翰), National Central University

Chun-Wei Tung (童俊維), National Health Research Institutes

Hsin-Min Wang (王新民), Academia Sinica

Jenq-Haur Wang (王正豪), National Taipei University of Technology

Yu-Cheng Wang (王昱晟), Lunghwa University of Science and Technology

Jheng-Long Wu (吳政隆), Soochow University

Shih-Hung Wu (吳世弘), Chaoyang University of Technology

Jui-Feng Yeh (葉瑞峰), National Chiayi University

Liang-Chih Yu (禹良治), Yuan Ze University

Messages from Conference Chairs

On behalf of the Conference Chairs, I would like to welcome you to the 34th Conference on Computational Linguistics and Speech Processing (ROCLING 2022), which will be held in Taipei, Taiwan, from November 21st to 22nd, 2022. ROCLING 2022 is jointly hosted by Taipei Medical University (TMU), National Pingtung University (NPTU), and the Association for Computational Linguistics and Chinese Language Processing (ACLCLP). The Conference is also supported by the National Science and Technology Council and the Ministry of Education.

ROCLING 2022 is of special significance during this particularly exciting period: our field has grown drastically with NLP gaining much interest and prominence in both research and industry, and the barrier to entry lowered considerably. With the easing of COVID-19 related measurements worldwide this year, we are finally able to come together and attend the conference in person to interact and enjoy the exchange of expertise.

This Conference would not have materialized without the dedication, guidance and assistance from the Organizing Committee. Many thanks to the Program Chairs, Prof. Jheng-Long Wu and Prof. Ming-Hsiang Su, the Demo Chair, Prof. Hen-Hsen Huang, the Special Session Chairs, Prof. Chin-Hung Chou and Yuan-Fu Liao, and the Shared Task Chair, Prof. Lung-Hao Lee for their coordination of the review process, which enables top quality research papers and informative talks to be presented during the conference. We also like to thank Prof. Yi-Fen Liu for her assistance in the publication of conference proceedings, which will be published by ACL Anthology.

We are also extremely grateful to all sponsors for their continuous and generous support. In addition, we would like to thank the chairs of previous conferences for their gracious help and advice, passing on all the know-how with much patience. We would also like to express our gratitude to the reviewers, workshop organizers, tutorial instructors, authors and presenters of the papers, and invited speakers. We thank all authors who have submitted their work for review. Your hard work makes this conference exciting and our community strong.

Finally, we would like to thank you, our participant, for making all efforts to attend the Conference from November 21st to 22nd, 2022. Please enjoy yourself, and We hope you will leave feeling scientifically engaged and happy with all the new connections you have made with like-minded peers.

Welcome and enjoy the conference!

Yung-Chun Chang, Taipei Medical University
Yi-Chin Huang, National Pingtung University
ROCLING 2022 Conference Chairs

Messages from Program Chairs

The excellent program and activities of ROCLING 2022 are the result of collaborative efforts of more than 40 program committee members and conference organizers. Each paper has been reviewed by 2 to 3 PC members, and we thank all of them for their insightful reviews, from which we can build an outstanding technical program. We would also like to thank the Demo Chair, Dr. Hen-Hsen Huang of Academia Sinica, for coordinating three excellent tutorials. We are very grateful to the Publication Chair, Prof. Yi-Fen Liu of the Feng Chia University, for editing the conference proceedings. We would also like to express our gratitude to the Special Session Chairs, Prof. Chin-Hung Chou of National Central University and Prof. Yuan-Fu Liao of National Yang Ming Chiao Tung University, and Shared Task Chair, Prof. Lung-Hao Lee of National Central University, for organizing the special session and shared task that enable the outreach of conference events to many important communities. Last but not least, we appreciate the contributions of Conference Co-chairs, Prof. Yung-Chun Chang of Taipei Medical University, and Prof. Yi-Chin Huang of National Pingtung University, to the construction of the conference website and event coordination.

Jheng-Long Wu, Soochow University
Ming-Hsiang Su, Soochow University
ROCLING 2022 Program Chairs

NLP Keynote by Prof. Makoto P. Kato

Matching Texts with Data for Evidence-based Information Retrieval

Speaker: Prof. Makoto P. Kato

Professor, The University of Tsukuba, Japan

Time: Monday, November 21, 2022, 09:00 - 10:00

Biography

Makoto P. Kato received his Ph.D. degree in Graduate School of Informatics from Kyoto University, Sakyo Ward, Yoshidahonmachi, in 2012. Currently, he is an associate professor of Faculty of Library, Information and Media Science, University of Tsukuba, Japan. In 2008, he was awarded 'WISE 2008 Kambayashi Best Paper Award' through the article 'Can Social Tagging Improve Web Image Search?' with other researchers. In 2010, he served as a JSPS Research Fellow in Japan Society for the Promotion of Science. During the period 2010 to 2012, he also served in Microsoft Research Asia Internship (under supervision by Dr. Tetsuya Sakai in WIT group), Microsoft Research Asia Internship (under supervision by Dr. Tetsuya Sakai in WSM group), and Microsoft Research Internship (under supervision by Dr. Susan Dumais in CLUES group). From 2012, he worked as an assistant professor in Graduate School of Informatics, Kyoto University, Japan. His research and teaching career began, and he worked as an associate professor from 2019 in Graduate School of Informatics, Kyoto University, Japan. His research interests include Information Retrieval, Web Mining, and Machine Learning, while he is an associate professor in Knowledge Acquisition System Laboratory (Kato Laboratory), University of Tsukuba, Japan.

Abstract

We are now facing the problem of misinformation and disinformation on the Web, and search engines are struggling to retrieve reliable information from a vast amount of Web data. One of the possible solutions to this problem is to find reliable evidences supporting a claim on the Web. But what are "reliable evidences"? They can include authorities' opinions, scientific papers, or wisdom of crowds. However, they are also sometimes subjective as they are outcomes produced by people.

This talk discusses some approaches incorporating another type of evidences that are very objective --- numerical data --- for reliable information access.

(1) Entity Retrieval based on Numerical Attributes. Entity retrieval is a task of retrieving entities for a given text query and usually based on text matching between the query and entity description. Our recent work attempted to match the query and numerical attributes of entities and produce explainable rankings. For example, our approach ranks cameras based on their numerical attributes such as resolution, f-number, and weight, in response to queries such as "camera for astrophotography" and "camera for hiking".

(2) Data Search. When people encounter suspicious claims on the Web, data can be reliable sources for the fact checking. NTCIR Data Search is an evaluation campaign that aims to foster data search research by developing an evaluation infrastructure and organizing shared tasks for data search. The first test collection for data search and some findings are introduced in this talk.

(3) Data Summarization. While the data search project attempts to develop a data search system for end users and help them make decisions based on data, it is still difficult for users to quickly interpret data. Therefore, data summarization techniques are also necessary to enable users to incorporate data in their information seeking process. Recent automatic visualization and text-based data summarization techniques are presented in this talk.

Speech Keynote by Prof. Junichi Yamagishi

Speech Synthesis Research 2.0

Speaker: Prof. Junichi Yamagishi

Professor, National Institute of Informatics, Japan

Time: Tuesday, November 22, 2022, 09:00 - 10:00

Biography

Junichi Yamagishi received the Ph.D. degree from Tokyo Institute of Technology in 2006 for a thesis that pioneered speaker-adaptive speech synthesis. He is currently a Professor with the National Institute of Informatics, Tokyo, Japan, and also a Senior Research Fellow with the Centre for Speech Technology Research, University of Edinburgh, Edinburgh, U.K. Since 2006, he has authored and co-authored more than 250 refereed papers in international journals and conferences. He was an area coordinator at Interspeech 2012. He was one of organizers for special sessions on "Spoofing and Countermeasures for Automatic Speaker Verification" at Interspeech 2013, "ASVspoof evaluation" at Interspeech 2015, "Voice conversion challenge 2016" at Interspeech 2016, "2nd ASVspoof evaluation" at Interspeech 2017, and "Voice conversion challenge 2018" at Speaker Odyssey 2018. He is currently an organizing committee for ASVspoof 2019, an organizing committee for ISCA the 10th ISCA Speech Synthesis Workshop 2019, a technical program committee for IEEE ASRU 2019, and an award committee for ISCA Speaker Odyssey 2020. He was a member of IEEE Speech and Language Technical Committee. He was also an Associate Editor of the IEEE/ACM TRANSACTIONS ON AUDIO, SPEECH, AND LANGUAGE PROCESSING and a Lead Guest Editor for the IEEE JOURNAL OF SELECTED

TOPICS IN SIGNAL PROCESSING special issue on Spoofing and Countermeasures for Automatic Speaker Verification. He is currently a guest editor for Computer Speech and Language special issue on speaker and language characterization and recognition: voice modeling, conversion, synthesis and ethical aspects. He also serves as a chairperson of ISCA SynSIG currently. He was the recipient of the Tejima Prize as the best Ph.D. thesis of Tokyo Institute of Technology in 2007. He received the Itakura Prize from the Acoustic Society of Japan in 2010, the Kiyasu Special Industrial Achievement Award from the Information Processing Society of Japan in 2013, the Young Scientists' Prize from the Minister of Education, Science and Technology in 2014, the JSPS Prize from Japan Society for the Promotion of Science in 2016, and Docomo mobile science award from Mobile communication fund in 2018.

Abstract

The Yamagishi Laboratory at the National Institute of Informatics researches text-to-speech (TTS) and voice conversion (VC) technologies. Having achieved TTS and VC methods that reproduce human-level naturalness and speaker similarity, we introduce three challenging projects we are currently working on as the next phase of our research.

(1) Rakugo speech synthesis [1] As an example of a challenging application of speech synthesis technology, especially an example of an entertainment application, we have concentrated on rakugo, a traditional Japanese performing art. We have been working on learning and reproducing the skills of a professional comic storyteller using speech synthesis. This project aims to achieve an "AI storyteller" that entertains listeners, entirely different from the conventional speech synthesis task, whose primary purpose is to convey information or answer questions. The main story of rakugo comprises conversations between characters, and various characters appear in the story. These characters are performed by a single rakugo storyteller, who changes their voice appropriately so the listeners can understand and entertain them. To reproduce such characteristics of rakugo voice by machine learning, performance data of rakugo and advanced modeling techniques are required. Therefore, we constructed a corpus of rakugo speech without any noise or audience sounds with the cooperation of an Edo-

style rakugo performer and modeled this data using deep learning. In addition, we benchmarked our system by comparing the generated Rakugo speech with performances by Rakugo storytellers of different ranks (“Zenza/前座," “Futatsume/二つ目," and “Shinuchi/真打") through subjective evaluation.

(2) Speech intelligibility enhancement [2] In remote communication, such as online conferencing, there are environmental background noises on both speaker and listener sides. Speech intelligibility enhancement is a technique to manipulate speech signals so as not to be masked by the noise on the listener's side while maintaining the volume. This is not a simple conversion task since "correct teacher data" does not exist. For this reason, deep learning has not been used in the past, and there has been no significant technological progress. However, various possible practical applications exist, such as intelligibility enhancement of station announcements. Therefore, we proposed a network structure called "iMetricGAN" and its learning method, in which complex and non-differentiable speech intelligibility and quality indexes are treated as output values of a discriminator in an adversarial generative network, the discriminator approximates the indexes and based on the approximated indexes, a generator is used to transform an input speech signal into an enhanced, easy-to-hear speech signal automatically. Subject experiments confirmed that this transformation significantly improves keyword recognition in noisy environments.

(3) Speaker Anonymization [3, 4] Now that it is becoming easier to build speech synthesis systems that digitally clone someone’s voice using ‘found' data on social media, there is a need to mask the speaker information in speech and other sensitive attributes that are appropriate to be protected. This is a new research topic; it has not yet been clearly defined how speaker anonymization can be achieved. We proposed a speaker anonymization method that combines speech synthesis and speaker recognition technologies. Our approach decomposes speech into three pieces of information: prosody, phoneme information, and a speaker embedding vector called X-vector, which is standardly used in speaker recognition and anonymizes the individuality of a speaker by averaging only the X-vector with K speakers. A neural vocoder is used to re-synthesize high-quality speech waveform. We also introduce a speech database and evaluation metrics to compare speaker anonymization methods.

References

[1] Shuhei Kato, Yusuke Yasuda, Xin Wang, Erica Cooper, Shinji Takaki, Junichi Yamagishi "Modeling of Rakugo Speech and Its Limitations: Toward Speech Synthesis That Entertains Audiences," IEEE Access, vol.8, pp.138149-138161, July 2020

[2] Haoyu Li, Junichi Yamagishi, "Multi-Metric Optimization Using Generative Adversarial Networks for Near-End Speech Intelligibility Enhancement," IEEE/ACM Transactions on Audio, Speech, and Language Processing, vol.29, pp.3000-3011, Sept 2021

[3] Fuming Fang, Xin Wang, Junichi Yamagishi, Isao Echizen, Massimiliano Todisco, Nicholas Evans, Jean-Francois Bonastre, "Speaker Anonymization Using X-vector and Neural Waveform Models," 10th ISCA Speech Synthesis Workshop (SSW10), Sept 2019

[4] Xiaoxiao Miao, Xin Wang, Erica Cooper, Junichi Yamagishi, Natalia Tomashenko, "Language-Independent Speaker Anonymization Approach using Self-Supervised Pre-Trained Models," Odyssey 2022: The Speaker and Language Recognition Workshop, June 2022

The 34th Conference on Computational Linguistics and Speech Processing (ROCLING 2022)
Taipei, Taiwan, November 21-22, 2022. The Association for Computational Linguistics and Chinese Language Processing

語言模型應用於中文手寫地址辨識 (Language Model Based Chinese Handwriting Address Recognition)

Chieh-Jen Wang, Yung-Ping Tien, Yun-Wei Hung
Service Systems Technology Center, Industrial Technology Research Institute
{chiehjen, JasonTien, joyce_h}@itri.org.tw

摘要

託運單中文手寫地址辨識是智慧物流領域自動化的重要挑戰，而中文手寫字的偵測與辨識是其中的核心。由於手寫字的書寫模式較印刷字複雜多變，辨識上容易誤判，且地址文字在託運單影像中占比小、文字排列緊密，易造成偵測上的困難，因此如何精準偵測託運單上的地址文字是本論文之研究重點。本論文提出託運單地址自動偵測及辨識系統，針對地址字元進行偵測與辨識，透過語言模型降低手寫字誤判的機率，提高辨識正確率。

Abstract

Chinese handwritten address recognition of consignment note is an important challenge of smart logistics automation. Chinese handwritten characters detection and recognition is the key technology for this application. Since the writing mode of handwritten characters is more complex and diverse than printed characters, it is easy misjudgment for recognition. Moreover, the address text occupies a small proportion in the image of the consignment note and arranged closely, which is easy to cause difficulties in detection. Therefore, how to detect the address text on the consignment note accurately is a focus of this paper. The consignment note address automatic detection and recognition system proposed in this paper detects and recognizes address characters, reduces the probability of misjudgment of Chinese handwriting recognition through language model, and improves the accuracy.

關鍵字：手寫辨識、地址辨識、語言模型

Keywords: handwritten recognition, address recognition, language model

1 緒論

新型態商業模式快速發展，加上疫情影響，消費者傾向線上購物，使得物流包裹快速增加，2020 上半年台灣進口包裹數量近五千萬件，為電商帶來 17.5%的銷售額成長。在流通的包裹中，手寫地址託運單佔比仍高，以台灣最大物流處理中心為例，臨櫃交寄託運單手寫地址佔 76%，物流中心每年需處理 500 萬件以上的手寫地址託運單。其託運單種類以紅單(50%)、三聯單(10%)及其他無特定格式之手寫或印刷(40%)為主，因傳統機器無法針對手寫地址進行有效的辨識，因此這些未數位化手寫託運單地址，仍需以大量人工判讀的方式對託運單地址進行分揀，造成人力負擔重，且易產生人為誤判。

即便物流業者開始引入自動分揀、分流系統，但在處理未數位化的手寫地址託運單時，仍需先以人工目視收件地址，將每個託運單的區域代碼輸入分揀機後，才能由機器進行分揀，人力負擔重。為解決物流中心依賴人工判讀託運單地址的問題，本論文提出一套運用自然語言處理及光學影像辨識技術的自動手寫託運單地址偵測及辨識系統，可快速判定託運單寄送區域，提高自動分揀效率。

欲建立自動化的託運單地址辨識系統，關鍵技術在於手寫字的偵測，由於手寫字的書寫模式較印刷字複雜多變，辨識上容易誤判，且地址文字在托運單中占比小、文字排列緊密，造成偵測上的困難，故如何精準偵測託運單上的地址文字是本論文之研發重點。

本研究擬運用自然語言處理技術、語言模型及光學影像辨識技術，針對託運單上的手寫地址進行辨識，建立託運單地址自動偵測及辨識系統。期待未來可協助物流處理中心達成託運單自動化判定分揀之目的，快速擷取託運單內的寄收件者、地址、電話、公司行號等資訊，加速物流行政處理速度，並減輕物流中心人工判讀託運單地址的負擔，提高託運單分揀效率。

未來除了物流相關產業，自動化的手寫辨識系統還可以擴展到其它不同的領域，例如：可整合 RPA（Robotic Process Automation）(Hofmann et al., 2020)應用，自動擷取訂單資料，利用自動化的手寫辨識技術，辨識不同格式訂單文件，替代人工進行鍵入、複製和貼上等繁瑣且耗時的操作。

2 文獻回顧

過去已經有一些學者對於地址辨識技術做過相關研究，主要是著重在地址語意剖析（Semantic Parser）(Z. Li et al., 2020)，以英文地址為例，通常只要能正確地使用空白斷詞，後續的拼寫校正及格式轉換通常就不會出問題，而不像中文地址常會有資訊錯誤或缺失的情況發生。這些地址剖析相關研究有基於辭典查找(Küçük Matci & Avdan, 2018)、隱藏式馬可夫模型(Hidden Markov Model, HMM) (X. Li et al., 2014)和條件隨機場(Conditional Random Field, CRF)(Arora, 2016; Sun, 2017)，但這幾種模式需要做特徵工程，倚賴專業領域知識去擷取特徵。近期研究(Abid et al., 2018; Sharma et al., 2018)則提出以深度學習為基礎的地址剖析，擺脫上述模型需要特徵工程的限制，也可以提升地址剖析的正確性。

有學者會針對地址文字內容的格式進行正規化(Sun, 2017)，讓所有文字都有統一的表現格式。以地址文字為例包括：阿拉伯數字、數字全形半形及中文數字等各種為了內容及格式統一的正規化。而不同地址型態會套用不同的正規化處理，例如：街路部分的數字要正規化成中文數字，巷弄號則是正規化成半形數字。

語言模型(Chen & Goodman, 1999)經常使用在許多自然語言處理方面的應用，如語音識別，機器翻譯，詞性標註，句法分析，手寫體識別和資訊檢索。人們長期在學習累積語言後有判斷合不合理與聯想的能力，語言模型就是利用機率大小來判斷句子合不合理。換句話說，語言模型描述一個字串 (word sequence, WS) 的機率。N-Gram (Jurafsky et al., 1999)語言模型是基於統計的語言模型算法，主要是將文本中之文字內容，取最靠近的 n 個字當作條件機率計算的先驗條件，形成長度是 n 的字詞片段序列，每個字詞片段及稱為 gram， 常見的 n -Gram 模型有 Unigram(1-gram)，Bigram(2-gram)，Trigram(3-gram)。 但語料庫無法含蓋人類古往今來說過的話，即語料庫的資料量通常不夠，因而許多字串出現的次數為零。神經網絡語言模型 (Neural-network-based language model, NNLM)(Park et al., 2018)。該神經網絡輸入一個字後，能夠輸出字庫中各個字為字串下一個字的機率。不同於 n -gram 統計語言模型從語料庫統計以換算機率，一個神經網絡預測下一個字的機率，是利用訓練的方式得到，如循環神經網絡 (Recurrent-neural-network-based, RNN) 語言模型(Xiao & Zhou, 2020)。

3 手寫地址辨識模型

手寫地址辨識模型系統架構如圖 1，可分成 3 個模組，包含：包裹攝影取像、托運單偵測和手寫辨識。利用高速攝影機，直接由輸送帶上拍攝包裹上托運單，再經由影像處理技術(Suri, 2000)，將托運單進行影像特徵擷取(Kumar & Bhatia, 2014)與旋轉校正(Yu et al., 2006)，最後再進行托運單偵測與手寫字辨識。手寫地址辨識系統模型會根據使用者回饋建議修正模型，讓模型辨識正確率隨著時間逐漸提升。

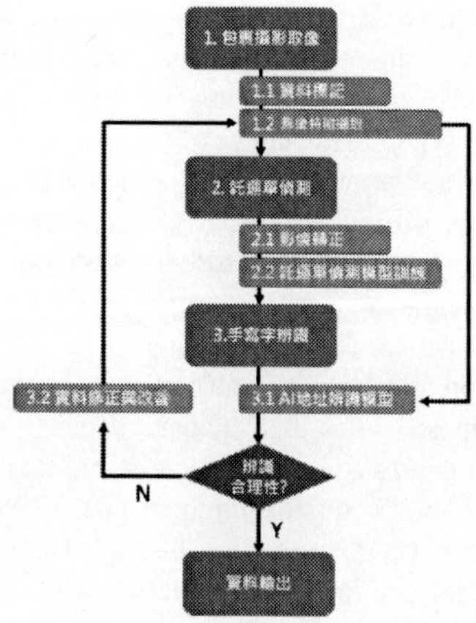

圖 1. 手寫地址辨識模型架構

	Google(美國)	ASTRI(香港)	蒙恬(台灣)	本研究(台灣)
偵測語言	包括英文、中文等 50 種語言	中文	中文、日文、韓文	中文(地址文字)
字元型態	手寫體、印刷體	手寫體	手寫體	手寫體、印刷體
技術	物件偵測、影像分類	影像分類	影像分類	影像分割、物件偵測、影像分類
功能	文字偵測、字元辨識	僅辨識無偵測	僅辨識無偵測	文字偵測、字元辨識
適用情境	適用於書籍或文件影像的解碼	僅適用於字元位置固定的申請表格	行動裝置或電腦的手寫輸入	適用於背景多元的託運單影像中判別地址資訊
優點	支援多種語言	支援手寫中文	支援手寫中文	支援手寫及印刷體的中文地址偵測辨識，正確率高
缺點	對託運單影像中字元的辨識度不高，正確率低	無法進行文字偵測，不適用託運單影像	無法進行文字偵測，不適用託運單影像	特針對中文地址字元進行辨識，通用性略窄

表 1. 全球光學影像辨識系統比較表

3.1 資料收集：託運單拍攝

本研究在台灣最大物流處理中心之物流輸送帶架設高速攝影機，自動拍攝包裹在輸送帶上的托運單，因為輸送帶周圍環境因素(如：輸送帶周圍光源不足與架設像機位子被限制)，相機取像有時會有文字模糊，或因相機取像定位偵測不佳，託運單無法完整拍攝等問題。

本研究總共收集原始影像 15 萬張(如圖 2. 左邊照片)，經過過濾上述問題的照片，再經由人工增加亮度、提高對比度的方式來做調整，有效樣本約 60%，約 9 萬張影像可用。

圖 2. 托運單原始與人工調整影像照片

3.2 託運單偵測

由於輸送帶上包裹並沒有固定的放置位置，也就是說託運單擺放位置並不是固定，因此如何擷取如包裹上面的托運單就是一個重要的議題。本研究透過 YOLO v4(Shafiee et al., 2017)進行託運單偵測， YOLO v4 架構中的 SPP(Spatial pyramid pooling) + PAN(Path Aggregation Network)，可解決小物件偵測問題，有效的偵測出包裹上託運單的位子如圖 3。

圖 3. 託運單偵測

3.3 手寫字辨識

手寫託運單地址辨識一直是相當困難的議題，除不同的人有不同的書寫風格之外，因少掉書寫筆畫順序等重要的特徵來協助辨識，使得離線(offline)手寫辨識相較在線(online)手寫辨識困難許多(Plamondon & Srihari, 2000)。現行文字辨識流程為先進行單一字元偵測如圖 4。再分析字元順序如圖 5。本研究使用 CRNN(Convolutional Recurrent Neural Network)(Shi et al., 2017)進行手寫字辨識；再針對是否有缺漏字等問題，透過地址語言模型進行比對，進行自動填補漏字及合理性驗證，以產出完整地址。

我們使用自然語言處理中語言模型(Chen & Goodman, 1999)，利用地址資料前後文關係建立先驗機率(Prior Probability)模型，自動填補漏字及更正誤判，解決因文字密集排列而造成的字元遺漏問題，語言模型訓練與校正的流程如下。

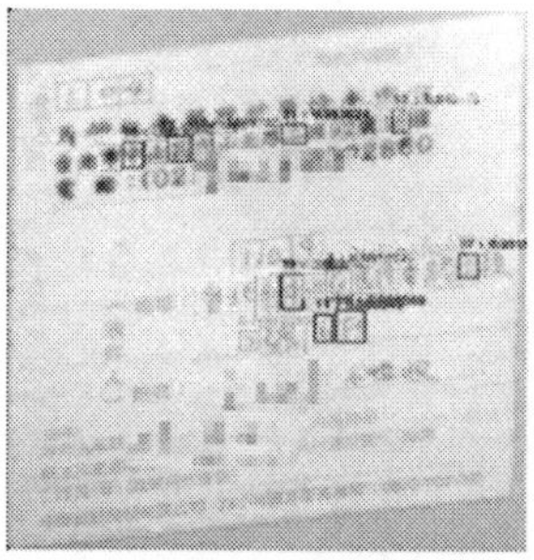

圖 4. 手寫字元偵測

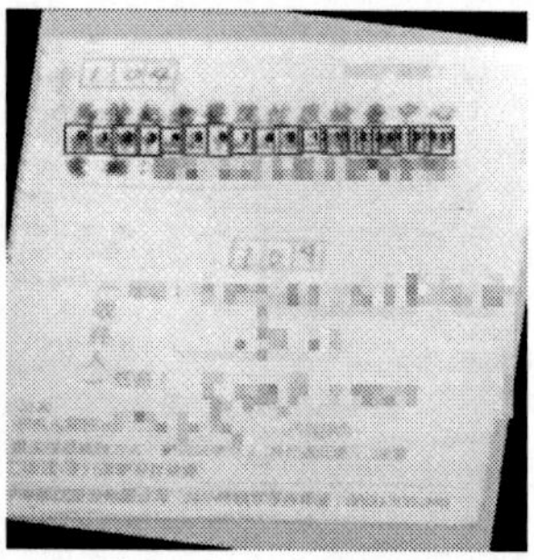

圖 5. 手寫字元排序

- 地址斷詞

地址斷詞採取 CKIP Transformers[1]為基礎架構，再憑藉著過去處理大量地址的經驗，優化成兼具效率及正確性的斷詞模組。輸入一地址資料，模組會產生斷詞地址資訊，如：縣市、鄉鎮市區、村里、路街道、巷弄號等地址斷詞結果。

舉例來說：“新竹縣竹東鎮中興路四段 195 號”，一般可能會斷成<新竹縣 竹東鎮 中興路 四段 195 號>，因為把‘中興路’當成斷詞的關鍵字，而我們則能成功斷成<新竹縣 竹東鎮 中興路四段 195 號>。

- 地址正規化

為了訓練語言模型，所以先將所有地址資料庫內的文字進行正規化，包括：阿拉伯數字、數字全形半形及中文數字等各種內容及格式統一的正規化。而不同地址型態會套用不同的正規化處理，例如：街路部分的數字要正規化成中文數字，巷弄號則是正規化成半形數字。

- 語言模型訓練

因為手寫字不同於印刷體文字，辨識出的地址通常都是有缺漏或是帶有些許錯誤，所以還是需要透過語言模型技術，比對輸入地址與校正基準語言模型中的地址，找一個最接近且唯一地址做為輸出的地址。本研究使用自己收集的地址資料外，也使用戶政司公開資料來訓練語言模型，利用 *n-gram* (Jurafsky et al., 1999)語言模型的編碼技術去達成高速的字串的校正比對，篩出候選地址後，再進行編輯距離（edit distance）的計算來找到最接近的候選地址。

4 效能評估

本研究主要有三個階段需要進行評估，如圖 6：包含托運單偵測、手寫字元偵測和手寫字元辨識。由地址資料庫中隨機挑選 6,000 張地址影像進行測試，文字影像標記字元數約達 10 萬字。

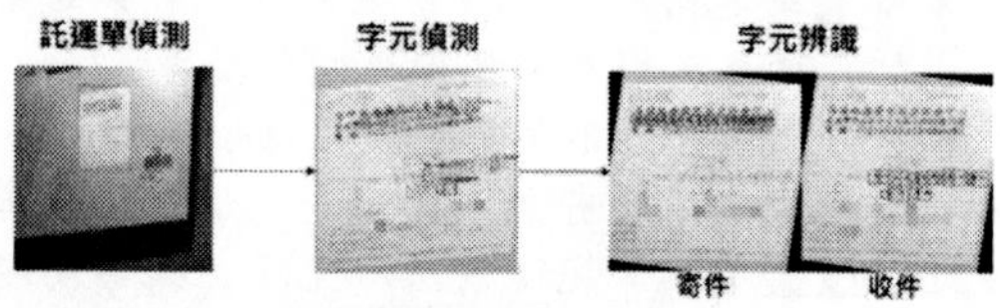

圖 6.三階段評估

我們使用正確率為評估指標，評估指標如公式如下：

$$\text{正確率} = \frac{\text{模型正確辨識字元數}}{\text{影像中的地址字元數}}$$

訓練過程正確率與損失率曲線如圖 7，可以觀察到隨著 epoch 增加，正確率跟著提升而損失率隨著下降。

在校能比較方面，我們使用目前業界辨識效能最好的 Google Cloud Vision API[2]當比較基準(Baseline)，系統效能如表 2，可以發現在托運單手寫字辨識應用，本研究所提出模型效能優於 Google Cloud Vision API，主要的原因可能是因為有針對手寫字與包裹托運單資料進行優化。有使用語言模型進行地址文字校正可以將正確率由 70%提升到 84%，可以發現使用語言模型進行地址校正對於系統效能是非常有幫助。

[1] https://github.com/ckiplab/ckip-transformers

[2] https://cloud.google.com/vision

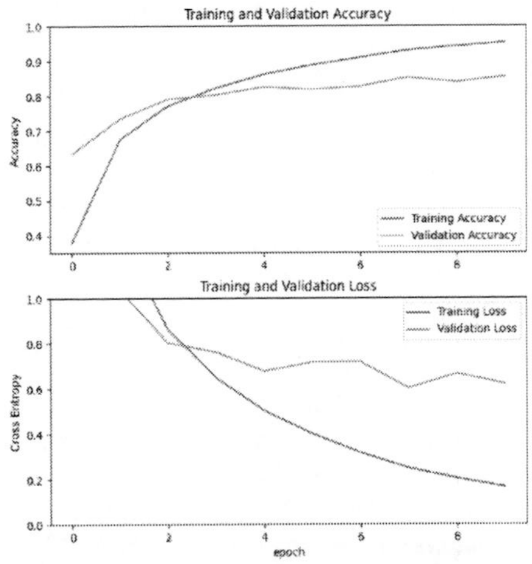

圖 7. 訓練過程正確率與損失率曲線如圖

	Google API	本研究	本研究(語言模型)
託運單偵測	---	82.74%	82.74%
字元偵測	70%	83.06%	83.06%
字元辨識	41.17%	70%	84%

表 2. 托運單手寫字辨識效能

對於辨識錯誤的案例如圖 8，系統會將「台」辨識為「6」或將「號」辨識為「路」，我們進行錯誤分析，發現因為手寫字撰寫較為擁擠、字跡草亂、有塗抹等情況，易造成文字辨識上的誤判。後續改善將以整行文字的模式進行偵測與擷取，先將以斷行的模式進行文字擷取後，再進行分析。用來改善字元定位並計算文字順序的問題，可降低文字定位失誤而產生的文字缺失問題。也可以嚐試調整物件偵測及文字辨識模型架構，建立相關模型再訓練機制，針對手寫字再進行資料蒐集與訓練。

• 台 → 6

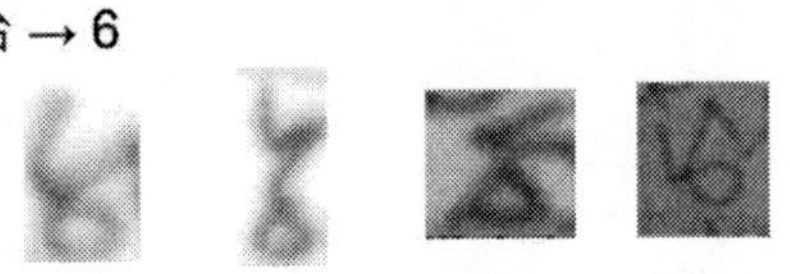

• 號 → 路

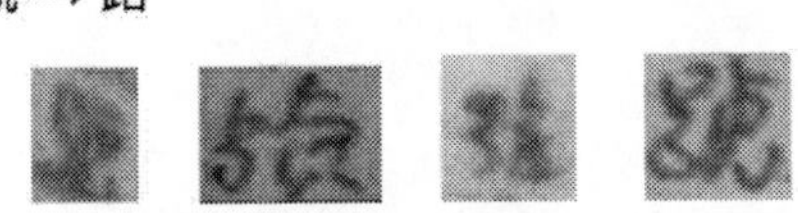

圖 8. 系統辨識錯誤實例

5 結論與未來規劃

現行包裹手寫地址佔比仍高，物流中心每年需處理 500 萬件以上的手寫地址包裹，因傳統機器無法針對手寫地址進行有效的辨識，因此這些未數位化手寫包裹地址，仍需以大量人工判讀的方式對包裹地址進行分揀，造成人力負擔重，且易產生誤判。

本研究建立自動化的包裹地址辨識系統，關鍵技術在於手寫字的偵測與辨識，由於手寫字的書寫模式較印刷字複雜多變，辨識上容易誤判，且地址文字在托運單中占比小、文字排列緊密，造成偵測上的困難，故如何精準偵測包裹上的地址文字是研發重點。

輸入包裹影像，手寫辨識系統先偵測託運單再進行字元偵測，根據字元偵測結果，計算影像傾斜角度並進行影像轉正，使用字元座標進行文字排序後，進行字元辨識並輔以語言模型根據地址關鍵字(縣、市、區等等)進行漏字判斷，自動填補漏字，最後輸出托運單地址。經過 6,000 筆測試資料驗證，模型效能優於 Google Cloud Vision API。

本研究運用人工智慧技術、小物件偵測及密集物件偵測技術，針對包裹託運單上的手寫地址進行辨識，建立包裹地址的自動偵測及辨識系統，期待未來可協助物流處理中心達成包裹自動化判定分揀之目的，並減輕物流中心人工判讀包裹地址的負擔，提高包裹分揀效率。

參考文獻

Abid, N., ul Hasan, A., & Shafait, F. (2018). DeepParse: A Trainable Postal Address Parser. *2018 Digital Image Computing: Techniques and Applications (DICTA)*, 1–8. https://doi.org/10.1109/DICTA.2018.8615844

Arora, N. (2016). Knock knock: Who's there? package delivery at the right address. *Proceedings of the Sixth International Conference on Emerging Databases: Technologies, Applications, and Theory*, 86–89. https://doi.org/10.1145/3007818.3007828

Chen, S. F., & Goodman, J. (1999). An empirical study of smoothing techniques for language modeling. *Computer Speech & Language*, *13*(4), 359–394. https://doi.org/10.1006/csla.1999.0128

Hofmann, P., Samp, C., & Urbach, N. (2020). Robotic process automation. *Electronic Markets*,

30(1), 99–106. https://doi.org/10.1007/s12525-019-00365-8

Jurafsky, D., Martin, J. H., Kehler, A., Linden, K. V., & Ward, N. (1999). *Speech and Language Processing: An Introduction to Natural Language Processing, Computational Linguistics and Speech Recognition*.

Küçük Matci, D., & Avdan, U. (2018). Address standardization using the natural language process for improving geocoding results. *Computers, Environment and Urban Systems*, *70*, 1–8. https://doi.org/10.1016/j.compenvurbsys.2018.01.009

Kumar, G., & Bhatia, P. K. (2014). A Detailed Review of Feature Extraction in Image Processing Systems. *2014 Fourth International Conference on Advanced Computing & Communication Technologies*, 5–12. https://doi.org/10.1109/ACCT.2014.74

Li, X., Kardes, H., Wang, X., & Sun, A. (2014). HMM-based Address Parsing with Massive Synthetic Training Data Generation. *Proceedings of the 4th International Workshop on Location and the Web*, 33–36. https://doi.org/10.1145/2663713.2664430

Li, Z., Qu, L., & Haffari, G. (2020). *Context Dependent Semantic Parsing: A Survey* (arXiv:2011.00797). arXiv. https://doi.org/10.48550/arXiv.2011.00797

Park, S., Song, J.-H., & Kim, Y. (2018). A Neural Language Model for Multi-Dimensional Textual Data based on CNN-LSTM Network. *2018 19th IEEE/ACIS International Conference on Software Engineering, Artificial Intelligence, Networking and Parallel/Distributed Computing (SNPD)*, 212–217. https://doi.org/10.1109/SNPD.2018.8441130

Plamondon, R., & Srihari, S. N. (2000). Online and off-line handwriting recognition: A comprehensive survey. *IEEE Transactions on Pattern Analysis and Machine Intelligence*, *22*(1), 63–84. https://doi.org/10.1109/34.824821

Shafiee, M. J., Chywl, B., Li, F., & Wong, A. (2017). *Fast YOLO: A Fast You Only Look Once System for Real-time Embedded Object Detection in Video* (arXiv:1709.05943). arXiv. https://doi.org/10.48550/arXiv.1709.05943

Sharma, S., Ratti, R., Arora, I., Solanki, A., & Bhatt, G. (2018). Automated Parsing of Geographical Addresses: A Multilayer Feedforward Neural Network Based Approach. *2018 IEEE 12th International Conference on Semantic Computing (ICSC)*, 123–130. https://doi.org/10.1109/ICSC.2018.00026

Shi, B., Bai, X., & Yao, C. (2017). An End-to-End Trainable Neural Network for Image-Based Sequence Recognition and Its Application to Scene Text Recognition. *IEEE Transactions on Pattern Analysis and Machine Intelligence*, *39*(11), 2298–2304. https://doi.org/10.1109/TPAMI.2016.2646371

Sun, W. (2017). Chinese named entity recognition using modified conditional random field on postal address. *2017 10th International Congress on Image and Signal Processing, BioMedical Engineering and Informatics (CISP-BMEI)*, 1–6. https://doi.org/10.1109/CISP-BMEI.2017.8302311

Suri, J. S. (2000). Computer Vision, Pattern Recognition and Image Processing in Left Ventricle Segmentation: The Last 50 Years. *Pattern Analysis & Applications*, *3*(3), 209–242. https://doi.org/10.1007/s100440070008

Xiao, J., & Zhou, Z. (2020). Research Progress of RNN Language Model. *2020 IEEE International Conference on Artificial Intelligence and Computer Applications (ICAICA)*, 1285–1288. https://doi.org/10.1109/ICAICA50127.2020.9182390

Yu, Z., Dong, J., Wei, Z., & Shen, J. (2006). A Fast Image Rotation Algorithm for Optical Character Recognition of Chinese Documents. *2006 International Conference on Communications, Circuits and Systems*, *1*, 485–489. https://doi.org/10.1109/ICCCAS.2006.284682

The 34th Conference on Computational Linguistics and Speech Processing (ROCLING 2022)
Taipei, Taiwan, November 21-22, 2022. The Association for Computational Linguistics and Chinese Language Processing

中文電影對話問答系統資料集
Chinese Movie Dialogue Question Answering Dataset

Shang-Bao Luo
Academia Sinica / Taiwan.
lowzhang@iis.sinica.edu.tw

Cheng-Chung Fan
Academia Sinica / Taiwan.
jjfan@iis.sinica.edu.tw

Kuan-Yu Chen
National Taiwan University of Science and Technology / Taiwan.
kychen@mail.ntust.edu.tw

Yu Tsao
Academia Sinica / Taiwan.
Yu.tsao@citi.sinica.edu.tw

Hsin-Min Wang
Academia Sinica / Taiwan.
whm@iis.sinica.edu.tw

Keh-Yih Su
Academia Sinica / Taiwan.
kysu@iis.sinica.edu.tw

摘要

本論文建構一個中文對話式問答資料集CMDQA。內容為中文電影資訊獲取的多輪對話場景，總共包含一萬筆對話，共約四萬輪對話。所有問題與背景文檔，皆由網路爬蟲從維基百科彙整而來。每個問題的答案都是其相關文檔內的某個片段。此外，為了模擬真實對話問答的情景，對話中會有代名詞的使用。因此，在CMDQA中，問答模型除了需自動地檢索相關文檔外，亦需處理代名詞與歷史資訊的問題。除了對話式多輪問答外，本資料集還可用於評估資訊檢索、機器閱讀理解與問題轉寫等任務的模型成效。除了CMDQA以外，本研究提供一個基礎系統並測試其效果。實驗顯示，基礎系統的效能與真人尚有相當大的差異，因此本資料集可對相關研究提供足夠的挑戰性。

Abstract

This paper constructs a Chinese dialogue-based information-seeking question answering dataset CMDQA, which is mainly applied to the scenario of getting Chinese movie related information. It contains 10K QA dialogs (40K turns in total). All questions and background documents are compiled from the Wikipedia via an Internet crawler. The answers to the questions are obtained via extracting the corresponding answer spans within the related text passage. In CMDQA, in addition to searching related documents, pronouns are also added to the question to better mimic the real dialog scenario. This dataset can test the individual performance of the information retrieval, the question answering and the question re-writing modules. This paper also provides a baseline system and shows its performance on this dataset. The experiments elucidate that it still has a big gap to catch the human performance. This dataset thus provides enough challenge for the researcher to conduct related research.

關鍵字：資訊獲取問答系統、對話式問答系統資料集、中文電影問答
Keywords: Information-Seeking Question Answering, Dialogue-based Question Answering Dataset, Chinese Movie QA

1 諸論

近年來，深度學習在資訊獲取問答(Information-seeking QA)的技術突飛猛進。這個任務目標是希望讓機器像人類一樣進行文檔閱讀，並根據使用者給出的問題在文檔中找出對應的答案。這個技術可以讓電腦幫助人類在大量文檔中找到想要的資訊，可以減輕資訊獲取的成本、加速資訊處理的速度以及提升資訊的利用率。此外，對話式的問答系統可進一步讓使用者以漸進式的方式來搜尋答案，使其更具親和性。

D	Document ID : 依照維基百科所蒐集之所有電影相關之文章，並給予相對應的 ID 表。	
Q_1	**凱雷特**寫的電影是什麼？	what is a film written by **Etgar Keret**?
A_1	9.99 美元	\$9.99
$Gold\ R_1$	凱雷特（希伯來語：אתגרקרררת，出生於 1967 年 8 月 20 日）是一位以色列作家，以其短篇小說、平面小說和影視劇本寫作而聞名。9.99 美元是一部 2008 年澳大利亞 …	Etgar Keret (Hebrew: אתגרקרררת, born August 20, 1967) is an Israeli writer known for his short stories, graphic novels, and scriptwriting for film and television. \$9.99 is a 2008 Australian …
Q_2	**這部電影**是哪一年上映的？	what was the release year of **this movie**?
A_2	2008	2008
$Gold\ R_2$	9.99 美元是一部 2008 年澳大利亞定格動作成人動畫片，由塔蒂婭·羅森塔爾（Tatia Rosenthal）撰寫和導演…	\$9.99 is a 2008 Australian stop-motion adult animated drama film written and directed by Tatia Rosenthal …

表 1. CMDQA 之題目範例

近年來問答系統已有大量研究與發展(Devlin et al., 2018; Zhu et al., 2021; Chakraborty et al., 2021)，本論文專注在對話式的資訊獲取問答系統。在尋求信息的對話中，系統與使用者彼此會反覆提問，以確定使用者真正想問的問題。對此種對話進行建模具有一定的挑戰性，因為問答模型需要去理解上下文、每輪對話的資訊、代名詞、歷史資訊與主題轉換的狀況，以便找出使用者真正想要的答案。目前在英文上，已建構了 CoQA (Siva et al., 2019)與 QuAC (Choi et al., 2018) 資料集，主要針對多種領域主題、共指、推理與不可回答的問題。

在對話式的問答系統中，常常會以代名詞來指代前輪對話中的專名實體(Named Entity)(Stent and Bangalore, 2010)。對於這種狀況，模型需要能夠解決上下文依賴關係的機制，來正確解釋後續問題的真正含意。在代名詞指涉的問題上，現有研究是透過問題轉寫(Question Rewriting, QR) (Elgohary et al., 2019; Liu et al., 2018; Vakulenko et al., 2021; Tredici et al., 2021)，將含糊資訊變成明確問題，以此來提高問答系統的效能。

此外，文檔搜尋式的問答系統(Yang et al., 2015; Qu et al., 2020; Longpre et al., 2021) 需要先從大量的背景文檔中找到回答問題所需的相關文檔，再根據相關文檔進行作答。由於文檔搜尋通常透過資訊檢索技術來完成，因此資訊檢索的成效會直接影響回答的品質。然而現有的中文問答資料集(Shao et al., 2018; Yiming et al., 2018; He et al., 2018; Zheng et al., 2019; Sun et al., 2019)，都沒有包含文檔搜尋部分，未能模擬真實問答中的情境，因此本篇論文特別針對此問題建構一個中文電影對話式資訊獲取問答資料集(*Chinese Movie Dialogue Question Answering Dataset*；簡稱 ***CMDQA***)。本資料集將公開供相關研究使用。

本資料集具有以下特點：

- 背景文檔從維基百科電影主題搜集而成，對話式問答系統需要先從大量文檔中篩選出與問題相關的文檔。
- 問答模型不能只使用單輪的文檔與問題來回答問題，還需考慮代名詞與歷史資訊來進行回答。
- 針對每個問題均有提供相關文檔，因此可作為資訊檢索任務的資料集，亦可簡化作為機器閱讀問答任務的資料集。
- 提供各種基礎模型，讓研究者可自由地抽換不同模型，與自行開發的模型相互搭配，並在本資料集上評估效能。

2 任務定義

在對話式多輪問答任務中，每一輪對話中會有一個問題，模型將根據問題、歷史對話內容以及相關文檔來回答這一輪對話的問題。因此，在第t輪對話中，整個問答系統可以表示為：

$$A_t = QA(Q_t, H_t, R_t) \quad (1)$$

$$H_t = [Q_1, A_1, Q_2, A_2, \dots, Q_{t-1}, A_{t-1}] \quad (2)$$

$$R_t = IR(H_t, Q_t) \quad (3)$$

其中A_t為問答系統依照當輪問題Q_t、相關文檔R_t與歷史資訊H_t所找出對應的答案。歷史

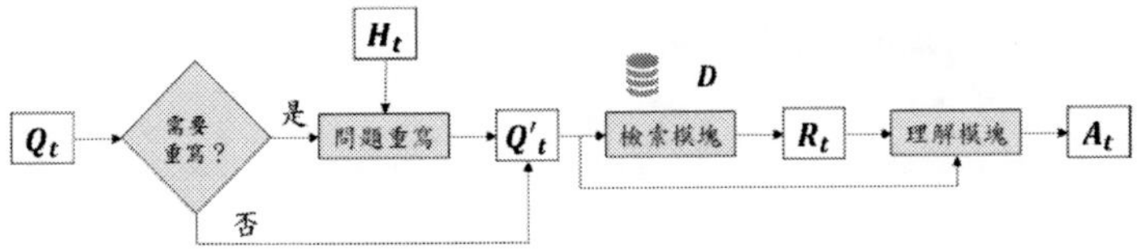

圖 1. CMDQA 之模型概述示意圖

資訊H_t為前$t-1$輪對話中出現過的問題$Q_{1:t-1}$與答案$A_{1:t-1}$。R_t為依照當輪問題Q_t，藉由資訊檢索系統所找出的相關文檔，並依此來回答當輪問題。其中相關的釋例，如表 1 所示。

3 資料蒐集

本論文主要受英文資料集 MovieQA (Tapaswi et al., 2016)啟發，依照英文頁面的維基百科資料來蒐集相關資料，搭配 Google 翻譯取得中文資料。接著由維基百科的標籤資料，透過規則式的模板來產生問題與答案。為了讓品質提升，再經由專名實體檢測與答案對齊等人工整理而得。參照 MovieQA，我們定義了七種標籤：電影、演員、導演、編劇、風格、年份與語言，並依標籤間的關係來建構問題、相關文檔及標準答案的組合。例如：問題提及**導演**，答案回答**電影**，主題就是**導演－電影**，標籤就是電影。針對各個標籤和主題設計的問題數量如表 2 與表 3 所示。

我們依照每一種主題之間的關聯性，將問題生成多輪對話的對話路徑(Dialogue Path)，並且從第二輪對話開始，都會將問題中的關鍵標籤進行代名詞化，讓整個對話情境更加擬真。原來的問題最後被篩選組出二至六輪的對話問題組，相關的資訊如表 4 所示。

4 基線系統概述

本基線系統(Baseline System)依照任務分為三大模塊，分別為檢索模塊、理解模塊與問題重寫模塊，整體示意圖如圖 1 所示。

4.1 檢索模塊

本論文採用 DPR (Karpukhin et al., 2020) 與 BM25 (Trotman et al., 2014)併用的作法(Ma et al., 2021)。資料集會提供每一個問題Q與對應的相關文檔$R \in D$，其中D為維基百科電影主題文檔集合。相關文檔R為問答系統回答問題Q時，檢索模塊認為相關的文檔。

標籤	訓練集	測試集	發展集
電影	12,409	3,675	2,875
演員	3,430	838	495
導演	4,074	1,093	650
編劇	4,880	724	704
風格	20	14	13
年份	101	98	94
語言	63	28	29

表 2. CMDQA 之標籤類別及問題數量

主題	訓練集	測試集	發展集
電影－演員	1,432	773	287
電影－導演	5,720	3,103	1,396
電影－風格	476	217	300
電影－語言	1,351	320	676
演員－電影	2,534	1,793	824
演員－編劇	3,546	732	1,645
演員－年分	7,579	1,597	3,045
編劇－電影	3,012	652	1,542
導演－電影	1,767	550	256

表 3. CMDQA 之主題類別及問題數量

對話輪	訓練集	測試集	發展集
單題數	27,426	9,737	9,971
兩輪	6,390	183	99
三輪	3,038	15	7
四輪	571	0	0
五輪	37	0	0
六輪	2	0	0
合計(多輪)	10,038	198	106

表 4. CMDQA 之多輪問答問題數量

4.2 理解模塊

本資料集回答問題的方式，以從相關文檔中擷取文本答案片段為主，故使用當前標準模型 BERT (Jiao et al., 2019) 為基礎來進行訓練與預測。以第t輪對話為例，輸入X_t的形式如下：

$$X_t = [CLS]q_{t,1}, \dots, q_{t,n}[SEP]r_{t,1}, \dots, r_{t,m}[SEP] \quad (4)$$

其中$R_t = \{r_{t,1}, \cdots, r_{t,m}\}$為檢索模型給予之相關文檔，$Q_t = \{q_{t,1}, \cdots, q_{t,n}\}$為第$t$輪對話所給予的問題。BERT透過$U$層轉換器(Transformer)，來獲得上下文資訊C：

$$C^0 = XW_{token} + W_{position} + W_{segment} \quad (5)$$

$$C^u = Transformer(C^{u-1}) \ \forall u \in [1, U] \quad (6)$$

其中W_{token}、$W_{position}$與$W_{segment}$為 BERT 所使用到的三種向量。最終透過全連結層FFN_{start}與FFN_{end}來產生答案片段出現在相關文檔中開始P^i_{start}與結束P^i_{end}位置的概率：

$$P^i_{start} = softmax(FFN_{start}(C^U)) \quad (7)$$

$$P^i_{end} = softmax(FFN_{end}(C^U)) \quad (8)$$

最終訓練目標如下：

$$(s, e) = \underset{s \le e}{\operatorname{argmax}} \, p^s_{start} p^e_{end} \quad (9)$$

即最大化正確的答案開始和結束位置的概率。

4.3 問題重寫模塊

本論文問題重寫採取基於規則的方式（如圖 2 所示）：以當前問題和歷史資訊為基準做分析，來選擇較合理的代名詞替換，並驗證代名詞轉換對於問答模型的影響。

首先將當輪問題Q_t透過句法分析，得出代名詞位置，並預測該代名詞為何種標籤。接著對歷史對話H_t的每一個問題與答案，依照七大標籤來提取關鍵詞後，以具相同標籤的關鍵詞來取代原本的代名詞，最終獲得當輪明確問題Q'_t。當具相同標籤的關鍵詞有多個時，挑選的順序是最近一輪的關鍵詞優先，且答案的關鍵詞優先於問題的關鍵詞。

5 基線模塊評估

5.1 資訊檢索

資訊檢索的實驗結果如表 5 所示。共有四種基礎模型，BM25 模型採用 PyLucene[1]與 Gensim (Rehurek and Sojka, 2011)的版本，表 5 中後者標記為 BM25*。DPR 模型則是採用 Pytorch (Paszke et al., 2017) 的版本[2]。最後 BMD

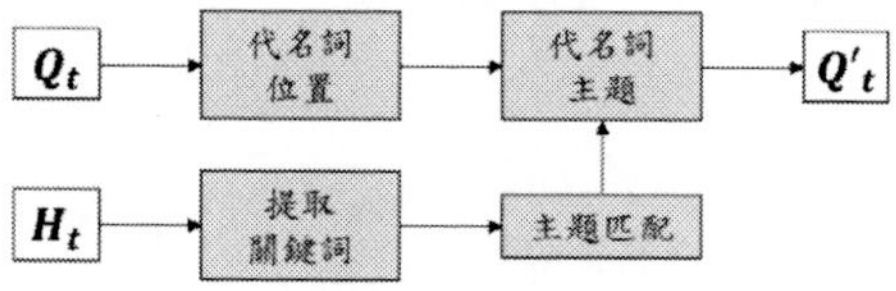

圖 2. 問題重寫之示意圖

(BM25+DPR)則是採用 DPR 與 BM25 模型，透過式(10)進行分數加權後，以最終的文檔s_{BMD}分數來進行篩選。

$$s_{BMD} = s_{DPR} + (1 - \alpha)s_{BM25} \quad (10)$$

訓練 CMDQA 的資訊檢索時，採取段落級(Paragraph-level)的方式來進行背景文檔的切割。呈現數據時，會將段落級的資料恢復成文檔級(Document-level)來進行預測與效能評比。

以召回率(Recall)為評估指標，可以發現在 BMD 的配置下有較好的結果，並且篩選的文檔的數量愈多，其召回率愈高。

5.2 問答模型

問答模型的實驗結果如表 6 所示。我們以 RoBERTa (Liu et al., 2019)為架構，並以中文預訓練模型[3]做為初始。由於簡體中文的預訓練模型使用較多的預訓練文本，我們的實驗皆是將正體中文轉換為簡體中文來進行。在整體訓練中，批次大小為 64、總期(Epoch)次數為 3、學習率為 3e-5。

由表 6 的實驗結果可以發現，在檢索相關文檔R的召回率愈高的情況下，問答模型的效能反而愈低。這主要是由於召回率愈高時，所需輸入問答模型的文字愈長，無關的內容也跟著變多，使得問答模型無法有效地抓取到正確的答案片段。

5.3 問題重寫

問題重寫的實驗結果如表 7 所示。本資料集提供三種不同的方法，說明如下：

- QR[ReA]將本輪問題Q_t的代名詞，直接以上一輪的答案A_{t-1}來進行取代。
- QR[ReQ]將本輪問題Q_t的代名詞，直接以上一輪的問題Q_{t-1}的關鍵詞來進行取

[1] https://cwiki.apache.org/confluence/display/lucene

[2] https://github.com/facebookresearch/DPR

[3] https://huggingface.co/hfl/chinese-roberta-wwm-ext

IR Module	訓練集			測試集			發展集		
	R@1	R@5	R@10	R@1	R@5	R@10	R@1	R@5	R@10
BM25	20.925	51.356	61.510	20.158	48.325	59.469	20.433	49.926	60.158
BM25*	19.492	50.826	62.917	26.740	55.298	65.555	23.278	51.513	63.199
DPR	54.120	75.776	79.435	44.613	72.558	77.963	46.447	71.023	76.206
BMD	68.359	86.955	88.384	62.131	88.022	90.785	63.912	87.223	90.412

表 5. CMDQA 之資訊檢索測試結果

QA Module	訓練集		測試集		發展集	
	EM	F1	EM	F1	EM	F1
Gold P	74.77	87.70	90.78	95.56	91.76	96.49
BM25 @ 1	25.01	44.99	26.72	41.35	25.87	43.49
BM25 @ 5	18.94	37.89	21.51	35.37	21.32	38.08
BM25 @ 10	16.22	34.56	18.42	31.60	18.77	35.61
DPR @ 1	38.36	53.27	31.84	47.43	29.07	48.41
DPR @ 5	24.87	34.91	22.88	37.05	20.72	39.11
DPR @ 10	24.31	38.93	22.52	36.51	20.33	38.59
BMD @ 1	45.61	62.36	40.22	56.56	39.29	58.31
BMD @ 5	29.68	46.71	30.11	44.63	28.68	46.10
BMD @ 10	28.64	44.54	28.35	42.99	26.42	44.05

表 6. CMDQA 之問答模型測試結果

代。此作法的理由為，當輪的問題常針對前一輪的問題進一步追問。

- QR[M]將本輪問題Q_t的代名詞，透過 4.3 節所描述的方法來進行取代。

問題重寫所採用的評估方法為：比較問題重寫後的問題與黃金問題(Gold Q)是否完全相同(Exact Match, EM)，或是採用機器翻譯常用的兩個指標 ROUGE-L 與 BLEU，其中 ROUGE-L 根據召回率衡量重寫後的質量，BLEU 則是根據精確度來進行評量。從表 7 可以看到，使用 EM 評估指標的結果非常不理想。這是因為本論文是將每一組原本的問題，利用不同的句法結構，改寫成相同意思的兩種問句(例如：A 導演曾經參與哪部電影？➔ 哪部電影由這個導演執導？)。因此，我們可以將這個任務視為一種摘要或轉寫，就可以透過機器翻譯常用的兩種指標來進行評估。

5.4 對話問答

多輪對話問答的實驗結果如表 8 所示。我們採用四種實驗設置，說明如下：

- 人工測試數據(Human Performance*)：從訓練、測試與發展集中各抽選 100 題進行人工評測的結果。
- 第一種設置(Gold P + Gold Q)：在完整多輪對話中，每一輪均使用包含答案的文檔(Gold P)與無歧義的問題(Gold Q)讓問答模型來回答。要注意的是，本論文提供的問答模型，只對單輪題目來進行訓練，並沒有針對對話式的架構來特別進行訓練。
- 第二種設置(BMD + Gold Q)：在完整多輪對話中，每一輪均使用無歧義的問題(Gold Q)讓 BMD 檢索模型去尋找相關文檔，最後由問答模型作答。其中@1-10 指的是將檢索回來的相關文檔串接 1 至 10 篇輸入問答模型。
- 第三種設置(BMD + Pron. Q)：在完整多輪對話中，除了第一輪的問題是無歧義的問題外，從第二輪開始，均使用含有代名詞的問題(Pron. Q)。並且每一輪中，BMD 檢索模型均直接使用該輪問題來尋找相關文檔，交給問答模型作答。我們認為此種狀況是最合乎真實情境的狀況。
- 第四種設置(BMD + Rewriting Q) ：與第三種設置相似，但在完整多輪對話中，第二輪起，含有代名詞的問題將透過

QR Module	訓練集			測試集			發展集		
	ROUGE-L	BLEU	EM	ROUGE-L	BLEU	EM	ROUGE-L	BLEU	EM
Original Q	42.683	16.49	0	43.241	14.846	0	42.291	17.289	0.885
QR[ReA]	44.706	18.089	0	45.585	17.834	0.173	45.773	19.974	1.22
QR[ReQ]	42.168	15.389	0.119	42.009	13.186	0	40.72	13.927	0
QR[M]	56.241	40.467	5.622	58.454	41.866	3.286	57.910	43.759	3.540

表 7. CMDQA 之問題重寫測試結果

Dialogue	訓練集			測試集			發展集		
	F1*	F1	EM	F1*	F1	EM	F1*	F1	EM
Human Performance*	88.619	88.246	80.851	89.421	89.990	76.595	86.123	87.026	78.723
Gold P + Gold Q	76.763	76.851	52.212	86.861	86.869	73.737	81.735	82.075	66.038
BMD@1+ Gold Q	45.776	46.019	17.543	43.309	43.434	15.152	49.772	49.686	19.811
BMD@5 + Gold Q	32.209	32.303	7.681	35.28	35.101	9.596	38.356	37.893	10.377
BMD@10 + Gold Q	31.257	31.265	7.362	33.333	33.165	8.586	35.16	35.063	10.377
BMD@1 + Pron. Q	19.676	20.614	0.309	21.898	21.886	0.505	23.288	23.428	0.943
BMD@5 + Pron. Q	15.582	16.228	0.199	18.248	18.182	0.505	17.808	18.082	0.000
BMD@10 + Pron. Q	13.145	13.674	0.004	13.382	13.384	0.505	20.548	20.440	0.000
BMD@1 + Rewriting Q	36.209	37.220	5.529	36.983	37.290	8.586	44.292	44.340	15.094
BMD@5 + Rewriting Q	21.842	22.282	2.740	21.655	21.717	4.545	28.767	28.302	8.491
BMD@10+ Rewriting Q	19.770	20.255	1.624	23.114	23.316	5.556	25.571	25.472	7.547

表 8. CMDQA 之多輪對話問答測試結果

QR[M]的方式將問題重寫後交給 BMD 去查找相關文檔及問答模型去進行作答。

本論文對於對話式多輪問答的評估方式分為三種：F1*、F1 與 EM。F1*為將全部多輪對話的所有題目分別計算 F1 再計算總平均。F1 與 EM 則是先分別計算每個多輪對話的平均 F1 與 EM 後，再按多輪對話的數量去計算平均。

觀察對話式多輪問答的結果(表 8)，可以發現，在第一種設置的狀況下，由於給予正確的文檔與無歧義的問題，於測試集與發展集在 EM 評估指標可分別達到 73.737%與66.038%。第二種設置探討的是：當需要搜尋相關文檔時，對於問答模型效能的影響。明顯可見的是，在沒有任何微調策略的情況下，問答模型於訓練、測試與發展集上，EM 皆達不到 20%。可見相關文檔搜尋是目前的瓶頸。第三種設置則是進一步探討當問句包含代名詞時，對於整體模型的影響。結果顯示問答模型幾乎已完全無法正確的回答。最後，第四種設置下的結果顯示，透過基礎系統提出的問題重寫方法，可提升約 15%~21%的 F1 分數與 5.22%~ 14.15%的 EM 分數。不過整體效能還是與第二種設置有一定的差距，換言之，本論文提出的資料集，是有一定的困難與挑戰性的。

6 總結

本論文構建一個中文電影對話式資訊獲取問答資料集。其中包含一萬個多輪對話(總計約四萬七千輪)。所有問題與背景文檔，皆由網路爬蟲從維基百科彙整而來。

本論文定義這類問題所需要的框架，依照當輪問題去背景文檔集搜尋相關文檔，並透過對話歷史資訊來改寫需要共指消解的問題，最終交給問答模型來回答當輪問題。

本論文依照上述的框架，提供各種模塊的基礎模型與個別效能。基線實驗結果顯示 CMDQA 資料集有一定的挑戰性與困難性。

未來規劃中，預計將擴充資料集中的問題類型，例如：多文本段與簡答題，讓 CMDQA 資料集更加完整與富有挑戰性。另外，會嘗試持續增加題目，讓測試集與發展集的題目分布更加均勻。

參考文獻

Adam Paszke, Sam Gross, Soumith Chintala and Gregory Chanan. 2017. Pytorch: Tensors and

Dynamic Neural Networks in Python with Strong Gpu Acceleration. PyTorch: Tensors and dynamic neural networks in Python with strong GPU acceleration, 6.

Ahmed Elgohary, Denis Peskov and Jordan Boyd-Graber. 2019. Can you unpack that? learning to rewrite questions-in-context.

Amanda J Stent and Srinivas Bangalore. 2010. Interaction between dialog structure and coreference resolution. In 2010 IEEE Spoken Language Technology Workshop, pages 342-347.

Andrew Trotman, Antti Puurula and Blake Burgess. 2014. Improvements to BM25 and language models examined. In Proceedings of the 2014 Australasian Document Computing Symposium, pages 58-65.

Chih Chieh Shao, Trois Liu, Yuting Lai, Yiying Tseng and Sam Tsai. 2018. DRCD: a Chinese Machine Reading Comprehension Dataset, arXiv:1806.00920.

Chujie Zheng, Minlie Huang, and Aixin Sun. 2019. ChID: A Large-scale Chinese IDiom Dataset for Cloze Test. In Proceedings of the 57th Annual Meeting of the Association for Computational Linguistics, pages 778–787, Florence, Italy. Association for Computational Linguistics.

Cui Yiming, Liu Ting, Che Wanxiang, Xiao Li, Chen Zhipeng, Ma Wentao, Wang Shijin and Hu Guoping. 2018. A Span-Extraction Dataset for Chinese Machine Reading Comprehension, arXiv:1810.07366.

Eunsol Choi, He He, Mohit Iyyer, Mark Yatskar, Wen-tau Yih, Yejin Choi, Percy Liang and Luke Zettlemoyer. 2018. QuAC : Question Answering in Context, arXiv:1808.07036.

Fengbin Zhu, Wenqiang Lei, Chao Wang, Jianming Zheng, Soujanya Poria and Tat-Seng Chua. 2021. Retrieving and reading : A comprehensive survey on open-domain question answering, arXiv:2101.00774.

Hengrui Liu, Wenge Rong, Libin Shi, Yuanxin Ouyang and Zhang Xiong. 2018. Question rewrite based dialogue response generation. In Proceedings of International Conference on Neural Information Processing, pages 169-180.

Jacob Devlin, Ming-Wei Chang, Kenton Lee and Kristina Toutanova. 2018. BERT: Pre-training of Deep Bidirectional Transformers for Language Understanding, arXiv:1810.04805.

Kai Sun, Dian Yu, Dong Yu and Claire Cardie. 2019. Probing prior knowledge needed in challenging chinese machine reading comprehension, aXiv:1904.09679.

Makarand Tapaswi, Yukun Zhu, Rainer Stiefelhagen, Antonio Torralba, Raquel Urtasun and Sanja Fidler. 2016. Movieqa: Understanding stories in movies through question-answering. In Proceedings of the IEEE conference on computer vision and pattern recognition, pages 4631-4640.

Marco Del Tredici, Gianni Barlacchi, Xiaoyu Shen, Weiwei Cheng and Adriá de Gispert. 2021. Question Rewriting for Open-Domain Conversational QA: Best Practices and Limitations. In Proceedings of the 30th ACM International Conference on Information & Knowledge Management, pages 2974-2978.

Nilesh Chakraborty, Denis Lukovnikov, Gaurav Maheshwari, Priyansh Trivedi, Jens Lehmann and Asja Fischer. 2021. Introduction to neural network-based question answering over knowledge graphs. Journal of the Wiley Interdisciplinary Reviews: Data Mining and Knowledge Discovery, 11(3):e1389.

Radim Rehurek and Petr Sojka. 2011. Gensim--python framework for vector space modelling. Journal of NLP Centre, Faculty of Informatics, Masaryk University, Brno, Czech Republic, 3(2).

Reddy, Siva, Danqi Chen, and Christopher D. Manning. 2019. Coqa: A Conversational Question Answering Challenge, In Proceedings of Association for Computational Linguistics, 7:249–266.

Shayne Longpre, Yi Lu and Joachim Daiber. 2021. MKQA: A linguistically diverse benchmark for multilingual open domain question answering. Journal of Transactions of the Association for Computational Linguistics, 9:1389-1406

Svitlana Vakulenko, Shayne Longpre, Zhucheng Tu and Raviteja Anantha. 2021. Question rewriting for conversational question answering. In Proceedings of the 14th ACM International Conference on Web Search and Data Mining, pages 355-363.

Vladimir Karpukhin, Barlas Oğuz, Sewon Min, Patrick Lewis, Ledell Wu, Sergey Edunov, Danqi Chen and Wen-tau Yih. 2020. Dense passage retrieval for open-domain question answering, aXiv:2004.4906.

Wei He, Kai Liu, Jing Liu, Yajuan Lyu, Shiqi Zhao, Xinyan Xiao, Yuan Liu, Yizhong Wang, Hua Wu, She Qiaoqiao, Liu Xuan, Wu Tian and Wang Haifeng. 2017. Dureader: a chinese machine reading comprehension dataset from real-world applications, arXiv:1711.05073.

Xiaoqi Jiao, Yichun Yin, Lifeng Shang, Xin Jiang, Xiao Chen, Linlin Li, Fang Wang and Qun Liu. 2019. Tinybert: Distilling bert for natural language understanding, arXiv:1909.10351.

Xueguang Ma, Kai Sun, Ronak Pradeep and Jimmy Lin. 2021. A replication study of dense passage retriever, arXiv:2104.05740.

Yi Yang, Wen-tau Yih and Christopher Meek. 2015. Wikiqa: A challenge dataset for open-domain question answering. In Proceedings of the 2015 conference on empirical methods in natural language processing, pages 2013-2018.

Yingqi Qu, Yuchen Ding, Jing Liu, Kai Liu, Ruiyang Ren, Wayne Xin Zhao, Daxiang Dong, Hua Wu and Haifeng Wang. 2020. RocketQA: An optimized training approach to dense passage retrieval for open-domain question answering, arXiv:2010.08191.

Yinhan Liu, Myle Ott, Naman Goyal, Jingfei Du, Mandar Joshi, Danqi Chen, Omer Levy, Mike Lewis, Luke Zettlemoyer and Veselin Stoyanov. 2019. Roberta: A robustly optimized bert pretraining approach, aXiv:1907.11692.

The 34th Conference on Computational Linguistics and Speech Processing (ROCLING 2022)
Taipei, Taiwan, November 21-22, 2022. The Association for Computational Linguistics and Chinese Language Processing

Unsupervised Text Summarization of Long Documents using Dependency-based Noun Phrases and Contextual Order Arrangement

Yen-Hao Huang[1], Hsiao-Yen Lan[2], Yi-Shin Chen[*]
Institute of Information Systems and Applications[1]
Department of Computer Science[2*]
National Tsing Hua University
Hsinchu, Taiwan
{yenhao0218[1], penny16335[2], yishin[*]}@gmail.com

Abstract

Unsupervised extractive summarization has recently gained importance since it does not require labeled data. Among unsupervised methods, graph-based approaches have achieved outstanding results. These methods represent each document by a graph, with sentences as nodes and word-level similarity among sentences as edges. Common words can easily lead to a strong connection between sentence nodes. Thus, sentences with many common words can be misinterpreted as salient sentences for a summary. This work addresses the common word issue with a phrase-level graph that (1) focuses on the *noun phrases* of a document based on grammar dependencies and (2) initializes edge weights by term-frequency within the target document and inverse document frequency over the *entire corpus*. The importance scores of noun phrases extracted from the graph are then used to select the most salient sentences. To preserve summary coherence, the order of the selected sentences is re-arranged by a flow-aware *orderBERT*. The results reveal that our unsupervised framework outperformed other extractive methods on ROUGE as well as two human evaluations for semantic similarity and summary coherence.

Keywords: Extractive Summarization, Graph, Dependency, Summary Coherence

1 Introduction

Text summarization helps in preserving and compressing representative information from long documents. This work aims at the extractive summarization, which condenses a document by extracting a few salient sentences. It produces fluent sentences with less training data than abstractive methods.

Most extractive summarization research focuses on supervised learning methods (Narayan et al., 2018; Dong et al., 2018; Yao et al., 2018; Wu and Hu, 2018; Liu and Lapata, 2019) to derive models for automatically observing salient sentences based on specified golden labels. Nonetheless, it is impractical to expect the availability of such high-quality training datasets. on the rich unpaired data. In this method, researchers model textual content into sentence-level (Erkan and Radev, 2004; Mihalcea and Tarau, 2004; Mallick et al., 2019; Zheng and Lapata, 2019) or hybrid (Tarau and Blanco, 2019) graphs and and adopt PageRank-based algorithms algorithm (Page et al., 1999) to retrieve the salient sentences in a document. Due to the characteristics of the graph, the extracted salient sentences are easily affected by common or function words that have high connectivities and are overestimated as key nodes. In addition, coherence is considered as an important attribute in summarization as it keeps the flow of concepts smooth and logical. However, few studies take coherence into consideration.

To address the above issues, this work assumes the major concepts in a document are expressed by key noun phrases and constructs a phrase-level graph specific for noun phrases that leverage grammar dependencies. With salient sentences extracted by key noun phrases, a sentence re-ordering step is applied to ensure the flow of concepts is contextually correct for the reader's understanding. There are two major steps in the proposed framework: *key noun phrase extraction* and *salient sentence extraction*, as shown in Figure 1. Our

[*]The corresponding author.

contributions are summarized as:

- An unsupervised extractive framework is proposed by constructing a novel phrase-level graph to obtain key noun phrases for salient sentence extraction. The proposed framework not only outperformed all extractive baselines on ROUGE, but also achieved results closer to the SOTA supervised transformer-based methods.
- The proposed orderBERT reorders the summary sentences with respect to sentence-level context, which improves 9% over using sentence's original position in a human-reader evaluation.
- The proposed noun phrase hyper relation extraction method can obtain more relations and less duplicates. These rich relations then provide more nodes and edges information to the phrase-level graph.

2 Key Noun Phrase Extraction

Keyphrases represent important information in sentences and documents but not all of them contribute the same amount of information. With noun phrases indicated as the most commonly occurring structures among different types of corpora (Le et al., 2016), the proposed method assumes that they potentially provide coverage of the major conceptual points of the document. By focusing on extracting key noun phrases from documents, this work proposes a graph-based keyphrase extraction for noun phrases in an unsupervised manner.

The key noun phrase extraction is separated into two steps: noun phrase hyper relation extraction and graph-based keyphrase scoring. The former is designed to extract the noun phrases along with the relations between them in a complete as possible manner according to the grammar dependency. To extract important noun phrases and avoid an undue influence of common words, further relations are adopted as a guide in constructing the dependency graph for specific noun phrases.

2.1 Noun Phrase Hyper Relation Extraction

In traditional relation extraction methods, noun phrases are extracted based on co-occurrence within a predefined window size, which might encounter a window size limitation; in other words, noun phrases whose relations are outside of the window size will be ignored. To overcome this limitation, this paper adapted the concept of open information extraction (OpenIE) to enable the extraction of both short and long relations between noun phases based on grammar relations, which is denoted by relation triples as in Definition 1.

Definition 1. *(Relation Triple). Let s, o, r, $\mathbf{N}$, and $\mathbf{NP}$ denote a subject, object, their relation, the set of nouns, and the set of noun phrases, respectively. The relation triple set $\mathbf{RT}$ is presented as follows:*

$$\mathbf{RT} = \{(s, r, o) | s, o \in \mathbf{N} \cup \mathbf{NP}\} \quad (1)$$

The goal of phrase relation extraction is to retrieve a set of triples **RT** from each sentence. However, existing OpenIE tools mainly focus on the direct relations between subjects, verbs, and objects. Consequently, complex relations cannot be captured, e.g. the intra-clause relation of two nouns and nested clauses. Except for adopting existing OpenIE tools, our approach proposes rules to capture complex relations based on the grammar dependencies as defined in Definition 2.

Definition 2. *(Grammar Dependency). Let ζ be the grammar dependency type between a source word γ and a target word τ in a given sentence st. A set of grammar dependencies $\mathbf{GD}_\zeta$ with type ζ in a given sentence st is presented as $\mathbf{GD}_\zeta^{st} = \{(\gamma, \tau)\}$.*

With the dependency parsing tool from Stanford CoreNLP (Manning et al., 2014), a set of dependencies $\mathbf{GD}^{st}$ and the corresponding word pairs are first extracted. In Figure 2, the extracted dependencies can be presented as $\mathbf{GD}^{st} = \{\mathbf{GD}^{st}_{\text{NSUBJ}}, \mathbf{GD}^{st}_{\text{CASE}}, \ldots, \mathbf{GD}^{st}_{\text{AMOD}}\}$, $\mathbf{GD}^{st}_{\text{CASE}} = \{(\text{success}, \text{for}), (\text{models}, \text{of})\}$. These dependencies $\mathbf{GD}^{st}$ are then used to construct the triples **RT** for each sentence by algorithms proposed in the following sections.

2.1.1 Inter-clause Relation

To extract relations in the same clause, the proposed procedures are shown below.

Definition 3. *(**RT** from Nominal Subjects). Let NSUBJ, OBJ, OBL, XCOMP, COP, and AUX*

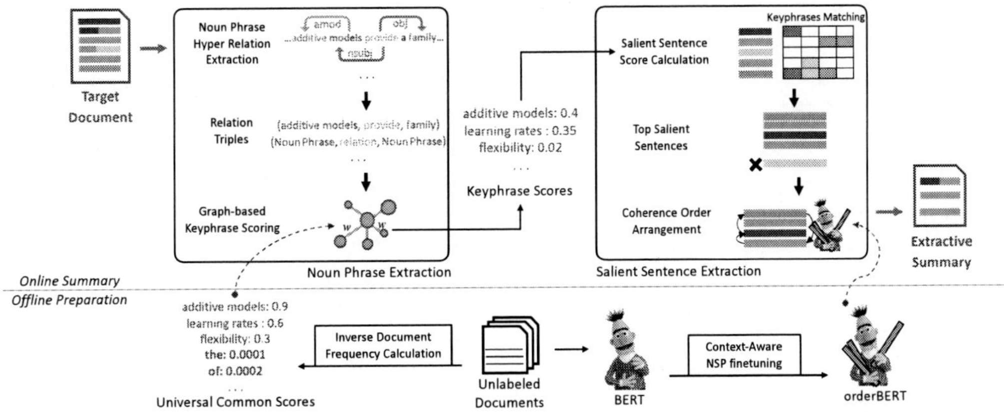

Figure 1: Overall framework flowchart

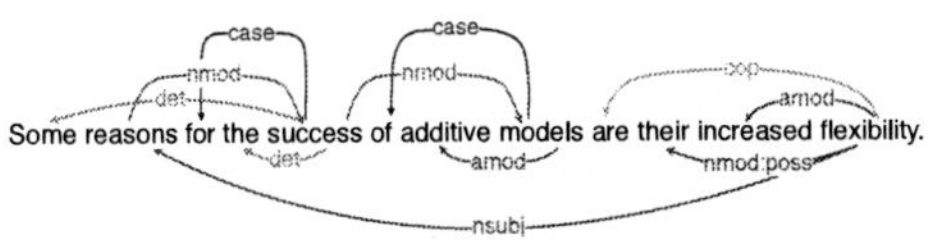

Figure 2: Example of dependency parsing

be the dependency types nominal subject, object, oblique nominal, open clausal complement, copula, and auxiliary. Let $\mathbf{GD}_{NSUBJ}$ *denote the set of grammar dependencies with type* NSUBJ*, where the set consists of two types of word pairs:* (γ_v, τ)*,* $(\gamma_v$ *is verb); and* (γ_n, τ)*,* $(\gamma_n$ *is noun). Let* $(\hat{\gamma_v}, \hat{\tau}) \in \mathbf{GD}_{OBJ} \cup \mathbf{GD}_{OBL}$*,* $(\tilde{\gamma_v}, \tilde{\tau}) \in \mathbf{GD}_{XOMP}$*, and* $(\check{\gamma}, \check{\tau}) \in \mathbf{GD}_{COP} \cup \mathbf{GD}_{AUX}$*. Triples can be extracted as follows:*

$$\mathbf{RT}^{NSUBJ}_{OBJ,OBL} = \{(\tau, \gamma_v, \hat{\tau}) | \gamma_v = \hat{\gamma_v}\} \quad (2)$$

$$\mathbf{RT}^{NSUBJ}_{XOMP} = \{(\tau, \tilde{\tau}, \hat{\tau}) | \gamma_v = \tilde{\gamma_v}, \tilde{\tau} = \hat{\gamma_v}\} \quad (3)$$

$$\mathbf{RT}^{NSUBJ}_{AUX,COP} = \{(\tau, \check{\gamma}, \gamma_n) | \gamma_n = \check{\tau}\} \quad (4)$$

Definition 4. *(***RT** *from Passive Nominal Subjects). Let* NSUBJ:P *denote the passive-nominal-subject type. Let* $(\gamma, \tau) \in \mathbf{GD}_{NSUBJ:P}$*,* $(\hat{\gamma}, \hat{\tau}) \in \mathbf{GD}_{OBL}$*, and* $(\tilde{\gamma}, \tilde{\tau}) \in \mathbf{GD}_{XOMP}$*. The triples can be extracted by*

$$\mathbf{RT}^{NSUBJ:P}_{OBL} = \{(\tau, \gamma, \hat{\tau}) | \gamma = \hat{\gamma}\} \quad (5)$$

$$\mathbf{RT}^{NSUBJ:P}_{XOMP} = \{(\tau, \gamma, \tilde{\tau}) | \gamma = \tilde{\gamma}\} \quad (6)$$

Definition 5. *(***RT** *from Nominal Modifier). Let* NMOD*,* CASE*,* PUNCT *be dependencies types nominal modifier, case marking, and punctuation, respectively. Let* $(\gamma, \tau) \in \mathbf{GD}_{NMOD}$ *and* $(\hat{\gamma}, \hat{\tau}) \in \mathbf{GD}_{CASE} \cup \mathbf{GD}_{PUNCT}$*. Triples are built as* $\mathbf{RT}^{NMOD} = \{(\gamma, \hat{\tau}, \tau) | \tau = \hat{\gamma}\}$*.*

Based on Definitions 3 to 5, these triples are first extracted and denoted as $\check{\mathbf{RT}}$ for bravity.

However, some relations are still missing after these extraction processes, such as relations between nouns and the corresponding appositions, which are ignored. Two algorithms in Definitions 6 and 7 are then proposed.

Definition 6. *(***RT** *from Conjunction). Let* CONJ *denote the conjunction dependency type and* $\tilde{\mathbf{RT}}$ *denote the set of all extracted triples. The triple set* $\mathbf{RT}^{CONJ}$ *is extracted based on Algorithm 1 for each* $(s, r, o) \in \tilde{\mathbf{RT}}$*.*

Algorithm 1 RT Construction from CONJ

```
for (γ, τ) ∈ GD_CONJ do
    if γ == r then
        if τ.isVerb() ∧ τ.hasNoSubject() then
            object ← getObj(GD_OBJ, τ)
            return (s, τ, object)
    else if γ == o then
        return (s, r, τ)
```

Definition 7. *(***RT** *from Appositional Modifier). Let* APPOS *denote the appositional-modifier dependency type. Let* $(\gamma, \tau) \in \mathbf{GD}_{APPOS}, (s, r, o) \in \tilde{RT}$*, and* ϕ *denote an empty relation word. The triples are built as* $\mathbf{RT}^{APPOS} = \{(\gamma, \phi, \tau) | \gamma = s \vee \gamma = o\}$*.*

2.1.2 Intra-clause Relation

For dependencies in the independence and subordinate clauses, the dependencies of which the object or subject in a subordinate clause provides complements for an independent clause are leveraged. Two subordinate clauses are considered and defined below.

Definition 8. *(***RT** *from Adjective Clausal Modifier of Noun). Let* ACL *be the adjective-clausal-modifier dependency type. Let* $(\gamma, \tau) \in \mathbf{GR}_{ACL}, (\hat{\gamma}, \hat{\tau}) \in \mathbf{GR}_{OBJ}$*. Triples are extracted as* $\mathbf{RT}^{ACL} = \{(\tau, \gamma, \hat{\tau}) | \gamma = \hat{\gamma}\}$*.*

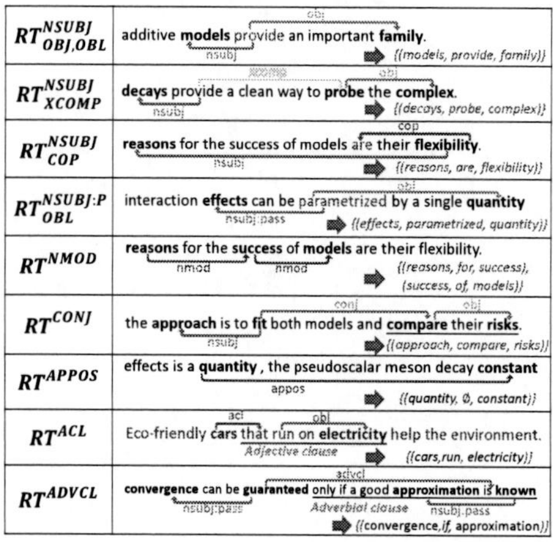

Figure 3: Examples of RT construction

Definition 9. *(**RT** from Adverbial Clause Modifier). Let* ADVCL *and* ADVMOD *be dependency types adverbial clause modifier and adverbial modifier, respectively. Let* $\tilde{\mathbf{RT}}$ *be all the extracted triples. The subsets of the triples are built by Algorithm 2 for each* $(\gamma, \tau) \in \mathbf{GR}_{\text{ADVCL}}$ *and all the triples are merged as* $\mathbf{RT}^{ADVCL}$.

Algorithm 2 RT Construction from ADVCL

```
tmpRT = ∅
for (s, r, o) ∈ RT do
    if γ == r then
        adverb ← getAdv(GR_ADVMOD, τ)
        object ← getObj(GR_OBJ ∪ GR_OBL, τ)
        tmpRT.add((s, adverb, object))
        continue
    for (γ̂, τ̂) ∈ GR_NSUBJ:P do
        if γ == γ̂ then
            object ← getObj(GR_OBJ ∪ GR_OBL, τ)
            adverb ← getAdv(GR_ADVMOD, τ)
            tmpRT.add((τ̂, adverb, object))
return tmpRT
```

As the adjective clauses provide extra information for the noun, there exists relations between the corresponding object of the verb in an adjective clause and the noun. Such relations could be extracted by Definition 8. For an adverbial clause, there are two major cases to be captured. First, all the extracted triples are considered, as an adverbial clause describes the conditions or reasons (such as *if* or *since*) for the action of a subject with regard to the corresponding object in the independent clause. Second, for a subject in the passive voice, it may not have a corresponding object and thus cannot be extracted by the previous methods. The details and an example are shown in Definition 9 and Figure 3, respectively. For brevity, all the extracted triples to this end are denoted as **RT**.

Lastly, due to the design of CoreNLP, the extracted (noun) words in **RT** are still uni-grams. To present the noun phrase, a uni-gram is combined with the previous word if there exists a grammar type for a compound or adjectival modifier. Let a target word be the subject s or object o from an extracted triple $(s, r, o) \in \mathbf{RT}$ of the sentence st. If the relation r between the target word and of any its previous word is compound, this work considers that this previous word is able to modify the meaning of the target word and, thus, combine these words.

2.2 Graph-based Keyphrase Extraction

Let $\mathbf{S}, \mathbf{R}$, and $\mathbf{O}$ denote the sets of subjects, relations, and objects in the extracted relation triples **RT** from all the sentences in a document, respectively, A bi-directional graph G is built as $G = (\mathbf{V}, \mathbf{E})$, where $\mathbf{V}$ represents noun phrase nodes and $\mathbf{E}$ denotes the edges, such that $\mathbf{V} = \mathbf{S} \cup \mathbf{O}$ and $\mathbf{E} = \mathbf{R}$.

With all the triples **RT** transformed into a graph G, a keyphrase extraction method is proposed to retrieve important noun phrases through this graph. The PageRank algorithm (Page et al., 1999) was adapted to score all the nodes in the graph. However, due to the nature of PageRank, the score of common phrases could be too high as they have more edges than other nodes. Thus, to avoid this common word issue, the term-frequency inverse document frequency (TFIDF) ratio was adapted for the edge weight in advance from all the training documents. It is computed by:

$$TFIDF(w) = log_2(freq(w)) * \log_2 \frac{|D|}{df(w)} \tag{7}$$

where $freq(w)$ denotes the frequency of word w in the source document, $|D|$ represents the number of total source documents in the collection, and $df(w)$ is the number of documents that contain the word w. It is worth noting that the although common words have lower IDF values, they still achieve high scores due to their overly high frequencies. The log function is thus adopted for $freq(w)$. The TFIDF scores are added into graph $G = (\mathbf{V}, \mathbf{E}, \Theta)$ as edge weights $\Theta = \{\theta\}$ by the following equation:

$$\theta_{i,j} = |Relation_{i,j}| * \frac{TFIDF_j}{TFIDF_i + TFIDF_j} \quad (8)$$

where $\theta_{i,j}$ is the edge weight, and $|Relation_{i,j}|$ is the number of relations among nodes v_i, v_j. PageRank is adopted in the end to obtain the importance scores for noun phrase nodes.

3 Salient Sentence Extraction

Consistent with our assumption that noun phrases potentially provide coverage of the major conceptual aspects of a document, the salient sentences are also selected based on these noun phrases with the corresponding importance scores derived by the weighted graph. In the following section, a context-aware BERT is derived to perform sentence reordering for the top salient scores in order to maintain summary coherence.

3.1 Salient Sentence Score Calculation

With important scores of noun phrases, they are utilized to calculate the salient score for each sentence in the document. Let $d = \{st_i\}$, $st_i = \{p_k\}$, $G^{(d)}$, and $\mathbf{V}^{(d)}$ be a document, sentence, graph, and set of nodes, respectively, where st_i represents the ith sentence in document d, p_k denotes the kth noun phrase in st_i, $G^{(d)}$ denotes the graph constructed by d, and $\mathbf{V}^{(d)} \in G^{(d)}$. Sum aggregation was applied to score the salience value for a given sentence:

$$Score_{sent_n} = \sum_{p_k \in (sent_n \cap \mathbf{V})} Score_{p_k} \quad (9)$$

where $Score_{p_k}$ is the importance score of noun phrase p_k calculated by $G^{(d)}$. Note that different sentence scoring methods were also proposed, such as the average aggregation, yet the sum aggregation performs the best.

3.2 Coherence Order Arrangement

With the salient score of each sentence in a document, sentences are ranked according to their scores. An intuitive solution to maintain the summary coherence in the extractive summarization is to reorder these top-n sentences according to their original position order in the source document (Zhong et al., 2020). However, the flow of selected sentences might be disrupted and, hence, damage the readability of the generated summary. With regard to the challenge, a flow-aware **orderBERT** is proposed for sentence order arrangement.

3.2.1 orderBERT

The orderBERT is a fine-tuned BERT by a modified objective of the next sentence prediction (NSP) (Devlin et al., 2019). Given a sentence pair (st_α, st_β), the goal of NSP is to predict whether the second sentence st_β is the sentence after the first sentence st_α.

In the original NSP, its negative samples are sentence pairs sampled from different documents. However, these training data may results in two objectives while pretraining: (1) BERT can successfully classify the "order" and "context" in which the given sentences are in the incorrect order or from different documents are classified as negative; instead, (2) it only predicts whether two input sentences originate from the same document or from different ones. It is difficult to ensure that BERT is aware of the order of the given sentences. Thus, this study finetunes BERT by the sentence order based on a **context-aware NSP fine-tuning** strategy. Specifically, as additional negative samples, a set of sentence pairs are constructed by inverse order of two consequent sentences within a single source article. The number of inverse-order false samples are set to be the same as the number of original consequent sentence pairs, as done in the original work (Devlin et al., 2019).

To this end, the training dataset contains (1) correct order consequent sentence pairs within a document (positive sample), (2) sentence pairs from different documents (negative sample), and (3) *inverse-order* consequent sentence pairs within a document (negative sample). With this training set, *orderBERT* was trained to predict whether the second sentence is next in order after the first sentence (Huang et al., 2021), thereby going beyond merely recognizing whether or not the sentences are from the same document. Note that this process remains unsupervised since its labels are obtained naturally from documents.

3.2.2 Summary Sentence Reordering

With the trained *orderBERT*, given a pivot sentence and a set of candidate sentences, we let orderBERT go through all the pairs of pivot sentence and candidates to obtain the most suitable candidate connected after the pivot sentence. Finally, given a set of salient sentences, *orderBERT* then maintains the coherence of summary by re-ordering the extracted salient sentences, as defined in Algorithm 3.

Overall, after the sentences reordering, a machine-generated extractive summary is obtained in an unsupervised manner, in which the summary comprises of n number of salient sentences from the original document. It is important to note that the salient sentences are selected based on the key noun-phrases and, thus, several important terminologies are present in each sentence of the summary. For the summary coherence, the improvement is not only contributed by sentence rearrangement step, the important terms (noun phrases) also play important role in connecting the concept through different sentences while the readers go through the summary.

Algorithm 3 Sentence Reordering

```
ST = Salient sentence list ordered by each one's original positions
st_pivot = ST.deque()
ordered_ST = [st_pivot]
while len(ST) ≠ 0 do
    st_pivot = GETNEXTBYORDERBERT(st_pivot, ST)
    ST.remove(st_pivot)
    ordered_ST.append(st_pivot)
return ordered_ST
```

4 Experimental Setup

4.1 Dataset and Preprocessing

This work focuses on long document summarization as the key concepts in long documents are more dispersed than in short ones. Two different long-document datasets, PubMed and arXiv from Cohan et al. (2018), were considered with the introductions as the source documents and their abstracts as the summaries. For pre-processing, documents with its introduction less than 10 sentences were removed, as there were an insufficient number of sentences from which to select. The statistics of the datasets are summarized in Table 1.

4.2 Baselines

To evaluate performance, we compared our framework with different baselines as follows: (a) **LEAD-5** and (b) **ORACLE** generally represent the lower-bound and upper-bound of extractive summarization tasks; for unsupervised methods, we adopted (c) **TextRank** (Mihalcea and Tarau, 2004) with co-occurrence relations with window size set at 2 for graph-based keyphrases and Equation 9 for sentences scores; (d) **DeepRank** (Tarau and Blanco, 2019) contains a word-sentence heterogeneous graph with PageRank for sentence scores; (e) **LexRank** (Erkan and Radev, 2004) is a sentence-level undirected graph with edge weight threshold set to 0.1 according to its paper and calculates a cosine similarity between sentences; and (f) **PacSum** (Zheng and Lapata, 2019) builds a sentence-level directed graph with TFIDF or BERT for the edge weights. For supervised methods, the following were adopted: (g) **Pointer Generator** (See et al., 2017) with attention and beam search algorithm; (h) **BertSum** (Liu and Lapata, 2019), three SOTA BERT-based models for both extractive and abstractive summarization that included BertExt, BertAbs, and BertExtAbs. The summary of each extractive method can contain at most 5 sentences.

For evaluation, ROUGE 1, 2, and L (Lin and Och, 2004) were first applied to examine the information-preserving capabilities. Secondly, a human evaluation of the coherence of the summaries was conducted.

5 Results and Discussion

5.1 Model Performance on ROUGE

The performance comparison for different methods on two datasets is demonstrated in Table 2. Overall, the proposed unsupervised keyword-based method outperformed all the extractive summarization baselines, including the SOTA transformer method, namely BertExt. For the BertAbs and BertExtAbs models that were trained under supervision, it is worth mentioning that our method still outperformed both of them with the PubMed dataset. As the size of the data in arXiv was ten times more than the PubMed dataset, BertAbs and BertExtAbs largely benefited from the supervised learning process; our methods then performed slightly worse than them. However, this still indicates that by leveraging key noun-phases using grammar de-

The 34th Conference on Computational Linguistics and Speech Processing (ROCLING 2022)
Taipei, Taiwan, November 21-22, 2022. The Association for Computational Linguistics and Chinese Language Processing

Dataset	# of Doc. train/valid/test	Avg. Abstract # word	Avg. Abstract # sentence	Avg. Introduction # word	Avg. Introduction # sentence	Avg. Doc. # word
PubMed	10k / 2k / 1.25k	201.9	6.8	1013.1	37.3	3224.4
arXiv	83k / 19.8k / 20k	177.7	6.6	1077.0	42.8	6913.8

Table 1: Dataset statistics

Method	Type	PubMed ROUGE-1	PubMed ROUGE-2	PubMed ROUGE-L	arXiv ROUGE-1	arXiv ROUGE-2	arXiv ROUGE-L
LEAD-5	*	0.2999	0.0865	0.2695	0.0137	0.0003	0.0137
ORACLE	*	0.4490	0.1817	0.3604	0.4610	0.1994	0.2784
TextRank	Unsup.	0.3514	0.0944	0.3115	0.3424	0.0972	0.3035
LexRank		**0.3936**	**0.1169**	**0.3469**	0.3592	0.1000	0.3151
DeepRank		0.3029	0.0651	0.2652	0.3257	0.0841	0.2861
PacSum (TFIDF)		**0.3650**	0.0904	**0.3237**	0.3835	0.1131	0.3341
PacSum (BERT)		0.3093	0.0677	0.2777	0.3595	0.1005	0.3146
Pointer Generator	Sup.	0.2999	0.0865	0.2695	0.3554	0.1255	0.3192
BertExt		0.3249	**0.1012**	0.2863	0.3829	0.1324	0.3311
BertAbs		0.3199	0.0730	0.2909	**0.4105**	**0.1512**	**0.3667**
BertExtAbs		0.3485	0.0802	0.3136	**0.4269**	**0.1598**	**0.3802**
Ours	**Unsup.**	**0.3999**	**0.1174**	**0.3504**	**0.4075**	**0.1347**	**0.3569**

Table 2: Overall performance on ROUGE

Method	Avg. # of Noun arXiv	Avg. # of Noun PubMed
DeepRank	29.3	35.6
LexRank	45.3	53.3
PacSum (TFIDF)	57.3	65.2
PacSum (BERT)	40.8	42.4
TextRank	38.8	49.0
Ours	**64.5**	**71.0**

Table 3: Noun usages of summaries

pendencies, there is a chance for unsupervised method to perform similarly to a supervised and pretrained method. In addition, one possible reason for the good performance with the more limited dataset (PubMed) was the usage of the grammar dependencies in constructing the graph for the keyphrases. Specifically, the rich grammar relations lay in the language usage implicitly, which allows our models to capture the key concepts of a document. The remaining evaluations focus on the comparisons among unsupervised baselines.

5.2 Noun for Information Preserving

As this work focuses on the representative noun phrases for concept preserving. Statistics were conveyed on the average frequencies of nouns from all graph-based baselines as shown in Table 3. This showed that the summary generated by our method contained mostly words that were nouns, which probably helped our method to preserve most of the concepts and obtain the best ROUGE performance.

5.3 Graph Construction Comparison

The other phrase-level method, TextRank, did not have as good a performance as ours. The only difference between our framework and TextRank is the way the phrase-level graph is constructed. Our framework utilizes rule-based relation extraction from grammar relations, while TextRank applies co-occurrence relations. To compare the differences, graphs were visualized with the same sentence as shown in Figure 4. In Figure 4a, there are only four adjective-noun combinations. The co-occurrence relations ignore many important relation between phrases due to the limited window size. In contrast, the graph by our method (Figure 4b) contains more relations between phrases that contributes to a dense graph and benefits for the keyword extraction.

As compared to a heterogeneous graph, DeepRank built a graph from both words and sentences. As there are many edges that connect from keyphrases to sentences, it results in the scores of important keyphrases being distributed uniformly to these sentences. The top-five salient sentences were examined as to whether they contained the top keyphrase. The average keyphrase counts in top-5 sentences from DeepRank were 0.748 and 0.864 while our method obtained 3.003 and 3.321 on arXiv and PubMed, respectively. This also indicates that it is better to separate phrases and sentences for summarization.

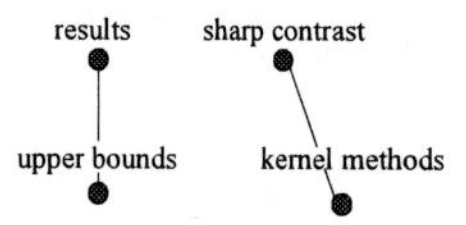

(a) Co-occurrence relation

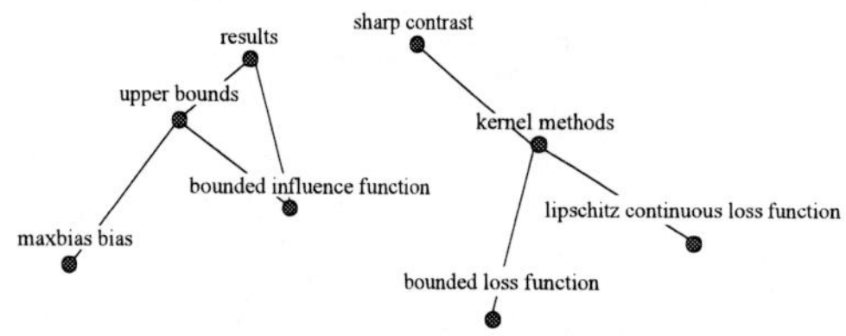

(b) Grammar dependency relation

Figure 4: Graphs built from an example sentence

5.4 Human Questionnaire Evaluation

Human evaluation was conducted on Amazon Mechanical Turk (AMT) to compare the semantic similarity to gold summary and coherence performance among baselines that had the best ROUGE score or was the most coherent. An abstract (golden summary) and multiple summaries from the baselines were provided for each question. There were a total of 10 documents that were randomly sampled from arXiv and PubMed in the same proportion and assigned to 100 AMT workers for evaluations. Note that 21 workers were discarded as they submit inattentive answers to the questionnaire including the behaviors of quick answering, the same answer for all questions, and wrong answer for the trap question. The results from both datasets are together in Table 4.

	Chose Ratio	
Method	Similarity	Coherence
LexRank	25.96%	28.79%
PacSum (TFIDF)	19.61%	19.33%
Ours + Orig. Pos.	27.22%	21.17%
Ours + orderBERT	27.21%	30.71%

Table 4: Percentage of human-preferred methods

From the semantic similarity question, our proposed methods outperform other unsupervised baselines. Noting that the sentences of two summaries generated by our methods are identical, only the orders are different. Therefore, their percentages are, therefore, almost the same–27.22% and 27.21%. It indicates that labelers struggled to select one of ours as the best semantic-similar summary from all options; with two of our methods together, most labelers selected our summaries as the most similar. For LexRank and PacSum (TFIDF), although they are comparable in ROUGE evaluation, the summaries by LexRank were more preferred by human readers.

With regard to summary coherence, with sentence re-ordering and key noun phrases, our method with *orderBERT* had better performance than others in terms of coherence evaluation. The results of two our methods also indicate a 9.5% improvement in coherence on the chosen ratio with the BERT reordering mechanism as compared to the summary that only reordered based on its original position (Ours + Orig. Pos.). Although adopting the original position for reordering works well in short document summarization, it may not be suitable to directly adopt for a long document. Interestingly, LexRank also obtained good results in the coherence questions. It is found that LexRank tends to select a few sentences with connecting/turning words that are helpful for coherence between sentences.

Example summaries are shown in Table 5. It is observed that the summary reordered by the original positions has multiple topic shifts and repetitions. The topic shifts from *model-checking problem* to *timed automata*, then to *model-checking problem*, and then to *timed automata* again. As for the summary by *orderBERT*, the topic first focuses on the *model-checking problem* and then provides the link between *timed automata* and *model-checking problem* instead of switching the topics between them. This shows that the original position method may produce topic gaps between salient sentences as there is more content in a long document. By reordering sentences at the sentence level, the mechanism with *orderBERT* could alleviate such an issue. Overall, the combined use of noun phrases and sentence reordering with *orderBERT* could provide better readability with respect to summary coherence than the other baselines.

5.5 Relation Extraction Comparison

To evaluate the proposed phrase extraction method, the latest OpenIE tool given by Stanford CoreNLP was compared as in Table 6.

For the Stanford CoreNLP tool, there was no triple extracted in Case 1 and all the results in Case 2 were almost the same. Al-

LexRank	For this class of parametric **timed automata**, they focus on the emptiness problem: are there concrete values for the parameters so that the automaton has an accepting run? they show that when only one clock is compared to parameters, the emptiness problem is decidable. The **model-checking problem** for **tctl** extended with parameters over discrete- and dense-**timed automata** (without parameters) is decidable. Unfortunately, in all those previous works, the parameters are only in the model (expressed as a timed automaton) or only in the property (expressed as a temporal logic formula). Nevertheless, when expressing a temporal property of a parametric system, it is natural to refer in the temporal formula to the parameters used in the system.
PacSum	In fact, the control has to leave *equation* at most *equation* time units after entering itand the control has to stay exactly *equation* time units in state *equation*. Let us consider the next three formulae for configuration *equation*, i.e. the control is in state *equation* and clock *equation* has value *equation*: a. *Equation* the parameter synthesis problem associated to formula *equation*, asks for which values of *equation* and *equation*, the formula is true at configuration *equation*. Formula *equation* formalizes the next question "in all the cases where the value assigned to parameter *equation* is greater than the value assigned to parameter *equation*, is it true that any cycle has a duration bounded by *equation*. On the positive side, we show that the **model-checking problem** becomes decidable and parameter synthesis problem is solvable for a fragment of logic where the equality is not allowed.
Ours +Orig.Pos.	In this paper, we further investigate the **model-checking problem** of real-time formalisms with parameters. For this class of parametric **timed automata**, they focus on the emptiness problem: Are there concrete values for the parameters so that the automaton has an accepting run? They show that when only one clock is compared to parameters, the emptiness problem is decidable. The **model-checking problem** for **tctl** extended with parameters over discrete- and dense-**timed automata** (without parameters) is decidable. In this paper, we study the **model-checking problem** of the logic **tctl** extended with parameters over the runs of a discrete-timed automaton with one parametric clock. On the negative side, we show that the **model-checking problem** of **tctl** extended with parameters is undecidable over **timed automata** with only one parametric clock.
Ours +order-BERT	In this paper, we further investigate the **model-checking problem** of real-time formalisms with parameters. On the negative side, we show that the **model-checking problem** of **tctl** extended with parameters is undecidable over **timed automata** with only one parametric clock. The **model-checking problem** for **tctl** extended with parameters over discrete- and dense-**timed automata** (without parameters) is decidable. In this paper, we study the **model-checking problem** of the logic **tctl** extended with parameters over the runs of a discrete-timed automaton with one parametric clock. For this class of parametric **timed automata**, they focus on the emptiness problem: Are there concrete values for the parameters so that the automaton has an accepting run? They show that when only one clock is compared to parameters, the emptiness problem is decidable.

Table 5: Example Summaries from Unsupervised Methods (Key noun-phrases are highlighted in bold).

Case 1	of such estimators belong to the large class of regularized kernel based methods over a reproducing kernel hilbert space.
CoreNLP	Not available.
Ours	(Examples, of, such estimators), (Examples, belong to, large class), (large class, of, regularized kernel), ...
Case 2	It is also a minimizer of the following optimization problem involving the original loss function .
CoreNLP	(It, is minimizer of, optimization problem), (It, is minimizer of, following optimization problem), (It, is also minimizer of, optimization problem), ...
Ours	(It, is minimizer), (minimizer, of, following optimization problem), (following optimization problem, involving, original loss function)

Table 6: Phrase Relation Extraction Comparison

though such duplication could be solved by post-processing, missing relations (such as the relation between a noun in a main clause and a noun in an adjective clause) were still not found. In addition, our framework could extract more useful triples from these cases.

6 Conclusion

In this research, a fully unsupervised framework is proposed for extractive summarization. The proposed method addresses the common word domination issue from a graph-based approach by using a phrase-level graph that focuses on key noun phrases based on grammar dependencies. The extracted key noun-phrases effectively capture the major concepts of a document and can be used to construct an extractive summary. Experiments showed that the proposed method outperformed all the extractive baselines, even for supervised methods. A human evaluation also showed that the use of keyphrases and sentence reordering successfully benefited the coherence of the summaries. In the future, we aim to adapt the proposed key noun-phrases for unsupervised abstractive summarization.

References

Arman Cohan, Franck Dernoncourt, Doo Soon Kim, Trung Bui, Seokhwan Kim, Walter Chang, and Nazli Goharian. 2018. A discourse-aware attention model for abstractive summarization of long documents. In *Proceedings of the 2018 Conference of the North American Chapter of the Association for Computational Linguistics: Human Language Technologies, Volume 2 (Short Papers)*, pages 615–621.

Jacob Devlin, Ming-Wei Chang, Kenton Lee, and Kristina Toutanova. 2019. BERT: Pre-training of deep bidirectional transformers for language understanding. In *Proceedings of the 2019 Conference of the North American Chapter of the Association for Computational Linguistics: Human Language Technologies, Volume 1 (Long and Short Papers)*, pages 4171–4186, Minneapolis, Minnesota. Association for Computational Linguistics.

Yue Dong, Yikang Shen, Eric Crawford, Herke van Hoof, and Jackie Chi Kit Cheung. 2018. BanditSum: Extractive summarization as a contextual bandit. In *Proceedings of the 2018 Conference on Empirical Methods in Natural Language Processing*, pages 3739–3748, Brussels, Belgium.

Günes Erkan and Dragomir R Radev. 2004. Lexrank: Graph-based lexical centrality as salience in text summarization. *Journal of artificial intelligence research*, 22:457–479.

Yen-Hao Huang, Ratana Pornvattanavichai, Fernando Henrique Calderon Alvarado, and Yi-Shin Chen. 2021. Unsupervised multi-document summarization for news corpus with key synonyms and contextual embeddings. In *Proceedings of the 33rd Conference on Computational Linguistics and Speech Processing (ROCLING)*, pages 192–201.

Tho Thi Ngoc Le, Minh Le Nguyen, and Akira Shimazu. 2016. Unsupervised keyphrase extraction: Introducing new kinds of words to keyphrases. In *Australasian Joint Conference on Artificial Intelligence*, pages 665–671. Springer.

Chin-Yew Lin and FJ Och. 2004. Looking for a few good metrics: Rouge and its evaluation. In *Ntcir Workshop*.

Yang Liu and Mirella Lapata. 2019. Text summarization with pretrained encoders. In *Proceedings of the 2019 Conference on Empirical Methods in Natural Language Processing and the 9th International Joint Conference on Natural Language Processing (EMNLP-IJCNLP)*, pages 3730–3740, Hong Kong, China. Association for Computational Linguistics.

Chirantana Mallick, Ajit Kumar Das, Madhurima Dutta, Asit Kumar Das, and Apurba Sarkar. 2019. Graph-based text summarization using modified textrank. In *Soft computing in data analytics*, pages 137–146. Springer Singapore, Singapore.

Christopher D. Manning, Mihai Surdeanu, John Bauer, Jenny Finkel, Steven J. Bethard, and David McClosky. 2014. The Stanford CoreNLP natural language processing toolkit. In *Association for Computational Linguistics (ACL) System Demonstrations*, pages 55–60.

Rada Mihalcea and Paul Tarau. 2004. Textrank: Bringing order into text. In *Proceedings of the 2004 conference on empirical methods in natural language processing*, pages 404–411.

Shashi Narayan, Shay B Cohen, and Mirella Lapata. 2018. Ranking sentences for extractive summarization with reinforcement learning. In *Proceedings of the 2018 Conference of the North American Chapter of the Association for Computational Linguistics: Human Language Technologies, Volume 1 (Long Papers)*, pages 1747–1759.

Lawrence Page, Sergey Brin, Rajeev Motwani, and Terry Winograd. 1999. The pagerank citation ranking: Bringing order to the web. Technical report, Stanford InfoLab.

Abigail See, Peter J Liu, and Christopher D Manning. 2017. Get to the point: Summarization with pointer-generator networks. In *Proceedings of the 55th Annual Meeting of the Association for Computational Linguistics (Volume 1: Long Papers)*, pages 1073–1083.

Paul Tarau and Eduardo Blanco. 2019. Dependency-based text graphs for keyphrase and summary extraction with applications to interactive content retrieval. *arXiv preprint arXiv:1909.09742*.

Yuxiang Wu and Baotian Hu. 2018. Learning to extract coherent summary via deep reinforcement learning. In *Thirty-Second AAAI Conference on Artificial Intelligence*.

Kaichun Yao, Libo Zhang, Tiejian Luo, and Yanjun Wu. 2018. Deep reinforcement learning for extractive document summarization. *Neurocomputing*, 284:52–62.

Hao Zheng and Mirella Lapata. 2019. Sentence centrality revisited for unsupervised summarization. In *Proceedings of the 57th Annual Meeting of the Association for Computational Linguistics*, pages 6236–6247.

Ming Zhong, Pengfei Liu, Yiran Chen, Danqing Wang, Xipeng Qiu, and Xuan-Jing Huang. 2020. Extractive summarization as text matching. In *Proceedings of the 58th Annual Meeting of the Association for Computational Linguistics*, pages 6197–6208.

The 34th Conference on Computational Linguistics and Speech Processing (ROCLING 2022)
Taipei, Taiwan, November 21-22, 2022. The Association for Computational Linguistics and Chinese Language Processing

運用響應式知識蒸餾機制增進中文多標籤文本分類效能
Enhancing Chinese Multi-Label Text Classification Performance with Response-based Knowledge Distillation

黃思齊 Szu-Chi Huang, 曹程富 Cheng-Fu Cao, 廖柏勛 Po-Hsun Liao
李龍豪 Lung-Hao Lee, 李柏磊 Po-Lei Lee, 徐國鎧 Kuo-Kai Shyu
國立中央大學 電機工程學系
Department of Electrical Engineering, National Central University
{110521103, 110521109, 110521086}@cc.ncu.edu.tw
{lhlee, pllee, kkshyu}@ee.ncu.edu.tw

摘要

資料類別不平衡存在長尾標籤問題，單獨的多標籤分類模型一次預測所有類別，針對個別標籤的最佳化十分困難，對於出現次數較少的長尾標籤效能通常不佳。本論文提出一種響應式知識蒸餾機制，將多個最佳化的二元模型作為教師網路，單一多標籤模型做為學生網路，改善多標籤模型在非平衡標籤的資料集分類效能。實驗資料來自 2,724 個中文健康照護文本，人工標記文章內容橫跨 9 個類別， 總共標籤數量是 8,731，平均每個樣本有 3.2 個標籤。實驗設定採用 5 折交互驗證，比較 TextRNN、TextCNN、HAN 和 GRU-att 模型，使用知識蒸餾機制與否的效能差異，結果顯示透過知識蒸餾機制能夠顯著提升單一多標籤分類模型的 micro-F1 約 2 至 3 %、macro-F1 約 4 至 6 %、weighted-F1 約 3 至 4 %，以及 subset accuracy 約 1 至 2 %。

Abstract

It's difficult to optimize individual label performance of multi-label text classification, especially in those imbalanced data containing long-tailed labels. Therefore, this study proposes a response-based knowledge distillation mechanism comprising a teacher model that optimizes binary classifiers of the corresponding labels and a student model that is a standalone multi-label classifier learning from distilled knowledge passed by the teacher model. A total of 2,724 Chinese healthcare texts were collected and manually annotated across nine defined labels, resulting in 8731 labels, each containing an average of 3.2 labels. We used 5-fold cross-validation to compare the performance of several multi-label models, including TextRNN, TextCNN, HAN, and GRU-att. Experimental results indicate that using the proposed knowledge distillation mechanism effectively improved the performance no matter which model was used, about 2-3% of micro-F1, 4-6% of macro-F1, 3-4% of weighted-F1 and 1-2% of subset accuracy for performance enhancement.

關鍵字：多標籤分類、長尾標籤、二元相關、知識蒸餾

Keywords: Multi-label classification, long-tailed labels, binary relevance, knowledge distillation

1 介紹

多標籤文本分類 (Multi-Label Text Classification) 廣泛用於許多應用，例如：廣告系統 (Agrawal et al., 2013)、情緒分析(Myagmar et al., 2019)、推薦系統 (Guo et al., 2016) 、幽默辨識 (Kao et al., 2021) 以及問答系統 (Chen et al., 2021)等。多標籤文本分類主要有兩種方法類型 (Tsoumakas and Katakis, 2007)，分別是 (1) 問題轉換：透過訓練多個二元分類模型來達成多重標籤分類，以及 (2) 訓練單一模型進行多重標籤分類。問題轉換類型可以透過調整類別權重(class weights) 的方式，針對單一類

別進行最佳化，提供更高的彈性 (Banerjee et al., 2019)，而當資料標籤不平衡時，訓練單一模型則難以最佳化各類別的預測效能。但訓練單一模型能夠依據標籤間的關聯性，或是潛在架構對模型進行優化，而問題轉換法則無法有效利用標籤間的相關性。

知識蒸餾 (knowledge distillation) 是一種將巨型的教師網路 (teacher net) 學習到的「知識」，轉移到較精簡的學生網路 (student net) 的深度學習技術 (Hinton et al., 2015)。我們假設最佳化多個二元分類器網路，在各類別上擁有比單一多標籤模型更佳的效能，將最佳化的多個二元分類器模型作為教師網路，單一多標籤模型作為學生網路進行訓練，目標是讓單一多標籤模型可以透過教師網路，在非平衡標籤資料上學習知識，用以改善單一多標籤模型在非平衡標籤上效能低落的缺點。

本篇論文提出利用知識蒸餾機制增進多標籤文本分類效能的方法，在中文健康照護文本上，驗證數個不同深度學習模型包含 TextRNN (Liu et al., 2016)、TextCNN (Liu et al., 2017)、HAN (Yang et al., 2016)、GRU-Att (Banerjee et al., 2019) 的效能差異，實驗結果顯示使用知識蒸餾機制與原先的單一多標籤分類模型相比，提升 2~3%的 micro-F1、4~6%的 macro-F1、3~4%的 weighted-F1 以及 1~2%的 subset accuracy。

2 相關研究

2.1 知識蒸餾

大規模的機器學習通常使用非常複雜的模型訓練，大量地計算導致模型參數量過大，同時也耗費計算資源。因此，Hinton (2015) 提出一種稱為「知識蒸餾」的模型壓縮方式，將繁瑣大型模型訓練完成後的知識，以「蒸餾」(distillation) 的方式，轉移到更適合使用的小型模型。知識蒸餾的種類可分為以下三種類型 (Gou et al., 2021)：

(1) Response-based

蒸餾的知識主要來源是教師模型的最終輸出層，通過使用損失函數 (loss function) 取得學生和教師模型的之間的差異，並在訓練過程中將損失最小化，最終讓學生模型能夠做出跟教師模型一樣的預測。

(2) Feature-based

主要是從教師模型神經網路的中間層中取得特徵，通過最小化教師和學生模型的特徵損失函數，訓練學生模型學習與教師模型相同的特徵。

(3) Relation-based

與 Feature-based 相似同樣都是從教師模型中取得特徵，差別在於先將特徵建立為圖形、矩陣、或是概率分佈圖，再與學生模型比較關係的差異，藉此訓練學生模型。

2.2 多標籤文本分類

多標籤文本分類與多元文本分類 (multi-class text classification) 都是具有兩個以上類別的分類任務。不同之處在於，多元分類每個標籤都是相互排斥的，分類標的樣本是從多個類別選擇一個。多標籤分類則可以為每個樣本分配多個不同標籤，而這些標籤並不相互排斥，這種分類方式也比較接近人類的思考，可以從多個角度來描述一件事物。

TextRNN 模型 (Liu et al., 2016) 採用長短期記憶神經網路 (Long Short-Term Memory, LSTM) 進行訓練。模型包含三個控制閘：輸入、輸出、遺忘，分別對應寫入、讀取以及遺忘的功能。透過這三個控制閘，模型能夠額外考慮前文的關係，使得當前的輸出不只受上一層輸入的影響，也受到同一層前一個輸出（即前文）的影響。

HAN 模型 (Yang et al., 2016) 使用 GRU 神經網路進行訓練。訓練時將 GRU 神經網路當作編碼器(word encoder)對每句話的詞語先進行注意力機制 (attention)，再疊上一層同樣的結構，用 GRU 對所有句子進行注意力機制，最後輸出分類結果。

TextCNN 模型 (Liu et al., 2017) 使用靜態（有微調）和非靜態（無微調）通道表示句子，並經過多個過濾器和特徵映射進行捲積，方便捕獲豐富的語義，同時採用動態最大池化 (dynamic max pooling)，生成多個特徵後，均分特徵的資訊，最後使用 dropout 和 Sigmoid 輸出分類。

GRU-Attention 模型 (Banerjee et al., 2019) 的結構便是在經過 GloVe (Pennington et al, 2014) 的預訓練後，將單詞序列輸入 GRU 之後進行注意力機制，最後線性結合最大池化(max-

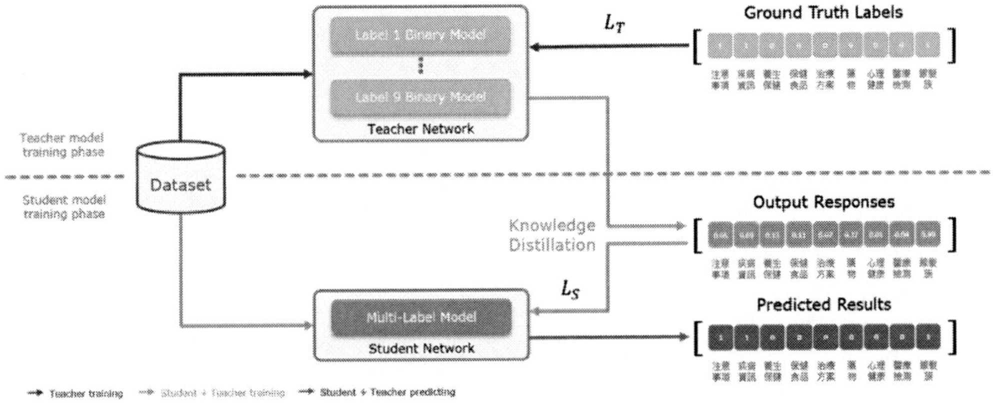

圖 1、基於知識蒸餾的多標籤分類模型訓練流程

pool) 和平均池化(mean-pool)的向量，並且輸出結果。

資料數量和分類標籤種類的增加，導致大部分資料通常集中在少數幾個標籤，多數的標籤只有極少數的資料，出現長尾 (long-tail) 效應。因此，我們提出一個響應式知識蒸餾的訓練方法，希望能改善長尾標籤的分類效能。

3 基於知識蒸餾的模型

我們提出一個基於知識蒸餾(Knowledge Distillation, KD) 的多標籤文本分類方法，目標是將二元分類器的優點應用在多標籤分類器上，用以改進單個多標籤分類器的效能。模型訓練流程如圖 1 所示，教師模型由多個二元分類模型組成，假設資料集有 n 個類別，就會有 n 個二元分類模型，學生模型則是一個多標籤分類模型。教師與學生所採用的模型架構皆相同，最大的差異在於模型最後一層的輸出數量。在訓練時，我們先訓練教師模型中的 N 個二元分類模型，針對相對應類別在驗證資料集的表現進行最佳化，以確保教師模型的效能，可以優於單個多標籤分類器的表現。然後，擁有最佳表現的教師模型會產生響應 (responses)，讓學生模型來學習。在學生模型訓練階段，學生預測目標是教師響應的機率值分佈，而不是目標標籤 (ground truth labels)，藉此，學生就能從老師的響應中得到損失值(loss)進行訓練。

我們在訓練教師模型時，透過類別權重 (class weights) 優化訓練時權重參數的更新。類別權重是一種常被用來處理資料不平衡問題的方法，對訓練集裡的每個類別加上一個權重。理論上，如果該類別的樣本數越多，那麼它被加上的權重就要越低；反之，樣本數越少的權重就給得越高。如此一來就會改變原本的損失函數，使得較多樣本數類別的損失函數變小，較少樣本數類別的損失函數變大。加上這個限制會迫使模型在訓練期間進行權重更新時，提升少樣本數類別(長尾標籤)的準確度，而樣本數多的類別則沒有明顯差異。

我們採用響應式(response-based) 知識蒸餾，此機制的主要想法為讓學生模型直接模仿教師模型所預測出來類別的機率分佈。我們使用 binary cross entropy 做為損失函數，因此教師模型中每個二元分類模型的損失函數 $L_T(y, z_t)$，加上類別權重 W 的損失函數變成加權平均，可以用方程式(1)表示，其中y_i代表第i個樣本的真實標籤值、z_i^t代表教師模型第i個樣本的輸出值。

$$L_T(y, z_t) = -\frac{1}{N}\sum_{i=1}^{N} W \cdot y_i \cdot \log(z_{s_i}) + (1 - y_i) \cdot \log(1 - z_{s_i}) \quad (1)$$

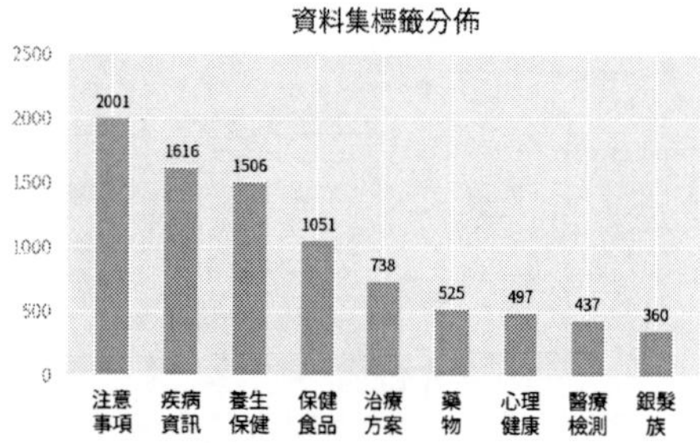

圖 2、資料集標籤分佈

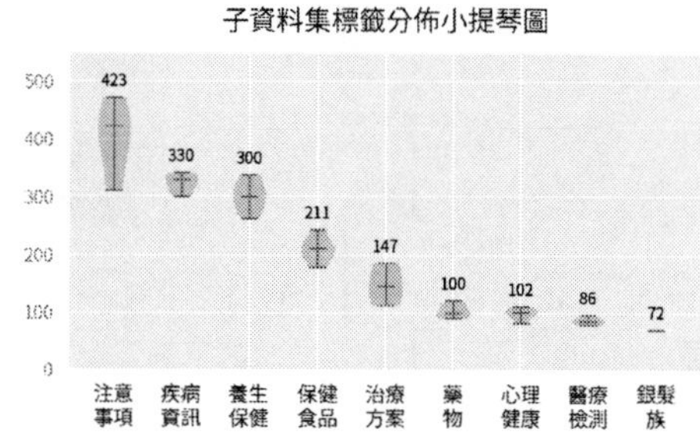

圖 3、子資料集標籤分佈

教師模型訓練完成後會對整個訓練資料集進行預測，產生各類別的機率分佈（響應），然後我們就可以用損失函數$L_S(z_t, z_s)$來訓練學生模型，其中z_s代表學生模型的輸出值。模型最後輸出的激活函數是 sigmoid，超過定義的門檻值(threshold)，即為模型的預測標籤。

$$L_S(y, z_t) = -\frac{1}{N}\sum_{i=1}^{N} y_i \cdot \log(z_{s_i}) + (1 - y_i) \cdot \log(1 - z_{s_i}) \quad (2)$$

4 實驗評估與結果

4.1 資料集

本研究實驗的資料來自網路爬取的中文健康照護網站，例如：康健雜誌、國家醫藥網路、健康醫療網等的文章內容，去除網頁標籤、圖片及詮釋資料(metadata)等雜訊，僅留下純文字內容做人工類別標記，整個資料集最終有 2,724 個文檔，橫跨 9 個類別標籤，包含：健康表現、心理健康、治療方案、醫療檢測、保健食品、注意事項、藥物和銀髮族，總共標籤數量是8,731，平均每個樣本有3.2個標籤。各標籤的樣本數量如圖 2 所示，「注意事項」這個標籤出現次數最多，佔整個資料集約 73%，而出現次數最少的標籤是「銀髮族」，僅佔約 13%。前半段 4 個類別出現的平均樣本數目是 1543.5，對比後半段的 4 個類別平均出現的樣本數是 454.8，落差約 3.4 倍，雖然類別標籤僅有 9 類，文本數目也還不夠多，整個資料集的標籤分佈不明顯，但還是可以看到存在長尾效應。

我們使用五折交叉驗證 (5-fold cross-validation)，分割資料集時，從最少樣本數的標籤開始隨機平均分配樣本至各子資料集，這樣能夠保證樣本數較少的標籤能夠在交叉驗證中被均分。圖 3 為分割後的子資料集標籤分佈的小提琴圖(violin plot)，圖中標示數值為中位數，可以看到與原資料集的分佈大致相同。

4.2 實驗設定

我們使用 Tensorflow 函式庫進行模型實作。所有文本使用 CKIP Transformer[1] 套件進行斷詞，模型輸入皆使用維度 300 的 Word2Vec (Mikolov et al., 2013)，並訓練在繁體中文維基百科語料庫[2]以及實驗資料集上。

我們分別比較不同深度學習模型，包含 TextRNN (Liu et al., 2016)、TextCNN (Liu et al., 2017)、HAN (Yang et al., 2016) 以及 GRU-Att (Banerjee et al., 2019)，導入知識蒸餾機制與否導致的效能差異。模型的訓練參數如下：文本長度 300 字元、Batch Size 32 (GRU-att 是 128) 、損失函數 Binary Cross Entropy、優化器 Adam、訓練迭代次數 30、早停法 patience 是 10、學習率 1e-3、輸出層激活函數 sigmoid 以及驗證集比率 15%。

每個模型比較以下三種不同訓練方法：

(1) 二元最佳化 (Binary Optimization)

[1] https://github.com/ckiplab/ckip-transformers

[2] https://dumps.wikimedia.org/zhwiki/latest/zhwiki-latest-pages-articles.xml.bz2

Model	Type	Micro F1	Macro F1	Weighted F1	Subset Accuracy
TextRNN	Binary Optimization (Teacher)	72.11	62.65	71.93	13.70
	Standalone Multi-label Classifier (Student)	71.09	57.15	68.82	15.85
	Knowledge Distillation (Teacher + Student)	**74.29**	**63.76**	**73.52**	**16.24**
TextCNN	Binary Optimization (Teacher)	75.89	**68.35**	75.48	18.75
	Standalone Multi-label Classifier (Student)	74.55	63.57	72.88	18.75
	Knowledge Distillation (Teacher + Student)	**76.80**	67.68	**75.72**	**19.70**
HAN	Binary Optimization (Teacher)	75.73	69.36	75.60	17.79
	Standalone Multi-label Classifier (Student)	74.63	66.08	73.66	19.10
	Knowledge Distillation (Teacher + Student)	**77.54**	**71.00**	**77.15**	**21.22**
GRU-Att	Binary Optimization (Teacher)	73.30	64.70	73.06	14.93
	Standalone Multi-label Classifier (Student)	71.90	61.44	70.88	14.69
	Knowledge Distillation (Teacher + Student)	**75.17**	**67.63**	**75.26**	**16.52**

表 1、多標籤分類模型實驗結果

知識蒸餾機制中單獨使用教師網路 (teacher net) 的作法。採用二元相關 (binary relevance) 轉換，各類別獨立訓練分類器調整類別權重，在最佳化二元相關轉換法的模型時，我們每個類別使用不同類別權重（0.05、0.1、0.5、1、2、3 和 5）訓練出多個模型，並選擇在驗證集表現最好的模型，最佳的權重值大致與標籤數量呈反比，標籤數越多類別權重愈小，反之，標籤數越少類別權重愈大。

(2) 單獨的多標籤分類模型 (Standalone Multi-label Classifier)

可以視為知識蒸餾機制中單獨使用學生網路 (student net) 的作法。輸入為 300 維的 Word2Vec (Mikolov et al., 2013)，直接使用真實標籤值計算模型的預測誤差訓練模型。

(3) 知識蒸餾機制 (Knowledge Distillation)

我們提出的基於知識蒸餾機制的多標籤分類模型訓練方式，包含教師網路和學生網路 (teacher net + student net)。先使用真實標籤值訓練出教師網絡，再以教師網路的預測值作為輸出響應，接著訓練學生網絡時，使用教師產生的響應計算預測誤差，使學生網路學習教師網路的行為。

我們使用 micro-F1、marco-F1、weighted-F1 以及 subset accuracy 評估模型的效能表現。micro-F1 不區分類別計算整體的 F1 分數。marco-F1 計算各類別 F1 分數的平均值。weighted-F1 計算各類別 F1 分數後，依據各類別的數量進行加權平均。subset accuracy 是最嚴格的評估指標，需要所有類別都是對的才判定是對，評估完全正確預測的比例。

4.3 實驗結果

表 2 為多標籤分類模型實驗結果。基於二元相關轉換訓練出來的模型，透過調整不同的類別權重進行最佳化後，在 micro-F1、macro-F1 與 weighted-F1，皆優於相同模型架構的單獨多標籤模型，表示二元最佳化的作法能夠做為教師模型，用以改進多標籤分類模型的分類效能。但二元相關轉換法訓練出的模型，

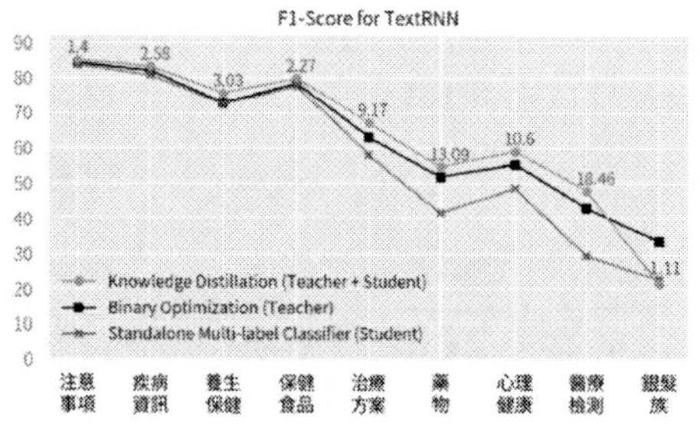

(a) TextRNN

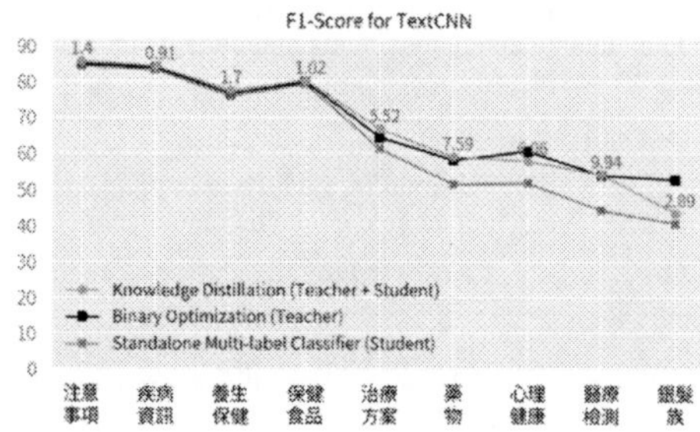

(b) TextCNN

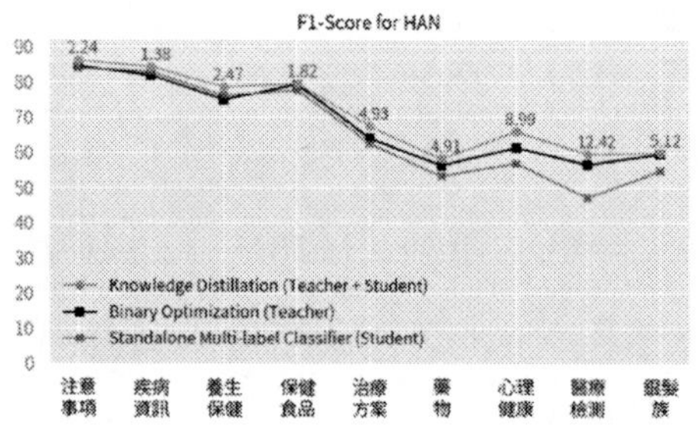

(c) HAN

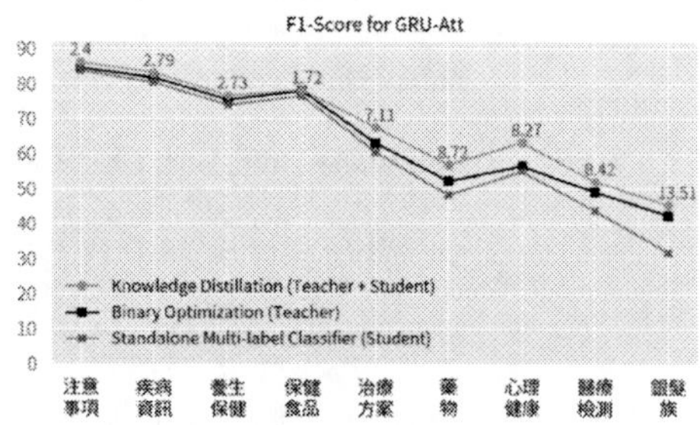

(d) GRU-Att

圖 4、 模型各類別標籤效能差異

沒辦法考慮類別間的相關性，導致要準確預測樣本的所有標籤較為困難，所以 subset accuracy 比多標籤模型低。

實驗結果顯示透過我們提出的知識蒸餾機制透訓練的多標籤模型，在不同模型架構下能夠顯著提升多標籤模型的性能 (p-value <0.01)，甚至與教師模型相比，因多標籤模型能夠在訓練的過程中獲取標籤間的相關性，相較於只有 0 或 1 的標籤值，機率值分佈擁有更多資訊，使得知識蒸餾的多標籤模型具有比二元最佳化的教師模型有更好的效能。

圖 4 為模型在不同訓練方法下，各類別標籤的 F1 (separated-F1)。我們可以看出二元相關轉換法訓練出的模型，因為每個分類器只需考慮單一類別，並且已透過不同類別權重進行最佳化，當訓練資料不平衡時，對效能的影響相對較小。

而多標籤分類模型在藥物、心理健康、醫療檢測、銀髮族等樣本數較少標籤，因為訓練資料不平衡造成分類效能明顯下降，但透過知識蒸餾訓練的多標籤模型，在這些長尾標籤相對於多樣本標籤能夠有更明顯的效能提升。

5 結論

我們提出基於知識蒸餾的多標籤分類模型訓練方法，將最佳化的二元相關轉換法作為教師網路，對多標籤分類模型進行響應式知識蒸餾，用以改善多標籤分類模型。實驗資料來自人工標記的 2,724 個多標籤中文健康照護文本，橫跨 9 個類別標籤，標籤數量是 8,731，平均每個樣本有 3.2 個標籤。實驗結果顯示使用知識蒸餾的訓練方法，在不同的深度學習模型，無論 micro-F1、macro-F1、weighted-F1 以及 subset accuracy 皆能有顯著的效能提升。

Acknowledgments

This work is partially supported by the National Science and Technology Council, Taiwan, under the grant MOST 111-2628-E-008-005-MY3.

References

Rahul Agrawal, Archit Gupta, Yashoteja Prabhu, and Manik Varma. 2013. Multi-label learning with millions of labels: recommending advertiser bid phrases for web pages. In *Proceedings of the 22nd International Conference on World Wide Web*, Association for Computing Machinery, pages 13–24. https://doi.org/10.1145/2488388.2488391

Siddhartha Banerjee, Cem Akkaya, Francisco Perez-Sorrosal, and Kostas Tsioutsiouliklis. 2019. Hierarchical transfer learning for multi-label text classification. In *Proceedings of the 57th Annual Meeting of the Association for Computational Linguistics.* Association for Computational Linguistics, pages 6295–6300. http://doi.org/10.18653/v1/P19-1633

Po-Han Chen, Yu-Xiang Zeng, and Lung-Hao Lee. 2021. Incorporating domain knowledge into language transformers for multi-Label classification of Chinese medical questions. In *Proceedings of the 33rd Conference on Computational Linguistics and Speech Processing.* Association for Computational Linguistics, pages 265–270.

Jianping Gou, Baosheng Yu, Stephen John Maybank, and Dacheng Tao. 2021. Knowledge distillation: a survey. *International Journal of Computer Vision*, 129:1789-1819. https://doi.org/10.1007/s11263-021-01453-z

Li Guo, Bo Jin, Ruiyun Yu, Cuili Yao, Chonglin Sun, and Degen Huang. 2016. Multi-label classification methods for green computing and application for mobile medical recommendations. *IEEE Access*, 4:3201-3209. https://doi.org/10.1109/ACCESS.2016.2578638

Geoffrey Hinton, Oriol Vinyals, and Jeff Dean. 2015. Distilling the knowledge in a neural network. arXiv preprint, arXiv:1503.02531 https://doi.org/10.48550/arXiv.1503.02531

Hao-Chuan Kao, Man-Chen Hung, Lung-Hao Lee, Yuen-Hsien Tseng. 2021. Multi-label classification of Chinese humor texts using hypergraph attention networks. In *Proceedings of the 33rd Conference on Computational Linguistics and Speech Processing.* Association for Computational Linguistics, pages 257–264.

Jingzhou Liu, Wei-Cheng Chang, Yuexin Wu, and Yiming Yang. 2017. Deep learning for extreme multi-label text classification. In *Proceedings of the 40th International ACM SIGIR Conference on Research and Development in Information Retrieval.* Association for Computing Machinery, pages 115-124 https://doi.org/10.1145/3077136.3080834

Pennington, Jeffrey, Richard Socher, and Christopher D. Manning. 2014. Glove: Global vectors for word representation. In *Proceedings of the 2014 Conference on Empirical Methods in Natural Language Processing*, pages 1532–1543. http://dx.doi.org/10.3115/v1/D14-1162

Pengfei Liu, Xipeng Qiu, and Xuanjing Huang. 2016. Recurrent neural network for text classification with multi-task learning. In *Proceedings of the 25th International Joint Conference on Artificial Intelligence.* pages 2873-2879. https://arxiv.org/abs/1605.05101

Batsergelen Myagmar, Jie Li, and Shigetomo Kimura. 2019. Cross-domain sentiment classification with bidirectional contextualized transformer language models. *IEEE Access*, 163219-163230. https://doi.org/10.1109/ACCESS.2019.2952360

Tomas Mikolov, Kai Chen, Greg Corrado, and Jeffrey Dean. 2013, Efficient estimation of word representations in Vector Space. *arXiv Preprint* arXiv:1301.3781 https://doi.org/10.48550/arXiv.1301.3781

Grigorios Tsoumakas, and Ioannis Katakis. 2007. Multi-label classification: an overview. *International Journal of Data Warehousing and Mining*, 3(3):1–13. https://doi.org/10.4018/jdwm.2007070101

Ran Wang, Xi'ao Su, Siyu Long, Xinyu Dai, Shujian Huang, and Jiajun Chen. 2021. Meta-LMTC: meta-learning for large-scale multi-label text classification. In *Proceedings of the 2021 Conference on Empirical Methods in Natural Language Processing.* Association for Computational Linguistics, pages 8633–8646. http://doi.org/10.18653/v1/2021.emnlp-main.679

Zichao Yang, Diyi Yang, Chris Dyer, Xiaodong He, Alex Smola, and Eduard Hovy. 2016. Hierarchical attention networks for document classification. In *Proceedings of the 2016 Conference of the North American Chapter of the Association for Computational Linguistics.* Association for Computational Linguistics, pages 1480–1489. http://doi.org/10.18653/v1/N16-1174

The 34th Conference on Computational Linguistics and Speech Processing (ROCLING 2022)
Taipei, Taiwan, November 21-22, 2022. The Association for Computational Linguistics and Chinese Language Processing

結合詞向量技術與分群演算法於信用卡商戶名稱辨識
Combining Word Vector Technique and Clustering Algorithm for Credit Card Merchant Detection

Fang-Ju Lee
Soochow University
Dept. of Data Science
rukolee@yahoo.com.tw

Ying-Chun Lo
Soochow University
Dept. of Data Science
ginny880530@gmail.com

Jheng-Long Wu
Soochow University
Dept. of Data Science
jlwu@gm.scu.edu.tw

摘要

透過客戶消費資料萃取相關之使用者行為，是蒐集客戶資訊的方式之一。現行文字探勘的領域中，大多以文本分類之相關研究為主，顯少有文本分群之研究主題。從非結構化之交易消費說明中，找尋字詞之間的關係，運用不同詞向量技術，突破分類需事先區分條件之限制，建立自動化辨識分析方法，提升分群之準確率。在本研究中將以銀行信用卡交易消費說明內容，進行 Jieba 中文斷詞並採用 Word2Vec 特徵值萃取，搭配基於密度分群法(DBSCAN)和階層分群法，交叉組合進行實驗。預測結果以 MUC、B³ 和 CEAF 之 F1 平均值 67.58%較為顯著。

Abstract

Extracting relevant user behaviors through customer's transaction description is one of the ways to collect customer information. In the current text mining field, most of the researches are mainly study text classification, and only few study text clusters. Find the relationship between letters and words in the unstructured transaction consumption description. Use Word Embedding and text mining technology to break through the limitation of classification conditions that need to be distinguished in advance, establish automatic identification and analysis methods, and improve the accuracy of grouping. In this study, use Jieba to segment Chinese words, were based on the content of credit card transaction description. Feature extractions of Word2Vec, combined with Density-Based Spatial Clustering of Applications with Noise (DBSCAN) and Hierarchical Agglomerative Clustering, cross-combination experiments. The prediction results of MUC, B³ and CEAF's F1 average of 67.58% are more significant

關鍵字：詞頻-逆向文件頻率、Word2Vec、BERT、餘弦相似度、分群演算法、密度分群法、K-平均演算法、階層分群法

Keywords: TF-IDF, Word2Vec, BERT, Cosine Similarity, Clustering Algorithms, DBSCAN, K-means, Hierarchical Clustering。

1 緒論

隨著科技的發展，台灣已漸漸踏入數位經濟時代，網際網路與電腦的結合，已開始應用在各項領域中，而其中又以金融業在應用上佔有先天之優勢，交易的數位化及電子化等等的商務模式，不僅改變人們的支付行為模式，也縮短了全球商家與消費者彼此間的距離。經由客戶支付行為模式的改變，可獲得更多客戶生活消費資訊，也能提供更優質的客戶服務以及與商戶合作的機會，例如：精準推播客戶喜好的商戶行銷活動、發掘新星商戶等。

本研究旨在運用自然語言處理 (Natural Language Processing, NLP) 、文字探勘及分群演算法等技術，有效的發展文本分群演算法增進於金融應用之發展，落實人工智慧技術於真實場景。本研究期望經由不同的處理技術和訓練模型之方法，從非結構化之交易消費說明中，找尋字詞之間的規則，發展出更為自動與廣泛的分析方法，其透過信用卡交易時，所顯示的商戶名稱，進而了解字詞間關係、語義和對命名實體的理解，並透過交

易的大量消費記錄，以獲得相似之實體商戶群體歸納，提升辨識效果和建立自動化命名實體歸納演算法。

我們將以探討詞向量技術應用於信用卡商戶名稱分群為主題，交易記錄限制於國內交易，並將交易分成 10 種類別，而其中為防範個資外洩之風險，排除了六類含有客戶個資之消費類別，例如，保險、3C 電信通訊、公共事業代繳等等。以小樣本資料進進行研究，尋求如何發展詞向量自動分群，並建立不同之模型並進行反覆驗證和評估，找出最佳模型以確認結果是否符合預期。

2 文獻回顧

隨著文字探勘的技術不斷在精進，機器跨越與人之間的語言障礙。近兩年來 BERT、ERNIE 等非監督式訓練之技術，在語言文字的判斷、語義的相似度、命名實體識別和情感的分析等 NLP 任務更有重大的突破。

2.1 命名實體識別

深度學習方法：隨著詞向量技術的發展，Mikolov 等 (2013) 提出 Continuous Bag-of-Words Model (CBOW) 與 Continuous Skip-gram Model (Skip-gram) 兩個模型結構，用於學習單詞的分佈式表示式，減少計算複雜度。而神經網絡的深度學習發展，始其更有效的處理 NLP 任務，如循環神經網絡 (Recurrent Neural Network) 擴展的 RNN-CRF、卷積神經網絡 (Convolutional Neural Network) 的 CNN-CRF。簡國峻與張嘉惠 (2019) 提出延伸記憶增強條件隨機場域於中文的命名實體擷取，利用門控卷積網路及雙向 GRU (Gated Recurrent Unit) 網路來增強記憶條件隨機場域，提升模型抓取長距離的文章資訊。藉由特徵探勘擷取命名實體的前後詞彙以及前綴後綴詞彙特徵 (Common Before、Common After、Entity Prefix、Entity Suffix , BAPS)，使模型可自動訓練的參數，自動調整詞向量及 BAPS 詞彙特徵，在社群資料中具穩定性和效能，高度依賴特徵設計，對於不同資料集是否有同樣效能值得再研究。而 BERT (Bidirectional Encoder Representations from Transformers) 是近年來較熱門的深度學習方法，許多研究指出 BERT 應用於自然語言上都有獲得不錯的成績。Gong 等 (2019) 將 CRF 層加到雙向 GRU 模型的隱藏層以限制每次的輸出，提高模型的識別性能 (BGRU-CRF model)，並將 Bert Embedding 和 Radical Embedding 串聯在一起做為輸入 Embedding 放入 BGRU-CRF 模型中。王子牛、姜猛、高建瓴與陳婭先(2019) 提出了基於 BERT 的神經網路方法進行命名實體辨識，結合 BERT 和 BiLSTM-CRF 模型，實驗結果均表示中文實體識別以無需添加任何特徵的方式，明顯提升了準確率、召回率和 F1 值。

2.2 字詞相似度

向量空間模型：李琳與李輝 (2018) 研究指出，已提出的非結構化文本相似度計算方法，主要包含基於詞袋 (Bag of Words, BOW) 模型、主題 (Topic) 模型、知識本體和詞向量等方法，然而這些模型方法仍有一些關鍵問題待解決。於是他們嘗試結合依存句法分析和詞嵌入方法，提出一種基於概念向量空間 (Concept Vector Space) 語義相似度的計算方法。曹錫 (2021) 使用 BERT、RoBERTa、ALBERT 三種預訓練語言模型，進行法律判決書案件情境相似檢索實驗，搭配餘弦相似度 (Cosine Similarity)、歐式距離 (Euclidean Distance) 和向量內積 (Inner Product) 三種演算法，以案由分群亂度 (Average Entropy of the Offence-charged Clustering, AEOC) 為指標評估，判斷檢索的優劣程度，其 AEOC 值愈小愈好，代表各分群內的類別蒐集愈收斂。

2.3 Bag-of-Word Model

TF-IDF (Term Frequency-Inverse Document Frequency) 是一種用於資訊檢索與文字探勘的傳統機器學習統計方法，用來評估一字詞對於一個檔案中的重要程度。王美淋(2020)提出結合擷取和萃取兩段式模型方式處理 NLP 任務，其實驗結果較 Transformer 良好。劉賢鈞 (2019) 以 Kaggle 的 Fake News 資料集進行預測假新聞之研究，使用 TF-IDF 找出文本的字詞特徵，並使用線性區別分析 (Linear Discriminant Analysis, LDA) 進行降維，搭配 Random Forests、XGBoost、Naïve Bayes 和羅吉斯迴歸四種分類進行比較，經實驗結果得知，以羅吉斯迴歸分類方法最佳，準確率高達 96.32%。TF-IDF 雖簡單、容易快速理解，但僅使用詞頻評估文章某一字詞的重要性，缺乏整體性；有時關鍵的字詞出現可能不多，無法表達字詞位置與上下文字的重要性。

2.4 分群模型評估

黃宇翔、王品鈞與方志強 (2017) 考量現今資料屬性為多樣式，為改善K-means演算法之處理效能，提出了將資料依數值、類別和順序三種屬性分別做 K-means，以取得較好之初始中心點後再進行組合找到質心。黃郁豪與張芳仁 (2017) 探討在網路資訊眾多的環境之下，如何讓閱讀者更容易獲取有興趣之相關文章，提升讀者點擊意願。研究以 Word2Vec 和 Doc2Vec 模型進行詞向量處理，並取每則新聞前 3%、5%、7%之 TF-IDF 權重較大為特徵關鍵字，與 Word2Vec 相乘轉換後產生新聞字詞向量，採用階層式聚合分群法將文章分群，以 Purity 和 Entropy 評估結果好壞。

3 研究方法

在本節中，我們將描述數據收集和清理、數據註釋、用於解決 NER 任務的模型和學習方法。

3.1 數據收集與清理

本研究以銀行 2020 年度信用卡交易消費為資料來源，銀行依據 VISA 與 MasterCard 國際組織所定義之行業代碼 (Merchant Category Code, MCC) 將資料區分為 15 大類，排除研究限制之含有客戶個人資料和國外消費，預計收集 10 萬筆國內十大消費類別，且不重複的刷卡消費交易記錄之樣本為本研究資料來源。為預防收集之消費類別筆數過少而無法抽樣取得全部消費類別之情形，單一消費類別之母體筆數占總筆數小於 2% 者全數收集，其他則依據母體筆數之比例抽樣收集。刷卡交易除了商戶名稱之外，多數含有分店資訊、使用的支付工具、分期期數或金額等訊息，以下將以各範例分別描述說明。

- 一般商戶
  同一商戶但在不同行銷通路或透過網購平台上架之賣家名稱內容，但商戶傳送交易的中文說明並無統一格式，如：「富邦 momo-EC」、「愛貝金流－momore25」
- 商戶且有分店或分期
  這類型資料常因交易消費說明過長，導致資料傳送時會將資料截斷，造成分店資訊不完整，如：「三灃－MoMo Paradise 復興牧」
- 可使用支付工具之商戶
  屬於非現金交易之掃碼行動支付或銀行與商戶自行開發之行動支付 APP 軟體，如：「全聯門市－PX Pay」、「街口電支－２派克脆皮雞排」。
- 提供自動加值功能之商戶或分店
  現行提供悠遊卡、一卡通 (iPASS) 和愛金卡 (i-cash) 三家公司之自動加值功能，如：「悠遊卡自動加值－比漾廣場摩斯漢堡」。

3.2 分群模型評估資料處理

為了讓資料在格式上能達成一致標準，處理內容含有分期資料的雜訊，移除不必要的資訊，以提升資料品質。在進行特徵植萃取前，本組使用 Jieba 與 CKIP Transformers 先行斷詞。

Transformer 多用於處理連續資料之任務，與 RNN 不相同的是，Transformer 不需要依照順序處理資料，因此減少了訓練時間，在近年的諸多 NER 任務中，Transformer 已取代了舊的遞歸神經網絡模型，迅速成為 NLP 問題的首選模型。

3.3 特徵值萃取

本研究以斷詞工具辨識內容中含有特定意義之名稱所產生的資料集，採用 TF (Term Frequency)、TF-IDF 以及 Word2Vec 三種方法進行文字轉特徵，萃取文本中關注的成分，並將這些詞句轉換為詞向量，以及 BERT 中文預訓練模型技術，計算其相似度供分群模型建立使用。

- TF、TF-IDF

依斷詞後的字詞，TF 採用計算字詞在消費說明內容中出現的次數、TF-IDF 以評估字詞在消費說明的重要程度產生關鍵詞，分別建立 TF 和 TF-IDF 不重複的字詞向量，分別產生特徵矩陣，供後續計算每筆記錄之間的相似度。

- Word2Vec

具有考慮上下文之特性，將字詞投射在向量空間，其訓練模型有 CBOW 和 Skip-gram 兩種，本研究採用 CBOW 模型架構，給定一個商戶名稱的前後鄰近的交易消費說明字詞，預測商戶名稱出現的機率。

- BERT

本研究採用 Cui 等人(2021) 提出的 Chinese-MacBERT-Base 預訓練模型，輸入資料集之每一筆商戶交易明細，訓練出每一筆 768 維詞向量的記錄，計算兩筆記錄之間的相似度，產生相似矩陣。

3.4 資料訓練與模型建置

本研究以四種特徵值方法分別計算消費說明資料彼此之間的相似度，依相似矩陣轉換成距離特徵資訊，作為密度聚類演算法 (DBSCAN)、DBSCAN + K-means 以及 DBSCAN + 階層分群法三種演算法之分群基準，將資料分成數個群集，目標找到群內差異小、群外差異大之群集，並配合特徵值萃取之技術，進行訓練與建立模型。

3.5 評估指標

本研究以共指消解作為評估方式，共指消解，是將文字中指向同一 Entity 的詞語劃分到同一個等價集的過程，其中被劃分的詞語稱為表述或指稱語（Mention），形成的等價集稱為共指鏈（Coreference Chain）。在共指消解中，指稱語包含：普通名詞、專有名詞和代詞，因此可以將顯性代詞消解看作是共指消解針對代詞的子問題。研究使用任務中最常使用之評估指標包括 MUC、B^3、CEAF 作為評估方式。

- MUC

MUC score 計算將預測的共指鏈映射到標註的共指鏈所需插入或者刪除的最少的鏈接數量，但 MUC 的缺點為無法衡量系統預測單例實體的性能。

- B^3

B^3 算法可以克服 MUC 的缺點，該算法主要是對每個 mention 分別計算 precision 和 recall，然後以所有 mention 的平均值作為最終的指標。

- CEAF

CEAF 是一種基於實體相似度的評估算法，相比於前兩個評估指標的算法更加直觀的表現評估共指簇劃分的好壞，就是對應地比較每個共指簇劃分。

3.6 相關參數設定

資料點之半徑距離會影響分群個數，而分群個數會直接影響結果。在 K-means 和 AGC 需事先設定群組個數，其分群數則由 DBSCAN 分群演算法而來。DBSCAN 依據不同之半徑距離ε、在ε之內最少有 1 個資料個數 (MinPts = 1)，計算可歸納為 n 個分群數。本研究以驗證集資料進行調參，並經由觀察不同特徵值方法之分群數遞減變化。下表為本研究所設定各特徵值萃取方法之參數。

特徵值方法	參數設定
TF	單詞在消費說明內容中出現的次數。
TF-IDF	重新計算 IDF 權重，若文檔不含關鍵詞時，無需對 IDF 做平滑 (不考慮分母為 0 的情形)。
Word2Vec	採用 CBOW 的方式，根據目標字的左右 5 個字進行預測，將訓練出對映到 300 維度空間的詞向量，迭代次數設定為 50 次。
BERT	Model 和 Tokenizer 採用 Chinese-Macbert-Base 預訓練模型，訓練出每一筆消費記錄之 768 維度空間的詞向量。

表 1. 特徵值萃取參數設定

分群演算法	參數設定
DBSCAN	半徑距離ε之內最少有 1 個資料個數。ε之範圍為 TF = 1.1~2.9，每次調整 0.2、TF-IDF = 1.1~2.9，每次調整 0.2、Word2Vec = 1.1~3.8，每次調整 0.3、BERT = 1.1~2.9，每次調整 0.2。距離計算方式使用預設值 Euclidean。依據上述參數設定，獲得 n 個 clusters

分群演算法	參數設定
DBKM	依據 DBSCAN 所以獲得 n 個分群數為參數，距離計算方式採用預設值 Euclidean，其隨機種子為 0
DBAGC	採用 CBOW 的方式，根據目標字的左右 5 個字進行預測，將訓練出對映到 300 維度空間的詞向量，迭代次數設定為 50 次。
BERT	依據 DBSCAN 所以獲得 n 個 clusters 為參數，資料點之間的距離採用 Euclidean 計算方式，群與群之間的距離則使用 Ward 方法。

表 2. 分群演算法參數設定

4 實驗結果

4.1 特徵值方法與演算法分析

依據斷詞工具加三種特徵值方法，以及 BERT 萃取特徵值結果，經由不同半徑距離所獲得之分群數，再依據表 2 分群演算法的參數設定，分別帶入 DBSCAN、DBKM、DBAGC 三種演算法，各自計算評估指標再取四種演算法 F1 平均值之最大值，作為 DBSCAN 半徑距離最佳參數設定，實驗結果分析如下圖 1 至圖 4。

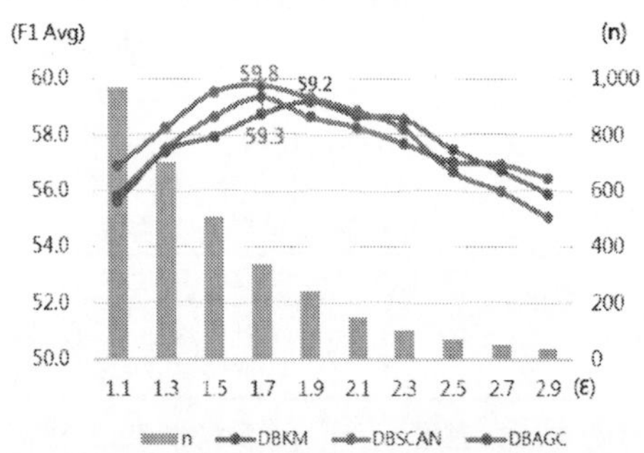

圖 1. TF 特徵值方法之評估結果

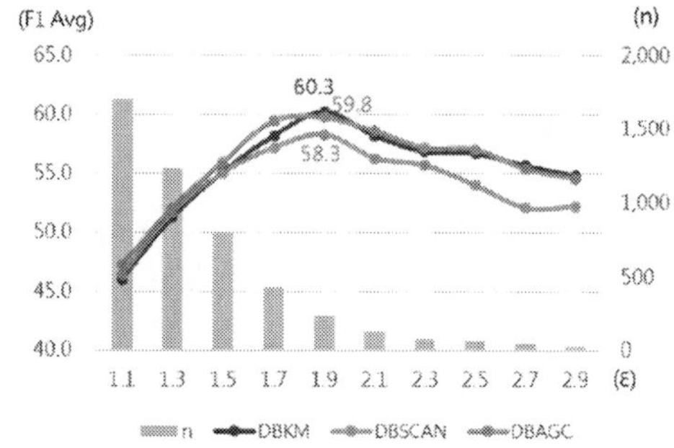

圖 2. TF-IDF 特徵值方法之評估結果

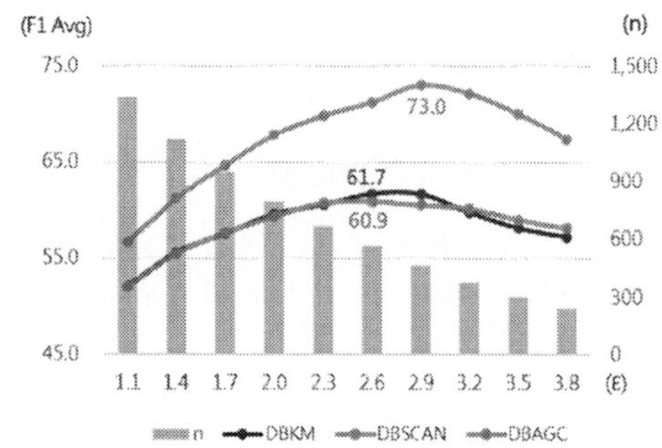

圖 3. Word2Vec 特徵值方法之評估結果

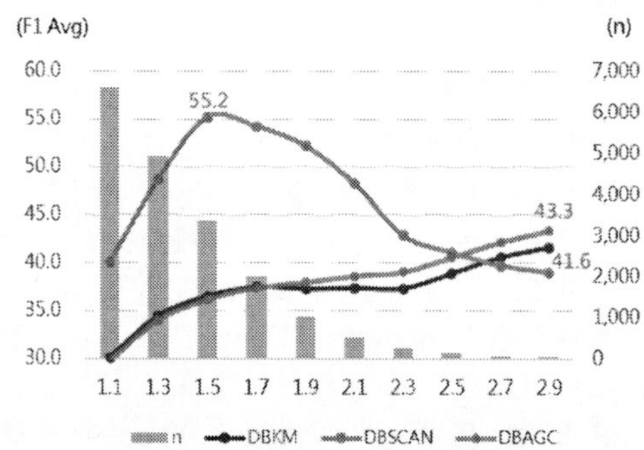

圖 4. BERT 特徵值方法之評估結果

TF 在半徑距離 1.9 時，DBKM 之 F1 為 59.2 最高；DBSCAN 和 DBAGC 在半徑距離 1.7 時均為最高，其 F1 分別為 59.8 和 59.3。三種演算法之 F1 平均值以 59.3 為最高，故 TF 特徵值方法最佳半徑距離設定為 1.7。

TF-ID 在半徑距離 1.9 時，DBKM、DBSCAN 和 DBAGC 之 F1 均最高，分別為 60.3、58.3 和 59.8。三種演算法之 F1 平均值為 59.4。可以發現 DBSCAN 之 F1 平均值計算結果均較低，且當分群數愈少時，F1 平均值比 DBKM 和 DBAGC 明顯較低，TF-IDF 較不適合 DBSCAN。

Word2Vec 在半徑距離 2.6 時，DBKM 之 F1 為 61.7 最高；DBSCAN 在半徑距離 2.9 時最高，其 F1 為 73.0； DBAGC 在半徑距離 2.6 時最高，其 F1 為 60.9。雖 DBKM 和 DBAGC 二種演算法之 F1 平均值計算結果相似，無明顯之差異，但三種演算法之 F1 平均值以 65.1 為最高，故 Word2Vec 最佳半徑距離設定為 2.9。

BERT 模型在半徑距離 2.9 時，DBKM 之 F1 為 41.6 最高；DBSCAN 在半徑距離 1.5 時最高，其 F1 為 55.2； DBAGC 在半徑距離 2.9 時最高，其 F1 為 43.3。DBSCAN 演算法對群數之多寡差異較為明顯，DBKM和DBAGC之計算結果較為相似，且可以發現群組數愈少其評估指標F1 平均值愈高。三種演算法之F1 平均值以 43.0 為最高，故 BERT 最佳半徑距離設定為 1.7。

BERT 模型訓練以學習完整句子為主，非以簡短之交易特店說明，雖然訓練集實驗結果以 DBSCAN 評估指標 F1 平均值 55.2%最高，DBKM 和 DBAGC 評估指標 F1 平均值均不超過 45%，整體而言此特徵值方法較不理想。

4.2 測試集結果

測試集正確商戶分群數為 264 分群數，其中單一商戶之分群數有 157 個，占正確總分群數 59.5%。由表 3 評估 F1 結果得知。

- 三種演算法的評估指標 F1 平均值與驗證集之實驗結果接近，以 Word2Vec 特徵值方法搭配 DBSCAN 演算法之 F1 平均值 67.58 最高。
- BERT 萃取特徵值方式受不同資料集筆數之多寡影響，依訓練集實驗結果之半徑距離進行測試，其分群數僅有 5 群，F1 平均值 36.93 最低。
- MUC 在不同特徵值方法搭配不同演算法之差異較不顯著，主要因 Precision 和 Recall 計算時，單一商戶之個數減 1 後相抵消失，評估指標無法計算含單一商戶之準確率。
- Word2Vec + DBSCAN 之分群數最多，其評估指標 B3 因排除單一商戶之分群，故 Precision 較 DBKM、DBAGC 偏低；評估指標 CEAF 經由調整後，包含單一商戶分群數，其 F1 較 TF-IDF + DBKM 和 TF + DBAGC 分別高出 30%和 20%；其中又以 TF-IDF+DBKM 之 Recall 為 10.56%最

演算法	DBKM				DBAGC				DBSCAN				DBSCAN			
特徵值	TF-IDF				TF				Word2Vec				BERT			
半徑距離	1.9				1.7				2.9				1.7			
總分群數	60				112				145				5			
單一商戶	0				4				93				2			
多個商戶	60				108				52				3			
評估指標	MUC	B^3	CEAF	平均	MUC	B^3	CEAF	平均	MUC	B^3	CEAF	平均	MUC	B^3	CEAF	平均
Precision	85.66	71.89	46.49	68.01	85.52	80.34	45.53	70.47	89.77	48.37	66.32	68.15	86.24	8.65	61.69	52.19
Recall	96.38	61.05	10.56	56.00	93.50	55.75	19.32	56.19	96.32	89.51	36.42	74.08	99.94	99.77	1.17	66.96
F1	90.70	66.03	17.22	57.98	89.33	65.83	27.13	60.76	92.93	62.80	47.02	67.58	92.58	15.93	2.29	36.93

表 3. 各模型於測試集之辨識效果評估結果

低，單一商戶分群數之多寡對 CEAF 影響最為明顯，是影響實驗結果主要原因。

- Word2Vec + DBSCAN 之 F1 平均值較 TF + DBAGC 高出 6.82%，亦較 TF-IDF + DBKM 高出 9.6%，其特徵值萃取之方法對評估結果具有影響力。

綜合整體研究測試結果得知，中文採用 Jieba 斷詞並以 Word2Vec 之特徵值萃取方式，搭配 DBSCAN 分群演算法之評估指標 F1 平均值 67.58%表現最佳；BERT 特徵值方法受限於模型訓練之方法不同，其測試結果表現最差。

5 結論

整體研究結果發現，Jieba 斷詞所訓練之 Word2Vec 模型，以 DBSCAN 演算法經由半徑距離設定，較容易獲得單一商戶之分群數，對於商戶名稱分群之效果最好，有助於自動分群之應用。依據 CEAF 評估指標可以發現，測試集正確商戶分群數為 264 個，DBSCAN 演算法預測之商戶分群數為 145 個，Recall 分數為 36.42；DBAGC 演算法預測之商戶分群數為 112 個，Recall 分數為 19.32；DBKM 演算法預測之商戶分群數為 60 個，Recall 分數為 10.56；正確分群數與預測分群數之差異多少，對於 CEAF 評估指標之 Recall 影響最為明顯。在 B^3 評估指標中，測試集正確商戶分群數中，多個商戶之分群數為 107 個；DBSCAN 演算法預測多個商戶之分群數為 52 個，Precision 分數為 48.37；DBKM 演算法預測多個商戶之分群數 60 個，Precision 分數為 71.89；DBAGC 演算法預測多個商戶之分群數為 108 個，Precision 分數為 80.34。多個商戶之分群數多寡，對於 B3 評估指標具有影響。若單一商戶(非連鎖) 較多時，其評估指標可能失去之可性度。

References

Bagga, A., & Baldwin, B. (1998). Algorithms for Scoring Coreference Chains. In The first international conference on language resources and evaluation workshop on linguistics coreference (Vol. 1, pp. 563-566).

Cui, Y., Che, W., Liu, T., Qin, B., & Yang, Z. (2021). Pre-training with whole word masking for chinese bert. IEEE/ACM Transactions on Audio, Speech, and Language Processing, 29, 3504-3514. doi:10.1109/TASLP.2021.3124365

Gong, C., Tang, J., Zhou, S., Hao, Z., & Wang, J. (2019). Chinese named entity recognition with bert. DEStech Transactions on Computer Science and Engineering. doi:10.12783/dtcse/cisnrc2019/33299

Lafferty, J., McCallum, A., & Pereira, F. C. N. (2001). Conditional random fields: Probabilistic models for segmenting and labeling sequence data.

Lee, K., He, L., & Zettlemoyer, L. (2018). Higher-order coreference resolution with coarse-to-fine inference. Proceedings of the 2018 conference of the North American chapter of the association for computational linguistics: human language technologies, volume 2 (short papers), 687–692. doi:10.18653/v1/N18-2108

Liu, Y. (2019). Fine-tune BERT for extractive summarization. arXiv:1903.10318.

Luo, X. (2005). On coreference resolution performance metrics. In Proceedings of Human Language Technology Conference and Conference on Empirical Methods in Natural Language Processing (pp. 25-32)

Mikolov, T., Chen, K., Corrado, G., & Dean, J. (2013). Efficient estimation of word representations in vector space. arXiv preprint arXiv:1301.3781.

Sun, Y., Wang, S., Li, Y., Feng, S., Tian, H., Wu, H., & Wang, H. (2020). ERNIE 2.0: A continual pre-training framework for language understanding. In Proceedings of the AAAI Conference on Artificial Intelligence (Vol. 34, No. 05, pp. 8968-8975). doi:10.1609/aaai.v34i05.6428

Vilain, M., Burger, J., Aberdeen, J., Connolly, D., & Hirschman, L. (1995). A model-theoretic coreference scoring scheme. In Sixth Message Understanding Conference (MUC-6): Proceedings of a Conference Held in Columbia, Maryland, November 6-8, 1995.

Xiao, X., Ye, S.-Z., Yu, L.-C., & Lai, K. R. (2017). 應用詞向量於語言樣式探勘之研究 (Mining Language Patterns Using Word Embeddings) [In Chinese]. In Proceedings of the 29th Conference on Computational Linguistics and Speech Processing (ROCLING 2017) (pp. 230-243)

Zhang, Z., Han, X., Liu, Z., Jiang, X., Sun, M., & Liu, Q. (2019). ERNIE: Enhanced language representation with informative entities. arXiv preprint arXiv:1905.07129.

王子牛, 姜猛, 高建瓴, & 陈娅先 (2019)。基于 BERT 的中文命名实体识别方法。计算机科学, 46(S2), 138-142。

王美淋 (2020)。結合擷取式與萃取式兩段式模型以增進摘要效能之研究。

车万翔, 刘挺, 秦兵, & 李生 (2004)。基于改进编辑距离的中文相似句子检索。高技术通讯, 14(7), 15–19。

吳政育, 陳冠宇 (2019)。EBSUM：基於 BERT 的強健性抽取式摘要法. 中文計算語言學期刊, 24(2), 19–35。

张占英, & 王中立. (2003)。中文文本中公司名简称的识别。许昌学院学报, 22(2), 99-101

李琳, & 李辉 (2018)。一种基于概念向量空间的文本相似度计算方法。数据分析与知识发现, 5。doi:10.11925/infotech.2096-3467.2018.0007

施瑞朗 (2018)。基于社交平台数据的文本分类算法研究。电子科技, 31(10), 69-70。doi:10. 16180 /j. cnki. issn1007 — 7820. 2018. 10. 016

胡若云, 孙钢, 丁麒, 沈然, & 谷泓杰 (2021)。基于雙向傳播框架的客服對話文本挖掘算法。沈阳工业大学学报。

郭家清, 蔡東風, 王智超, & 劉浩公 (2007)。一種基于條件隨機場的人名識別方法. Journal of Communication and Computer, 4(2), 22–25。

黃宇翔, 王品鈞, & 方志強 (2017)。混合型資料集的 K-means 分群演算法。電子商務學報, 19(1), 1–28。doi:10.6188/JEB.2017.19(1).01

黃郁豪, & 張芳仁 (2017)。新聞分群方法之比較研究及應用 (Doctoral dissertation)。

簡國峻, 張嘉惠 (2019)。應用記憶增強條件隨機場域與之深度學習及自動化詞彙特徵於中文命名實體辨識之研究。中文計算語言學期刊, 24(1), 1–14.

The 34th Conference on Computational Linguistics and Speech Processing (ROCLING 2022)
Taipei, Taiwan, November 21-22, 2022. The Association for Computational Linguistics and Chinese Language Processing

臺灣口音中英雙語之多語者影音合成系統
Taiwanese-Accented Mandarin and English Multi-Speaker Talking-Face Synthesis System

Chia-Hsuan Lin, Jian-Peng Liao, Cho-Chun Hsieh
Kai-Chun Liao and Chun-Hsin Wu
Department of Computer Science and Information Engineering
National University of Kaohsiung, Taiwan
{a1085512, a1085508, a1085540, a1085520}@mail.nuk.edu.tw
wuch@nuk.edu.tw

摘要

本論文提出一個多語者影音合成系統，結合語音複製與嘴型同步技術，透過取得任意語者短暫的説話語音及影像片段，以零樣本之遷移學習，來實現可即時翻譯的文字轉人物説話影像。除此之外，我們利用開源語料集訓練了多個臺灣口音的模型，同時也提出使用注音作爲合成器之文字嵌入的方式，來提升系統合成中英交雜語句的能力。透過此系統，使用者便可創造出豐富的應用，且此技術之研究與應用，在影音合成領域具有相當的新穎性。

Abstract

This paper proposes a multi-speaker talking-face synthesis system. The system incorporates voice cloning and lip-syncing technology to achieve text-to-talking-face generation by acquiring audio and video clips of any speaker and using zero-shot transfer learning. In addition, we used open-source corpora to train several Taiwanese-accented models and proposed using Mandarin Phonetic Symbols (Bopomofo) as the character embedding of the synthesizer to improve the system's ability to synthesize Chinese-English code-switched sentences. Through our system, users can create rich applications. Also, the research on this technology is novel in the audiovisual speech synthesis field.

關鍵字：多語者語音合成、語者驗證、語音複製、語碼轉換、嘴型同步、人物説話影像

Keywords: Multi-Speaker TTS, Speaker Verification, Voice Cloning, Code-Switching, Lip-Syncing, Talking-Face Generation

1 緒論

隨著人工智慧技術的蓬勃發展，大量人機互動相關的應用如雨後春筍般出現。而文字轉語音技術便扮演了一個不可或缺的角色，相關的研究也成了熱門的議題。現今，普通的單語者語音合成技術已經非常成熟了，如 Google、Microsoft 與 AWS 等皆有提供相關的應用程式介面（Application Programming Interface，API）服務可供使用。有了這樣的基礎後，眾多研究便希望可以將其延伸，發展出多語者語音合成系統。

爲了要實現多語者語音合成，並能應用在沒有見過的目標語者上，亦即達到語音複製（Voice Cloning）的效果，可透過引入語者驗證（Speaker Verification）機制到文字轉語音系統中的方式，也就是取一小段目標語者的聲音，再利用遷移學習來合成與目標語者相似的語音。該方法同時解決了訓練單語者語音合成模型，需要同一名語者大量語音資料的困難。然而目前大多數的研究都僅限在英文等外語，缺乏有效且實用的中文內容，同時臺灣口音的中文語音研究更是稀少。

有鑑於此，我們透過訓練影響口音最主要的合成器模型，並實驗了多組語料集，其中包含一個全臺灣口音中文語音的公開語料集 Common Voice Corpus[1]，藉此提出了一個臺灣口音的零樣本多語者語音合成系統（見圖 1），只需要參考短暫的目標人聲，便可複製目標語者之聲音，以產生任意內容的語音。我們也嘗試以注音來建立合成器中的字元嵌入（Character Embedding），並進行中英混雜語句合成的開發，有了語音複製的技術後，我們還可以將電腦生成的語音，利用嘴型同步（Lip-Syncing）的方式來合成出人物説話影像。

整合語音複製文字轉語音（Text-to-Speech，TTS）與嘴型同步，我們便可以建立一個文字轉人物説話影像合成系統，透過輸入目標文字、目標語者之語音與人臉（圖片或影片），即可產生目標語者在説目標文字的影像。我們亦加入了語音辨識和語言翻譯模組，可以辨識語者説話的原始內容，再進行中英雙向翻譯，使目標語者説出不同語言。透過該系統，能創

[1]https://commonvoice.mozilla.org

The 34th Conference on Computational Linguistics and Speech Processing (ROCLING 2022)
Taipei, Taiwan, November 21-22, 2022. The Association for Computational Linguistics and Chinese Language Processing

圖 1. SemiTrue 系統介面

造出豐富的應用，如多國語言電影的配音工作、演講錄音生成講者跨語影像等，而此技術的應用在臺灣可說是前所未見的。

本文之架構分成第 1 章簡述研究之內容，第 2 章介紹該領域的相關工作，第 3 章說明系統設計，第 4 章設置實驗來驗證成果，最後第 5 章爲本研究之結論。

2 相關工作

語音合成可以從文字來產生自然且可以理解的語音內容，而若要測量語音合成品質，主要有兩個重要的依據：可理解性及自然度。在語音合成技術發展的歷史中，經歷了許多的改進與演變，目前最爲熱門的技術，是基於神經網路的端到端語音合成 (Wang et al., 2017; Shen et al., 2018)，能在有限資料的背景下，合成出逼真的語音 (Ning et al., 2019; Tan et al., 2021)。在此基礎上，許多關於多語者語音合成的想法被提出，包括建立語者編碼，並訓練多個語者、利用語者驗證 (Jia et al., 2018; Lőrincz et al., 2021; Neekhara et al., 2021)，來實現語音複製，或者透過語音轉換 (Zhang et al., 2019; Casanova et al., 2022) 來改變語者的聲音。而隨者全球化發展，很多人會同時使用多種語言，如中英夾雜的語句，這類可支援語碼轉換（Code-Switching）的語音合成系統 (Hung et al., 2019; Zhou et al., 2020)，也成了熱門的研究重點。

在中文語音合成領域，也有不少的研究出現 (Cheng and Chen, 2019; Hung et al., 2019; Wang and Chen, 2020; Wang and Huang, 2021)，其中 Wang and Huang, 2021 在改進 Tacotron 架構的同時，提供了有關語者驗證和語音轉換，來實現語音複製的實作。 Wang and Chen, 2020 針對臺灣口音的中文語音合成進行了研究，但未支援中英混雜語句的合成。

雖然中文語音合成的研究日漸增多，但卻鮮少有研究將文字轉語音合成與人物說話影像生成的領域結合，即便是外國有類似之研究 (Song et al., 2022)，也沒有包含語音複製的功能，我們的研究涉及了在語音領域的多項研究重點，包含臺灣口音、中文語音合成、語音複製以及語碼轉換等，而配合人物說話影像生成領域中嘴形同步技術，而提出的文字轉人物說話影像合成系統，實屬相當創新的概念，值得進一步研究發展。

3 系統設計

本研究提出了一個文字轉人物說話影像合成系統，並將其命名爲 SemiTrue。在本系統中，使用者可以選擇設定輸入語言、輸出語言、目標文字、3～8 秒的目標語音以及目標人臉，其中目標人臉允許是圖片，或是長度大於合成音訊的影片。若是選擇輸入圖片，在最終所呈現的人物說話影像，則大部分會是靜態的，僅有嘴部區域會隨音訊內容而產生變化。另外，語音、圖片與影像皆有支援多種常見的格式，但在音訊進入系統後會被轉成 WAV 格式，而圖片或影像則會被自動縮放爲適當的大小，以利後續的合成工作。除了透過使用者上傳自定義的目標語音與目標人臉外，系統中已有事先載入好預設的語音與人臉，使用者僅需要輸入任意文字，就能合成出人物說話影像。

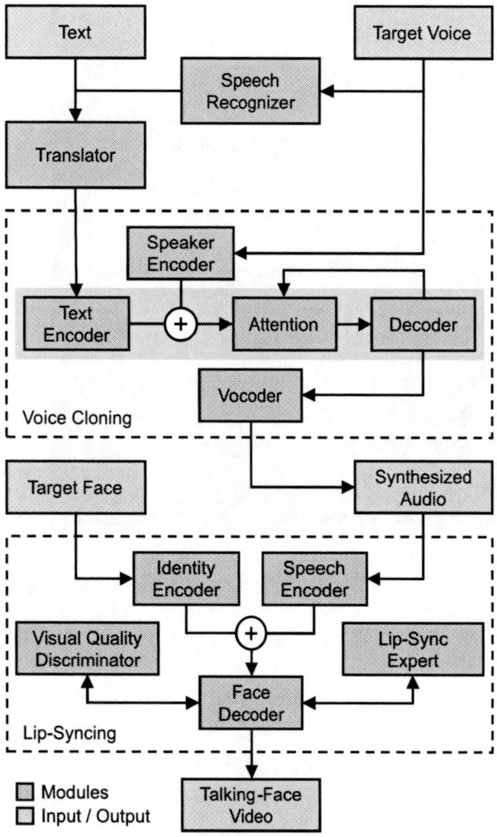

圖 2. SemiTrue 系統架構

SemiTrue 的整體架構，大致可以區分成以下四個模組：語音辨識、翻譯、語音複製以及嘴型同步。SemiTrue 整合了多個開源專案，並利用 FastAPI[2] 實作成網頁 API 服務，供使用者以網路請求的方式，來進行語音和影像的合成。同時，我們也建置了網頁前端，以圖形使用者介面來展現系統的功能。

SemiTrue 的運作流程如圖 2 所示，先將目標文字與目標音訊，依照輸出語言的不同，輸入語音複製模組中對應語言的複製器，來產生合成音訊，再將合成音訊與目標人臉之圖像或影像輸入嘴型同步模組 (見圖 3)，最終得到一段人物說話影像。在系統處理的過程中，根據不同使用者的需求，輸入之語音可以進行語音辨識，轉成文字內容，再進行文字翻譯後，才放入語音複製模組。如此一來就可以使目標人物，以其聲音說出不同語言的翻譯內容。

在後面的幾個小節中，我們將針對 SemiTrue 的四個模組，進行更詳細的說明。

[2]https://fastapi.tiangolo.com/

3.1 語音辨識模組

核心的文字轉人物說話影像功能，主要是透過使用者手動輸入目標文字，來作爲合成語音的文字來源。但在部分情境中，如僅有會議錄音，而無會議逐字稿的情況下，要合成出講者的語音及影像，甚至是進行語言的轉換，就會顯得較爲麻煩。有鑑於此，SemiTrue 另外加入了語音辨識模組，並利用了 Google 雲端平台的 Speech-to-Text API[3]，故在語音辨識穩定度與準確度上，能有一定程度的品質。

3.2 翻譯模組

SemiTrue 還可對使用者輸入的內容進行翻譯。舉例來說，使用者可將一段英文演講者的原始音訊輸入系統中，並經由語音辨識模組辨識其說話內容成英語原文，再透過翻譯模組將英文語句翻譯成中文語句，最後才進入到語音複製模組進行後續的複製工作。該模組的實作則使用了 Google Translate API[4] 進行翻譯。

3.3 語音複製模組

SemiTrue 語音複製模組的實作，大部分是基於 Jemine, 2019 的 Real-Time Voice Cloning[5] (RTVC) 與其在中文的版本 MockingBird[6] 修改而來的。RTVC 的設計是源自於一個零樣本語音複製框架 (Jia et al., 2018)，其架構大致由一個三階段管線構成，分別爲語者編碼器 (Speaker Encoder)、合成器 (Synthesizer) 與聲碼器 (Vocoder)，下文將分別介紹這三個階段的設計與我們改進的地方。

3.3.1 語者編碼器

爲了要實現語音複製，系統需要分離出不同語者的聲音特徵，合成器才可依此特徵產生出不同音色的人聲，這樣的方式稱作語者驗證。而要區分不同語者聲音的特徵，可以透過一個向量來表示，因此語者編碼器便負責從目標語音中抽取其特徵，包括音色、聲調、字詞發音，來形成語者嵌入向量，供後面的合成器使用。

RTVC 使用 GE2E (Wan et al., 2018) 方法來實現語者驗證，該模型將聲音轉換後的對數梅爾頻譜資訊，映射到一個固定的嵌入向量，以此來區分語者。一開始，目標語音被轉換成 40-Channel 的對數梅爾頻譜資訊，透過特徵萃取得到特徵向量，再經過 3 層 LSTM 組成之 768 個單元網路後，輸出 256 維的向量，再套用 L2 正規化，才能取得語者嵌入向量。

[3]https://cloud.google.com/speech-to-text
[4]https://cloud.google.com/translate
[5]https://github.com/CorentinJ/Real-Time-Voice-Cloning
[6]https://github.com/babysor/MockingBird

The 34th Conference on Computational Linguistics and Speech Processing (ROCLING 2022)
Taipei, Taiwan, November 21-22, 2022. The Association for Computational Linguistics and Chinese Language Processing

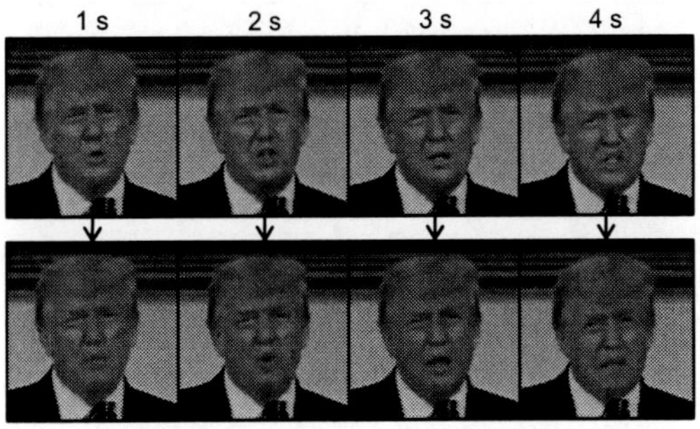

圖 3. 原始影像與嘴型同步後影像之比較

Method	Character Embedding
Pinyin	mei3 li4 de5 tai2 wan1
Bopomofo	ㄇㄟˇ ㄌㄧˋ ㄉㄜ˙ ㄊㄞˊ ㄨㄢ

表 1. 「美麗的臺灣」的字元嵌入

Method	Character Embedding
Pinyin	Hello，shi4 jie4 ！
Bopomofo	Hello，ㄕˋ ㄐㄧㄝˋ ！

表 2. 「Hello，世界 !」的字元嵌入

3.3.2 合成器

合成器部分採用了 Tacotron 2 (Shen et al., 2018) 的架構，其基本上是由文字編碼器、注意力層與解碼器所組成。文字編碼器輸入部分，可以選擇使用語音的文字符號（Grapheme），或者聲音符號（Phoneme）的串列，並將結果與目標語者的語者嵌入向量串接，使嵌入的內容得以傳給注意力層與解碼器，最後產生合成語音的梅爾頻譜資訊。該架構可以使模型將輸入文字映射到每個字音上，也可加快模型收斂的速度，並從訓練資料中學習生僻字詞與專有名詞的發音。

SemiTrue 在合成英文語句時，使用 RTVC 的設計，以文字符號序列輸入文字編碼器，該序列會映射到 26 個英文字母及常用標點符號。合成中文語句時，原本 MockingBird 採用了漢語拼音的聲音符號輸入方式，拼音由英文字母組合成發音，聲調則以數字表示，字與字之間以空白分隔，但在本研究的 SemiTrue 系統中，提出改以注音作爲聲音符號輸入，其中包含了 37 個注音、4 種聲調（一聲沒有標記）與標點符號。主要是因爲原 MockingBird 中的字元嵌入採用拼音，而拼音的聲音符號會與英文的文字符號重疊，使其不能應用於中英混雜的語句。基於此問題，我們設計了一個中英混雜的版本，輸入的映射序列含有 37 個注音符號、26 個英文字母、阿拉伯數字 0～9 及常用標點符號。在表 1 與表 2 中顯示了輸入的文字被轉爲字元嵌入符號的範例。

爲了抑制背景雜訊與強化複製人聲的韻律及音色，又加入了全域風格標籤（Global Style Token）(Wang et al., 2018)。原本在 TTS 系統中，若要學習語者的語調及風格，就必須提供上下文的風格關係，即便如此也難以評估是否爲正確的聲音風格，而全域風格標籤在訓練時，不需要任何實際的標籤，而是讓內部架構自行決定風格的樣式。也正是因爲沒有固定的標籤，可以讓系統實現多樣化的風格，且更可適應於長句子的合成上。

3.3.3 聲碼器

從前面的合成器，只能得到語音的梅爾頻譜資訊，並不是一般可以直接聆聽的語音文件，因此聲碼器主要的工作便是將梅爾頻譜資訊轉換成聲音波型，也就可以產生普通 WAV 格式的語音檔案。現今聲碼器的發展相當多元，有很多不同的實作，而每個方法都有其優缺點，因此 SemiTrue 加入了三種基於神經網路的聲碼器：WaveRNN (Kalchbrenner et al., 2018)、HiFi-GAN (Kong et al., 2020)、Fre-GAN (Kim et al., 2021) 以及一個基於演算法的聲碼器：Griffin-Lim，下文將對這四種聲碼器進行簡略的介紹。

WaveRNN：利用 Tacotron 時一般會配合 WaveNet 作爲聲碼器，WaveNet 使用自回歸（Auto-Regression）的方式生成聲音，根據前一刻的輸出來預測下一刻的數値，因採用多層架構，讓 WaveNet 可以生成高品質的自然人聲，但也因爲其高複雜度，進而導致生成速度緩慢，不適合在實際應用場景中使用。於是 WaveRNN 便針對生成速度做優化，透過將模型簡化與序列調整，使其可僅依靠 CPU 運算，來實現語音合成。

HiFi-GAN：使用生成對抗網路（Generative Adversarial Network）作爲模型基礎，與 Mel-GAN (Kumar et al., 2019) 較爲相似，其中包含了一個生成器與兩個鑑別器：多週期鑑別器（Multi-Period Discriminator）和多尺度鑑別器（Multi-Scale Discriminator），以此來強化 GAN 評斷眞實語音的能力。

Fre-GAN：在 HiFi-GAN 的基礎上，改良了生成器與鑑別器，採用 RCG（Resolution-Connected Generator）與 RWD（Resolution-Wise Discriminator）。而 Fre-GAN 最核心的改進是：傳統中在採樣時，使用了如平均池化等方法，會損失高頻區域，而 Fre-GAN 則選擇使用離散小波變換，可以完整保留聲音的所有資訊。

Synthesizer Model	Phonetic Method	Corpus
MockingBird	Pinyin	aidatatang_200zh + AISHELL-3
CV8-75K	Pinyin	Common Voice 8.0
Chinese-Hybrid	Pinyin	Common Voice 8.0 + aidatatang_200zh
Bopomofo	Bopomofo	Common Voice 8.0
Code-Switching	Bopomofo	Common Voice 8.0 + VCTK

表 3. 模型的字元嵌入方式與使用之語料集

Griffin-Lim：基於演算法的經典聲碼器，利用短時距傅立葉變換的大小，來重建聲音訊號。該演算法簡單且高效，但因爲 Griffin-Lim 在生成時沒有使用神經網路，所以在語音的合成品質較遜於上面所提及的聲碼器。

3.4 嘴型同步模組

對於 SemiTrue 嘴型同步模組的建構，本研究參考 Wav2Lip (Prajwal et al., 2020) 的方法與實作。Wav2Lip 主要針對一段人物說話影像，依據輸入語音的資訊，來產生與該語音同步的人物嘴型，並置換掉原始影片中人物的嘴部區域，最終產生出自然且準確的嘴型同步影像。

Wav2Lip 改進了由 Prajwal et al., 2019 所提出的方案，藉由引入了一個預訓練的嘴型同步鑑別器（Pretrained Lip-Sync Discriminator），其專注於調整嘴型同步的效果，並回饋到下一次生成，以此來提高嘴型同步的精準度，雖然透過嘴型同步鑑別器能夠產生準確的嘴形，卻可能會在連續影像中導致嘴部區域的模糊以及瑕疵。因此，Wav2Lip 又加入了一個影像品質鑑別器（Visual Quality Discriminator）作爲輔助，透過考慮連續多個影格，修正嘴型同步鑑別器所導致的模糊問題，進一步提升了影像的品質。同時，又因爲 Wav2Lip 是透過讀入語音頻譜資訊來生成影像的，使其可以運用於任何目標人臉與任何語言的人聲，即便是透過 TTS 合成出來的語音也沒問題，這使相當適合應用於我們的系統，來產生指定目標人物的說話影像。

Wav2Lip 的架構區分爲生成器與鑑別器兩部份，而生成器又可以再細分爲三個區塊，分別是人物編碼器（Identity Encoder）、語音編碼器（Speech Encoder）與臉部解碼器（Face Decoder）。在實際運作時，嘴型同步模組需要輸入目標人臉，與經由語音複製模組所產生的合成語音，之後系統會隨機挑選目標人臉影像中的一部分參照片段，與另一段移除嘴部區域後的片段，並將兩個片段連接在一起，作爲人物編碼器的輸入，產生出臉部嵌入向量。而合成音訊的梅爾頻譜資訊，則會進入語音編碼器來產生語音嵌入向量。將臉部嵌入向量與語音嵌入向量合成後，再送入臉部解碼器中，依目標人物的特徵來產生相應的嘴型同步影片，生成結果經過嘴型同步鑑別器與影像品質鑑別器來評斷生成品質，最終合成人物說話影像。

4 實驗

4.1 研究方法

在本章節中，我們將探討語音複製與嘴型同步的品質及效能，並針對中文語音合成部分，比較 MockingBird 與我們提出之改進方案的差異，包括使用拼音字元嵌入、使用注音字元嵌入、混合語料集、中文混雜語句之四個模型（見表 3），又以其中一個模型去探討：搭配 WaveRNN、HiFi-GAN、Fre-GAN 與 Griffin-Lim 聲碼器對語音合成效果的影響。爲了評斷 SemiTrue 所合成之人物說話影像的整體效果，我們也對比了同一名語者之原始影片、英文語句合成與中文語句合成的語音品質、相似程度與嘴型同步品質。

鑒於 Wang et al., 2017 等多篇論文都是以平均意見分數（Mean Opinion Score，MOS）(P.800.2, 2016) 來評斷影音之品質，因此，我們將不具標籤之語音及影像，整理成問卷的形式，每段語音或影像以最差 1 分至最佳 5 分進行匿名評分，來取得其平均意見分數。

另外，我們參考了 Jia et al., 2018 與 Wang and Huang, 2021 的實驗，透過語者相似度分析圖來檢視，不同語者間的離異性與語音複製的相似程度，及使用梅爾頻譜圖來觀察，中英混雜版本與純中文版本在合成效果上之差別，以提供除了合成語音經人類觀測的主觀評分外，較爲客觀的驗證方法。

4.2 模型訓練

SemiTrue 語音複製模組的架構中，包含語者編碼器、合成器與聲碼器，其中影響合成品質及口音最大的是合成器模型。若期望合成語音可以更貼近臺灣人的口音特色，必須使用含有臺灣口音的語料集來進行合成器模型的訓練。下文即列出了 SemiTrue 與 MockingBird 有使用到的語料集。

Common Voice Corpus：由 Mozilla 發行的開源多語言語音資料集，任何人都可以提供錄音，固定每 3 個月發布新版本。SemiTrue 大部分的模型是採用華語（臺灣）第 8 版進行訓練的，該版本有 1,695 名語者提供上萬筆共 89 小時的錄音。

NER-Trs-Vol1[7]：臺灣口音中文語料集，由北科大教育電台廣播節目錄製音檔組成，經過人工校正、切割並整理。因爲每段錄音時間較長，不宜用作訓練，故我們抽取其中一部分用作實驗中驗證的語音。

VCTK[8]：全英語之語料集，包含 110 名不同口音的語者，每位語者約提供 400 句朗讀報紙、演講段落的錄音，我們用於訓練中英混雜語句的英語部分。

Aidatatang_200zh[9]：中文北京口音普通話語料集，錄音主要爲多名語者在安靜室內透過 Android 與 iOS 手機錄製而成的，長達 200 小時，爲 MockingBird 作者訓練模型的語料集。

AISHELL-3[10]：中文北京口音普通話語料集，採用高保眞度麥克風錄製，經過嚴格的品質檢驗，包含 218 名語者，共 85 小時的錄音，爲 MockingBird 作者訓練模型的語料集。

爲了實驗拼音字元嵌入符號、注音字元嵌入符號、混和口音語料集、中英混雜語句合成的效果，我們分別訓練了四個模型，並命名爲 CV8-75K、Bopomofo、Chinese-Hybrid 與 Code-Switching，加上 MockingBird 作者提供的模型作爲對照組。特別要注意的是，在訓練 Code-Switching 模型時，因爲沒有大量乾淨的中英混雜語料集，於是採用了中文與英文語料集交錯訓練的方式。

4.3 實驗結果

原本 256 維的語者嵌入向量經過 UMAP (McInnes et al., 2018) 方法降維後，形成了可視化的圖表。透過這個分群，可從客觀的角度得知語料集中的語者聲音，經過 SemiTrue 的語者編碼器可以被有效的區分開來，其中圖 4 顯示出語者編碼器可以清晰的分離男女語者的聲音，而圖 5 則進一步顯示出同性別語者間，也能達成有效的分群，且經過合成後的語音也被分在同一群中，即語音複製的效果可以更貼近目標人聲。

在語音與影像合成品質部分，最終我們收集到了 120 份問卷回應，經過統計得到了測試資料的平均意見分數。表 4 中比較了四種合成器模型的語音品質，其中我們所訓練的三個

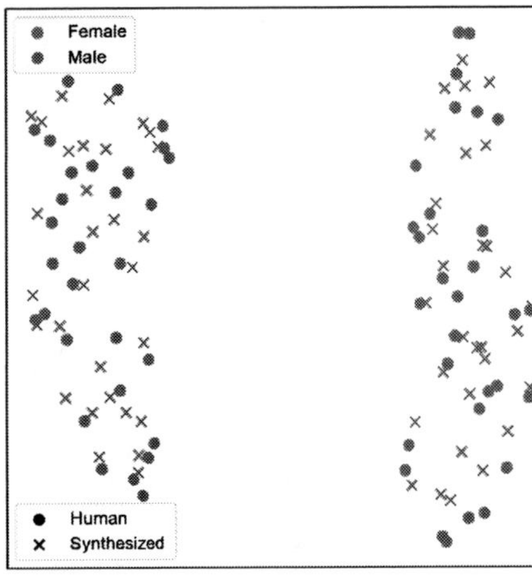

圖 4. 男女語者聲音分群的語者相似度分析

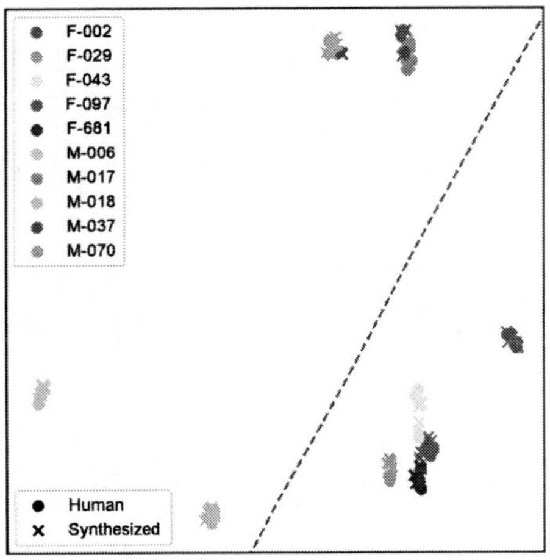

圖 5. 不同語者聲音分群的語者相似度分析（左上爲男性語者，右下爲女性語者）

合成器模型，皆取得了比 MockingBird 更高的分數。而如表 5 中所示，在不同聲碼器之間，又以 WaveRNN 取得 3.8 分較高。

從表 4 的結果可發現，用注音作爲文字嵌入符號的想法是可行的，故我們進一步以梅爾頻譜圖來觀察中英混雜模型 Code-Switching 的合成效果是否也有所提升。我們使用 MockingBird、CV8-75K、Bopomofo 與 Code-Switching 四個模型生成一段中英混雜語句「我明天要報五篇 Paper」後得到了語音的梅爾頻譜圖（見圖 6）。仔細觀察其中「Paper」部分的頻譜，因爲 MockingBird 與 CV8-75K 使了用拼音，故合成英文字時容易造成映射與中文拼音衝突，因此不論是用什麼語料集訓練，採用拼音方案，都較容易導致頻譜顯示模糊。反觀 Code-Switching 分離了

[7]http://www.aclclp.org.tw/use_mat_c.php#ner_edu
[8]https://datashare.ed.ac.uk/handle/10283/3443
[9]https://openslr.org/62
[10]https://www.openslr.org/93

Synthesizer Model	MOS
MockingBird + WaveRNN	2.43±0.19
CV8-75K + WaveRNN	3.80±0.16
Chinese-Hybrid + WaveRNN	2.82±0.17
Bopomofo + WaveRNN	4.13±0.16

表 4. 以不同模型合成之語音的平均意見分數

Vocoder Model	MOS
CV8-75K + WaveRNN	3.80±0.16
CV8-75K + HiFi-GAN	3.77±0.16
CV8-75K + Fre-GAN	3.32±0.16
CV8-75K + Griffin-Lim	2.92±0.17

表 5. 以不同聲碼器合成之語音的平均意見分數

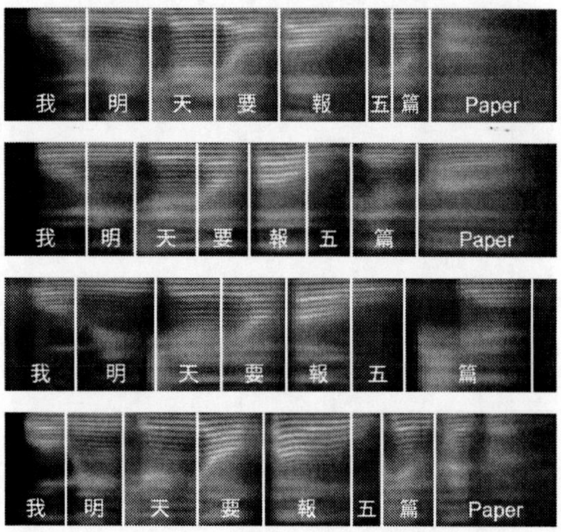

圖 6. 以不同模型合成之語音的梅爾頻譜圖（由上而下分別爲 MockingBird、CV8-75K、Bopomofo、Code-Switching 模型）

中文與英文的字元嵌入，使其可以讀出當中夾雜的英文字，這也反映出了較爲清晰的頻譜。另外，因爲 Bopomofo 的字元嵌入不含英文字母，故合成時系統會直接剪掉英文的部分。

在 SemiTrue 整體合成品質部分，我們使用前美國總統唐納·川普（Donald Trump）的演講影片作爲輸入，合成一段英文語句及一段中文語句，並比較其語音品質、相似程度與嘴型同步品質，結果呈現於表 6 中。透過比較原始影片、英文語句及中文語句合成影片之平均意見分數差異，可以發現中英語之說話影像的語音與嘴型同步品質，皆達到了一定水準，受測者對這些影像之嘴型同步品質所給出的分數與原始影片相當接近，惟中文語音之相似度較爲差強人意，因與原始影片的語言不同，僅取得受測者認爲「普通」的評價。

Case	Criteria	MOS
Original Video	Audio Quality	4.39±0.15
	Voice Similarity	4.35±0.16
	Lip-Sync Quality	4.23±0.17
English	Audio Quality	3.97±0.16
	Voice Similarity	3.90±0.16
	Lip-Sync Quality	4.24±0.15
Mandarin	Audio Quality	3.47±0.16
	Voice Similarity	2.91±0.19
	Lip-Sync Quality	3.79±0.17

表 6. 系統整體品質的平均意見分數

Case	Inference Time
Audio only	8.31 s
Audio + Image	13.30 s
Audio + Video	22.10 s

表 7. 不同合成方案的推論時間

另外在評估系統運作效能上，我們針對僅進行語音複製、語音複製配合以圖片合成影像、語音複製配合以影片合成影像，這三種情形在搭載 RTX2060 圖形處理器的設備上，以合成器模型 CV8-75K，並搭配合成品質最佳，但生成時間最長的聲碼器 WaveRNN，生成語句「任何人有三百萬美金都能參加慈善撲克大賽」，所消耗的時間進行統計，結果顯示於表 7。從表中可見，上述三種情況的生成時間呈現遞增，語音複製配合以影片合成影像，共用了 22.1 秒進行推論，但若僅進行語音複製則可在 8.31 秒完成，從以上的數據可看出我們的系統，在推論時間上有良好的表現。

5 結論

在本研究中提出了一個基於零樣本學習的 SemiTrue 多語者影音合成系統，其中包含了兩個主要改進。首先，我們利用臺灣口音語料集來訓練語音合成模型，且經匿名問卷調查後，得到了較高之平均意見分數，故使用我們的模型合成出的語音，確實更能令受測者感覺到自然與流暢。除此之外，我們以注音符號來表示合成器中的字元嵌入，從而在中英語句的英文部分，獲得了更清晰的梅爾頻譜圖，使系統具備初步合成中英混雜語句的能力。本研究仍有許多值得改進的地方，未來我們會朝向提升混雜語句能力的方向研究，最終期望在單一模型中，合成出自然且逼真的雙語語音。

Acknowledgments

特別感謝國家實驗研究院資安卓越中心規劃建置計畫、台灣人工智慧學校，提供運算資源，協助本研究順利進行。

References

Edresson Casanova, Julian Weber, Christopher D Shulby, Arnaldo Candido Junior, Eren Gölge, and Moacir A Ponti. 2022. YourTTS: Towards zero-shot multi-speaker TTS and zero-shot voice conversion for everyone. In *Proceedings of the 39th International Conference on Machine Learning*, volume 162 of *Proceedings of Machine Learning Research*, pages 2709–2720. PMLR.

An-Chieh Cheng and Chia-Ping Chen. 2019. 即時中文語音合成系統 (Real-time Mandarin speech synthesis system). In *Proceedings of the 31st Conference on Computational Linguistics and Speech Processing (ROCLING 2019)*, pages 256–265, New Taipei City, Taiwan. The Association for Computational Linguistics and Chinese Language Processing (ACLCLP).

Yi-Hsiang Hung, Yi-Chin Huang, and Guang-Feng Deng. 2019. 應用文脈分析於中英夾雜語音合成系統 (Linguistic analysis for English/Mandarin speech synthesis system). In *Proceedings of the 31st Conference on Computational Linguistics and Speech Processing (ROCLING 2019)*, pages 368–377, New Taipei City, Taiwan. The Association for Computational Linguistics and Chinese Language Processing (ACLCLP).

Corentin Jemine. 2019. Real-time voice cloning. Master's thesis, University of Liége, Liége, Belgium.

Ye Jia, Yu Zhang, Ron Weiss, Quan Wang, Jonathan Shen, Fei Ren, zhifeng Chen, Patrick Nguyen, Ruoming Pang, Ignacio Lopez Moreno, and Yonghui Wu. 2018. Transfer learning from speaker verification to multispeaker text-to-speech synthesis. In *Advances in Neural Information Processing Systems*, volume 31. Curran Associates, Inc.

Nal Kalchbrenner, Erich Elsen, Karen Simonyan, Seb Noury, Norman Casagrande, Edward Lockhart, Florian Stimberg, Aaron van den Oord, Sander Dieleman, and Koray Kavukcuoglu. 2018. Efficient neural audio synthesis. In *Proceedings of the 35th International Conference on Machine Learning*, volume 80 of *Proceedings of Machine Learning Research*, pages 2410–2419. PMLR.

Ji-Hoon Kim, Sang-Hoon Lee, Ji-Hyun Lee, and Seong-Whan Lee. 2021. Fre-GAN: Adversarial frequency-consistent audio synthesis. In *Proc. Interspeech 2021*, pages 2197–2201.

Jungil Kong, Jaehyeon Kim, and Jaekyoung Bae. 2020. HiFi-GAN: Generative adversarial networks for efficient and high fidelity speech synthesis. In *Advances in Neural Information Processing Systems*, volume 33, pages 17022–17033. Curran Associates, Inc.

Kundan Kumar, Rithesh Kumar, Thibault de Boissiere, Lucas Gestin, Wei Zhen Teoh, Jose Sotelo, Alexandre de Brébisson, Yoshua Bengio, and Aaron C Courville. 2019. MelGAN: Generative adversarial networks for conditional waveform synthesis. In *Advances in Neural Information Processing Systems*, volume 32. Curran Associates, Inc.

Beáta Lőrincz, Adriana Stan, and Mircea Giurgiu. 2021. Speaker verification-derived loss and data augmentation for DNN-based multispeaker speech synthesis. In *2021 29th European Signal Processing Conference (EUSIPCO)*, pages 26–30. IEEE.

Leland McInnes, John Healy, and James Melville. 2018. Umap: Uniform manifold approximation and projection for dimension reduction.

Paarth Neekhara, Jason Li, and Boris Ginsburg. 2021. Adapting TTS models for new speakers using transfer learning.

Yishuang Ning, Sheng He, Zhiyong Wu, Chunxiao Xing, and Liang-Jie Zhang. 2019. A review of deep learning based speech synthesis. *Applied Sciences*, 9(19).

Recommendation P.800.2. 2016. Mean opinion score interpretation and reporting. Technical Report P.800.2 E 40885, ITU-T, Geneva Switzerland.

K R Prajwal, Rudrabha Mukhopadhyay, Vinay P. Namboodiri, and C V Jawahar. 2020. A lip sync expert is all you need for speech to lip generation in the wild. In *Proceedings of the 28th ACM International Conference on Multimedia*, MM '20, pages 484–492, New York, NY, USA. Association for Computing Machinery.

K R Prajwal, Rudrabha Mukhopadhyay, Jerin Philip, Abhishek Jha, Vinay Namboodiri, and C V Jawahar. 2019. Towards automatic face-to-face translation. In *Proceedings of the 27th ACM International Conference on Multimedia*, MM '19, New York, NY, USA. ACM.

Jonathan Shen, Ruoming Pang, Ron J. Weiss, Mike Schuster, Navdeep Jaitly, Zongheng Yang, Zhifeng Chen, Yu Zhang, Yuxuan Wang, Rj Skerrv-Ryan, Rif A. Saurous, Yannis Agiomvrgiannakis, and Yonghui Wu. 2018. Natural TTS synthesis by conditioning wavenet on MEL spectrogram predictions. In *2018 IEEE International Conference on Acoustics, Speech and Signal Processing (ICASSP)*, pages 4779–4783.

Hyoung-Kyu Song, Sang Hoon Woo, Junhyeok Lee, Seungmin Yang, Hyunjae Cho, Youseong Lee, Dongho Choi, and Kang-wook Kim. 2022. Talking face generation with multilingual TTS. In *Proceedings of the IEEE/CVF Conference on Computer Vision and Pattern Recognition (CVPR)*, pages 21425–21430.

Xu Tan, Tao Qin, Frank Soong, and Tie-Yan Liu. 2021. A survey on neural speech synthesis.

Li Wan, Quan Wang, Alan Papir, and Ignacio Lopez Moreno. 2018. Generalized end-to-end loss for speaker verification. In *2018 IEEE International Conference on Acoustics, Speech and Signal Processing (ICASSP)*, pages 4879–4883. IEEE.

Sheng-Yao Wang and Yi-Chin Huang. 2021. Incorporating speaker embedding and post-filter network for improving speaker similarity of personalized speech synthesis system. In *Proceedings of the 33rd Conference on Computational Linguistics and Speech Processing (ROCLING 2021)*, pages 326–332, Taoyuan, Taiwan. The Association for Computational Linguistics and Chinese Language Processing (ACLCLP).

Yih-Wen Wang and Chia-Ping Chen. 2020. Real-time single-speaker Taiwanese-accented Mandarin speech synthesis system. In *Proceedings of the 32nd Conference on Computational Linguistics and Speech Processing (ROCLING 2020)*, pages 87–101, Taipei, Taiwan. The Association for Computational Linguistics and Chinese Language Processing (ACLCLP).

Yuxuan Wang, R.J. Skerry-Ryan, Daisy Stanton, Yonghui Wu, Ron J. Weiss, Navdeep Jaitly, Zongheng Yang, Ying Xiao, Zhifeng Chen, Samy Bengio, Quoc Le, Yannis Agiomyrgiannakis, Rob Clark, and Rif A. Saurous. 2017. Tacotron: Towards end-to-end speech synthesis. In *Proc. Interspeech 2017*, pages 4006–4010.

Yuxuan Wang, Daisy Stanton, Yu Zhang, RJ-Skerry Ryan, Eric Battenberg, Joel Shor, Ying Xiao, Ye Jia, Fei Ren, and Rif A. Saurous. 2018. Style tokens: Unsupervised style modeling, control and transfer in end-to-end speech synthesis. In *Proceedings of the 35th International Conference on Machine Learning*, volume 80 of *Proceedings of Machine Learning Research*, pages 5180–5189. PMLR.

Yu Zhang, Ron J. Weiss, Heiga Zen, Yonghui Wu, Zhifeng Chen, RJ Skerry-Ryan, Ye Jia, Andrew Rosenberg, and Bhuvana Ramabhadran. 2019. Learning to speak fluently in a foreign language: Multilingual speech synthesis and cross-language voice cloning.

Xuehao Zhou, Xiaohai Tian, Grandee Lee, Rohan Kumar Das, and Haizhou Li. 2020. End-to-end code-switching TTS with cross-lingual language model. In *ICASSP 2020 - 2020 IEEE International Conference on Acoustics, Speech and Signal Processing (ICASSP)*, pages 7614–7618. IEEE.

The 34th Conference on Computational Linguistics and Speech Processing (ROCLING 2022)
Taipei, Taiwan, November 21-22, 2022. The Association for Computational Linguistics and Chinese Language Processing

Is Character Trigram Overlapping Ratio Still the Best Similarity Measure for Aligning Sentences in a Paraphrased Corpus?

Aleksandra Smolka
SNHCC TIGP
Institute of Information Science
Academia Sinica
aleksandra.smolka@hotmail.com

Jason S. Chang
Department of Computer Science
National Tsing Hua University
jason@nlplab.cc

Hsin-Min Wang
Institute of Information Science
Academia Sinica
whm@iis.sinica.edu.tw

Keh-Yih Su
Institute of Information Science
Academia Sinica
kysu@iis.sinica.edu.tw

Abstract

Sentence alignment is an essential step in studying the mapping among different language expressions, and the *character trigram* overlapping ratio was reported to be the most effective similarity measure in aligning sentences in the text simplification dataset. However, the appropriateness of each similarity measure depends on the characteristics of the corpus to be aligned. This paper studies if the character trigram is still a suitable similarity measure for the task of aligning sentences in a paragraph paraphrasing corpus. We compare several embedding-based and non-embeddings model-agnostic similarity measures, including those that have not been studied previously. The evaluation is conducted on parallel paragraphs sampled from the Webis-CPC-11 corpus, which is a paragraph paraphrasing dataset. Our results show that modern BERT-based measures such as Sentence-BERT or BERTScore can lead to significant improvement in this task.

Keywords: sentence alignment, sentence similarity, sentence embedding

1 Introduction

Monolingual text matching is necessary for many downstream applications, such as Paraphrase Identification and Extraction (Qiu et al., 2006), Question Answering (Weiss et al., 2021), Natural Language Inference (MacCartney et al., 2008), and Text Generation (Barzilay and McKeown, 2005). Take the QA task as an example, identifying the text fragments that match the given question within the associated passage is often required for locating the desired answer.

However, modern neural-network (NN) approaches to text matching often suffer from certain limitations when two sequences contain considerably different lexicons or diverse grammatical structures (McCoy et al., 2019). For example, when the verb "*decide*" in the sentence "*They **decided** to go*" is nominalized to the noun "*decision*" in its paraphrase "*They **made a decision** to go*", the popular word embedding similarity approach might fail as the embedding-vectors of "*decide*" and "*decision*" are quite different [1]. Another example is a pair of sentences "*A cat is chasing a dog.*" and "*A dog is chasing a cat.*", which contain the same set of lexicons and syntactic structure but with opposite meanings.

Furthermore, the NN approaches frequently fail while the matching involves multi-word expressions, or when expressions require compositionality handling (Blevins et al., 2018; Hupkes et al., 2020; Zhou et al., 2020). For example, it is difficult to match expressions "*put off*" and "*procrastinate*" using basic word embeddings, as the real meaning of the idiom "*put off*" is not the sum of the meanings of its tokens.

We found that the limitations of NN models in text matching could be greatly alleviated by utilizing lexico-syntactic paraphrasing patterns such as $[_{VP}[_{VBN}[see]_{NP}[X_1]]] \rightarrow [_{S}[_{NP}[X_1]_{VP}[_{VBD}[be]$

[1] The nearest semantic associates of the verb *decide* based on the cosine similarity between the word2vec vectors (trained on English Wikipedia) are those verbs such as: *choose* (0.64), *opt* (0.62), *persuade* (0.61), *want* (0.58), *refuse* (0.57), *insist* (0.56). However, the noun *decision* only has a similarity score 0.512, which means that its similarity to the verb *decide* is even less than that between *decide* and its quasi-antonymous *refuse*.

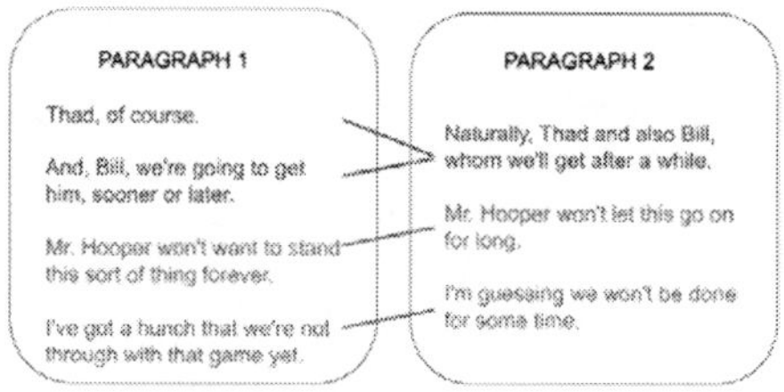

Figure 1: Sentence alignment for extracting paraphrased sentence-pairs. Sentences pairs in green are those we want to extract; sentences in red are in multi-to-one relation and do not constitute sentential paraphrases.

$_{VP}$*[observe]]]*[2], which denotes the conversion from active to passive voice for the phrase pair "*see the lion*" and "*the lion was observed*". Since some key lexicons are involved in the pattern, it would be difficult to exhaustively list such patterns by a human. It is preferable to automatically extract them from a large paraphrase corpus.

To collect such lexico-syntactic patterns, a high-quality paraphrased sentence-pair dataset is essential. Unfortunately, current *sentence-aligned* paraphrase datasets (e.g., MRPC (Dolan and Brockett, 2005), PPDB (Ganitkevitch et al., 2013), and QQP (Aghaebrahimian, 2017)) are too trivial for this task, as they mainly contain lexical paraphrases that could be easily handled by a NN. On the other hand, some *paragraph-aligned* paraphrase corpora, containing different human translations from the same source text, fit our needs well. To utilize those paragraph-aligned paraphrase corpora, monolingual sentence alignment is the first step in retrieving the desired patterns.

Figure 1 shows how a correct sentence alignment could help extract paraphrased sentence pairs from longer paraphrased texts. Unless we correctly identify which sentences are in 1-to-1 relationships (green in the figure), we cannot correctly identify the desired paraphrased pattern.

Monolingual sentence alignment approaches could be classified into two categories: *model-based* approaches (e.g., Jiang et al., 2020), which adopt specific models to encode the input sentences and perform alignment, and *model-agnostic* approaches (Štajner et al., 2018), which can be directly applied to the selected dataset, without the necessity of training a neural model in advance. In our work, we focus on model-agnostic approaches, as they do not require additional labeled data to train the model.

The downside of previous model-agnostic approaches (Štajner et al., 2017; 2018) is that they only test the early word2vec word embeddings, and do not explore those more advanced NN approaches such as Sentence-BERT (Reimers and Gurevych, 2019) and BERTScore (Zhang et al., 2020). Also, they are mainly evaluated on Text Simplification (TS) datasets, which are different from our paraphrasing datasets.

In the TS dataset, the original and the simplified text often share a considerable number of keywords, which remain unchanged and are rarely substituted with synonyms. However, this property does not hold in our paraphrasing corpus, as its paraphrasing expressions usually possess diverse syntactic structures with many different lexical items.

Therefore, we suspect that the character trigram overlapping ratio, reported as the best for monolingual sentence alignment in previous works (Štajner et al., 2017; 2018), would not perform best on our data. Since our paraphrasing corpus contains considerably different lexicons and word order, the string-based method such as character ngram similarity would lose its edge. Previously reported text similarity measures thus should be re-evaluated for our task, and more advanced NN approaches should be explored.

In this work, we not only compare various previously reported text similarity measures on a paraphrased paragraph corpus but also additionally test some new measures based on the most recent NN sentence embedding methods. We utilize those above measures with two sentence alignment approaches: simple greedy match (e.g., Štajner et al. 2018), and sequence match (Gale and Church, 1993; Barzilay and McKeown, 2001). We conduct the evaluation on a manually annotated sentence-aligned dataset with 400 paraphrased paragraph pairs randomly sampled from the multiple translation corpus Webis-CPC-11 (Burrows et al., 2013).

Our contributions include:

(1) To the best of our knowledge, we present the first study on aligning sentences on a paragraph paraphrased corpus;
(2) We show that character trigram similarity is not the best measure for aligning

[2] The structure is annotated in bracketed form analogically to phrase-parsing annotation and X_i, $i = 1, 2, \ldots$ marks matching variables. We use the same tagset as that adopted in Penn Treebank (Marcus et al., 1993)

paraphrasing corpora. Instead, BERT-based embedding methods achieve significantly better results even without fine-tuning on the target dataset;

(3) We test several NN-related sentence similarity measures (other than word2vector) that have not been evaluated before for model-agnostic monolingual sentence alignment;

(4) We confirm and expand the observation of Choi et al., (2021), showing that [CLS] token representation is not necessarily superior to averaging individual word vectors for sentence representation while aligning paraphrased text under BERT.

2 Sentence Alignment Procedure

Our sentence alignment procedure is implemented with two main elements: (1) selecting an appropriate search mechanism (either *Bi-Directional Best Match* or *Sequence Match*); (2) adopting a specified sentence similarity measure, either string- or embedding-based.

2.1 Search Mechanisms

We adopt two approaches to conduct sentence alignment: Directional Best Match and Sequence Match.

2.1.1 Bi-directional Best Match

This is a simple greedy approach that ignores the adjacency and dependency information within sentences during matching. We adopt an approach similar to that reported in Štajner et al. (2018). However, in addition to *Uni-directional* Best Match adopted by Štajner et al. (2018), we also test *Bi-directional* Best Match, where we align the sentences bi-directionally. We believe that the bi-directional approach will be more applicable in our case since our data is symmetric, while the data tested in Štajner et al. (2018) is not.

In both versions, we take two sets of sentences as the input and calculate the similarity of each sentence pair that can be formed between these two sets. Based on the sentence similarity scores, for each sentence in one set, we select the sentence from the second set that possesses the highest similarity score, forming a set of sentence pairs. In the uni-directional version, those pairs are directly selected as the final alignments.

In contrast, for the bi-directional approach, we additionally repeat the same selection procedure from the opposite direction for each sentence in the second set to form another set of sentence pairs. Afterward, we take the intersection of these two sets to obtain the final aligned sentence pairs.

2.1.2 Sequence Match

Based on the selected similarity measure, this approach adopts dynamic programming to find out the best alignment sequence among the sentences within the given paragraph pair (Gale and Church, 1993; Barzilay and McKeown, 2001).

2.2 Similarity Measures

The text similarity measures adopted in our experiments fall into two main categories: (a) string-based approaches, in which the similarity is calculated purely based on the sentence strings; (b) embedding-based approaches, in which a neural model is first used to convert each sentence into its corresponding embedding-vector, and then the cosine similarity between these two sentence embedding-vectors is taken as the sentence similarity.

2.2.1 String-Based Sentence Similarity

We adopt two different overlapping ratios: (1) *Character ngram*, which is reported as the state-of-art on the text simplification corpus (Štajner, 2018), and (2) *token string*, which is commonly used in sentence alignment tasks (e.g., Barzilay and McKeown, 2001).

Character Ngram

We follow Štajner et al. (2018) to calculate the ngram similarity based on the *Character Ngram Similarity* model with tf-idf weighting (adapted from McNamee and Mayfield (2004)). We experiment with different ngram sizes (1 to 5) and use NGRAM to refer to this measure. We add Laplace smoothing to account for those unseen ngrams in the test set. The final similarity is calculated by taking cosine similarity.

Token String

For calculating token-based sentence similarity, we use the following token overlap formula:

$$similarity_{token} = \frac{|tokens_1 \cap tokens_2|}{|tokens_1| + |tokens_2|} \quad (1)$$

where $tokens_1$ is the set of tokens in the first sentence, $tokens_2$ is the set of tokens in the second sentence, and the function | | specifies the cardinality of the token set. We consider two different normalization mechanisms for comparing two tokens: (1) converting the strings into their associated lemmas before comparison (abbreviated as TOKENstring); (2) also taking synonyms as exactly matched lemmas during comparison (abbreviated as TOKENsyn). Token lemmas for each sentence are retrieved using an automatic tokenizer and lemmatizer (Qi et al., 2020). Synonymic relationships are taken from WordNet (Fellbaum, 1998).

2.2.2 Embedding-Based Sentence Similarity

We adopt three different approaches to calculate the similarity score between two sentences: (1) *word-embedding* based, where we first look up the word embedding-vector for every token in each sentence from a pretrained model and then combine them into their associated sentence embedding-vector by vector averaging (Putra and Tokunaga, 2017). Afterward, we calculate the similarity between the two obtained sentence embedding vectors. (2) *sentence-embedding* based, where we use a model, such as BERT (Devlin et al., 2019) or Sentence-BERT (Reimers and Gurevych, 2019), to directly embed a sentence into its associated sentence-embedding. We then calculate the similarity between these two sentence embedding vectors. (3) *BERTScore* (Zhang et al., 2020), which uses BERT to directly generate the similarity value between two sentences.

Word-embedding Similarity

For directly retrieving the token-associated embedding vector from a pretrained embedding lookup table, we test both word2vec (Mikolov et al., 2013) and Glove (Pennington et al., 2014) embeddings. Additionally, we also test contextualized word embeddings retrieved from BERT (Devlin et al., 2019).

Moreover, while it is common to use the [CLS] token yielded by the BERT encoder to represent the whole encoded sentence, recent works note that this might not be the best solution for all downstream tasks (Choi et al., 2021). We therefore additionally test the following approach: generate the sentence embedding via averaging the contextual word embeddings retrieved from the BERT model.

Regardless of the way of selecting word embedding, we combine the associated embedding vectors into the corresponding sentence representation by taking an average over them (Putra and Tokunaga, 2017). The sentence similarity is then calculated as the cosine similarity between the two sentence embedding vectors.

Among various types of word-embedding, only Word2vec is tested by Štajner et al. (2018). But it was reported not the best one in their experiments (the best one is character trigram in their task).

Sentence-embedding Similarity

Another way to generate the sentence-embedding is to adopt BERT to transform all its associated token-embeddings into it. We test two methods of obtaining sentence representation via BERT. First, we take the [CLS] token from the BERT to represent the whole sentence. Alternatively, we use Sentence-BERT (Reimers and Gurevych, 2019), which is an alternative method of obtaining sentence representation from BERT-type models, suggested as a better alternative for directly adopting [CLS] token embedding. We use Sentence-BERT to separately obtain a single embedding for each sentence in the pair. The sentence similarity is then calculated between two obtained sentence embedding vectors.

BERTScore

Last, we can directly generate the desired similarity value among two sentences by adopting the BERTScore (Zhang et al., 2020) approach, which is originally developed as an automatic evaluation metric for comparing various text generation systems. This approach first uses BERT to obtain the word embeddings of all input tokens. The pairwise similarity is then calculated for each possible token pair. Afterward, for each token from the first input sequence (i.e., the sentence from the "*original*" paragraph), BERTScore finds its matching token in the second sequence (i.e., the sentence from the "*paraphrased*" paragraph) via greedy search. Last, it calculates both precision and recall based on the matching result.

As BERTScore is designed to evaluate the similarity between the ground truth and the generated text, we thought it should be also suitable for measuring the sentence similarity for our task. Typically, BERTScore will report precision, recall, and f1-score at the same time. We take each of these values to represent a specific sentence pair similarity measure; and we refer to them as BERTprec, BERTrec, and BERTf1, respectively.

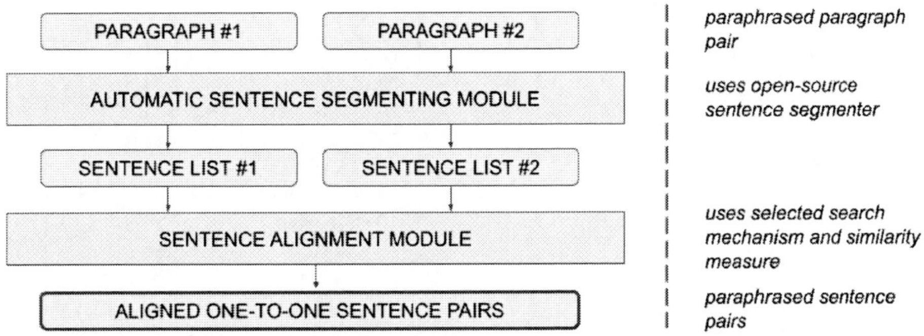

Figure 2: Operation flow for obtaining one-to-one sentence alignment within paraphrased paragraph pairs.

3 Experiments

Figure 2 shows the operation flow adopted in the experiments. Taking a pair of paraphrased paragraphs as input, the paragraphs are first preprocessed and split into sentences. Then, we use the sentence alignment module with the selected search mechanism and similarity measure to generate the desired sentence alignments. Those one-to-one sentence alignments are then extracted and output as the answer.

Following subsections give details of the experiment setting and results.

3.1 Dataset

We randomly sampled 400 paragraph pairs from the Webis-CPC-11 corpus (out of which 7 were found to be incorrectly marked as paraphrases and removed from the evaluation data). However, for checking if we can automatically detect if the given paragraph pair is a paraphrased one, we still reserve them as additional data on which we can experiment with a method of filtering out such undesired input.

As all tested similarity measures are model-agnostic, we do not require a training set. Therefore, we split all the aligned paragraph pairs (i.e., excluding those non-paraphrased pairs) into the development set and the test set with a 1:7 ratio. As a result, we end up with 48 paragraph pairs in the development set and 345 paragraph pairs in the test set. We use the development set for selecting hyper-parameters such as similarity cutting threshold and alignment type probabilities for the Gale-Church algorithm (Gale and Church, 1993).

Table 1 gives the associated dataset statistics. Within them, 566 1-to-1 paraphrased sentence pairs (77% among all aligned passage pairs) exist in the test set. This set of 1-to-1 sentence pairs (i.e., sentential paraphrases) is the desired output in our task and the ground truth for our evaluation.

3.2 Pre-processing

Because the Webis-CPC dataset only contains un-segmented paragraphs, it must be first converted into a collection of sentences. We use an off-the-shelf sentence segmenter (Qi et al., 2020) to split each paragraph into sentences. The output is thus two sets of sentences, one for each of the paragraphs.

3.3 Experiment Settings

Since the character trigram is reported as the best measure by Štajner et al. (2018), and no easily applicable code is released, we re-implement it as our baseline. The character ngram similarity is calculated as described by Štajner et al. (2018), including the tf-idf weighting adopted in the

	all	dev	test
#input paraphrased paragraph-pairs	393	48	345
#input non-paraphrased pairs (dataset errors)	7	2	5
avg. paragraph length (#sentences)	2.3	2.4	2.3
paragraph range (# sentences)	1-7	1-6	1-7
avg. sentence length (#tokens)	20.9	19.3	21.1
# 1-1 alignments (ground truth)	633 (77%)	67 (77%)	566 (77%)

Table 1: Dataset Statistics (without non-paraphrase cases). #Min-#Max specifies the range.

measure	% on the test set			Best
	prec	rec	F1	TH
NGRAM(n=1)*	77.8	82.2	79.9	0.3
NGRAM(n=2)*	77.8	82.2	79.9	0.3
NGRAM(n=3)	79.9	72.5	76.1	0.3
NGRAM(n=4)	77.8	82.2	79.9	0.3
NGRAM(n=5)	77.8	82.2	79.9	0.3
TOKENstring*	83.7	73.1	78.1	0.2
TOKENsyn	77.1	71.5	74.2	0.1
W2V	79.7	74.5	77.0	0.8
GLOVE	73.5	81.2	77.1	0.95
BERTword*	78.5	**87.0**	**82.5**	0.75
BERTcls	81.9	67.9	74.3	0.9
SBERTbert	75.2	90.8	82.3	0.6
SBERTalbert	82.9	70.7	76.9	0.35
SBERTmini*	78.4	85.2	81.6	0.6
BERTprec*	86.5	72.9	79.1	0.9
BERTrec*	83.5	74.9	80.4	0.9
BERTf1	**86.8**	74.9	80.4	0.9

Table 2: Alignment results for the Uni-directional Best Match strategy across all similarity measures. TH is the threshold value, selected on the development set based on the f1 value for each measure. The asterisk * marks the metrics that outperforms NGRAM baseline (n=3) with $p \leq 0.05$.

measure	% on the test set			Best
	prec	rec	F1	TH
NGRAM(n=1)	80.5	81.8	81.1	0.3
NGRAM(n=2)	80.5	81.8	81.1	0.3
NGRAM(n=3)	78.9	87.0	82.7	0.1
NGRAM(n=4)	80.5	81.8	81.1	0.3
NGRAM(n=5)	80.5	81.8	81.1	0.3
TOKENstring	84.7	73.1	78.5	0.2
TOKENsyn	78.6	81.8	80.2	0.05
W2V	81.1	87.6	84.2	0.6
GLOVE	79.7	78.0	78.8	0.95
BERTword	82.3	86.4	84.3	0.75
BERTcls	**86.2**	66.5	75.1	0.9
SBERTbert	79.1	88.6	83.6	0.6
SBERTalbert	80.6	89.8	84.9	0.25
SBERTmini*	80.7	90.2	**85.1**	0.25
BERTprec	80.9	88.2	84.4	0.85
BERTrec	79.7	88.2	83.7	0.85
BERTf1	79.9	**90.8**	85.0	0.9

Table 3: Alignment results for the Bi-directional Best Match strategy across all similarity measures. TH is the threshold value, selected on the development set based on the F1 value for each measure. The asterisk * marks the metrics that outperforms NGRAM baseline (n=3) with $p \leq 0.05$.

original work. We do not test our implementation on the original data adopted by them, as they only used human evaluation, without indicating which dataset was used for evaluation. Therefore, directly verifying our implementation with their results is impossible.

When experimenting with various search mechanisms, we additionally impose similarity score thresholding, which filters out those obtained 1-1 sentence pairs with their similarities below the specified threshold. The threshold value is selected for each similarity measure separately, based on the development set results.

For the approach of adopting [CLS] for sentence representation, we use a pretrained BERT-base model (Devlin et al., 2019). For the Sentence-BERT approach, we test three different pretrained versions released by an open resource[3]: BERT (Devlin et al., 2019; abbreviated as SBERTbert), ALBERT-mini (Lan et al., 2020; abbreviated as SBERTalbert), and MiniLM (Wang et al., 2020; abbreviated as SBERTmini). Among them, SBERTbert is trained with various *Natural Language Inference* data sets; in contrast, the last two versions are trained on various paraphrasing datasets [4]. The pre-trained model used for calculating the BERTScore is ROBERTA-Large (Liu et al., 2019).[5]

3.4 Various Experiments

We measure precision, recall, and F1-score for the two alignment strategies with various similarity measures. Furthermore, we use the McNemar test (Dietterich, 1998) to check if a given configuration (i.e., the adopted search mechanism and the specified similarity measure) yields significantly different results from the baseline (taking $p \leq 0.05$ as the significance test threshold).

We test the following measures: (A) **String-based** similarities: including character ngram similarity with *n* from 1 to 5 (NGRAM), and token overlap similarity calculated with either token strings (TOKENstring) or token synonyms (TOKENsyn); (B) **Embedding-based** similarities: (1) word embedding-based similarities calculated with word2vec (W2V), Glove (GLOVE) and BERTbase (BERTword) embeddings; (2) sentence embedding-based similarity: (i) using [CLS] token yielded by BERTbase model (BERTcls), and (ii)

[3] https://huggingface.co/sentence-transformers

[4] The list of specific datasets used was not published by the open-source authors.

[5] https://github.com/Tiiiger/bert_score

measure	% on the test set			Best
	prec	rec	F1	TH
NGRAM(n=1)*	89.1	83.4	86.1	0.2
NGRAM(n=2)*	89.1	83.4	86.1	0.2
NGRAM(n=3)	89.7	84.2	86.9	0.1
NGRAM(n=4)*	89.1	83.4	86.1	0.2
NGRAM(n=5)*	89.1	83.4	86.1	0.2
TOKENstring	**92.7**	81.6	86.8	0.15
TOKENsyn	86.2	86.9	86.3	0
W2V	87.6	87.6	87.6	0.45
GLOVE	87.3	85.2	86.2	0.9
BERTword	91.5	82.2	86.6	0.75
BERTcls	92.3	81.4	86.5	0.85
SBERTbert*	89.8	**87.8**	**88.8**	0.6
SBERTalbert	91.1	85.8	88.3	0.25
SBERTmini	87.8	86.8	87.3	0.25
BERTprec	90.0	86.8	88.4	0.85
BERTrec*	89.9	87.6	88.7	0.85
BERTf1*	90.1	87.4	88.7	0.85

Table 4: Alignment results for the *Sequence Match* strategy across all similarity measures. *TH* is the threshold value, selected from the development set based on the F1 value for each measure. The asterisk * marks the metrics that outperforms NGRAM baseline (n=3) with $p \leq 0.05$.

Sentence-BERT embeddings with three different pretraining models (SBERTbert, SBERTalbert, and SBERTmini); (C) **BERTScore** with precision (BERTprec), recall (BERTrec) and F1-score (BERTf1).

Tables 2-4 compare all similarity measures under the *Best Match* (*Uni-* and *Bi-directional*, separately) strategy and the *Sequence Match* strategy, respectively. For each measure, we only report the results with the best threshold value, which is selected on the development set based on the F1 value. The threshold for each specific similarity measure is different and is noted in the corresponding table. Measures that outperform the character trigram baseline in a significant manner are marked with the asterisk *.

Overall, comparing the best result of each approach, the sequence match approach (with the best F1-score equaling 88.8%) outperforms both best match approaches (the best F1-score of 85.1% is from the bi-directional mode). We conjecture the sequence match performs the best as it additionally considers the adjacency and dependency information within sentences during matching.

Moreover, the Uni-directional Best Match approach performed the worst (only with 82.5% best F1) as expected. Since our data is symmetric, the matching results would be more reliable if the alignment is considered from both directions.

measure	mean	L-CI (0.95)	#pairs
NGRAM(n=3)	0.547	0.530	5
TOKENstring	0.221	0.214	4
TOKENsyn	0.141	0.136	4
SBERTbert	0.541	0.522	3
SBERTalbert	0.411	0.391	3
SBERTmini*	0.339	0.321	6
BERTprec*	0.914	0.911	**7**
BERTrec	0.917	0.914	5
BERTf1*	0.915	0.913	5

Table 5: Results of filtering out non-paraphrased paragraph pairs based on the 0.95 confidence interval. *Mean* is the mean similarity value for all (393) paraphrased paragraph pairs; *L-CI* is the left boundary of the Confidence Interval, and *#pairs* is the number of non-paraphrased pairs that fall outside the confidence interval (out of 7). Results with $p \leq 0.05$ are marked with the asterisk *.

Furthermore, the best similarity measure varies under different search mechanisms. In the sequence match approach, three BERT-type measures (i.e., SBERTbert (88.8% F1), BERTrec (88.7% F1), and BERTf1 (88.7% F1)) significantly outperform the baseline. The SentenceBERT measure performs best, surpassing the character-trigram baseline method by 1.9% (88.8% vs. 86.9%) because it is trained to encode the overall sentence meaning, not the specific meaning of individual tokens, which fits our task well. Similarly, BERTScore also delivers good results because it is directly trained to measure the similarity between two sequences.

On the other hand, in the bi-directional best match approach, the best result is again obtained by the Sentence-BERT measure (SBERTmini) with the best F1-score 85.1%, significantly outperforming the character ngram similarity measure at 82.7%. Also, both SBERTalbert and BERTf1 measures outperform the baseline with *$p<0.06$*. We believe that the above reasons given for the sequence match approach also apply here.

Last, in the uni-directional best match approach, several tested measures significantly outperform the baseline (76.1%), including BERTword (82.5%), SBERTbert (82.3%), SBERTmini (81.6%), BERTf1(80.4%), NGRAM with $n \neq 3$ (79.9%), BERTrec (79.7%), BERTprec (79.1%) and TOKENstring (78.1%). The measures that perform best in this search mechanism are again mostly those that encode the sentence as a whole, similar to other search mechanisms.

We additionally note that in both versions of the Best Match approach, BERTword is significantly better (84.3% and 82.5% for bi- and uni-directional, respectively) than that is calculated with the [CLS] token embedding (BERTcls, 75.1%, and 74.3%). This is in line with the observation from Choi et al. (2021), who noted that interpreting the [CLS] token embedding as the sentence representation might be inferior to combining the individual sub-word embeddings obtained from BERT.

3.5 Exploring Features for Non-paraphrased Paragraph-pair Detection

Since the Webis-CPC-11 paraphrasing dataset is found to contain some non-paraphrased paragraph pairs (a total of 7 pairs are found among 400 pairs sampled), we also want to check if it is possible to automatically detect those outliers. As the paragraph is just a longer passage in comparison with the sentence, we expect that the measures adopted to calculate the sentence similarity could be also applied to evaluate the paragraph similarity. We thus further test whether the measures adopted for sentence alignment are discriminative enough to filter out those incorrectly annotated paragraph pairs (i.e., non-paraphrased pairs found).

We calculate paragraph similarity via the same approaches conducted for evaluating the sentence similarity and test some similarity measures which perform better for the sentence case (including Sentence-BERT, BERTScore, etc.). We fit the similarity values from all paraphrased paragraph pairs for each measure with specific normal distribution and then calculate its 0.95 confidence interval to check whether the non-paraphrased paragraphs can be detected as outliers outside this interval.

Table 5 shows the left boundary value of the 0.95 Confidence Interval as well as the number of non-paraphrased paragraph pairs (out of 7 in the data) that fall below this interval. We found that all non-paraphrased paragraphs can be detected as outliers and filtered out using BERTprec (with the nearest outlier sitting at p=0.01). It thus confirms the feasibility of adopting BERTprec for automatically filtering out those annotation errors.

4 Error Analysis

We analyzed 50 errors generated by our best approach (i.e., Sequence Match with SBERTmini), and categorized them based on their associated error sources: (1) mistaking 1-n mapping for 1-1 (46%); (2) associated with incorrect sentence boundary (26%), in which the sentences are split incorrectly before conducting alignment (e.g., a sentence is incorrectly split into two sequences by the sentence segmenter); (3) paraphrased sentences take different sequence-orders within two given paragraphs (16%); (4) others (12%), of which it is difficult to attribute each error to a specific reason.

The first error category, incorrectly marking 1-n alignment as 1-1, is likely due to two reasons. First, those proposed similarity measures are still incapable of truly reflecting the semantic similarity between two sentences when they are paraphrased in an abstract way; as a result, they might incorrectly convert a golden 1-n mapping into a 1-1 mapping. Second, because the alignment is selected based on the sentence similarity and the probability of each alignment type on the development set, the model has a preference for extracting 1-1 alignments as they are most common in the dataset (cf. Table 1).

The second error category (i.e., with incorrect sentence boundary) occurs when the pre-processing module incorrectly split the sentences within one of the input paragraphs. Finally, the last type of error is caused by the sequence search mechanism, which assumes all paraphrased passage pairs follow the same relative order within each paragraph. If this assumption is violated in the given paragraph pair, it will always return an incorrect answer.

5 Related Work

Sentence Alignment Mechanisms

Works on sentence alignment started with bilingual data (Brown et al., 1991; Gale and Church, 1993) adopted to train the statistical machine translation model. Monolingual sentence alignment appeared much later. Most of them are conducted on comparable corpora for developing text-to-text generation systems (e.g., Barzilay and Elhadad, 2003; Nelken and Shieber, 2006). Subsequently, it is also applied in the text simplification task (e.g., Hwang et al., 2015).

Based on the adopted search mechanism, both mono- and bilingual sentence alignment techniques can be split into greedy search (e.g., Brown et al., 1991; Hwang et al., 2015; Štajner et al., 2018) or sequence search (e.g., Gale and Church, 1993, Barzilay and McKeown, 2001).

Those previously reported monolingual alignment approaches are mainly model-agnostic, and adopt various similarity measures (Hwang et al., 2015; Štajner et al., 2018), as there is no need to additionally prepare annotated training data. As the development of NN progressed, model-dependent approaches (Huang et al., 2018; Jiang et al., 2020) also emerge, as they can deliver better performance with the cost of annotating a training dataset.

Sentence Similarity Measures

The early adopted sentence similarity measures are mostly string-based, including sentence-level tf-idf (Nelken and Shieber, 2006) or shared tokens (Barzilay and McKeown, 2001; Ganitkevitch et al., 2013). Later, to increase the possibility of recognizing those non-identical strings with similar semantic meanings, new methods are introduced: such as Word-Net similarity (e.g., Hatzivassiloglou et al., 1999), which use external resources to augment the matching scope by looking up their synsets, and WikNet similarity (Hwang et al., 2015), which is a semantic similarity based on Wiktionary.

Those embedding-based approaches appeared in literature only recently, using latent variable models (Guo and Diab, 2012) or neural models (Mueller and Thyagaraja, 2016; Neculoiu et al., 2016; Štajner et al., 2018).

6 Conclusions

We have presented the first comparison among various model-agnostic similarity measures used for aligning sentences among paraphrased paragraphs. For most cases, we find that embedding-based similarity measures outperform the string-based approaches (including the previous SOTA character trigram approach tested on the TS dataset), and sentence-embedding-based methods are preferable to the word-embedding-based methods for most search mechanisms except the uni-directional greedy matching.

Additionally, our results have shown that in calculating the similarity for sentence alignment, word vector averaging is better than adopting the [CLS] token when retrieving a representation of a whole sentence from a BERT-based model.

References

Ahmad Aghaebrahimian. 2017. Quora Question Answer Dataset. *Text, Speech, and Dialogue.* Springer International Publishing, pages 66-73. https://doi.org/10.1007/978-3-319-64206-2_8

Regina Barzilay and Noemie Elhadad. 2003. Sentence Alignment for Monolingual Comparable Corpora. In *Proceedings of the 2003 Conference on Empirical Methods in Natural Language Processing*, pages 25–32. https://aclanthology.org/W03-1004

Regina Barzilay and Kathleen R. McKeown. 2001. Extracting paraphrases from a parallel corpus. In *Proceedings of the 39th Annual Meeting on Association for Computational Linguistics (ACL '01)*, pages 50–57. Association for Computational Linguistics. https://doi.org/10.3115/1073012.1073020

Regina Barzilay and Kathleen R McKeown. 2005. Sentence fusion for multidocument news summarization. *Computational Linguistics.* https://doi.org/10.1162/089120105774321091

Vuk Batanović and Dragan Bojić. 2016. Using Part-of-Speech Tags as Deep-Syntax Indicators in Determining Short-Text Semantic Similarity. *Computer Science and Information Systems.* 2015; 12(1):1–31. https://doi.org/10.2298/CSIS131127082B

Terra Blevins, Omer Levy, and Luke Zettlemoyer. 2018. Deep RNNs Encode Soft Hierarchical Syntax. In *Proceedings of the 56th Annual Meeting of the Association for Computational Linguistics (Volume 2: Short Papers)*, Melbourne, Australia. Association for Computational Linguistics, pages 14–19. http://dx.doi.org/10.18653/v1/P18-2003

Piotr Bojanowski, Edouard Grave, Armand Joulin, and Tomas Mikolov. 2017. Enriching Word Vectors with Subword Information. *Transactions of the Association for Computational Linguistics*, 5:135–146. https://doi.org/10.1162/tacl_a_00051

Peter F. Brown, Jennifer C. Lai, and Robert L. Mercer. 1991. Aligning Sentences in Parallel Corpora. In *29th Annual Meeting of the Association for Computational Linguistics*, Berkeley, California, USA. Association for Computational Linguistics, pages 169–176. http://dx.doi.org/10.3115/981344.981366

Steven Burrows, Martin Potthast, and Benno Stein. 2013. Paraphrase Acquisition via Crowdsourcing and Machine Learning. In *Transactions on Intelligent Systems and Technology* (ACM TIST), pages 1-21. https://doi.org/10.1145/2483669.2483676

Xiaoqiang Chi, Yang Xiang and Ruchao Shen. 2020. Paraphrase Detection with Dependency Embedding. In *2020 4th International Conference on Computer Science and Artificial Intelligence (CSAI 2020)*, December 11-13, 2020, Zhuhai,

China. ACM, New York, NY, USA, 6. https://doi.org/10.1145/3445815.3445850

Hyunjin Choi, Judong Kim, Seongho Joe, and Youngjune Gwon. 2020. Evaluation of BERT and ALBERT Sentence Embedding Performance on Downstream NLP Tasks. In *Proceedings of the* 25th *International Conference on Pattern Recognition (ICPR 2020).* https://doi.org/10.48550/arXiv.2101.1064

Jacob Devlin, Ming-Wei Chang, Kenton Lee, and Kristina Toutanova. 2019. BERT: Pre-training of Deep Bidirectional Transformers for Language Understanding. In *Proceedings of the 2019 Conference of the North American Chapter of the Association for Computational Linguistics: Human Language Technologies, Volume 1 (Long and Short Papers)*, pages 4171–4186. Association for Computational Linguistics. http://dx.doi.org/10.18653/v1/N19-1423

Thomas G. Dietterich. 1998. Approximate Statistical Tests for Comparing Supervised Classification Learning Algorithms. *Neural Computation.* 10 (7): pages 1895–1923. https://doi.org/10.1162/089976698300017197

William B. Dolan and Chris Brockett. 2005. Automatically Constructing a Corpus of Sentential Paraphrases. In *Proceedings of the Third International Workshop on Paraphrasing (IWP2005).* https://aclanthology.org/I05-5002

Ying Ding, Junhui Li, Zhengxian Gong and Guodong Zhou. 2020. Improving neural sentence alignment with word translation. *Frontiers of Computer Science.* 15, 151302. https://doi.org/10.1007/s11704-019-9164-3

Mamdouh Farouk. 2019. Measuring Sentences Similarity: A Survey. *Indian Journal of Science and Technology*, Vol 12(25), July 2019. https://doi.org/10.17485/ijst/2019/v12i25/143977

Christiane Fellbaum. 1998 (ed.). *WordNet: An Electronic Lexical Database.* Cambridge, MA: MIT Press. https://doi.org/10.7551/mitpress/7287.001.0001

William A. Gale and Kenneth W. Church. 1993. A Program for Aligning Sentences in Bilingual Corpora. *Computational Linguistics*, 19(1):75–102. https://aclanthology.org/J93-1004

Juri Ganitkevitch, Benjamin Van Durme, and Chris Callison-Burch. 2013. PPDB: The Paraphrase Database. In *Proceedings of the 2013 Conference of the North American Chapter of the Association for Computational Linguistics: Human Language Technologies*, Atlanta, Georgia. Association for Computational Linguistics, pages 758–764. ttps://aclanthology.org/N13-1092

Hannaneh Hajishirzi, Wen-tau Yih, and Aleksander Kolcz. 2010. Adaptive near-duplicate detection via similarity learning. In *Proceedings of the Association for Computing Machinery Special Interest Group in Information Retrieval (ACM SIGIR)*, pages 419–426. https://doi.org/10.1145/1835449.1835520

Vasileios Hatzivassiloglou, Judith L. Klavans, and Eleazar Eskin. 1999. Detecting Text Similarity over Short Passages: Exploring Linguistic Feature Combinations via Machine Learning. In *1999 Joint SIGDAT Conference on Empirical Methods in Natural Language Processing and Very Large Corpora.* https://aclanthology.org/W99-0625

Andrew Hickl and Jeremy Bensley. 2007. A Discourse Commitment-Based Framework for Recognizing Textual Entailment. In *Proceedings of the ACL-PASCAL Workshop on Textual Entailment and Paraphrasing*, Prague. Association for Computational Linguistics, pages 171-176. https://aclanthology.org/W07-1428

Tsutomu Hirao, Jun Suzuki, Hideki Isozaki, and Eisaku Maeda. 2004. Dependency-based Sentence Alignment for Multiple Document Summarization. In *COLING 2004: Proceedings of the 20th International Conference on Computational Linguistics*, pages 446–452. https://doi.org/10.3115/1220355.1220419

Yonghui Huang, Yunhui Li, Yi Luan. 2018. *Monolingual sentence matching for text simplification.* Computing Research Repository, arXiv:1809.08703. Version 1. https://doi.org/10.48550/arXiv.1809.08703

Dieuwke Hupkes, Verna Dankers, Mathijs Mul, and Elia Bruni. 2020. Compositionality Decomposed: How do Neural Networks Generalise? (Extended Abstract). In *Proceedings of the Twenty-Ninth International Joint Conference on Artificial Intelligence.* International Joint Conferences on Artificial Intelligence Organization, pages 5065-5069. https://doi.org/10.24963/ijcai.2020/708

William Hwang, Hannaneh Hajishirzi, Mari Ostendorf, and Wei Wu. 2015. Aligning Sentences from Standard Wikipedia to Simple Wikipedia. In *Proceedings of the 2015 Conference of the North American Chapter of the Association for Computational Linguistics: Human Language Technologies*, Denver, Colorado. Association for Computational Linguistics, pages 211–217. http://dx.doi.org/10.3115/v1/N15-1022

Chao Jiang, Mounica Maddela, Wuwei Lan, Yang Zhong, and Wei Xu. 2020. Neural CRF Model for Sentence Alignment in Text Simplification. In *Proceedings of the 58th Annual Meeting of the Association for Computational Linguistics*, Online. Association for Computational Linguistics, , pages

7943–7960. http://dx.doi.org/10.18653/v1/2020.acl-main.709

Jonas Mueller and Aditya Thyagarajan. 2016. Siamese recurrent architectures for learning sentence similarity. In *Proceedings of the Thirtieth AAAI Conference on Artificial Intelligence (AAAI'16)*. AAAI Press, pages 2786–2792. https://www.aaai.org/ocs/index.php/AAAI/AAAI16/paper/view/12195

Paul Neculoiu, Maarten Versteegh, and Mihai Rotaru. 2016. Learning Text Similarity with Siamese Recurrent Networks. In *Proceedings of the 1st Workshop on Representation Learning for NLP*, , Berlin, Germany. Association for Computational Linguistics, pages 148–157. http://dx.doi.org/10.18653/v1/W16-1617

Rani Nelken and Stuart M. Shieber. 2006. Towards Robust Context-Sensitive Sentence Alignment for Monolingual Corpora. In *11th Conference of the European Chapter of the Association for Computational Linguistics*, Trento, Italy. Association for Computational Linguistics, pages 161–168. https://aclanthology.org/E06-1021

Zhenzhong Lan, Mingda Chen, Sebastian Goodman, Kevin Gimpel, Piyush Sharma, and Radu Soricut. 2020. ALBERT: A Lite BERT for Self-supervised Learning of Language Representations. In *Proceedings of 8th International Conference on Learning Representations (ICLR 2020)*, Addis Ababa, Ethiopia, April 26-30, 2020. https://doi.org/10.48550/arXiv.1909.11942

Yinhan Liu, Myle Ott, Naman Goyal, Jingfei Du, Mandar Joshi, Danqi Chen, Omer Levy, Mike Lewis, Luke Zettlemoyer, and Veselin Stoyanov. 2019. *RoBERTa: A Robustly Optimized BERT Pretraining Approach*. Computing Research Repository, arXiv:1907.11692. Version 1. https://doi.org/10.48550/arXiv.1907.11692

Bill MacCartney and Christopher D. Manning. 2008. Modeling Semantic Containment and Exclusion in Natural Language Inference. In *Proceedings of the 22nd International Conference on Computational Linguistics (Coling 2008)*, Manchester, UK. Coling 2008 Organizing Committee, pages 521–528. https://aclanthology.org/C08-1066

Mitchell P. Marcus, Beatrice Santorini, and Mary Ann Marcinkiewicz. 1993. Building a Large Annotated Corpus of English: The Penn Treebank. *Computational Linguistics*, 19(2):313–330. https://aclanthology.org/J93-2004

Paul McNamee and James Mayfield. 2004. Character N-Gram Tokenization for European Language Text Retrieval. *Information Retrieval 7* (2004): 73-97. https://doi.org/10.1023/B:INRT.0000009441.78971.be

Tom McCoy, Ellie Pavlick, and Tal Linzen. 2019. Right for the Wrong Reasons: Diagnosing Syntactic Heuristics in Natural Language Inference. In *Proceedings of the 57th Annual Meeting of the Association for Computational Linguistics. Association for Computational Linguistics*, pages 3428–3448. http://dx.doi.org/10.18653/v1/P19-1334

Tomas Mikolov, Kai Chen, Greg Corrado, and Jeffrey Dean. 2013. Efficient Estimation of Word Representations in Vector Space. In *1st International Conference on Learning Representations, ICLR 2013, Scottsdale, Arizona, USA, May 2-4, 2013, Workshop Track Proceedings*. https://doi.org/10.48550/arXiv.1301.3781

Jessica Ouyang and Kathy McKeown. 2019. Neural Network Alignment for Sentential Paraphrases. In *Proceedings of the 57th Annual Meeting of the Association for Computational Linguistics*, Florence, Italy. Association for Computational Linguistics, pages 4724–4735. http://dx.doi.org/10.18653/v1/P19-1467

Şaziye Betül Özateş, Arzucan Özgür, and Dragomir Radev. 2016. Sentence Similarity based on Dependency Tree Kernels for Multi-document Summarization. In *Proceedings of the Tenth International Conference on Language Resources and Evaluation (LREC'16)*, Portorož, Slovenia. European Language Resources Association (ELRA), pages 2833–2838. https://aclanthology.org/L16-1452

Matteo Pagliardini, Prakhar Gupta, and Martin Jaggi. 2018. Unsupervised Learning of Sentence Embeddings Using Compositional n-Gram Features. In *Proceedings of the 2018 Conference of the North American Chapter of the Association for Computational Linguistics: Human Language Technologies, Volume 1 (Long Papers)*, New Orleans, Louisiana. Association for Computational Linguistics, pages 528–540. http://dx.doi.org/10.18653/v1/N18-1049

Jeffrey Pennington, Richard Socher, and Christopher Manning. 2014. GloVe: Global Vectors for Word Representation. In *Proceedings of the 2014 Conference on Empirical Methods in Natural Language Processing (EMNLP)*, Doha, Qatar. Association for Computational Linguistics, pages 1532–1543. http://dx.doi.org/10.3115/v1/D14-1162

Jan Wira Gotama Putra and Takenobu Tokunaga. 2017. Evaluating text coherence based on semantic similarity graph. In *Proceedings of TextGraphs-11: the Workshop on Graph-based Methods for Natural Language Processing*, Vancouver, Canada. Association for Computational Linguistics, pages 76–85. http://dx.doi.org/10.18653/v1/W17-2410

Nils Reimers and Iryna Gurevych. 2019. Sentence-BERT: Sentence Embeddings using Siamese BERT-Networks. In *Proceedings of the 2019 Conference on Empirical Methods in Natural Language Processing and the 9th International Joint Conference on Natural Language Processing (EMNLP-IJCNLP)*, Hong Kong, China. Association for Computational Linguistics, pages 3982–3992. http://dx.doi.org/10.18653/v1/D19-1410

Sanja Štajner, Marc Franco-Salvador, Paolo Rosso, and Simone Paolo Ponzetto. 2018. CATS: A Tool for Customized Alignment of Text Simplification Corpora. In *Proceedings of the Eleventh International Conference on Language Resources and Evaluation (LREC 2018)*, Miyazaki, Japan. European Language Resources Association (ELRA). https://aclanthology.org/L18-1615

Sanja Štajner, Marc Franco-Salvador, Simone Paolo Ponzetto, Paolo Rosso, and Heiner Stuckenschmidt. 2017. Sentence Alignment Methods for Improving Text Simplification Systems. In *Proceedings of the 55th Annual Meeting of the Association for Computational Linguistics (Volume 2: Short Papers)*, Vancouver, Canada. Association for Computational Linguistics, pages 97–102. http://dx.doi.org/10.18653/v1/P17-2016

Peng Qi, Yuhao Zhang, Yuhui Zhang, Jason Bolton, and Christopher D. Manning. 2020. Stanza: A Python Natural Language Processing Toolkit for Many Human Languages. In *Proceedings of the 58th Annual Meeting of the Association for Computational Linguistics: System Demonstrations*, Online. Association for Computational Linguistics, pages 101–108. http://dx.doi.org/10.18653/v1/2020.acl-demos.14

Long Qiu, Min-Yen Kan, and Tat-Seng Chua. 2006. Paraphrase Recognition via Dissimilarity Significance Classification. In *Proceedings of the 2006 Conference on Empirical Methods in Natural Language Processing*, Sydney, Australia. Association for Computational Linguistics, pages 18–26. https://aclanthology.org/W06-1603

Wenhui Wang, Furu Wei, Li Dong, Hangbo Bao, Nan Yang, Ming Zhou. 2020. MiniLM: Deep Self-Attention Distillation for Task-Agnostic Compression of Pre-Trained Transformers. In *Proceedings of the 34th International Conference on Neural Information Processing Systems (NIPS'20)*. Curran Associates Inc., Red Hook, NY, USA, Article 485, pages 5776–5788. https://dl.acm.org/doi/abs/10.5555/3495724.3496209

Daniela Brook Weiss, Paul Roit, Ayal Klein, Ori Ernst, and Ido Dagan. 2021. QA-Align: Representing Cross-Text Content Overlap by Aligning Question-Answer Propositions. In *Proceedings of the 2021 Conference on Empirical Methods in Natural Language Processing*, Online and Punta Cana, Dominican Republic. Association for Computational Linguistics, pages 9879–9894. http://dx.doi.org/10.18653/v1/2021.emnlp-main.778

Bernard Lewis Welch. 1947. The generalization of 'STUDENT'S' problem when several different population variances are involved. *Biometrika*, Volume 34, Issue 1-2, pages 28–35. doi: 10.1093/biomet/34.1-2.28

Zhibiao Wu and Martha Palmer. 1994. Verb Semantics and Lexical Selection. In 32nd Annual Meeting of the Association for Computational Linguistics, Las Cruces, New Mexico, USA. Association for Computational Linguistics, pages 133–138. http://dx.doi.org/10.3115/981732.981751

Junru Zhou, Zhuosheng Zhang, and Hai Zhao. 2020. LIMIT-BERT: Linguistic Informed Multi-Task BERT. In Findings of the Association for Computational Linguistics: EMNLP 2020. Association for Computational Linguistics, pages 4450–4461. http://dx.doi.org/10.18653/v1/2020.findings-emnlp.399

The 34th Conference on Computational Linguistics and Speech Processing (ROCLING 2022)
Taipei, Taiwan, November 21-22, 2022. The Association for Computational Linguistics and Chinese Language Processing

基於 RoBERTa 的中藥命名實體識別模型
(RoBERTa-based Traditional Chinese Medicine Named Entity Recognition Model)

Ming-Hsiang Su, Chin-Wei Lee, Chi-Lun Hsu and Ruei-Cyuan Su
Department of Data Science, Soochow University, Taipei, Taiwan
{huntfox.su,vivibank888, laurenhsu31,70613rex}@gmail.com

摘要

本研究構建了一個命名實體識別，並將其應用於中藥名稱和疾病名稱的識別，其結果可進一步用於人機對話系統，為人們提供正確的中藥用藥提醒。首先，本研究利用網路爬蟲整理網路資源，成為中藥命名實體語料庫，收集了 1097 篇文章，1412 個疾病名稱和 38714 個中藥名稱。然後，我們使用中藥名稱和BIO標籤方法對每篇文章進行標註。最後，本研究用 BiLSTM 和 CRF 對 BERT、ALBERT、RoBERTa、GPT2 進行訓練和評估。實驗結果表明，RoBERTa 結合 BiLSTM 和 CRF 的 NER 系統取得了最好的系統性能，其中精準率為 0.96，召回率為 0.96，F1-score 為 0.96。

Abstract

In this study, a named entity recognition was constructed and applied to the identification of Chinese medicine names and disease names. The results can be further used in a human-machine dialogue system to provide people with correct Chinese medicine medication reminders. First, this study uses web crawlers to sort out web resources into a Chinese medicine named entity corpus, collecting 1097 articles, 1412 disease names and 38714 Chinese medicine names. Then, we annotated each article using TCM name and BIO tagging method. Finally, this study trains and evaluates BERT, ALBERT, RoBERTa, GPT2 with BiLSTM and CRF. The experimental results show that RoBERTa's NER system combining BiLSTM and CRF achieves the best system performance, with a precision rate of 0.96, a recall rate of 0.96, and an F1-score of 0.96.

關鍵字：中藥、疾病、命名實體識別模型
Keywords: Traditional Chinese Medicine, Disease, Named Entity Recognition Model

1 Introduction

中藥(Traditional Chinese Medicine, TCM) 是中華民族傳統藥物的總稱，根據中醫理論指導下應用的藥物 (Wiki, 2022)。台灣擁有一個融合了傳統中藥和西藥的多元化醫療環境，中藥對保健和慢性病的作用近來逐漸受到公眾的重視，中藥的使用也得到了廣泛的普及 (顏秋蘭等人, 2020; 葉明功, 2020)。民眾普遍認為中藥溫和，沒有副作用。因此，人們經常在沒有醫生處方的情況下到中藥店購買中藥，或者聽地下電台誇大療效，購買相關中藥產品，而忽視了中藥的安全性 (楊榮季, 2012)。根據統計，約有 88.2%的大眾在過去一年中有過購買和服用中藥的經歷 (顏秋蘭等人, 2020)。然而，市場上存在著各種非法的藥品廣告和不合格的產品。國人的用藥習慣不正確，往往會加重肝腎負擔，甚至誤用、混用、中西藥相互作用，導致藥物的療效或毒性發生變化，對健康的影響是不可低估的。王海征等人 (王海征等人, 2015) 研究指出銀髮族患者病情複雜，慢性病居多，加上認為中藥其中以銀髮族用藥錯誤所造成的健康影響最為嚴重。在 520 例用藥錯誤中，以用法、用量錯誤為最高，佔了 48.5%。在聊天過程中，如何提供人們正確的中藥使用方式及用藥資訊，以避免因錯誤用藥造成健康惡化，是對話系統值得研究的議題。

深度學習是目前機器學習領域最具前瞻性的方法，如對話理解 (Su et al., 2018)、對話回應生成 (Su et al., 2019)、圖像分類 (Chhillar et al., 2020) 或語音翻譯 (McCarthy et al., 2020) 等成功案例。具深度學習模型的機器，可以從大量的數據中自行摸索出潛在的抽象規則，而不需要他人的指導。鑒於近年來深度學習出色的識別能力，本研究將應用深度學習技術於中藥命名實體識別(Named Entity Recognition, NER)，從而提供對話系統與人的互動，並提醒避免用藥錯誤。目前，中藥領域的語料庫還沒有像中文或英文語料庫那樣多樣化和豐富，這大大增加了中藥命名實體識別的難度。如果能夠克服中藥命名實體識別的問題，就有可能正確識別人機對話中人們提到的藥名，這對後續用藥提醒回應的生成有很大的幫助。對於中藥領域，目前還沒有適合使用的中藥公共知識庫。如果能通過網路爬蟲將網路資源整理成中藥知識庫，包括各種類型的中藥和中藥處方及療效，將對對話系統和問答系統有很大幫助。

現今，在命名實體識別任務中，主要採用基於循環神經網路(Recurrent Neural Network, RNN)的方法 (Chiu & Nichols, 2016; Lample et al., 2016) 作為序列標註的模型，並輔以字元級的詞向量或有其他文本特徵。Chiu 和 Nichols (Chiu & Nichols, 2016) 在序列標註模型中使用了雙向長短期記憶循環神經網路(Bidirectional Long Short-Term Memory, Bi-LSTM)。在循環神經網路輸出後，使用人工網路來確定哪些電流應該被標記。命名實體，作者使用字元級模型使用了具有一些字元特徵的卷積神經網路 (Convolutional Neural Network, CNN)，例如首字母是否大寫。

而 Lample et al. (Lample et al., 2016) 使用一層條件隨機域 (Conditional Random Fields, CRF)來判斷當前的標註結果。他們利用 CRF 的特點，讓前一個時間點的標註結果影響當前的標註，從而提高準確率。另一方面，字元層面的編碼也發生了變化，他們在字元層面使用了預先訓練好的詞向量語另一個雙向的長短期循環神經網路。最後，他們將原始單詞向量語字元級向量連接起來，作為單詞的代表向量。除了使用 RNN 來判斷命名實體外，Strubell et al. (Strubell et al., 2017) 使用疊代擴張卷積神經網路 (Iterated Dilated Convolutional Neural Networks, ID-CNN)來處理命名實體以達到加速的目的。他們通過卷積網路的特殊結構，解決了卷積網路不適合於序列標註的缺點。

NER 系統通常通過將其輸出與人類注釋進行比較來評估，這可以通過精確匹配來量化。NER 涉及到實體邊界和實體類型，通過精確匹配評估，只有當時體邊界和實體類型都與基礎事實相匹配時，命名實體才被認為是正確的 (Tjong et al., 2003; Pradhan et al., 2012; Li et al., 2020)。由於大多數NER系統涉及多種實體類型，因此通常需要評估所有實體類型的性能，這方面通常使用兩種方法，宏觀平均的 F-score 和微觀平均的 F-score，宏觀平均 F-score 是針對每個實體類型獨立計算的，然後取其平均值。微觀平均 F-score 將所有類別的實體貢獻彙總，計算出一個平均值。後者可能會受到語料庫中大類別識別實體質量的嚴重影響。

2 Dataset Collection

在台灣，雖然人們經常使用中藥來保養身體，但很少有人整理中藥數據集來訓練 NER 模型。在本研究中，採用爬蟲從 KingNet 網站 (KingNet, 2022) 和 CloudTCM 網站 (CloudTCM, 2022) 檢索中藥數據。對於中藥和處方的種類，根據其名稱、功效、用法、禁忌等，自動整理成適合NER模型的中藥數據集。在 KingNet 網站上，共收集了 730 篇文章，包含 678,846 個單詞;而在 CloudTCM 網站上，共收集了 367 篇文章，包含 1,219,168 單詞。中藥名稱和處方名稱的例子見 Table1。然後本研究採用內-外-開始 (IOB) 進行標註，我們將中藥名稱標註為 ”B-TMC” 和 “I-TMC”，症狀標註為 “B-SYMP” 和 “I-SYMP”，其他標註為 “O”。例如，”人蔘的安神益智功效主要表現在促進學習記憶方面。適量人蔘可安神舒眠，緩解壓力” 被標為 “人 B-TMC” 和 “蔘 I-TMC”，其他的則被標為 ”O”。

中藥名稱	白芷、薄荷、人蔘等。
處方名稱	桂枝湯、溫脾湯、清脾飲等。

Table 1: 中藥名稱和處方名稱的例子。

3 Proposed Methods

3.1 Word Embedding

語言模型預訓練已被證明在改善許多自然語言處理任務方面是有效的 (Devlin, 2018)。這些任務包括句子級任務和標記級任務，如自然語言推理和 NER。在本研究中，我們使用 Bidirectional Encoder Representations from

The 34th Conference on Computational Linguistics and Speech Processing (ROCLING 2022)
Taipei, Taiwan, November 21-22, 2022. The Association for Computational Linguistics and Chinese Language Processing

Transformers (BERT) 作為詞嵌入模型，其中 BERT 是 Google AI 團隊近年來發布的自然語言預訓練模型。

BERT 是一種自然語言預訓練模型，與其他預訓練語言模型相比，它的訓練方法更加新穎。它採用 Transformer 的編碼器雙向連接，在訓練雙向語言模型時採用兩個無監督的預測任務，即遮罩語言模型 (Masked Language Model, MLM) 和下一句預測 (Next Sentence Prediction, NSP)。雙向和單向的區別主要是由於單詞語言表現的訓練方向不同。單向語言模型會根據每個詞的左邊或右邊的詞來訓練每個詞的語言表示。例如，假設你想得到”我訪問了銀行帳戶”句子中”銀行”這個詞的語言表示。單向語言模型根據”銀行”左邊的”我訪問了”而不是”銀行”右邊的”帳戶”來訓練”銀行”這個詞。對於雙向語言模型，通過考慮”我訪問了”和”帳戶”來訓練該詞的詞嵌入。一個好的詞語語言表現對於 Natural language processing (NLP) 任務非常重要，而雙向語言模型可以讀取雙向訊息，所以詞語的語言表現會比單向的好。

但 BERT 的作者解釋說，一般語言模型的雙向發展可能是因為它可以間接地 ”看到自己”，所以預測單詞時只需要直接考慮它的已知上下文訊息，為了解決雙向語言模型面臨的問題，BERT 提出了在預測單詞的任務中加入遮罩的訓練技術，將輸入句子中 15%的單詞遮罩，並預測這些遮罩的單詞。該任務實例如 Table 2 所示。如何選擇遮擋的比例是一個問題。首先，如果所選單詞 100% 被遮擋，會導致模型只通過遮擋來學習上下文語言表現。對於未被遮擋的詞，很難學習到好的語言表現。其次，由於遮擋本身並不出現在實際的預測階段，為了迫使模型關注所有的詞，一定比例的被選中的詞並設有被遮罩，而是被替換成其他的詞或者保持不變。通過這種訓練機制，模型可以學習到更好的上下文語言表現。

Input:
The man [MASK1] to [MASK2] store
Label:
[MASK1] = went ; [MASK2] = store

Table 2: 遮罩語言模型預測人物的例子。

BERT 訓練策略中加入的另一項創新是其他語言模型沒有考慮的兩個句子之間的關係，這也是許多自然語言任務的一個重要特徵。因此，為了讓模型學習句子之間的關係，將給出兩個句子 A 和 B，模型將判斷 B 是否是真實語料庫中 A 的下一句。任務實例見 Table 3，預測兩個句子間的關聯學習深度雙向的上下文表示。此外，BERT 還有實驗表明，在模型的輸出中加入線性層，通過微調可以在各種自然語言處理任務中表現良好，適用於自然語言任務，如情感分類或問題回答。BERT 的輸入是標記嵌入、分段嵌入、位置嵌入，如 Figure 1 所示，還有兩個特殊符號[CLS]、[SEP]。[CLS]可用於後續的自然語言分類任務，而[SEP]則用於區分兩個句子。

有許多基於 BERT 的改進模型，包括 ALBERT (Lan et al., 2019)，RoBERTa (Liu et al., 2019) 和 GPT2 (Lagler, 2013)。本研究將評估這些不同的模型，以獲得 NER 系統的最佳性能。

Input:
The man went to the store [SEP] he bought a gallon of milk
Label:
IsNext
Input:
The man went to the store [SEP] penguins are flightless birds
Label:
NotNext

Table 3: 下一句話預測任務的例子。

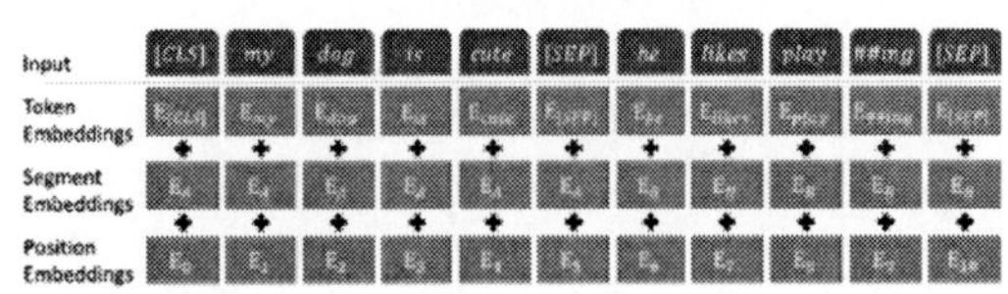

Figure 1: BERT 輸入表示的示意圖。

3.2 Bi-LSTM

長短期記憶 (Long Short-Term Memory, LSTM) 是一種特殊的 RNN。與傳統的 RNN 不同，LSTM 使用三個不同的閥來控制單元的狀態。這些閥是輸入閥、遺忘閥和輸出閥。這三個閥在 Figure 2 中分別三個綠框表示。

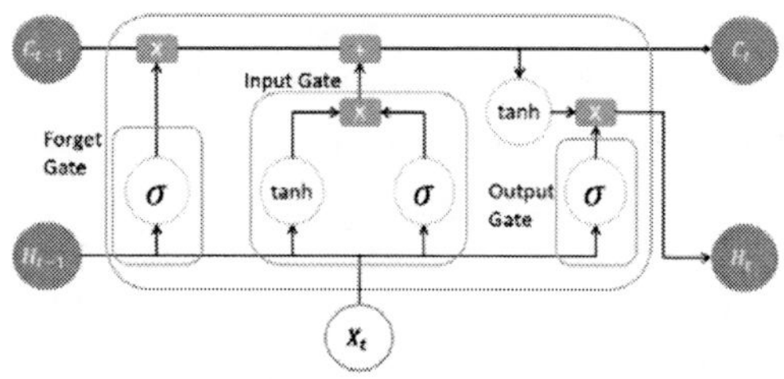

Figure 2: LSTM 模型的示意圖。

遺忘閥通過 (1) 來控制遺忘，其中W_f和U_i代表要與前一個時間點的輸出和當前輸入相乘的權重矩陣，h_{t-1}代表前一個時間點的輸出，X_t代表當前輸入，b_f代表偏移量向量，所得的f_t可以決定哪些訊息應該被遺忘。輸入閥分為兩小部分，一部分稱為候選狀態向量$\tilde{\boldsymbol{c}}_t$和輸入閥向量$\boldsymbol{i}_t$，操作方法為 (2) 和 (3)，其中W_c, W_i, U_c 和 U_i代表權重矩陣，$\boldsymbol{b}_c$和 $\boldsymbol{b}_i$代表偏移量向量。

用這兩個向量$\tilde{\boldsymbol{c}}_t$和 $\boldsymbol{i}_t$來控制多少個單元狀態受到當前輸入的影響，新的單元狀態$\boldsymbol{c}_t$將由f_t, $\boldsymbol{c}_{t-1}$, $\boldsymbol{i}_t$和 $\tilde{\boldsymbol{c}}_t$決定，如 (4) 所示。輸出閥是為了控制將輸出多少個單元狀態，如(5)所示，這也是由當前的輸入$\boldsymbol{X}_t$和前一輪的輸出h_{t-1}決定的。最後，本輪的輸出向量h_t取決於本輪的單元狀態$\boldsymbol{c}_t$和輸出閥的向量$\boldsymbol{o}_t$，如(6)所示。由於這些閥的機制，LSTM 可以記住長期的依賴關係。

$$f_t = \sigma(W_f h_{t-1} + U_i X_t + \boldsymbol{b}_f) \quad (1)$$
$$\tilde{\boldsymbol{c}}_t = tanh(W_c h_{t-1} + U_c X_t + \boldsymbol{b}_c) \quad (2)$$
$$\boldsymbol{i}_t = \sigma(W_i h_{t-1} + U_i X_t + \boldsymbol{b}_i) \quad (3)$$
$$\boldsymbol{c}_t = f_t \boldsymbol{c}_{t-1} + \boldsymbol{i}_t \tilde{\boldsymbol{c}}_t \quad (4)$$
$$\boldsymbol{o}_t = \sigma(W_o \boldsymbol{h}_{t-1} + U_o \boldsymbol{X}_t + \boldsymbol{b}_o) \quad (5)$$
$$\boldsymbol{h}_t = \boldsymbol{o}_t * \tanh(\boldsymbol{c}_t) \quad (6)$$

大多數LSTM的輸出會是一個或多個向量，與地面實況相比，得到兩者之間的誤差，然後通過隨機梯度下降或其他優化算法矩陣更新網路中的權重。由於網路中存在多個閥，大大降低了部分分化過程中梯度消失或爆炸的可能性，這是 LSTM 比一般 RNN 的優勢。Bi-LSTM 是一種雙向 LSTM，其結構圖如 Figure 3 所示。Bi-LSTM 用於學習時間序列的依賴關係，通過訓練輸入閥、遺忘閥和輸出閥的權重來學習序列輸入中應該注意的關鍵點。

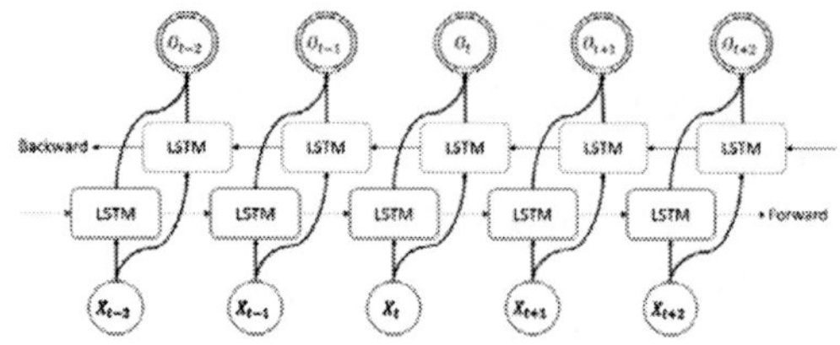

Figure 3: Bi-LSTM 模型的示意圖。

3.3 CRF

輸入序列中的每個向量進入 Bi-LSTM，並與前一個時間點的隱藏向量相匹配，判斷當前時間點的輸出。這個輸出將作為特徵進入 CRF 層，並讓 CRF 學習每個權重的特徵函數，如 Figure 4 所示。CRF 的訓練方法主要有兩個步驟。第一步是由訓練數據集生成特徵函數，並初始化每個特徵函數對應的權重。第二步是使用最大似然估計、梯度下降等方法來更新每個特徵函數的權重，直到權重變化收斂。以 Bi-LSTM 和 CRF 作為 NER 模型，對於 CRF 來說，Bi-LSTM 在每個時間點的輸出序列就是 CRF 的觀察向量，可以將命名實體的標註序列與 CRF 預測的序列進行比較，計算出誤差函數的梯度。通過反向傳播算法，這個誤差梯度被反饋給 Bi-LSTM 和 CRF，權重可以被更新以最小化誤差。

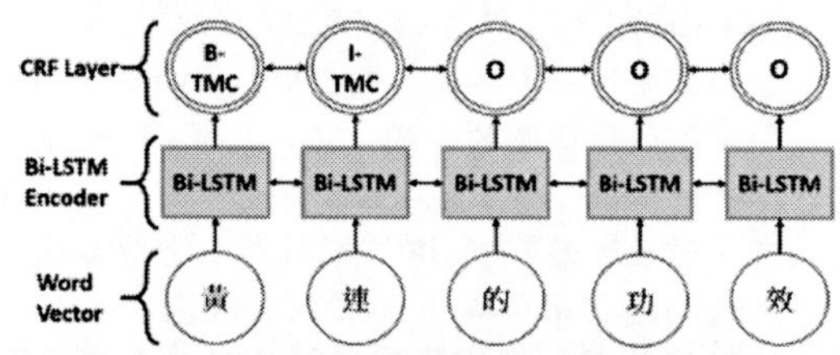

Figure 4: NER 模型的示意圖。

4 Experimental Results and Discussion

本研究針對命名實體識別任務提出了 BERT, Bi-LSTM 和 CRF 串聯模型，用 BERT 表示單句的訊息關係，然後通過 Bi- LSTM 和 CRF 模型判斷命名實體的標註位置。本研究比較了 BERT、ALBERT、RoBERTA 和 GPT2 結合 Bi-LSTM 和 CRF 模型的性能，以確定最終 NER 系統的架構。測試集的實驗結果表明，BERT 的精確度為 0.86，召回率為 0.91，F1-score 為 0.89; ALBERT 的精確度為 0.93，召回率為 0.94，

F1-score 為 0.93; RoBERTA 的精確度為 0.96，召回率為 0.96，F1-score 為 0.96; GPT2 的精確度為 0.93，召回率為 0.92，F1-score 為 0.92。

Table 4 和 Table 5 分別顯示了不同模型在 TMC、SYMP 標籤、微觀平均值、宏觀平均值和加權平均值上的實驗結果。實驗結果顯示，RoBERTa 模型優於 BERT、ALBERT 和 GPT2 模型。我們認為，在我們收集的 TCM 語料庫中，RoBERTa 模型更能夠提取語料相關的訊息，這導致了最佳的整體性能。

	BERT			ALBERT		
	P	R	F1	P	R	F1
SYMP	0.66	0.83	0.74	0.89	0.88	0.88
TMC	0.5	0.56	0.53	0.68	0.75	0.71
micro avg	0.86	0.91	0.89	0.93	0.94	0.93
macro avg	0.79	0.85	0.82	0.89	0.9	0.9
weighted avg	0.88	0.91	0.89	0.93	0.94	0.94

P: 精確度; **R**: 召回率; **F1**: F1-score

Table 4: 對 BERT 和 ALBERT 的評估。

	RoBERTa			GPT2		
	P	R	F1	P	R	F1
SYMP	**0.92**	**0.91**	**0.92**	0.82	0.79	0.81
TMC	**0.8**	**0.79**	**0.79**	0.66	0.62	0.64
micro avg	**0.96**	**0.96**	**0.96**	0.93	0.92	0.92
macro avg	**0.93**	**0.92**	**0.93**	0.87	0.85	0.86
weighted avg	**0.96**	**0.96**	**0.96**	0.93	0.92	0.92

P: 精確度; **R**: 召回率; **F1**: F1-score

Table 5: 對 RoBERTa 和 GPT2 的評估。

5 Conclusion and future work

在這項研究中，構建了命名實體識別模型，並將其應用於中藥名稱和疾病名稱的識別。其結果可進一步用於人機對話系統，為人們提供正確的中藥用藥提醒。此外，本研究利用網路爬蟲將網路資源整理成中藥命名實體語料庫，共包括 1097 篇文章、1412 個疾病名稱和 38714 個中藥名稱。然後我們用中藥名稱和BIO標籤方法對每篇文章進行標籤。最後，實驗結果表明，RoBERTa 組合 Bi-LSTM 和 CRF 的 NER 系統取得了最好的系統性能，其中精準度為 0.96，召回率為 0.96，F1-score 為 0.96。

在未來的工作中，我們希望能獲得更多的中藥對話數據集，以便我們能訓練出更適合對話系統的 NER 系統。此外，我們還希望在 NER 系統中加入自我注意力的機制，以提高系統性能。最後，我們希望擴大 NER 的標籤，使 NER 能夠識別更多語中藥有關的命名實體。

References

王海征, 林曉蘭, 張鵬, 王雅葳, and 陳文強. 2015. 老年患者中藥用藥錯誤報告 520 例分析. *藥物不良反應雜誌*. 17(5): 353.

楊榮季. 2012. 「老人」及「婦女」醫學保健之用藥安全調查與知能研究. *行政院衛生署中醫藥年報*, 1(6): 1-120.

顏秋蘭, 黃林煌和葉明功. 2020. 藥師介入提升民眾中醫藥就醫用藥安全. *藥學雜誌*, 29(3).

葉明功. 2020. 中醫藥就醫用藥之停、看、聽、選、用專業. 南投醫院. Retrieved October 12, 2020, from https://www.nant.mohw.gov.tw/public/ufile/c909c79547bd1528856c92f9a08e9361.pdf.

Ankit Chhillar, Sanjeev Thakur, and Ajay Rana. 2020. Survey of Plant Disease Detection Using Image Classification Techniques. In *Proceedings of the 8th International Conference on Reliability, Infocom Technologies and Optimization (ICRITO)*, pp. 1339-1344.

Arya D. McCarthy, Puzon Liezl, and Pino Juan. 2020. SkinAugment: auto-encoding speaker conversions for automatic speech translation. In *Proceedings of IEEE International Conference on Acoustics, Speech and Signal Processing (ICASSP)*, pp. 7924-7928.

Chiu, Jason PC, and Eric Nichols. 2016. Named entity recognition with bidirectional LSTM-CNNs. *Transactions of the Association for Computational Linguistics*, 4: 357-370.

CloudTCM website, Retrieved October 11, 2022, from https://cloudtcm.com/

Emma Strubell, Patrick Verga, David Belanger, and Andrew McCallum. 2017. Fast and Accurate Entity Recognition with Iterated Dilated Convolutions. In *Proceedings of the conference on Empirical Methods in Natural Language Processing*, pp. 2670-2680.

Erik F. Tjong Kim Sang, and Fien De Meulder. 2003. Introduction to the CoNLL-2003 shared task: language-independent named entity recognition. In *Proceedings of the 7th conference on Natural language learning at HLT-NAACL 2003-Volume 4*, pp. 142-147.

Guillaume Lample, Miguel Ballesteros, Sandeep Subramanian, Kazuya Kawakami, and Chris Dyer. 2016. Neural architectures for named entity recognition. In *Proceedings of the Conference of the North American Chapter of the Association for*

Computational Linguistics: Human Language Technologies, pp. 260-270, 2016.

Jacob Devlin, Ming-Wei Chang, Kenton Lee, and Kristina Toutanova. 2018. Bert: Pre-training of deep bidirectional transformers for language understanding. *arXiv preprint* arXiv:1810.04805, 2018.

Jing Li, Aixin Sun, Jianglei Han, and Chenliang Li. 2020. A survey on deep learning for named entity recognition. *IEEE Transactions on Knowledge and Data Engineering*, 34(1): 50-70.

K. Lagler, Schindelegger, Michael, Böhm, Johannes, Krásná, Hana, and T. Nilsson. 2013. GPT2: Empirical slant delay model for radio space geodetic techniques. *Geophysical research letters*, 40(6): 1069-1073.

KingNet website, Retrieved October 11, 2022, from https://www.kingnet.com.tw/tcm/

Ming-Hsiang Su, Chung-Hsien Wu, Kun-Yi Huang, and Chu-Kwang Chen. 2018. Attention-based dialog state tracking for conversational interview coaching. In *Proceedings of 2018 IEEE International Conference on Acoustics, Speech and Signal Processing (ICASSP)*, pp. 6144-6148.

Ming-Hsiang Su, Chung-Hsien Wu, and Liang-Yu Chen. 2019. Attention-Based Response Generation Using Parallel Double Q-Learning for Dialog Policy Decision in a Conversational System. *IEEE/ACM Transactions on Audio, Speech, and Language Processing*, 28: 131-143.

Sameer Pradhan, Alessandro Moschitti, Nianwen Xue, Olga Uryupina, and Yuchen Zhang. 2012. CoNLL-2012 shared task: Modeling multilingual unrestricted coreference in OntoNotes. In *Proceedings of the Joint Conference on EMNLP and CoNLL-Shared Task*, pp. 1-40.

Wiki. Traditional Chinese medicine. Retrieved October 11, 2022, from https://en.wikipedia.org/wiki/Traditional_Chinese_medicine.

Yinhan Liu, Myle Ott, Naman Goyal, Jingfei Du, Mandar Joshi, Danqi Chen, Omer Levy, Mike Lewis, Luke Zettlemoyer, and Veselin Stoyanov. 2019. Roberta: A robustly optimized Bert pretraining approach. *arXiv preprint* arXiv:1907.11692, 2019.

Zhenzhong Lan, Mingda Chen, Sebastian Goodman, Kevin Gimpel, Piyush Sharma, and Radu Soricut. 2019. Albert: A lite Bert for self-supervised learning of language representations. *arXiv preprint* arXiv:1909.11942.

The 34th Conference on Computational Linguistics and Speech Processing (ROCLING 2022)
Taipei, Taiwan, November 21-22, 2022. The Association for Computational Linguistics and Chinese Language Processing

運用不同音訊長度於遷移式學習以提升電鋸聲音識別能力之研究
A Study on Using Different Audio Lengths in Transfer Learning for Improving Chainsaw Sound Recognition

張家瑋 Jia-Wei Chang
jiaweichang.gary@gmail.com

胡忠雲 Zhong-Yun Hu
e871223eeee@gmail.com

國立臺中科技大學資訊工程系
Department of Computer Science and Information Engineering
National Taichung University of Science and Technology

摘要

在山林中，由於聲音的多元複雜及環境中諸多的雜訊，電鋸聲音的識別是富有挑戰性的任務。本研究認為以不同的聲音長度對於模型的訓練結果可能有所差異，故以簡易的 LeNet 模型結合了平均池化層設計出能夠接受任意長度音訊的識別模型。本研究主要分析不同聲音長度對於模型訓練之影響以及短至長與長至短音訊的遷移學習結果。本實驗皆以 ESC-10 資料集來訓練模型並以自行蒐集的電鋸聲資料集驗證模型的準確度。實驗結果表明(1)以 1 秒、3 秒、5 秒資料集分別訓練的三個模型，在 1 秒、3 秒與 5 秒的電鋸聲驗證集中，各達到 74%~78%、74%~77%與 79%~83%的準確度。(2)以 1 秒→3 秒→5 秒的 ESC-10 資料遷移學習的模型於 1 秒、3 秒與 5 秒電鋸聲驗證集中分別達到 85.28%、88.67%與 91.8%準確度，均較原訓練方法有所明顯提升。(3)在遷移式學習中，相較於長至短秒數的遷移訓練，以短至長秒數的遷移訓練得到了較佳的結果；尤其在 5 秒的電鋸聲驗證集中相差了 14%的準確度。

Abstract

Chainsaw sound recognition is a challenging task because of the complexity of sound and the excessive noises in mountain environments. This study aims to discuss the influence of different sound lengths on the accuracy of model training. Therefore, this study used LeNet, a simple model with few parameters, and adopted the design of average pooling to enable the proposed models to receive audio of any length. In performance comparison, we mainly compared the influence of different audio lengths and further tested the transfer learning from short-to-long and long-to-short audio. In experiments, we used the ESC-10 dataset for training models and validated their performance via the self-collected chainsaw-audio dataset. The experimental results show that (a) the models trained with different audio lengths (1s, 3s, and 5s) have accuracy from 74%~78%, 74%~77%, and 79%~83% on the self-collected dataset. (b) The generalization of the previous models is significantly improved by transfer learning, the models achieved 85.28%, 88.67%, and 91.8% of accuracy. (c) In transfer learning, the model learned from short-to-long audios can achieve better results than that learned from long-to-short audios, especially being differed 14% of accuracy on 5s chainsaw-audios.

關鍵字：聲音辨識、環境聲音分類、電鋸聲音識別、遷移學習

Keywords: Voice Recognition, Environmental Sound Classification, Chainsaw Sound Recognition, Transfer Learning

1 緒論

近年來對於環境保護的意識逐漸在社會大眾中受到重視，其中針對森林的相關議題除了天災的野火、土石流，就是針對人為因素的防範，在人為的事件中對於森林破壞度最大的就是盜伐，透過監視器或是人工巡邏對於保護一個森林來說成本以及保護力度都不足

夠，但如果透過聲音監控的方式，可以將布置防護網的成本降低，也可以更加即時的反應盜伐事件的發生。這個任務是屬於環境聲音分類(Environmental Sound Classification, ESC)的範疇，在進行環境聲音分類的任務之前需要將聲音經過預處理，預處理的方法有很多，也能取得許多不同的特徵以供模型使用。過零率(Zhang and Kuo, 2001)、小波特徵(Valero and Alías, 2012)、梅爾倒頻譜係數(MFCC)(Uzkent et al., 2012)。目前機器學習與深度學習已經被廣泛的應用於環境聲音分類任務上。支持向量機(Support Vector Machine，SVM) (Chu et al., 2009; Piczak, 2015b)、隨機森林分類器(Random Forest Classifier，RF) (Piczak, 2015b)、高斯混合模型(Gausasian Mixture Model，GMM) (Piczak, 2015b; Dhanalakshmi et al., 2011)都是經典的機械學習方法。但是機器學習一開始的訓練很耗費時間和成本。如果沒有充足的資料，難以訓練出可用的模型。近年來，深度學習技術已被很好的應用於從聲音信號中提取高辨識度特徵以執行環境聲音分類。提取有用特徵以及對於細微聲音仍然保持良好的泛化能力使深度學習成為了環境聲音分類的首選方式。環境聲音分類與語音辨識任務的不同之處在於，環境聲音分類所要識別的聲音通常都是零散的，同一類的聲音所轉換出的頻譜圖可能表現出相當大的落差，聲音模式可以是連續的、不規則的、瞬間的、而且大部分會包含許多吵雜或是無聲的幀，我們輸入的聲音長度也有可能不同。並且如果需要將模型應用於森林之中的小型監控設備，對於模型的大小、複雜度以及聲音的長度都有較大的限制，因此本篇論文想要研究在一個簡單的模型中，所以本篇嘗試透過改變訓練時的音訊秒數以進行遷移式學習(Zhuang et al., 2020; Liao et al., 2021; Hung and Chang., 2021)來研究模型針對訓練集外的電鋸聲音判斷的敏感度。本研究其餘章節的組織如下：第二節說明本研究會使用之環境聲音模型原始架構相關工作，第三節介紹本研究所使用的資料集以及解釋本研究實行之方法論，第四節為本研究模型訓練結果比較以及模型對於資料集音訊外的聲音判斷能力結果，第五章對實驗結果進行相關討論，第六章總結本研究結果。

2 相關研究

本章節介紹使用基於深度學習的模型進行環經聲音分類的相關工作。

2.1 將頻譜圖應用於 CNN

由於將音訊轉換成頻譜圖後能得到二維的特徵，所以頻譜圖一直是聲音深度學習模型喜歡使用的預處理方式。在 CNN 問世後(Piczak, 2015a)首次提出將頻譜圖特徵作為輸入並執行 ESC 的 2D-CNN，根據研究結果表示與 SVM、RF、GMM 等機器學習模型相比 PiczakCNN 顯著的提高了辨識的準確度，受到 PiczakCNN 的啟發，愈來愈多的人將頻譜圖輸入不同的 CNN 模型，也有人結合了預訓練網路都得到了極佳的效果(如 GoogleNet(Szegedy et al., 2015)和 AlexNet(Krizhevsky et al., 2012))。

2.2 LeNet-5

本篇研究所使用之模型參考自 LeNet-5(LeCun et al., 2015)並進行一些修改以符合訓練任務需求，在 90 年代，由於 SVM 等算法的發展，深度學習的發展受到了很大的阻礙。但 LeCun 等人(LeCun et al., 2015)堅持不懈，依然在該領域苦苦研究。1998 年，LeCun 提出了 LeNet-5 網絡用來解決手寫識別的問題。LeNet-5 被譽為是卷積神經網絡的「Hello Word」，足以見到這篇論文的重要性。該模型共有 7 層，共有 3 個卷基層、2 個平均池化層以及 2 個全連接層。

2.3 二元自適應均值池化層

要進行本篇想研究的方案之前，需要先想辦法使模型能輸入不同維度大小的聲音資訊，於是在原有模型卷積層後展平層之前加入了 AdaptiveAvgPool2d 此方法的使用概念類似於全域性池化層(Global Average Pooling, GAP)(Lin et al., 2013)，使模型能輸入不同維度的聲音資料，正常的平均池化需要自己計算窗口以及步伐，但 AdaptiveAvgPool2d 能夠只輸入想要輸出的資料維度大小，它會自動的計算窗口以及步伐使得輸出格式符合模型要求。

2.4 遷移學習

在某些領域中標籤的標記昂貴，導致訓練資料的不足，容易使訓練出來的模型發生過擬合的狀況，也就是對於訓練資料外的資料泛化能力不足，導致模型沒有實務價值，遷移學習中有兩個常用的方法，特徵萃取和微調，特徵萃取是指先以預先訓練好的模型作為資料特徵提取的部分，為目標任務提取有用的特徵，微調技術是將原有任務訓練好的模型以及參數應用於目標訓練任務，使目標訓練任務能有較佳的初始梯度位置進行訓練，能達到較快收斂以及增加準確度的功效，遷移式學習在過去的研究取得不錯的成果，因此本篇研究提出的模型訓練方式便基於微調技術，研究是否能夠在不改變模型複雜度的情況透過改變輸入音訊長度進行遷移訓練以此提升準確度。

3 方法論

3.1 資料集

- ESC-10 資料集(Piczak et al., 2015b):

ESC-10 資料集為 ESC-50 資料集的子集，內包含400個室內外環境錄音的標記集合，適用於環境聲音分類的基準測試方法，該數據集的音訊都是由 5 秒長的紀錄組成，採樣率為 44100Hz，被平均分類為 10 個類別，其中一類為電鋸聲，每個類別都有 40 條音訊，此數據集內的標籤已預先安排了 5-fold 以進行交叉驗證，確保同一原始源文件的片段包含在同一個 fold 中。

- 電鋸聲音集：

本研究自行蒐集的包含電鋸聲音的聲音片段，沒有包含任何來自 ESC-10、ESC-50 的音訊資料，數據集的音訊都是由 5 秒長的紀錄組成，採樣率為 44100Hz，特別一提的是這些片段不全是乾淨的電鋸聲，以模擬在現實中需要判斷時會有雜音的情況。

3.2 透過不同秒數進行訓練模型之架構

本章共有四個小節，第一小節說明資料預處理，第二小節介紹模型實做細節以及實驗的參數設定，第三小節說明實驗設計，第四小節說明實驗環境與超參數設定。

3.2.1 資料預處理

從給定的聲學訊號中提取了頻譜圖特徵。採樣率為 44100Hz，帧移設置為 512，窗口長度為 2048，濾波器個數為 128，最高頻率為 22050，最低頻率為 20。在此研究中使用了 Python 中的 Libroas 庫(McFee et al., 2015)來提取頻譜訊號，由於本研究想要透過不同秒數來訓練模型以及進行遷移式訓練，想要提取短中長三種不同長度以做出區別所以選擇了 1 秒、3 秒、5 秒。轉換出來的特徵大小分別為(128,87,1)、(128,259,1)、(128,431,1)。由於聲音都是 5 秒片段，所以提取 1 秒及 3 秒聲音時資料分別會增加 5 倍及 3 倍，圖 1 表示聲音片段提取的方式。本實驗設計了兩種模型訓練方式分別為：(1)正常的 ESC-10 標籤，標籤由 0 至 9 共 10 個標籤進行分類，以及(2)將電鋸聲以外的聲音標籤都設為 0，電鋸聲標籤設為 1，進行二元分類。

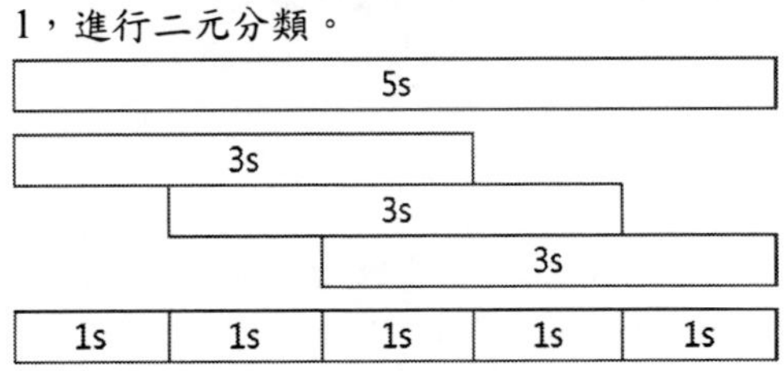

圖 1: 不同聲音長度之提取示意圖

3.2.2 模型實做細節以及實驗的參數設定

圖 2 展示了本篇研究所使用之模型架構。模型相關參數如下。

- A1:輸入大小為(1, 128, W)，W 為 1 秒、三秒以及 5 秒轉換成頻譜圖後的寬度。
- A2:為一個 2D-CNN 卷積層，輸入通道數為 1，輸出通道數為 16，kernel_size 為 5，stride 為 1，padding 為 0。
- A3:為一個最大池化層，kernel_size 為 2，stride 為 2，padding 為 0。
- A4:為一個 2D-CNN 卷積層，輸入通道數為 16，輸出通道數為 32，kernel_size 為 5，stride 為 1，padding 為 0。
- A5:為一個最大池化層，kernel_size 為 2，stride 為 2，padding 為 0。

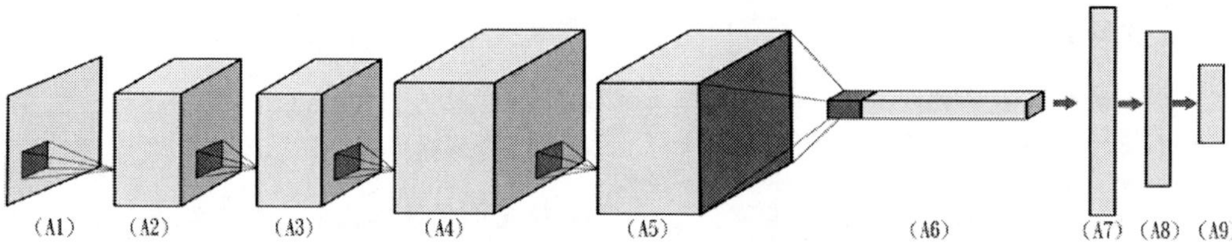

圖 2: LeNet 結合 Global Average Pooling 之模型架構圖

- A6:為一個二元自適應平均池化層，依照通道方向進行自適應平均池化，輸出為一為陣列長度 32。
- A7:為全連接層，節點數為 120。
- A8:為全連接層，節點數為 84。
- A9:為全連接層，節點數為 10 或者 2，依照實驗項目而定。

3.2.3 實驗設計

本研究以不同長度 (1 秒、3 秒、5 秒) 的 ESC-10 資料集來訓練模型，並將訓練好的三個模型分別使用本研究自行蒐集電鋸聲資料集之 1 秒、3 秒與 5 秒的音檔來驗證電鋸聲之識別能力。本研究著重於(1)觀察不同長度聲音的訓練對於準確度的影響；(2)依照秒數由短到長(1秒→3秒→5秒)與由長到短(5秒→3秒→1秒)的方式進行遷移學習訓練，並與先前的模型進行比較。其中，模型訓練統一使用 ESC-10 資料集以 5-Fold 交叉驗證來進行；而圖 3 至圖 6 的模型效能比較，則統一使用本研究自行蒐集之電鋸資料集，該資料集中不包含 ESC-10 之電鋸音檔。

3.2.4 實驗環境與超參數設定

所有模型都是在具有 8GB RAM 和 NVIDIA GeForce RTX3060 6G GPU 上進行開發及運行，所提出之實驗方法使用在 Windows10 作業系統上運行 Python 的開源 Pytorch 1.12 庫開發。批次大小為 64，使用 Adam 優化器 (Kingma and Ba, 2014)用於優化，學習率為 0.0002 每訓練 10 次將學習率降為原來的一半，損失函數方法為交叉熵(CrossEntropy Loss) (Zhang and Sabuncu, 2018)，共訓練 30 次，遷移式訓練的部分就是將模型以上述參數用不同長度音訊資料重複訓練。

4 實驗結果

本章節將實驗結果分為兩個階段，第一階段式模型正常訓練的結果，第二階段為模型進行遷移式訓練的結果。圖 3、圖 4 與圖 5 中的長條皆代表 5-fold 驗證的平均準確度，長條上的誤差線高點為 5-fold 裡最高準確度，低點為 5-fold 裡最低準確度。

4.1.1 模型依二元分類訓練後的準確度

圖 3 為模型使用二元分類為最終結果進行訓練後分別餵入不同秒數的判斷準確度。模型共有 3 個 分別以 1 秒、3 秒、5 秒進行訓練，並都餵入 1 秒、3 秒、5 秒進行預測。3 個模型對於 1 秒測試音訊分別有 53.52%、60.04%、53.68%的準確度，都高於 3 秒測試音訊的 49.47%、55.4%、44.87%，以及五秒測試音訊的 44%、50%、39.8%，結果來說二元分類模型對於電鋸聲音預測準確度最高的是以 1 秒進行預測。

4.1.2 模型依 ESC-10 分類訓練後的準確度

圖 4 為模型使用 ESC-10 分類為最終結果進行訓練後分別餵入不同秒數的判斷準確度。模型共有 3 個 分別以 1 秒、三秒、5 秒進行訓練，並都餵入 1 秒、3 秒、5 秒進行預測。3 個模型對於 1 秒測試音訊分別有 74.16%、74.16%、79.32%的準確度，3 秒測試音訊分別有 78.2%、76.13%、83.53%的準確度，5 秒測試音訊分別有 78.8%、77.6%、83.2%的準確度，結果來說不管幾秒訓練的模型，模型對於不同秒數的測試資料預測的準確度都差不多，但可以看出使用 5 秒進行訓練的模型準確度較高，在測試資料方面餵入較長秒數的預測準確度普遍較高，而且所有的預測準確度都比都比使用二元預測的方式高很多。

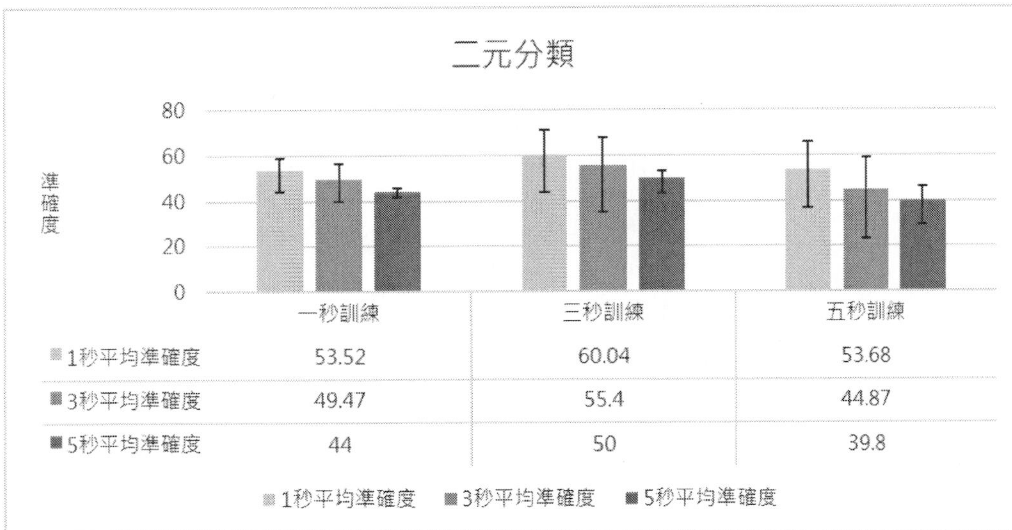

圖 3: 使用二元分類訓練後的準確度直方圖，模型分別以 1 秒、3 秒以及 5 秒進行單獨訓練，並且使用 1 秒、3 秒以及 5 秒的測試音訊進行準確度測試。

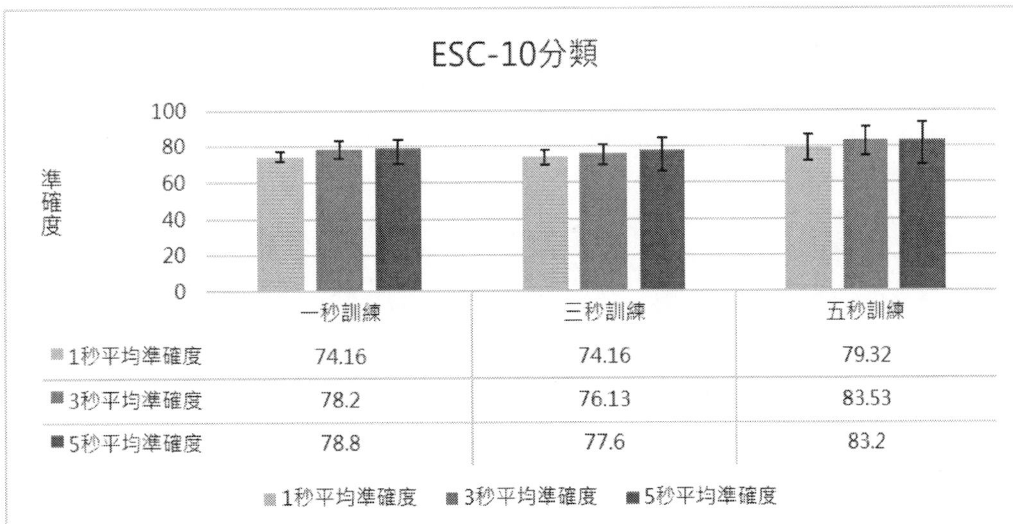

圖 4: 使用 ESC-10 分類訓練後的準確度直方圖，模型分別以 1 秒、3 秒以及 5 秒進行單獨訓練，並且使用 1 秒、3 秒以及 5 秒的測試音訊進行準確度測試。

4.2 模型使用遷移式訓練後的準確度

圖 5 為模型使用遷移式訓練後的準確度，模型分別以(1 秒→3 秒→5 秒)進行訓練，以及(5 秒→3 秒→1 秒)秒進行訓練，並都餵入 1 秒，3 秒，5 秒進行預測。2 個模型對於 1 秒測試音訊分別有 85.28%、74.52%的準確度，3 秒測試音訊分別有 88.67%、77.06%的準確度，五秒測試音訊分別有 91.8%、77.8%的準確度。與圖 4 表現最好的模型相比，以 5 秒進行訓練的模型的測試數據進行比較，可以發現將秒數由小到大(1 秒→3 秒→5 秒)進行訓練的模型，在 5 秒音訊的準確度提升了 8.6%，3 秒音訊提升了 5.14%，1 秒音訊提升了 5.96%，由大到小(5 秒→3 秒→1 秒)進行訓練的模型表現出較差結果的，而且在各秒數的準確度比起圖 4 中的任何模型都沒有進步。

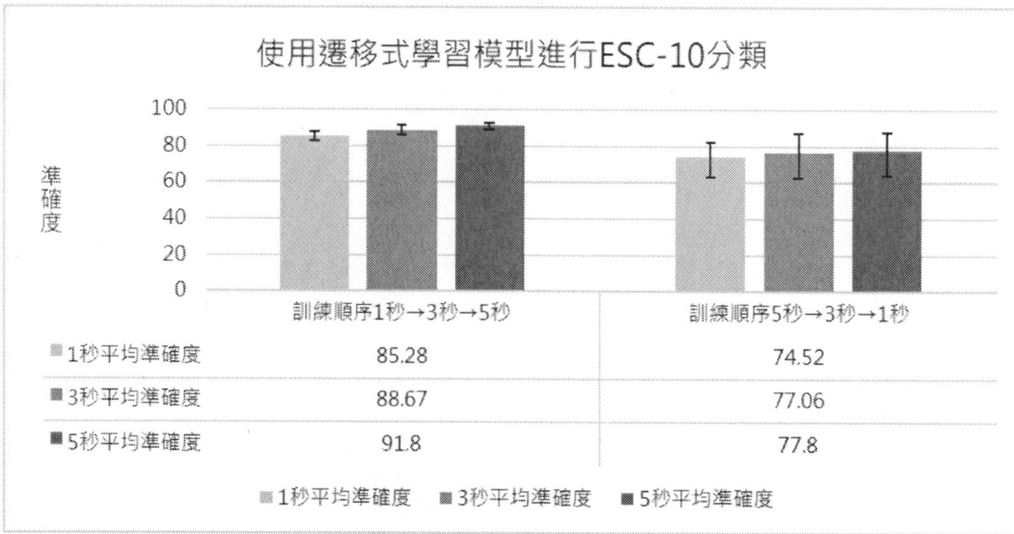

圖 5: 使用遷移式學習後模型進行 ESC-10 分類的準確度直方圖，模型分別以(1 秒→3 秒→5 秒)以及(5 秒→3 秒→1 秒)的順序進行遷移式學習，並且使用 1 秒、3 秒以及 5 秒的測試音訊進行準確度測試。

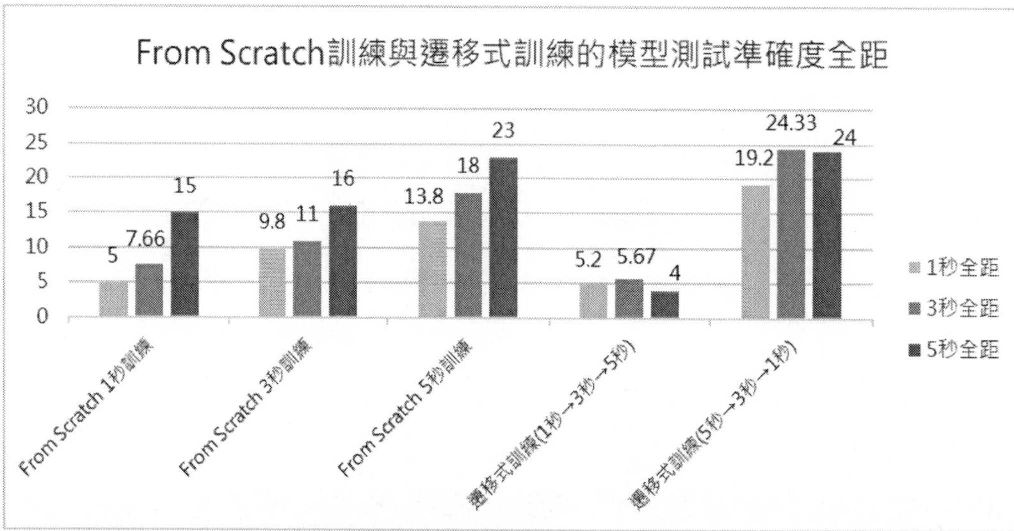

圖 6: 分別使用 From Scratch 以及遷移式學習訓練模型進行 ESC-10 分類 K-Fold 的預測準確度全距直方圖，模型分別以 1 秒、3 秒以及 5 秒進行單獨訓練以及(1 秒→3 秒→5 秒)、(5 秒→3 秒→1 秒)的順序進行遷移式學習，並且使用 1 秒、3 秒以及 5 秒的測試音訊進行預測值全距計算。對於 K-Fold 的預測準確度全距，全距計算方式為把 K-Fold 中預測最高準確度的值減去預測最低準確度的值。

4.3 模型使用遷移式訓練後對於 K-Fold 的預測全距

圖 6 為模型使用遷移式訓練後對於 K-Fold 的預測值全距，計算方式為將 K-Fold 預測最高準確度的值減去預測最低準確度的值。前三個模型為沒有經過遷移式學習只使用單一秒數(1 秒、3 秒、5 秒)進行訓練的模型，1 秒預測準確度值全距分別為 5%、7.66%、15%，3 秒預測準確度全距分別為 9.8%、11%、16%，5 秒預測準確度全距分別為 13.8%、18%、23%，後面為兩個模型使用遷移式訓練後的準確度，模型分別以(1 秒→3 秒→5 秒)進行訓練，以及(5 秒→3 秒→1 秒)秒進行，1 秒預測準確度全距分別為 5.2%、19.2%，3 秒預測準確度全距分別為 5.67%、24.32%，5 秒預測準確度全距分別為 4%、2.4%，訓練結果來說可以看到以(1 秒→3 秒→5 秒)進行遷移式訓練後

能有效的降低預測值全距，並且從圖 4 以及圖 5 的準確度中可以看到在降低全距的同時還可以大量的提升準確度，對於 5 秒的測試資料提升了 8.6%的準確度並降低了高達 19%的全距，對於 3 秒的測試資料提升了 5.14%的準確度並降低了 12.33%的全距，對於 1 秒的測試資料提升了 5.96%的準確度並降低了 8.6%的全距，研究表明遷移式訓練出來的模型增加了對於音訊特徵的提取性能增加了模型的泛化性還能提升模型判斷的準確度。

5 討論

從實驗結果可以看到以二元分類的方式進行訓練的模型成效不佳，推測是因為訓練時的資料分布太過偏斜因為餵進去的資料不是電鋸聲以及電鋸聲的音訊比例是 9 比 1 導致模型泛化能力降低，以正常 ESC-10 標籤進行訓練的模型就算用與訓練時使用的秒數不同的音訊進行判斷也有相當的準確度，有意思的是可以看到給予模型較長秒數進行預測的準確度普遍較高不管模型是用幾秒訓練的，但是這兩個訓練方式可以看到在 5-Fold 的準確度差異較大最高準確度與最低準確度差異較大，表現較好的以 ESC-10 分類的模型在輸入較長秒數進行預測時的最高最低準確度相差最多。使用遷移式訓練的模型中以遞增秒數方式進行訓練可以看到其在 5 秒的判斷準確度較高，3 秒、1 秒也有所提升，以遞減秒數方式進行訓練可以看到所有的判斷準確度都沒有進步而且誤差變大了，1 秒預測準確度全距分別為 5.2%、19.2%，3 秒預測準確度全距分別為 5.67%、24.32%，5 秒預測準確度全距分別為 4%、2.4%，所以經過研究表示，如果要將模型使用不同長度音訊進行遷移式訓練，從短音訊訓練到長音訊能得到較佳的結果，如果由長音訊訓練至短音訊並不會提升判斷的準確度，並且提高了模型的誤差，從短音訊訓練到長音訊其最高準確度與最低準確度差異明顯變小，因此正確的遷移式學習的確對於電鋸聲音的識別有所裨益。

6 結論

本研究提出一個問題使模型能接受不同於訓練音訊長度的音訊進行預測以及探討遷移式學習對於此種模型的幫助，不同訓練秒數對於模型的泛化能力的比較，實驗比較了兩種不同的標註方式以及在表現較好的標註方式上進一步的使用遷移式學習進行訓練，結果證明了模型能有效的進行泛化對於不同於訓練音訊長度的音訊也有著不差的準確度，在遷移式學習方面可以看到這種訓練方式能有效的提升模型的泛化能力以及準確度。

References

Chu, S., Narayanan, S., & Kuo, C. C. J. (2009). Environmental sound recognition with time–frequency audio features. IEEE Transactions on Audio, Speech, and Language Processing, 17(6), 1142-1158.

Dhanalakshmi, P., Palanivel, S., & Ramalingam, V. (2011). Classification of audio signals using AANN and GMM. Applied soft computing, 11(1), 716-723.

Hung, J. C., & Chang, J. W. (2021). Multi-level transfer learning for improving the performance of deep neural networks: theory and practice from the tasks of facial emotion recognition and named entity recognition. Applied Soft Computing, 109, 107491.

Kingma, D. P., & Ba, J. (2014). Adam: A method for stochastic optimization. arXiv preprint arXiv:1412.6980.

Krizhevsky, A., Sutskever, I., & Hinton, G. E. (2012). Imagenet classification with deep convolutional neural networks. Advances in neural information processing systems, 25.

LeCun, Y., Bottou, L., Bengio, Y., & Haffner, P. (1998). Gradient-based learning applied to document recognition. Proceedings of the IEEE, 86(11), 2278-2324.

Liao, J. Y., Lin, Y. H., Lin, K. C., & Chang, J. W. (2021, December). 以遷移學習改善深度神經網路模型於中文歌詞情緒辨識 (Using Transfer Learning to Improve Deep Neural Networks for Lyrics Emotion Recognition in Chinese). In International Journal of Computational Linguistics & Chinese Language Processing, Volume 26, Number 2, December 2021.

Lin, M., Chen, Q., & Yan, S. (2013). Network in network. arXiv preprint arXiv:1312.4400.

McFee, B., Raffel, C., Liang, D., Ellis, D. P., McVicar, M., Battenberg, E., & Nieto, O. (2015, July). librosa: Audio and music signal analysis in python. In Proceedings of the 14th python in science conference (Vol. 8, pp. 18-25).

Piczak, K. J. (2015a, September). Environmental sound classification with convolutional neural networks. In 2015 IEEE 25th international workshop on machine learning for signal processing (MLSP) (pp. 1-6). IEEE.

Piczak, K. J. (2015b, October). ESC: Dataset for environmental sound classification. In Proceedings of the 23rd ACM international conference on Multimedia (pp. 1015-1018).

Szegedy, C., Liu, W., Jia, Y., Sermanet, P., Reed, S., Anguelov, D., ... & Rabinovich, A. (2015). Going deeper with convolutions. In Proceedings of the IEEE conference on computer vision and pattern recognition (pp. 1-9).

Uzkent, B., Barkana, B. D., & Cevikalp, H. (2012). Non-speech environmental sound classification using SVMs with a new set of features. International Journal of Innovative Computing, Information and Control, 8(5), 3511-3524.

Valero, X., & Alías, F. (2012, August). Gammatone wavelet features for sound classification in surveillance applications. In 2012 Proceedings of the 20th European Signal Processing Conference (EUSIPCO) (pp. 1658-1662). IEEE.

Zhang, T., & Kuo, C. C. J. (2001). Audio content analysis for online audiovisual data segmentation and classification. IEEE Transactions on speech and audio processing, 9(4), 441-457.

Zhang, Z., & Sabuncu, M. (2018). Generalized cross entropy loss for training deep neural networks with noisy labels. Advances in neural information processing systems, 31.

Zhuang, F., Qi, Z., Duan, K., Xi, D., Zhu, Y., Zhu, H., ... & He, Q. (2020). A comprehensive survey on transfer learning. Proceedings of the IEEE, 109(1), 43-76.

The 34th Conference on Computational Linguistics and Speech Processing (ROCLING 2022)
Taipei, Taiwan, November 21-22, 2022. The Association for Computational Linguistics and Chinese Language Processing

Using Grammatical and Semantic Correction Model to Improve Chinese-to-Taiwanese Machine Translation Fluency

Yuan-Han Li
nck10509@gmail.com

Chung-Ping Young
dryncku@gmail.com

Wen-Hsiang Lu
whlu@mail.ncku.edu.tw

National Cheng Kung University
Department of Computer Science and Engineering

Abstract

Currently, there are three major issues to tackle in Chinese-to-Taiwanese machine translation: multi-pronunciation Taiwanese words, unknown words, and Chinese-to-Taiwanese grammatical and semantic transformation. Recent studies have mostly focused on the issues of multi-pronunciation Taiwanese words and unknown words, while very few research papers focus on grammatical and semantic transformation. However, there exist grammatical rules exclusive to Taiwanese that, if not translated properly, would cause the result to feel unnatural to native speakers and potentially twist the original meaning of the sentence, even with the right words and pronunciations. Therefore, this study collects and organizes a few common Taiwanese sentence structures and grammar rules, then creates a grammar and semantic correction model for Chinese-to-Taiwanese machine translation, which would detect and correct grammatical and semantic discrepancies between the two languages, thus improving translation fluency.

Keywords: Machine translation, Taiwanese grammatical rules, Lexical transformation, Syntactic transformation, Chinese-to-Taiwanese

1 Introduction

Machine translation systems are being increasingly used across multiple fields, such as businesses, tourism and medical industries. These systems can translate multiple languages like English, Chinese, Japanese and even obscure traditional languages such as Swahili and Croatian. Taiwanese machine translation is likewise gaining importance as the government becomes more aware of its historical and cultural importance, thus setting out to digitally preserve the language. There has been multiple research papers on Chinese-to-Taiwanese (henceforth referred to as C2T) machine translation, usually focusing on the issues of multi-pronunciation words and unknown words translation. However, despite the importance of grammatical and semantic differences between languages in machine translation, it has been observed that papers that integrate them into C2T translation systems are comparatively rare, which results in the output of C2T systems losing fluency and potentially the original meanings of the original Chinese input. As such, this paper proposes a grammatical and semantic error detection and correction model, which can improve C2T translation fluency by correcting the discrepancies between Chinese and Taiwanese grammar.

2 Related Work

Considering the importance of machine translation (Raad, 2020; Panayiotou et al., 2020; Kapoor et al., 2019), researchers begin to apply rule-based (Hurskainen and Tiedemann, 2017), statistical (Och et al., 1999; Koehn et al., 2003), and neural machine translation (Sutskever et al., 2014; Vaswani et al., 2017) technology to various languages, including C2T translation models (Lin and Chen, 1999), in order to tackle various recurring issues in this field, such as choosing the correct pronunciation for multi-pronunciation words and unknown words.

For multi-pronunciation words, (Wu, 2015) extracts the features of each word in the input sentence, such as part-of-speech (POS) and semantic meaning, then employ feature models

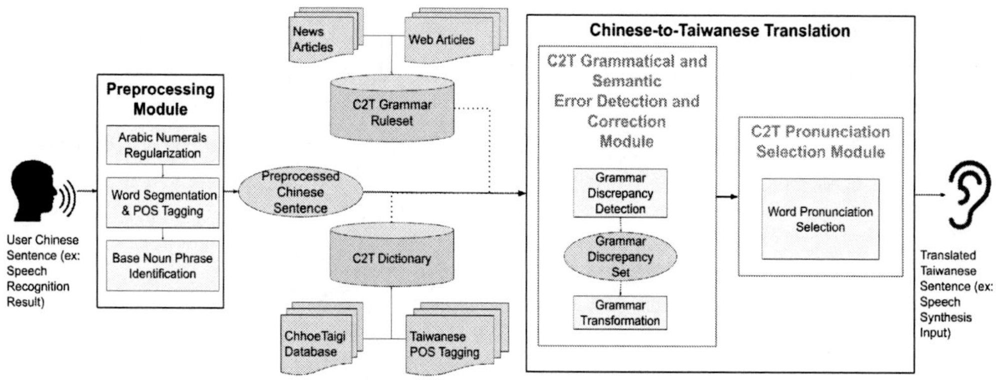

Figure 1: System architecture of C2T machine translation using grammatical and semantic correction model

based on word features of co-occurring words and layered structure to select the most suitable translation rule for the Chinese words. For unknown words, (Chen, 2015) uses a mixed model which utilizes the prefix and suffix of words, pronunciation, word subsets, etc. to statistically analyze the corresponding Taiwanese pronunciation of unknown words in Chinese sentences. (Huang, 2015) also attempts to resolve insertion/deletion issues in C2T translation by compiling a set of insertion/deletion rules, calculate the confidence scores, then combine Naïve-Bayes and CRF statistical models to perform machine learning, improving the fluency of the Taiwanese translation output.

(Hsu et al., 2020), on the other hand, uses a Convolutional Neural Network (CNN) deep learning model, the C2T-pronunciation parallel corpus iCorpus and a precompiled Chinese-Taiwanese parallel dictionary to create a Chinese-character-to-Taiwanese-pinyin module and perform whole-sentence translation. However, the paper does not focus on the issues of multi-pronunciation words and unknown words encountered during C2T translation.

In comparison to the issues of multi-pronunciation words and unknown words pronunciation, C2T grammatical and semantic level issues, such as structural transformation or split Chinese words, are less commonly explored in these research papers. As such, this paper explores sentence structure transformation based on Taiwanese grammar.

3 Methods

3.1 System Architecture

Figure 1 shows the architecture of the C2T translation model using grammatical and semantic correction model. The system consists of two major modules: the preprocessing module, which regularizes numeral words in the Chinese sentence input, performs word segmentation and part-of-speech(POS) tagging, and identifies base noun phrases (BNP) in the input sentences, and the C2T translation module, which detects and corrects grammatical and semantic errors in Chinese sentences into their Taiwanese counterparts, then translates each word in the sentences. A detailed introduction will be listed in the following sections.

3.2 Preprocessing Module

To perform grammatical and semantic error correction (such as word-order transformation) and pronunciation selection in later modules, the C2T translation system in this study uses a preprocessing module that not only performs word segmentation and POS tagging, but also correct certain errors in user input sentences that are not strictly tied to grammatical errors, but nevertheless affect translation accuracy and fluency. These errors are described below.

(1) Arabic Numerals Regularization The preprocessing module regularizes Arabic numeral by transforming them into either traditional Chinese or modern Chinese depending on the semantic meaning. Traditional Chinese

Pronunciation type	Numeral type	Examples
Modern pronunciations	Number + Unit word	117 片 → 一百十七片、2 盒 → 二盒
	Time/Date	5 月 17 日 → 五月十七日
Classical pronunciations	Phone numbers	防疫專線 0800-001922 → 防疫專線控捌控控-控控一玖貳貳
Ordinal pronunciations	Ordinals (第 + Number + Unit word)	第 2 名 → 第貳名、第 5 位 → 第五位

Table 1: Common Arabic numerals examples and their corresponding pronunciation

(壹 ～ 玖，控) would be used for classical Taiwanese numerals, while modern Chinese (一 ～ 九，零) would be used for modern Taiwanese numerals. Table 1 shows some common Arabic numerals examples and their corresponding pronunciation.

(2) Word Segmentation and POS Tagging To select the correct pronunciation and retrieve the information needed for grammatical transformation, the module uses the CKIP word segmentation/ POS tagging system to segment the Chinese sentence input and perform POS tagging in preparation for the pronunciation selection process.

(3) Base Noun Phrase (BNP) Identification Some segments involved during sentence structure word reordering, especially noun subjects and objects, usually have phrases as their minimal unit. The Hanlp toolkit is able to use dependency parsing to obtain the noun phrases within a sentence. As such, the module also employs Hanlp toolkit to identify the noun phrases in a given Chinese input sentence so that the C2T grammatical and semantic error detection and correction module can successfully detect and revise the errors found during input. For example, in Taiwanese, "志明跑步比隔壁教室的阿甘跑得快" is translated as "志明走了 khah 隔壁教室 ê 阿甘緊". The phrase "隔壁教室的阿甘" is a complete object noun phrase that has its position swapped with "比" and "跑得".

3.3 Chinese-to-Taiwanese Translation

The translation module incorporates information from the precompiled C2T dictionary and grammar ruleset, and consists of two components: C2T grammatical and semantic error detection and correction module and C2T pronunciation selection module. Each component of the translation module will be detailed in the following sections.

3.3.1 C2T dictionary

Figure 2 shows the structure of the dictionary used in this system. The dictionary uses the pronunciations taken from the Taiwanese Common Words Dictionary by MOE and the Chhoetaigi Taiwanese corpus organized by public sources. Since some Taiwanese pronunciations for words in Chhoetaigi Taiwanese corpus are not commonly used in the modern age, they are filtered out while the rest are compiled into the new C2T dictionary.

Each entry contains a Chinese word, the corresponding Taiwanese pronunciation, the part of speech (POS) of the Chinese word and whether the pronunciation is considered classical (文言) or modern (白話) (Table 2) .

Chinese word	Taiwanese Pronunciation	POS	Wenbai
香	hiong	N;	文
	hiunn	N;	白
	phang	Adj;	白
端午節	bah-tsàng-tseh ; gōo-gueh-tseh	N;	白

Table 2: Taiwanese words entries in C2T dictionary

For words with multiple accepted translations, such as "端午節" as either "bah-tsàng-tseh" or "gōo-gueh-tseh " (Table 2), all translations are compiled into the same entry.

Index	對應華語	音讀	詞性	文白	註解
58	丁	ting	N;		
59	七	tshit	Neu;Adj;		
60	九	káu	Neu;Adj;	白	
61	九	kiú	Neu;	文	
62	完	liáu	V;F;	白	
64	二	jī	Neu;	文	
65	二	nn̂g	Neu;	白	
66	人	lâng	N;		
67	入	jip	V;		
68	八	pat	Neu;	文	
69	八	peh	Neu;	白	
	……				

Figure 2: C2T dictionary corpus

The pronunciation selection module would use these criteria to decide on the translation of Chinese words in a given input sentence.

3.3.2 Chinese-Taiwanese Grammatical Ruleset

Figure 3 shows the types and amount of Chinese-Taiwanese grammatical and semantic differences occurring in news articles. This study collects Taiwanese grammatical rules from news articles, web articles, and Wikipedia, and compiles them into eight major categories for the C2T grammatical error detection and correction module ruleset. Furthermore, 16259 Chinese sentences are extracted from 1851 news articles, with empty strings and repeated sentences removed, in order to analyze the appearance frequency of each type of grammatical differences between Chinese and Taiwanese sentences.

3.3.3 C2T Grammatical and Semantic Error Detection and Correction Module

The preprocessed Chinese sentence would be sent to the grammatical and semantic error detection and correction module to undergo grammatical transformation. The module would output a set of grammatical discrepancies found in the Chinese sentence based on the compiled Taiwanese sentence structure and grammatical rules, then perform word switching or word order revision depending on the corresponding error revision method for each rule. The output of the module is a sentence that complies to Taiwanese grammar. A few of these grammatical rules are listed in Table 3.

3.3.4 C2T Pronunciation Selection Module

After the grammatical and semantic error detection and correction module transforms the Chinese sentence to better fit Taiwanese grammar, the sentence would be inputted into C2T pronunciation selection module. The module would then select the correct pronunciation of each Chinese word by looking up the dictionary for its POS, corresponding Chinese entry and Wenbai pronunciation, and output the translated sentence.

(1) Abbreviation Word Restoration: In news articles, certain Chinese words tend to be abbreviated, like “因爲” being abbreviated as “因”, “但是” as “但” and “可以” as “可”. However, since native Taiwanese speakers usually speak the whole original word, the module would restore them into their original forms based on the semantic context so that they can be properly translated.

(2) Word Pronunciation Selection: For each word in the input sentence, if there are multiple Taiwanese translation entries that fit the POS of the original word, the module would prioritize entries with modern pronunciation. Otherwise, it chooses the entry with the smallest index number. For word entries with multiple pronunciations, the module chooses the first pronunciation. Unknown words are translated by dissecting them into characters and translating them separately. In addition, some words have suffixes with unique meanings, and the module would translate them separately from the main word. The algorithm of the pronunciation selection module is described below in Algorithm 1.

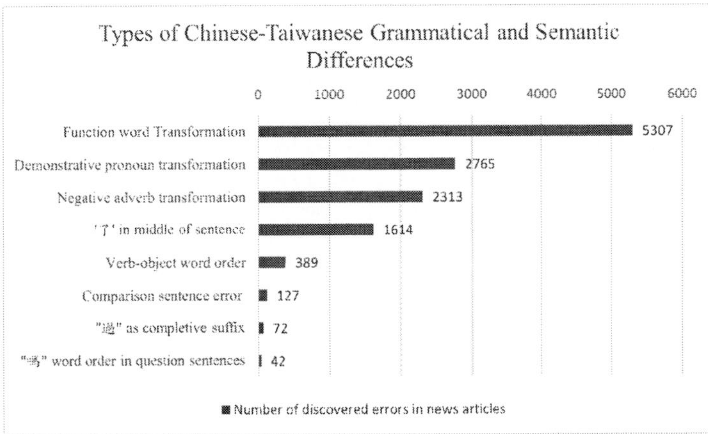

Figure 3: Types of Chinese-Taiwanese grammatical and semantic differences

Grammatical differences	Transformation rule(s)	Examples
“共” sentences (kā sentence)	function words such as “把, 向, 跟” → “kā”	• 他向老爸借兩百萬 → I kā lāu-pē tsioh nn̄g pah-bān • 醫生跟你說要多喝水 → I-sing kā lí kóng ài ke lim-tsuí • 大家把小偷抓到警察局了 →Tak-ke kā tshat-á liah-khì kíng-tshat-kiok--ah
“了” at the end of sentences	“了” → “--ah”	• 燈光照到他了 → Ting-hué tsiò-tioh i--ah • 我找到她了 → Guá tshuē-tioh i--ah • 他把飲料買回來了 → I kā liâng-tsuí bé-tńg-lâi--ah
Negative adverb translation	不 +V. → m̄ (毋)+V. 不 +Adj. → bô (無) +Adj.	• 這裡是不穩定的環境 → Tsia sī bô ún-tīng ê khuân-kíng • 我不知道 → Guá m̄-tsai-iánn • 他不聽我的話 → I m̄ thiann guá ê uē
Basic comparison sentences	A + 比 +B + adj → A + khah + adj + B	• 女兒比兒子貼心 →Tsa-bóo-kiánn khah tah-sim tsa-poo-kiánn • 他比你高一點兒 → I khah lò lí tsit-sut-á • 你比他好不到哪兒去 → Lí khah-hó i bô-guā-tsē
“了” preceded by verb	V.+ 了 → ū (有) + V.	• 弟弟買了一台機車 → Sió-tī ū bé tsit tâi oo-tóo-bái • 媽媽吃了一粒蘋果 → A-bú ū tsiah tsit-liap phōng-kó • 她贏了五百元 → I ū iânn gōo-pah khoo
“嗎” word order in question sentences	Translate “嗎”as “kám” (敢), and advance its position to right after the subject	• 他知道這件事嗎?→ I kám tsai-iánn tsit-khuán tāi-tsì? • 你找到它了嗎? → Lí kám tshuē-tioh i--ah? • 那件事情很困難嗎? → Hit-kiānn tāi-tsì kám tsiok khùn-lân?

Table 3: C2T grammatical differences and transformation rules

Algorithm 1 Pronunciation Selection

```
for Every Chinese word in segmented sentence input do
    if Word has special suffix then
        Translate the suffix separately
    else
        Check the number of entries with the same Chinese word and POS
        if Word has 1 corresponding entry then
            Apply word as translation
        else if Word has multiple corresponding entries then
            Select entry with smallest index number
        else
            Translate each character separately
        end if
    end if
end for
```

4 Experimental Results

4.1 Dataset and Evaluation Metrics

To evaluate the system built for this study, thirty news articles are selected and divided into 5 categories: social, lifestyle, economics, weather and technology, each with 6 articles. In total, 265 sentences and 8667 words from the articles are used to test the C2T machine translation system. For the grammatical and semantic error detection and correction module, grammatical correction rate is utilized as evaluation criteria, which is defined as:

> Grammatical correction rate $= a/b$, where a is the number of grammatical errors detected and corrected by the module, and b is the number of grammatical errors in news article Chinese sentences

For the pronunciation selection module, Word Error Rate (WER) is utilized as the evaluation criteria. Its formula is defined below:

> WER $= x/y$, where x is the number of erroneously translated words, and y is the number of total words

The results of each experiment are listed in Table 4 and Table 5.

In addition, 10 sentences from the dataset are selected to evaluate the C2T system in this paper (henceforth referred to as 公跨拳) against 3 other baseline systems: the C2T machine translation system developed by NCKU (Pan, 2021), the popular Ithuan Dopaiji Taiwanese translation system [1], and the translation system developed by Hsu et al., available at National Chiao Tung University Speech Communication Lab (NCTU SCL) website[2]. The comparison results are shown in Table 6.

Amongst the example sentences chosen, it is observed that the NCKU, Ithuan and NCTU SCL systems are all unable to translate arabic numerals correctly, in addition to not being able to correct grammatical errors, in particular errors that involve word order transformation, such as the positional differences between the question particle "嗎" and its Taiwanese counterpart "敢". For example, in the sentence "5000 元的藍牙耳機讓我眞的會好奇，眞的有這個價值嗎", 公跨拳 translates "5000" into "gōo-tshing" and successfully moves the question particle "嗎" to immediately after the invisible subject "這", both of which the other three systems failed to revise.

4.2 Error Analysis

4.2.1 C2T Grammatical and Semantic Error Detection and Correction Module

(1) "共" Sentences Translation Error In the C2T error correction module, prepositions like "把、跟、向" are transformed into their corresponding Taiwanese word "共" (kā), however there is one exception for "向": if there is a directional word following "向", such as "上" and "下", then even though "向" is still a preposition, it also contains the semantic meaning "朝... 方向" alongside the properties of a verb, therefore it should be translated as "hiòng" rather than "kā".

(2) "了" Particle Transformation Error The particle "了" has different transformation rules depending on its position. For instance, when "了" is placed in the middle of the sentence and after a verb, it may semantically mean "completion of an action", in which case

[1] https://suisiann.ithuan.tw/
[2] http://tts001.iptcloud.net:8804/

Grammatical rules	Function word transformation	Negative Adverb Translation	Demonstrative pronoun Translation	Comparison sentences word order revision
Number of appearances	85	36	44	2
Number of correctly revised errors	78	33	43	1
Grammatical rules	**“了” in middle of sentence**	**“嗎” word order in question sentences**	**“過” as verb suffix**	**Verb-object word order revision**
Number of appearances	14	3	1	3
Number of correctly revised errors	9	1	1	0
Grammatical correction rate = 87.6%				

Table 4: Grammatical and semantic error detection and correction module experiment result

Total Words	Number of erroneously translated words	Number of missing words	Number of untranslated words	Number of extra inserted words	Number of erroneously positioned words
8667	865	30	20	69	26
WER ≈ 11.7%					

Table 5: Pronunciation selection module experiment result

“了” is translated as “有” (ū) and switches positions with the verb before it. In verbs with an adverb inserted in the middle like “上錯了菜”, however, “了” can be seen as a particle without meaning and be omitted, yet our correction module only swaps “了” with the word before it without considering its POS, creating erroneous transformations like “上有錯菜”.

4.2.2 C2T Pronunciation Selection Module

In the C2T pronunciation selection module, aside from failing to translate words not included in the dictionary corpus, there are also instances observed in which new words not in the original Chinese sentence are supposed to be inserted into the Taiwanese translation to improve semantic fluency. Examples include “見巡邏車經過時”, in which an extra word “到” is inserted after “見” in the Taiwanese translation as “看到巡邏車經過時”, and instances in which an additional unit word is inserted between a Chinese number directly followed by a noun, such as “四人” being translated into Taiwanese as “四個人”, with an additional unit word “個” inserted between “四” and “人”.

5 Conclusion and Future Work

This paper focuses on correcting grammatical and syntactic differences between Chinese and Taiwanese encountered during C2T machine translation by building a grammatical and semantic error detection and correction module, which can transform the grammar of the Chinese sentence inputs into their corresponding Taiwanese sentence structures in accordance

System name	WER	Translation sample sentence 1: 男子酒測值高達0.83毫克，被依公共危險罪送辦。	Translation sample sentence 2: 5000 元的藍牙耳機讓我真的會好奇，真的有這個價值嗎？
NCKU	39.2%	lâm-tsú tsiú tshik tat kuân-kàu X.XX hô-khik ，pī i kong-kiōng guî-hiám tsuē sàng pān 。	XXXX guân ê nâ gê hī ki niū guá ū-iánn ē-hiáu hònn-kî ，ū-iánn iú tse ê kè-tat kiám？
Ithuan	32.8%	lâm-tsú tsiú tshik tat ko tat 0.83 hô-khik,pī i kong-kiōng guî-hiám tsuē sàng pān.	5000 guân ê nâ gê hīnn-ki niū guá tsin tik ē hònn-kî,tsin ê Ū tsit kò kè-tat má?
NCTU SCL	20%	tsa1 poo1 tsiu2 tshik4 tat8 kuan5 kau3 phi5 khi3 sam1 ho5 khik4 , pi7 an3 kong1 kiong7 hui5 hiam2 tsue7 sang3 pan7 .	tiat8 si7 tsin1 guan5 e5 lam5 ge5 hi7 ki1 hoo7 gua2 tsin1 e5 hue7 honn3 ki5 , tsin1 e5 u7 tsit4 e5 ke3 tat8 ma1？
公跨麥	8%	tsa-poo-tsiú-tshik-tit kuân-kàu **khòng-tiám-pat-sam-hô-khik**， hōo i kong-kiōng-guî-hiám-tsuē sàng-pān 。	**gōo-tshing-khoo**-ê lâm-gâ-ní-ki hōo guá ū-iánn ē hònn-kî, kám ū-iánn ū tsit tsit-ê-kè-tat ?

Table 6: C2T translation system performance evaluation. The NCTU SCL system uses numbers to denote Taiwanese tone, while the other three systems use Tailuo tone symbols. (Blue words are translations of numeral words, and red words denote grammatical discrepancies between Chinese and Taiwanese. We denote the revised errors in bold words.)

with the grammatical rules of the target language.

Experiment proves that a grammatical and semantic error detection and correction module can successfully improve translation fluency of C2T machine translation. The correction module can be widely used in areas that require machine translation, and would greatly contribute to meetings, tourism, language education, elder care, AI, etc.

Future work would include expanding the dictionary to include more words exclusive to Chinese which are found in news articles, such as technical terms, and idioms. In addition, for some Chinese words and sentence structures, translating them into Taiwanese and transforming the grammatical structure requires deeper knowledge of the original semantic meaning. Sometimes the translation result may be structured differently from the original, and this issue would also be explored in the future. Lastly, the grammatical transformation rules and words used in this paper may not be commonly used by native Taiwanese speakers, since translating from Chinese to Taiwanese is relatively lax. As such, a field survey may be conducted in the future to collect native speakers' opinions and feedback on the results of this translation system to help it output sentences that better fit the users' daily usage habits.

References

Shih-Hsiang Chen. 2015. Decision for pronunciation of out-of-vocabularies in a mandarin to taiwanese text-to-speech system. Master's thesis, National Chung Hsing University.

Wen-Han Hsu, Cheng-Jung Tseng, Yuan-Fu Liao, Wern-Jun Wang, and Chen-Ming Pan. 2020. A preliminary study on deep learning-based Chinese text to Taiwanese speech synthesis system. In *International Journal of Computational Linguistics & Chinese Language Processing, Volume 25, Number 2, December 2020*, Taipei, Taiwan. Association for Computational Linguistics and Chinese Language Processing.

Chih-Chao Huang. 2015. A study on example-based mandarin-taiwanese machine translation. Master's thesis, National Taiwan Ocean University.

Arvi Hurskainen and Jörg Tiedemann. 2017. Rule-based machine translation from English to Finnish. In *Proceedings of the Second Conference on Machine Translation*, pages 323–329, Copenhagen, Denmark. Association for Computational Linguistics.

Ravish Kapoor, Angela Truong, Catherine Vu, and Dam-Thuy Truong. 2019. Successful verbal communication using google translate to facilitate awake intubation of a patient with a language barrier: A case report. *A A Practice*, 14:1.

Philipp Koehn, Franz J. Och, and Daniel Marcu. 2003. Statistical phrase-based translation. In *Proceedings of the 2003 Human Language Technology Conference of the North American Chapter of the Association for Computational Linguistics*, pages 127–133.

Chuan-Jie Lin and Hsin-Hsi Chen. 1999. A Mandarin to Taiwanese Min Nan machine translation system with speech synthesis of Taiwanese Min Nan. In *International Journal of Computational Linguistics & Chinese Language Processing, Volume 4, Number 1, February 1999*, pages 59–84.

Franz Josef Och, Christoph Tillmann, and Hermann Ney. 1999. Improved alignment models for statistical machine translation. In *1999 Joint SIGDAT Conference on Empirical Methods in Natural Language Processing and Very Large Corpora*.

Guan-Xun Pan. 2021. Taiwanese speech synthesis system based on taiwanese tone sandhi and implementation of chinese to taiwanese translation. Master's thesis, National Cheng Kung University. Unpublished thesis.

Anita Panayiotou, Kerry Hwang, Sue Williams, Terence Chong, Dina Logiudice, Betty Haralambous, Xiaoping Lin, Emiliano Zucchi, Monita Mascitti, Anita Goh, Emily You, and Frances Batchelor. 2020. The perceptions of translation apps for everyday health care in healthcare workers and older people: A multi-method study. *Journal of Clinical Nursing*, 29.

Bareq Raad. 2020. The role of machine translation in language learning. *Academic Research International*, 7:2348–7666.

Ilya Sutskever, Oriol Vinyals, and Quoc V. Le. 2014. Sequence to sequence learning with neural networks. *CoRR*, abs/1409.3215.

Ashish Vaswani, Noam Shazeer, Niki Parmar, Jakob Uszkoreit, Llion Jones, Aidan N Gomez, L ukasz Kaiser, and Illia Polosukhin. 2017. Attention is all you need. In *Advances in Neural Information Processing Systems*, volume 30. Curran Associates, Inc.

Shi-Yao Wu. 2015. Combing a multi-feature model and a layer approach in solving the polysemy problem in a chinese to taiwanese tts system. Master's thesis, National Chung Hsing University.

The 34th Conference on Computational Linguistics and Speech Processing (ROCLING 2022)
Taipei, Taiwan, November 21-22, 2022. The Association for Computational Linguistics and Chinese Language Processing

探討語者驗證系統中特徵處理模組與注意力機制
Investigation of feature processing modules and attention mechanisms in speaker verification system

陳廷威 **Ting-Wei Chen**, 林威廷 **Wei-Ting Lin**, 陳嘉平 **Chia-Ping Chen**
國立中山大學資訊工程學系
National Sun Yat-sen University
Department of Computer Science and Engineering
{m103040017, m093040020}@student.nsysu.edu.tw,
cpchen@cse.nsysu.edu.tw
呂仲理 **Chung-Li Lu**, 詹博丞 **Bo-Cheng Chan**, 鄭羽涵 **Yu-Han Cheng**,
莊向峰 **Hsiang-Feng Chuang**, 陳威妤 **Wei-Yu Chen**
中華電信研究院
Chunghwa Telecom Laboratories
{chungli, cbc, henacheng, gotop, weiweichen}@cht.com.tw

摘要

本論文建構並替換不同的音訊特徵前處理模組與注意力機制來改進語者驗證系統。我們使用了基於 ECAPA-TDNN 所改進的模型作爲基準模型，並透過替換與組合不同的前處理模組與注意力機制來進行比較，以選出最佳的組合作爲論文提出的最終模型。訓練上我們使用了 VoxCeleb 2 資料集進行訓練，並使用多個測試集來測試模型的表現。最終模型在 VoxSRC2022 驗證集中對比基準模型有 16% 的進步幅度，成功在語者驗證系統上取得了更好的成效。

Abstract

In this paper, we use several combinations of feature front-end modules and attention mechanisms to improve the performance of our speaker verification system. An updated version of ECAPA-TDNN is chosen as a baseline. We replace and integrate different feature front-end and attention mechanism modules to compare and find the most effective model design, and this model would be our final system. We use VoxCeleb 2 dataset as our training set, and test the performance of our models on several test sets. With our final proposed model, we improved performance by 16% over baseline on VoxSRC2022 valudation set, achieving better results for our speaker verification system.

關鍵字：語者驗證、前處理模組、注意力機制、時延神經網路

Keywords: speaker verification, front-end module, attention mechanism, Time Delay Neural Network

1 緒論

隨著資訊科技的日新月異，大量的數位化資訊充斥在我們的生活當中，透過各式各樣新穎的設備，任何事物、資料都可以被電子化的儲存，並隨時傳送到地球上的任何地方，這使得人們得以跳脫固有的時間與空間上限制，能以更爲宏觀的視角來探索這個世界。然而，當每個人對這些通訊設備的依賴度越來越高時，個人資訊被不合法的洩漏、利用的情形也日漸增加，如何保護自身的資訊安全是一個非常迫切的議題。

語者辨識技術便是其中一項在近年來越來越受到重視的資訊防護方法，藉由這項技術，我們可以將語者的聲紋特徵轉換成具有語者特徵的嵌入向量，透過比對這個嵌入向量來對當前語者的身分進行確認，以防止個人資訊被僞造及竊取。

近年來，有許多過去在圖像領域發光發熱的模型結構被帶入到聲學領域當中，並爲語者驗證技術帶來了極大的突破，像是以時延神經網路（Time Delay Neural Network, TDNN）作爲主幹，並在其中引入了 Res2Net (Gao et al., 2019) 多分支卷積結構與 SENet (Hu et al., 2018) 注意力機制的與基於傳統二維卷積神經網路建構的 ResNet (He et al., 2016a)，兩者都在近年的語者驗證競賽中取得亮眼的表

現。而鑒於兩種截然不同架構都在競賽上取得優秀的成果，希望能夠集合兩種架構優點的新型架構被研究出來，也就是 ECAPA CNN-TDNN (Thienpondt et al., 2021)。在該模型中，ResNet 結構被設計爲 ECAPA-TDNN 的前處理模組，用於降低輸入音檔特徵頻譜圖在頻率軸上的偏移，透過卷積操作重組與保留較重要之特徵訊息。該結構在實驗上進一步的提高模型的表現，並爲語者驗證模型的變化性增加了更多的可能性。

在本篇論文中，我們使用基於 ECAPA-TDNN 架構進行改進的 Improving ECAPA-TDNN (Zhang et al., 2021) 做爲基底，透過修改部份結構以提出 IM ECAPA-TDNN 做爲本次的基準模型，並將其依照 ECAPA CNN-TDNN 的架構設計進行擴增。我們的實驗與分析集中在不同的前處理模組以及注意力機制上。首先，我們會將前處理模組替換爲不同的結構進行訓練，除了原始的 CNN 結構外，我們另外實驗了預激活的 CNN 結構以及導入兩個維度注意力的 MFA 模組 (Liu et al., 2022)。之後我們會取這三組模型中表現較好的模型替換其中使用的注意力機制，將原有的 SE 模組分別替換成 CBAM 模組 (Woo et al., 2018) 以及 GC 模組 (Cao et al., 2019)。在我們的最終模型中，使用了預激活的 2D CNN 模組作爲前處理模組以及 CBAM 模組作爲模型的注意力機制，在 Voxceleb 1-O、Voxceleb 1-E、Voxceleb 1-H 及 VoxSRC2022 測試集上都實現了比起基準模型更好的表現。

本文主要分爲五個部份，第一部份爲緒論；第二部份爲研究方法，會介紹使用到的資料前處理方法、模型架構、特徵前處理模組以及注意力機制；第三部份爲實驗設置，說明實驗所使用到的資料集、參數設置以及評估準則；第四部份爲實驗結果，會比較不同前處理模組與注意力機制的實驗數據，並根據實驗結果進行分析與討論；第五部份爲結論。

2 研究方法

在這個章節我們將會詳細的講解本次實驗所使用到的各種方法，包含對輸入音檔進行的處理、主幹模型架構的細節、不同前處理模組以及不同注意力機制的介紹。實驗上我們使用了 VoxSRC 官方所提供的訓練工具 (Chung et al., 2020) 進行訓練，並以 IM ECAPA-TDNN 做爲基準模型，透過結合不同的前處理模組以及注意力機制觀察這些改動對模型效能所造成的影響。

2.1 資料前處理

爲了提高模型的強健性以及避免產生過度擬和（overfitting）的狀況，我們利用了資料增強的方法增加訓練資料的多樣性。透過對訓練音檔加入噪音跟迴響，能夠有效的提昇模型的泛化能力，使其在推論階段的表現更加優秀。而在將音檔轉換爲特徵向量方面，在參考了近年競賽中各隊伍的作法後，我們選用梅爾頻譜作爲主要聲學特徵。

2.1.1 資料增強

我們使用了兩種用於資料增強的資料集來對我們的訓練資料進行強化。首先是透過 MUSAN 資料集 (Snyder et al., 2015) 來爲輸入音檔加入噪音，在 MUSAN 資料集中共分成了三個部份，分別爲語音（speech）、音樂（music），以及噪音（noise），語音部份的內容全都是來自公共場合中的背景說話聲，包含朗讀書本章節以及美國政府部門聽證會等等，語音部份總共由 12 種語言組成，其中以英語的比例爲最多；音樂部份的內容包含了多種不同時期、流派的音樂，比如有傳統流派的巴洛克、浪漫、古典音樂，也有流行流派的爵士、藍調、嘻哈音樂等等；噪音部份的內容則包含了科技性噪音（如撥號音、傳眞機噪音等）以及環境聲音（如雷聲、雨聲、動物噪音等），有些檔案也會有包含模糊的人群噪音。另一個則是利用 RIR（Room Impulse Response，空間脈衝響應）資料集 (Ko et al., 2017) 將音檔加入迴響（Reverberate），在 RIR 資料集中有眞實與模擬的聲音資料，我們只會使用模擬的空間音進行資料增強。

2.1.2 聲紋特徵擷取

我們使用 80 維的梅爾頻譜（Mel-filter bank features，FBank features）作爲我們的主要聲學特徵，理由是相較於梅爾倒頻譜係數（Mel-Frequency Cepstral Coefficients，MFCC）來說，梅爾頻譜因爲沒有經過 DCT 變換，使得其保留了更多的聲音訊號資訊，能夠在分析語者特徵上取得更好的結果。

2.2 模型架構

在 ECAPA-TDNN 推出之後，得益於優秀的多層聚合策略以及多尺度特徵卷積，該模型在各個語者驗證競賽中都取得優秀的表現，許多人也以其架構作爲基底進行不同程度的改良。本篇論文我們以基於 ECAPA-TDNN 改進的 Improving ECAPA-TDNN 作爲基底，配合後續實驗進行調整，降低了模型計算量並維持相近之模型表現。我們把修改後的模型命名爲

IM ECAPA-TDNN，並將其作爲本篇論文中的基準模型。

2.2.1 Improving ECAPA-TDNN

Improving ECAPA-TDNN 是基於 ECAPA-TDNN 所設計的一個改進版本。在該模型中，Zhang et al.使用了帶有 SE 注意力機制的 SC-Block (Liu et al., 2020) 取代了原始架構主幹網路裡的 Res2Block，通過 SC-Block 所帶有的自校準計算及分割卷積來獲得更大的感受野（receptive field）及上下文的空間注意力，以此避免特徵中不必要的資訊，並在 SC-Block 後面接上 SE-Block，透過注意力機制使有效特徵圖（feature map）權重要大於低效的特徵圖。Zhang et al.還在每一層 SE-SC-Block 之間插入聚合（aggregation）層的結構，用來將不同分辨率的特徵串接整合並降採樣爲下一層 SE-SC-Block 的輸入大小。這些聚合層會與原始 ECAPA-TDNN 的多層聚合方法結合，使模型成爲一個階層式的聚合結構，也就是每一層 SE-SC-Block 的輸出都會作爲之後每一層聚合層的輸入，而越接近模型尾端的聚合層就會融合越多不同分辨率的特徵，以提取更具語者資訊的嵌入向量。

2.2.2 IM ECAPA-TDNN

我們以 Improving ECAPA-TDNN 作爲基底進行修改，最主要的改動便是我們減去了一層聚合層結構，與此同時也減去了一層的 SE-SC-Block，並將第一層 TDNN 結構的輸出也作爲後面各聚合層的輸入，修改後的模型如圖 1 所示。我們想要透過聚合層來將保留更多特徵資訊的第一層 TDNN 輸出向量一併與後面每一層的 SE-SC-Block 的輸出向量進行特徵重組，以此來獲取更多的語者特徵訊息；而將 SE-SC-Block 及聚合層各減少一層的主要是考量到實驗彈性，由於首層 TDNN 的輸出會加入到每一層聚合層當中進行特徵重組，若是保留原有的四層結構，在替換前處理模組以及注意力機制的實驗上便會出現硬體限制的情況發生。基於以上原因，我們對原始的 Improving ECAPA-TDNN 進行了修改，並將修改後的模型命名爲 IM ECAPA-TDNN。

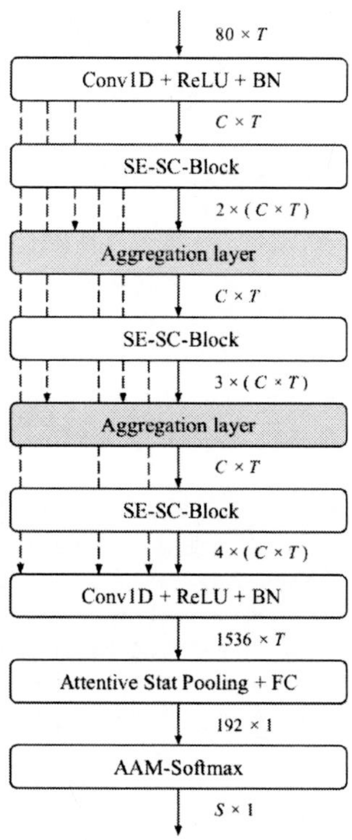

圖 1. 修改提出的 IM ECAPA-TDNN。其中 C 表示通道數，T 表示音框數，S 表示分類與者數量。

2.3 特徵前處理模組

在 ECAPA CNN-TDNN 的研究成果中，通過將輸入音檔的特徵頻譜圖先傳入前處理模組中進行特徵重組，再將重組後的特徵圖在通道及頻率維度攤平（flatten），使其作爲一般輸入傳入 ECAPA-TDNN 進行訓練能夠有效的提高模型表現，因此我們將這個設計加入基準模型當中。我們在 IM ECAPA-TDNN 前面實作了 3 種不同結構的前處理模組進行實驗，分別爲原始論文中的 2D CNN 模組、經過預激活（pre-activation）修改的 2D CNN 模組，以及引入兩維度注意力 MFA 模組。

2.3.1 2D CNN 模組

爲原始在 ECAPA CNN-TDNN 中所使用的前處理模組，通過一般的二維卷積與 ResNet 結構中的 ResBlock 進行組合而成，在實做上我們還有在 ResBlock 中加入 SE 模組，整體結構如圖 2 所示。由於實驗環境以及訓練時間等因素考量，我們將 residual block 的通道數下調爲 64 以降低模型大小，同時參照原始模型設定將第一個及最後一個二維卷積的步幅（stride）設置爲 2 來增加計算效率。

2.3.2 預激活的 2D CNN 模組

我們參考了 (He et al., 2016b) 中對殘差網路的研究結果，在該研究中表明當在 ResBlock 的捷徑連結（shortcut connection）上進行任何操作都會降低模型的表現；同時若是將模型中的激活函數從傳統的後激活（post-activation）改爲預激活（pre-activation），能夠使模型更易於訓練，並有效的提高模型的泛化度。基於上述研究結果，我們將 2D CNN 模組中

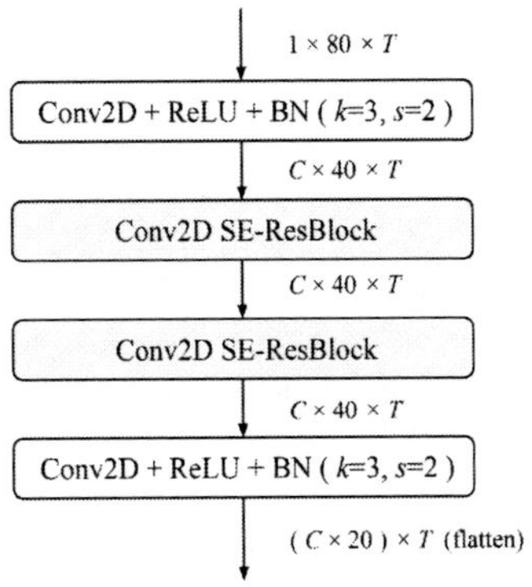

圖 2. 2D CNN 模組。其中 C 表示通道數，T 表示音框數。而卷積中的 k 與 s 表示卷積核大小及步伐長度。

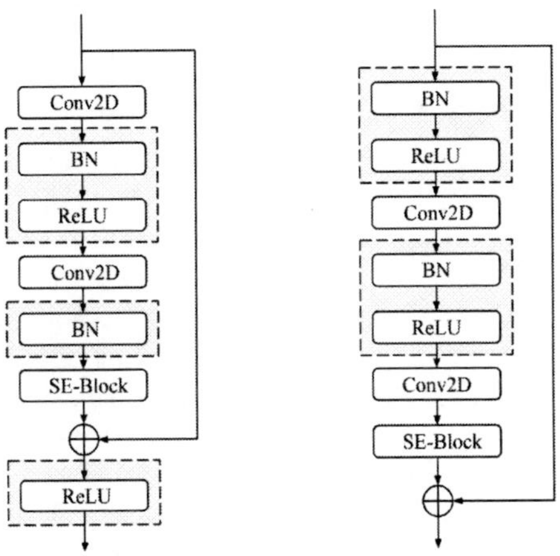

(a) original (b) pre-activation

圖 3. 原始 SE-ResBlock 與預激活結構之比較。⊕ 表示元素對應相加。

ResBlock 的結構順序進行調整，新結構與舊結構比較如圖 3 所示。

2.3.3 MFA 模組

MFA 模組是 Liu et al.在 MFA-TDNN 中設計用來取代 2D CNN 模組的新結構，其中使用了一個 Res2Block 變體來取代 ResBlock，這個變體是在傳統的 Res2Block 中改進了兩個新結構，也就是雙通道多尺度模組（dual-pathway multi-scale module）以頻率及通道注意力模組（frequency-channel attention module），模組結構如圖 4 所示。雙通道多尺度模組的做法是在 Res2Block 中的每個分支卷積後額外再進行一個 TDNN 模組的卷積，並且這個模組的輸出會傳入到另一個分支當中，這就與 Res2Net 原有的卷積輸出形成了雙通道

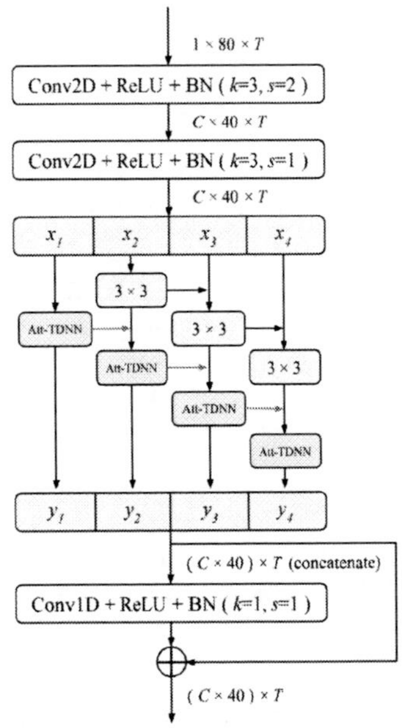

圖 4. MFA 模組。其中 C 表示通道數，T 表示音框數，卷積中的 k 與 s 表示卷積核大小及步伐長度，⊕ 表示元素對應相加。

輸入到另一個分支中進行計算。頻率及通道注意力模組則是建構在前面提到的 TDNN 模組當中，結構如圖 5。其整體的概念其實與 SE 模組相似，不同的是特徵向量通過全局平均池化（Global average pooling，GAP）後是會留下頻率以及通道兩個維度的平面向量，接著將此向量攤平進行 SE 模組中激發（excitation）計算，最後再將激發後的向量重塑（reshape）回原來的平面向量並且作爲權重值乘回原始的特徵向量。

2.4 注意力機制

在原始的 ECAPA-TDNN 及後續的各個改進版本中，不論如何修改、擴增網路結構，其中都會引入注意力機制來提高模型整體的表現。就我們的基準模型以及 2D CNN 模組中使用到的 SE 模組來説，SE 模組會對特徵向量操作後取得特徵向量各通道不同的權重，透過權重，我們可以抑制特徵中不重要的資訊，並有效的將重要的特徵資訊給凸顯出來。而考慮到在 SE 模組問世至今，已有許多後起之秀在各大競賽中脫穎而出，藉由自身獨特的結構設計進一步增強注意力機制在模型上的影響，我們在此替換並比較包含 SE 模組在內，共計 3 種不同結構的注意力機制在本次語者驗證系統上的表現，要替換成的模組分別是 CBAM 模組以及 GC 模組。關於這些注意力模組的詳細結構請見圖 6。而由於 MFA 模組中自身較特

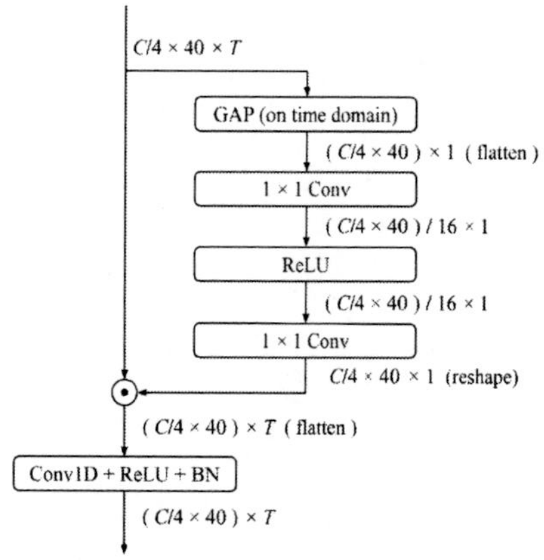

圖 5. MFA 模組中的 Att-TDNN 模組之結構。其中 C 表示通道數，T 表示音框數，$\odot$ 表示元素對應相乘。

殊的注意力設計，我們並不會替換 MFA 模組當中使用的注意力機制。

2.4.1 SE 模組

SE（Squeeze and Excitation）模組爲原始結構中所使用的注意力機制模組，模型結構如圖 6(a) 所示。其透過壓縮（squeeze）與激發（excitation）兩步驟來計算不同通道的權重。首先是壓縮，輸入特徵會對通道以外的維度進行全局平均池化計算，以取得各個通道的記述子（descriptor）；再來是激發，各通道的記述子會輸入兩層卷積層中進行降維升維的操作，來學習不同通道記述子的重要程度，並透過 sigmoid 函數將其轉換成通道權重乘回原始特徵向量當中。

2.4.2 CBAM 模組

CBAM（Convolutional Block Attention Module）模組是基於 SE 模組的擴展，模型結構如圖 6(b) 所示。其在計算完通道權重之後，會接著計算空間權重以突顯更重要的空間特徵。同時在兩種權重的計算當中除了使用全局平均池化之外，還會使用全局最大池化（Global map pooling，GMP）來取得更多不同的資訊。

2.4.3 GC 模組

GC（Global Context）模組是將 SE 模組與 Non-local 模組 (Wang et al., 2018) 進行結合而成，模型結構如圖 6(c) 所示。鑑於 Non-local 模組優秀的上下文建模（context modeling）能力與 SE 模組輕量的計算結構， Cao et al.通過簡化 Non-local 模組，然後將 Non-local 模組的特徵轉換層修改爲類 SE 模組的結構以融合兩模組的優點。透過這樣的設計，GC 模組在各項電腦視覺領域的競賽當中皆有不俗的表現。

3 實驗設置

這個章節我們會介紹本論文實驗中所使用到的訓練資料集以及測試資料集，也會詳細描述模型在訓練中所設置的各項超參數，並說明最終用來評估模型表現的準則。

3.1 資料集

我們使用 VoxCeleb 2 (Chung et al., 2018) 中 dev 的部份作爲我們的訓練資料集，並使用以 VoxCeleb 1 (Nagrani et al., 2017) 資料集音檔所組成的 VoxCeleb 1-O/E/H 測試集以及 VoxSRC 2022 的驗證集作爲本次模型的測試集。我們並沒有使用語音活性偵測（Voice activity detection，VAD）對實驗音檔進行調整。

3.2 參數設置

爲了公平比較模型表現，所有模型皆套用了相同的訓練策略進行訓練：使用 Adam 優化器（optimizer）調整神經網路參數，初始學習率爲 1e-03，每 10 個 epoch 會減少 25%。使用 AAM-Softmax 作爲損失函數，其中 margin 設爲 2，scale 設爲 30。訓練期間應用權重衰減來防止模型過度擬合，將值設爲 2e-05。訓練時的 batch size 設置爲 256，並訓練 100 個 epoch 取其中最好的模型參數。主幹網路 IM ECAPA-TDNN 中的通道數量皆設置爲 512，語者嵌入的輸出大小設置爲 192；在前處理模組方面，2D CNN 模組不論是否爲預激活其通道大小都設置爲 64，而 MFA 模組基於模型大小則設爲 32。

3.3 評估準則

我們以等錯誤率（Equal Error Rate, EER）以及最小檢測成本函數（Minimum Detection Cost Function, MinDCF）作爲我們評估系統表現的準則。其中最小檢測成本函數依照 VoxSRC 2022 設定的標準，將參數設置爲 C_{miss}=1、C_{fasle}=1、P_{target}=0.05。我們並沒有使用任何分數正規化方法對分數進行調整。

4 實驗結果

Architecture	VoxCeleb1-O		VoxSRC2022 val	
	EER(%)	minDCF	EER(%)	minDCF
ECAPA-TDNN (Re-implemented)	1.3770	0.0931	**3.6735**	0.2479
IM ECAPA-TDNN	**1.2600**	**0.0849**	3.6824	**0.2462**

表 1. IM ECAPA-TDNN 與 ECAPA-TDNN 在最簡單及最困難的資料集上之表現比較

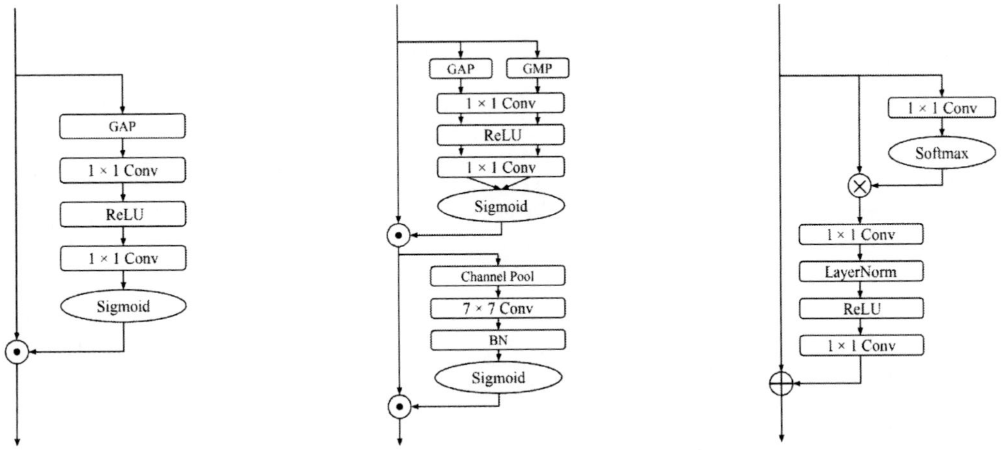

(a) SE 模組　(b) CBAM 模組　(c) GC 模組

圖 6. 不同注意力機制模組之結構。⊙ 表示元素對應相乘，⊗ 表示矩陣相乘，⊕ 表示元素對應相加。

Architecture	VoxCeleb1-O		VoxCeleb1-E		VoxCeleb1-H		VoxSRC2022 val	
	EER(%)	minDCF	EER(%)	minDCF	EER(%)	minDCF	EER(%)	minDCF
IM ECAPA-TDNN (baseline)	1.2600	0.0849	1.4733	0.0941	2.6891	0.1621	3.6824	0.2462
不同的前處理模組								
IM ECAPA CNN-TDNN	1.1218	0.0886	1.2763	0.0825	**2.3318**	0.1475	**3.2230**	0.2144
IM ECAPA CNN-TDNN (pre-act)	**1.0424**	**0.0739**	1.2646	0.0831	2.3518	**0.1415**	3.4471	0.2198
IM ECAPA MFA-TDNN	**1.0424**	0.0797	**1.2632**	**0.0813**	2.3526	0.1439	3.2535	**0.2118**
不同的注意力機制								
IM ECAPA CNN-TDNN (pre-act) with SE	**1.0424**	**0.0739**	1.2646	0.0831	2.3518	**0.1415**	3.4471	0.2198
IM ECAPA CNN-TDNN (pre-act) with CBAM	1.1484	0.0817	**1.2507**	**0.0821**	**2.3500**	0.1437	**3.1160**	**0.2053**
IM ECAPA CNN-TDNN (pre-act) with GC	1.2552	0.0992	1.3807	0.0926	2.5533	0.1551	3.4990	0.2282

表 2. 不同模型在各測試集上的表現比較

我們首先比對了原始 ECAPA-TDNN 與本次作爲基準模型的 IM ECAPA-TDNN 在最簡單的 VoxCeleb1-O 及最困難的 VoxSRC2022 驗證集上的表現，其結果如表 1 所示。可以看到經過修改後的 IM ECAPA-TDNN 雖然在困難資料集上的表現與原始 ECAPA-TDNN 相差無多，但在簡單資料集上明顯是更爲優秀的一方。

接著我們會分別討論不同的前處理模組以及不同的注意力機制對模型表現所造成的影響，並將表現最好的組合做爲我們的最終模型。所有模型在各個測試集上的詳細結果如表 2 所示。

4.1 前處理模組的比較

在加入了前處理模組之後，所有的模型相較於基準模型都有顯著的進步。相比於 2D CNN 模組在各個資料集上都有穩定的發揮，預激活的 2D CNN 模組雖然在相對簡單的 Voxceleb1-O 測試集上明顯優於原始的 2D CNN 模組，但是其在複雜度越高的測試集上表現卻較爲差勁，我們認爲主要是由於我們使用了輕量的 IM ECAPA-TDNN 作爲主幹網路，而在 (He et al., 2016b) 中表明了預激活的 ResBlock 要在深層的網路結構中才能發揮效果，所以才造成預激活 2D CNN 模組在複雜測試集上表現不佳的原因。而 MFA 模組得益於其多尺度多維度注意力的卷積結構，其在簡單的測試集上可以做到與使用預激活 2D CNN 模組一樣優異的表現，並在複雜的測試集上表現相對穩定。

4.2 注意力機制的比較

考慮到 MFA 模組本身自帶的注意力機制無法輕易變動，我們在 2D CNN 模組中選擇了預激活的版本替換其注意力模組，來觀察各注意力機制對模型表現造成的影響。SE 模組在相對簡單的 Voxceleb1-O 測試集上依舊有著較佳的表現，但是 CBAM 模組在其他更爲複雜資料集對比另外兩個注意力模組都有著更優秀的結果。會有這樣的差異我們認爲是因爲 CBAM 模型引入空間注意力能夠有效的將更多重要的語者特徵突顯出來，且相比 SE 模組只做了全局平均池化，CBAM 還加入了全局最大池化進行計算以取得不同方面的資訊，這些設計讓模型能夠在複雜的測試集上擷取更細微的特徵進行辨識，進而提高了辨識結果的表現；對比 CBAM 的優異表現，GC 模組反而在所有測試集的表現都不突出，會有這樣的問題我們認爲是模組的設計與 TDNN 結構衝突，將模組結構硬是改寫爲相容 TDNN 反而造成擷取特徵時產生冗餘的資訊，導致 GC 模組連 SE 模組的表現都達不到。

4.3 最終提出模型

根據我們上述的實驗結果，我們將帶有預激活 2D CNN 前處理模組，並替換注意力機制爲 CBAM 的 IM ECAPA-TDNN，即表 2 中的 IM ECAPA CNN-TDNN (pre-act) with CBAM 做爲我們的最終提出模型。相比與基準模型，我們的最終模型在各測試集上都有明顯的進步，以最複雜的 VoxSRC2022 驗證集來說，最終模型在 EER 值與 minDCF 值上分別有 15.4% 以及 16.6% 的進步幅度。

5 結論

本論文提出了基於 Improving ECAPA-TDNN 修改的 IM ECAPA-TDNN 結構作爲我們的基準模型，並透過結合不同的前處理模組以及調整注意力機制來對模型表現進行進一步的強化。我們提出的最終模型通過結合預激活的 2D CNN 前處理模組與替換注意力機制爲 CBAM 模組，在各項測試集上的表現對比基準模型都有著大幅提昇。未來我們將會以此爲依據來修改其他更加複雜的主幹網路，希望能夠藉此來進一步的提昇我們語者驗證系統的效能。

References

Yue Cao, Jiarui Xu, Stephen Lin, Fangyun Wei, and Han Hu. 2019. Gcnet: Non-local networks meet squeeze-excitation networks and beyond.

Joon Son Chung, Jaesung Huh, Seongkyu Mun, Minjae Lee, Hee Soo Heo, Soyeon Choe, Chiheon Ham, Sunghwan Jung, Bong-Jin Lee, and Icksang Han. 2020. In defence of metric learning for speaker recognition. In *Proc. Interspeech*.

Joon Son Chung, Arsha Nagrani, and Andrew Zisserman. 2018. Voxceleb2: Deep speaker recognition. *CoRR*, abs/1806.05622.

Shang-Hua Gao, Ming-Ming Cheng, Kai Zhao, Xin-Yu Zhang, Ming-Hsuan Yang, and Philip Torr. 2019. Res2net: A new multi-scale backbone architecture. *IEEE transactions on pattern analysis and machine intelligence*, 43(2):652–662.

Kaiming He, Xiangyu Zhang, Shaoqing Ren, and Jian Sun. 2016a. Deep residual learning for image recognition. In *2016 IEEE Conference on Computer Vision and Pattern Recognition (CVPR)*, pages 770–778.

Kaiming He, Xiangyu Zhang, Shaoqing Ren, and Jian Sun. 2016b. Identity mappings in deep residual networks.

Jie Hu, Li Shen, and Gang Sun. 2018. Squeeze-and-excitation networks. In *2018 IEEE/CVF Conference on Computer Vision and Pattern Recognition*, pages 7132–7141.

Tom Ko, Vijayaditya Peddinti, Daniel Povey, Michael L. Seltzer, and Sanjeev Khudanpur. 2017. A study on data augmentation of reverberant speech for robust speech recognition. In *2017 IEEE International Conference on Acoustics, Speech and Signal Processing (ICASSP)*, pages 5220–5224.

Jiang-Jiang Liu, Qibin Hou, Ming-Ming Cheng, Changhu Wang, and Jiashi Feng. 2020. Improving convolutional networks with self-calibrated convolutions. In *2020 IEEE/CVF Conference on Computer Vision and Pattern Recognition (CVPR)*, pages 10093–10102.

Tianchi Liu, Rohan Kumar Das, Kong Aik Lee, and Haizhou Li. 2022. Mfa: Tdnn with multi-scale frequency-channel attention for text-independent speaker verification with short utterances. In *ICASSP 2022-2022 IEEE International Conference on Acoustics, Speech and Signal Processing (ICASSP)*, pages 7517–7521. IEEE.

Arsha Nagrani, Joon Son Chung, and Andrew Zisserman. 2017. VoxCeleb: A large-scale speaker identification dataset. In *Interspeech 2017*. ISCA.

David Snyder, Guoguo Chen, and Daniel Povey. 2015. Musan: A music, speech, and noise corpus.

Jenthe Thienpondt, Brecht Desplanques, and Kris Demuynck. 2021. Integrating frequency translational invariance in tdnns and frequency positional information in 2d resnets to enhance speaker verification. *arXiv preprint arXiv:2104.02370*.

Xiaolong Wang, Ross Girshick, Abhinav Gupta, and Kaiming He. 2018. Non-local neural networks. In *2018 IEEE/CVF Conference on Computer Vision and Pattern Recognition*, pages 7794–7803.

Sanghyun Woo, Jongchan Park, Joon-Young Lee, and In So Kweon. 2018. Cbam: Convolutional block attention module.

Yu-Jia Zhang, Yih-Wen Wang, Chia-Ping Chen, Chung-Li Lu, and Bo-Cheng Chan. 2021. Improving Time Delay Neural Network Based Speaker Recognition with Convolutional Block and Feature Aggregation Methods. In *Proc. Interspeech 2021*, pages 76–80.

The 34th Conference on Computational Linguistics and Speech Processing (ROCLING 2022)
Taipei, Taiwan, November 21-22, 2022. The Association for Computational Linguistics and Chinese Language Processing

使用離散小波轉換特徵於 Conv-TasNet 語音強化模型的初步研究
A Preliminary Study of the Application of Discrete Wavelet Transform Features in Conv-TasNet Speech Enhancement Model

陳彥同
Yan-Tong Chen
暨南大學電機系
National Chi Nan University
s109323508@mail1.ncnu.edu.tw

吳宗泰
Zong-Tai Wu
暨南大學電機系
National Chi Nan University
s110323503@mail1.ncnu.edu.tw

洪志偉
Jeih-Weih Hung
暨南大學電機系
National Chi Nan University
jwhung@ncnu.edu.tw

摘要

當前基於深度類神經網路架構之語音強化模型，常使用時域特徵來加以學習其模型參數，時域特徵如同經典的頻域特徵一般，能夠使所得模型達到優異的語音強化效果。基於此概念，本研究主要是探討如何從時域的語音中提取資訊、以在語音強化中創建更有效的特徵。我們提出了在時域中擷取短時間的子頻帶信號，並將它們融合成為單一特徵。具體方法是應用離散小波變換對每個輸入的音框信號進行分解、以獲得子頻帶信號，並對這些信號進行投影融合處理以創建最終小波域特徵。對應的融合處理法稱為雙投影融合(bi-projection fusion, BPF)法。同時，我們將藉由離散小波轉換之融合小波域特徵與原始時域特徵加以整合、來學習一高效的語音強化網路：全卷積時域音頻分離網路 (Conv-TasNet)，藉此來強化受雜訊干擾的語音訊號、提升其品質與可讀性。

我們在 VoiceBank-DEMAND 與 VoiceBank-QUT 兩個語音強化資料集上進行了評估實驗，初步結果表明，所提出的方法比原始單純使用時域特徵的 Conv-TasNet 實現了更高的客觀語音品質和可讀性指標，表明融合小波域特徵可以輔助原時域特徵、從輸入的雜訊語音中學習一個更有效的 Conv-TasNet 網路、達到更佳的語音強化效果。

Abstract

Nowadays, time-domain features have been widely used in speech enhancement (SE) networks like frequency-domain features to achieve excellent performance in eliminating noise from input utterances. This study primarily investigates how to extract information from time-domain utterances to create more effective features in speech enhancement. We present employing sub-signals dwelled in multiple acoustic frequency bands in time domain and integrating them into a unified feature set. We propose using the discrete wavelet transform (DWT) to decompose each input frame signal to obtain sub-band signals, and a projection fusion process is performed on these signals to create the ultimate features. The corresponding fusion strategy is the bi-projection fusion (BPF). In short, BPF exploits the sigmoid function to create ratio masks for two feature sources. The concatenation of fused DWT features and time features serves as the encoder output of a celebrated SE framework, fully-convolutional time-domain audio separation network (Conv-TasNet), to estimate the mask and then produce the enhanced time-domain utterances.

The evaluation experiments are conducted on the VoiceBank-DEMAND and VoiceBank-QUT tasks. The experimental results reveal that the proposed method achieves higher speech quality and intelligibility than the original Conv-TasNet that uses time features only, indicating that the fusion of DWT features created from the input utterances can benefit time features to learn a superior Conv-TasNet in speech enhancement.

The 34th Conference on Computational Linguistics and Speech Processing (ROCLING 2022)
Taipei, Taiwan, November 21-22, 2022. The Association for Computational Linguistics and Chinese Language Processing

關鍵字：語音強化、離散小波轉換、跨域、雙投影融合、全卷積時頻分離網路

Keywords: speech enhancement, discrete wavelet transform, cross-domain, temporal speech sequence, Conv-TasNet, bi-projection fusion

1 簡介

現今的語音處理技術已成功集成到智能 3C 設備、實現語音辨識、交互式語音聊天、智能機器人的語音指令控制、汽車或機車的語音控制等功能於眾多網路和多媒體視聽設備中。然而，在拓展語音相關之應用上，仍然存在許多關鍵性的挑戰。從信號處理的角度來看，雜訊(noise)干擾是信號傳輸和語音處理的首要問題之一。正如 2021 年暢銷書(Kahneman, 2021)中所述，雜訊(noise)和偏差(bias)是精準估測與決策上兩個主要的錯誤來源。然而，與偏差相比，雜訊的隨機性使其準確估測的可能性大大降低，從而加深了處理雜訊的難度。雖然這主要是對人類判斷的敘述，但它似乎同樣適用於基於機器之自動語音信號處理所面臨的處境。

在對應語音中的雜訊之各種議題中，語音強化 (speech enhancement, SE) (Philipos C. Loizou,2013)應可謂最直接的處理機制，其針對接收到的語音訊號加以處理、目標為提升輸出語音訊號的訊雜比(signal-to-noise ratio, SNR)，或改善語音的品質(quality)和可讀性(intelligibility)，使人們或機器更容易接受和理解語音訊號。傳統的語音強化演算法主要依賴於語音或雜訊的統計特性建構模型，然而它們在非穩態雜訊場景中的表現通常較差，主因之一在於非穩態的訊號特性較難以統計形式加以精準估測。

近十年來，由於深度學習和深度神經網路(deep neural networks, DNN)(Ian Goodfellow et al., 2016) 的理論與應用的飛快進步，學者和專家藉由 DNN 來建構語音強化的模型，與傳統基於統計的語音強化法相較，基於 DNN 的方法效果通常優異許多、特別是在非穩態的雜訊場景中。

在諸多基於 DNN 的語音強化法中，全摺積時域音訊分離網路法 (Conv-TasNet)(Yi Luo and Nima Mesgarani, 2019)相當著名且高效，因此廣為學者所探討並加以延伸。Conv-TasNet 採用編碼器串接解碼器(encoder-decoder)的架構，並應用堆疊的一維擴張卷積塊(dilated convolutional block)來執行其中的遮罩估測網路(mask estimation network)。原始的 Conv-TasNet 在編碼器端使用可訓練之一維卷積層來創建時域特徵，以作為編碼器輸出。而跨域時間卷積網路法(CD-TCN)(Fu-An Chao et al., 2019)則 進一步採用頻域特徵，結合時域特徵作為編碼器輸出。實驗結果表明，相較於使用單一時域的 Conv-TasNet，使用跨域特徵（時域與頻域）的 CD-TCN 達到更佳的語音強化效能。

在本研究中，我們參考了 CD-TCN 的方法脈絡，嘗試通過添加另一個特徵源來改進 Conv-TasNet，而這個特徵源來自輸入之音框訊號的離散小波變換 (discrete wavelet transform, DWT)(Stephane Mallat,2019)。我們使用 DWT 創建子頻帶特徵，然後將這些子頻帶特徵加以融合(fusion)、成為小波域特徵，最後將此小波域特徵與時域特徵加以串接、作為 Conv-TasNet 的編碼器輸出，我們參照了 CD-TCN 的方法，將其二元投影融合法(bi-projection fusion, BPF)用於小波子頻帶特徵的融合上。

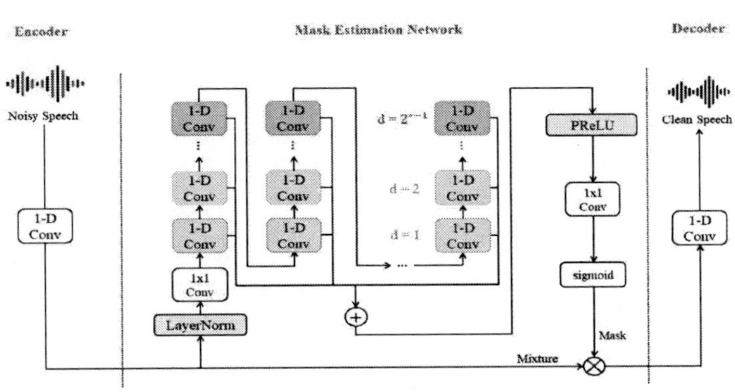

圖一. 原始 Conv-TasNet 的流程圖（編碼端使用時域特徵）

我們將所提之新方法在 VoiceBank-DEMAND 和 VoiceBank-QUT 數據集上進行評估，初步實驗結果表明，所提出之新型跨域（小波域與時域）的 Conv-TasNet 模型在客觀語音品質和語音可讀性指標上，都呈現了優異的語音強化性能、優於單一時域的 Conv-TasNet 法，另外，藉由與 Conv-TasNet 架構類似、但於遮罩估測網路更細緻的 DPTNet (Jingjing Chen, 2020)模型之評估，我們也驗證了所提之小波域特徵的優越性。

2 提出之新方法

原始使用時域特徵作為編碼器輸出的 Conv-TasNet 其流程圖如圖一所示。我們看到其包含了編碼器、遮罩估測網路與解碼器三部分。在這裡，我們主要是針對其編碼器加以變化，提出採用小波域特徵的求取法、並將小波域特徵與時域特徵相結合，作為此網路的編碼器特徵。 這個新方法主要包括以下步驟：

2.1 建立時域特徵與一階離散小波特徵

從單通道麥克風接收到的受雜訊干擾的語音信號 y[n]可以表示如下：

$$y[n] = h[n] * x[n] + d[n], \quad (1)$$

其中$x[n]$是乾淨的語音信號，$h[n]$是對應於通道效應或混響的捲積性雜訊，$d[n]$則是加成性雜訊，而n是時間索引。在這裡，我們忽略卷積性雜訊$h[n]$，專注處理加成性雜訊$d[n]$所干擾之語音訊號，以重建乾淨語音信號$x[n]$為目的的語音強化模型。

根據語音其短時穩態的特性，我們將輸入語音信號$y[n]$切割成M個長度為L的音框訊號，各音框訊號以向量 $\mathbf{x}_k \in \mathbb{R}^{L\times 1}$表示，其中 k為音框索引(frame index)。 因此，我們將各音框之向量橫排、構成一個原始資料矩陣 $X \in \mathbb{R}^{L\times M}$ 。

(1) 時域特徵

我們將輸入之原始資料矩陣 X 通過可訓練之一維卷積層運算，使其原本為L維的行向量x_k轉換為 N 維向量，橫向串接後得到時域特徵矩陣$\boldsymbol{W_T} \in \mathbb{R}^{N\times M}$，公式如下：

$$W_T = H(UX), \quad (2)$$

其中$U \in \mathbb{R}^{N\times L}$ 為N個時域轉換的編碼器基底(basis)向量直排而成，即為卷積層之 kernel 函數，H 是一個非線性函數，如 ReLU 函數，以確保輸出 W_T的每項都是大於或等於零。

(2) 一階離散小波特徵

首先，我們對矩陣X的每一個行向量$\mathbf{x}_k$執行一階離散小波變換，得到其近似項係數(approximation coefficients)與細節項係數(detail coefficients)，如下式所示：

$$[\mathbf{c}_k^A, \mathbf{c}_k^D] = \boldsymbol{DWT}(X), \quad (3)$$

其中$\boldsymbol{DWT}(\cdot)$代表一階離散小波變換，$\mathbf{c}_k^A$和 $\mathbf{c}_k^D$分別是近似項係數和細節項係數，可以看作是原始序列$\mathbf{x}_k$的低通(lowpass)子頻帶和高通(highpass)子頻帶。二者之頻寬都大約等於原始序列頻寬的一半，而它們的點數減為$\mathbf{x}_k$點數的一半，即$\frac{L}{2}$。

我們將高通與低通之各音框子頻帶信號分別橫排再一起、產生兩個特徵矩陣C_A和C_D，大小為 $\frac{L}{2} \times K$，它們的行向量分別為$\mathbf{c}_k^A$和$\mathbf{c}_k^D$。之後，我們使用一維可訓練卷積層（連同非線性函數H）進一步處理C_A和C_D，以生成大小為$N \times M$的兩個矩陣W_A和W_D，兩者與時域特徵矩陣W_T大小相同。 其運算公式為：

$$W_A = H(U_A C_A), \; W_D = H(U_D C_D), \quad (4)$$

其中U_A和U_D分別表示C_A和C_D對應的一維卷積層運算矩陣。

2.2 彙整時域特徵和小波域特徵

到目前為止，我們有三個特徵矩陣：W_T（時域特徵）、W_A（小波域低頻特徵）和W_D（小波域高頻特徵）。它們的尺寸相同。在這裡，我們提出了三種方法來彙整它們，以建構最終的編碼器輸出矩陣W_E，它們的流程圖分別繪製於圖二(a)、圖二(b)與圖三(b)。三個方法分述如下：

相加 (addition)

首先，最直觀的彙整方式是將W_E設為三個矩陣的加權和：

$$W_E = 0.5W_T + 0.25W_A + 0.25W_D, \quad (5)$$

此步驟由圖一(a)所示。由此可看出最終的特徵矩陣W_E與每個分量矩陣的尺寸一致。

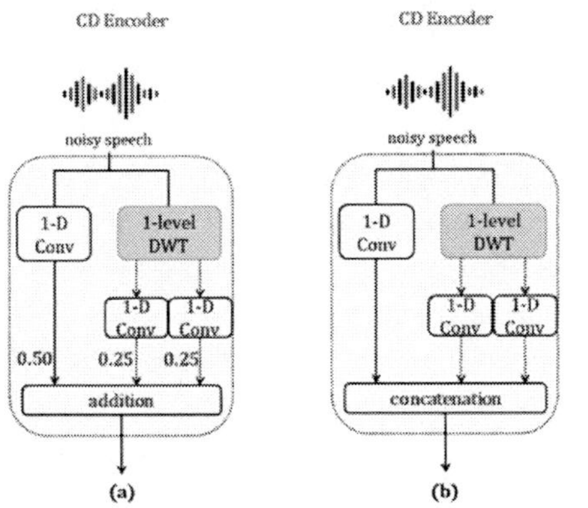

圖二. 更新後的 Conv-TasNet 編碼器部分示意圖，通過(a) 相加，或 (b)串接來彙整時域和小波域特徵

串接 (concatenation)

另一種直觀的彙整方式是將三個矩陣橫向串接：

$$W_E = [W_T; W_A; W_D], \tag{6}$$

此步驟由圖一(b)所示。由此可看出最終的特徵矩陣W_E相對於每個分量矩陣而言，項數變為 3 倍

先融合再串接 (fusion and concatenation)

為了更有效地提取與整合兩個小波域特徵W_A和W_D的資訊，我們利用文獻(Fu-En Wang, 2020)所使用的二元投影融合法(bi-projection fusion, BPF) 將二者相融合。 BPF 已被用於集成時域和頻域特徵，並在 CD-TCN 法(Fu-An Chao et al., 2019) 中有優異的表現。此外，語音訊號中的低通成分和高通成分對應至不同的資訊、受雜訊影響也可能不同。例如，低通特徵W_A通常對應更多母音的成分，而高通特徵W_D可能對應到子音。此外，在常見的雜訊干擾場景中，低通特徵W_A的訊雜比 (signal-to-noise ratio, SNR) 通常高於低通特徵W_D（因為語音的低頻成分能量通常較大）。因此，BPF 模塊的兩個互補性遮罩矩陣（各項非負且二矩陣相同位置的二項和為 1）應適合用於融合這兩個不同頻帶的特徵來強化語音。

使用 BPF 法融合兩特徵的步驟如下：首先，我們串接W_A與W_D作為一個可訓練之卷積層的輸入，求取一遮罩(mask) M:

$$M = \sigma(\Psi_M([W_A; W_D], \theta_M)), \tag{7}$$

其中σ是 sigmoid 函數，Ψ_M是卷積投影層運算，其參數為θ_M。 接著，我們將M和$1-M$與W_A和W_D分別相點乘，進而相加以生成小波域融合特徵：

$$W_{DWT} = M \odot W_A + (1-M) \odot W_D, \tag{8}$$

其中 $\odot$是點乘運算。

最後，我們橫向串接小波域融合 特徵和時域特徵以得到最終的特徵矩陣W_E：

$$W_E = [W_T; W_{DWT}], \tag{9}$$

因此，矩陣W_E的項數是各域特徵矩陣的兩倍。

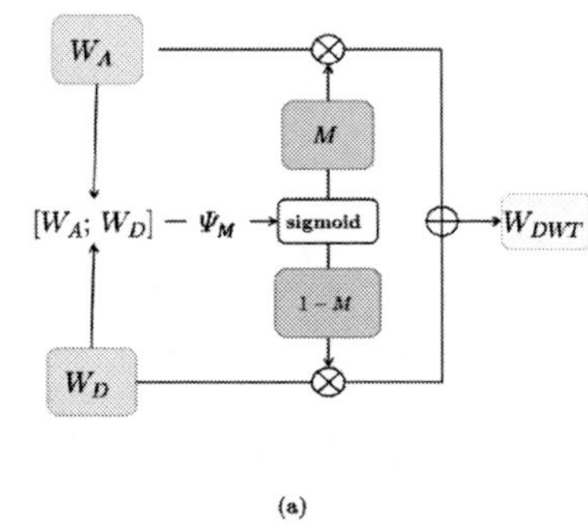

圖三. (a) 融合高頻與低頻之小波域特徵的 BPF 模塊

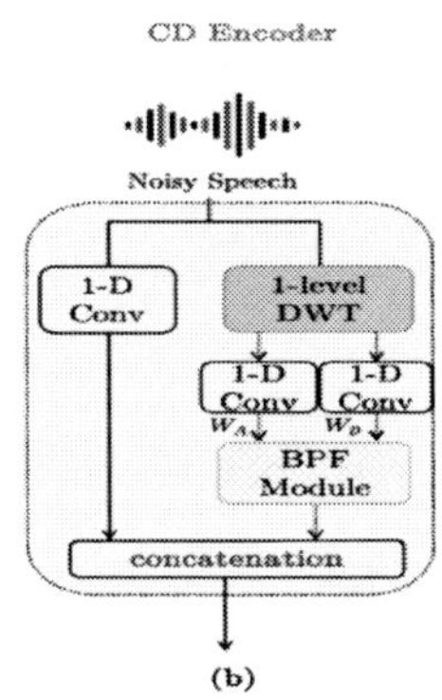

(b) 更新後的 Conv-TasNet 編碼器部分示意圖，通過先融合再串接來彙整時域和小波域特徵

3 評估實驗與結果討論

3.1 實驗設置

我們首先使用 VoiceBank-DEMAND [9,10] 之資料集任務來評估我們提出的新方法，其中 語音訊號來自 VoiceBank 語料庫 (Christophe Veaux et al., 2013)、而摻入的雜訊則來自 DEMAND 資料庫(Joachim Thiemann et al., 2013)。擷取自 Voicebank 語料庫，訓練集包括 28 個語者的 11,572 個語句，測試集包則包括 2 個語者的 824 個語句，訓練集語句由

DEMAND 資料庫中的十種雜訊所混合、其訊雜比(SNR)有四種：0、5、10 和 15 dB。測試集語句則分別以四種訊雜比、摻入五種來自 DEMAND 的雜訊：2.5、7.5、12.5 和 17.5 dB。此外，我們從訓練集中挑選 200 個語句作為驗證集。

為了進一步研究所提出方法的一般化能力(generalization capability)，我們建立了另一個測試集。該測試集使用與原始測試集相同的乾淨語音，但是摻入 QUT-NOISE 資料庫(Dean et al., 2010) 的不同類型的非穩態雜訊、以建構相對於 VoiceBank-DEMAND 任務更加複雜的場景，

且其面對的是訓練模型時未見的雜訊環境(unseen noise)，該測試集之訊雜比分別設為 -5、0、5 和 15 dB，我們稱之為 VoiceBank-QUI 資料集任務。在細項參數設定上，我們使用 db2 小波函數來實現所提方法中的離散小波轉換。對於 Conv-TasNet，我們使用的超參數：個別波段(repat)之捲積塊個數 X = 8、總波段數 R = 3、bottleneck 中的通道數B = 128、個別捲積塊中的通道數H = 256、在 skip-connection 路經之1 × 1 卷積塊的通道數 S = 128、以及捲積塊中的 kernel 大小 P = 3，此設置與文獻(Yi Luo and Nima Mesgarani, 2019) 中的最佳設置的唯一不同，是將參數 H的值減半，來加快訓練與測試之速度。

在評估語音強化的效能上，我們分別使用了 PESQ 分數(Antony W. Rix et al., 2001)作為語音品質(quality)的客觀指標、STOI 分數(Cees H. Taal et al., 2016)作為語音可讀性(intelligibility)的客觀指標、SI-SNR 分數(Yusuf Isik et al., 2016)作為度量語音失真的客觀指標，PESQ 分數介於-0.5 與 4.5 之間，STOI 分數介於 0 與 1 之間，三者分數越高皆代表語音強化效能越好。

3.2 實驗結果及討論

3.2.1 使用不同特徵之 Conv-TasNet

我們藉由各種不同的特徵來評估 Conv-TasNet 法。這些特徵包含原始的時域特徵、CD-TCN 使用的時域與頻域之融合特徵、以及我們提出的三種時域與小波域之彙整特徵。相對應的測試集其 PESQ、STOI 和 SI-SNR 分數如表一所示。從這張表中，我們可看出以下幾點：

1. 在 DEMAND 雜訊場景下，與未處理的基礎實驗相比，這裡使用之對應不同特徵的

特徵域	整合方式	VoiceBank 測試集 (Conv-TasNet)					
		DEMAND			QUT-NOISE		
		PESQ	STOI	SI-SNR	PESQ	STOI	SI-SNR
未處理（基礎實驗）		1.970	0.921	8.445	1.247	0.784	3.876
時域	–	2.618	0.943	19.500	1.908	0.860	13.694
時域及頻域	–	2.648	0.942	**19.712**	**1.936**	**0.863**	13.779
時域及小波域	相加	**2.681**	0.942	19.352*	1.922	0.858*	13.645*
	連接	2.669	0.942	19.609	1.932	0.861	13.775
	先融合再串接	2.668	**0.943**	19.496*	**1.936**	0.862	**13.824**

表一. 各種特徵運用於 Conv-TasNet 法、在 DEMAND 與 QUT 雜訊場景下所得的語音強化評估指標值

特徵域	整合方式	VoiceBank 測試集 (DPTNet)					
		DEMAND			QUT-NOISE		
		PESQ	STOI	SI-SNR	PESQ	STOI	SI-SNR
未處理		1.970	0.921	8.445	1.247	0.784	3.876
時域	–	2.549	0.935	19.080	1.804	0.845	12.802
時域及頻域	–	**2.782**	**0.946**	**19.963**	2.019	0.870	14.500
時域及小波域	**先融合再串接**	2.724	0.945	19.960	**2.044**	**0.873**	**14.543**

表二. 各種特徵運用於 DPTNet 法、在 DEMAND 與 QUT 雜訊場景下所得的語音強化評估指標值

Conv-TasNet 法都達到明顯更佳的 PESQ 和 SI-SNR 分數，反映了這些特徵對應之 Conv-TasNet 其優異的語音強化能力。相比之下，它們對於STOI指標的改進較少，可能是因為基礎實驗對應的 STOI 分數已經高達 0.921（滿分為 1）。相對而言，在 QUT 雜訊場景中，各種特徵之 Conv-TasNet 法在三個指標(PESQ, STOI 與 SI-SNR)上都能有效提升。

2. 當 Conv-TasNet 法運用於 DEMAND 雜訊場景與 QUI 雜訊場景中，使用單一時域特徵相較於使用時域與頻域之融合特徵、以及三種時域與小波域之彙整特徵，對應的 PESQ 與 SI-SNR 分數大部分都較低，此顯示了頻域與小波域特徵都能補強原始時域特徵、使 Conv-TasNet 法達到更好的效果。
3. 相較於時域與頻域之融合特徵，三種時域與小波域之彙整特徵在 DEMAND 雜訊場景下得到較顯著的 PESQ 提升，而在 QUI 場景下則各有優劣。
4. 若比較所提出的三種時域與小波域之彙整特徵，在比較單純的 DEMAND 場景中，簡易的相加整合法可得到最佳的 PESQ 分數，而先融合再串接的整合法則在較複雜的 QUI 場景中得到較佳的 PESQ 與 STOI 分數，背後可能的原因是，先融合再串接之整合法的特徵數目是相加整合法的特徵數目的 2 倍，且前者有更多的模型參數（如 BPF 模型之參數）需學習，在單純的 DEMAND 場景中較容易使所學習之 Conv-TasNet 模型產生過擬合(over-fitting)的不良現象，但在未知且非穩態雜訊的 QUI 場景中，則是先融合再串接之整合法表現較佳。

3.2.2 使用不同特徵之 DPTNet

為了驗證所提之小波域特徵對於語音強化模型的效能，在這裡，我們額外採用一個與 Conv-TasNet 法架構相似、但其中的遮罩估測模組採用更細緻安排的架構，即 DPTNet 法(Jingjing Chen, 2020)，其主要參照當今效能卓越之 Transformer 架構(Ashish Vaswani et al., 20117)來構建其遮罩估測模組。類似 3.1 章節的安排，我們藉由相同的資料集安排，使用不同種類的編碼器特徵來訓練與測試 DPTNet 效能，其得到的實驗結果如表二所示，特別註明的是，為了簡單起見，這裡我們只採用了「先融合再串接」的方法求時域與小波域之彙整特徵。

1. 相較於表一與表二的結果，正如預期的那樣，除了時域特徵外，所有種類的編碼特徵在 DPTNet 中都比在 Conv-TasNet 中提供更好的 PESQ 分數。我們認為其可能的原因在於，在時間特徵的情況下，DPTNet 未最佳化之超參數設定造成不如 Conv-TasNet 的結果。
2. 相較於單一使用時域特徵，當與頻域特徵與小波域特徵分別與時間特徵相結合時，DPTNet 在三種語音強化指標上都有明顯的進步，由此可驗證頻域與小波域特徵對於時域特徵的加成性。
3. 若和時域與頻域之融合特徵相比較，時域與小波域之彙整特徵在 DEMAND 雜訊場景下其 PESQ 分數較低、STOI 與 SI-SNR 的分數則較高。然而在 QU 雜訊場景下，時域與小波域之彙整特徵則在三個指標(PESQ, STOI 與 SI-SNR)上都優於時域與頻域之融合特徵，此結果也大致與 Conv-TasNet 法的觀察類似，即採用「先融合再串接」的方法求時域與小波域之彙整特徵，在 QUT 此未知且非穩態雜訊的雜訊場景中表現幾乎是最佳的。

綜合上述的實驗結果，我們可看到，所提出的小波域特徵，在 Conv-TasNet 與 DPTNet 這兩種語音強化模型上，都能有效與原始時域特徵相加成、以達到更佳的語音強化效果，雖然在與時域特徵結合時，小波域特徵與頻域特徵對應上的效果各有優劣，然而本研究是凸顯小波域特徵在與時域特徵的整合上，是頻域特徵的另一個有效選擇，亦即小波域特徵和頻域特徵的加入都能有效改善 Conv-TasNet 與 DPTNet 這些著名的語音強化模型的效能。

3.3 時頻圖之比較

除了語音強化的各項指標外，這裡我們額外使用語句的強度時頻圖 (magnitude spectrogram)來驗證所提之時域與小波域彙整特徵藉由 Conv-TasNet 所呈現的消噪(denoising)效能。在圖四中，我們分別呈現了一段語句在(a)乾淨環境、(b)雜訊環境、(c)雜訊環境但經時域特徵對應的 Conv-TasNet 強化

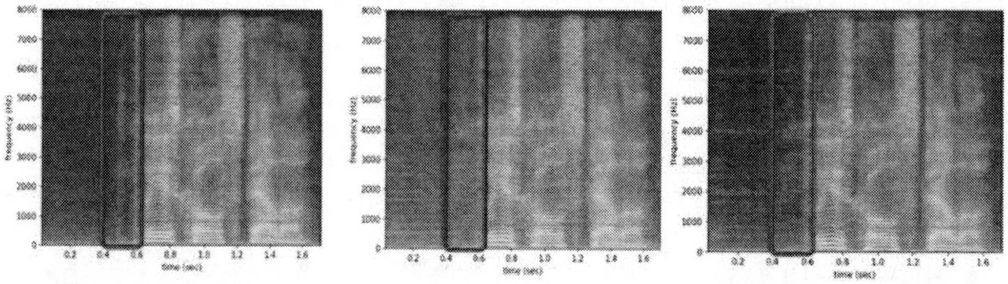

(a) clean (b) noisy (c) enhanced by time-domain Conv-TasNet

圖四. 各種場景下的語音強度時頻圖：(a)乾淨環境、(b)雜訊干擾 (c)雜訊干擾且由時域特徵對應之 Conv-TasNet 強化

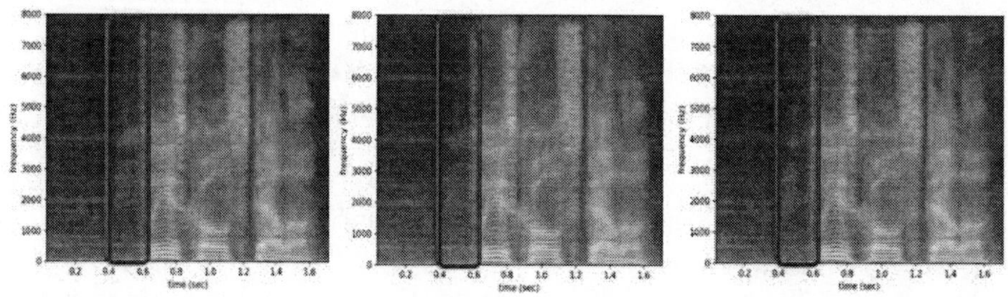

(a) addition (b) concatenation (c) fusion and concatenation

圖五. 不同時域與小波域之彙整特徵對應的 Conv-TasNet 強化所得之強度時頻圖：(a) 相加法 (b) 連接法 (c) 先融合再連接法

後所得到的強度時頻圖，而圖五則分別對應了原圖四(b)之雜訊干擾語句經過三種時域與小波域之彙整特徵對應的 Conv-TasNet 強化所得之時頻圖強度。比較這些強度時頻圖，我們可以觀察到：

1. 雜訊的摻入對於乾淨語音造成顯著的干擾，特別是在前段的無聲片段中，時頻圖呈現的失真相當明顯。
2. 時域特徵對應的 Conv-TasNet 法能有效減少雜訊造成的時頻圖失真，如圖中的紅框所包含的區域，雜訊成分大幅減少。
3. 與雜訊語音時頻圖相較，三種時域與小波域之彙整特徵對應的 Conv-TasNet 也能帶來顯著的雜訊抑制，從紅框所包含的區域，我們看到第三種彙整法（先融合再串接）似乎比其他兩種彙整法達到更佳的雜訊抑制效果。

4 結論

在這項研究中，我們主要關注於處理語音信號中的雜訊干擾，進而討論一些著名的基於深度學習的語音強化法，並提出使用離散小波轉換為語音強化模型建立特徵。藉由廣泛使用於語音強化實驗的 VoiceBank-DEMAND 和 VoiceBank-QUT 兩種語料庫，我們評估了兩種語音強化模型架構 Conv-TasNet 和 DPTNet，在其上運用我們所提之小波域特徵整合原始時域特徵。初步實驗表明，小波域特徵可以有效與時域特徵相加成，使 Conv-TasNet 與 DPTNet 的語音強化效能更佳，特別是在提升語音的品質指標上。在未來的規劃中，我們將嘗試把小波域特徵應用於其他進階的語音強化模型、如 FullSubNet 與 MANNER 中，觀測其表現，同時也將使用更大型的語音資料評估任務（如 DNS challenge）來評估本研究所提之新方法的效能。

References

Ashish Vaswani et al., "Attention is all you need," *in Proc. NIPS*, 2017

Antony W. Rix, John G. Beerends, Michael P. Hollier and Andries P. Hekstra, "Perceptual evaluation of speech quality (PESQ) – a new method for speech quality assessment of telephone networks and codecs," *in Proc. ICASSP*, 2001.

Cees H. Taal, Richard C. Hendriks, Richard Heusdens, Jesper Jensen, "An algorithm for intelligibility prediction of time–frequency weighted noisy speech," *IEEE Trans on Audio, Speech, and Language Processing*, 2011.

Christophe Veaux, Junichi Yamagishi and Simon King, "The voice bank corpus: Design, collection and data analysis of a large regional accent speech database," *in Proc. O-COCOSDA/CASLRE*, 2013

Dean, David and Sridharan, Sridha and Vogt, Robert and Mason, Michael. "The QUT-NOISETIMIT corpus for the evaluation of voice activity detection algorithms," *in Proc. Interspeech*, 2010.

Fu-An Chao, Jeih-weih Hung and Berlin Chen, "Cross-Domain Single-Channel Speech Enhancement Model with BI-Projection Fusion Module for Noise-Robust ASR," *in Proc. ICME*, 2021.

Fu-En Wang et al., "BiFuse: Monocular 360° depth estimation via bi-projection fusion," *in Proc. CVPR*, 2020

Ian Goodfellow, Yoshua Bengio and Aaron Courville, "Deep learning," *MIT Press*, 2016

Jingjing Chen, Qirong Mao, Dong Liu, "Dual-Path Transformer Network: Direct Context-Aware Modeling for End-to-End Monaural Speech Separation," *in Proc. Interspeech*, 2020

Joachim Thiemann, Nobutaka Ito, and Emmanuel Vincent, "Demand: a collection of multi-channel recordings of acoustic noise in diverse environments," *in Proc. ICA*, 2013

Kahneman, D., Sibony, O., and Sunstein, C. R. "Noise: a flaw in human judgment," *First edition, New York, Little, Brown Spark*, 2021

Philipos C. Loizou, "Speech Enhancement: Theory and Practice," *CRC Press*, 2013

Stephane Mallat, "A Wavelet Tour of Signal Processing," *2nd ed., San Diego, CA: Academic*, 1999

Yi Luo and Nima Mesgarani, "Conv-TasNet: Surpassing Ideal Time–Frequency Magnitude Masking for Speech Separation," *IEEE/ACM Trans on Audio, Speech, and Language Processing*, 2019.

Yusuf Isik, Jonathan Le Roux, Zhuo Chen, Shinji Watanabe, and John R. Hershey, "Single-channel multi-speaker separation using deep clustering," *in Proc. Interspeech*, 2016

The 34th Conference on Computational Linguistics and Speech Processing (ROCLING 2022)
Taipei, Taiwan, November 21-22, 2022. The Association for Computational Linguistics and Chinese Language Processing

藉由壓縮性之頻譜損失函數以學習 DEMUCS 語音強化模型之初步研究
Exploiting the compressed spectral loss for the learning of the DEMUCS speech enhancement network

戴麒恩	洪啟瑋	洪志偉
Chi-En Dai	Qi-Wei Hong	Jeih-Weih Hung
暨南大學電機系	暨南大學電機系	暨南大學電機系
National Chi Nan University	National Chi Nan University	National Chi Nan University
s108323060@mail1.ncnu.edu.tw	s108323024@mail1.ncnu.edu.tw	jwhung@ncnu.edu.tw

摘要

本研究針對著名的 DEMUCS 語音強化模型、藉由修改其訓練時所需的損失函數，來提升其效能。DEMUCS 由 Facebook 團隊開發，主要由卷積層組成其編碼模組與解碼模組，而兩模組之間則以長短時記憶模型來對編碼模組之輸出加以分解或降噪。雖然 DEMUCS 是一個純時域處理的語音強化架構，其訓練所使用的損失函數，卻同時涵蓋了時域和頻域的特徵，其中頻域上的特徵即為訊號經短時間傅立葉轉換所得的頻譜。

我們探討當 DEMUCS 之損失函數中的頻譜其強度值做壓縮時，對於所訓練而得的模型其效能是否有明顯的改變，我們採用的壓縮運算主要是對頻譜強度取一個小於一的正冪次方值，或對頻譜強度取其對數值。

當在 VoiceBank-DEMAND 之資料集上進行評估實驗時，初步結果表明，上述之壓縮運算為取正冪次方值時，其損失函數能使所學習的 DEMUCS 模型比原 DEMUCS 模型更有效地提升測試語音的客觀品質與可讀性指標(PESQ 與 STOI)，充分顯示引入次方壓縮性的頻譜強度於損失函數中能得到語音強化效能更佳的 DEMUCS 模型。相較而言，當壓縮運算為對數函數時，則沒有改進的效果。

Abstract

This study aims to improve a highly effective speech enhancement technique, DEMUCS, by revising the respective loss function in learning. DEMUCS, developed by Facebook Team, is built on the Wave-U-Net and consists of convolutional layer encoding and decoding blocks with an LSTM layer in between. Although DEMUCS processes the input speech utterance purely in the time (wave) domain, the applied loss function consists of wave-domain L1 distance and multi-scale short-time-Fourier-transform (STFT) loss. That is, both time- and frequency-domain features are taken into consideration in the learning of DEMUCS.

In this study, we present revising the STFT loss in DEMUCS by employing the compressed magnitude spectrogram. The compression is done by either the power-law operation with a positive exponent less than one, or the logarithmic operation.

We evaluate the presented novel framework on the VoiceBank-DEMAND database and task. The preliminary experimental results suggest that DEMUCS containing the power-law compressed magnitude spectral loss outperforms the original DEMUCS by providing the test utterances with higher objective quality and intelligibility scores (PESQ and STOI). Relatively, the logarithm compressed magnitude spectral loss does not benefit DEMUCS. Therefore, we reveal that DEMUCS can be further improved by properly revising the STFT terms of its loss function.

關鍵字：語音強化、DEMUCS、短時傅立葉轉換、損失函 數、壓縮頻譜損失、對數頻譜距離、感知語音品質、短時語音可讀性

Keywords: speech enhancement, DEMUCS, STFT, loss function, compressed spectral loss, logarithmic spectral distance, PESQ, STOI

The 34th Conference on Computational Linguistics and Speech Processing (ROCLING 2022)
Taipei, Taiwan, November 21-22, 2022. The Association for Computational Linguistics and Chinese Language Processing

1 簡介

語音強化 (speech enhancement, SE) 目的在於抑制語音中的加成性雜訊、通道干擾或混響、以優化語音的品質或可讀性。現今，由於語音分析技術的高度發展，逐漸落實於智慧生活的諸多應用，例如手機的語音輸入、語音檢索、語音操控機器人、助聽器等，但雜訊的存在使這些應用或設備無法精準捕捉原始乾淨語音之資訊、進而限制了語音技術在實用性上的擴展，因此直接在接收端抑制雜訊的語音強化技術相當重要性。

經典的語音強化技術通常是基於語音或雜訊干擾的統計特性以建構模型，如頻譜消去法(spectral subtraction) (Boll, 1979)、維納濾波法(Wiener filter) (Scalart and Filho, 1996)、卡爾曼濾波法(Kalman filter) (Dionelis and Brookes, 2018)等，為了在處理上減少延遲，它們所擷取的訊號通常較短、其統計特性無法精準呈現，進而限制了這些技術的效能，且其在非穩態的雜訊環境中表現通常較差。

近年來由於深度類神經網路(deep neural network, DNN) (Goodfellow et al., 2016; Hinton et al., 2012)之理論及技術的高度發展，基於DNN 的語音強化技術也如雨後春筍地不斷湧現，且其在非穩態雜訊場影中的強化效能通常優於經典之基於統計特性的方法。一般來說，基於 DNN 之語音強化法，根據其對於輸入語音之特徵擷取的角度，大致可分為兩類：時頻域(time-frequency domain, T-F domain)法和端到端(end-to-end)的時域(time domain)法(Luo and Mesgarani, 2019; Yin et al., 2020)，二類型的方法在不同的雜訊場景或語音資料的表現各有優劣。時頻域法通常藉由短時傅立葉轉換(short-time Fourier transform, STFT) 對輸入語音創建時頻圖(spectrogram)，亦稱時頻域(T-F)特徵，在對這些 T-F 特徵加以消噪或強化後，進而用反短時離散傅立葉轉換(inverse STFT)重建原始的時域訊號波形(waveform)。可是使用 STFT 建構的時頻域特徵可能存在缺點或限制：首先，STFT 是一種固定的訊號轉換法（使用固定的弦波基底），相較於時域法其基底是由資料學習而得，時頻域法未必較佳。其次，時頻法對於乾淨語音之頻譜的相位成分通常無法精準的重建。

在諸多時域的語音強化法中，由 Facebook 團隊所研發的 DEMUCS 法(Defossez et al., 2019; Defossez et al., 2020)（全名：Deep Extractor for Music Sources with extra unlabeled data remixed）效能相當優異且廣為使用，它原本的目標是對於不同音源的混合分離成個音源，但也可以直接用於語音強化上（相當於把雜訊看成與乾淨語音不同的另一個音源）。它主要是由卷積層搭配跳躍連接(skip connection)的 U-net 模組來組成其編碼器-解碼器架構，而其訓練所使用的損失函數則主要包含了兩項：時域（或稱波域：wave domain）上的損失及時頻域上的損失，後者之時頻域所用特徵即為 STFT 求得的時頻圖。

諸多文獻(Ephraim and Malah, 1985; Yu and Deng, 2015)提到，人耳對於語音強度之感知程度(perceptual nature)是近似於一對數函數，亦即人耳感知的語音強度的提升程度不及真實語音強度的提升程度，可謂是人耳自我保護的機制、避免為太大聲的語音傷害。在語音強化與強健語音辨識的領域，許多方法(Lee et al., 2018; Braun and Ivan Tashev, 2021)皆利用這個特點、將語音頻譜之強度取對數或取小於一的正次方值，壓縮其動態範圍(dynamic range)，多數因而得到更佳的效果。在近期的研究(Hong et al., 2022; Wu et al., 2022)中，也提出了直接使用客觀語音品質指標(PESQ) (Ruder, 2017)與語音可讀性指標(STOI) (V-Botinhao et al., 2016)來監測 DEMUCS 在訓練上的收斂程度，而使 DEMUCS 達到適度提升的效果。

基於上述觀察，本研究提出：將 DEMUCS 訓練時在損失函數中所使用的短時傅立葉轉換求得的各個音框頻譜強度做動態壓縮，探討此壓縮的運算是否能使訓練而得的 DEMUCS 法在語音強化上的表現更佳，整體示意圖如圖一所示。我們分別使用前述的取冪次方值與取對數的壓縮法。值得一提的是，相較於最近的研究(Hong et al., 2022; Wu et al., 2022)、語音品質與可讀性指標只用於監測 DEMUCS 的收斂程度、而沒有實際加入其損失函數求其梯度來更新模型參數，這裡所提的頻譜強度動態壓縮法則藉由更動 DEMUCS 的損失函數直接參與其模型參數的訓練。而當上述的更新法藉由 VoiceBank-DEMAND 資料集來實現評估時，我們初步發現此更新版的 DEMUCS 相較於原 DEMUCS 能夠達到更佳的客觀語音強化指標、亦即 PESQ 與 STOI 值。

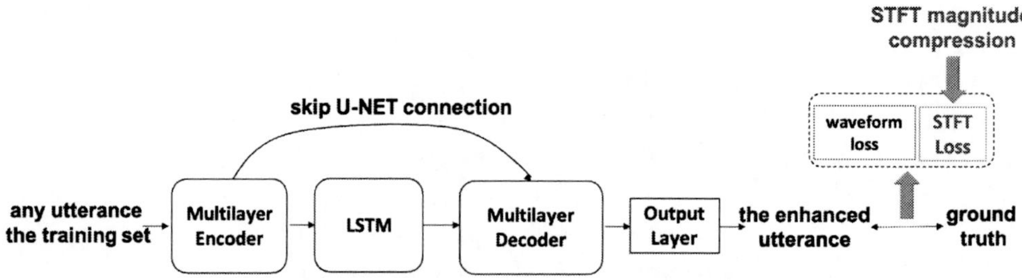

圖一: DEMUCS 訓練流程、及本文所提之處理 STFT 頻譜強度的壓縮用於損失函數

在之後的章節中，我們將先簡要介紹 DEMUCS 法的流程，接著陳述我們提出之更動損失函數的新方法，隨後是實驗環境介紹、實驗結果呈現分析與討論，最後則是結論與未來展望。

2 DEMUCS 法簡要介紹

最初，DEMUCS 是為多音源分離而設計。它主要是由卷積層搭配跳躍連接(skip connection)的 U-net 模組來組成其編碼器-解碼器架構，其中搭配了長短時記憶模型(LSTM)用於修改編碼器輸出來分離音源，當 DEMUCS 應用於單聲道語音強化時，我們將 DEMUCS 的輸入與輸出通道數設置為 1、直接以乾淨語音為逼近的真實目標(ground truth)。關於 DEMUCS 模型安排的細節，可參考文獻(Defossez et al., 2019; Defossez et al., 2020)。

在原始 DEMUCS 網路模型的學習中，用以最小化的損失函數包括了在（時域）波形上的 L1 損失和（時頻域）多解析度短時傳立葉轉換(multi-resolution STFT)之頻譜損失。對任一其長度（點數）為T的輸入訊號，其增強後的時域訊號$\boldsymbol{y}$和原始乾淨的語音信號$\tilde{\boldsymbol{y}}$之間的損失函數表示為：

$$L_{DEMUCS}(\boldsymbol{y},\tilde{\boldsymbol{y}}) = \frac{1}{T}\|\boldsymbol{y}-\tilde{\boldsymbol{y}}\|_1 + \sum_i L_{stft}^{(i)}(\boldsymbol{y},\tilde{\boldsymbol{y}}), \quad (1)$$

其中$\|.\|_1$是 L1 範數運算，而式子右邊第一項是時域波形上的 L1 損失，第二項是多解析度時頻域上的損失和，下標 "$stft$"為短時間傅立葉轉換(STFT)，上標“(i)”是對應不同音框長度(frame size)與音框平移(frame shift)的索引(index)。此外，第二項中個別索引(i)項的$L_{stft}^{(i)}(\boldsymbol{y},\tilde{\boldsymbol{y}})$又包含兩部分：頻譜收斂(spectral convergence, 以下標sc表示)之損失$L_{sc}(\boldsymbol{y},\tilde{\boldsymbol{y}})$和頻譜強度(spectral magnitude, 以下標mag表示)之損失$L_{mag}(\boldsymbol{y},\tilde{\boldsymbol{y}})$，呈現如下式：

$$L_{stft}(\boldsymbol{y},\tilde{\boldsymbol{y}}) = L_{sc}(\boldsymbol{y},\tilde{\boldsymbol{y}}) + L_{mag}(\boldsymbol{y},\tilde{\boldsymbol{y}}), \quad (2)$$

其中

$$L_{sc}(\boldsymbol{y},\tilde{\boldsymbol{y}}) = \frac{\||STFT(\boldsymbol{y})|-|STFT(\tilde{\boldsymbol{y}})|\|_F}{\|STFT(\boldsymbol{y})\|_F}, \quad (3)$$

而

$$L_{mag}(\boldsymbol{y},\tilde{\boldsymbol{y}}) = \frac{1}{T}\left\|\log\left(\frac{|STFT(\boldsymbol{y})|}{|STFT(\tilde{\boldsymbol{y}})|}\right)\right\|_1, \quad (4)$$

其中$STFT(.)$是求取音框之頻譜的短時間傅立葉轉換(short-time Fourier transform), $|.|$是逐項(element-wise)取絕對值的運算，$\|.\|_F$是 Frobenius 範數運算。

3 提出之新方法

DEMUCS 網路訓練中使用的損失函數綜合衡量了強化語音與其原始乾淨語音在時域與頻域上的差異。一般而言，修改損失函數的做法有兩種：第一種是在原損失函數上加上其他的損失函數並取加權，而第二種是對原始損失函數中的個別項目作修改，我們採取的是第二種，其相對第一種修改法的可能好處是在訓練中求取損失函數之梯度時，運算複雜度的增加幅度較小。

我們具體的作法是將 DEMUCS 原損失函數中使用的短時傅立葉轉換求得的音框頻譜的強度做壓縮(compression)，使其動態範圍(dynamic range)降低，這樣的潛在優點是：一方面可模擬人耳對於音量強度的感知效應（感知強度的變化低於真實強度的變化），另一方面也有助於避免訓練模型時，損失函數之梯度下降值過大導致不易收斂至最佳值的問題(Ruder, 2017)。

參照文獻 (Braun and Ivan Tashev, 2021)，我們使用兩種強度壓縮的運算。第一種是乘冪運算，且使用的冪次方值為小於一的正數，即 $f(x) = x^r, 0 < r < 1$。第二種則是使用 log1p 函數，即 $f(x) = \text{log1p}(x) = \log(1 + x)$，其中取對數前加一的目的是使函數的最小值為 0，而非負無窮大（當 $x \geq 0$ 時）。

根據使用乘冪運算的壓縮法，我們將原(3)與(4)式修改為：

$$\hat{L}_{sc}(\boldsymbol{y}, \tilde{\boldsymbol{y}}) = \frac{\| |STFT(\boldsymbol{y})|^r - |STFT(\tilde{\boldsymbol{y}})|^r \|_F}{\| |STFT(\boldsymbol{y})|^r \|_F}, \tag{5}$$

$$\hat{L}_{mag}(\boldsymbol{y}, \tilde{\boldsymbol{y}}) = \frac{1}{T} \left\| \log \left(\frac{|STFT(\boldsymbol{y})|^r}{|STFT(\tilde{\boldsymbol{y}})|^r} \right) \right\|_1, \tag{6}$$

其中的次方值 $0 < r < 1$。值得注意的是，雖然原式(3)中的 $STFT(\boldsymbol{y})$ 項是複數陣列，但它的 Frobenius 範數 $\|STFT(\boldsymbol{y})\|_F$ 只和 $STFT(\boldsymbol{y})$ 其中每項的絕對值 $|STFT(\tilde{\boldsymbol{y}})|$ 有關，亦即 $\|STFT(\boldsymbol{y})\|_F = \| |STFT(\boldsymbol{y})| \|_F$，因此，式(5)中的分母項可以直接表達成 $\| |STFT(\boldsymbol{y})|^r \|_F$。

同理，對於第二種使用 $\text{log1p}\ (x) = \log(x + 1)$ 函數的壓縮法，我們將原式(3)與式(4)修改為：

$$\hat{L}_{sc}(\boldsymbol{y}, \tilde{\boldsymbol{y}}) = \frac{\|\text{log1p}\ |STFT(\boldsymbol{y})|) - \text{log1p}\ (|STFT(\tilde{\boldsymbol{y}})|)\|_F}{\|\text{log1p}\ (|STFT(\boldsymbol{y})|)\|_F}, \tag{7}$$

$$\hat{L}_{mag}(\boldsymbol{y}, \tilde{\boldsymbol{y}}) = \frac{1}{T} \left\| \log \left(\frac{\text{log1p}(|STFT(\boldsymbol{y})|)}{\text{log1p}(|STFT(\tilde{\boldsymbol{y}})|)} \right) \right\|_1, \tag{8}$$

在更動式(3)(4)、如式(5)(6)或是式(7)(8)，我們將式(2) 對應的時頻域損失更新為：

$$\hat{L}_{stft}(\boldsymbol{y}, \tilde{\boldsymbol{y}}) = \hat{L}_{sc}(\boldsymbol{y}, \tilde{\boldsymbol{y}}) + \hat{L}_{mag}(\boldsymbol{y}, \tilde{\boldsymbol{y}}), \tag{9}$$

其中 $\hat{L}_{sc}(\boldsymbol{y}, \tilde{\boldsymbol{y}})$ 與 $\hat{L}_{mag}(\boldsymbol{y}, \tilde{\boldsymbol{y}})$ 分別如式(5)(6)、或是式(7)(8)所示，則 DEMUCS 使用之整體的損失函數可以更動為：

$$\hat{L}_{DEMUCS}(\boldsymbol{y}, \tilde{\boldsymbol{y}}) = \frac{1}{T}\|\boldsymbol{y} - \tilde{\boldsymbol{y}}\|_1 + \sum_i \hat{L}_{stft}^{(i)}(\boldsymbol{y}, \tilde{\boldsymbol{y}}), \tag{10}$$

其中更動的 $\hat{L}_{stft}^{(i)}(\boldsymbol{y}, \tilde{\boldsymbol{y}})$ 項來自式(9)。

4 實驗設定

我們使用 VoiceBank-DEMAND 語料庫(V-Botinhao et al., 2016; Thiemann et al., 2013)來評估我們所提的新方法、對於相對應的 DEMUCS 模型進行訓練與測試，所使用之乾淨無干擾的語句和雜訊分別來自 VoiceBank(V-Botinhao et al., 2016) 和 DEMAND (Thiemann et al., 2013)語料庫。訓練集包含了 28 個語者所生成的 11,572 個語句，其中摻入 10 種雜訊、訊雜比(SNR)分別為 0, 5, 10 與 15 dB，測試集則包含 2 個語者所生成的 824 個語句、摻入與訓練集不同之另 5 種雜訊、訊雜比(SNR)分別為 2.5, 7.5, 12.5 與 17.5 dB。此外，我們從訓練集中挑出 742 個語句作為驗證集。

我們採用文獻(Defossez et al., 2020)所介紹之具因果性(causal)的 DEMUCS 架構，學習迭代次數(epoch)設為 300，批量設為 32，其他參數設置，分別是 $U = 4$, $S = 4$, $K = 8$, $L = 5$ 及 $H = 48$。依照式(5)-(8)，我們分別訓練對應至不同損失函數之 DEMUCS 模型。在測試上，我們使用客觀語音品質指標 PESQ (Rix et al., 2001)和可讀性指標 STOI (Taal et al., 2011)來評估強化後的語音，PESQ 分數介於-0.5 與 4.5 之間，STOI 分數介於 0 與 1 之間，三者分數越高皆代表語音強化效能越好。

5 實驗結果與討論

我們探討使用頻譜強度壓縮對應之 DEMUCS，其中，乘冪運算其冪次方 r 值分別設為 0.1, 0.3, 0.5 與 0.7，另外，為了觀察頻譜強度壓縮的逆運算、亦即將頻譜強度伸展對 DEMUCS 帶來的效應，我們額外求得冪次方 $r = 1.1$ 對應的 DEMUCS 模型。使用乘冪運算與對數函數 log1p 之頻譜強度壓縮之 DEMUCS 對測試集強化所對應的 PESQ 與 STOI 指標數據列於表一，從此表我們有了以下的觀察：

1. 未任何強化處理之基礎實驗結果都遠比理想值差(PESQ 上限為 4.5，STOI 上限為 1)，足見雜訊干擾對於語音的破壞程度，而這裡所有的 DEMUCS 法都能得到較佳的 PESQ 與 STOI 分數，可見它們確實都能有效強化語音。
2. 對於使用小於 1 之冪次方 r 的頻譜壓縮之 DEMUCS 而言，它們幾乎都比原始

DEMUCS ($r = 1$)得到更佳的PESQ與STOI分數，例如當$r = 0.3$時，PESQ與STOI值為 3.006 與 0.949 為最佳，超越原始DEMUCS的2.923與0.947，這與文獻[13]所得到的結果大致相符，其頻譜強度其壓縮冪次設為 0.3 時語音強化效能也是最好。我們也觀察到，當壓縮冪次r從原始的1逐漸變小至0.3時，PESQ都有顯著的提升、STOI則維持或是小幅提升。而r值從0.3降為 0.1 時，雖然其 PESQ 變差，但仍高達2.988，超越原始 DEMUCS ($r = 1$)的 2.923。這些結果充分顯示了我們所提出、在DEMUCS的損失函數使用冪次壓縮頻譜強度確實能提升 DEMUCS 的語音強化效能。

3. 當冪次值$r = 1.1$時，頻譜強度的動態範圍反而變大，實驗結果顯示，其反而使DEMUCS對應的PESQ分數下降，因此，延展頻譜強度的損失函數並無法改進DEMUCS。

若使用 log1p 函數來做頻譜強度壓縮時，其PESQ與STOI的分數都明顯變差，基於log1p函數與取冪次方皆有相似的壓縮輸出之動態範圍的效果，此結果令我們有些意外，可能的原因是當使用 log1p 函數時，在式(8)所呈現的頻譜強度損失連用了兩次的 log 函數、它可能對於頻譜強度造成過度壓縮而使對應的損失值失去鑑別力，在未來的研究裡，我們將對此問題進一步探討其解決方向。

		PESQ	STOI
基礎實驗（未處理）		1.970	0.921
原始 DEMUCS ($r = 1$)		2.923	0.947
使用冪次壓縮頻譜強度之 DEMUCS	$r = 0.1$	**2.988**	**0.948**
	$r = 0.3$	**<u>3.006</u>**	**0.949**
	$r = 0.5$	**2.979**	**0.948**
	$r = 0.7$	**2.974**	0.947
	$r = 1.1$	2.910*	0.947
使用 log1p 函數壓縮頻譜強度之 DEMUCS		2.735*	0.943*

表 1: 原始 DEMUCS 與各種壓縮頻譜強度之DEMUCS法對應的PESQ與STOI值

除了語音強化的相關評估數據外，我們也使用強度時頻圖(magnitude spectrogram)來驗證各方法在消噪上的效能，圖二(a)-(f)繪製了一VoiceBank 的語音在各種環境下所得的強度時頻圖，首先，圖二(a)(b)分別對應乾淨環境與

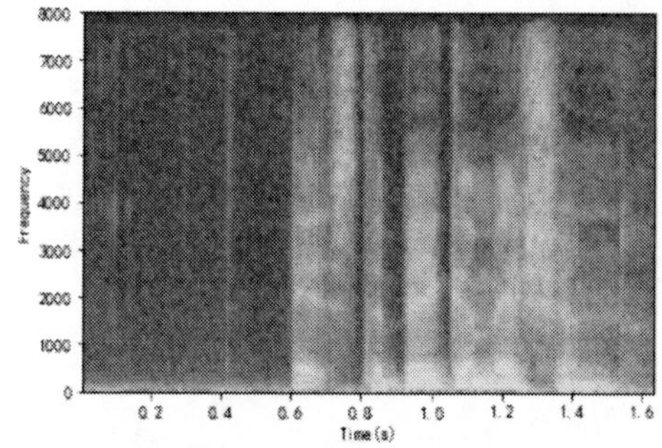

(a) clean

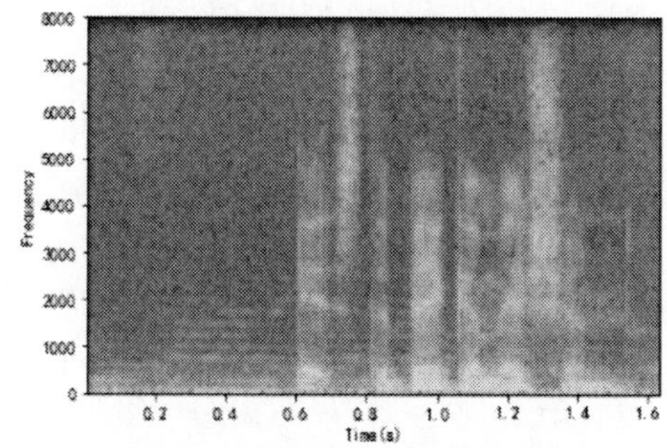

(b) noisy

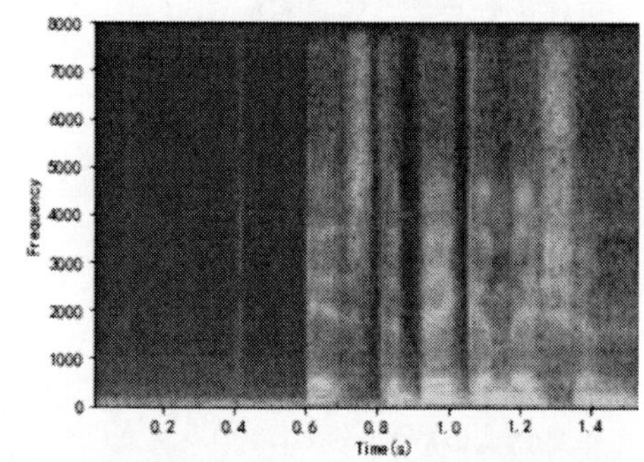

(c) enhanced by original DEMUCS

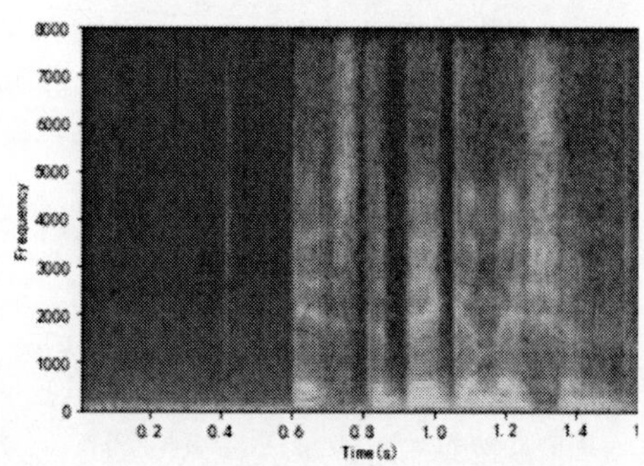

(d) enhanced by DEMUCS with power r = 0.3

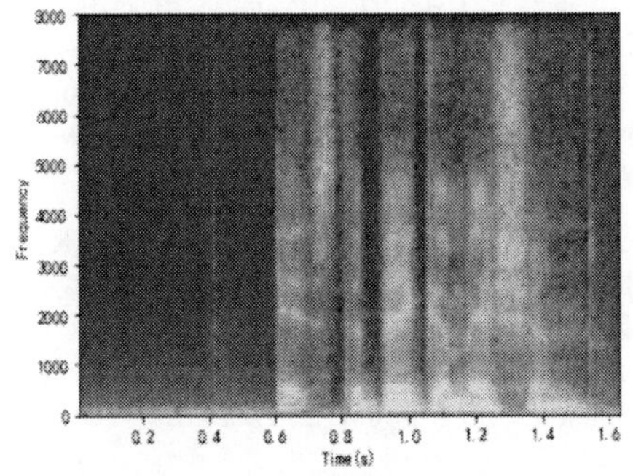

(e) enhanced by DEMUCS with power r = 1.1

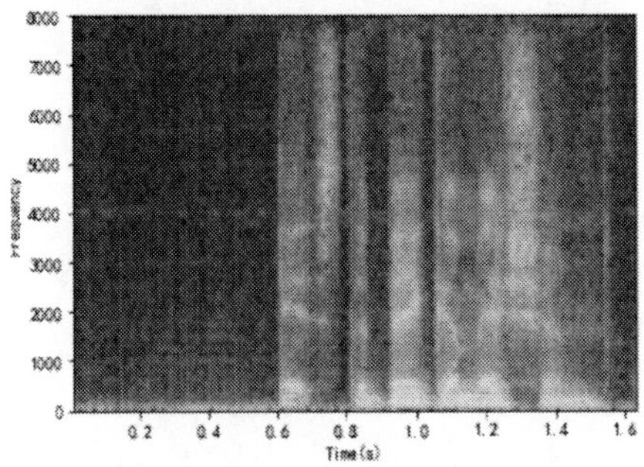

(f) enhanced by DEMUCS with log1p compression

圖二：一段語音在不同環境下的強度時頻圖：(a)乾淨、(b)雜訊干擾、(c) 雜訊干擾但使用原始DEMUCS強化、(d)雜訊干擾但使用冪次為0.3 作頻譜壓縮之DEMUCS強化、 (e) 雜訊干擾但使用冪次為1.1作頻譜壓縮之DEMUCS強化、(f)雜訊干擾但使用 log1p 函數作頻譜壓縮之DEMUCS強化

雜訊環境，我們看到雜訊對於語音的時頻圖造成明顯的失真。其次，圖二(c)(d)為雜訊語音（圖二(b)）經過原始DEMUCS與冪次為0.3之頻譜壓縮之 DEMUCS 對應的時頻圖，將它們與圖二(a)(b)相比較，我們可看到雜訊被有效地抑制，然而似乎比圖(a)顯示的乾淨語音時頻圖更"乾淨"一些，意味著可能部分語音也被當作雜訊被消除或減低。圖二(e)(f)為雜訊語音（圖二(b)）經過冪次為 1.1 之頻譜延展與使用 log1p 函數壓縮之 DEMUCS 對應的時頻圖，它們似乎顯示不僅雜訊抑制、許多語音成分也被消除，例如在圖二(a)中 0.4 秒附近有一個短暫的語音頻譜成分，它在圖(f)中幾乎已經不見了。這呼應了之前的結果、即使用log1p 函數做頻譜壓縮反而會造成DEMUCS效能的退步。

6. 結論與未來展望

此研究提出在訓練 DEMUCS 的損失函數時，預先對其 STFT 頻譜強度進行壓縮，藉此模擬人耳效應、提升其收斂穩定度以期提升DEMUCS 語音強化的表現。我們藉由冪次方運算以及對數(log1p)運算分別來壓縮短時間頻譜強度。初步實驗結果顯示，當損失函數引用了冪次方運算壓縮之時頻圖，能使訓練而得的 DEMUCS 對輸入語音造就更佳的語音品質與可讀性，而對數運算的壓縮則表現不如預期。在未來的研究裡，我們會探討對數運算壓縮表現不佳的原因，同時，我們也將驗證上述的壓縮頻譜強度於其他類別的語音強化法是否也能發揮類似的效能、並進一步探究最佳化壓縮的方法。

參考文獻

Steven Boll, “Suppression of acoustic noise in speech using spectral subtraction,” *IEEE Trans. on Acoustics, Speech and Signal Processing*, 1979.

Pascal Scalart and Jozue VIEIRA Filho, “Speech enhancement based on a priori signal to noise estimation,” *in Proc. ICASSP*, 1996

Nikolaos Dionelis and Mike Brookes, "Speech Enhancement Using Kalman Filtering in the Logarithmic Bark Power Spectral Domain," *in Proc. EUSIPCO*, 2018

Ian Goodfellow, Yoshua Bengio and Aaron Courville, “Deep learning,” *MIT Press*, 2016

Geoffrey Hinton, Li Deng, Dong Yu, George E. Dahl et al., “Deep neural networks for acoustic modeling in speech Recognition: the shared views of four research groups,” *IEEE Signal Processing Magazine*, 2012,

Yi Luo and Nima Mesgarani, “Conv-tasnet: Surpassing ideal time–frequency magnitude masking for speech separation,” *IEEE/ACM transactions on audio, speech, and language processing*, 2019.

Dacheng Yin, Chong Luo, Zhiwei Hong and Wenjun Zeng, “Phasen: A phase-and-harmonics-aware speech enhancement network,” *in Proceedings AAAI*, 2020.

Alexandre Defossez, Nicloas Usunier, Leo’n Bottu and Francis Bach, “Music source separation in the waveform domain,” *arXiv:1911.13254*, 2019.

Alexandre Defossez, Gabriel Synnaeve and Yossi Adi, “Real time speech enhancement in the waveform domain,” *in Proc. Interspeech*, 2020

Yariv Ephraim, David Malah, “Speech enhancement using a minimum mean-square error log-spectral amplitude estimator,” *IEEE Transactions on Acoustics, Speech, and Signal Processing*, 1985.

Dong Yu, Li Deng, "Automatic Speech Recognition: A Deep Learning Approach," *London: Springer*, 2015.

Jinkyu Lee, Jan Skoglund, Turaj Shabestary, Hong-Goo Kang, "Phase-sensitive joint learning algorithms for deep learning-based speech enhancement," *IEEE Signal Processing Letters*, 2018.

Sebastian Braun, Ivan Tashev, “A consolidated view of loss functions for supervised deep learning-based speech enhancement”, *in Proc. TSP*, 2021.

Qi-Wei Hong, Chi-En Dai, Hui-Chun Hsu, Zong-Tai Wu, Jeih-Weih Hung, "Leveraging the perceptual metric loss to improve the DEMUCS system in speech enhancement", *in Proc. ICASI*, 2022

Zong-Tai Wu; Yan-Tong Chen; Jeih-weih Hung, "Improving the performance of DEMUCS in speech enhancement with the perceptual metric loss", in Proc. ICCE-TW, 2022Sebastian Ruder, "An overview of gradient descent optimization algorithms", *arXiv:1609.04747v2,* 2017.

Cassia Valentini-Botinhao, Xin Wang, Shinji Takaki, Junichi Yamagishi, “Investigating RNN-based speech enhancement methods for noise-robust text-to-speech,” *in Proc. SSW*, 2016.

Joachim Thiemann, Nobutaka Ito, Emmanuel Vincen, “Demand: a collection of multi-channel recordings of acoustic noise in diverse environments,” *in Proc. ICA*, 2013

Antony W. Rix, John G. Beerends, Michael P. Hollier and Andries P. Hekstra, “Perceptual evaluation of speech quality (PESQ) – a new method for speech quality assessment of telephone networks and codecs,” *in Proc. ICASSP*, 2001.

Cees H. Taal, Richard C. Hendriks, Richard Heusdens, and Jesper Jensen, “An algorithm for intelligibility prediction of time–frequency weighted noisy speech,” *IEEE Trans. on Audio, Speech, and Language Processing*, 2011.

The 34th Conference on Computational Linguistics and Speech Processing (ROCLING 2022)
Taipei, Taiwan, November 21-22, 2022. The Association for Computational Linguistics and Chinese Language Processing

以機器學習與規則方法辨識中文民事裁判書結構
Using Machine Learning and Pattern-Based Methods for Identifying Elements in Chinese Judgment Documents of Civil Cases

林泓任 Hong-Ren Lin　劉威志 Wei-Zhi Liu　劉昭麟 Chao-Lin Liu　楊婕 Chieh Yang
國立政治大學資訊科學系
Department of Computer Science, National Chengchi University
{109753156, 109753157, chaolin}@g.nccu.edu.tw, 05141343@gm.scu.edu.tw

摘要

在建構法學資訊相關的分類模型或是推薦系統時，提供模型關於語料中與任務相關的輔助訊息有助於提升模型的效能及運算結果的可解釋性。在本研究中，我們選擇以人工智慧應用於法學資訊中較少見的民事訴訟案件作為研究對象。我們將「給付扶養費」相關的判決書依照其結構的功能性，找出聲請人所提出的主張、相對人所提出的答辯、法院對案件的見解及法院所引用的法條這四個部分，並從中抽取出該案件訴訟兩造的主要爭點。

Abstract

Providing structural information about civil cases for judgement prediction systems or recommendation systems can enhance the efficiency of the inference procedures and the justifiability of produced results. In this research, we focus on the civil cases about alimony, which is a relatively uncommon choice in current applications of artificial intelligence in law. We attempt to identify the statements for four types of legal functions in judgement documents, i.e., the pleadings of the applicants, the responses of the opposite parties, the opinions of the courts, and uses of laws to reach the final decisions. In addition, we also try to identify the conflicting issues between the plaintiffs and the defendants in the judgement documents.

關鍵字：民事案件、給付扶養費、文章結構分類

Keywords: civil cases, the issues of alimony, legal element identification

1 緒論

要讓使用者能接受演算法所提供的推薦項目，提供推薦理由是很重要的一件事。Mumford et al. (2021) 曾在研究中提到 "*without an explanation of why the case was so classified, the adjudicator has no reason to follow.*"，意即如果無法說明案件結果是如何被分類出來，那法官也沒有理由去採信模型所提出來的決策。
為了讓電腦產生的案件預測結果能被使用者接受或是提升電腦的預測能力，建立讓電腦理解及能夠解釋法律文件細節的核心能力是有必要的。

因此，我們的研究主旨在提供法律文件中各段落、句子在裁判書中的作用。我們選擇將裁判書內文依照文章結構的功能性分類為四個大類，分別是：1.聲請人提出的主張、2.相對人提出的答辯、3.法院在判決中所引用的法條、4.法院對該案件的見解與裁判，在往後的文章中會簡稱為C1、C2、C3、C4。除了將裁判書依其文章結構中的功能性分出四大類外我們也希望能找出案情的爭議點，在完成四大類後我們會找出裁判書中的爭點，其為法院對於案情爭點的說明以及裁判，並將這類型的句子簡稱為C5。

不過這些標籤在我們所取得的裁判書資料中是不存在的，因此本研究中會先建構一套使用規則與正規表示法(regular expressions)的技術來對特定範圍內的裁判書以段落為單位達成初步的自動標記，並透過段落的自動標記轉出換成對句子的預標記，以此訓練模型將C1、C2、C3、C4的標記推廣到其他無法直接使用規則標記方法的段落上。如此一來可以針對各別部分建立推薦系統使推薦系統更

有說服力，也可應用於裁判結果預測或其他法學資訊的相關應用研究上。

使用以規則自動標記的預標記建立對裁判書文章架構的分類系統後，我們會透過藉由法學領域專家的標記來驗證我們的分類系統成效，並對比以專家人工標記訓練的分類模型與自動標記系統建立的分類模型對前述四分類任務的差距。

完成C1、C2、C3、C4四分類系統後，我們將文章架構分類器推廣到第5個分類，也就是爭點的部分。此分類法官會描述聲請人與相對人所提出的主張中的爭議點，並加以說明、裁判。其都存在於C4類別中，但C5中會描述到聲請人或相對人所提出的主張，因此也容易與C1、C2的分類混淆。

後續內容會介紹我們針對台灣民事案件裁判書所做的前處理、如何切割段落及斷句，並說明如何轉換成我們模型的輸入資料並探討以不同前後短句句數訓練的成效差異及若將模型加深、複雜化能對分類效果帶來的提升；之後以一開始針對處理的裁判書類型以外的裁判書搭配專家人工標記的結果驗證模型。確認完能在不同段落數的裁判書生效後將分類工作推廣到更進一步的案件爭點分類、搜尋工作上。此外我們也會比較一些既有模型設定上的差異以及基於前面C1、C2這種易與C5混淆段落的驗證。

2 相關研究

過往，將人工智慧技術應用於法學資訊在國外已經有很長的一段歷史，最早的研討會可追溯到1987年 (Bench-Capon et al., 2012)。而常見的法學資訊相關研究可分為判決書結果及刑度預測、類似案件推薦、法律問答系統等 (Zhong et al., 2020)。

其中，Lin et al. (2012) 的研究中透過 CRF (conditional-random field)模型對刑事案件判決書中的量刑因子進行自動標記並應用於判決結果及刑度的預測上。建構命名實體辨識 (NER, named-entity recognition)系統時，根據 Chen et al.(2020)的研究指出，提供模型相關判決書額外的法律資訊也是有助於提升模型的。

綜合 Zhong et al. (2020)的研究整理及先前提及的研究，為了讓電腦產生的案件預測結果能被使用者接受或是提升電腦的預測能力，建立讓電腦理解及能夠解釋法律文件細節的能力是有必要的。因此在 Chalkidis et al. (2021) 的研究中，透過已經標註好段落與法院判決間的關係的資料，讓模型抽取到與法院作出判斷相關聯的段落時就給予額外的獎勵來建構可解釋性的法律預測模型。

但我們所使用來自於台灣司法院開放平台[1]所公開的裁判書資料，其並不具有這些額外的法律相關資訊的標記。而且在民事案件的裁判書中，也不像刑事案件有較為明確的量刑因子與法律用語，台灣相關研究的數量也較為少見，不過近期也有針對將 AI 技術應用於民事案件可行性的相關研究 (Ho, 2021)。

因此我們又參考了 de Buy Wenniger et al. (2020) 的研究，其研究中讓文章輸入模型時將句子附加上依照其在文章節中的功能所給予的標記提升了預測成效；說明了文章結構影響分類結果，也啟發我們開始從各個段落及文句在裁判書中所具有的功能性開始著手。而 Li et al. (2019) 的研究中，將中國的刑事訴訟裁判書分成三個部分，分別為描述被告過往是否有其他犯罪紀錄的段落、該次案件的犯罪事實、法院對於案件做出的裁定，並透過注意力機制將關於被告犯罪紀錄的描述以及該次案件犯罪事實結合起來得到了能更好預測法院裁定結果的模型。

因此我們將初步目標放在區分出民事案件中的段落及句子在文章結構上的功能性，依此建構一套透過規則與正規表示法來自動找出裁判書中的C1、C2、C3、C4標記並以此為基礎訓練以句為單位的分類模型，並驗證這個方法的可行性。

在 C5，也就是爭點類別的搜尋中，我們參考了 Xu et al. (2021) 所提出的研究。他們其中一項研究是將案件全文中的句子分類為IRC與non IRC 兩種，其中 IRC 的部分包含有 I，是法院在該案件中所要裁決的問題、還有C是法院對I所做出的裁決，而最後的R是法院說明如何得出結論的句子；此一部分恰好為我們緒論中提到要尋找的爭點與爭點的說明，也就是被我們所定義為 C5 這個類別的句子，因

[1] https://opendata.judicial.gov.tw

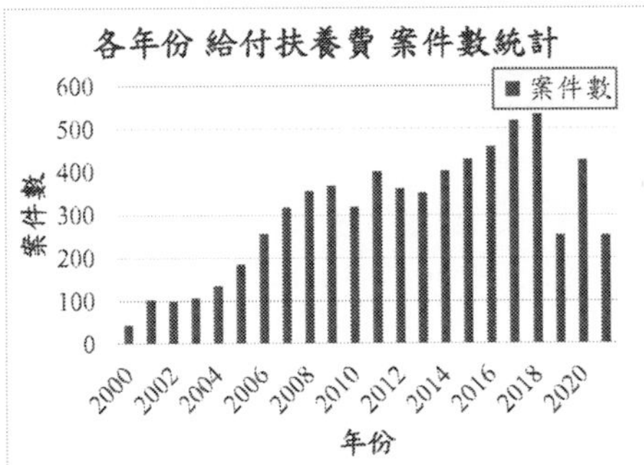

圖 1. 各年分給付扶養費案件數統計

此我們同樣會使用分類模型的方式來嘗試找到我們所定義的 C5 類別。

3 問題定義與假設

我們研究的目標是處理台灣司法院開放平台上關於民事訴訟，且案由為給付扶養費的案件，將裁判書中的句子及段落依照其在文章結構中的功能性區分出 C1、C2、C3、C4 這四種類別，因此我們嘗試將其視作針對裁判書中各句子的分類任務。

除了上面四種類別外，我們也希望能找出案件的爭點，與 Xu et al. (2021) 提出研究不同的是，他們將在整篇裁判書中挑出少量的 IRC 段落並將其他段落視為 non-IRC，而在我們的觀察中，這類段落會包含在 C4 類別的句子之中，因此我們透過 5 分類的模型從裁判書中找出本次案件的 C5 類別，也就是爭點，並且同時給予模型目標句子的前後句做為參考。

在我們所定義的 C5 相關的句子中會包含法官對爭點的說明，也就是聲請人與相對人所提出的事證中有所衝突的部分，因此這類句子會與前述聲請人提出的主張或相對人的答辯容易產生混淆，所以我們也會嘗試從 C4 類別中被分類器錯誤分類為 C1、C2 的句子中找出 C5。

4 資料前處理

我們所使用的資料主要來自於台灣的司法院開放平台上所公開，擷取其中自 2000 年到 2021 年的裁判書。因台灣司法院開放平台網站每月會更新公開的裁判書，所以相關文件總數會是浮動的數值。自 2000 年至 2021 年份間，案由為給付扶養費的裁判書數量統計如圖 1，21 年間總數共 6679 篇裁判書。

4.1 語料挑選

台灣司法院對於所公開的裁判書，在撰寫上並沒有嚴格限制格式。因此我們會透過一些規則及正規表示法來濾除多餘的部分取出我們所需要的段落。

裁判書中裁判字號、日期、案由會在固定的位置，可以藉由判斷開頭行數關鍵字對其進行整理。其中，我們透過找出裁判書上的案由並篩選出其案由為給付扶養費的案件。除此之外，還有許多單純筆錄、上訴的案件不會包含緒論中所定義的四項結構標簽，因此在前處理中也會將這方面的裁判書濾除。

4.2 語料清理

篩選完給付扶養費相關裁判書後，我們會進一步清理裁判書的內文。在裁判書內文中除了裁判字號、日期、案由、聲請人和相對人姓名外，便是裁判書內文。

以我們主要研究對象，案由為給付扶養費的案件為例；內文會包含有主文及理由 (或是事實、事實與理由) 段落。其中主文是紀錄法院最後的裁判結果，而事實與理由段落則會包含有聲請人在訴訟中提出的聲明、相對人所提出的抗辯、還有法院對裁判結果的說明及所引用的法條，也就是緒論中所定義的 C1、C2、C3、C4 四種分類。

因此我們主要分析的語料便是裁判書中的事實與理由段落。我們會透過前面裁判書固定段落中的聲請人、相對人姓名做紀錄並屏蔽掉事實與理由段落中的聲請人、相對人姓名部分。之後透過正規表示法找出裁判書中數字相關的用語，如金額、年分、生日，將其取代為某金額、某年、某月這種較為模糊的用語。除此之外，我們也會藉由中研院開源的工具 CKIP 對初步處理過後的文句以其中的 NER 工具找出各段落的人名、地名、組織部分，將其替換為某人 1、某人 2 這種形式後才應用於後續分類任務。

4.3 段落裁切與斷句

進一步分析後發現，裁判書中會固定使用幾種章節標號來區分段落，我們整理其使用的章節標號用來切割裁判書大段落的依據。

壹、，貳、，參、，肆、…
㈠, ㈡, ㈢, ㈣, ㈤ …
（一），（二），（三），（四），…
一、，二、，三、，四、…
㊀, ㊁, ㊂, ㊃…

表 1. 裁判書中常見章節符號

透過如上表 1 所示的章節符號切割出大段落後，圖 2 是我們統計從 2000 年至 2021 年底為止，案由為給付扶養費的裁判書，各種不同大段落數所包含的裁判書數量。此處的裁判書並未濾除語料清理段落所說不合要求的裁判書。

除了切割大段落外，我們藉由「，、；。：」五種標點符號作為斷句，將大段落切割成數句短句，並保留每句短句的標點符號。其短句長度分布區間如圖 3 所示，大部分的短句長度會在 32 個字以內。

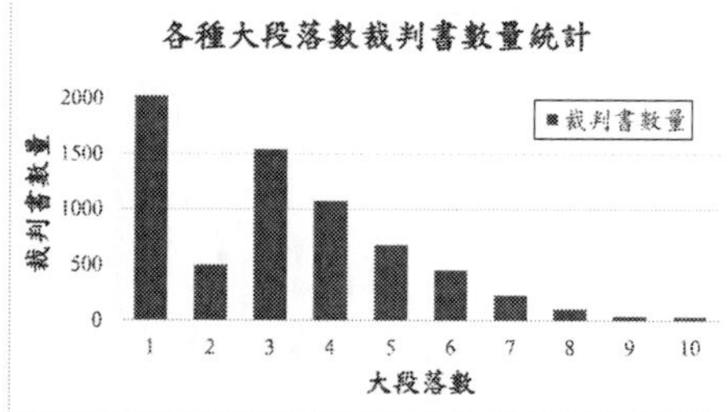

圖 2. 各種不同大段落數裁判書數量統計

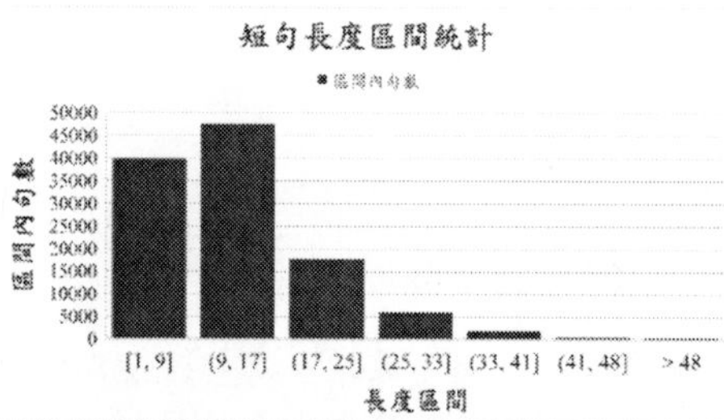

圖 3. 短句長度區間統計

5 實驗設計

在我們的實驗中，挑選前述語料中大段落數為 4 或 5 的 1629 篇裁判書作為初步的研究對象，因我們觀察各種不同段落數的裁判書後發現在這兩種大段落數的裁判書，撰寫上是較有規律的。透過語料清理段落所提到的清理過程後剩餘 814 篇裁判書。

5.1 資料標記

我們分別使用兩種方法來對資料進行標記。在初期實驗，我們並不具有任何語料的標記，因此藉由規則與正規表示法來做為針對特定段落數裁判書自動標記的手段。

以前處理段落所述的大段落來做為分界，首先，C4 的段落可能出現在裁判書事實與理由段落的開頭，而且在 C4 的段落中可以同時找到“(本|法)院”及“(判斷|心證|據)”這些強烈暗示該段落為法院用語的詞組。

而描述聲請人主張與相對人抗辯內容的 C1、C2 段落，C1 的段落總是會安排在 C2 的段落之前，且開頭會分別提到“聲請人聲起略以”、“相對人答辯略以”這類直接提及聲請人及相對人的詞彙，可藉此區分出 C1、C2 的段落。

當法官要描述所引用的法條，也就是 C3 的段落，會以“按”作為開頭。但 C3 的段落可能混雜在 C4 中的其中一個小段落中，因此需要針對 C4、C3 的小段落額外去做排除與區別。這種依靠規則與正規表示法對裁判書中段落進行標記的方式後續會簡稱為規則標記。在得到大段落的規則標記資料後，我們會藉由前面段落裁切與斷句章節中所提到的方法，將大段落中的文字切割為短句，並將每句短句視為與該大段落相同的標籤做為規則標記資料使用。

除了上述規則標記的方法外，我們也聘請法學院畢業的專任助理對這些裁判書的句子進行標記。這些經過專家人工判斷與標記後的方式，我們往後會簡稱為人工標記。

5.2 分類模型與參數設定

本次研究主軸並非針對已有的資料集提出更進一步的改善，而是提出一個新的、對於法律資訊相關研究有所幫助的成果，並非改善既有的分類任務，因此分類器會應用既有的工具及模型來組成。

其中我們使用了 TensorFlow[2]的框架，並以其下 TensorFlow Hub[3]所包裝好的，由 Google

[2] https://www.tensorflow.org/
[3] https://www.tensorflow.org/hub

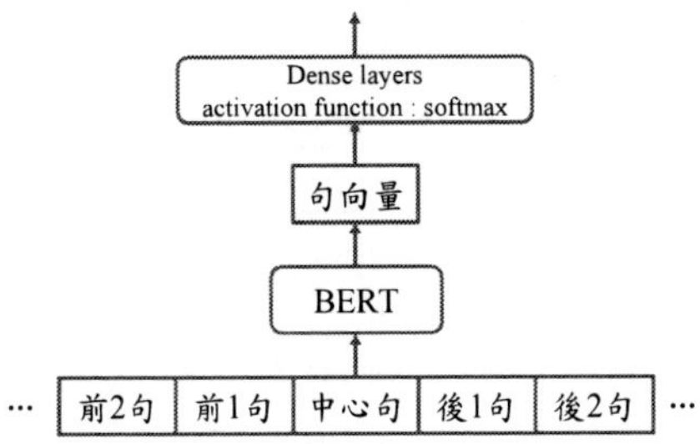

圖 4. 分類模型示意圖

所開源的預訓練模型BERT[4]針對中文做預訓練的 bert_zh_L-12_H-768_A-12 接上一層的全連接層，並且在訓練中會對 BERT 進行 fine tune。而訓練時會以 TensorFlow 內建的 adamw 作為優化器 (optimizer)，將起始的學習率設定為 5e-5。並使用 TensorFlow 框架內建的 sparse categorical cross entropy 作為損失函數 (loss function)，此外因為硬體限制所以 batch size 設定為 16；若驗證資料的 loss 連續四次沒有下降則停止訓練。

輸入資料除目標句子外，也就是中心句外，也會提供模型額外的前後各 n 句句子，我們會嘗試設定 n 值，從最小為 1 到最大為 5。輸入 BERT 前會使用 BERT 內建的 token "[SEP]"做為前後各個輸入句的分隔及連接，模型設計如圖 4 所示；並取其中較好的結果嘗試 Rao et al. (2018) 提出的 sentence representations LSTM 概念。往後會將該模型簡稱為 SR-LSTM，此部分會在往後章節詳細介紹。

實驗時，使用 scikit-learn[5]套件中的工具，以裁判書為單位隨機挑選 20%的篇數做為測試資料，剩餘 80%的篇章中取 20%做為訓練過程的驗證資料，80%做為模型的訓練資料。

雖然僅 814 篇裁判書，但若以句子為單位，我們每次實驗會有 70000、18000、23000 筆以上的訓練、驗證及測試資料，這些資料的數量會受到 random seed 選取的影響而浮動。

為了避免數據洩露的問題，所有的資料都是以裁判書為單位切割出大段落後，以大段落為範圍來生成包含有前後不同句數的資料。也就是每次輸入的 n 句短句會以裁判書的大段落為範圍，不會輸入不同大段落的短句，若是前或後短句不足則會以 "[PAD] "替代之。

BERT + Dense					
	n 句前後文				
	1	2	3	4	5
C1	0.724	0.777	0.743	0.750	0.756
C2	0.545	0.594	0.524	0.542	0.468
C3	0.875	0.858	0.815	0.809	0.790
C4	0.833	0.852	0.815	0.797	0.761
macro F_1	0.744	0.770	0.724	0.724	0.694

表 2. 人工標記測試資料驗證規則標記訓練的模型

BERT + Dense					
	n 句前後文				
	1	2	3	4	5
C1	0.723	0.767	0.740	0.744	0.743
C2	0.529	0.565	0.518	0.523	0.440
C3	0.783	0.777	0.749	0.742	0.740
C4	0.772	0.785	0.766	0.744	0.708
macro F_1	0.702	0.723	0.694	0.688	0.658

表 3. 規則標記測試資料驗證規則標記訓練的模型

6 實驗結果

我們首先會實驗以實驗設計段落提出的規則標記方法來對裁判書進行 C1、C2、C3、C4 四分類，之後分別以規則標記及人工標記的資料進行測試，確認初步的規則標記結合深度學習方法可行之後以人工標記資料訓練模型並與我們規則標記訓練出來的模型進行對比。

除了四分類模型外我們也會拓展到五分類，透過五分類模型來找出裁判書中的爭點，以及依靠爭點句特性設想出的方法實驗結果。

6.1 以規則標記資料訓練句的四分類模型

這個章節我們會使用前面資料標記章節所述的規則標記資料做為訓練資料的模型，並且分別使用人工標記及規則標記的方式對測試資料進行標記後測試模型效果。

以表 2 與表 3 分別呈現測試資料以人工標記及規則標記後的 F_1 score。

[4] https://github.com/google-research/bert

[5] https://scikit-learn.org/

BERT + Dense					
	n句前後文				
	1	2	3	4	5
C1	0.741	0.745	0.728	0.759	0.758
C2	0.559	0.562	0.504	0.538	0.490
C3	0.788	0.788	0.774	0.767	0.757
C4	0.783	0.788	0.776	0.779	0.778
macro F_1	0.718	0.721	0.696	0.711	0.696

表 4. 人工標記測試資料驗證人工標記訓練的模型

BERT + Dense					
	n句前後文				
	1	2	3	4	5
C1	0.763	0.767	0.748	0.785	0.784
C2	0.581	0.592	0.531	0.577	0.534
C3	0.936	0.928	0.920	0.928	0.904
C4	0.874	0.878	0.868	0.883	0.875
macro F_1	0.788	0.791	0.766	0.793	0.774

表 5 規則標記測試資料驗證人工標記訓練的模型

令人意外的是，就算是以規則標記的訓練資料訓練模型，在人工標記的測試資料上整體都維持有比在規則標記的測試資料上更高的 F_1 score。推測是因為在大方向上規則標記的方式有成功找出與專家所給的標記相符合的意見，但其中仍有許多不完善的地方會造成規則標記的方式在少數場合無法得到正確的標記，使其中含有額外的雜訊使得規則標記的測試資料整體 F_1 score 都比人工標記的測試資料還略低 0.03 到 0.05 之間。

另外，在 n=2 時在 macro F_1 上有最佳的分數，之後隨著前後句句數增長反而略微下降，在此猜測或許是過多的不夠精確的標記配上前後文反而令分類模型混淆。

6.2 以人工標記資料訓練句的四分類模型

這個章節中我們透過使用經由法律領域專家標記資料做為訓練資料的模型。表 4 與表 5 分別為以人工標記的測試資料測試及以規則標記的測試資料測試的 F_1 score。

BERT + SR-LSTM				
	人工標記		規則標記	
	n句前後文		n句前後文	
	2	4	2	4
C1	0.752	0.806	0.729	0.770
C2	0.494	0.620	0.478	0.582
C3	0.933	0.938	0.786	0.783
C4	0.875	0.898	0.783	0.794
macro F_1	0.763	0.816	0.694	0.732

表 6. 人工標記訓練資料訓練 SR-LSTM

BERT + SR-LSTM				
	人工標記		規則標記	
	n句前後文		n句前後文	
	2	4	2	4
C1	0.742	0.778	0.735	0.778
C2	0.529	0.602	0.515	0.595
C3	0.867	0.865	0.782	0.788
C4	0.839	0.851	0.777	0.796
macro F_1	0.744	0.774	0.702	0.739

表 7. 規則標記訓練資料訓練 SR-LSTM

以規則標記的測試資料整體趨勢與先前實驗相似，皆是在 n=2 時 F_1 score 最高。但 n=4 時不管是規則標記或人工標記的測試資料皆有所上升，在人工標記的測試資料中 F_1 score 是分數最高的。

考量兩個實驗的結果，後續實驗會先以 n=2 與 n=4 的句數為主要實驗目標進行實驗與驗證。

6.3 SR-LSTM 模型四分類測試

表 6 與表 7 分別整理測試多次以人工標記或規則標記的訓練資料訓練 SR-LSTM 後各類別的 macro F_1 score 以及整體 4 項類別的 macro F_1 score。

除了前面實驗使用的直觀的 BERT 接上單層的全連接層進行分類外，我們模仿(Rao et al., 2018)所提出的 SR-LSTM 模型概念，以 BERT 輸出詞向量做為嵌入層後交由與輸入句數數量相同、彼此獨立的 LSTM 將詞向量轉換成句向量。此處每個短句會輸入同一個 BERT 內，但短句間的關係並不透過 BERT 處理，而是使用 BERT 下一層的 LSTM。BERT 下一層的每

SR-LSTM 5 分類實驗						
		人工標記				
		C1	C2	C3	C4	C5
預測結果	C1	3361	305	104	237	9
	C2	293	1434	4	319	35
	C3	1	1	4596	183	3
	C4	760	354	315	7991	302
	C5	94	36	13	1027	1096

表 8. SR-LSTM(n=4) 5 分類結果混淆矩陣

SR-LSTM 5 分類實驗					
	人工標記				
	C1	C2	C3	C4	C5
macro F_1	0.810	0.620	0.934	0.826	0.627

表 9. SR-LSTM(n=4) 5 分類 macro F_1 score

個 LSTM 彼此獨立，且其 unit 數皆會參考前面 BERT 所輸出的詞向量長度，設定為和句向量長度相同的 unit 數。之後交由另外一層獨立的 LSTM 處理分類問題，因這層 LSTM 主要處理前一層 LSTM 所整理出來的句向量，因此 unit 數設定與前一層獨立 LSTM 數量相同，意即若 n=9 的 SR-LSTM 模型，則第一層會有 9 個獨立的 LSTM 將詞向量處理為句向量，並由第二層 unit 數為 9 的 LSTM 接受處理過後的句向量來輸出分類問題的答案。這一 SR-LSTM 模型在訓練時也會同時使用訓練資料對 BERT 進行 fine tune。

與單純使用 BERT 加上一層全連接層不同的是，所有 SR-LSTM 的結果皆呈現 n=4 的時候有著比 n=2 時更好的 F_1 score 且 n=4 時有著目前最好的 F_1 score，因此後續延伸實驗會以 SR-LSTM 為主要的分類模型。

6.4 延伸實驗與假設驗證

除了嘗試依照句子在裁判書中的功能性將其分類為 C1、C2、C3、C4 四個類別外，我們也嘗試從裁判書中使用分類器及按照我們對徵點句的假設嘗試找出爭點。

6.4.1 五分類測試

文章開頭提到，我們除了希望完成裁判書中文章架構的功能性分類外，也想要從中整理出該次判決的爭點以幫助使用者能更快更輕鬆的理解裁判書，因此我們先使用最直觀的方式，將問題轉換成一個 5 分類問題，並選擇以先前有最高 macro F_1 score 的 SR-LSTM，並同樣設置前後句數 n=4 來做為五分類測試的實驗模型。

我們目前尚未找出能以規則標記爭點的方式，因此此處的訓練資料、驗證資料、測試資料都會使用專家人工標記的資料為主。下表 8 顯示了其中最接近整體 10 次實驗平均的某次其混淆矩陣，另外表 9 則是與先前相同，進行 10 次實驗後整理 5 分類模型的 macro F_1 score。

其中 C1、C2、C3 的部分與原先 4 分類實驗中並無太大差異，而 C5 則與開頭的假設類似，有部分 C5 句子會與 C1、C2 混淆，而可能因為 C5 大多是參雜在 C4 類別句子之中的一段描述，因此極易與 C4 的句子混淆。

6.4.2 從易混淆句子中搜尋爭點

此外我們也嘗試使用先前的假設為概念，將各個大段落中的句子分為 C1、C2、C3、C4 後，將大段落的分類視為其中句子分類標記最多相同類型，並從被分為 C4 的大段落中檢查其中 C1、C2 的句子是否屬於爭點。

不幸的是，在初步的嘗試中準確率及召回率分別只有 0.16 與 0.04。

6.4.3 以大段落數為 6 的文章驗證 4 分類模型

如表 10 所見，我們挑選了相同案由不過大段落數為 6 的裁判書，這些裁判書通過相同的前處理後仍有 322 篇，並且依照相同的前處理方式處理大段落數為 6 的裁判書資料，以此驗證先前兩種訓練資料訓練出來的模型能應用於不同大段落數的裁判書上。

SR-LSTM (n=4)		
測試資料	人工標記	
訓練資料	人工	規則
C1	0.772	0.737
C2	0.654	0.622
C3	0.934	0.846
C4	0.888	0.840
macro F_1	0.812	0.761

表 10. 以大段落總數為 6 的人工標記資料驗證

BERT + Dense 前後各 4 句				
訓練資料	人工標記		規則標記	
測試資料	人工	規則	人工	規則
C1	0.272	0.261	0.308	0.300
C2	0.223	0.205	0.166	0.163
C3	0.805	0.688	0.777	0.684
C4	0.751	0.663	0.739	0.656
macro F_1	0.513	0.454	0.497	0.451

表 11. BERT + Dense (n=4)模型，不對 BERT 進行 fine tune

6.4.4 驗證 BERT fine tune 效果

我們嘗試類似 (Zhang et al., 2021) 中所提出的實驗，比較不對 BERT 進行 fine tune 對預測結果的影響。如表 11 所示，若不讓 BERT 對訓練資料進行 fine tune，可以看到 macro F_1 從 0.79 降低到 0.51 左右。

7 結語

對於人工智慧應用於法律資訊的推薦系統亦或是判決預測系統來說，告訴使用者電腦做出該推薦或是預測的原因及正當性是有必要的。

本篇文章中我們比較了使用不同方式來將原始裁判書整理成依照文章架構的功能性上具有意義的段落及句子，並將這問題轉換成分類問題並比較其成效。以目前的成果看來初步的 C1、C2、C3、C4 這 4 大類別的分類上已有不錯的效果。但 C5，也就是爭點的抽取或分類仍有改善空間。

此外，也驗證了規則標記的概念可以應用在無法與專家配合標記資料時快速得到具有一定可靠度的標記；這方面標記是有能力提升下游更應用面的任務，如判決預測任務的準確率及可解釋性。

8 致謝

本研究承國科會研究計畫 107-2221-E-004-009-MY3 與 110-2221-E-004-008-MY3 與國立政治大學高教深耕校內補助計畫 111H124D-13 之部分補助，謹此致謝。

參考文獻

Trevor Bench-Capon, Michał Araszkiewicz, Kevin Ashley, et al.. 2012. A history of AI and Law in 50 papers: 25 years of the international conference on AI and Law. *Artif Intell Law 20*, pages 215–319. https://doi.org/10.1007/s10506-012-9131-x

Yanguang Chen, Yuanyuan Sun, Zhihao Yang, and Hongfei Lin. 2020. Join entity and relation extraction for legal documents with legal feature enhancement. In *Proceedings of the 28th International Conference on Computational Linguistics*, pages 1561–1571. https://doi.org/10.18653/v1/2020.coling-main.137

Gideon Maillette de Buy Wenniger, Thomas van Dongen, Eleri Aedmaa, Herbert Teun Kruitbosch, Edwin A. Valentijn, and Lambert Schomaker. 2020. Structure-tags improve text classification for scholarly document quality prediction. In *Proceedings of the First Workshop on Scholarly Document Processing*, pages 158–167. https://aclanthology.org/2020.sdp-1.18/

Yi Feng, Chuanyi Li, and Vincent Ng. 2022. Legal judgment prediction via event extraction with constraints. In *Proceedings of the 60th Annual Meeting of the Association for Computational Linguistics (Volume 1: Long Papers)*. pages 648–664.
https://doi.org/10.18653/v1/2022.acl-long.48

Jim-How Ho. 2021. AI 引入民事程序可行性之研究 (The feasibility research on introducing artificial intelligence into civil procedures) [In Chinese]. Doctoral Dissertation, Department of Information Management, National Taiwan University of Science and Technology.
https://hdl.handle.net/11296/pkvh27

Wan-Chen Lin, Tsung-Ting Kuo, Tung-Jia Chang, Chueh-An Yen, Chao-Ju Chen, and Shou-de Lin. 2012. Exploiting machine learning models for Chinese legal documents labeling, case classification, and sentencing prediction. *International Journal of Computational Linguistics and Chinese Language Processing, vol. 17, no. 4*, pages 49–68.
https://aclanthology.org/O12-5004.pdf

Shang Li, Hongli Zhang, Lin Ye, Xiaoding Guo, and Binxing Fang. 2019. Mann: A multichannel attentive neural network for legal judgment prediction. *IEEE Access*, pages 151144 – 151155. https://ieeexplore.ieee.org/document/8861054

Jack Mumford, Katie Atkinson, and Trevor Bench Capon. 2021. Machine learning and legal argument. In *Proceedings of the 21st Workshop on Computational Models of Natural Argument*, pages 47–56. https://core.ac.uk/display/477904310

Guozheng Rao, Weihang Huang, Zhiyong Feng, and Qiong Cong. 2018. LSTM with sentence representations for document-level sentiment classification. *Neurocomputing*, 308, pages 49–57. https://doi.org/10.1016/j.neucom.2018.04.045

Huihui Xu, Jaromir Savelka, and Kevin D Ashley. 2021. Accounting for sentence position and legal domain sentence embedding in learning to classify case sentences. In *Legal Knowledge and Information Systems*, · pages 33–42. https://ebooks.iospress.nl/doi/10.3233/FAIA210314

Haoxi Zhong, Chaojun Xiao, Cunchao Tu, Tianyang Zhang, Zhiyuan Liu, and Maosong Sun. 2020. How does NLP benefit legal system: A summary of legal artificial intelligence. In *Proceedings of the 58th Annual Meeting of the Association for Computational Linguistics*, pages 5218–5230. https://aclanthology.org/2020.acl-main.466/

The 34th Conference on Computational Linguistics and Speech Processing (ROCLING 2022)
Taipei, Taiwan, November 21-22, 2022. The Association for Computational Linguistics and Chinese Language Processing

中英文語碼轉換語音合成系統開發
Development of Mandarin-English code-switching speech synthesis system

練欣柔 Hsin-Jou Lien, 黃立宇 Li-Yu Huang, 陳嘉平 Chia-Ping Chen
國立中山大學資訊工程學系
National Sun Yat-sen University
Department of Computer Science and Engineering
m103040105@nsysu.edu.tw, m093040070@nsysu.edu.tw, cpchen@cse.nsysu.edu.tw

摘要

本論文提出中英文語碼轉換語音合成系統。爲了使系統可專注於學習不同語言間的內容，利用已統一語者風格的多語言人工資料集進行訓練。之後在合成器中加入語言向量，以增加系統對多語言的掌握。此外對輸入的中、英文分別進行不同的前處理，將中文進行斷詞且轉爲漢語拼音，藉此增加語音的自然度，且減輕學習時的複雜度，也透過數字正規化判斷句子中的阿拉伯數字，是否需要加上數字單位。英文部份則對複雜的頭字語進行讀音判斷與轉換。

Abstract

In this paper, the Mandarin-English code-switching speech synthesis system has been proposed. To focus on learning the content information between two languages, the training dataset is multilingual artificial dataset whose speaker style is unified. Adding language embedding into the system helps it be more adaptive to multilingual dataset. Besides, text preprocessing is applied and be used in different way which depends on the languages. Word segmentation and text-to-pinyin are the text preprocessing for Mandarin, which not only improves the fluency but also reduces the learning complexity. Number normalization decides whether the arabic numerals in sentence needs to add the digits. The preprocessing for English is acronym conversion which decides the pronunciation of acronym.

關鍵字：語音合成、語碼轉換、資料前處理

Keywords: speech synthesize, code-switching, text preprocessing

1 緒論

語碼轉換（Code-switching）是指在一句話或多句話裡，含有一種以上的語言被交替使用，這種情況在現今社會中十分常見，爲因應這種趨勢，語音合成系統也朝著多語言（Multilingual）的方向發展。現今的語料多爲單語言，較少有同一語者的多語言語料，這導致語碼轉換在訓練時會遇到許多問題，像是語者無法合成非母語的語句，亦或是語者隨著句子語言轉換而改變的狀況。爲解決上述問題，我們參考任意語者風格中英文語音合成系統 (Wang, 2021)，做爲我們的資料生成模型，給予系統一個參考音檔，其可生成與參考音檔相同語者風格的聲音訊號，藉此系統統一多語言資料集的語者風格，以建置多語言語音合成系統。

在本文中，使用 FastSpeech2 (Ren et al., 2020) 做爲合成器，將編碼器與解碼器改爲 (Gulati et al., 2020) 所提出的 Conformer 架構，聲碼器使用 HiFi-GAN (Kong et al., 2020)。此外爲增加系統對於多語言的掌握，於合成器中加上語言向量（language embedding），並爲句子依中、英文編上語言 ID（language ID），而語碼轉換的句子無法直接以單一語言 ID 表示，對此在實驗中進行了處理。

我們發現因中文數量龐大、字詞讀音多變，因此將中文字轉換爲漢語拼音，降低系統學習時的複雜度。此外也發現交雜在中文句子中的阿拉伯數字，有需要數字單位與否的問題，於是對此進行正規化。而在英文中經常使用的頭字語，是指將一句話或較長的名詞，縮寫成連續大寫字母，其發音分爲字母讀音或視爲新單字，要系統完整學習所有的英文頭字語是較爲困難的，我們創建頭字語字典，以便進行分類讀音方式，並進行轉換，我們透過對文本進行資料前處理，以降低複雜度，提升中文、英文語音合成之正確率。

論文之其餘章節安排如下，章節二：研究方法描述系統架構、改進方法及文字前處理；章節三：實驗設置描述資料集與模型參數設定；章節四：實驗結果對基礎架構與改進後的系統進行比較；章節五：總結我們系統的優點和未來的改進方向。

2 研究方法

以 Conformer-FastSpeech2 加上語言向量作爲模型架構，爲了提升中、英文語音合成的品質，分別對輸入的中文和英文文本做不同的前處理。在中文方面，使用中文斷詞、文字轉拼音與數字正規化，英文則執行縮寫讀法判斷與轉換，並且針對語碼轉換做語言 ID 編碼，與因中、英文語速差異進行的調整。

2.1 多語言語音合成系統

在本文中，使用 FastSpeech2 (Ren et al., 2020) 做爲合成器，聲碼器使用 HiFi-GAN (Kong et al., 2020)。

FastSpeech2 是一個非自迴歸 (Non-autoregressive) 的模型，可用更短的時間合成出與自迴歸 (Auto-regressive) 模型相同品質的語音。架構中的編碼器和解碼器使用 Transformer 架構，在我們系統中將 Transformer 改爲 Conformer (Gulati et al., 2020)，並命名爲 Conformer-FastSpeech2（CFS2）。Conformer 結合了 Transformer 和卷積模組 (Convolution module) 以增強效果，其網路包含前饋神經網路（Feed Forward Module）、多頭自注意力機制（Multi-Head Attention Module）、卷積模組、層正歸化（Layer Normalization)。系統架構如圖 1，而圖右半邊則爲 Conformer 的架構。

在架構中加入語言向量，並將其和 phoneme embedding 串接在一起做爲編碼器的輸入。藉此提升系統合成多語言的表現，另外，依照資料的語言給予編號，稱爲語言 ID，使用 0 和 1 爲 language ID 分別表示英文與中文。

2.2 中文資料前處理

由於人們在交談時是有些微停頓的，爲了讓系統學習語音這些細節，我們首先使用了一個 python 工具名爲 Jieba (Sun, 2012) 進行中文斷詞（Word segmentation），當中共有四種不同的斷詞模式，實驗中使用預設的精確模式，利用將符號置於斷詞處，以表示語句中的停頓，進而提升語音的自然度。此外 Jieba 工具可自行匯入符合使用者需求的字典，實驗中將 CKIP team (Ma and Chen, 2005) 的字典匯入，以提升斷詞的準確度，也將 CLMAD (Bai et al., 2018) 整理成另一份擴充字典，當系統應用於特殊領域時可匯入。

然而因爲中文字本身數量龐大、字詞讀音多變，要系統學習所有的字詞是過於複雜的，因此不可直接將其作爲輸入。於是我們利用 pypinyin 將中文字轉換成漢語拼音，其爲一個

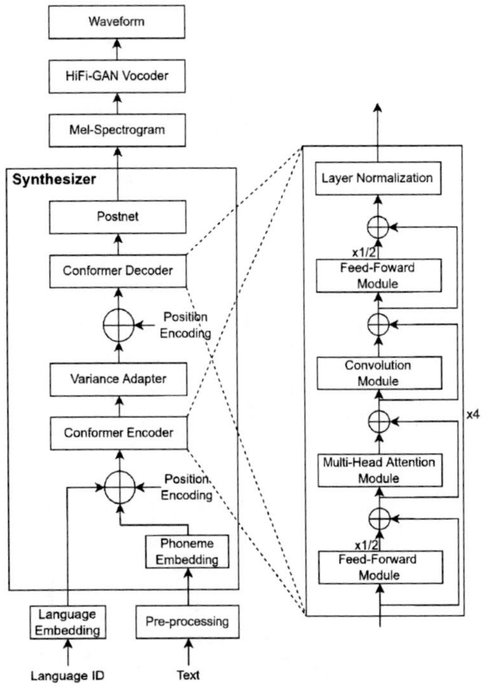

圖 1. Conformer-FastSpeech2 系統架構圖，基於 FastSpeech2 加入語言向量，右半邊爲 Conformer 的架構，其基於 Transformer 架構再加上卷積模組以增強效果。

grapheme-to-phoneme（G2P）的 python 工具，以英文表示拼音，並用數字表示聲調（Tone)，藉由此拼音組合的轉換簡單化中文的表示，使系統可以用較簡單的方式學習中文的發音。表 1 爲中文斷詞及文字轉拼音的範例。

此外我們還發現，當阿拉伯數字若在中文句子中時，會有是否需要唸出數字單位的差異，數字單位是指個、十、百、千、萬等。因此我們參考 [1]Chinese Text Normalization 作爲基礎概念，其做法爲將數字的常用情況進行分類，並以 Regular Expression 對數字找出相對應的模式，再判斷是否需加上數字單位，然而我們對模式內容進行修改，使其更貼近我們所需，共有五大種模式，表 2 爲各模式的例子及正規化後的結果。

2.3 針對語碼轉換之處理

在訓練階段，使用英文和中文兩種語言 ID 進行語言向量。然而在合成階段，若輸入爲語碼轉換的文本，無法單純以中文或英文予以編號。爲此設立編定語言 ID 於語碼轉換文本之方法，如圖 2 所示，首先依語言分段輸入的

[1]https://github.com/speechio/chinese_text_normalization

前處理方法	文本狀態
原始文本	明天不會下雨
中文斷詞	明天 * 不會 * 下雨
文字轉拼音	ming2 tian1 * bu4 hui4 * xia4 yu3*。.

表 1. 中文資料前處理。先對文本進行中文斷詞，再將其轉換爲漢語拼音。

文本，計算各分段的字元長度，藉由相對位置予以對應的語言 ID 且進行語言向量。分段後的文本分別進行資料前處理，再進行音素向量（phoneme embedding）作爲編碼器的輸入。最後將編碼器輸出的隱藏特徵序列（hidden state sequence），和語言向量的輸出相加，獲得新的隱藏特徵序列進行後續的訓練。

由於中、英文資料集的語速差異，導致系統在合成語碼轉換之句子時，會有英文部份語速較快而感到不自然的問題。FastSpeech2 架構中的 Length Regulator，有一參數 α 可調整 duration predictor 輸出的時長（duration）大小，藉此改變梅爾頻譜圖的隱藏特徵序列長度，α 預設爲 1。若 $\alpha = 1.5$，表示將時長序列乘上 1.5 倍，進而使隱藏特徵序列拉長 1.5 倍，即爲放慢速度。搭配語言 ID，即可透過相對位置單獨調整英文的速度。兩者差異如圖 3。左圖爲無搭配語言 ID，針對整個序列進行調整。右圖則爲單獨對英文進行調整，將英文部份的時長與 α 相乘，四捨五入，獲得新的時長序列。

2.4 英文資料前處理

英文的頭字語可細分爲 acronym 和 initialism，兩者的差異是縮寫後的單字該如何發音。acronym 指將縮寫後的單字讀爲一個新的詞，例如：NASA 會讀做 "na-suh"，FOMO 讀做 "fow-mow"，而 initialism 則是指在發音上只念字母的讀音，而非視爲一個新的詞，像是 FBI、NBA、BBC 等。然而由於頭字語爲 acronym 或是 initialism，較難單純以文字進行分類，這導致系統難以學習，因此我們收集大量的頭字語，自行建立了一個頭字語字典，當輸入的文本含有全大寫的英文時，搜尋字典確認此輸入是否爲 initialism，若是，則將字母轉換爲相似讀音，以增加合成的正確性，若非則不做更改，舉例來說，當 BBC 經確認是 initialism ，會轉換爲 "bee bee ci"，FBI 則會轉換爲 "ef bee I"。

3 實驗設置

在實驗中的資料集分爲原始資料集，以及利用資料生成系統所生成的人工資料集，此外使用

模式名稱	範例文本	正規化結果
Date	1986 年 8 月 18 日	一九八六年八月十八日
	1997/9/15	一九九七年九月十五日
Money	19588 元	一萬九千五百八十八元
Phone 手機	0919114115	零九一九一一四一一五
Phone 市話	02-2720-8889	零二二七二零八八八九
percentage	62%	百分之六十二
cardinal 量詞	1999 個蘋果	一千九百九十九個蘋果
	130 顆球	一百三十顆球
	124000 瓶水	十二萬四千瓶水
cardinal 編號	學號是 103040100	學號是一零三零四零一零零
cardinal 純數	175.5 公分	一百七十五點五公分

表 2. 輸入的文本以 Regular Expression 找出相對應的模式，判斷是否要加上數字單位或其他處理。

ESPnet2 (Watanabe et al., 2018) 做爲開發工具協助開發。

3.1 資料集

- 原始資料集：使用的資料集包含中文語料 AISHELL3 (Shi et al., 2020) 及英文語料 VCTK (Yamagishi et al., 2019) ，在實驗中發現無需使用全部的資料，即可訓練出一個品質相當的系統，減少資料量亦可減少整體訓練時間，因此各選取了 30 名語者的資料做爲我們實驗用的資料集，時長約爲整體資料集的四分之一，並命名爲 AISHELL3-thirty 和 VCTK-thirty，資料集的詳細資訊如表 3 所示。

- 人工資料集: 參考任一語者風格中英文語音合成系統 (Wang, 2021)，作爲我們的資料生成系統。選用 AISHELL3 資料集中的一個音檔作爲參考音檔，並使用 AISHELL3-thirty 和 VCTK-thirty 的文本作爲生成資料時的文本，藉此生成與參考音檔相同語者風格的多語言資料集，將其稱爲 Generated-multi，共 25,362 筆音檔，共 15.6 小時，如表 3 所示。

3.2 訓練設定

本文使用 ESPnet2 (Watanabe et al., 2018) 作爲開發的工具。CFS2 的訓練集爲多語言的 Generated-multi，架構中的 Conformer 編碼器和解碼器 kernel size 分別爲 7 及 31，padding 爲 3 與 15，優化器（Optimizer）使用 Adam (Kingma and Ba, 2014)，學習率（Learning rate）設定爲 1。因爲我們的系統爲多語言的語音合成系統，爲了使聲碼器可將多語言的梅爾頻譜圖轉爲聲音訊號，HiFi-GAN 聲碼器利用 AISHELL3-thirty 和 VCTK-thirty 資料集進行訓練，批量大小（Batch size）設定爲 32，使用 Adam 作爲優化器，學習率設定爲 0.0002。

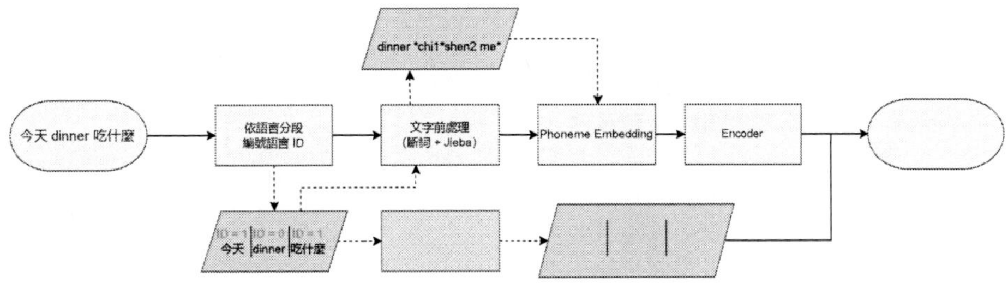

圖 2. 語碼轉換語言向量流程圖，LanEmb 表示語言向量。將輸入文本依語言分段並編號語言 ID，每段依序進行資料前處理、音素向量，將結果做爲編碼器的輸入。對語言 ID 進行語言向量，將輸出與編碼器的輸出相加。

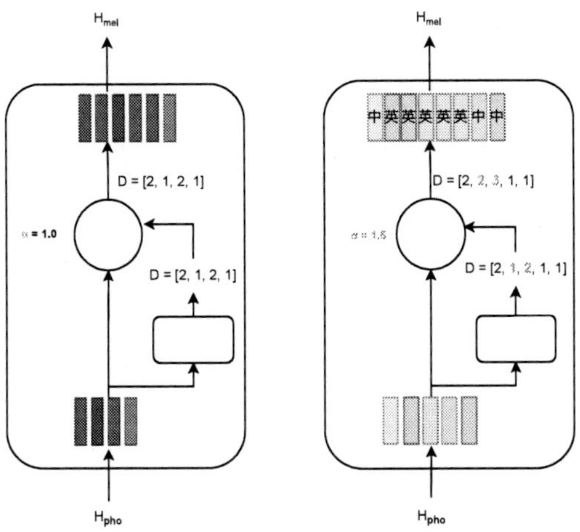

圖 3. Length Regulator 的作法。以 Length Regulator 中之參數 α 調整隱藏特徵序列長度架構圖。D 表示時長（duration），H_{pho} 表示 phoneme 的隱藏特徵，H_{mel} 爲梅爾頻譜圖的隱藏特徵。右側爲依語言 ID 選取要調整的時長元素，再將元素乘上 α 後四捨五入，得到新的時長以調整序列長度，左側則爲對全部序列進行調整。

4 實驗結果與分析

本實驗採用平均意見分數（Mean Opinion Score, MOS）作爲評估機制，分數區間爲 0（低）～5（高），針對語音的整體品質進行評分，包含了流暢度、人聲相似度和有無雜訊等。隨機選取各實驗所需要的文本進行合成，由我們研究室中的 11 位研究人員參與聆聽，並對各合成語音進行評分，最後將所有分數平均做爲結果。

4.1 生成資料集的品質

對 3.1 生成資料集 Generated-multi 與原始資料集 AISHELL3-thirty 和 VCTK-thirty 進行比較，以確保此生成資料集的品質，由表 4 所示，可得生成資料集的分數皆在 4 分以上，表示使用生成的方式依然可獲得不錯的聲音訊號，以此資料集訓練合成器是可行的。

資料集	音檔數量	總時長（小時）
VCTK-thirty	11, 654	22.5
AISHELL3-thirty	13, 708	19
Generate-multi	25, 362	15.6

表 3. 資料集詳細資訊。包含選取三十位語者的 VCTK-thirty 和 AISHLLE3-thirty，及生成資料集 Generate-multi。

資料集	MOS	
	英文	中文
VCTK-thirty	4.46 ± 0.22	-
AISHELL3-thirty	-	4.73 ± 0.17
Generated-multi	4.28 ± 0.31	4.09 ± 0.62

表 4. 資料集的 MOS。基於 VCTK-thirty 和 AISHELL3-thirty 的文本做爲生成 Generated-multi 時的文本。比較生成資料集的語音品質，生成的資料集分數在 4 分以上。

語言	資料前處理流程	w/o	MOS
中	中文斷詞	w/o	4.50 ± 0.11
		w/	4.52 ± 0.18
	數字正規化	w/o	4.02 ± 0.40
		w/	4.45 ± 0.20
英	頭字語處理	w/o	3.69 ± 0.20
		w/	3.99 ± 0.15

表 5. 有無進行前處理的 MOS。比較有無前處理的語音訊號品質，處理後的品質，皆有所提升。

4.2 資料前處理結果

由於兩種語言是分開進行資料前處理，因此在 MOS 評分，將中、英文前處理的效果分開進行比較。中文文本在訓練時皆轉爲漢語拼音，於是用於評分的文本皆有經過文字轉拼音，以便系統合成，由表 5 可知，文本進行中文斷詞後，MOS 有些微的增加，另外，進行評估數字正規化的文本，爲突顯正規化的效果，文本皆選用含有阿拉伯數字的中文句子，正規化後 MOS 分數由 4.02 提高到了 4.45，分數大幅的提升了，由此可知，數字正規化對於文本的重要。在英文結果的部份，選用在英文句中含有連續大寫的文本，用以評估處理頭字語的效果，然而在加入頭字語處理後，MOS 分數由 3.69 增加至 3.99，由結果可知透過前處理能提升合成之品質。

5 結論

我們建立的中英文語碼轉換語音合成系統，其有相當不錯的表現，透過中、英文的資料前處理大幅提升語音的品質，尤其是中文的數字正規化與英文的頭字語處理，分別由 4.02 上升至 4.45，及 3.69 至 3.99，不過整體系統依舊有進步的空間，因此，未來也將持續改進語碼轉換中，中英文的語音流暢度，以及以建立一個可分離語者資訊，單純學習文本資訊的編碼器爲目標，無需再使用生成模型生成的資料集進行訓練，依然可合成多語言語碼轉換的句子。

References

Ye Bai, Jianhua Tao, Jiangyan Yi, Zhengqi Wen, and Cunhang Fan. 2018. Clmad: A chinese language model adaptation dataset. In *2018 11th International Symposium on Chinese Spoken Language Processing (ISCSLP)*, pages 275–279.

Anmol Gulati, James Qin, Chung-Cheng Chiu, Niki Parmar, Yu Zhang, Jiahui Yu, Wei Han, Shibo Wang, Zhengdong Zhang, Yonghui Wu, et al. 2020. Conformer: Convolution-augmented transformer for speech recognition. *arXiv preprint arXiv:2005.08100*.

Diederik P Kingma and Jimmy Ba. 2014. Adam: A method for stochastic optimization. *arXiv preprint arXiv:1412.6980*.

Jungil Kong, Jaehyeon Kim, and Jaekyoung Bae. 2020. Hifi-gan: Generative adversarial networks for efficient and high fidelity speech synthesis. *Advances in Neural Information Processing Systems*, 33:17022–17033.

Wei-Yun Ma and Keh-Jiann Chen. 2005. Design of ckip chinese word segmentation system. *Chinese and Oriental Languages Information Processing Society*, 14(3):235–249.

Yi Ren, Chenxu Hu, Xu Tan, Tao Qin, Sheng Zhao, Zhou Zhao, and Tie-Yan Liu. 2020. Fastspeech 2: Fast and high-quality end-to-end text to speech. *arXiv preprint arXiv:2006.04558*.

Yao Shi, Hui Bu, Xin Xu, Shaoji Zhang, and Ming Li. 2020. Aishell-3: A multi-speaker mandarin tts corpus and the baselines. *arXiv preprint arXiv:2010.11567*.

J Sun. 2012. Jieba chinese word segmentation tool.

Yih-Wen Wang. 2021. Integrating hidden speaker and style information to multi-lingual and code-switching speech synthesis. `https://hdl.handle.net/11296/du785x`.

Shinji Watanabe, Takaaki Hori, Shigeki Karita, Tomoki Hayashi, Jiro Nishitoba, Yuya Unno, Nelson Enrique Yalta Soplin, Jahn Heymann, Matthew Wiesner, Nanxin Chen, et al. 2018. Espnet: End-to-end speech processing toolkit. *arXiv preprint arXiv:1804.00015*.

Junichi Yamagishi, Christophe Veaux, Kirsten MacDonald, et al. 2019. Cstr vctk corpus: English multi-speaker corpus for cstr voice cloning toolkit (version 0.92).

The 34th Conference on Computational Linguistics and Speech Processing (ROCLING 2022)
Taipei, Taiwan, November 21-22, 2022. The Association for Computational Linguistics and Chinese Language Processing

老年扶養費請求案件之准駁及扶養金額預測
Predicting Judgments and Grants for Civil Cases of Alimony for the Elderly

劉威志 Wei-Zhi Liu **吳柏憲 Po-Hsien Wu**

林泓任 Hong-Ren Lin **劉昭麟 Chao-Lin Liu**

國立政治大學資訊科學系
Department of Computer Science, National Chengchi University
{109753157, 111753120, 109753156, chaolin }@g.nccu.edu.tw

摘要

有鑒於近年請求扶養費民事訴訟案件逐年上升之趨勢，考慮伴隨著調解件數增長，未來量能或將難以負荷，本研究將以斷詞及向量化後之段落以 logistic regression 為基礎提出扶養費准駁預測模型，同時提出使用 model tree 建構扶養金額預測模型，以期未來能在庭外調解時提供一相對客觀的試算結果供有扶養費爭議之兩造參考並儘早達成共識，亦或給予法官參考數據輔助以期能加速判決之進程，進而減少司法資源的浪費。

Abstract

The needs for mediation are increasing rapidly along with the increasing number of cases of the alimony for the elderly in recent years. Offering a prediction mechanism for predicting the outcomes of some prospective lawsuits may alleviate the workload of the mediation courts. This research aims to offer the predictions for the judgments and the granted alimony for the plaintiffs of such civil cases in Chinese, based on our analysis of results of the past lawsuits. We hope that the results can be helpful for both the involved parties and the courts. To build the current system, we segment and vectorize the texts of the judgement documents, and apply the logistic regression and model tree models for predicting the judgments and for estimating the granted alimony of the cases, respectively.

關鍵字：判決預測、民事案件, 給付扶養費

Keywords: legal judgment prediction, civil case, the issues of alimony

1 引言

有鑒於請求給付扶養費訴訟有逐年增加趨勢，人工智慧於法律領域之相關應用日漸重要，於是本研究提出二個與扶養費金裁判相關之預測模型，分別為「請求准駁預測模型」和「扶養金額預測模型」，前者預測一案件是否通過或駁回扶養請求；後者則預測一案件之扶養金裁判金額。

本研究採用自民國 89 年至民國 110 年間與扶養費相關案件過濾上訴、離婚及協議相關案件，進行扶養金准駁預測與金額預測。

本文所提「兩造」為扶養金額案件中請求扶養之「聲請人」與被請求扶養之「相對人」此二身份，其可能為配偶、父母、子女亦或手足等關係，此類家事案件往往在調解中關於「是否具扶養義務」與「扶養金額是否適當」有所爭執及論點攻防，因此我們針對兩造主張部分進行准駁預測；針對相關客觀特徵進行金額預測，供兩造及法官參考，以利加速調解及裁判之進程。

實驗中會先擷取特定段落即兩造主張之段落，進行斷詞與向量化之前處理，再使用准駁預測模型進行訓練與預測案件是 (准許請求) 否 (駁回請求) 通過扶養金額之聲請。針對「不同預測模型」及「是否模糊化」進行 F_1 score 比較。

其次，關於扶養金額預測部分會先進行相關特徵之提取，諸如：聲請人現居地月均支出、聲請人每月補助、聲請人每月要求之金

額等 (詳見本文段落 7)，以利進行初步試算，再使用其他特徵，如：相對人經濟狀況及兩造關係 (是否具相應扶養義務) 等特徵進行輔助調整 (詳見本文段落 8.2)，並得出最終預測金額結果。

關於實驗結果比較，我們採用：僅給予特徵提取之 scikit-learn[1]的 linear regression、只使用 model tree 進行預測區分且每個區塊單純使用 scikit-learn 的 linear regression 及本文模型，三者進行比較，以比對「是否使用 model tree」、「是否使用多種預測方式」之 mean absolute error (以下簡稱 MAE) 結果優劣。

關於文章架構，本文段落 2 提及關於本實驗的相關研究；段落 3 敘述本實驗的資料來源與篩選；段落 4 講述准駁預測之前處理；段落 5 則介紹准駁預測模型實驗設計；段落 6 則為准駁預測實驗結果比較。段落 7 陳述扶養金預測之前處理與特徵提取；段落 8 則介紹金額預測模型設計；段落 9 為金額預測模型實驗結果比較；段落 10 為上述二模型之實驗總結；段落 11 則為本文結語。

2 相關研究

人工智慧技術應用於法律領域不論在國內或國外都有許多的前沿研究，其應用層面有很多方向，而應用於裁判預測上更是數不勝數，目前在這領域中以刑事案件為主流，以國內為例：像是林婉真等 (2012) 提出將構成特徵要素作為特徵，利用 additive regression 預測強盜及恐嚇取財之量刑結果。然而裁判預測應用在民事案件上目前是相對少見的。

以民事案件來說近期有何君豪 (2021) 提出導入機器學習演算法的建議，再依據繁簡分流理論進行導入 AI 法官的民事訴訟類型選擇，希望能為我國民事訴訟導入 AI 法官提供具體可行的藍圖。王道維等提出 AI 輔助親權判決預測[2]，其系統藉由輸入夫妻雙方的有利與不利條件後，進行小孩的監護權判給某一方之機率預測。而黃詩淳等 (2020) 的研究則是在探討直接將法律裁判原文輸入機器後，觀察機器能否了解法官的語意並進行親權酌定。

Muhlenbach et al. (2020) 的贍養費裁判預測，該研究在避免過多的法律特徵與避免使用較不具解釋性之 AI 模型的前提下，提出利用隨機森林 (random forest) 與回歸模型對於離婚案件中的贍養費進行預測。

而黃詩淳 (2022) 同時提出透過特徵提取來進行分類決策樹與回歸決策樹之扶養預測，其與本研究相似於預測應用方面，不過其中的特徵提取與模型則有所不同，本研究受到前者 Muhlenbach et al.之啟發，選擇家事案件中給付扶養費判例作為實驗對象並以兩造主張為基礎提出同請求通過與否關聯之准駁預測模型，以及試算通過數額之扶養金額預測模型，並在提取相對客觀及有限的特徵且避免缺乏解釋性之前提下建構其 model tree (Malerba et al., 2004) 分支條件，再根據林玠鋒 (2015) 對於酌定扶養費的研究去改善與調整我們的預測模型，望能在提供預測結果時亦提出令人信服之特徵解釋。

3 資料來源與篩選實驗對象

本研究使用的資料主要來自臺灣司法院資料開放平臺[3]，收集了自民國 89 年 1 月起至民國 110 年 12 月之裁判書。裁判書為 JSON格式檔案，其key值會包含「案由、裁判字號、裁判年份、裁判書內文」等，因此本實驗選用案由含有「扶養費」但不包含「返還扶養費代墊款」及「酌減扶養費」之案件，其再進行篩選，篩選規則如下：將裁判字號含有「抗、上、高等、最高、婚」等字眼，因此類字號屬於上訴、抗告審、程序事由與其他類型案件，這些案件並非在本實驗研究範圍內，並過濾裁判書內文中段落不足或未有提及兩造主張之案件，以利後續准駁預測模型訓練。

根據上述過濾條件得出基本語料共1,930案件，即是准駁預測模型之實驗對象，其中未通過數量則為 983件；通過案件數量為947件。

[1] https://scikit-learn.org/stable/

[2] https://custodyprediction.herokuapp.com/userPredict

[3] https://opendata.judicial.gov.tw

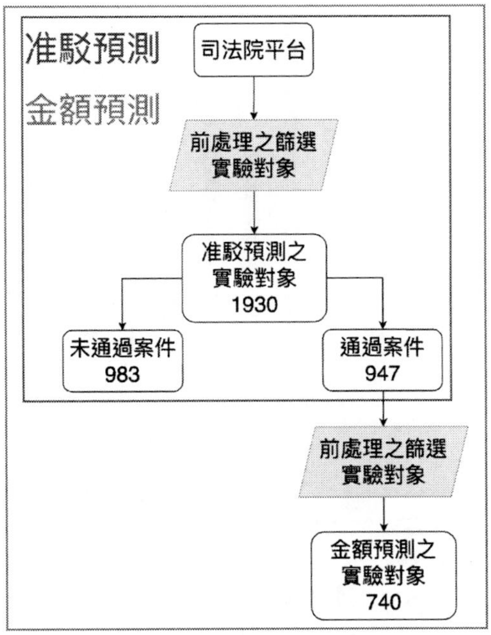

圖 1. 實驗對象之過濾

故會對通過案件中再對具私下調解或協議性質及一次性給付之案件進行過濾，過濾後所剩案件為742件，即本文金額預測模型之實驗對象。其流程如圖1。

4 准駁預測之前處理

經由前段所述之資料篩選過後須要再對裁判書內文做進一步地清理以得出實驗所需資料。裁判書內文含有主文及理由 (或是事實、事實及理由要領等詞語) 之標題段落，而主文段落為記錄法院最終裁判結果；理由段落則會含有兩造的主張 (即聲請人的聲明和相對人的抗辯) 與法院裁判之理由等，其中實驗所需的輸入資料來自理由段落，而標記資料則來自主文段落。

4.1 資料擷取

裁判書在撰寫上未有嚴格限制，經過分析後我們發現每個標題內的段落會以多種章節標號做條列敘述，如：「『壹、』、『㊀』、

例子	識別標籤	替換文字
劉大明	PERSON	某人
文山區	LOC	某地
台北市	GPE	某地

表 1. 命名實體替換標籤

『(一)』、『甲、』」等，因此透過正規表示式法 (regular expressions) 將理由段落切割成各個章節段落，在經觀察案例後得出法官會以特定的格式來描述聲請人或相對人的主張段落，通常以「聲請人意指略以」或「相對人則以」等來進行開頭，因此我們以其來擷取主張內容即為本研究提出的准駁預測模型所使用的輸入資料。

4.2 資料模糊化與向量化

為了搭配後續的向量化，要先將切割好兩造主張之段落經中研院開源的工具CKIP[4]進行斷詞與命名實體辨識 (named-entity recognition, NER)，將主張段落進行斷詞時，會先設置強迫斷詞之詞彙，例如：聲請人、相對人、本件、略以等，以避免出現斷詞錯誤。又因裁判書的內容會出現地點、人名、時間等特殊資訊，不利推廣到所有案件，於是將地名與人名改成「某地」和「某人」如表 1，然而時間的部分未用命名實體辨識，因套件會將年齡也歸類為時間，故時間的替換是用正規表示式法來抽取並替換成「某時」，接著進入後續向量轉換。

其中將主張段落透過兩種方法來進行文字向量化，包含 TF-IDF[5]與 Sentence-BERT (Nils Reimers et al., 2019)，以下簡稱 SBERT[6]。前者透過統計文件中的詞頻 (term frequency) 以及逆向文件頻率 (inverse document frequency)，將兩者分數相乘得其評估分數同時也視其為向量。而後者是使用了孿生網路 (siamese network) 及三連體網路 (triplet network) 為架構，比較多種目標函數及整合特徵向量的方法，最終可直接輸出該句之句向量 (sentence embedding)，以利後續實驗進行。

[4] https://ckip.iis.sinica.edu.tw
[5] http://scikit-learn.org/stable/modules/generated/sklearn.feature_extraction.text.TfidfVectorizer.html
[6] https://www.sbert.net

Vectorize	Model	Blur	F1 score
TF-IDF	naïve-Bayes	F	0.612
TF-IDF	naïve-Bayes	T	0.632
TF-IDF	Logistic	F	0.669
TF-IDF	Logistic	T	0.788
SBERT_AVG	NN	F	0.660
SBERT_AVG	NN	T	0.690
SBERT + LSTM	NN	F	0.555
SBERT + LSTM	NN	T	0.649

表 2. 准駁預測模型模型比較

5 准駁預測模型實驗設計

由於法官會參考兩造說法及所提的相關事證後進行裁判，因此我們擷取出兩造主張之段落後，經由上段提及之向量化方式來進行向量轉換。望能透過不同向量化的方法及搭配不同的預測模型，從中找到較適合扶養金准駁預測之模型，實驗中的資料切割都是以 8 比 2 的方式來進行切分訓練資料與測試資料。

5.1 向量化設定

透過 scikit-learn 的 TF-IDF 進行向量轉換時，會設置停用詞來避免統計無意義的詞彙，其維度在是否使用模糊化的效果下分別約為 18,000 多維與 24,000 多維。

SBERT 之預訓練模型本實驗選用"distiluse-base-multilingual-cased-v1"因其訓練資料才有使用繁體中文且表現較其他也有使用繁體中文的預訓練模型來得佳，不過由於 SBERT 會有字數上的限制 (128 個字)，所以會將主張段落以「。！？；」四種標點符號進行斷句將其切割成多個句子，並進一步向量轉換得出多個句向量，其向量維度為 512 維。

5.2 准駁預測模型參數設定

TF-IDF 向量化方式會搭配 scikit-learn 提供的 naïve-Bayes 與 logistic regression 來進行預測通過與否，其參數按照預設值進行訓練。而 SBERT 向量化方式則會將多個句向量進行平均加總或用 LSTM 進行串接，其串接方式會以最多句子數之段落為基準，若有段落句子數小於其數量則會進行 padding，以其能不影響訓練又能不失去最多句子數之資訊，接著使用 PyTorch[7]之框架進行准駁預測訓練，其中會以 Adam 為優化器，並將起始的學習率設定為 2e-3，loss function 使用 PyTorch 提供的 Binary Cross Entropy，batch_size 設為 32，epoch 則設為 10。

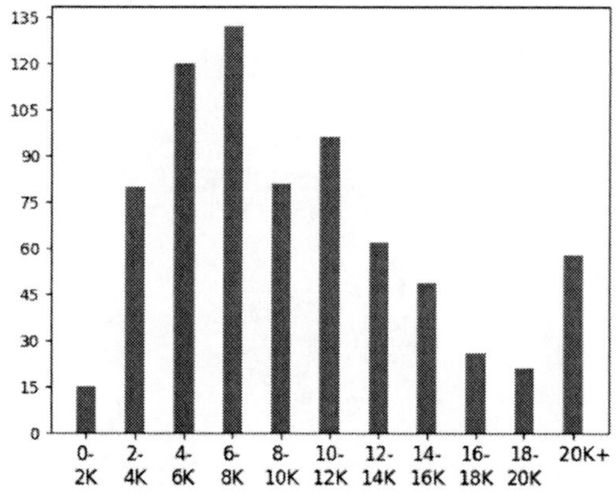

圖 2. 為真實扶養金額分佈

6 准駁預測模型結果

預測結果如表2所示。由下表可見，在資料規模較小的情況下，TF-IDF 搭配 logistic regression 會較 SBERT轉換向量來得好，其 F_1 score 會來到 0.788。

理論上當新案例進入該准駁預測模型後，若判斷為不駁回者才繼續進入下文所提之扶養金額預測模型，但此研究為了更準確地建構金額預測模型，故不採用准駁預測模型模型判斷後分類為通過之案例，而是採用真實通過且經前段 (本文段落 3) 所提條件過濾之案例。

7 扶養金額預測之前處理與特徵提取

圖 2 為真實扶養金額分佈圖，真實扶養金額之均值為 9606.95 元，其中扶養金的金額預測我們以客觀特徵為基礎並以「按月給付」之金

[7] https://pytorch.org/tutorials/beginner/basics/buildmodel_tutorial.html

特徵名稱	簡稱	定義
Consume	C	聲請人現居地平均每人每月消費支出、最低消費基準
Grant	G	聲請人每月補助金
Others	O	聲請人每月額外所需開銷
Ask	A	聲請人請求之金額
Persons	P	相對人數
numChilds	N	具扶養義務之人數
Income	I	相對人之每月收入總和
Estate	E	相對人之財產總和
n_income	N_I	扶養義務人之每月收入總和
n_estate	N_E	扶養義務人之財產總和

表 3. 主要特徵

額為主要預測結果，其中若相對人為複數時，實驗中會視多個相對人合併為一個相對人，因此將主文段落中所有相對人各自「按月給付」之金額進行加總，作為模型預測之對照真值。

再以人工進行8種主要客觀特徵之提取，會使用此8種主要特徵的原因在於觀察到法院裁判之理由段落是以這些特徵為主要考量計算，但由於此模型望能在將來提供兩造進行調解，而此階段並不會有法官參與，因此所謂客觀特徵便是在避免擷取到法院裁判之理由段落中法官的考量，其會根據自己的心證得出聲請人所需的扶養金額。而採用人工提取特徵是為了確保提取之準確，避免給予模型不正確的特徵值，提取概要如以下所述。

Consume，以下簡稱 C，以行政院公佈之各縣市人月均消[8]為基準，代表聲請人每月之可能開銷。

Grant，以下簡稱 G，以裁判書中聲請人自承或法官依職權調閱補助領取紀錄，係代表聲請人每月可用於補貼開銷之金額。

Others，以下簡稱 O，以聲請人自承並附以相關物證 (如收據) 或人證 (傳換證人之證稱)，其表聲請人每月額外開銷，以上三者係構成聲請人每月開銷之主要客觀特徵。

Ask，以下簡稱 A，則為聲請人主觀認定每月所須之生活所資。

Persons，以下簡稱 P、Numchilds，以下簡稱 N，則分別為該案件中相對人數及具扶養義務人數，可用於計算案件中相對人須負擔扶養金額之比例，因此本模型首先會對上述特徵進行判斷預測其可能之初步裁判金額。

Income，以下簡稱 I、Estate 以下簡稱 E，分別代表相對人月收及財產，皆為法官依職權調閱之年度財產所得申報資料，即相對人之財力狀況與負擔能力，並可能影響扶養金額調整，因此本模型會採用客觀數據 (行政院公佈之國民所得中位數[9]及基本薪資[10]) 及其他特徵來進行來對初步裁判金額進行分類，區分是否需進一步調整。

N_income，以下簡稱 N_I、N_estate，以下簡稱 N_E，代表扶養義務人之財力狀況即負擔能力，並可能影響扶養金額調整，最終調整之部分會採用 N_I, N_E 及聲請人離家等其他客觀特徵來進行來對需調整案件之裁判金額進行最終調整。

以上主要特徵資訊整理如表 3，其次林玠鋒 (2015) 有提出法官會因聲請人的不良行為或相對人的財力狀況而對扶養金額有所調整[11]，因此我們將其稱為輔助特徵，並將其整理如表 4 所示。

然而在實務上並不會預先有判決書，所以我們假設在庭外調解時，兩造可如實告訴此模型相關特徵，而在庭上調解時由法官依職權調取資料以及關係人之證詞進而抽取該特徵來進行預測。

8 金額預測模型設計

本實驗金額預測模型即為一 model tree，透過特定規則將案件歸屬於某個分支，若分到最

8 https://www.stat.gov.tw/ct.asp?xItem=40875&ctNode=511&mp=4

9 https://www.dgbas.gov.tw/ct.asp?xItem=47996&ctNode=5624

10 https://www.mol.gov.tw/1607/28162/28166/28180/28182/28184/29016/

11 民法 1115、1118、1118-1、1119，家事事件法 99~103、107.1、126

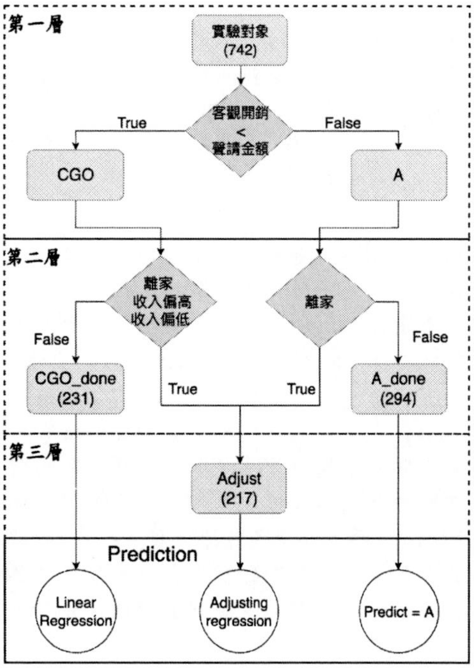

圖 3. 金額預測模型架構

終節點時則進入該節點的預測模型，各層功能大致上為：試算初步裁判金額、決定是否進一步調整金額、需調整者對其進行調整，大致架構如下列各點所述及圖 3 所示。

8.1 Model tree 各層設計

P 第一層先試算出聲請人每月客觀所需開銷 (C − G + O) 再乘以相對人對於具扶養義務人之佔比 (P/N)，稱其為客觀金額。

$$客觀金額 = (C-G+O)\frac{P}{N} \quad (1)$$

並與 A 進行比較大小，若試算金額較小則歸為「CGO」，反之則歸為「A」，若兩者相同則歸為「A」，依此區分出 「CGO」 及「A」兩部份。

第二層則繼前一層區分出「CGO」和「A」後，要再進一步區分是否需進行調整，區分條件如下：「CGO」部分的案件會考量聲請人是否有離家、賭博、酗酒及家暴等事由，且以訴訟開始年份之國民最低薪資與中位數薪資判斷相對人之財力狀況。

「A」部分則因聲請人要求已比客觀數據來得低(見圖 3 第一層判斷)，若非聲請人對相對人有未盡扶養之事實，法官不太會再根據相

特徵名稱	簡稱	定義
Adjust_label_1	A1	聲請人是否有不良嗜好或積欠債務
Adjust_label_2	A2	聲請人是否被相對人家暴
Adjust_label_3	A3	聲請人是否有家暴行為
Adjust_label_4	A4	聲請人是否離家未善盡照顧相對人
Higher income	H_I	相對人人均月薪是否比該年薪資中位數高
Lower income	L_I	相對人人均月薪是否比該年最低薪資低
Rate of Income	R_I	$\frac{I/P}{N\_I/N}$
Rate of Estate	R_E	$\frac{E/P}{N\_E/N}$

表 4. 輔助特徵

對人財力狀況進行調整，因此只針對聲請人有離家、賭博、酗酒及家暴等事由進行判斷。

若判斷後不需調整則歸為「Done」其預測結果即為初步預測金額，反之則歸為「Adjust」便會進入下一層進行調整。

關於第三層，除上述二層提及之主要特徵外，會再多增加考量聲請人之不良行為或相對人之於所有具扶養義務人財力比較等 8 個輔助特徵 (參考表 4)，以此針對「Adjust」之預測金額進行調整。最終該模型呈現三個分支並在各分支使用不同預測方式，最後會將各分支 MAE 進行加權計算以得出整體模型之結果。

8.2 Model tree 各分支對應預測方式介紹

關於上段所提三分支之預測方式如下：

「A_done」分支中案件已比相對客觀之主要特徵來得低，表示聲請人可能已考量其他因素後所提出的聲請金額，且法官無其他理由進行上調，而下調者則應會在第二層 (圖 3) 區分至「Adjust」故可直接採用聲請人要求之金額作為最終預測之結果。

關於「CGO_done」，由於以客觀特徵試算出的金額仍可能有些微波動，故會將此分支以 8 比 2 方式切割訓練資料與測試資料並丟入 scikit-learn 的 linear regression 進行隨機 split 訓練，其回歸預測即為最終預測之結果。

Data_group (num)	Only SKL LinearRegs.	SKL with M.T.	本文模型
Ask_done (294)	-	1961.45	1351.29
CGO_done (231)	-	1935.77	1935.77
Adjust (217)	-	3170.60	3033.98
Total (742)	2751.78	2310.73	2028.02

表5. 各模型MAE比較

「Adjust」分支模型我們以倍率調整的構思進行設計，因此我們提出：

$$Predict_i = X_i * \prod_{j=1}^{8} Features_j^{weight_j} \quad (2)$$

，不過我們會進行對數轉換，轉換成：

$$\log Predict_i = \log X_i + \sum_{j=1}^{8} weight_j * \log Features_j \quad (3)$$

以利進行回歸預測，其中 i為案件，X_i為初步預測金額。

以下進行舉例說明，假設第三層train完後的 weight=[0.2, 0.3, -0.5, -0.6, 0.1, -0.2, 0, 0.4]，且某案件第一層初步預測結果為100又該案輔助特徵=[1, 1, 1, 2, 1, 1, 1.2, 1.2]，則其調整為：

$$100 \times 1^{.2} \times 1^{.3} \times 1^{-.5} \times 2^{-.6} \times 1^{.1} \times 1^{-.2} \times 1.2^{0} \times 1.2^{.4}$$
$$= 100 \times (1 \times 1 \times 1 \times 0.66 \times 1 \times 1 \times 1 \times 1.0756)$$
$$\approx 70.96$$

並將70.96作為最終預測結果。

當前六者 (A1 到 A4, H_I, L_I)為是時，標註為 2，為否則標註為 1；後二者 (R_I, R_E)則如表 4 之計算。

由上述舉例可見當特定輔助特徵之 training weight 為 0 或其標註為 1 時並不會影響調整，故我們利用此對數特性提出該分支模型。.

9 扶養金額預測結果比較

本研究以不用model tree且單純使用scikit-learn的 linear regression (以下簡稱 Only SKL LinearRegs.)、使用model tree且每個分支一樣單純使用scikit-learn的linear regression (以下簡稱 SKL with M.T.) 及本文模型進行實驗結果比較。

Only SKL LinearRegs.採用全部通過案件資料及上述提及之特徵，並不使用 model tree 進行分支故只有總合之結果；SKL with M.T. 則使用 model tree 且各分支進行相同迴歸預測 (scikit-learn 的 linear regression) 並將其結果以各分支判例數量加權計算總和結果；本文模型則為使用 model tree 但各分支皆不同預測方式 (詳見本文 9.1 到 9.3 段落)，再以各分支判例數量加權計算總和結果，所有預測模型皆以 8 比 2 進行分割，並採 1000 次隨機 split 實驗結果之 MAE 平均，再將三者進行比較，其 MAE 比較結果如下表所示 (表 5)。

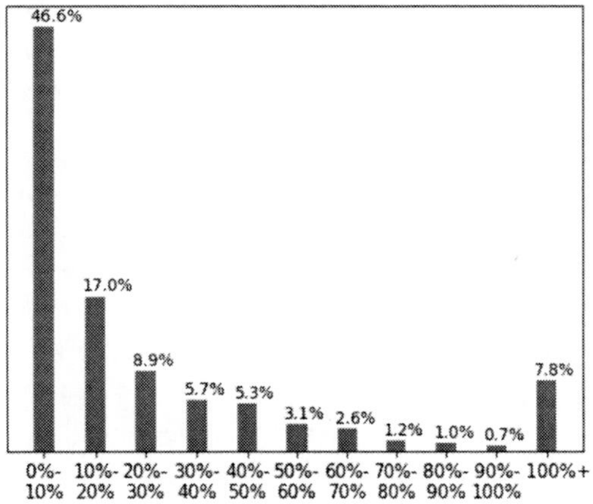

圖4. AE與真實值之比值

由表 5 可見，從整體的 MAE 比較可看出不使用 model tree (即 Only SKL LinearRegs.) 與使用 model tree (即 SKL with M.T.)，相比後者有較好的表現；且單純使用 model tree (即 SKL with M.T.) 與針對不同區塊使用對應之預測方式及調整 (即本文模型)，本文模型的結果也較前者優秀。

圖 4 則展現我們提出的模型預測值與真實答案誤差之比值統計，可看出超過六成可以控制在 20%以內。

10 實驗總結

關於准駁預測模型部分，針對所選之比較模型與前處理仍有以下可改良之部份：

對於 TF-IDF 應可增加對於相似詞進行統一化之前處理，以避免不同詞頻之近似字詞導致不同向量結果，進而影響准駁預測之可能。而對於 SBERT 模型，由於採用句向量，可能抹平主張之特徵段落而導致預測與模型學習不易，因此，採用 SBERT 搭配 LSTM 及

SBERT 加權平均當作深度學習之代表，並得出「TF-IDF 搭配 logistic regression 會較 SBERT 轉換向量來得好」此一結論或有不夠周全之處。

關於金額預測模型部分，我們採用盡可能客觀且常見之特徵，如：行政院主計處公告之當地月均消、相對人年度申報所得、聲請人是否曾家暴相對人等，以期能在有限且僅裁判書所提之特徵 (8 個主要特徵與 8 個輔助特徵)亦不過擬合 (overfit)的前提下進行訓練與預測，但仍有以下考量不足之處：

本實驗將所有相對人之扶養金額進行加總預測，而非針對個別相對人進行預測，因此無法在相對人為複數且扶養義務不盡相同時進行準確預測。關於金額預測模型中第三層部分，盡可能採用較為通用而直觀之輔助特徵，如：聲請人是否曾家暴相對人等 (表 4. A1 到 A4 部分)，但為了不造成過擬合亦可能有缺漏之輔助特徵，故儘管成效較僅使用 linear regression 之結果佳，不過仍有進步空間。

11 結語

儘管如上段所言，兩模型於設計或結果上仍有缺漏亦可進步之處，但我們仍望提供未來請求扶養費案件中之兩造乃至法官一客觀參考基準，或能在不久之將來對於相關輔助應用有所貢獻。

致謝

本研究承國科會研究計畫 107-2221-E-004-009 -MY3 與 110-2221-E-004-008-MY3 與國立政治大學高教深耕校內補助計畫 111H124D-13 之部分補助，謹此致謝。

參考文獻

Jim-How Ho. 2021. AI 引入民事程序可行性之研究 (The feasibility research on introducing artificial intelligence into civil procedures) [In Chinese]. Doctoral Dissertation, Department of Information Management, National Taiwan University of Science and Technology. https://hdl.handle.net/11296/pkvh27.

黃詩淳和邵軒磊. 2020. 以人工智慧讀取親權酌定裁判文本: 自然語言與文字探勘之實踐. *臺大法學論叢 NTULawJournal*, 49 (1): 196-218.

黃詩淳. 2022. 老親扶養費酌定裁判之實證研究. *台灣大學數位智能法院、法律科技與接近正義研討會.*

林玠鋒. 2015. 論家事財產法上法院之裁量調控 - 以扶養費、家庭生活費用及贍養費之酌付為中心 (Regulation of the Judicial Discretion in Domestic Property Law：Focusing on the Determination of Maintenance, Living Expenses of the Household, and Alimony) [In Chinese]. *國立政治大學法律學系所.* https://thesis.lib.nccu.edu.tw/cgi-bin/gs32/gsweb.cgi?o=dallcdr&s=id=%22G0096651501%22.&searchmode=basic#XXXX.

Wan-Chen Lin, Tsung-Ting Kuo, Tung-Jia Chang, Chueh-An Yen, Chao-Ju Chen, and Shou-de Lin. 2012. 利用機器學習於中文法律文件之標記、案件分類及量刑預測 (Exploiting Machine Learning Models for Chinese Legal Documents Labeling, Case Classification, and Sentencing Prediction)[In Chinese]. In *Proceedings of the 24th Conference on Computational Linguistics and Speech Processing (ROCLING 2012)*, pages 140–141. https://aclanthology.org/O12-1013/.

Donato Malerba, Floriana Esposito, Michelangelo Ceci and Annalisa Appice. 2004. Top-down induction of model trees with regression and splitting nodes. In *IEEE Transactions on Pattern Analysis and Machine Intelligence (Volume: 26, Issue: 5, May 2004).* https://ieeexplore.ieee.org/stamp/stamp.jsp?tp=&arnumber=1273937&isnumber=28505.

Fabrice Muhlenbach, Long Nguyen Phuoc and Isabelle Sayn. 2020. Predicting Court Decisions for Alimony: Avoiding Extra-legal Factors in Decision made by Judges and Not Understandable AI Models. arXiv:2007.04824.

Nils Reimers, Iryna Gurevych. 2019. Sentence-BERT: Sentence Embeddings using Siamese BERT-Network. arXiv:1908.10084.

The 34th Conference on Computational Linguistics and Speech Processing (ROCLING 2022)
Taipei, Taiwan, November 21-22, 2022. The Association for Computational Linguistics and Chinese Language Processing

結構性重參數化 VGG 架構之輕量化聲音事件偵測模型
Lightweight Sound Event Detection Model with RepVGG Architecture

劉家全 Chia-Chuan Liu, 黃頌仁 Sung-Jen Huang, 陳嘉平 Chia-Ping Chen
國立中山大學資訊工程學系
National Sun Yat-sen University
Department of Computer Science and Engineering
{m103040063, m093040011}@student.nsysu.edu.tw,
cpchen@cse.nsysu.edu.tw
呂仲理 Chung-Li Lu, 詹博丞 Bo-Cheng Chan, 鄭羽涵 Yu-Han Cheng,
莊向峰 Hsiang-Feng Chuang, 陳威妤 Wei-Yu Chen
中華電信研究院
Chunghwa Telecom Laboratories
{chungli, cbc, henacheng, gotop, weiweichen}@cht.com.tw

摘要

本文中提出以模型輕量化為目標的聲音事件偵測 RepVGGRNN 模型。其於卷積層使用 RepVGG 卷積塊，透過殘差連接的網路結構使模型達到良好的效能，並於模型訓練完畢後透過結構重參數化使得卷積參數得以縮減。此外，其於訓練階段合併使用知識蒸餾及均值教師模型之訓練方法進一步提昇輕量化模型之預測準確度。RepVGGRNN 在 DCASE 2022 Task4 驗證集中，PSDS(Polyphonic sound event detection score)-scenario 1, 2 分別以 40.8%, 67.7% 優於官方 baseline 系統所達到的 34.4%, 57.2%，並在模型參數量上，RepVGGRNN 使用的參數量約為 49.6 萬，僅 baseline 系統之 44.6%。

Abstract

In this paper, we proposed RepVGGRNN, which is a light weight sound event detection model. We use RepVGG convolution blocks in the convolution part to improve performance, and re-parameterize the RepVGG blocks after the model is trained to reduce the parameters of the convolution layers. To further improve the accuracy of the model, we incorporated both the mean teacher method and knowledge distillation to train the lightweight model. The proposed system achieves PSDS (Polyphonic sound event detection score)-scenario 1, 2 of 40.8% and 67.7% outperforms the baseline system of 34.4% and 57.2% on the DCASE 2022 Task4 validation dataset. The quantity of the parameters in the proposed system is about 49.6K, only 44.6% of the baseline system.

關鍵字：聲音事件偵測、輕量化模型、知識蒸餾

Keywords: Sound event detection, Light weight model, Knowledge distillation

1 緒論

聲音事件偵測主要是利用機器來辨識聲音訊號中是否存在特定事件，而機器除了辨識音訊中的事件類別外，亦需標註事件發生的起始時間與終止時間，隨著 DCASE challenge Task4 競賽的舉行，此研究項目亦成為了熱門的音訊處理研究主題之一，許多企業如三星 (Chen et al., 2022), LG(Kim and Yang, 2022) 亦一同參與競賽。在應用上，隨著移動端裝置及物聯網裝置的興起，結合聲音事件偵測的應用如 smart home, smart speaker 也隨之提出，為日常生活帶來諸多便利性，但受限於硬體上的限制，使得需要高度運算資源的高複雜網路模型不利於佈署在這些裝置上，像是中國語音技術團隊 (Zheng et al., 2021) 在卷積層採用多分支卷積注意力機制，使得模型推論時占用較大的記憶體空間與計算量，而日本名古屋大學團隊 (Miyazaki et al., 2020) 使用 CNN 與 Transformer 結構，使得模型推論一筆音檔時需要較高的運算成本，這些網路模型雖然在事件偵測上有著高度的準確度，但其高

度運算需求之特性亦可能影響使用者的體驗。在本篇論文中，我們以模型輕量化爲目標提出 RepVGGRNN 模型，此模型在架構上採用近年來 DCASE challenge Task4 參賽隊伍主流採用的 CRNN 結構，並在 CNN 的部分參考 RepVGG (Ding et al., 2021) 卷積塊，於訓練時使用多分支殘差連接 (He et al., 2016) 協助訓練卷積層參數，並在訓練完畢後透過結構重參數化將 RepVGG 精簡爲 VGG (Simonyan and Zisserman, 2014) 使得模型整體推論時僅使用單一分支 3×3 卷積層進行運算，相較於 MobileNet (Howard et al., 2017) 透過深度可分離式卷積 (Depthwise separable convolution) 減少參數量，RepVGG 則是應用結構重參數化將原先複雜的多分支卷積簡化爲單一分支卷積達到模型參數與運算時間上的縮減。除了模型結構上的精進，我們於訓練階段中合併使用知識蒸餾 (Hinton et al., 2015) 與均值教師模型 (Tarvainen and Valpola, 2017) 之訓練方法來改善輕量化模型不易於訓練的問題，使整體模型兼具輕量及高準確性等特色。本文中其餘的章節將如下編排：章節二：研究方法，描述了模型架構與訓練方式；章節三：實驗設置，描述網路參數之設置以及評估指標；章節四：實驗結果，對比 RepVGGRNN 與 baseline 模型、預訓練模型之間的差異；章節五：結論，總結了我們所提出系統的特色。

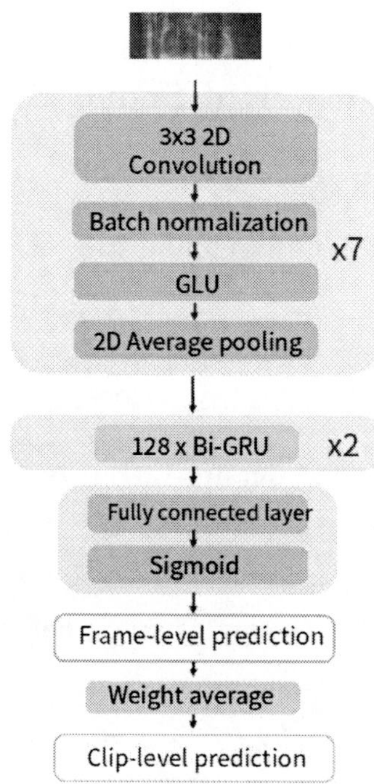

圖 1. Baseline 系統：整體爲 CRNN 模型，輸入特徵會先經 7 層卷積網路進行特徵擷取，並透過 2 層雙向門控循環單元與全連階層產生強預測結果與弱預測結果。

2 研究方法

本章節描述 baseline 與 RepVGGRNN 模型之間架構上的差異，後者於卷積層中使用 RepVGG 卷積塊使得模型在訓練階段透過不同分支卷積得以學習多尺度特徵擷取，除了模型本身的架構外，我們於訓練階段合併使用知識蒸餾及均值教師模型提高資料本身的使用度，進一步提升模型本身的效能，並且使用 mixup (Zhang et al., 2017) 資料增強來減緩模型過擬合等現象。

2.1 Baseline 模型

本文中以 DCASE Task4 官方所提供的 CRNN 模型 (Turpault et al., 2019) 作爲 baseline 系統，模型整體如圖 1 所示使用 7 層卷積網路層連接 2 層循環網路層，在卷積層的部分，每層使用 3×3 大小的卷積核，各層濾波器的數量分別爲 16, 32, 64, 128, 128, 128, 128 個，並以門控線性單元 (Gated Linear Unit,GLU) 作爲激勵函數, 以及在各層卷積層中使用批標準化 (Batch normalization) 與 dropout ，最後，每層卷積層運算完畢後會再進行平均池化，平均池化視窗的大小依序爲 2×2, 2×2, 1×2, 1×2, 1×2, 1×2 與 1×2。在循環網路層的部分爲 2 層雙向門控循環單元 (Bidirectional Gated Recurrent Unit) ，各層具 128 個神經元，最後透過一層全連接層與 S 型函數 (Sigmoid function) 產生該筆輸入音檔的強標註預測 (Strong prediction)，此預測結果包含了預測的事件類別與該事件所發生的時間界線，接著將強標註預測依各類時間維度使用注意力池化 (Attention pooling) 取權重平均來產生該筆音檔的弱標註預測 (Weak prediction)，此預測結果相比於強標註預測，僅包含事件類別而無時間界線上的註記。

2.2 RepVGGRNN 模型

因應模型輕量化的目標，我們透過修改 baseline 系統的架構來達到減少參數量的效果，在卷積層中，層數由原先的 7 層縮減至 5 層，並在結構上參考 RepVGG 卷積塊，內部結構如圖 2 所示，單一卷積層於訓練時包含了 3 個分支，分別爲 3×3 卷積, 1×1 卷積與恆等層，並且各卷積皆連接批標準化層，與 residual network 殘差連接的網路設計相似，各分支的輸出會進行加總並在運用線性整流函數 (Rectified Linear Unit, ReLU) 後作爲 RepVGG 卷

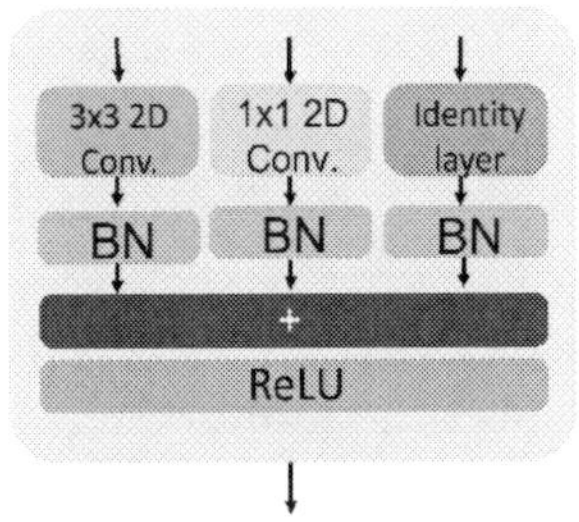

圖 2. RepVGG 卷積塊：訓練階段時共有三個分支卷積，依卷積核的大小分爲 3×3、1×1 與恆等層。

積塊的輸出。多分支卷積相比於單一分支在模型推論時通常佔用了較大的記憶體空間，因此 RepVGG 卷積塊在模型訓練完畢後再透過結構重參數化 (Structure re-parameterization) 將 1×1 卷積分支, 恆等分支合併至 3×3 卷積分支來縮小空間佔用率及整體模型的參數量，結構重參數化共分爲三個步驟 (1) 將各分支卷積所連接之批標準化層合併至卷積層中，以 RepVGG 中的 3×3 卷積分支爲例，令其輸入維度、輸出維度分別爲 c_{in}, c_{out} ，卷積核爲 $W\in R^{c_{out}\times c_{in}\times3\times3}$，輸入特徵及輸出特徵分別爲 $F\in R^{N\times c_{in}\times T\times F}$ 與 $\hat{F}\in R^{N\times c_{out}\times T'\times F'}$ ，當中的 N 爲批次中的資料筆數且 T, F 爲時間維度與頻率維度大小，則該分支卷積輸出 $\hat{F}$ 各 *channel* 維度特徵 $\hat{F}_{:,i,:,:}\ \forall i, 1\leq i\leq c_{out}$ 爲第 i 個卷積核 $W_{i,:,:,:}$ 與輸入特徵 F 經卷積運算與標準化後的結果，如以下等式：

$$\hat{F}_{:,i,:,:}=\gamma_i\frac{(W_{i,:,:,:}*F)-\mu_i}{\sqrt{\sigma_i^2+\epsilon}}+\beta_i \quad (1)$$

，其中 γ_i , μ_i , σ_i^2 , β_i 表示第 i 個 *channel* 其批標準化層之參數，而 $*$ 爲卷積運算子，爲了將批標準化層之參數合併至卷積層中，令 $W'_{i,:,:,:}$ 與 β'_i 分別爲第 i 個卷稽核在合併批標準化後的參數與偏差值爲以下等式：

$$W'_{i,:,:,:}=\frac{\gamma_i}{\sqrt{\sigma_i^2+\epsilon}}W_{i,:,:,:} \quad (2)$$

$$\beta'_i=\beta_i-\frac{\gamma_i\mu_i}{\sqrt{\sigma_i^2+\epsilon}} \quad (3)$$

，則此時可將公式 1 透過 W'_i, β'_i 簡化爲

$$\hat{F}_{:,i,:,:}=W'_{i,:,:,:}*F+\beta'_i \quad (4)$$

完成批標準化參數的合併 (2) 將合併批標準化層之 1×1 卷積層、恆等層透過補 0 的方式將卷積核擴張爲 3×3 卷積 (3) 將擴張完成的卷積透過卷積運算之可加性將 1×1 卷積, 恆等層之參數合併至 3×3 卷積中以完成結構重參數化，經上述步驟後即可將原先多分支的卷積合併爲單一 3×3 卷積，整體流程可參考圖 3。RepVGG 原作者在卷積層之輸入特徵維度與輸出特徵維度不相同時並無使用恆等層，因此我們稍微了修改其設置，當輸入特徵圖的維度與輸出特徵圖的維度不相同時恆等層會以 3×3 卷積層做取代，使其整體網路保有三分支卷積的結構。RepVGGRNN 各層卷積的濾波器數量爲 16, 32, 64, 128, 128 個，並且在前三層中皆堆疊了兩層的 RepVGG 卷積塊，後兩層中各僅使用一層。循環網路層的部分我們將 baseline 中的 2 層雙向門控循環單元縮減至 1 層，而全連接層的部分與 baseline 系統相同，並以強標籤預測與弱標籤預測來作爲模型最終的輸出。

2.3 合併知識蒸餾與均值教師模型

有鑑於網路模型在縮減架構的同時也犧牲了精準度上的表現，因此我們透過合併使用知識蒸餾與均值教師模型來協助輕量化模型進行訓練，使得輕量化模型除了保有輕巧的特色外，亦能維持住相當水準的性能。

知識蒸餾是模型壓縮經常使用到的訓練方法，利用預訓練好的高複雜度模型 (我們稱爲預訓練教師模型) 來引導低複雜度模型 (我們稱爲學生模型) 進行訓練，使得預訓練教師模型具有的高精準度與泛化能力能夠遷移至學生模型上，而均值教師模型是近年來半監督式學習 (Semi-supervised learning) 中主流使用的訓練方法，與知識蒸餾間的相似之處在於，均值教師模型亦存在老師模型與學生模型的概念，不同的是在均值教師模型當中，兩者是完全相同的網路模型，而在訓練時，透過對於同一筆輸入資料之輸出，學生模型的預測除了需貼近眞實標注資料外，也必須與老師模型之預測結果相近，透過保持學生模型與老師模型間的一致性，也使得未具有標注的資料被充分的利用。在實做中，我們合併使用了知識蒸餾與均值教師模型，使用了三個模型分別爲預訓練教師模型與均值教師結構的 RepVGGRNN 模型，使得模型在訓練初期透過預訓練教師模型提供可靠的預測標籤供學生模型進行參考，而在均值教師結構的模型中透過移動平均更新的方式，使均值教師模型更近一步提升精準度。我們令均值教師中學生模型的預測結果與三者計算差值，分別爲 (1) 眞實標籤 (爲 Supervised loss) (2) 預訓練教師模型的預測結果 (爲 Knowledge distillation loss) (3) 均值教師模型中老師模型的預測結果 (爲

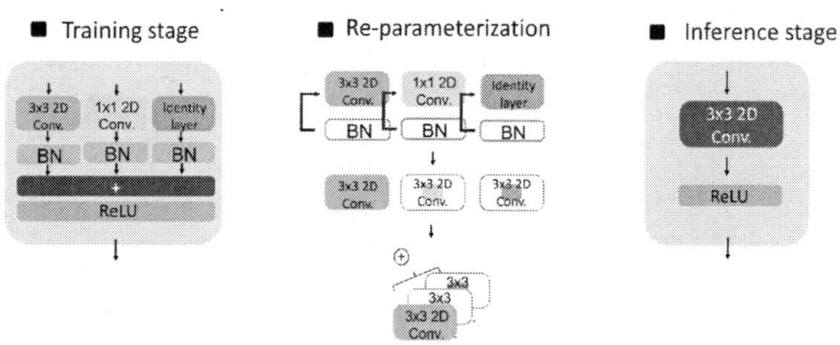

圖 3. RepVGG 重參數化：當模型訓練完畢後 RepVGG 透過結構重參數化將 1×1 卷積、恆等層之參數合併至 3×3 卷積層中，使其變爲單一分支卷積結構。

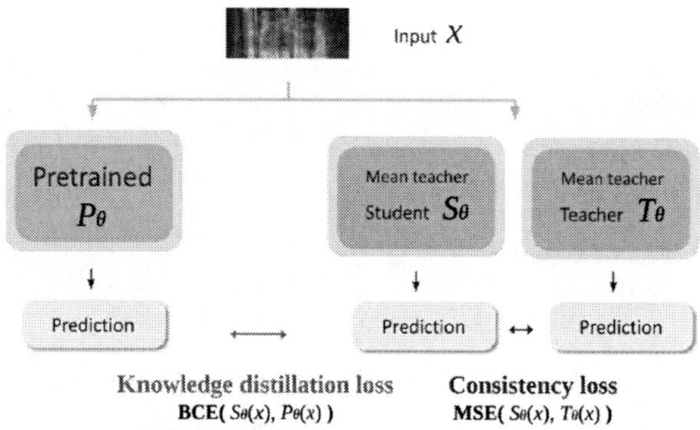

圖 4. 合併知識蒸餾與均值教師模型：學生模型在損失函數的計算上共有三個來源，分別是與 Ground-truth 之間的差值、預訓練模型之輸出間的差值以及均值教師模型中教師模型之間的差值。

Consistency loss) ，其損失函數如下:

$$L_{student} = L_{Supervised} + L_{KD} + L_{Consistency} * w \quad (5)$$

。由於均值教師模型於訓練初期有著較差的準確性，所以其權重 w 會先設爲 0，隨著訓練的進行再逐步調高其權重。在參數的更新中，僅有學生模型會參與反向傳播的更新，待更新完畢後再以指數移動平均 (Exponential moving average) 之方式利用學生模型之參數更新教師模型，如下公式:

$$\theta'_t = \alpha\theta'_{t-1} + (1-\alpha)\theta_t \quad (6)$$

，其中，θ'、θ 分別代表教師模型與學生模型之參數，t 代表當前的訓練 step ，而 α 是介於 0 至 1 之間的權重，整體訓練流程可參考圖 4 。

2.4 預訓練教師模型

預訓練教師模型使用的是 VGGSKCCT 模型，該模型於卷積層使用殘差連接使得模型在有較深的卷積層數下也能減緩梯度消失的現象而有較佳的效能，並於卷積層間使用選擇性內核單元 (Selective kernel unit) (Li et al., 2019) ，透過不同大小的卷積核與注意力機制使得模型在不同事件的偵測準確率上能有效的提昇。整體模型之溫度參數 (Temperature parameter) 設置爲 2，並使用不同資料增強方式與 fusion 多個訓練結果來進一步提升模型效能，模型 fusion 的數量爲 3 個。

2.5 資料增強

模型訓練時對原始資料進行輕微的擾動可減緩過擬合的現象，我們參照了 DCASE Task4 所使用的資料增強方式，對同一批中的強標籤註記資料與弱標籤註記資料各自隨機成對進行 mixup，過程如下列公式所示:

$$x' = \lambda x_i + (1-\lambda)x_j \quad (7)$$

$$y' = \lambda y_i + (1-\lambda)y_j \quad (8)$$

，x_i 與 x_j 爲隨機兩筆同一批且具同性質標籤之資料，而 y_i 與 y_j 爲其各自的眞實標籤，經過介於 0 至 1 之間的權重係數 λ 進行線性組合後，所得 x' 與 y' 即爲經過 mixup 所得之資料與標籤。

3 實驗設置

本節將描述實驗所採用的相關設置，包括：模型所使用的訓練集與測試集、特徵前處理方式、整體訓練時中的學習率設置及模型所採用的評估指標等。

3.1 資料集

	資料筆數	類型	原始採樣率
強標籤訓練集	13470	眞實錄製或合成	44.1kHz/16kHz
弱標籤訓練集	1578	眞實錄製	44.1kHz
無標籤訓練集	10000	眞實錄製	44.1kHz
強標籤驗證集	1168	眞實錄製	44.1kHz
公開測試集	699	眞實錄製	44.1kHz

表 1. DESED 訓練集與測試集其資料筆數、類型與原始採樣率

資料集使用 DCASE 2022 Task4 提供的 DESED(Domestic Environment Sound Event Detection dataset) 資料集做爲模型的訓練與評估。每筆音檔的長度爲 10 秒，依標籤註記種類的不同分爲 (1) 強標籤資料: 音檔標籤包含了事件類別並註記事件的起始時間與終止時間 (2) 弱標籤資料: 音檔的標籤僅註記事件的類別 (3) 無標籤資料: 音檔沒有提供任何相關的標籤註記。各類音檔筆數分別爲 13470、1578、10000 筆。

測試集以 DESED 提供的驗證集 (Validation dataset) 與公開測試集 (Public evaluation dataset) 作爲模型的評估，各測試集中的資料筆數分別爲 1168 筆與 692 筆，並且每筆音檔皆具有強標籤的注記，詳細內容如表 1。

3.2 音訊特徵擷取

由於 DESED 資料集中的音檔存在採樣率、聲道不一致與音檔長度存在不一致的情形，因此我們使用 librosa 套件將所有音檔統一爲 16000 Hz、單聲道並透過補 0 之方式將各音檔長度塡補至 12 秒，並將波型訊號 (Waveform) 轉換爲梅爾頻譜圖 (Mel-spectrogram) 並取 log 作爲網路模型的輸入，在參數設置上，我們以窗口大小 (Window size) 爲 2048、框擷取步伐 (Hop length) 爲 256 進行短時傅立葉變換，最後經由 128 個梅爾濾波器 (Mel-filter bank) 產生維度大小爲 751(時間維度)、128(頻率維度) 的梅爾頻譜圖。

3.3 參數設置

所有的實驗結果皆使用相同的參數設置，每個網路模型皆訓練 200 個 epoch ，在優化器的部分我們使用 ADAM 演算法，並於前 50 個 epoch 應用 exponential warm-up 策略，初始學習率會以趨近於 0 的極小值隨著訓練步伐的增加而遞增，至第 50 個 epoch 時學習率會遞增至最大值 0.001。

3.4 評估指標

Polyphonic sound event detection score (PSDS)(Bilen et al., 2020) 適用於評估模型於多類別聲音事件預測上的準確性，其在模型預測與眞實標籤之間依序透過 (1) 檢測容差標準 (Detection Tolerance Criterion): 事件預測標籤與眞實標籤間的交集是否超過 DTC 門檻 (2) 眞實標籤交集標準 (Ground Truth intersection Criterion): 眞實標籤是否存在 (通過 DTC 門檻的) 事件預測標籤與其交集超過 GTC 門檻 (3) 交叉觸發容差標準 (Cross-Trigger Tolerance Criterion): 事件預測標籤在時間上的預測正確但類別錯誤，分別計算眞陽性 (True positive): 通過 DTC 與 GTC 的事件、僞陽性 (False positive): 未通過 DTC 的事件、與跨類別觸發事件 (Cross-Trigger): 未通過 DTC 但通過 CTTC 的事件，接著再透過 TP, FP 與 CT 來計算最終的 PSDS。我們參考 DCASE 2022 task 4 的參數設置，使用兩個參數設置分別爲 PSDS-scenario1(簡稱 PSDS-1) 與 PSDS-scenario2(簡稱 PSDS-2) 來作爲指標，分別將三者門檻比率分別設置爲 0.7、0.7、0，該參數對於事件預測在時間區間的精準度上有著較高的要求，而後者則是設爲 0.1、0.1、0.3，著重於事件類別預測的正確性。

除了模型的效能外我們也評估了模型的資源使用量，分別統計了模型的參數量與浮點數運算次數 (Floating Point Operations, FLOPs)，前者分析模型於記憶體空間之佔用量，後者則是評估模型推論時之計算複雜度。使用的套件是 Pytorch 第三方函式庫 THop，此套件可用於統計 Pytorch 模型上的參數量及浮點數運算資訊，我們使用當中的 profile 函式統計模型之參數量與模型推論一筆 10 秒鐘音檔所需的 FLOPs 作爲實驗結果之數據。

4 實驗結果

我們比較了 RepVGGRNN 分別與 baseline、VGGSKCCT 及 DCASE 2022 Task4 競賽第一名模型於效能及資源使用量間的差異。Baseline 系統的實驗結果是由我們使用官方提供的程式碼重新訓練而取得，而 DCASE 2022 Task4 第一名模型是使用官方所公佈的數據結果。此外，若模型以均值教師模型訓練，則 PSDS 分數取學生模型與教師模型各別 (PSDS-1)+(PSDS-2) 較高者爲代表。

Model	Validation dataset		Public evaluation dataset	
	PSDS-1	PSDS-2	PSDS-1	PSDS-2
Baseline(Provided by DCASE Task4)	0.344	0.572	0.385	0.546
依不同訓練方式				
RepVGGRNN(均值教師模型)	0.370	0.620	0.421	0.660
RepVGGRNN(知識蒸餾)	0.388	0.654	0.441	0.687
RepVGGRNN(合併均值教師與知識蒸餾)	**0.408**	**0.677**	**0.447**	**0.688**
預訓練教師模型				
VGGSKCCT	0.426	0.670	0.489	0.712
DCASE 2022 Task 4 第一名模型				
Ebbers UPB task4_4	0.492	0.721	-	-

表 2. 模型效能比較：呈現 baseline、RepVGGRNN、VGGSKCCT 與 DCASE 2022 Task 4 第一名模型於驗證集與公開測試集下的 PSDS 結果。

模型	參數量	浮點運算次數
VGGRNN	$4.974*10^5$	$5.418*10^8$
RepVGGRNN(Training)	$6.283*10^5$	$7.515*10^8$
RepVGGRNN(Inference)	$4.965*10^5$	$5.279*10^8$

表 3. 重參數化之比較：RepVGGRNN 重參數化前、後與 VGGRNN 在參數量與浮點運算次數中的差異，當中的數值以科學記號來表示，並將實數部份之小數點第三位以下之數值進行無條件捨去。

Model	參數量	浮點運算次數
Baseline	$1.112*10^6$	$9.309*10^8$
RepVGGRNN	$4.965*10^5$	$5.279*10^8$
VGGSKCCT	$7.485*10^6$	$1.07*10^{10}$
Ebbers UPB task4 _ 4	$1.34*10^8$	-

表 4. 各類模型資源使用量的比較：呈現各類模型在參數量與浮點數運算次數的差異。

4.1 效能比較

表 2 爲 RepVGGRNN 依訓練方式之不同，分別使用 (1) 均值教師模型 (2) 知識蒸餾 (3) 合併使用均值教師模型與知識蒸餾之 PSDS。此外，Ebbers UPB task4_4 系統數據以 DCASE Task 4 官方公佈之結果作爲呈現，因爲提交系統並沒有上傳公開驗證集上的結果，因此沒有列出該數據。在驗證集與公開驗證集中，RepVGGRNN 以均值教師模型方式訓練下，其 PSDS 要高於 baseline 系統，若使用 VGGSKCCT 透過知識蒸餾方式訓練 RepVGGRNN ，其 PSDS-1、PSDS-2 皆有所成長，由此可知利用預訓練模型提供的高準確度預測相比於均值教師模型，可使學生模型有著較佳的訓練效果，若更進一步使用知識蒸餾並維持 RepVGGRNN 之均值教師模型訓練方式，在預測效能上相比於僅使用均值教師模型，在驗證集中 PSDS-1 由 0.370 提昇至 0.408，而 PSDS-2 亦由 0.620 提昇至 0.677 ，顯示了除了預訓練模型所提供的參考預測外，均值教師模型中的教師模型參數是以學生模型參數透過指數移動平均方式來更新，因此教師模型相比於學生模型既學習到了當前資料特徵之分佈，亦較大程度的保留過往資料所學習到的特徵，使得教師模型較不易受到離群資料的影響而降低在常態資料上的預測，進一步增進模型效能。最後，RepVGGRNN 與 DCASE 2022 Task 4 第一名的模型 Ebbers UPB task4_4 相比，雖然 RepVGGRNN 透過模型架構與訓練方式的改進來提升精準度，但受限於模型本身的規模與訓練資料的使用，在預測的準確度上仍有著較大的落差。

4.2 VGG 與 RepVGG 重參數化之差異

表 3 呈現了 RepVGGRNN 進行結構重參數化前、後與一般 VGGRNN 在資源使用量之差異，當中的 VGGRNN 是將 RepVGGRNN 中的 RepVGG 替換爲 VGG 而得，若卷積層中的 RepVGG 堆疊了兩層即以同樣堆疊兩層卷積之 VGG 替代，若僅有一層 RepVGG 則以單一層卷積層取代，使兩模型在卷積層的深度相同。在參數量上，由於合併了各 RepVGG 層中的 1×1 卷積、恆等層中的 3×3 卷積與批標準化層中的參數至 3×3 卷積後，RepVGGRNN 的參數量由原先的 62.8 萬縮減至 49.6 萬，減少的幅度約爲 20.9%，並且浮點運算次數亦由 7.515 億次降至 5.279 億次，幅度爲 29.8%，顯示模型整體透過合併卷積與批標準化的方式可達到參數量與運算量的縮減。而與一般 VGG 相比，重參數化後的 RepVGGRNN 因批標準化層皆融合進了卷積層，雖然在參數量上減少的幅度不大但在整體運算量有著相對明顯的降低，由 $5.418*10^8$ 降至 $5.279*10^8$，縮減的幅度約爲 2.7%。

4.3 資源使用量比較

表 4 列出四者模型於推論時之資源使用量，當中的數據以科學記號方式表達，同時對實數位小數點第三位以下的數進行無條件捨去，其中，VGGSKCCT 因爲使用 3 個架構相同的模型做 fusion ，因此其參數量與計算量以單一模型之數據的 3 倍作爲實驗結果數據。首先比較參數量，RepVGGRNN 與 baseline 、VGGSKCCT 與 Ebbers UPB task 4_4 相比皆爲其中最少者，總參數量約爲 49.6 萬個，僅使用 baseline 參數量約 111.2 萬之 44.6%，顯示了 RepVGGRNN 透過整體架構的縮減仍可以相對較少的參數量達到接近 baseline 系統的效能，與 VGGSKCCT 系統相比，僅約其 748.5 萬參數量之 6.6%，且是 Ebbers UPB task 4_4 系統 1.34 億參數量之 0.3% 。除了空間上的占用量外，運算量亦爲輕量化模型所需縮減的目標之一，RepVGGRNN 之運算量爲三個模型中最少者，其處理單一筆資料共需約 5.279 億次浮點運算，爲 baseline 9.309 億次運算之 56.7%，且爲 VGGSKCCT 所需 107 億次運算之 8.7%，可見 RepVGGRNN 模型在重參數化與縮減模型層數後，其在資源使用上具有相當的優勢。

5 結論

近年來隨著移動式裝置的普及，結合深度學習的移動端應用亦隨之而發展，除了網路模型本身的效能外，硬體資源使用的情形如記憶體使用量、續航力與運算需求亦是模型部屬所考量的方向，透過我們的實驗結果可見，RepVGGRNN 在驗證集中以 PSDS-1 , PSDS-2 分別爲 0.408% , 0.677% 皆高於 baseline 系統所達到的 0.344%, 0.572% ，且在資源使率中其參數量僅使用約 49.6 萬個，少於 baseline 系統所具有的 111.2 萬個參數，顯示了相比於 baseline 系統，其兼具了高準確性及輕量化的特色。在未來，希望能持續增進系統並在移動端裝置實踐聲音事件偵測之相關應用。

References

Çağdaş Bilen, Giacomo Ferroni, Francesco Tuveri, Juan Azcarreta, and Sacha Krstulović. 2020. A framework for the robust evaluation of sound event detection. In *ICASSP 2020-2020 IEEE International Conference on Acoustics, Speech and Signal Processing (ICASSP)*, pages 61–65. IEEE.

Minjun Chen, Tian Wang, Jun Shao, Yiqi Tang, Yangyang Liu, Bo Peng, Jie Chen, and Xi Shao. 2022. Dcase 2022 challenge task4 technical report. Technical report, DCASE2022 Challenge.

Xiaohan Ding, Xiangyu Zhang, Ningning Ma, Jungong Han, Guiguang Ding, and Jian Sun. 2021. Repvgg: Making vgg-style convnets great again. In *Proceedings of the IEEE/CVF Conference on Computer Vision and Pattern Recognition*, pages 13733–13742.

Kaiming He, Xiangyu Zhang, Shaoqing Ren, and Jian Sun. 2016. Deep residual learning for image recognition. In *Proceedings of the IEEE conference on computer vision and pattern recognition*, pages 770–778.

Geoffrey Hinton, Oriol Vinyals, Jeff Dean, et al. 2015. Distilling the knowledge in a neural network. *arXiv preprint arXiv:1503.02531*, 2(7).

Andrew G Howard, Menglong Zhu, Bo Chen, Dmitry Kalenichenko, Weijun Wang, Tobias Weyand, Marco Andreetto, and Hartwig Adam. 2017. Mobilenets: Efficient convolutional neural networks for mobile vision applications. *arXiv preprint arXiv:1704.04861*.

Changmin Kim and Siyoung Yang. 2022. Sound event detection system using fixmatch for dcase 2022 challenge task 4. Technical report, DCASE2022 Challenge.

Xiang Li, Wenhai Wang, Xiaolin Hu, and Jian Yang. 2019. Selective kernel networks. In *Proceedings of the IEEE/CVF conference on computer vision and pattern recognition*, pages 510–519.

Koichi Miyazaki, Tatsuya Komatsu, Tomoki Hayashi, Shinji Watanabe, Tomoki Toda, and Kazuya Takeda. 2020. Convolution-augmented transformer for semi-supervised sound event detection. Technical report, DCASE2020 Challenge.

Karen Simonyan and Andrew Zisserman. 2014. Very deep convolutional networks for large-scale image recognition. *arXiv preprint arXiv:1409.1556*.

Antti Tarvainen and Harri Valpola. 2017. Mean teachers are better role models: Weight-averaged consistency targets improve semi-supervised deep learning results. *Advances in neural information processing systems*, 30.

Nicolas Turpault, Romain Serizel, Justin Salamon, and Ankit Parag Shah. 2019. Sound event detection in domestic environments with weakly labeled data and soundscape synthesis.

Hongyi Zhang, Moustapha Cisse, Yann N Dauphin, and David Lopez-Paz. 2017. mixup: Beyond empirical risk minimization. *arXiv preprint arXiv:1710.09412*.

Xu Zheng, Han Chen, and Yan Song. 2021. Zheng ustc team's submission for dcase2021 task4 — semi-supervised sound event detection. Technical report, DCASE2021 Challenge.

The 34th Conference on Computational Linguistics and Speech Processing (ROCLING 2022)
Taipei, Taiwan, November 21-22, 2022. The Association for Computational Linguistics and Chinese Language Processing

Analyzing discourse functions with acoustic features and phone embeddings: non-lexical items in Taiwan Mandarin

Pin-Er Chen
National Taiwan University
cckk2913@gmail.com

Yu-Hsiang Tseng
National Taiwan University
seantyh@gmail.com

Chi-Wei Wang
National Taiwan University
r09142007@ntu.edu.tw

Fang-Chi Yeh
National Tsing Hua University
fangchiyeh2000@gmail.com

Shu-Kai Hsieh
National Taiwan University
shukaihsieh@ntu.edu.tw

Abstract

Non-lexical items are expressive devices used in conversations that are not words but are nevertheless meaningful. These items play crucial roles, such as signaling turn-taking or marking stances in interactions. However, as the non-lexical items do not stably correspond to written or phonological forms, past studies tend to focus on studying their acoustic properties, such as pitches and durations. In this paper, we investigate the discourse functions of non-lexical items through their acoustic properties and the phone embeddings extracted from a deep learning model. Firstly, we create a non-lexical item dataset based on the interpellation video clips from Taiwan's Legislative Yuan. Then, we manually identify the non-lexical items and their discourse functions in the videos. Next, we analyze the acoustic properties of those items through statistical modeling and building classifiers based on phone embeddings extracted from a phone recognition model. We show that (1) the discourse functions have significant effects on the acoustic features; and (2) the classifiers built on phone embeddings perform better than the ones on conventional acoustic properties. These results suggest that phone embeddings may reflect the phonetic variations crucial in differentiating the discourse functions of non-lexical items.

Keywords: non-lexical item, discourse function, acoustic property, acoustic representation, pragmatics

1 Introduction

People's everyday interactions include sounds that are not verbal words in the traditional sense. These sounds, such as sighs, sniffs, and grunts, are used in indexing the turn-taking in dialogues, marking stance, showing affections, and expressing roles and meanings in conversations (Dingemanse, 2020). Examples of these *non-lexical items* are *un-huh* in English as a marker showing understanding and attentiveness, while the single syllable *uh* and *um* act as fillers and disfluency markers (Ward, 2006; Buschmeier et al., 2011).

While these non-lexical items are important linguistically, they pose an interesting challenge to linguistic inquiry. Non-lexical items do not belong to a major word class, and some do not conform to the language's phonological requirements (Keevallik and Ogden, 2020). Moreover, while the phonetic properties of non-lexical items could be generally described, they are nevertheless "phonetically underspecified."(Keating, 1988) For example, in the study of "moan" in board game interactions, Hofstetter (2020) found "moans" involve phonetic properties related to open vowels, irrespective of their frontness, backness, or roundedness. The study suggests that a non-lexical item can not be represented as a single phonetic symbol; instead, it may refer to the vowel space for which we do not have a general phonetic symbol. Some studies, therefore, analyze these items in terms of their acoustic properties: the components' sound (Ward, 2006), the fundamental frequencies, durations, and intensities. (Shan, 2021; Ballier and Chlébowski, 2021).

In contrast to the conventional acoustic property analysis, an alternative approach to analyzing non-lexical items is through the acoustic representations learned by data-driven methods. These methods include deep learning models mapping the audio segments to the latent embedding space from acoustic data in a (self-)supervised fashion (Li et al., 2020; Xu et al., 2021; Baevski et al., 2020). Although the models are not explicitly trained to represent the similarities among phonetic features, studies nonetheless find the audio segments with similar linguistic properties are closer together in the embedding space (Ma et al., 2021; Cormac English et al., 2022; Silfverberg et al., 2021). Therefore, these phonetic representations may already encode the phonetic variability of non-lexical items to reflect their different discourse functions.

This study thus aims to investigate how the acoustic properties contribute to the non-lexical items' discourse functions and how the phone embeddings extracted from the deep learning model help differentiate those functions. The rest of the paper is organized as follows. We first review related works on discourse markers and how they are analyzed with acoustic properties (Sec. 2). Next, we describe our dataset on non-lexical items (Sec. 3) in Taiwan Mandarin, in which we manually identify the items and annotate their discourse functions in interpellation video clips of Taiwan's Legislative Yuan. Finally, based on the dataset, we conduct the acoustic property analysis (Sec. 4) and build classifiers based on the phone embeddings extracted from a deep learning model (Sec. 5). Finally, Section 6 concludes the paper.

2 Related Works

2.1 Discourse Marker

Discourse markers (hereafter, DMs) has received increasing attention since Schiffrin (1987, p. 31) initially defined them as "sequentially dependent elements which bracket units of talk." However, little consensus has been not only on the terminology[1] of DMs but on the classification frameworks. Schiffrin (1987) has proposed that DMs form a category composed of phrases, conjunctions, and interjections, and that they have a part in discourse coherence considering different planes of talk.[2] Additionally, DMs can also serve as identifiers of participation status, speaker's assumptions, or hearer's knowledgement (Schiffrin, 1987; Schwenter, 1996; Fraser, 1999).

Despite that earlier research considered DMs as text-connective items bonding to syntactic structures, Fischer (2006, p. 9) defined DMs as devices involved in "turn-taking, interpersonal management, topic structure, and participation frameworks." Subsequently, Diewald (2006, 2013) suggested that DMs demonstrate pragmatic functions, manage discourse in a syntactically-independent way, and present their polyfunctionality in discourse (c.f. Fraser, 2009; Hansen, 2006; Németh, 2022).

Although numerous analyses were conducted on the pragmatic functions of DMs, they focused mostly on the associations with semantic senses and syntactic structures (e.g., Aijmer, 2011; Crible, 2017; Ford and Thompson, 1996). That is, studies of the connections between the discourse functions and the phonological information of DMs are relatively few.

2.2 Acoustic Property

The previous works which interwove DMs and their acoustic properties were mainly on the pragmatic-prosodic interface. Shan (2021) and Zhao and Wang (2019) investigated the Mandarin Chinese DMs, 你知道 *ni zhidao* 'you know' and 你不知道 *ni bu zhidao* 'you don't know', respectively. While Shan (2021) analyzed on duration, tempo, intensity, and fundamental frequencies (i.e., pitch, hereinafter F_0), Zhao and Wang (2019) examined the speech tempo, mean F_0 frequencies, and pitch accents of the DMs. In general, they have found correlations between the discourse functions and the acoustic properties. Moreover, Tseng et al. (2006) have suggested that connectors are predictable from speech prosody; most 'redundant prosodic fillers' are duration-triggered and manifested through

[1] For instance, discourse marker (Jucker and Ziv, 1998; Schiffrin, 1987); discourse particles (Aijmer, 2002; Fischer, 2006); pragmatic marker (Brinton, 1996); among others

[2] Schiffrin has suggested the five planes of talk: the Exchange structure (ES), Action structure (AS), Ideational structure (IdS), Participation framework (PF), and Information state (InS). More details can be seen in Schiffrin (2005), Maschler and Schiffrin (2015), and Hamilton et al. (2015).

narrowed F_0 ranges, whereas 'obligatory discourse markers' are syntax-triggered and manifested through widened F_0 ranges and resets.

The acoustic properties and their relevance to the pragmatic functions of DMs have also been analyzed cross-linguistically (e.g., Cabarrão et al., 2018; Raso and Vieira, 2016; Gonen et al., 2015; Beňuš, 2014). Referring to Wu et al. (2021), the phonetic variations of DMs in French are likely to appear in spontaneous speech and undergo phonetic reduction, considering their shorter mean phone duration and a rather centralized vowel space. Additionally, Schubotz et al. (2015) investigates the common English construction *you know* in terms of its duration, which is likely to be affected by the residuals of speech rate.

In addition to acoustic properties, past studies also examined the phonetic representations learned with data-driven methods. For example, Silfverberg et al. (2021) studied phonological alternations of Finnish consonant gradation with vector representations retrieved from RNN models. Other studies also tried to learn dense vector representations purely from text using grapheme-to-phoneme mappings with CBOW and SkipGram models (O'Neill and Carson-Berndsen, 2019). Notably, recent studies found transformer-based speech processing models (Baevski et al., 2020; Hsu et al., 2021), while not explicitly modeling phonetic properties, encoded the phonetic categorization information in the model representations, such as vowels and consonants, or fricatives and stops (Ma et al., 2021; Cormac English et al., 2022).

Tracing back to the former sections, previous literature on DMs mostly concentrated on their status at the semantic-pragmatic interface. The reviewed acoustic-related research, however, focused on those construction-wise DMs, and not to mention that the analyzed acoustic properties were limited to suprasegmental features, such as pitch and duration. In this case, the potential phonetic-pragmatic interrelationship of non-lexical items is yet to be elaborated.

3 Non-lexical Items Dataset

First, we used four interpellation video clips from Taiwan' s Legislative Yuan.[3]. Audio tracks were then extracted from the clips, converted into 16 bit `WAV` format, and resampled with 22kHz sampling rates. The overall data comprise separate interpellation of two male and two female legislators, each ranging 6-8 minutes. The equal number of genders was to balance potential gender differences in the utterances.

Secondly, the audio segments of non-lexical items (e.g., *uh, em,* and *ho*) were annotated by three native speakers via Praat 6.2.03 (Boersma and Weenink, 2021). Each non-lexical item acquired two tags, one for functional *Role* and one for pragmatic *Meaning*. Referring to Ward (2006), we defined the six candidates of *Role* as follows:

- `BACKCHANNEL`, which occurs repetitively and shows the agreement of the hearer; it often overlaps the main channel[4] of the utterance.
- `CFT (Clause-final token)`, which occurs in the sentence-final position and ends certain turn of talk.
- `DISFLUENCY`, which refers to the onset or coda of a word that can hardly be recognized due to its discoursal incompleteness.
- `FILLER`, which serves as a connector between two sentences or a sentence-initial particle of the speaker.
- `RESPONSE`, which occurs in the main channel and often indicates a flippant attitude.
- `OTHER`, which represents the non-lexical item not belonging to the above types.

Similarly, we summarized the following eight candidates for *Meaning*. It is noted that certain non-lexical items may carry multiple pragmatic meanings, and that the candidates below are not mutually exclusive. Thus, one non-lexical item is allowed to be annotated with multiple *Meaning* tags.

[3]The clips were downloaded from the Parliament TV website (https://www.parliamentarytv.org.tw/) and encoded as AAC, H.264

[4]see also Heinz (2003), Li et al. (2010), and McNely (2009) among others.

- `authority`. The speaker demonstrates his profession, personal experience, or intention in the speech.
- `control`. The speaker is in control of knowing exactly what to say or do next.
- `concern`. The speaker lacks confidence in his own words or tries to show respect to the audience.
- `thought`. The speaker takes the words (from himself or the other participant) as involving or meriting thought.
- `dissatisfaction`. The speaker is unsatisfied with his own words, the conversation, or the other participant.
- `new information`. The speaker wants to express that he has received new information; the speaker successfully lets the other participant understand the topic of the speech.
- `old ground`. The speaker is expecting to move on to the next topic since he has already acknowledged the current one.
- `neutral`.

In sum, a total of 143 non-lexical items produced by the legislators were manually annotated. We then moved on to extract the acoustic properties for the dataset.

4 Acoustic Property Analysis

With the assumption that the discourse functions may encode phonological variations, we illustrated our data collection and the annotation for non-lexical items in Sec. 3. The following sections (4.1 and 4.2) then present the analyses and results of acoustic properties.

4.1 Property Extraction

For each non-lexical item, we retrieved six conventional acoustic properties: mean pitch, duration, F1, F2, F3, and nasality, via customized Praat scripts (Styler, 2017). As formant frequencies construct the vowel space, F1 is determined by the vowel height, F2 is determined by the vowel backness, and F3 is determined by the vowel roundness.[5]

In terms of nasality, it can be quantified by ***a1-p1*** (for high vowels such as [i, u, y]) or ***a1-p0*** values (for non-high vowels such as [a, o, ə, e]). Since most of the annotated non-lexical items are realized and transcribed with non-high vowels, only the ***a1-p0*** values were considered. While ***a1*** stands for the amplitudes (in *dB*) of F1, ***p0*** stands for the amplitude of the nasal peak below F1 (Chen, 1997; Cho et al., 2017; Chiu and Lu, 2021).

Subsequently, to build up the most comprehensive acoustic properties, the values of F1, F2, F3 frequencies and ***a1-p0*** amplitude for each annotated non-lexical item were measured at 5 different time-points (i.e., the 10%, 30%, 50%, 70%, 90% time-points within each item interval). The retrieved acoustic data for 715 tokens[6] were processed and modified into machine-readable forms using the **pandas** package (The Pandas Development Team, 2020) in Python 3.8.9 (Python Core Team, 2021).

The statistical analysis was performed via the `lmerTest` package (Kuznetsova et al., 2017) in R 4.2.1 (R Core Team, 2022). Some factors contain rare categories were therefore re-coded. Specifically in the candidates of *Role*, `DISFLUENCY` and `RESPONSE` in were merged into `OTHER`, considering their extremely few occurrences. As for the candidates of *Meaning*, the items with multiple candidate tags were recoded as `complex`. The `OTHER` and `complex` were set as references in *Role* and *Meaning* factors, respectively. Finally, Box-Cox transformations (Box and Cox, 1964) were applied to each response variable to reduce the non-normalities in the distributions.

4.2 Evaluations

To explore the effect of discourse functions on the acoustic properties, we conduct statistical analyses with linear mixed-effects models and classification tasks with SVM.

Statistical Modeling. Apart from the two discourse functions (*Role* and *Meaning*), we also take *Transcriptions* into consideration. As *Transcriptions*, annotated for segment-identification, reflects the annotators' perception for each non-lexical item, it is likely a

[5]The higher the F1, the lower the vowel; the higher the F2, the more anterior the vowel; the lower the F3, the rounder the vowel (Flanagan, 1955; Lindblom and Studdert-Kennedy, 1967).

[6]Each 143 annotated non-lexical items were measured at 5 different points, resulting in 715 tokens.

	Chiq	Df	p-value
Duration	83.79	9	<.001 ***
Pitch	124.66	9	<.001 ***
F1	10.12	9	.341
F2	20.32	9	.016 *
F3	7.62	9	.573
Nasality	15.29	9	.083

Table 1: Model comparisons of linear mixed-effects in different response variables. The comparisons are between the base model, which only contains transcription and random intercepts, and the full model, which additionally includes discourse function predictors. For brevity, only comparison statistics are shown. * $p < 0.05$, ** $p < 0.01$, *** $p < 0.001$.

control variable that poses significant effects on the properties. Thus, for the evaluation of each acoustic property, we actually compare two models: one full linear mixed-effects model (composed of *Role*, *Meaning*, and *Transcriptions*) as well as one counterpart baseline model (composed of only *Transcriptions*).

Table 1 illustrates the sequential (Type I) ANOVA results for the linear mixed-effects models, in which one specific acoustic property is used as the dependent variable. Specifically, the acoustic properties that reach statistical significance among the model comparisons are `Duration`, `Pitch`, and `F2`, suggesting that certain types of roles and meanings present additional effects on acoustic properties, after controlled for the transcriptions. These results imply acoustic properties help differentiate discourse functions.

To further examine such possibility, Table 2 compiles the fixed-effect results of the full linear mixed-effects models for the acoustic properties, where the discourse functions[7] are the predictors. We find that `Pitch` shows the most significance when predicting both discourse functions, which corresponds to the previous works introduced in Sec. 2.2. Yet, `Duration` and `F2` are only capable of predicting certain types of *Meaning* and without any overlap. Not to mention the other three acoustic properties (i.e., `F1`, `F3`, and `Nasality`) which did not show any statistical significance.

To sum up, the overall effectiveness of the linear mixed-effects models for the acoustic properties to predict the discourse functions remain questionable. In the following section, we go on to the implementation of the alternative model, the Support Vector Machines (SVM).

Support Vector Machines Support Vector Machines (SVM) model is implemented for the classification tasks, in which the acoustic properties are used in prediction of discourse functions. As we assume that the discourse functions may reflect in the phonological variations of the non-lexical items, linear models such as SVM are applicable.

We use random 70-30 splits for training and testing data. While the training data comprise 500 tokens, the testing data comprise 215 tokens. A random guessing model, serving as a *the-most-frequent baseline*, is also implemented for comparison. It calculates the frequency distributions of all discourse functions, and then it invariably predicts the most frequent class. We use the accuracy, precision, recall, and F1-score to evaluate the performance of the two models.

Table 3 shows that both models, based on the acoustic properties, find it harder to predict *Meaning* than *Role*. Specifically, the `acoustics` achieved slightly better accuracy (.48) and precision (.09) than the baseline (.38 and .04). In the prediction of *Role*, however, the performance of the models was very similar. It implies that the `acoustics` in fact does not acquire much advantage in predicting discourse functions. This observation is consistent with the results of the previous liner mixed-effects model, in which we found few correlations between the acoustic properties and the discourse functions. Therefore, we attempt to find other presentations of phonological variations that may better capture the candidates of discourse functions with higher accuracy.

5 Phone embeddings

As the conventional acoustic properties did not show promising results of capturing the

[7]Notice that the aforementioned `BACKCHANNEL` (as *Role*) and `concern` (as *Meaning*) only exist in the supplementary annotation for those non-lexical items produced by the administrative officers in opposition to the legislators. Data are reserved for the future studies.

	Duration	Pitch	F1	F2	F3	Nasality
(transcriptions)			--			
CFT	0.034	12.04***	35.68	6.28	10 169.4	4.03
FILLER	0.042	14.92***	2.67	1.22	10 913.4	5.67
authority	−0.016	3.87**	3.98	2.29***	−6832.3	2.52
control	−0.013	0.16	3.49	7.87	2345.1	0.18
dissatisfaction	−0.052	−10.07***	45.70	3.16**	−9942.1	4.08
neutral	−0.016	0.05	58.17	1.58*	1948.2	0.30
new information	−0.267**	10.17***	−40.21	1.65	−5134.1	−2.71
old ground	−0.003	0.82	−4.51	1.31	3383.3	0.13
thought	−0.288***	−2.36	97.46	1.55	2643.0	2.75

Table 2: Parameter estimates of discourse functions in the linear-mixed effect models. The variables of transcriptions are included in all models, but their estimates are not shown in the table for brevity. Response variables are Box-Cox transformed, the parameters are therefore in the transformed scale. * $p < 0.05$, ** $p < 0.01$, *** $p < 0.001$.

Role	Acc	Pr	Rc	F1
acoustics	.76	.15	.20	.17
acoustics-base	.76	.15	.20	.17
Meaning	Acc	Pr	Rc	F1
acoustics	.48	.09	.14	.11
acoustics-base	.38	.04	.10	.06

Table 3: Evaluation of acoustic models

discourse functions, we reached out to phonetic vector representations, in which the phonological variations of non-lexical items might be encoded.

Instead of the common end-to-end models trained on waveforms and language-specific transcriptions in ASR tasks, we chose the *Allosaurus* model by Li et al. (2020)[8] for retrieving the phone embeddings. Specifically, the Allosaurus is an universal phone recognizer integrating an ASR encoder with an allophone layer, in which language-independent phone distributions are directly recognized and mapped into language-dependent phoneme distributions.

We first examine the phone embeddings learned by the phone recognition model. In the video clips collected in Section 3, the model automatically identifies 29,218 phones in the conversations. To investigate the phone organizations in the embedding space, we then extract the bi-LSTM representations[9] with which model predicts the phones as phone embeddings. Next, we average these embeddings by their predicted phones and obtain 34 phone centroids in the embedding space. We follow the literature (Cormac English et al., 2022) and conduct hierarchical clustering with Ward linkage based on the Euclidean distances between the centroids. The clustering results are shown in Figure 1a and Figure 1b. We not only observe clear clusters of vowels and consonants but observe that the fricatives and stops tend to be close to each other with similar phonetic properties. The patterns suggest that the phone embeddings might reflect the phonetic variations in our conversation data.

Moreover, we inspect the clustering structure of recognized phones that occurred in the non-lexical items. Figure 1c shows the two-dimensional t-SNE (Pedregosa et al., 2011) visualization of the 640-dimension phone embeddings obtained from Allosaurus. The same phones tend to form distinct clusters, and the general distinction between vowels and consonants is still observed in the figure. It indicates that the embeddings may represent their corresponding phonetic properties. As Li et al. (2020) have shown in their studies, Allosaurus has the advantage of multilingual phone recog-

[8]https://github.com/xinjli/allosaurus

[9]Referring to the comments from the reviewers, the bi-LSTM representations are used as the phone embeddings considering their better performance than the other representations (i.e., the 40-dimension MFCCs and the phone logits) generated by Allosaurus.

(a)

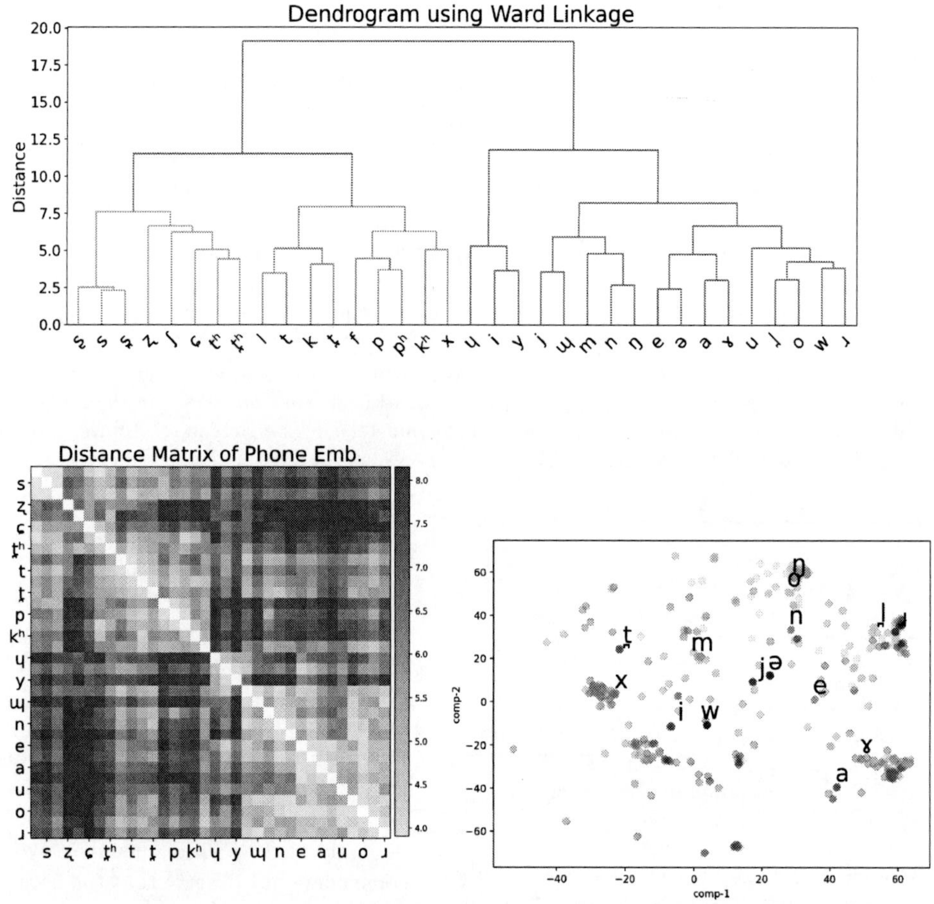

(b) (c)

Figure 1: (a) The dendrogram of the hierarchical clustering with Ward linkage. The links are color-coded for visual references. Generally, the top left and right branches loosely correspond to consonants and (semi-)vowels. The leftmost branch (orange) are mostly fricatives (e.g., s, ʂ, ɕ); the one on the right (green) includes stops (e.g., k, t, p). (b) The distance matrix shows a consistent pattern with the one in the dendrogram. (c) The t-SNE projection of the phones in non-lexical items. Only the most-frequent 15 phones are shown for clarity. IPA symbols mark the median points of each category.

nition and involves more phonological knowledge. It is thus appropriate for us to leverage these phone embeddings, by which the discourse functions of non-lexical items may be encoded.

5.1 Classification Task

The output data by Allosaurus (i.e., the phone embeddings and phoneme transcriptions) are aligned with our annotations of discourse functions for non-lexical items. It is noted that only the phoneme, whose timestamp matches the 715 tokens of non-lexical items, are kept for the classification tasks. The data is split randomly 70-30 into training and testing datasets as in Section 4.2.

We also implement a linear SVM model and a random guessing model serving as a *the-most-frequent baseline* for the classification tasks.[10] The only difference here is that we replace use the acoustic properties with the phone embedding vectors to predict the candidates of the discourse functions.

[10]Regarding the comments from the reviewers, the

Role	Acc	Pr	Rc	F1
`phone emb.`	.92	.96	.87	.91
`baseline`	.78	.16	.20	.18
Meaning	Acc	Pr	Rc	F1
`phone emb.`	.77	.84	.68	.72
`baseline`	.42	.05	.11	.07

Table 4: Evaluation of classifiers based on phone embeddings

5.2 Evaluation Results

As shown in the upper part of Table 4, **`phone emb.`** stands out with the highest accuracy (.92) and precision (.96) in prediction of *Role*. While `baseline` presents the accuracy of .78, the acoustic models (see Table 3) show even lower accuracies (.76) and precision (.15). As for predicting *Meaning*, **`phone emb.`** significantly outperforms its baseline and remains the highest in accuracy (.77) and precision (.84) among all models. In general, **`phone emb.`** presents superior performance than the other models in prediction of both discourse functions.

Moreover, both models (i.e., `acoustics` and `phone emb.`) are better at predicting *Role* than *Meaning*, likely due to the fact that *Meaning* comprises more types of candidates and internally more equal distribution. In this case, the gap between the accuracies of `phone emb.` (i.e., between .92 and .77) is still the smallest among the models. This suggests that our model is better at capturing the discourse functions by using the phone embeddings, the phonetic realizations, than the statistical acoustic properties.

6 Conclusion

This paper focuses on the phonetic-pragmatic interrelationship of non-lexical discourse markers in Taiwan Mandarin. As we assume that the discourse functions may be captured by the phonological variations, we firstly analyzed on the common acoustic properties (i.e., duration, nasality, mean pitch, F1, F2, and F3), followed by the classification tasks considering the 640d-phone embeddings. In comparison with the conventional acoustic properties, the model using phonetic realizations performs better in prediction of the functional *Role* and pragmatic *Meaning* of the non-lexical items. The result is consistent with our hypotheses that the phonetic realizations, embeddings via deep learning, encode certain phonological variations of non-lexical items and correlate with their discourse functions.

linear SVM model and the model baseline are adopted to not only display the data distributions but highlight the results of Allosaurus, as we mainly focus on whether the phone representations really help us explore non-lexical items. Based on the results, we did find the the model using phonetic realizations performs better in predicting the discourse functions, and we expect future research to develop better representations and state-of-the-art models that allow us to describe non-lexical items more appropriately.

Acknowledgments

We sincerely thank the three native-speakers for the annotation work and the two anonymous reviewers whose comments and suggestions have helped us clarify the technical details in the paper.

References

Karin Aijmer. 2002. *English discourse particles: evidence from a corpus.* Number 10 in Studies in corpus linguistics. Benjamins, Amsterdam.

Karin Aijmer. 2011. Well i'm not sure i think···the use of well by non-native speakers. *International Journal of Corpus Linguistics*, 16:231–254.

Alexei Baevski, Yuhao Zhou, Abdelrahman Mohamed, and Michael Auli. 2020. wav2vec 2.0: A framework for self-supervised learning of speech representations. *Advances in Neural Information Processing Systems*, 33:12449–12460.

Nicolas Ballier and Aurélie Chlébowski. 2021. "see what i mean, huh?" evaluating visual inspection of f0 tracking in nasal grunts. In *Interspeech 2021*, pages 376–380. ISCA.

Štefan Beňuš. 2014. Conversational entrainment in the use of discourse markers. In *Recent Advances of Neural Network Models and Applications*, pages 345–352. Springer.

Paul Boersma and David Weenink. 2021. Praat: Doing phonetics by computer [computer program] version 6.2.03, retrieved 23 august 2022 from http://www.praat.org/.

George EP Box and David R Cox. 1964. An analysis of transformations. *Journal of the Royal Statistical Society: Series B (Methodological)*, 26(2):211–243.

Laurel J. Brinton. 1996. *Pragmatic markers in English: grammaticalization and discourse functions.* Number 19 in Topics in English linguistics. Mouton de Gruyter, Berlin ; New York.

Hendrik Buschmeier, Zofia Malisz, Marcin Włodarczak, Stefan Kopp, and Petra Wagner. 2011. Are you sure you're paying attention?'-uh-huh'communicating understanding as a marker of attentiveness. In *Twelfth Annual Conference of the International Speech Communication Association.*

Vera Cabarrão, Helena Moniz, Fernando Batista, Jaime Ferreira, Isabel Trancoso, and Ana Isabel Mata. 2018. Cross-domain analysis of discourse markers in european portuguese. *Dialogue & Discourse*, 9(1):79–106.

Marilyn Y Chen. 1997. Acoustic correlates of english and french nasalized vowels. *The Journal of the Acoustical Society of America*, 102(4):2360–2370.

Chenhao Chiu and Yu-An Lu. 2021. Articulatory evidence for the syllable-final nasal merging in taiwan mandarin. *Language and Speech*, 64(4):771–789.

Taehong Cho, Daejin Kim, and Sahyang Kim. 2017. Prosodically-conditioned fine-tuning of coarticulatory vowel nasalization in english. *Journal of Phonetics*, 64:71–89.

Patrick Cormac English, John D. Kelleher, and Julie Carson-Berndsen. 2022. Domain-informed probing of wav2vec 2.0 embeddings for phonetic features. In *Proceedings of the 19th SIGMORPHON Workshop on Computational Research in Phonetics, Phonology, and Morphology*, pages 83–91, Seattle, Washington. Association for Computational Linguistics.

Ludivine Crible. 2017. *Discourse Markers and (Dis) fluency across Registers.* Ph.D. thesis, Université de Berne.

Gabriele Diewald. 2006. Discourse particles and modal particles as grammatical elements. *Approaches to Discourse Particles*, pages 403–425.

Gabriele Diewald. 2013. "same same but different" - modal particles, discourse markers and the art (and purpose) of categorization. *Discourse Markers and Modal Particles. Categorization and Description*, pages 19–46. Cited By :34.

Mark Dingemanse. 2020. Between sound and speech: Liminal signs in interaction. *Research on Language and Social Interaction*, 53(1):188–196.

Kerstin Fischer. 2006. Towards an understanding of the spectrum of approaches to discourse particles: introduction. In Fischer, editor, *Approaches to discourse particles*, number 1 in Studies in pragmatics, pages 1–20. Elsevier, Oxford.

James L Flanagan. 1955. A difference limen for vowel formant frequency. *The journal of the Acoustical Society of America*, 27(3):613–617.

C Ford and S Thompson. 1996. Interactional units in conversation: Syntactic, intonational and pragmatic resources. *Interaction and grammar*, (13):134.

Bruce Fraser. 1999. What are discourse markers? *Journal of Pragmatics*, 31(7):931–952.

Bruce Fraser. 2009. An account of discourse markers. *International Review of Pragmatics*, 1:293–320.

Einat Gonen, Zohar Livnat, and Noam Amir. 2015. The discourse marker axshav ('now') in spontaneous spoken hebrew: Discursive and prosodic features. *Journal of Pragmatics*, 89:69–84.

Heidi E Hamilton, Deborah Tannen, and Deborah Schiffrin. 2015. *The handbook of discourse analysis.* John Wiley & Sons.

Maj-Britt Mosegaard Hansen. 2006. *A dynamic polysemy approach to the lexical semantics of discourse markers: (with an exemplary analysis of French toujours*, number 1 in Studies in pragmatics, pages 21–41. Elsevier, Netherlands.

Bettina Heinz. 2003. Backchannel responses as strategic responses in bilingual speakers' conversations. *Journal of pragmatics*, 35(7):1113–1142.

Emily Hofstetter. 2020. Nonlexical "moans" : Response cries in board game interactions. *Research on Language and Social Interaction*, 53(1):42–65.

Wei-Ning Hsu, Benjamin Bolte, Yao-Hung Hubert Tsai, Kushal Lakhotia, Ruslan Salakhutdinov, and Abdelrahman Mohamed. 2021. Hubert: Self-supervised speech representation learning by masked prediction of hidden units. *IEEE/ACM Transactions on Audio, Speech, and Language Processing*, 29:3451–3460.

A.H. Jucker and Y. Ziv. 1998. *Discourse Markers: Descriptions and Theory.* New series]. Lightning Source Incorporated.

Patricia A. Keating. 1988. Underspecification in phonetics. *Phonology*, 5(2):275–292.

Leelo Keevallik and Richard Ogden. 2020. Sounds on the margins of language at the heart of interaction. *Research on Language and Social Interaction*, 53(1):1–18.

Alexandra Kuznetsova, Per B. Brockhoff, and Rune H. B. Christensen. 2017. lmerTest package: Tests in linear mixed effects models. *Journal of Statistical Software*, 82(13):1–26.

Han Z Li, Yanping Cui, and Zhizhang Wang. 2010. Backchannel responses and enjoyment of the conversation: The more does not necessarily mean the better. *International journal of psychological studies*, 2(1):25.

Xinjian Li, Siddharth Dalmia, Juncheng Li, Matthew Lee, Patrick Littell, Jiali Yao, Antonios Anastasopoulos, David Mortensen, Graham Neubig, Alan Black, and Florian Metze. 2020. Universal phone recognition with a multilingual allophone system. pages 8249–8253.

Björn EF Lindblom and Michael Studdert-Kennedy. 1967. On the role of formant transitions in vowel recognition. *The Journal of the Acoustical society of America*, 42(4):830–843.

Danni Ma, Neville Ryant, and Mark Liberman. 2021. Probing acoustic representations for phonetic properties. In *ICASSP 2021 - 2021 IEEE International Conference on Acoustics, Speech and Signal Processing (ICASSP)*, pages 311–315.

Yael Maschler and Deborah Schiffrin. 2015. Discourse markers language, meaning, and context. *The handbook of discourse analysis*, pages 189–221.

Brian McNely. 2009. Backchannel persistence and collaborative meaning-making. In *Proceedings of the 27th ACM international conference on Design of communication*, pages 297–304.

Zsuzsanna Németh. 2022. The conversation-organising role of the non-lexical sound öö in hungarian. *Journal of Pragmatics*, 194:23–35.

Emma O'Neill and Julie Carson-Berndsen. 2019. The effect of phoneme distribution on perceptual similarity in english. In *The 20th Annual Conference of the International Speech Communication Association (Interspeech 2019), Graz, Austria, 15-19 September 2019.* ISCA.

Fabian Pedregosa, Gaël Varoquaux, Alexandre Gramfort, Vincent Michel, Bertrand Thirion, Olivier Grisel, Mathieu Blondel, Peter Prettenhofer, Ron Weiss, Vincent Dubourg, et al. 2011. Scikit-learn: Machine learning in python. *Journal of machine learning research*, 12(Oct):2825–2830.

Python Core Team. 2021. *Python: A dynamic, open source programming language.* Python Software Foundation. Python version 3.8.9.

R Core Team. 2022. *R: A Language and Environment for Statistical Computing.* R Foundation for Statistical Computing, Vienna, Austria.

Tommaso Raso and Marcelo Vieira. 2016. A description of dialogic units/discourse markers in spontaneous speech corpora based on phonetic parameters. *CHIMERA Romance corpora and linguistic studies*, 3:221.

Deborah Schiffrin. 1987. *Discourse Markers.* Studies in Interactional Sociolinguistics. Cambridge University Press.

Deborah Schiffrin. 2005. Discourse markers: Language, meaning, and context. *The handbook of discourse analysis*, pages 54–75.

Louise Schubotz, Nelleke Oostdijk, and Mirjam Ernestus. 2015. Y' know vs. you know: What phonetic reduction can tell us about pragmatic function. In *S. Lestrade, P. de Swart & L. Hogeweg (Eds.). Addenda. Artikelen voor Ad Foolen.*, pages 261–280. Nijmegen: Radboud Universiteit Nijmegen.

Scott A. Schwenter. 1996. Some reflections on o sea: A discourse marker in spanish. *Journal of Pragmatics*, 25(6):855–874.

Yi Shan. 2021. Investigating the interaction between prosody and pragmatics quantitatively: A case study of the chinese discourse marker ni zhidao ("you know"). *Frontiers in psychology*, 12.

Miikka Silfverberg, Francis Tyers, Garrett Nicolai, and Mans Hulden. 2021. Do RNN states encode abstract phonological alternations? In *Proceedings of the 2021 Conference of the North American Chapter of the Association for Computational Linguistics: Human Language Technologies*, pages 5501–5513, Online. Association for Computational Linguistics.

Will Styler. 2017. On the acoustical features of vowel nasality in english and french. *The Journal of the Acoustical Society of America*, 142(4):2469–2482.

The Pandas Development Team. 2020. *pandas-dev/pandas: Pandas.*

Chiu-yu Tseng, Zhao-yu Su, Chun-Hsiang Chang, and Chia-hung Tai. 2006. Prosodic fillers and discourse markers–discourse prosody and text prediction. In *Tonal Aspects of Languages.*

Nigel Ward. 2006. Non-lexical conversational sounds in American English. *Pragmatics & Cognition*, 14(1):129–182.

Yaru Wu, Mathilde Hutin, Ioana Vasilescu, Lori Lamel, Martine Adda-Decker, Liesbeth Degand, et al. 2021. Fine phonetic details for discourse marker disambiguation: a corpus-based investigation. In *The 10th Workshop on Disfluency in Spontaneous Speech (DiSS 2021).*

Qiantong Xu, Alexei Baevski, and Michael Auli. 2021. Simple and effective zero-shot cross-lingual phoneme recognition. *arXiv preprint arXiv:2109.11680.*

Beibei Zhao and Gaowu Wang. 2019. The prosodic features of the mandarin discourse marker nibuzhidao under different functions. In

Proceedings of the 3rd International Conference on Art Design, Language, and Humanities.

The 34th Conference on Computational Linguistics and Speech Processing (ROCLING 2022)
Taipei, Taiwan, November 21-22, 2022. The Association for Computational Linguistics and Chinese Language Processing

A Dimensional Valence-Arousal-Irony Dataset for Chinese Sentence and Context

Sheng-Wei Huang
Soochow University
Dept. of Data Science
kiwihwung11@gmail.com

Wei-Yi Chung
Soochow University
Dept. of Data Science
hwork0511@gmail.com

Yu-Hsuan Wu
Soochow University
Dept. of Data Science
ikaroskasane@gmail.com

Chen-Chia Yu
The University of Edinburgh
School of PPLS
alisonyu119@gmail.com

Jheng-Long Wu
Soochow University
Dept. of Data Science
jlwu@gm.scu.edu.tw

Abstract

Chinese multi-dimensional sentiment detection is a challenging task with a considerable impact on semantic understanding. Past irony datasets are utilized to annotate sentiment type of whole sentences of irony. It does not provide the corresponding intensity of valence and arousal on the sentences and context. However, an ironic statement is defined as a statement whose apparent meaning is the opposite of its actual meaning. This means that in order to understand the actual meaning of a sentence, contextual information is needed. Therefore, the dimensional sentiment intensities of ironic sentences and context are important issues in the natural language processing field. This paper creates the extended NTU irony corpus, which includes valence, arousal and irony intensities on sentence-level; and valence and arousal intensities on context-level, called Chinese Dimensional Valence-Arousal-Irony (CDVAI) dataset. Therefore, this paper analyzes the annotation difference between the human annotators and uses a deep learning model such as BERT to evaluate the prediction performances on CDVAI corpus.

Keywords: Irony annotation, Dimensional valance-arousal-irony, Sentiment analysis, Deep learning

1 Introduction

The popularity of social media has made the exchange of opinions more frequent, and users not only use narratives but also widely use irony, metaphors and other special expressions when commenting on online forums. In the past, the literature has compiled research on irony detection (Joshi et al., 2017). Although most of the literature lacks a clear and consistent definition of irony, one of the most common features of irony is the inversion of the literal meaning and the semantic turn of the context. In Chinese irony, the contrast between positive and negative emotions is often used to indicate the difference between sentences and contexts. This emotional contrast is often used to achieve sarcastic expressions (Veale & Hao, 2010). For example "Great, it's raining, but I didn't bring an umbrella....", the context "it's raining, but I didn't bring an umbrella...." is a negative emotion, keyword "Great" is a positive emotion. This emotional contrast enables the expression of irony. In order to improve the performance on the irony recognition task, this study argues that context must be considered to match the characteristics of ironic sentences. As the grammatical structure of the above-mentioned irony suggests, irony emotion detection is quite difficult in natural language processing (NLP).

As a result, past research on irony detection is rare, and the work of emotion analysis turned to the study of characteristics of irony language (Colston, 2019). With the development of machine learning, some studies have gradually begun to use its methods to predict the degree of irony (Chia et al., 2021). However, due to the limitation of annotation, most of them predict only the degree of irony of the whole sentence (Dimovska et al., 2018) instead of considering the expression differences of the context as mentioned above.

In order to improve machine learning of identifying the intensity of irony, scholars have proposed to annotate these structural features or use feature selection to screen important irony spans when studying irony in the English language. (Kumar & Harish, 2019). However, grammatical structures can differ in different languages, and the improvement of irony detection performance cannot be handled in the same way. Long et al. (2019) proposed the usage of capitalized words as a hint of irony in English. Such a method is not suitable for learning features of irony in Chinese, as the notion of capitalization does not exist in the Chinese language. In conclusion, while these rules have been thoroughly studied in English, their applicability to Chinese is an inappropriate approach. Although some scholars are studying Chinese irony rules (Jia et al., 2019), there are few datasets that are quantified and annotated based on these rules. In conclusion, considering the multi-dimensional Valence-Arousal-Irony (VAI) Irony Sentences and Context Dataset, it is possible to identify the true meaning of ironic sentences and the emotional state of the sender, which also contributes to the field of Chinese NLP.

The construction of the existing VAI corpus was carried out with the efforts of Xie et al. (2021). Its contribution is to show that the VAI indicator has the characteristics of mutual influence. The biggest difference between the corpus established in this study and Xie et al. is that the context is considered and annotated with VA.

Based on Tang's (Tang & Chen, 2014) open data on irony sentences, this study proposes to add sentence-level valence, arousal and irony annotations, and context-level valance annotations to the ironic sentences provided by the dataset. This annotation method provides a way to judge the difference in context and semantics in the subsequent analysis of irony sentences. By quantifying emotional indicators, the degree of irony is more clearly understood. This augmented CDVAI dataset is the first dataset to do sentiment annotations for irony context.

Furthermore, this paper proposes a deep learning model based on the work of Devlin et al. (2018), Bidirectional Encoder Representations from Transformers (BERT) to learn the dimensional VAI on the ironic sentences and dimensional VA on ironic contexts. The experimental models include (1) using a linear layer with pre-trained BERT to predict dimensional VAI on sentence and context; (2) sum hidden features of corresponding the context from pre-trained BERT (3) concatenate two hidden features of BERT from sentence and context, respectively.

2 Related works

Metaphor is a feature of irony, which can be expressed as the use of exaggerated keywords with positive emotions to describe things with negative emotions, which also makes the apparent meaning of the sentence opposite to the actual meaning that the speaker expects or wants to convey. It is also frequently used in satirical sentences. Since irony is not commonly used in official documents, most researchers turn to social media platforms for data collection and analysis (Lestari, 2019). Due to different research perspectives, the definition of irony is often adjusted. However, researchers have reached a basic consensus in the process of exploration, that is, the basic feature of irony. "Irony is an expression in which the true meaning is the opposite of the literal meaning" (Li & Huang, 2020) Li et al. (2020) proposed an Irony Identification Program (IIP) to identify whether a sentence is ironic during the annotation process. Using IIP, they studied the semantic relations in the grammatical structure of irony according to the context. The above research provides support for the definition of irony in this study.

English has few corpora for VAI, and most of them are only for VA (valence and arousal). In a recent study, Preoţiuc-Pietro et al. (2016) established and annotated the VA tags for Facebook posts. They used the Likert nine-point scale to annotate and found that the two indicators of VA had a high correlation. In addition, in the construction of the irony corpus, Bosco et al. (2013) proposed the corpus Senti-TUT to mark the irony and emotional expression of tweets on Twitter. Their work includes positive and negative emotions, emotional expression, and irony. The corpus considers the concept of valence instead of focusing only on irony. Gosh et al. (2015) Annotate figurative language such as irony, satire, and metaphor on a 11-point scale at SemEval-2015 Task 11 and recruit annotators using a crowdsourcing platform. In addition, there are still many foreign languages for the construction of VA or I corpus, but literature that comprehensively considers all three aspects (which is VAI corpus) is very rare.

While few studies consider and label all three indicators simultaneously (VAI), there is a correlation among the three indicators, and the following studies demonstrate the need to do so. The effect of irony on human emotions was found in the study of Pfeifer (Pfeifer & Lai, 2021). Regardless of contextual emotion, people who use irony are considered to be in a less negative and less excited state of mind. The study by Xie et al. (Xie et al., 2021). found that stronger irony expressions may have lower valence (more negative) and higher arousal levels, respectively.

Research on Chinese Irony Corpus Xiang et al. (2020) constructed a corpus for irony. The Ciron dataset they built contains 8.7K Weibo posts. The study only annotated the degree of irony of sentences in the corpus without considering the context. NTU Irony Corpus (Tang & Chen, 2014) has released that it only provides the ironic sentences and context, but without other sentiment scores such as sentence-level VAI. Lack of carry out more subtle emotional labeling for the internal grammatical structure, which is impossible to understand clearly on the emotional transitions and semantic changes in the sentences. Therefore, the corpus provided in this paper has a greater advantage in understanding the structure of ironic sentences.

In the follow-up application in the field of irony, Rangwani et al. (2018) considered emojis, which are often used on Twitter, as a factor when annotating ironic sentences to improve the results. CNN (Convolutional Neural Network) is implemented to pre-train the emoji, and XGBoost model is applied for classification. Naseem et al. (2020) proposed a T-Dice model based on the transformer model to judge post valence, irony and irony classification. It was then connected to Bi-LSTM (Bi-directional Long Short-Term Memory) to classify emotions, and its accuracy surpassed the most advanced methods at that time. Xiang et al Xiang et al. found that the effect of BERT is better than that of GRU in the experimental results of the Ciron dataset they built. Lu et al. (2020) improved the Bi-GRU model based on BERT in the Chinese sentiment analysis task to achieve the best results. To sum up, in recent years, no matter in sentiment analysis or in irony recognition tasks, LSTM and other models that can connect the information of the entire sentence have achieved better results, and based on models with attention mechanisms such as BERT or transformers can make the overall model achieves the best results. In summary, this paper will use BERT as the basis to identify the VAI of the sentence and the VA of the context.

3 CDVAI dataset

This paper annotates and extends the NTU irony corpus to a dimensional valence-arousal-irony, called CDVAI. NTU irony corpus provides ironic sentences and their ironic context. The annotation tasks are the VAI intensity of the sentence and the VA intensity of the context, respectively. Li and Huang (Li & Huang, 2020) analyzed the sentence structure of Chinese irony based on the existing corpus, and proposed that context is an important information for judging irony. Based on its findings and the sentence structure within the NTU irony corpus, this study defines irony as "irony is an expression in which the true meaning is the opposite of the literal meaning." Context is the true meaning of the sentence (usually a negative description), while ironic keywords (usually positive descriptions) are required to make the literal meaning contrary to the context.

3.1 Dimensional VAI annotation

The paper proposes that the VAI score were rated from 1 to 5. The detailed annotation processes as follow:

- **Valence:** Lower valence scores indicate more negative emotions (1-2 points), whereas higher valence scores indicate more positive emotions (4-5 points), and 3 is neutral, representing no emotion or inability to judge .
- **Arousal:** A lower arousal score indicates a lower degree of intensity. A score of 0 is an objective description of absolutely no emotion. For example: “I am a student.” A score of 1 is close to an objective description, or it is more difficult to judge whether there is emotion. A score of 2 means that the annotator can feel the emotion from the sentence, but there is no emotion word. A score of 3 and above will be given to posts with explicit emotional words or phrases. Emotional words such as sad,

annoyed, lost, happy, etc. can clearly describe the emotional state. A score of 4 means that the annotator can clearly feel strong emotions in the sentence, such as madness, rage, excitement, etc. In addition to exaggerated rhetoric, posts may contain violent words, such as aggressive language. A score of 5 indicates extreme choice of words, words with discrimination, hatred, or words with obvious manic emotions. For example: "Great, the class report is going to be with that pathetic nerd!"

- **Irony:** The judging criterion of irony is as follows. The annotator reads a sentence and judges whether the true meaning is the opposite of the literal meaning. Most of the sentences in NTU irony corpus use negative descriptions as the context, and positive descriptions as the keywords that constitute irony sentences. This study believes that the judgment of irony intensity can be determined according to the difference between the positive degree of irony keywords and the negative degree of context. In this paper, the positive degree of various ironic keywords appearing in the corpus is summarized as: wonderful > great > very good > good. The larger the gap between the positive degree of the ironic keyword and the negative degree of the context, the higher the degree of irony, and vice versa. A score of 1 indicates that the irony keyword of the sentence has a small gap with the context, or the context is close to an objective description. Example: Good, it's raining. A score of 2 indicates that there is a moderate gap between ironic keywords and context. A score of 3 means that there is a clear gap between the ironic keywords and the context. A score of 4 means that there is a big gap between the ironic keywords and the context. A score of 5 indicates that there is a great gap between ironic keywords and context. The sentence may contain discriminatory or morally unacceptable metaphors, such as sexual innuendo.

3.2 Annotated result analysis

After screening the NTU Irony Corpus, the paper left a total of 1004 sentences, of which 843 sentences with irony context needed to be annotated. Each sample was annotated by three annotators. The annotators consist of postgraduate students and an undergraduate student, all of them are native Chinese speakers and ages between 20 and 25. Due to the intrinsic bias of subjectivity of different annotators, taking the average of 3 annotators as the gold standard.

This study believes that it is most reasonable to label the three indicators of VAI with a score system, because human cognition of emotional intensity is closer to continuous scores than classification. From the unavoidable bias among annotators, we know that even if the scoring criteria are well-defined, there are differences in judging the same sentence. The meaning of the labeling criterion in this study is to set the standard score line and to concretize the vague definition of intensity. Therefore, the traditional classification consensus algorithm such as kappa value does not meet the assumptions of this study, so the mean absolute error (MAE) metric is used to evaluate the annotation quality of each annotator. The MAE among the three annotators ranged from 0.05 to 0.31 in sentence-level valance, 0.25 to 0.41 in arousal, 0.22 to 0.56 in irony. The valance at the context level is between 0.07 and 0.4. Arousal is between 0.15 and 0.65. It can be seen from the above that the difference between the labeling scores of the three annotators is very small, which proves that the labeling is effective.

- **For example:**

Score of a sentence: valence: 1, arousal: 5, irony: 4

Score of a context: valence: 1, arousal: 5

Sentence: "*很好 (applause)工廠的廠務小姐已經來上班好多好多年了,跟我說她不會用 outlook 發會議通知!! ㄍㄋㄋ勒!!妳的薪水也給我我就幫你發通知!!" ("Very good (applause) The factory manager of the factory has been coming to work for many years. She told me that she doesn't know how to use Outlook to send meeting notices!! mother fucker!! Give me your salary and I will send the notices for you!!")*

Context: "*工廠的廠務小姐已經來上班好多好多年了,跟我說她不會用 outlook 發會議通知!!" ("The factory manager of the factory has* *been coming to work for many years. She told me that she doesn't know how to use Outlook to send meeting notices!!")*

Judgement: In terms of judging the valence, this post contains extremely negative emotions, such as "*mother fucker!! Give me your salary and I will sent a notice for you!!*". It is clear that the emotions manifested by the swear words and complaints are highly negative. As for the Arousal label, the post contains a clear sense of manic and abuse language. Thus, the Arousal label is given a score of 5 points. The post carries the irony keyword "*very good*", which is a minimal positive description. However, according to the description of the sender, the incident was judged to be a serious one because it caused serious discomfort and negative emotions. In addition to the irony keyword, this sentence contains other irony spans, such as "*Give me your salary and I will send a notice for you.*", so it is given a high score of 4 points in irony. Since the sentiment of the context is like the whole, the dimensional VA score is the same as the sentence.

3.3 Statistics of annotated result

The previous chapters have described the importance of the structure and context of ironic sentences. Next, this study extends the sentiment labeling based on Tang's (Tang & Chen, 2014) open data on irony sentences, which is the only dataset with labelled irony contexts. There are a total of 1004 sentences, of which 843 sentences have context. Table 1 shows the annotated CDVAI dataset in different levels and sentiment. Since the data is mainly ironic, the valence values are all negative. Considering that there are many emotions in the sentence, the arousal focuses on points 2, 3 and 4. The arousal of context is distributed to a lower score after the irony keyword is removed, because irony keywords usually have exaggerated expressions, resulting in a higher arousal. The irony distribution is more even, but because higher scores indicate more serious factual differences, there are still relatively few high scores.

Level	Sentiment	0	1	2	3	4	5
Sentence	Valence	0	380	624	0	0	0
	Arousal	0	60	406	369	150	46
	Irony	0	181	428	310	75	20
Context	Valence	0	302	516	25	0	0
	Arousal	56	279	264	161	76	26

Table 1: Score frequency of all sentiments.

4 Model performance evaluation

In order to verify the labeling consistency of this study and the feasibility of irony detection, this study uses a deep learning model to predict indicators. Table 2 shows the general statistics of CDVAI dataset. As a benchmark data for deep learning model, the dataset is split using Stratified sampling to get the training, validation, and the testing set. The ratio of train set and test set is 7:3, and validation set is split from train set and the ratio is 9:1.

dataset	Sentence-level	Context-level
Training set	632	531
Validation set	71	59
Testing set	301	253

Table 2: Statistics of the proposed CDVAI dataset.

4.1 Prediction models

The dataset already has manually annotated contexts. Then this paper uses the pretrained BERT model as an encoder and performs VAI score prediction. The sentence will enter the encoder to obtain hidden features and to predict the VAI score through the linear layer. The VA score prediction on context-level has three approaches. (1) M1: After entering the encoder, the VA score is predicted through a linear layer. (2) M2: The position of the context in the sentence can be located, so after entering the encoder, the hidden features of the location of the context is used to enter the linear layer to predict VA score. (3) M3: Enter the sentence and context into the encoder, respectively, and concatenate two hidden features from two hidden features and enter the linear layer to predict the VA score.

This study compares four BERT models pre-trained on a Chinese corpus and two on a multilingual corpus to find the best results, such as PM1: *ckiplab/albert-base-chinese* is trained using the Zhwiki corpus; PM2: *hfl/chinese-macbert-base* uses Wikipedia simplified and traditional Chinese as the corpus to train the model; PM3: *shibing624/macbert4csc-base-chinese* is trained using the SIGHAN typo correction corpus; and PM4: *uer/chinese_roberta_L-4_H-256* is pre-trained from UER-py. Using multilingual corpus to train models, such as PM5: *bert-base-multilingual-uncased* is trained using the Wikipedia corpus, and PM6: *flax-community/alberti-bert-base-multilingual-case* is trained using the PULPO literary poetry corpus.

4.2 Experimental settings

Since the annotation of the CDVAI dataset uses the irony context in it to enhance the model's understanding of contextual emotional changes, it is necessary to use the context span feature for additional context VA prediction. Thus, the paper uses BERT as the experimental mode. The parameters are shown in Table 3. In addition to predicting the VAI of the sentence, the average feature of the context span is also used to predict the VA of the context. Each pre-trained model uses the same parameters, except the learning rate value, context has a smaller starting value than the sentence, which is due to the information of the context is less than the sentence, so a smaller learning rate should be tried.

Parameter	Value
Optimizer	Adam
Learning rate - sentence-level	4e-4, 4e-5, 4e-6
Learning rate - context-level	4e-5, 4e-6, 4e-7
Number of epochs	50

Table 3: Parameter settings of BERT models.

4.3 Experimental results

The prediction performance of dimensional VAI score on sentence-level is shown in Table 4. The MAEs of all models are less than 0.4. The model has the best MAE indicator. MAE is all greater than 0.5, one possible reason for the relatively poor performance is that the determination of excitement is not limited to the intensity of the word, but is annotated according to the overall situation of the described event. Therefore, it is difficult for the model to learn the degree of arousal. The irony result is similar to arousal, the MAEs of all models are greater than 0.5. The possible reason why it is difficult for the model to learn irony is that the degree of irony is not limited to a single ironic word, there may be multiple ironic information in a sentence.

Model	Valence	Arousal	Irony
PM1	**0.319**	0.532	0.548
PM2	0.347	0.522	0.522
PM3	0.339	0.526	0.532
PM4	0.334	0.532	0.533
PM5	0.353	0.536	0.520
PM6	0.332	0.529	0.526

Table 4: Prediction performance of dimensional VAI score on sentence-level.

The prediction performance of dimensional VA score on context-level is shown in Table 5. Valence of context-level also performs quite well. Regardless of the method, the MAE is around 0.45. However, it is worth noting that the second method is not better than the first method to extract the hidden features of the corresponding position of the context and sum up the prediction. However, the prediction effect of M3 after connecting the hidden features of the sentence and context is better in some model scores. However, in most results, the effect of M1 is still better. It is speculated that the reason is that M2 and M3 will increase the amount of noise when predicting the value. The overall effect of Arousal of context is worse than that of valence, and the MAE of any method is about 0.8. However, it is worth noting that M3 achieves better results in most models in arousal prediction. And the difference is very small with M1. It can be speculated that M3 considers the information of the entire sentence and context to help predict the degree of arousal. Compared with M1, M2 has little difference in the results of most models. It can be seen that M2 is less helpful for predicting the degree of arousal.

Model	Valence			Arousal		
	M1	M2	M3	M1	M2	M3
PM1	0.438	0.452	0.456	0.813	0.835	0.787
PM2	0.431	0.451	0.422	0.819	0.817	0.793
PM3	0.401	0.451	0.422	0.743	0.817	0.793
PM4	0.417	0.463	0.438	0.767	0.857	0.788
PM5	0.425	0.438	0.388	0.829	0.824	0.799
PM6	0.429	0.433	0.432	0.847	0.84	0.806

Table 5: Prediction performance of dimensional VA score on context-level.

Analysis of the above cases shows that irony detection is a challenging task. The main problem encountered by the BERT model is difficult to infer the speaker's intention. The lack of common sense carried by the model also affects its judgement. There is also no way to judge the importance and severity of the incidents described in the posts, which makes it difficult for the model to identify the level of irony accurately.

4.4 Error analysis

Based on the performance of BERT model, we present a few incorrect prediction cases below.

- **Example:**
  Sentence: *"很好...連喇叭都壞了 X-(" ("Very good.... even the speakers are broken X-(")*
  Context: *"連喇叭都壞了" ("even the speakers are broken")*
  Judgement: The prediction results are shown in Table 6. The reason why the model judges the valence to be "1.21" may be that it judges "連", "壞了" (*"even, broken")* as negative words. However, the post only indicated that the speakers are broken, which is usually not perceived as highly negative. The lack of common sense may have led to the failure to detect its valence correctly. In terms of irony, the prediction score is relatively large. It is speculated that because the judgment of valence is relatively negative and the term "很好" (*"very good")* is positive, there is a large emotional gap. The model therefore yields a higher irony score. However, the sentence has no other span that emphasizes irony, so the annotated score is lower.

	Sentence-level			Context-level	
	V	**A**	**I**	**V**	**A**
Annotated	2	3	1	2	3
Predicted	1.71	3.45	1.94	1.63	1.97

Table 6: Predict results of example 1.

5 Conclusion

The paper introduced the CDVAI dataset which extended from NTU irony corpus. It contains multi-index sentiment annotation and irony context sentiment annotation, which is helpful for developing Chinese irony computational methods of detection that allow the model to learn sentimental changes and differences in context. The experimental results showed that the annotation of CDVAI dataset provides a learning direction for the BERT model as the basic model, so that the model can understand the irony structure. And the third method proposed in this paper, connecting the sentence with the context and then predicting, can effectively improve the effect of the model predicting arousal of context.

CDVAI dataset does not have enough examples for machine learning experiments, and there is no way to cover a considerable number of fields and complete ironic sentence patterns. Nevertheless, the paper is suitable to use as guide data to obtain more samples or as a template for labeling guidelines. Furthermore, the proposed CDVAI dataset could be combined with other ironic corpora to extend the training sample size so that machine learning algorithms would be improved in the future.

References

Castor, A. and Pollux, L. E. (1992). The use of user modelling to guide inference and learning. *Applied Intelligence*, 2(1):37–53.

Ghosh, A., Li, G., Veale, T., Rosso, P., Shutova, E., Barnden, J., & Reyes, A. (2015, June). Semeval-2015 task 11: Sentiment analysis of figurative language in twitter. In Proceedings of the 9th international workshop on semantic evaluation (SemEval 2015) (pp. 470-478).

Grandchercheur, L.B. (1983). Vers une modélisation cognitive de l'être et du néant. In S.G Paris, G.M. Olson, & H.W. Stevenson (Eds.), *Fondement des Sciences Cognitives*. Hillsdale, NJ: Lawrence Erlbaum Associates (pp. 6—38).

Strötgen, J. and Gertz, M. (2012). Temporal tagging on different domains: Challenges, strategies, and gold standards. In *Proceedings of the Eight International Conference on Language Resources and Evaluation (LREC 2012)* (pp.3746–3753).

Superman, S., Batman, B., Catwoman, C., and Spiderman, S. (2000). Superheroes experiences with books. *The Phantom Editors Associates, Gotham City, 20th edition.*

Bosco, C., Patti, V., & Bolioli, A. (2013). Developing corpora for sentiment analysis: The case of irony and senti-tut. *IEEE Intelligent Systems, 28*(2), 55-63.

Colston, H. L. (2019). Irony as indirectness cross-linguistically: On the scope of generic mechanisms. In *Indirect Reports and Pragmatics in the World Languages* (pp. 109-131). Springer.

Devlin, J., Chang, M.W., Lee, K., & Toutanova, K. (2018). BERT: Pre-training of Deep Bidirectional Transformers for Language Understanding. Computation and Language. arXiv:1810.04805. Version 2.

Dimovska, J., Angelovska, M., Gjorgjevikj, D., & Madjarov, G. (2018). Sarcasm and irony detection in english tweets. *International Conference on Telecommunications* (pp. 120-131). Springer, Cham.

Jia, X., Deng, Z., Min, F., & Liu, D. (2019). Three-way decisions based feature fusion for Chinese irony detection. *International Journal of Approximate Reasoning, 113*, 324-335.

Joshi, A., Bhattacharyya, P., & Carman, M. J. (2017). Automatic sarcasm detection: A survey. *ACM Computing Surveys (CSUR), 50*(5), 1-22.

Kumar, H., & Harish, B. (2019). Automatic irony detection using feature fusion and ensemble classifier. *International Journal of Interactive Multimedia & Artificial Intelligence, 5*(7).

Lestari, W. (2019). Irony analysis of Memes on Instagram social media. *PIONEER: Journal of Language and Literature, 10*(2), 114-123.

Li, A.-R., & Huang, C.-R. (2020). A method of modern Chinese irony detection. *In From Minimal Contrast to Meaning Construct* (pp. 273-288). Springer.

Long, Y., Xiang, R., Lu, Q., Huang, C.-R., & Li, M. (2019). Improving attention model based on cognition grounded data for sentiment analysis. *IEEE transactions on affective computing.*

Lu, Q., Zhu, Z., Xu, F., Zhang, D., Wu, W., & Guo, Q. (2020). Bi-GRU sentiment classification for chinese based on grammar rules and bert. *International Journal of Computational Intelligence Systems.*

Naseem, U., Razzak, I., Eklund, P., & Musial, K. (2020). Towards improved deep contextual embedding for the identification of irony and sarcasm. *2020 International Joint Conference on Neural Networks (IJCNN)* (pp. 1-7). IEEE.

Pfeifer, V. A., & Lai, V. T. (2021). The comprehension of irony in high and low emotional contexts. *Canadian Journal of Experimental Psychology/Revue canadienne de psychologie expérimentale.*

Preoţiuc-Pietro, D., Schwartz, H. A., Park, G., Eichstaedt, J., Kern, M., Ungar, L., & Shulman, E. (2016). Modelling valence and arousal in facebook posts. *Proceedings of the 7th workshop on computational approaches to subjectivity, sentiment and social media analysis* (pp. 9-15).

Rangwani, H., Kulshreshtha, D., & Singh, A. K. (2018). Nlprl-iitbhu at semeval-2018 task 3: Combining linguistic features and emoji pre-trained cnn for irony detection in tweets. *Proceedings of the 12th international workshop on semantic evaluation* (pp. 638-642).

Tang, Y.-j., & Chen, H.-H. (2014). Chinese irony corpus construction and ironic structure analysis. *Proceedings of COLING 2014, the 25th International Conference on Computational Linguistics: Technical Papers* (pp. 1269-1278).

Veale, T., & Hao, Y. (2010). Detecting ironic intent in creative comparisons. In *ECAI 2010* (pp. 765-770). IOS Press.

Xiang, R., Gao, X., Long, Y., Li, A., Chersoni, E., Lu, Q., & Huang, C.-R. (2020). Ciron: a new benchmark dataset for Chinese irony detection. *Proceedings of the 12th Language Resources and Evaluation Conference* (pp. 5714-5720).

Xie, H., Lin, W., Lin, S., Wang, J., & Yu, L.-C. (2021). A multi-dimensional relation model for dimensional sentiment analysis. *Information Sciences,* 579, 832-844.

The 34th Conference on Computational Linguistics and Speech Processing (ROCLING 2022)
Taipei, Taiwan, November 21-22, 2022. The Association for Computational Linguistics and Chinese Language Processing

智慧未來休憩港灣應用服務：以高雄亞灣爲例建構複合休憩知識圖譜
Intelligent Future Recreation Harbor Application Service: Taking Kaohsiung Asia New Bay as an Example to Construct a Composite Recreational Knowledge Graph

吳典志 Dian-Zhi Wu[1], 呂昱德 Yu-De Lu[1], 董家銘 Chia-Ming Tung[1], 黃柏洋 Bo-Yang Huang[1]
黃薰慧 Hsun-Hui Huang[2], 林謙德 Chien-Der Lin[2], 盧文祥 Wen-Hsiang Lu[1]
資訊工程學系, 成功大學[1]
地方創生處, 資訊工業策進會[2]
{ P76101495, ne6101068, P78081065, P76091666 }@gs.ncku.edu.tw
{ beatrice, chiender }@iii.org.tw, whlu@ncku.edu.tw

摘要

有鑑於台灣目前針對港灣休憩的整體專屬規劃服務缺少，多樣的海洋休憩活動和海上景點觀光也未能統合市港週遭服務進行規劃發展，加上針對港灣休憩服務進行軟硬整合而發展的新型態產品及應用服務不多，以及台灣的港灣休憩服務相關產業正面臨數位轉型挑戰。因此資策會提出創新「智慧未來休憩港灣應用服務」計畫，並委託本團隊以高雄亞灣爲主要實證場域，提出複合休憩知識建構模型，運用多來源知識圖譜建構與推論技術推薦適切的休憩服務資訊，讓遊客能夠享受最佳的擬眞智慧人機感知互動服務體驗。

Abstract

In view of the lack of overall specialized design services for harbour recreation in Taiwan nowadays, various marine recreational activities and marine scenic spots haven't yet been planned and developed in the integration of services around the city and harbour. As there are not many state-of-the-art products and application services, and Taiwan's harbour leisure services-related industries are facing the challenge of digital transformation. Institute for Information Industry proposed an innovative "Smart Future Recreational Harbour Application Service" project, taking Kaohsiung Asia's New Bay Area as the main field of demonstration, Using multi-source knowledge graph integration and inference technology to recommend appropriate recreational service information, as a result, tourists can enjoy the best virtual reality intelligent human-machine interactive service experience during their trip.

關鍵字：高雄亞灣、港灣休憩、知識圖譜、智慧人機互動服務體驗、複合休憩知識建構模型

Keywords: Kaohsiung Asia New Bay Area, Harbour Recreation, Knowledge Graph, Intelligent Human-Machine Interactive Service Experience, Complex Rest Knowledge Construction Model

1 緒論

1.1 背景

本研究爲因應經濟部技術處法人科專分項計畫「智慧未來休憩港灣應用服務」需要，本團隊提出複合休憩知識建構模型，擷取非結構化資料並建構港灣休憩知識圖譜，同時設計開發合適的知識圖譜建構框架於港灣休憩智慧應用服務的技術研究。

1.2 動機

「智慧未來休憩港灣應用服務」計畫主要有鑑於台灣目前針對港灣休憩的整體規劃服務缺少，多樣的海洋休憩活動和海上景點觀光也未能統合市港週遭服務進行規劃發展。此外，針對港灣休憩服務進行軟硬整合而發展的新型態產品及應用服務不多，以及台灣的港灣休憩服務相關產業面臨數位轉型挑戰，需要藉由新興科技的導入。

因此，本計畫預計將整合高效能、高附加價值及高創新應用之服務與產品發展之綜合考量，規劃發展以「港灣體感科技旅遊」爲主軸、高雄亞灣爲主要實證場域，並融入元宇宙虛擬體驗進行核心技術研發，以完成遊艇載具爲主的實船串接模擬機連動與環境擬眞體驗之即時擬眞智慧人機感知系統，提供使用者線上線下遊艇休憩體感模擬與跨域共遊體驗。打造全台首創體感港灣休憩服務，讓民眾體驗遊艇航行環境的眞實呈現和港灣休憩即時互動服務內容，滿足遊艇休憩活動的擬眞互動感需求，對海洋活動不再陌生畏懼、近而產生興趣。

1.3 方法

本計畫之系統架構圖如圖1所示，首先蒐集選定景點官方網站 (詳見3.1) 的網頁資訊，同時結合高雄市政府公開資訊平台[1]以及高雄港務

[1]高雄市政府公開資訊平台

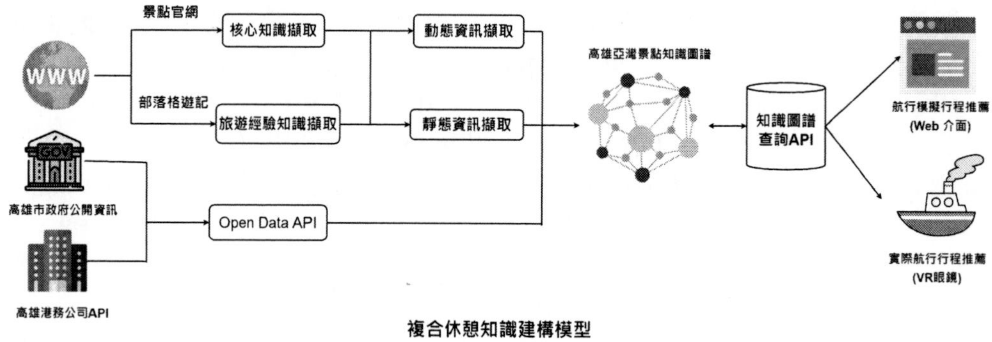

圖 1: 系統架構圖

公司[2]提供的港區船席現況 API 作爲資料集，所蒐集的資料包含結構化、半結構化及非結構化資料，本研究提出複合休憩知識建構模型，擷取非結構化資料並建構港灣休憩知識圖譜，同時設計開發合適的知識圖譜建構框架於港灣休憩智慧應用服務的技術研究。

2 相關研究

2.1 知識圖譜建構

Google 於 2012 年提出知識圖譜的概念[3]，利用語意檢索從許多來源進行資訊蒐集並將其加入 Google Search 服務以優化其搜尋引擎。知識圖譜基本組成由「實體-關係-實體」三元組所建成，實體概念或詞彙代表節點 (node)、以關係代表邊 (edge)。透過自然語言處理 (Natural Language Processing, NLP) 的技術將文章內容進行分析以取出節點與邊的語意關係並建構出龐大的網路結構。知識圖譜的建構主要可以分成兩類，分別是通用型知識圖譜以及特定領域型知識圖譜，通用型知識圖譜最早可以追溯至 WordNet (Miller, 1992)，WordNet 是一個英文的語意網路，在 WordNet 中，名詞、動詞、形容詞和副詞各自被組織成一個同義詞的集合 (synsets)，每個同義詞集合都代表一個基本的語義概念，並且這些集合之間也由各種關係連接形成網絡，後續基於 WordNet 的結構又衍生出許多不同的語言的語意網路甚至是多語言的語義網路，通用型知識圖譜除了常見的用於表達詞彙的定義、詞彙間的關係的語義網路以外，Vrandečić and Krötzsch (2014)，利用維基百科的資料建構了 WikiData 知識庫，藉由維基百科的共同協作性、多語性等特性，保證了知識圖譜的知識量會隨著時間持續擴增。另一方面，知識圖譜也被廣泛應用在多個特定領域，例如醫療領域 (Gatta et al., 2017; Rastogi and Zaki, 2020)、教育領域 (Aliyu et al., 2020; Chen et al., 2018) 或是本計畫的主題旅遊領域。(Ling, 2020) 以中國的泰山作爲核心景點並蒐集相關的景點資訊，例如文化背景、自然資源等等，建構出泰山旅遊導覽知識圖譜，DBtravel(Calleja et al., 2018) 利用擷取 Wikitravel[4]中的網頁資訊，並透過 Wikitravel 網頁中的特定 html 標籤結構建構出知識圖譜。目前現有之旅遊導覽知識圖譜大都多依賴於旅遊網站等結構化資料，這些客觀資訊較難反映出一個景點眞實的旅遊經驗，本計畫將引入部落客遊記，當作使用者可參考的主觀資訊。

2.2 旅遊推薦系統

推薦系統近年來非常流行，最常見的應用在於電商平台，透過分析使用者的購買紀錄、瀏覽紀錄等資訊，用來預測並推薦消費者的偏好商品，促成交易 (Jain and Hegade, 2021; Zhao et al., 2022)。而隨著人們對於生活便利的強烈追求，更多領域引入了推薦系統，例如本計畫的旅遊領域，而使用知識圖譜進行旅遊行程推薦的系統更是少見，(Ling, 2020) 以泰山爲核心景點建構知識圖譜並透過分析使用者的基本資訊、情境資訊、行爲資訊去推薦使用者適合的泰山周遭景點或導覽資訊。本計畫則是以高雄亞灣爲核心景點。

3 方法

本研究整合網際網路資源、高雄市政府公開資訊平台及高雄港務公司船舶停靠資訊 API 以擷取亞灣休憩知識圖譜所需知識。

如圖1所示網際網路資源包含選定景點的官方網站資源爲核心知識擷取的內容及景點相關之部落格遊記文章爲旅遊經驗知識擷取的內容。

[2]高雄港區停泊現況資訊

[3]Introducing the Knowledge Graph: things, not strings

[4]Wikitravel

選定景點	選定景點
亞灣遊艇碼頭	高雄展覽館
高雄 85 大樓	高雄港埠旅運中心
流行音樂中心-鯨魚堤岸	流行音樂中心-音浪塔
駁二藝術特區	蓬萊商港區 (棧庫群)
哈瑪星鐵道文化園區	新濱碼頭
鼓山輪渡站	鼓山漁港
哨船頭遊艇碼頭	西子灣風景區
打狗英國領事館文化園區	高雄燈塔
旗津輪渡站	旗津老街
旗后漁港	海軍第四造船廠
夢時代購物中心	

表 1: 亞灣 21 景點

- 核心知識:
  官方網站將依資料特性區分爲景點基本資訊的靜態資訊及最新消息、活動及展演等各類活動的動態資訊。動態資訊將另行開發排程程式定期更新，並依活動啓迄日期進行知識圖譜的內容更新，進行中的活動可因活動日期已結束而修改其活動類別，同時也會新增圖譜內不存在的新增活動，以維護知識圖譜內容的正確性。

- 旅遊經驗:
  本研究提出複合休憩知識建構模型分析及擷取部落格與選定景點有關之遊記以擷取旅遊經驗，輔以高雄市政府及高雄港務公司之公開資訊分別可提供餐館類別、住宿等級及高雄港船舶停靠資訊，以用於知識圖譜查詢回應清單及未來應用於 VR 以提供遊船於港區航行之數位分身以呈現與現實船隻活動相同視覺。

3.1 資料集

本研究由資策會選定高雄亞灣週邊景點爲知識圖譜建構範圍如表1所列 21 個景點。景點資訊主要蒐集官方網站、旅遊網站景點介紹資訊 (交通、住宿、美食等) 以及痞客邦中與表1有關之部落格遊記文章內容。

除前述網站資源外，本研究另行整理附近景點、餐廳及住宿等三類詞庫，以供複合休憩知識建構模型提升實體詞標記之正確性。餐廳清單選自愛食記網站中所列位於高雄的餐廳及其分類；附近景點之詞庫則蒐集 Tripadvisor 中所列與高雄港相關但排除計畫選定之 21 個景點之亞灣附近景點；住宿的詞庫則是匯整高雄市政府資料開放平台提供之高雄市民宿資料、高雄市一般旅館資料及 Tripadvisor 中所列高雄住宿所匯整之詞庫。

實體詞	HTML 擷取規則
簡介	article
	div.entry-content
	div.ContentPlaceHolder1
營業時間	div.day
	div.time
地址	div.location
	footer-address
電話	div.phone
	footer-address
	data.top.info
活動開始日期	div.starttime
	valid-dates
活動結束日期	div.endtime
	valid-dates
活動內文	thecontent
	entry-content
圖片	img
	img.BigImg

表 2: 景點核心知識擷取規則範例

3.2 景點核心知識建構

景點核心知識擷取的內容以各景點官方網站爲主要知識來源，官網資料依其內容尚可分爲靜態景點介紹之基本資訊及隨時間推移而有所變動的動態訊息，包含最新消息、展覽資訊及活動等訊息。擷取景點核心資訊所使用的規則依如表2所示，依其活動時間及查詢時間動態連結成爲景點的歷史活動、現在活動及未來活動等知識。以下將以網站內容的形態區分靜態知識與動態知識擷取的方法:

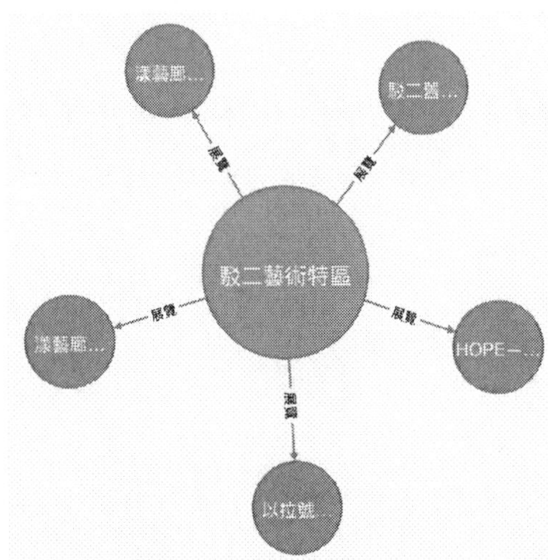

圖 2: 知識圖譜節點與關連範例

3.2.1 靜態知識擷取

知識圖譜的基本單元爲「實體-關連-實體」，較常以句子中所擷取的名詞爲實體詞來源，而動詞則是關連的來源，透過知識圖譜單元可建構出網狀如圖2的圖譜，在此範例中以駁二藝術特區串連各個展覽活動。

資料集所列景點官方網站這類型的內容其異動的頻率較低且能夠利用 HTML 標籤來擷取建構圖譜所需要的知識來源，並經由分析與擷取出文章句子中的實體詞及其關連以建立知識單元。

經過觀察各景點的網站原始碼，因各網站的開發與使用語言各不相同，因此本研究無法利用統一的 HTML 標籤來進行資料擷取，需依照各網站設定擷取資料的 HTML 使用規則，表2所列乃目前針對已蒐集的網站所建立的知識擷取規則。

圖 3: 駁二藝術特區最新活動截圖
https://pier2.org/activity/info/1035/

3.2.2 動態知識擷取

動態知識的來源爲各官網的最新消息、展演及活動等有特定時效的知識，以圖3駁二藝術特區網站的最新活動消息爲例，最新資訊的標題、簡介、開放時間，利用取出 HTML Tag 中所包含的 starttime 及 endtime 而獲得活動"駁遊路" 的開始日期爲 2022/09/03 與結束日期爲 2022/09/04，加上網站 Title 取得活動名稱爲「小人類 x 駁遊路 - 駁二蓬萊倉庫 | 駁二藝術特區」而建立活動名稱與開始與結束日期的知識。

3.3 旅遊經驗知識建構

本研究針對部落格旅遊文章內容的知識擷取重點定位在遊記中所提的延伸附近景點、餐飲美食及住宿，以供建立知識圖譜查詢應用的推薦清單。遊記的文章內容與景點官網的內容有較大的結構性差異，遊記主要以 Content 的內容爲知識擷取來源而屬於處理非結構化文件。爲提升知識擷取的效能，本研究提出複合休憩知識建構模型 (Complex Rest Knowledge Construction Model, CRKC) 來分析遊記內文。CRKC 主要整合二大知識擷取方法，一爲以自建的附近景點、餐廳及住宿三類詞庫搭配 CKIP CoreNLP 之複合休憩知識建構模型-實體詞辨識 (CRKC-NER) 以取得本研究感興趣的實體-關係-實體。另一方法則是應用 CKIP 中文句法剖析結果歸納出可識別主詞與受詞之語意角色集之複合休憩知識建構模型-句法剖析 (CRKC-Parser)。

3.3.1 複合休憩知識建構模型-實體詞辨識 (CRKC-NER)

本研究爲有效提升擷取旅遊經驗的知識，鎖定這類文章中提及的景點、餐飲及住宿等三類以供後續知識圖譜的推薦應用。因此，本研究以人工方式整理前述三類的正式名稱、同義詞、縮寫等建構出三類的詞庫，以提升實體詞辨識之準確率。以下分別說明每一類別詞庫建立的方法:

- 附近景點:
  此類詞庫的主要來源爲 TripAdvisor 並加入遊記中所見的景點一般常用詞、簡稱等所組成的詞庫。例如在 TripAdvisor 中搜尋"駁二藝術特區" 的景點，可以獲得" 誠品書店-駁二店"、" 北極殿"、" 大銘高級腕錶" 等 200 個附近景點。

- 餐廳: 愛食記網站中羅列台灣各地區最新、最流行的美食餐廳，並可了解網友對餐廳的評價及連結至部落客專業食記。因此本研究選定愛食記-高雄地區的餐廳爲此類詞庫的資料來源。

- 住宿: 民宿與飯店的詞庫建立主要參考高雄市政府公開資料平台中所列的星級飯店、民宿清單及 TripAdvisor 而來。例如公開資料的高雄民宿可獲得民宿的登記編號、中文名稱、地址、電話及房間總數等資料，一般旅館資料可取得類別、星等、旅宿名稱、地址、電話、房間數、電子郵件、網址、經緯度等資訊。

3.3.2 複合休憩知識建構模型-句法剖析 (CRKC-Parser)

本研究利用 CKIP Parser[5] 對部落格文章進行中文句法剖析，並經由觀察許多文章及分析句法語意角色內容以整合歸納出表3的內容來連結語意角色與主詞及受詞的關係。並應用於演算法1的主詞語意角色集 (Subject Semantic Role, SSR) 及受詞語意角色集 (Object Semantic Role,

[5] CKIP 中文剖析. **http://parser.iis.sinica.edu.tw/**

OSR) 二項變數中。

如圖4所示。以「頂樓空中花園俯瞰高雄展覽館與高雄港」爲例，可擷取出語意角色爲 agent 的主詞片語" 頂樓空中花園" 及語意角色爲 goal 的地方詞片語" 高雄展覽館與高雄港" 搭配剖析樹所得的動詞" 俯瞰" 而組成知識圖譜所需的 SVO 三元組。

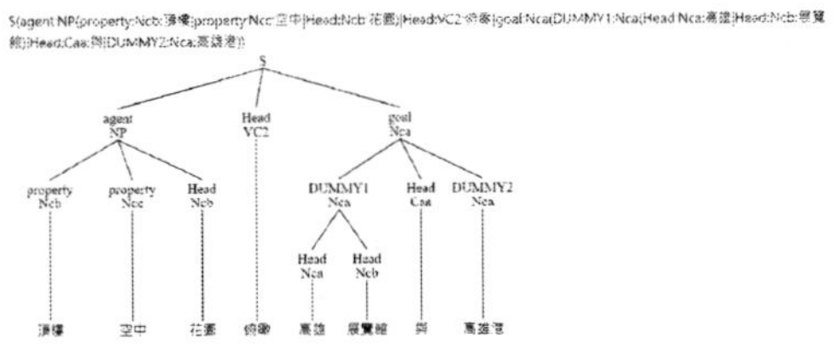

圖 4: CKIP 中文剖析樹

關係類型	語意角色標籤
主詞關係	Agent Causer Experiencer Topic Theme(句首)
受詞關係	Benefactor Goal Target Theme(句尾) Range

表 3: 語意角色之主詞及受詞關係

4 實驗

本章節將介紹初步實驗結果，4.1 說明已蒐集的資料集數量；4.2 說明景點核心知識圖譜的建構過程與結果；4.3 說明旅遊經驗知識圖譜的建置成果；4.4 則舉例說明提出方法的錯誤分析。

4.1 資料集

本研究依所列的 21 項景點之官方網站、旅遊網站之景點介紹、市政府旅遊觀光局處資料以建立靜態景點知識、動態展覽與活動及個人旅遊經驗及推薦等資料來建構出本研究所需的景點核心與旅遊經驗知識圖譜，目前已蒐集的各類文章如表4所示。

資料來源	資料類型	數量
景點資訊	靜態	11
	動態	228
部落格遊記	靜態	1100

表 4: 資料集分布

Algorithm 1 剖析樹語意角色節點知識擷取法

Input: Sentence parsing result SP
Output: Subject S, Extracted Object O, Extracted Object V

```
SSR: Semantic role set of subject [agent, causer, experiencer, topic, theme (句首)]
OSR: Semantic role set of object [benefactor, goal, target, theme (句尾)]
V_POS: Verb POS tagging set [VA, VAC, VB, VC, VCL, VD,...]
S ←[]
O ←[]
V ←[]
for token_i in SP do
    for token_i in SSR do
        S ←token_i
    end for
    for token_i in OSR do
        O ←token_i
    end for
    if token_i belong to "HEAD" && "V_POS" then
        V ←token_i
    end if
end for
```

爲了優化亞灣休憩的知識圖譜建構，特別蒐集整理部落格文章內提到亞灣周遭並排除表1所列 21 景點的景點、餐廳及住宿之清單建構亞灣休憩延伸詞庫，以擷取出更多的知識，表5爲附近景點、餐廳及住宿三類詞庫的資料來源及人工整理之數量，未來將可透過人工方式新增詞庫內容。

資料標籤	資料來源	數量
附近景點	Tripadvisor	636
餐廳	愛食記-高雄	5813
住宿/飯店	Tripadvisor + 市府公開資料平台	342

表 5: 資料集分布

4.2 中文斷詞及詞性標記效能評估

中文斷詞與詞性標記的結果將影響後續知識擷取的成果，本研究隨機挑選部落格文章句子並使用史丹佛 CoreNLP[6]及中研院中文詞庫小組提供的 CKIP CoreNLP[7]、CKIP Transformers[8]套線上展示系統來比較各系統斷詞與詞性標記結果。

[6]Stanford NLP Group
[7]CKIP CoreNLP
[8]CKIP Transformers

圖5爲 CKIP CoreNLP 斷詞結果，可見斷詞的結果可以比較貼近台灣的用詞，例如雞排、西子灣、狠腳色等詞彙。CKIP Transformers 所得的斷詞結果與 CKIP CoreNLP 相同。相同的句子使用史丹佛 NLP Group 的分析後可得到如圖6的結果，可以發現在斷詞部份就產出較多的錯誤。錯詞的斷詞包含林媽媽雞、排、西子、灣、個狠腳色。因此，本研究後續主要使用 CKIP CoreNLP 來進行中文斷詞及詞性標記。

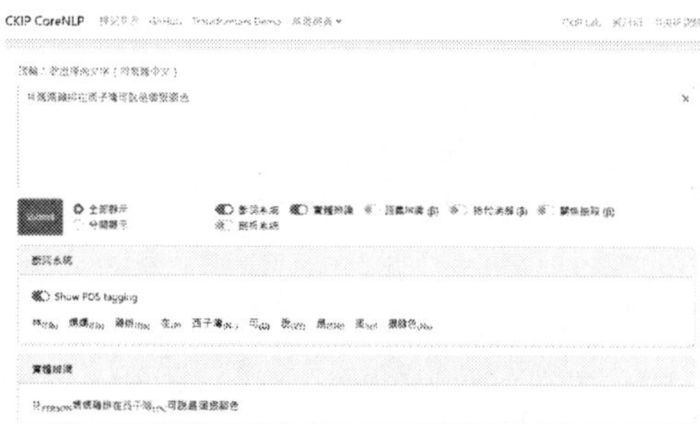

圖 5: CKIP CoreNLP 斷詞範例

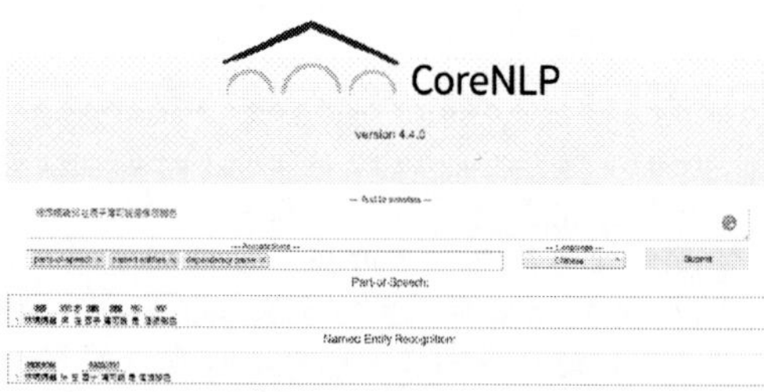

圖 6: Stanford CoreNLP 斷詞範例

4.3 旅遊經驗知識建構效能評估

4.3.1 實體詞擷取效能評估

實體詞擷取的結果將可影響知識擷取的結果，本研究評比 Stanford CoreNLP、CKIP Transformers、CKIP CoreNLP 及本研究提出之 CRKC-NER，由表6可了解 CRKC-NER 可獲得最佳的實體詞擷取結果。

方法	Precision	Recall	F1
Stanford CoreNLP	0.56	0.41	0.47
CKIP Transformers	0.67	0.93	0.78
CKIP CoreNLP	0.71	0.87	0.78
CRKC-NER	0.94	0.73	0.82

表 6: 實體詞擷取方法效能比較

舉例" 新濱駅前將高雄的舊三和銀行改建成咖啡店，是高捷西子灣/輕軌哈瑪星站很受歡迎的高雄咖啡廳" 應該要能正確辨識出的實體詞有" 新濱駅前"、" 高雄"、" 三和銀行"、" 高捷西子灣/輕軌哈瑪星站"、" 高雄咖啡廳" 等實體詞。

利用前述四種方法比較實體詞擷取結果，表7可以看到 Stanford CoreNLP 僅能正確辨識一個實體詞，CKIP Transformers 與 CKIP CKIP CoreNLP 二者辨識實體詞的數量一樣，但實體詞有些許落差。例如 Transformers 可以正確辨識出" 三和銀行"，但 CoreNLP 則無法辨識出相同的實體詞，但 CoreNLP 可以正確辨識" 高雄咖啡廳" 而 Transformers 則只能辨識出" 高雄"，CRKC-NER 則因多加詞庫的影響，僅有" 新濱駅前" 未識別出。" 新濱駅前" 實體詞正確的名稱是" 新濱・駅前"，此爲一家新開幕的餐酒館。經由維護詞庫將" 新濱・駅前" 及其同義詞" 新濱駅前" 加入餐廳類別的詞庫後 CRKC-NER 即可辨識出五個實體詞。

方法	正確	類別錯誤	未識別
Stanford CoreNLP	1	3	1
CKIP Transformers	3	1	1
CKIP CoreNLP	3	1	1
CRKC-NER	4	0	1

表 7: 例句" 新濱駅前將高雄的舊三和銀行改建成咖啡店，是高捷西子灣/輕軌哈瑪星站很受歡迎的高雄咖啡廳" 實體詞擷取方法的正確詞彙比較

4.3.2 「實體-關連-實體」關係擷取效能評估

爲驗證本研究提出的 CRKC-Parser 於旅遊經驗知識擷取的成果，使用 Stanford CoreNLP 提供的 Dependency Parser 所擷取到的實體詞及其關連來取得「實體-關連-實體」的關係進行效能評比。本研究隨機選取資料集中的 50 個句子來進行效能評比，比較結果如表8所示。可發現當作對照組的 Stanford CoreNLP 的方法對於實體的擷取結果較不理想，例如「駁二藝術特區原本是舊倉庫」經由 Stanford Core NLP 處理後取得一個 PERSON 的實體詞" 駁二藝術特區"，而 CKIP 則取得一個行政區的實體詞" 駁二藝術特區"，相較之下 CKIP 較能貼近在地使用體驗。

方法	Precision	Recall	F1
Stanford CoreNLP	0.26	0.18	0.21
CRKC-Parser	0.63	0.35	0.45

表 8: 旅遊經驗知識建構之「實體-關連-實體」關係擷取效能評估

4.4 亞灣休憩知識圖譜建構與系統展示

本研究目前初步利用駁二藝術特區、高雄展覽館等景點來蒐集官網、遊記文章以建立知識圖

The 34th Conference on Computational Linguistics and Speech Processing (ROCLING 2022)
Taipei, Taiwan, November 21-22, 2022. The Association for Computational Linguistics and Chinese Language Processing

譜的雛形系統並利用 Neo4j 建構出本系統的核心可視化知識圖譜，可視化的呈現可提供人員可以方便快速的查閱知識圖譜所有節點與關係，圖7即爲以哈瑪星鐵道文化園區爲中心所展示的圖譜節點與關係，系統維護人員可容易的查看目前知識圖譜的內容及可透過 API 進行人爲的圖譜知識節點與關係的新增、刪除與修改等維護作業。目前進度已蒐集高雄展覽館、駁二藝術特區、哈瑪星鐵道文化園區等 5 個主要的景點進行初期建構與驗證。

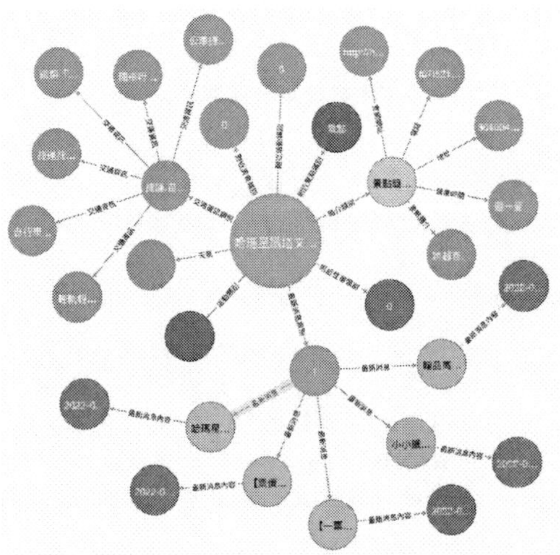

圖 7: 可視化知識圖譜

本系統設計一套三階知識圖譜查詢的 API 邏輯以降低前端應用程式查詢時需要回傳大量資料，以加速系統的回應時間。詳細的 API 設計邏輯如下：

- L1-景點基本資訊: 本階層目的在提供遊客該景點基本簡介及連結的知識，包含景點交通、住宿、餐飲及活動、展覽等類別供遊客深入探索。
  - 輸入: 高雄展覽館
  - 輸出:
    * 高雄展覽館 (KEC) 位於亞洲新灣區核心，是台灣第一座多功能的臨港會展中心，由經濟部投資興建，安益國際展覽集團營運，致力打造一個國際商業與貿易的平台，推動產業聚落永續發展，引領會展城市經濟邁向另一個高峰。多功能的室內、户外以及水岸活動空間及會議中心，可激發創意盡情馳騁，全方位滿足會展需求。2021 年導入 5G 專頻專網建設與創新會展應用，轉型爲高科技多功能場域，以「場館即平台、科技即服務」的新目標定位，透過會展商務推廣，推動產業數位轉型，發展成爲 5G AIoT 科技新創應用商機拓展的大平台。
    * 官 網:https://www.kecc.com.tw/zh-tw/kec
    * 地址: 高雄市前鎮區成功二路 39 號
    * 電話:07-2131188
    * 營業時間: 週一至週日:10：00 - 18：00
    * 活動: 現在活動、歷史活動、未來活動
    * 交通: 汽車、捷運、公車
    * 美食類別: 中式料理、日本料理、韓式料理、美式料理、義式料理、泰式料理、港式料理
    * 附近住宿: 一星級、二星級、三星級、四星級、五星級、其他
- L2-景點 + 類別: 本階層主要回應使用者於 L1 點選感興趣的類別資訊，例如使用者想了解高雄展覽館附近五星級住宿的相關資訊，前端應用程式將以高雄展覽館 + 五星級來進行第二階知識查詢。
  - 輸入: 高雄展覽館 + 五星級
  - 輸出:
    * 名稱: 英迪格酒店、漢來大飯店
- L3-景點行程項目詳細資訊: 第三階層顯示內容爲使用者所選定景點及特定項目的完整資訊。
  - 輸入: 高雄展覽館 + 五星級 + 漢來大飯店
  - 輸出:
    * 官網:https://www.grand-hilai.com/
    * 房間數:540 間
    * 簡介: 漢來大飯店座落於高雄繁華的商業中心，樓高 186 公尺，可俯瞰大高雄全景，擁有三千多件隨處可見的古董藝術珍品、540 間舒適客房、13 家中西餐廳及 1000 個停車位。距離高鐵站只要 20 分鐘車程；步行至捷運站也僅需 15 分鐘。館內除了住宿、餐飲、會議、宴客的功能之外，還結合了精品雲集的漢神百貨，並符合一次購足的便利。充滿新古典主義風格的大廳，古董藝術品

遍佈全館，呈現壯麗典雅的設計風格。房內採用穩重大方的原木材質，加以現代感的簡潔線條設計與歐洲古典紋飾，呈現出尊貴優雅的氣質。打開窗簾，高雄港的美麗景緻盡收眼底，不但令人驚艷，更造就了漢來大飯店的無價！

* 地址: 高雄市前金區成功一路 266 號
* 電話:(07)215-7266

4.5 知識擷取錯誤分析

針對本研究利用 CKIP 中文剖析樹搭配演算法進行 SVO 擷取的過程目前仍有些問題待解決。

- 單一句子，多重剖析樹:
首先是中文剖析系統會自動利用標點符號進行字串的分割，因此一句較長的句子會先依標點符號斷開後解析成多個剖析樹，在未使用自然語言處理的搭配詞 (Collocation) 的方法前會得到較差的知識擷取成果。表9爲錯誤的例句。以第一句範例「走到底就會抵達駁二藝術特區，經過高雄港牌樓，倉庫群就在眼前」所取得的剖析樹只能擷取語意角色爲 goal 的受詞「駁二藝術特區」，該句並無法擷取到屬於主詞的語意角色，而「經過高雄港牌樓」及「倉庫群就在眼前」分別只能得到動詞片語及名詞片語的剖析樹。

- 缺少明顯主詞或主詞不明確:
第二類錯誤是句子沒有明顯的主詞或是主詞不明顯時也容易造成擷取 SVO 時的錯誤，第二句範例「房間能看見 85 大樓與高雄流行音樂中心」，人工分析時會將房間當成主詞、看見是動詞而 85 大樓及高雄流行音樂中心則爲受詞，但 CKIP 剖析樹得到的是一個動詞片語，房間被辨識爲地方詞而非主詞，動詞及受詞則與人工標記結果相同。因此需考量將地方詞加入演算法判斷主詞及受詞的規則中並以該詞出現的位置來決定標記成主詞或受詞才可擷取到預期的知識。

例句	正確結果	分析結果
走到底就會抵達駁二藝術特區，經過高雄港牌樓，倉庫群就在眼前	倉庫群 (s)/就 (v)/在眼前 (o)	抵達 (v) 駁二藝術特區 (o)
房間能看見 85 大樓與高雄流行音樂中心」	房間 (s)/看見 (v)/85 大樓與高雄流行音樂中心 (o)	85 大樓與高雄流行音樂中心 (o)

表 9: SVO 剖析知識擷取錯誤分析範例

5 結論

本研究提出複合休憩知識建構模型，結合 HTML 標籤及整合 CKIP 中文剖析樹、語意角色之旅遊經驗知識擷取演算法以建構符合計畫需求之高雄港灣休憩知識圖譜。目前仍在持續蒐集各景點官網、旅遊網站及遊記經驗等資料並持續建構中，以達期末成果展示之所需。複合休憩知識建構模型未來仍有優化、改進之處:

- 引入搭配詞:
遊記經驗的文章中的景點與內文較易出現字句過長的現象，目前的建構方法尚無法擷取出適當的知識單元，未來將加入搭配詞 (Collocation) 的機制來串連文章前後句的關係，提高主詞擷取成功的機率。

- 動態資訊定期更新與維護:
景點官網的動態資訊需要定期更新與維護，需要排程程式定期取得各網站的最新消息、展演及活動等資訊並更新知識圖譜內容，以確保圖譜內知識的正確性。

- 知識圖譜維護機制:
本研究已設計一套可經由人工維護知識圖譜內容的方法，待景點資訊建構完成後將接續完成此一維護介面，使得知識能夠建立、應用及解釋，對於錯誤學習的知識也可經由人工校正，以健全知識圖譜內容。

References

Ismail Aliyu, A. F. D. Kana2, and Salisu Aliyu. 2020. Development of knowledge graph for university courses management. volume arXiv:2004.00071, pages 1–4. International Journal of Education and Management Engineering.

Pablo Calleja, Freddy Priyatna, Nandana Mihindukulasooriya, and Mariano Rico. 2018. *DBtravel: A Tourism-Oriented Semantic Graph: ICWE 2018 International Workshops, MATWEP, EnWot, KD-WEB, WEOD, TourismKG, Cáceres, Spain, June 5, 2018, Revised Selected Papers*, pages 206–212.

Penghe Chen, Yu Lu, Vincent W. Zheng, and Xiyang Chen. 2018. Knowedu: A system to construct knowledge graph for education. volume 6, pages 1–4. IEEE Access.

Roberto Gatta, Mauro Vallati, and Lenkowicz. 2017. Generating and comparing knowledge graphs of medical processes using pminer. pages 1–4. K-CAP.

Sourabh Jain and Prakash Hegade. 2021. E-commerce product recommendation based on product specification and similarity. In *2021 International Conference on Innovation and Intelligence for Informatics, Computing, and Technologies (3ICT)*, pages 620–625.

Feng Ling. 2020. Design of tourism intelligent recommendation model of mount tai scenic area based on knowledge graph. pages 241–244.

George A. Miller. 1992. Wordnet: a lexical database for english. volume Speech and Natural Language: Proceedings of a Workshop Held at Harriman, New York, February 23-26, 1992, pages 23–26.

Nidhi Rastogi and Mohammed J. Zaki. 2020. Personal health knowledge graphs for patients. volume arXiv:2004.00071, pages 1–4.

Denny Vrandečić and Markus Krötzsch. 2014. Wikidata: A free collaborative knowledgebase. *Communications of the ACM*, 57:78–85.

Kai Zhao, Yukun Zheng, Tao Zhuang, Xiang Li, and Xiaoyi Zeng. 2022. Joint learning of e-commerce search and recommendation with a unified graph neural network. WSDM '22, page 1461—1469, New York, NY, USA. Association for Computing Machinery.

The 34th Conference on Computational Linguistics and Speech Processing (ROCLING 2022)
Taipei, Taiwan, November 21-22, 2022. The Association for Computational Linguistics and Chinese Language Processing

HanTrans: An Empirical Study on Cross-Era Transferability of Chinese Pre-trained Language Model (預訓練語言模型在漢語上的跨時代學習能力)

Chin-Tung Lin
Academia Sinica
cindylin@iis.sinica.edu.tw

Wei-Yun Ma
Academia Sinica
ma@iis.sinica.edu.tw

摘要

近年來預訓練的語言模型在自然語言處理中蔚爲風潮，以 BERT (Bidirectional Encoder Representations form Transformers) 模型爲代表，其掩碼語言建模 (masked-language modeling, MLM) 被廣泛應用於大型語言模型的預訓練，使得後續微調 (fine tuning) 後的模型即可在下游任務有很好的表現。然而，在預訓練的語料中，相比於簡體中文，繁體中文只佔了很少的比例，尤其缺乏古漢語（上古、中古、近代等）的語料。這使得古漢語的自然語言處理一直沒有適切的大型預訓練模型可用。基於此，我們訓練與發佈了一個專爲古漢語打造的 BERT 系列模型。我們的預訓練語言模型與原本的中文 BERT 系列模型相比，能夠成功降低了古漢語的 perplexity 分數。同時，我們也進一步開發了不同時代的分詞與詞類標記的模型，並探究其對於跨時代語料的遷移學習能力。最後，我們將不同時代模型的人稱代名詞詞向量 (word embedding) 進行降維，觀察其不同時代的變異情形。我們的程式碼發布在`https://github.com/ckiplab/han-transformers`。

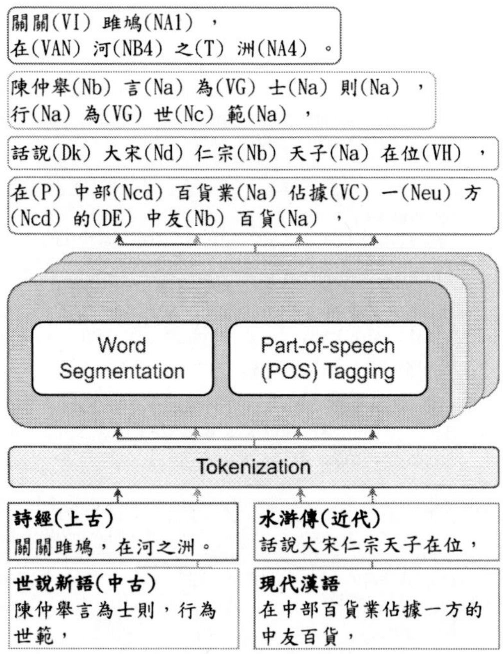

Figure 1: 漢語分詞和詞類標記範例，我們使用四個時代的漢語語料預訓練語言模型，同時應用在分詞和詞類標記的下游任務上。

Abstract

The pre-trained language model has recently dominated most downstream tasks in the NLP area. Particularly, bidirectional Encoder Representations from Transformers (BERT) is the most iconic pre-trained language model among the NLP tasks. Their proposed masked-language modeling (MLM) is an indispensable part of the existing pre-trained language models. Those outperformed models for downstream tasks benefited directly from the large training corpus in the pre-training stage. However, their training corpus for modern traditional Chinese was light. Most of all, the ancient Chinese corpus is still disappearance in the pre-training stage. Therefore, we aim to address this problem by transforming the annotation data of ancient Chinese into BERT style training corpus. Then we propose a pre-trained Oldhan Chinese BERT model for the NLP community. Our proposed model outperforms the original BERT model by significantly reducing perplexity scores in masked-language modeling (MLM). Also, our fine-tuning models improve F1 scores on word segmentation and part-of-speech tasks. Then we comprehensively study zero-shot cross-eras ability in the BERT model. Finally, we visualize and investigate personal pronouns in the embedding space of ancient Chinese records from four eras. We have released our code at `https://github.com/ckiplab/han-transformers`.

The 34th Conference on Computational Linguistics and Speech Processing (ROCLING 2022)
Taipei, Taiwan, November 21-22, 2022. The Association for Computational Linguistics and Chinese Language Processing

關鍵字：漢語、預訓練語言模型、零樣本跨時代學習

Keywords: Chinese Language Model, Zero-shot Cross-Era Transfer Learning

1 緒論

近年自然語言處理 (Natural Language Processing, NLP) 領域中，大型預訓練的語言模型 (Kenton and Toutanova, 2019; Radford et al., 2019; Raffel et al., 2020) 在許多下游任務中均取得優異的表現。多語言的預訓練模型 (Kenton and Toutanova, 2019; Xue et al., 2021) 也日益出現，能夠支援中文的自然語言處理。常見的中文下游任務包含問答系統 (Shao et al., 2018; Cui et al., 2019)、機器翻譯 (Sennrich et al., 2016)、文本情感分析 (Pontiki et al., 2016; Tan and Zhang, 2008)、文本摘要 (Hu et al., 2015)、詞性標記 (Xue et al., 2005) 和中文分词 (Emerson, 2005; Jin and Chen, 2008) 等等。

得益於多語言的預訓練資料，(Pires et al., 2019) 發現以 104 種語言預訓練的 Multilingual BERT (mBERT) 有 zero-shot 的跨語言學習能力。以中文問答系統爲例，(Hsu et al., 2019) 實驗得出英文問答資料上做微調的 BERT 模型，測試於中文的問答資料上就能得到不錯的 F1 值。而同時使用中文和英文的問答資料做微調，比單獨使用中文的資料表現有更高的 F1 值。然而多語言的預訓練模型同時也受限於預訓練階段不同語言文本的資料量多寡，與多資源的語言相比之下，下游任務在少資源語言上表現較爲不佳，舉例來說，mBERT (Pires et al., 2019) 的預訓練資料中最多的是英文 (21%)，因此在 XNLI (Conneau et al., 2018) 的任務上英文有最好的表現，相比之下簡體中文差了大約五個百分點。在現存大部分預訓練語言模型以英文語料爲主的情況下，增加中文的預訓練語料來提升中文下游任務的成績，有著迫切的需求。

簡體中文的領域有已經發布的 MacBERT (Cui et al., 2021) 使用大量簡體中文語料做爲預訓練文本，在各個中文下游任務比原始 BERT 模型 (Kenton and Toutanova, 2019) 有更好的成績，然而在繁體中文的領域中，這部分較爲缺乏。特別在古漢語的部分，據我們所知，還未有專門爲其打造的預訓練語言模型。因此，在這份工作中，我們使用古漢語的語料對 BERT 系列模型做預訓練，並開發了不同時代的分詞與詞類標記的模型。同時，基於上述多語言預訓練給我們的啓示，我們擬探究中文不同時代的語料訓練出來的模型是否具有遷移能力，以及綜合不同時代的語料一起訓練是否會有助於各時代的下游任務表現等問題。

斷詞和詞性標註 (擷取自堯典)
乃 (DL) 命 (VF) 羲 (NB1) 和 (NB1) ，
欽若 (VH1N) 昊天 (NA1) ；
歷 (DA) 象 (VP) 日月 (NB2) 星辰 (NA2) ，
敬 (DV) 授 (VD) 人時 (NA5) 。

Table 1: 漢語語料庫標註資料

針對上述需求與問題，我們使用中央研究院的四個時代的漢語文本語料庫作爲預訓練的資料，並使用其對應的標記語料做爲下遊任務的調適訓練和測試，包含上古漢語[1](先秦到西漢)、中古漢語[2](東漢魏晉南北朝)、近代漢語[3](唐五代以後) 和現代漢語平衡語料庫[4]。各時代標記語料均含有人爲標記的斷詞和詞類，如表1所示，第一行的「乃」是關聯副詞、「命」是複雜雙賓動詞 (外動複)，而第二行開頭的「欽若」是兩個中文字組成的狀態不及物動詞 (内靜)，我們使用這些標記資料來做中文的分詞與詞類標記任務。透過這四個時代的 BERT 預訓練與微調訓練，我們擬探討不同時代語料能否互相增進學習表現。實驗發現，對於分詞任務，不同時代語料的確能夠互相增進學習，證明模型的遷移能力，而對於詞類標記任務，由於詞類標記在四個時代的標記分類不盡相同，像是上古語料中有 382 種 (89%) 詞類標記並未在其他三個時代語料出現，因此我們發現詞類標記任務就不具備這樣的遷移能力。

之後的章節中，第2章將介紹如何將中央研究院的漢語標記語料庫轉換成 BERT 模型 (Kenton and Toutanova, 2019) 的資料型態，我們撰寫程式轉換三種任務對應的不同輸入和標記型態。之後在第3章講解我們三種模型的訓練方法，使用我們資料集預訓練中文語言模型，以及分別微調 (Fine-Tune) 預訓練模型在兩個下游任務模型。接著我們在第4章節介紹我們設計的實驗。最後第5章中列出實驗結果，除了三種模型在不同時代資料集的交叉測試結果和討論，我們也對不同時代的人稱代詞 (personal pronouns) 在語言模型的詞嵌入 (word embedding) 向量空間中的表現進行觀察與分析。本論文主要有以下四種貢獻：

[1]http://lingcorpus.iis.sinica.edu.tw/cgi-bin/kiwi/akiwi/kiwi.sh

[2]http://lingcorpus.iis.sinica.edu.tw/cgi-bin/kiwi/dkiwi/kiwi.sh

[3]http://lingcorpus.iis.sinica.edu.tw/cgi-bin/kiwi/pkiwi/kiwi.sh

[4]http://asbc.iis.sinica.edu.tw/

詞語	詞類	頻率	Vocab. set
一	S	2108	一
一	VH1	23	## 夫
一	VP	47	## 旦
一夫	NA1	2	## 再
一旦	NA5	3	## 氣

Table 2: 轉換標記資料成 BERT 字彙表

Domain	#Lexicons	Size of Vocab.
上古	41595	8781
中古	25956	7448
近代	36906	8660
現代	144655	12563

Table 3: 四個時代字彙統計

- 使用四個時代的漢語語料來預訓練語言模型，其中使用古漢語語料是自然語言處理領域的首次嘗試。我們預訓練的語言模型符合 HuggingFace 平台上 transformers 套件的使用格式，進一步促進繁體中文語言處理的研究發展。

- 微調預訓練語言模型在下游任務，包含中文分詞與詞類標記任務，古漢語的自動化分詞與標記能幫助歷史語言方面的研究。

- 啓發於 (Pires et al., 2019; Hsu et al., 2019) 發現語言模型在下游任務有 zero-shot 的跨語言學習能力。我們想觀察語言模型在我們的兩個下游任務上是否有 zero-shot 跨時代漢語學習能力。實驗發現在中古語料數量最少的情況下，拿訓練在近代語料上的分詞模型直接測試在中古語料上，和使用中古語料訓練的分詞模型相比達到可競爭的 F1 分數，發現模型具有 zero-shot 跨時代漢語學習能力。

- 視覺化語言模型中人稱代詞的詞嵌入向量，觀察漢語人稱代詞裡詞跟詞 (例如「濃」和「吾」)，在四個時代詞空間裡相對位置的一致性。

2 資料處理

2.1 建立模型字彙表

我們撰寫程式將漢語語料庫提供的詞語表轉成 BERT 格式的字彙表 (如表2)，這些在字彙表中的字詞 (token) 可以重組成表2左邊的所有詞語。BERT 的字彙表使用 Google NMT (Wu et al., 2016) 提出的 WordPiece 斷詞方法，將原來的 words 拆成更小微度的 wordpieces，可以有效處理不在字典裡頭的詞語。而中文方面是字符單位 (character-level) 的斷詞，有 ## 前綴的字詞即爲 wordpieces。如下表2的「一夫」，長度爲 2 個字符，由「一」和「## 夫」兩個字詞組成。

轉換完成的數量集大小如表3所示，原本上古中有 41595 個詞語 (Lexicon)，我們將之轉換縮減成總共 8781 個字詞的 BERT 字彙表，也就是這 8781 個字詞即可表示左邊的 41595 種詞語。中古、近代和現代分別將各自的詞語從 25956、36906 和 144655 透過我們的程式轉成 7448、8660 和 12563 個字詞。四個資料集合計有 37452 個字詞，這些字詞可以完整表示原本四個時代漢語的所有詞語。

Original annotation						
曰若 (T) 稽 (VC2) 古 (NA5) ： 帝堯 (NB1) 曰 (VG) 放動 (NB1) 。						
斷詞	曰	若	稽	古	：	
分詞	B	I	B	B	B	
詞類	T	T	VC2	NA5	-	
斷詞	帝	堯	曰	放	動	。
分詞	B	I	B	B	I	B
詞類	NB1	NB1	VG	NB1	NB1	-

Table 4: 斷詞和詞性標註訓練範例

2.2 建立分詞和詞類標記訓練資料

我們撰寫程式將漢語語料庫提供的分詞和詞類標記資料轉換成模型訓練資料，如表4所示。最上面是語料庫提供的人工標記資料，下面是我們轉換完成的分詞任務和詞類標記任務的模型訓練資料，分詞模型的標記轉成以 BIO 格式來表示。「曰若稽古：」是一句話，而其中「曰若」是古漢語中的一個詞，所以分詞任務裡，「曰」是這個詞的 beginning，「若」則是 inside。當模型輸入「曰若稽古：」時，我們希望分詞模型輸出「BIBBB」。而詞類標記模型對每個字詞標記對應的詞性，於是我們期望詞類標記模型輸出「T T VC2 NA5」。表示「曰若」(T) 是語助詞，「稽」(VC2) 是準動作單賓動詞 (準外動)，「古」(Na5) 是時間詞。

2.3 新增古漢語字彙到實驗模型

我們將轉換完的古漢語字彙表新增到實驗模型，擴充原模型的中文詞彙表，實驗模型裡新增的四個時代詞彙字詞個數如表5所示。我們的實驗總共實作和比較在五種模型上，其中三個 ckiplab/開頭的模型 (表5上方) 是中文詞庫小組[5]之前只訓練在現代的語料上 (ZhWiki

[5]https://github.com/ckiplab/ckip-transformers

Model	上古	中古	近代	現代
ckiplab/albert-tiny-chinese	2673	1041	941	2635
ckiplab/albert-base-chinese	2673	1041	941	2635
ckiplab/bert-base-chinese	2673	1041	941	2635
roberta-base (Liu et al., 2019)	8781	7444	8660	12563
bert-base-uncased (Kenton and Toutanova, 2019)	8371	6983	8212	12134

Table 5: 實驗模型擴充後的字彙數量

輸入句子	則必有穿窬拑楗、抽箕踰備之姦； 爲孔子之窮於陳、蔡而廢六藝，
新增字詞前	‘則’, ‘必’, ‘有’, ‘穿’, ‘[UNK]’, ‘[UNK]’, ‘[UNK]’, ‘、’, ‘抽’, ‘箕’, ‘[UNK]’, ‘備’, ‘之’, ‘姦’, ‘；’ (from ckiplab/bert-base-chinese) ‘[UNK]’, ‘[UNK]’, ‘子’, ‘之’, ‘[UNK]’, ‘[UNK]’, ‘陳’, ‘、’, ‘[UNK]’, ‘[UNK]’, ‘[UNK]’, ‘[UNK]’, ‘[UNK]’, ‘，’ (from bert-base-uncased)
新增字詞後 (我們模型)	‘則’, ‘必’, ‘有’, ‘穿’, ‘[UNK]’, ‘拑’, ‘楗’, ‘、’, ‘抽’, ‘箕’, ‘踰’, ‘備’, ‘之’, ‘姦’, ‘；’ ‘爲’, ‘孔’, ‘子’, ‘之’, ‘窮’, ‘於’, ‘陳’, ‘、’, ‘蔡’, ‘而’, ‘廢’, ‘六’, ‘藝’, ‘，’

Table 6: 新增字詞 (tokens) 前後的模型斷詞結果

與 CNA 資料集)。另外我們挑選兩個 BERT 的系列模型（表5下方），可以發現 bert-base-uncased (Kenton and Toutanova, 2019) 模型在作者的原始訓練資料中已含有部分中文字彙表，而 roberta (Liu et al., 2019) 的模型完全沒看過中文資料，因此我們轉換完成的字彙表被完全擴充到 roberta 的模型字彙表中。

新增古漢語字詞到模型後，輸入的文句會先經由模型的 tokenizer 做斷詞處理，在 BERT 模型中不認識的字詞會以「[UNK]」表示。如表6所示，當輸入「則必有穿窬拑楗、抽箕踰備之姦;」到 ckiplab/bert-base-chinese 模型時，因爲新增字詞前模型不認識「窬」、「拑」、「楗」和「踰」，所以斷詞結果皆顯示爲「[UNK]」，在語言模型內映射這四個字到向量空間時，皆以「[UNK]」對應的詞嵌入向量表示，導致模型理解混亂。而在我們新增從漢語語料庫提供的 Lexicon 轉成的字詞到模型後，表6最下列在這個範例中模型多認識了「拑」、「楗」和「踰」三個字。而輸入「爲孔子之窮於陳、蔡而廢六藝，」到 bert-base-uncased 模型時，可以發現這輸入範例中原始模型認識的中文字非常少，只有「子」、「之」、「陳」以及標點符號 (表6中間)，在我們新增字詞到模型後，此範例所有的中文字都成功斷詞，在之後模型裡能以各字詞獨有的詞嵌入向量表示。

3 方法

3.1 中文語言模型

我們採用 (Kenton and Toutanova, 2019) 預訓練語言模型的方法，稱爲 Masked LM (Masked Language Modeling) 的訓練技巧，目的是訓練詞嵌入向量來學習雙向的語言資訊。以表6舉例，當我們輸入文句「曰若稽古：帝堯曰放勳。」時，在 Masked LM 中，在斷詞後的 11 個字詞中，每個字詞有 15% 的機率被替換成「[MASK]」，而模型的目標是預測出被遮起來的原字詞是什麼。在這個任務目標上，模型必須得理解「[MASK]」前後兩端的語言資訊才能正確推論出原本被我們替換成「[MASK]」的字詞原本是什麼，因此可以訓練出有雙向資訊的上下文詞嵌入向量。

依照原始 BERT(Kenton and Toutanova, 2019) 的說法，如果將所有選定的 token 皆替換成「[MASK]」，會導致模型學到只需要在遇到「[MASK]」時才做預測，其他的字詞皆視作上下文來訓練。因此實作上，作者設定的是 15% 被選定替換的 tokens 中，80% 替換成「[MASK]」、10% 是字彙表中隨機的 token 和 10% 保留原本的 token。我們也依循此設定進行古漢語文字的 Masked LM 訓練。

我們將四個時代的資料以 10:1:1 的比例切割爲訓練資料集 (train)、開發資料集 (dev) 和測試資料集 (test set)，各資料集句子數量如表7所示。在訓練階段時使用訓練資料集來做訓練，每 500 個訓練步數使用開發資料集做測試並將表現最好的模型儲存下來。訓練完成後，我們統一測試於各時代測試集上作爲實驗結果。表7中最下方的 merge，是我們合併四個時代的資料集來訓練模型，並分別測試在四個時代的測試資料集上。

The 34th Conference on Computational Linguistics and Speech Processing (ROCLING 2022)
Taipei, Taiwan, November 21-22, 2022. The Association for Computational Linguistics and Chinese Language Processing

Domain	Train	Develop	Test
上古	460170	43890	43060
中古	262395	22688	31277
近代	698749	61934	76106
現代	1175516	109715	110718
Merge	2596830	238227	-

Table 7: 語言模型訓練資料

Dataset	Train	Develop	Test
上古	3274921	326074	325511
中古	2169011	214735	220383
近代	6511768	645702	659317
現代	15824246	1576439	-

Table 8: 分詞標記模型訓練資料

3.2 中文分詞模型

當模型輸入表9的斷詞結果（以中文字符爲單位），分詞模型會對每個字詞輸出 IBO 格式的標記結果，如表9中間所示。分詞訓練的任務上，對每一個字詞做分類，區分是 B、I 或 O。最後經過後處理將 BI 標記對應中文字串轉成我們要的分詞結果，如表9最下行所示。當輸入句子「朱儒問徑天高於脩人，」後我們可以得到分詞結果，其中「朱儒」、「問」、「徑」、「天高」、「於」、「脩人」、「，」分別可視爲一個中文詞語。最後模型訓練資料的統計結果如表8，以句子爲單位做資料集切割 (比例與3.1語言模型訓練相同)，之後每一筆資料以詞語作爲單位。

3.3 詞類標記模型

詞類標記任務和分詞任務相同，同樣可視爲以字詞爲單位的分類問題。但不同於分詞模型只有 B、I 和 O 共三種類別，四個時代語料中總共包含 518 種詞類類別。上古語料使用當中 428 種詞類爲最多，因爲在漢語語料庫人工標記時，對上古語料的動詞後有加註字母來表示語境和特徵。而中古、近代和現代資料集則分別使用 98、98、76 種詞語標記。圖2表示他們標記的分布情形。詞類標記任務如表9所示，當輸入句子「朱儒問徑天高於脩人，」後模型會輸出每個字的詞類標記，幫助我們理解句中每個詞語的作用。如範例所示：「朱儒」(NA1) 是有生名詞，「問」(VE) 是後接句賓或動詞組的動作及物動詞 (外動子)，「徑」(U) 是待分析詞句，「天高」(NI) 是抽象名詞及衍生名詞，「於」(P) 是介詞，最後「脩人」(NA1) 是有生名詞。得知古漢語中一句話裡每個詞的作用後，能更方便我們理解此句含意。模型訓練資料統計結果如表10，以句爲單位使用之前語言模型訓練同樣的資料集切割，每一筆訓練資料如表4所示。

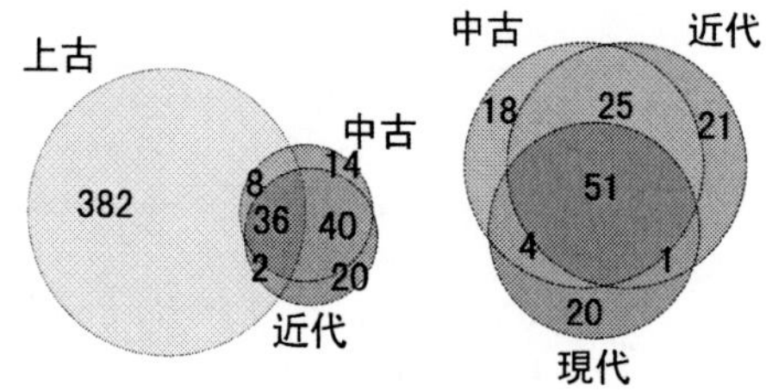

Figure 2: 各時代語料中詞類標記集

4 實驗模型

所有實驗模型的大小皆使用 (Kenton and Toutanova, 2019) 中定義，例如 BERT-base 就是總共 12 層、768 維的 hidden vector、12 個 self attention head 等基於 transformer 架構的模型。我們實驗總共包含三種類別 (baseline, our indiv., our merge) 的模型，以訓練資料作爲區分方式，訓練完成後皆分開測試於四個時代的測試集上來進行比較。

4.1 之前發表模型 (baseline)

在預訓練語言模型、分詞和詞類標記等三個任務上，直接取用原發表模型的參數初始化任務模型，不進行任何訓練且凍結此任務模型的參數。經過模型的 inference 模式，在四個時代的測試資料集上進行測試，此結果作爲我們的 baseline 模型，跟後面兩種經由我們訓練後的模型結果作比較。

4.2 訓練於獨立時代語料模型 (our indiv.)

首先，在模型初始化上，我們的預訓練語言模型使用已發佈的 BERT 的參數初始化，而分詞和詞類標記等下游任務則用我們預訓練好的 bert-base-han-chinese 模型初始化。接著進行微調 (Fine-Tune)，分別經由我們四個時代的資料集做訓練，同時在訓練當中透過同時代的開發資料集選出表現最好的模型 checkpoint。在這個方法中，每個時代都會訓練出各自的模型，以我們的 bert-base-han-chinese 舉例 (表11中間)，對應上古、中古、近代和現代都有一個各自微調的 bert-base-han-chinese 模型，總共有四個模型，各自測試其對應時代的測試集。

4.3 訓練於合併時代語料模型 (our merge)

模型初始化方式同4.2，不同的是訓練時使用的資料集，三個任務的訓練和開發資料集分

輸入句子	朱儒問徑天高於脩人，									
斷詞結果	朱	儒	問	徑	天	高	於	脩	人	，
詞類模型輸出	NA1	NA1	VE	U	NI	NI	P	NA1	NA1	-
分詞模型輸出	B	I	B	B	B	I	B	B	I	B
後處理結果	朱儒 (NA1) 問 (VE) 徑 (U) 天高 (NI) 於 (P) 脩人 (NA1) ，									

Table 9: 分詞標記和詞類標記範例

Dataset	Train	Develop	Test
上古	459910	43859	42877
中古	262271	22668	31260
近代	698746	61933	76106
現代	1175516	109715	110718
Merge	2596443	238175	-

Table 10: 詞類標記模型訓練資料

別使用表7、8和10最下方的合併 (merge) 資料集。不同於獨立時代語料的模型，我們的 bert-base-han-chinese 只有一個模型。

5 實驗結果與討論

這章節是我們的實驗結果，在語言模型上，含有在混淆度上測試的結果和視覺化人稱代詞的分析。之後對兩個下游任務上有 F1 分數的結果和 zero-shot 跨時代學習能力的討論。

5.1 語言模型

語言模型在各時代語料測試集上的結果如表11所示。粗體是各時代語料上最好的結果。最上方是 baseline 模型，包括 google 的 BERT 模型和來自 ckiplab 發布的繁體中文語言模型。ckiplab 的三個 BERT 系列模型只訓練在現代的語料上 (ZhWiki 與 CNA 資料集)，因此在現代測試集上表現不錯，但在上古、中古和近代測試集上都明顯表現不佳。

表11中間是4.2提到的獨立時代語料訓練結果，與 ckiplab 的模型相比，在同樣訓練於現代語料上，表現最好的 bert-base 模型降低 4.23 的混淆度 (8.85 vs 4.61)。而在上古、中古和近代三個時代測試集上跟 baseline 相比皆有顯著的進步，例如上古原本 bert-base 模型的混淆度高達 233.64，經過上古資料的訓練後，我們的 bert-base 模型能降到 24.76。

最下方是使用我們合併的四個時代資料集進行訓練，可發現整體趨勢上，除了 albert-tiny 模型之外，merge 資料集訓練的模型表現較佳，雖然以 bert-base 來看，測試於上古和近代輸給各自時代訓練的模型，但差距並不大 (上古差 6.42、近代差 2.24)，在中古有 9.39 的進步，在資料集數量大的現代語料上也有 0.11 的些微進步，而在 roberta-base 模型上，上古和中古皆有進步，但近代和現代略輸 0.36 和 1.44，但整體結果上 merge 資料的確對語言模型訓練有一定的幫助，在中古資料集數量最少的情況下 (表7)，在中古測試集上 merge 的好處尤爲明顯。在後續的實驗中，雖然整體是 roberta-base 模型較好，但考慮到 bert-base 模型與其相差不大，而且是唯一全部贏過 baseline 的模型 (roberta-base 在現代上比 baseline 差)，因此在下游任務初始化我們皆選用 merge 的 bert-base-han-chinese。

語言模型交叉測試在不同時代語料上，如表12所示，可以發現在同樣模型 (皆爲 bert-base) 下，整體來看 merge 的結果最好，四個時代皆贏過我們的 baseline 模型。與獨立時代語料訓練相比，merge 模型另一個優點是，使用上不需背景知識先判斷資料隸屬於哪個時代來使用對應的時代模型。

5.2 向量空間中的人稱代詞

我們對訓練好的語言模型詞向量空間做分析，挑選人稱代詞做 PCA 和 t-SNE 降維，結果如圖3所示。當中包含第一人稱的「余、我、吾」，第二人稱的「你、汝、儂」，第三人稱的「他、伊、之」。模型挑選 google 的 bert-base-chinese 和分別訓練於四個不同時代資料集 (our indiv.) 的模型。圖3左邊 PCA 降維可以看到同一個詞在不同時代的模型距離相近，如右下角的「儂」和左上角的「吾」和「汝」，表示同樣的詞在不同時代中相對於其他詞有相似的詞嵌入位置。圖3右邊經由 t-SNE 降維的結果，可以觀察到類似同心圓的分布，最中間最聚集的是 google/bert-base-chinese 模型，由內往外分別是上古 (橘)、現代 (紫)、中古 (綠) 和近代 (紅)。

5.3 分詞模型

分詞標記的實驗結果如表13所示。表13最上方是中文詞庫小組之前發布的中文分詞模型，作爲我們的 baseline，在現代測試集上有最好的表現，但在其他三個時代語料上卻表現很差。我們的分詞模型使用5.1預訓練完成的 our/bert-base-han-chinese(merge) 初始化

Language Model	Train-set	Test-set, Perplexity↓			
		上古	中古	近代	現代
google/bert-base-chinese	-	167.7257	268.6131	187.615	10.5801
ckiplab/albert-tiny-chinese		627.9473	780.1218	563.2704	34.9042
ckiplab/albert-base-chinese		359.8375	520.2965	388.5624	39.7566
ckiplab/bert-base-chinese		233.6394	405.9008	278.7069	8.8521
our/albert-tiny-han-chinese	our indiv. 上古/中古/近代/現代	48.0267	139.6061	79.7592	13.0466
our/albert-base-han-chinese		37.0239	112.6525	65.0357	7.4371
our/bert-base-han-chinese		24.7588	70.6244	46.8308	4.6143
our/roberta-base-han-chinese		20.9822	64.5587	**30.6159**	12.3762
our/albert-tiny-han-chinese	our merge	68.7009	107.9195	93.0871	14.2858
our/albert-base-han-chinese		50.7889	87.0224	74.4756	7.6285
our/bert-base-han-chinese		31.1807	61.2381	49.0672	**4.5017**
our/roberta-base-han-chinese		**20.6797**	**37.5194**	30.9787	13.8190

Table 11: 預訓練語言模型在各時代測試集上的混淆度分數, 數字越小越好。最上方是我們的 baseline 模型，挑選原始 google 發布的 bert-base-chinese 模型和三個來自中文詞庫小組發布的預訓練語言模型，不進行訓練 (zero-shot) 測試在四個時代語料上。中間部份是我們使用獨立時代語料訓練完成的語言模型，模型訓練集和測試集皆來自同一時代語料。最下方是我們合併四個時代語料訓練的語言模型，統一使用四個時代合併的語料進行訓練，再分別測試於四個時代測試集的結果。

Language Model	Train-set	Test-set, Perplexity↓			
		上古	中古	近代	現代
ckiplab/bert-base-chinese	-	233.6394	405.9008	278.7069	8.8521
our/bert-base-han-chinese	上古	**24.7588**	87.8176	297.1111	60.3993
	中古	67.861	70.6244	133.0536	23.0125
	近代	69.1364	77.4154	**46.8308**	20.4289
	現代	118.8596	163.6896	146.5959	4.6143
	merge	31.1807	**61.2381**	49.0672	**4.5017**

Table 12: 交叉測試同架構語言模型在不同時代測試集上的混淆度分數

WS Model	Train-set	Test-set, F1↑			
		上古	中古	近代	現代
ckiplab/bert-base-chinese-ws	-	86.5698	82.9115	84.3213	**98.1325**
our/bert-base-han-chinese-ws	上古	**97.6090**	88.5734	83.2877	70.3772
	中古	92.6402	**92.6538**	89.4803	78.3827
	近代	90.8651	92.1861	**94.6495**	81.2143
	現代	87.0234	83.5810	84.9370	96.9446
	merge	97.4537	91.9990	94.0970	96.7314

Table 13: 交叉測試中文分詞模型在不同時代語料上的 F1 分數

POS Model	Train-set	Test-set, F1↑			
		上古	中古	近代	現代
our/bert-base-han-chinese-pos	上古	**91.2945**	-	-	-
	中古	7.3662	**80.4896**	11.3371	10.2577
	近代	6.4794	14.3653	**88.6580**	0.5316
	現代	11.9895	11.0775	0.4033	**93.2813**
	merge	88.8772	42.4369	86.9093	92.9012

Table 14: 交叉測試詞類標記模型在不同時代與語料上的 F1 分數

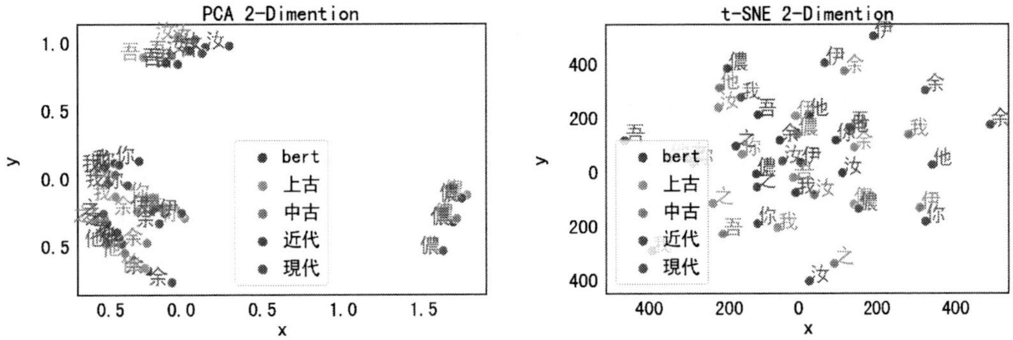

Figure 3: 左圖、右圖分別是對不同人稱代詞的 embedding 做 PCA、t-SNE 降維的視覺化，測試於五種模型，包含原始 bert-base-chinese 與我們分別使用四個時代資料集訓練的語言模型。

Number of POS types				
上古	中古	近代	現代	merge
428	98	98	76	518

Table 15: 各資料集的詞類標記數量

參數，之後使用各自時代的資料集做訓練，再交叉測試於四個時代的測試集上。粗體字表示上古、中古、近代和現代測試集上最好的結果，F1 分數愈高愈好。從表13中，我們可以發現各自時代訓練的模型表現最好，例如在上古測試集中表現最好的是單獨訓練於上古資料集的模型，有趣的是使用近代資料集訓練的模型測試在中古測試集上也表現不錯。整體來看我們可以得知不同時代語料對模型訓練影響很大，語料的時間跨度跟 performance 影響成正比。舉例來說，上古與現代的語料誕生時間距離最久，反映在模型表現上，訓練在上古的模型測試在現代資料上有最大的差距（27.26%）。

5.4 詞類標記模型

詞類標記模型的表現如表14所示，可以發現如同分詞模型的結果 (表13)，單獨時代語料訓練的模型在同時代語料上有最好的表現。但與5.3不同的是，獨立時代語料訓練完的模型並沒有跨時代學習的能力，我們推測原因是：詞類標記任務與分詞任務雖然都是分類問題，但分詞任務的輸出只有三個類別 (BIO)，且四個時代皆是同樣的；但詞類標記任務在表10和圖2可以發現各時代語料的類別集合皆不完全相同，尤其在上古的部分，所有 428 個類別裡有高達 382 個 (89%) 的類別是它自己獨有的，因此訓練在上古的詞類標記模型完全無法應用在其他三個時代。而其他三個時代單獨訓練的模型測試在不同時代測試集上表現也大幅下降。相對來看，則可以發現 merge 的模型整體來看較爲穩定，雖然受限於資料數量不平衡的原因 (表10)，在中古數量最少的情況下，導致 merge 的模型測試在中古上表現較差。

5.5 零樣本跨時代學習能力

綜合表7、8和10來看，可以發現訓練數量是現代最多、近代次之，而中古最少。在這樣的環境下，語言模型的結果 (表12) 可以看到只訓練在近代語料的模型，直接應用在中古語料上 (77.41)，比訓練在中古且測試在中古語料的結果 (70.62) 還要更好，而使用 merge 資料訓練的結果測試在中古語料上則有最好的成績 (61.24)。分詞模型的結果 (表13) 也可以看到訓練在近代的模型測試在中古語料上也有可競爭的 F1 分數 (92.19 vs 92.65)。我們由此推測模型的確在漢語上，具有零樣本 (zero-shot) 跨時代學習的能力。唯一例外的是詞類標記模型，受限於不同時代的類別相差過大，因此無法成功跨時代語料學習。

6 結論

現今已發布的預訓練語言模型裡，大多數都是基於英文的模型，在其他語言中建構強大預訓練語言模型的嘗試較少。在古漢語這塊，更是完全沒有可使用的模型。因此我們考量到自然語言處理領域上，目前繁體中文的缺乏和古漢語的缺失。我們使用包含四個不同時代的漢語語料庫來預訓練語言模型，同時成功應用在分詞和詞類標記的下游任務上。除此之外，Bert 架構模型除了之前研究發現的零樣本跨語言學習能力外，在我們的實驗中發現語言模型在掩碼詞 (masked word) 預測和分詞任務上都具有零樣本跨時代學習能力。最後我們使用 PCA 和 t-SNE 對四個時代的人稱代詞詞向量降維並視覺化呈現，發現不同時代模型中詞跟詞之間有相同的相對位置關係。在未來的研究上，不同於 Bert 是基於 encoder 的模型，我們可以嘗試使用現存的其他基於文字生成的模型。

Acknowledgments

本研究由中央研究院數位人文研究計畫 (2379-111237j) 贊助支持。古漢語標記語料由中央研究院語言所提供，特此感謝。感謝國研院國網中心提供計算與儲存資源，協助本研究順利進行。

References

Alexis Conneau, Ruty Rinott, Guillaume Lample, Adina Williams, Samuel Bowman, Holger Schwenk, and Veselin Stoyanov. 2018. XNLI: Evaluating cross-lingual sentence representations. In *Proceedings of the 2018 Conference on Empirical Methods in Natural Language Processing*, pages 2475–2485.

Yiming Cui, Wanxiang Che, Ting Liu, Bing Qin, and Ziqing Yang. 2021. Pre-training with whole word masking for chinese bert. *IEEE/ACM Transactions on Audio, Speech, and Language Processing*, 29:3504–3514.

Yiming Cui, Ting Liu, Wanxiang Che, Li Xiao, Zhipeng Chen, Wentao Ma, Shijin Wang, and Guoping Hu. 2019. A span-extraction dataset for Chinese machine reading comprehension. In *Proceedings of the 2019 Conference on Empirical Methods in Natural Language Processing and the 9th International Joint Conference on Natural Language Processing (EMNLP-IJCNLP)*, pages 5883–5889.

Thomas Emerson. 2005. The second international chinese word segmentation bakeoff. In *Proceedings of the fourth SIGHAN workshop on Chinese language Processing*.

Tsung-Yuan Hsu, Chi-Liang Liu, and Hung-yi Lee. 2019. Zero-shot reading comprehension by cross-lingual transfer learning with multi-lingual language representation model. In *Proceedings of the 2019 Conference on Empirical Methods in Natural Language Processing and the 9th International Joint Conference on Natural Language Processing (EMNLP-IJCNLP)*, pages 5933–5940.

Baotian Hu, Qingcai Chen, and Fangze Zhu. 2015. LCSTS: A large scale Chinese short text summarization dataset. In *Proceedings of the 2015 Conference on Empirical Methods in Natural Language Processing*, pages 1967–1972.

Guangjin Jin and Xiao Chen. 2008. The fourth international chinese language processing bakeoff: Chinese word segmentation, named entity recognition and chinese pos tagging. In *Proceedings of the sixth SIGHAN workshop on Chinese language processing*.

Jacob Devlin Ming-Wei Chang Kenton and Lee Kristina Toutanova. 2019. Bert: Pre-training of deep bidirectional transformers for language understanding. In *Proceedings of naacL-HLT*, pages 4171–4186.

Yinhan Liu, Myle Ott, Naman Goyal, Jingfei Du, Mandar Joshi, Danqi Chen, Omer Levy, Mike Lewis, Luke Zettlemoyer, and Veselin Stoyanov. 2019. Roberta: A robustly optimized bert pretraining approach. *arXiv preprint arXiv:1907.11692*.

Telmo Pires, Eva Schlinger, and Dan Garrette. 2019. How multilingual is multilingual BERT? In *Proceedings of the 57th Annual Meeting of the Association for Computational Linguistics*, pages 4996–5001.

Maria Pontiki, Dimitrios Galanis, Haris Papageorgiou, Ion Androutsopoulos, Suresh Manandhar, Mohammad Al-Smadi, Mahmoud Al-Ayyoub, Yanyan Zhao, Bing Qin, Orphée De Clercq, et al. 2016. Semeval-2016 task 5: Aspect based sentiment analysis. In *International workshop on semantic evaluation*, pages 19–30.

Alec Radford, Jeffrey Wu, Rewon Child, David Luan, Dario Amodei, Ilya Sutskever, et al. 2019. Language models are unsupervised multitask learners. *OpenAI blog*, 1(8):9.

Colin Raffel, Noam Shazeer, Adam Roberts, Katherine Lee, Sharan Narang, Michael Matena, Yanqi Zhou, Wei Li, Peter J Liu, et al. 2020. Exploring the limits of transfer learning with a unified text-to-text transformer. *J. Mach. Learn. Res.*, 21(140):1–67.

Rico Sennrich, Barry Haddow, and Alexandra Birch. 2016. Edinburgh neural machine translation systems for WMT 16. In *Proceedings of the First Conference on Machine Translation: Volume 2, Shared Task Papers*, pages 371–376, Berlin, Germany. Association for Computational Linguistics.

Chih Chieh Shao, Trois Liu, Yuting Lai, Yiying Tseng, and Sam Tsai. 2018. Drcd: a chinese machine reading comprehension dataset. *arXiv preprint arXiv:1806.00920*.

Songbo Tan and Jin Zhang. 2008. An empirical study of sentiment analysis for chinese documents. *Expert Systems with applications*, 34(4):2622–2629.

Yonghui Wu, Mike Schuster, Zhifeng Chen, Quoc V Le, Mohammad Norouzi, Wolfgang Macherey, Maxim Krikun, Yuan Cao, Qin Gao, Klaus Macherey, et al. 2016. Google's neural machine translation system: Bridging the gap between human and machine translation. *arXiv preprint arXiv:1609.08144*.

Linting Xue, Noah Constant, Adam Roberts, Mihir Kale, Rami Al-Rfou, Aditya Siddhant, Aditya Barua, and Colin Raffel. 2021. mT5: A massively multilingual pre-trained text-to-text transformer. In *Proceedings of the 2021 Conference of the North American Chapter of the Association for Computational Linguistics: Human Language Technologies*, pages 483–498.

Naiwen Xue, Fei Xia, Fu-Dong Chiou, and Marta Palmer. 2005. The penn chinese treebank: Phrase structure annotation of a large corpus. *Natural language engineering*, 11(2):207–238.

The 34th Conference on Computational Linguistics and Speech Processing (ROCLING 2022)
Taipei, Taiwan, November 21-22, 2022. The Association for Computational Linguistics and Chinese Language Processing

自動口說評估於英語作為第二語言學習者的初步研究

A Preliminary Study on Automated Speaking Assessment of English as a Second Language (ESL) Students

吳姿儀 Tzu-I Wu[1], 羅天宏 Tien-Hong Lo[1], 趙福安 Fu-An Chao[2], 宋曜廷 Yao-Ting Sung[3], 陳柏琳 Berlin Chen[1]

[1] 國立台灣師範大學資訊工程學系
[1]Department of Computer Science and Information Engineering, National Taiwan Normal University
[2] 國立台灣師範大學心理與教育測驗研究發展中心
[2]Research Center for Psychological and Educational Testing, National Taiwan Normal University
[3] 國立台灣師範大學教育與心理輔導學系
[3]Department of Educational Psychology and Counseling, National Normal Taiwan University

{61047087s, teinhonglo, fuann, sungtc, berlin}@ntnu.edu.tw

摘要

為順應國際化潮流，大學生對於國際交流以及英語授課所需之英文口說有越來越迫切的需求。本論文旨在發展自動化英語評測系統，並初探臺灣大學生之英語精熟程度。基於近期在臺灣所蒐集的口說語料，我們藉由一套自動語音辨識(Automatic Speech Recognition, ASR)系統，將語音轉寫成文字並擷取其中聲學特徵，最後使用機器學習模型來挑選適用的特徵以預測學生英語口說精熟度(English Speaking Proficiency)。經一系列所蒐集的臺灣大學生口說測驗語料的實驗和分析顯示，使用機器學習方法來進行自動英語口說能力分級，能較專家人工分級有更高的穩定性。

Abstract

Due to the surge in global demand for English as a second language (ESL), developments of automated methods for grading speaking proficiency have gained considerable attention. This paper aims to present a computerized regime of grading the spontaneous spoken language for ESL learners. Based on the speech corpus of ESL learners recently collected in Taiwan, we first extract multi-view features (e.g., pronunciation, fluency, and prosody features) from either automatic speech recognition (ASR) transcription or audio signals. These extracted features are, in turn, fed into a tree-based classifier to produce a new set of indicative features as the input of the automated assessment system, viz. the grader. Finally, we use different machine learning models to predict ESL learners' respective speaking proficiency and map the result into the corresponding CEFR level. The experimental results and analysis conducted on the speech corpus of ESL learners in Taiwan show that our approach holds great potential for use in automated speaking assessment, meanwhile offering more reliable predictive results than the human experts.

關鍵字：自動發音檢測、英語能力分級

Keywords: automated speaking assessment, grader, CEFR

1 緒論 (Introduction)

為增加國際競爭力，臺灣的大學校園裡需要用到英語口說的情境大幅增加，舉凡國際交流以及全英語授課(English as a Medium of Instruction, EMI)，其中對於英文的口說能力的教學與測驗也有迫切的需求。根據過往經驗，學習者會使用線上的英語口說教學資源練習英語，而近年主流的應用程式[1,2]，在其口說練習中，題目以朗讀的發音練習為主，並使用自動語音辨識 (Automatic Speech Recognition, ASR)檢視語者的音素(Phoneme)發音是否與系統中的母語語者的發音資料相同，來提供語者發音正確與否的回饋。

而劍橋自動化語言教學與評估中心(Institute for Automated Language Teaching and Assessment, ALTA)所發展的 Speak & Improve

[1] ELSA SPEAK: https://elsaspeak.com/en/

[2] EF Hello: https://tw.hello.ef.com/

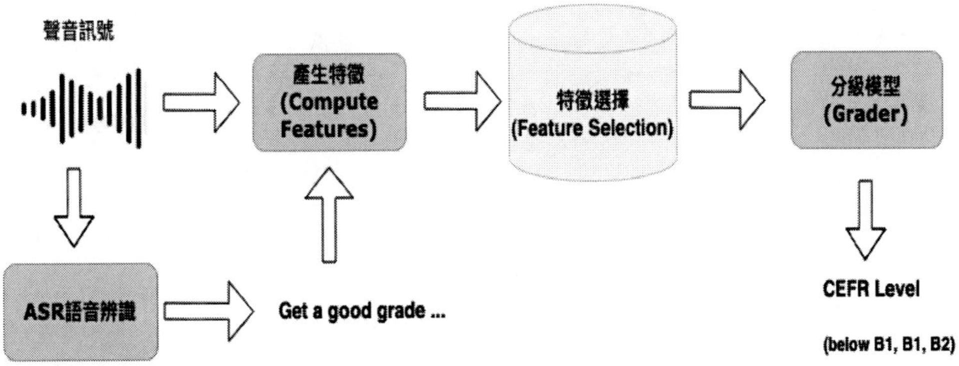

圖 1. 自動化英語精熟度系統

網站[3]，則提供更進階的口說練習，使用者會需要回答一連串的問題，經過系統分析，並得到以歐洲共同語言標準 (Common European Framework of Reference for Language, CEFR) 為分級的英語程度級數。相較於只考慮發音正確性的朗讀測驗，此系統需考量更全面的面向(如單詞使用 、文法等)來取得整體式評分 (Holistic Scoring)。

受到上述多元的英語口說工具啟發，本研究想發展英語評測平臺以初探臺灣大學生的英語音韻程度。我們希望藉由多樣的特徵以及迴歸與分類模型來客觀地預測受試臺灣大學生的英語音韻精熟度，發展適合臺灣本地大學生的英語口說評量平臺，以歐洲通用語言參考框架 (CEFR) 作為標準，有效地為其分析英語口說能力表現且分級，並期許大學生能透過平臺的回饋，使之成為自我英語口說精進之依據。

2 相關研究 (Related Work)

目前國外已有很多針對非母語語者之英語口說自動化測驗的研究，其文獻多半以自動化評分為目標，並使用多元測驗的題型來研究口說精熟度的特徵。

Zechner et al. (2011) 於口說測驗中「朗讀」的任務上，藉由自動產生音韻特徵 (Prosodic Features) 來預測非母語人士英語精熟度分數，因為是朗讀文本，所以相較於一般口說測驗中「回答問題」的題型，在語音辨識上的複雜程度相對較低。而 Knill et al. (2018) 使用 ASR 轉錄的文字資訊，探討了 ASR 的表現對於口說測驗中回答問題之題型所造成的影響。由於 ASR 錯誤率會影響到自動化口說評分系統的結果，因此他們嘗試改進 ASR 轉錄文本上的單詞錯誤率(Word Error Rate, WER)，並納入其他語音相關特徵，以豐富其自動化口說評分系統。Craighead et al. (2020) 則僅基於來自 ASR 獲得的轉錄文本，使用多目標訓練的預訓練語言模型(Pretrained Language Model)，來為學習者評分。

除了使用文本作為英文精熟度分析基礎之外，也有一些文獻加入聲音或視覺特徵來預測不同任務上的英語口說精熟度。在人與機器的對話測驗上，Litman et al. (2018) 使用如 F0, 能量 (Power) 的聲音特徵來為非母語的英文口說精熟度評分。而在口說問答自動化評估的研究，Wang et al. (2018) 使用能量 (Energy) 作為其口說測驗訓練模型基準的輸入特徵之一。Saeki et al.(2021) 在為面試任務的口說任務上，使用詞彙、聲學以及視覺特徵，由類神經網路訓練並預測非母語口說語者的 CEFR 分級，其中的聲學特徵是使用音高 (Pitch) 和能量 (Power) ，而其實驗結果顯示結合詞彙及聲學特徵就能取得很好的正確率。

從前述的研究都顯示出從 ASR 與這些聲學特徵都能提升自動化為非母語學習者評價口說精熟度的有效性。而我們的自動化評測系

[3] Speak&Improve：https://speakandimprove.com/

統主要建立於聲音特徵上，會使用從 ASR 聲學模型獲得的以音段為級別的 (Segmental level) 特徵，與跨音段的超音段 (Suprasegmental level) 特徵，來處理從語言角度所分類之各面向特徵，並作為預測受試者英語程度的輸入特徵。

3 方法 (Method)

本研究中，方法的架構如圖 1。一共分成三個階段：第一階段，是使用預先訓練好的 ASR 模型與原始聲音訊號抽取聲音特徵；第二階段，使用極限樹 (Extra Tree) 來挑選適用於本任務之聲音特徵；第三階段，使用機器學習模型來預測受試臺灣大學生的音韻精熟度。在後續章節，我們將本論文所使用的方法拆分為特徵、特徵選擇，以及分級模型個別描述。

3.1 特徵 (Features)

綜合前述研究的成果，我們將此次任務的音韻特徵分成發音 (Pronunciation) 、流暢度 (Fluency) 與韻律 (Prosody) 面向，如表 1。在所有三個面向底下的特徵皆屬於聲音特徵，在發音與流暢度面向的特徵都是由 ASR 聲學模型將音訊以及文本對齊來獲得。而韻律面向的聲學特徵是從聲音訊號所抽取，以語音學的定義來看，韻律面向需包含發音長短、音量以及音高三種要素，而我們分別能藉由持續時間、能量以及基本頻率來獲得此資訊，而值得注意的是，本次任務尚未考量持續時間與韻律面向之關係，因此未納入表 1 之韻律分類中。在研究不同面向的特徵時，不同面向之間採用的特徵向量可能互有重疊，像是音素/字詞的信心分數 (Phone/Word Confidence) ，能同時成為探討發音和流暢度的要素之一。

3.1.1 發音 (Pronunciation)

英文非母語的學習者往往會將其母語的發音法連帶應用到英文上，進而產生發音誤差。若以音素來說明，其通常可被分為三類，分別是替代 (Substitutions) 、增加 (Insertion) 、刪除 (Deletion) 。母語的發音限制往往會觸發替代跟刪除這兩類錯誤，其中刪除對聽者的理解影響最大；替代則是使用類母語的發音去說其他語言 (Chen, 2016) 。

面向	特徵
發音 (Pronunciation)	Word/Phone Confidence
流暢度 (Fluency)	Silence
	Long Silence
	Disfluency
	Word/Phone Duration
	Word/ Phone Confidence
韻律 (Prosody)	F0
	Energy

表 1. 本研究音韻特徵

為了檢視發音誤差，我們使用音素與單詞級別的發音良好度 (Goodness of Pronunciation, GOP) (Witt and Young, 2000) 作為音段級別 (Segmental level) 特徵以計算信心分數，藉由取事後機率對數之持續時間標準化的方法，比對 ASR 所識別的文字和英文為母語者的發音模型。以 GOP 在音素級別的發音良好度公式為例：

$$GOP(r,n) \equiv \frac{\log P\left(X_{r,n} \middle| Y_{r,n}\right)}{T_{r,n}} \quad (1)$$

在 GOP 中，$Y_{r,n}$為語者所產生的音素；$X_{r,n}$為相應的目標聲學段落；$T_{r,n}$為聲學段落所經歷的時間範圍數量，其中r與n表示第r個語句中的第n個音素。

而受試者的總體發音與 ASR 模型的差異越大，獲得信心分數就越低。其中原因可能是發音不清楚或不正確，或是不流暢和語法錯誤。因此，信心分數可以反應非母語人士的英語熟練程度，發音較好的受試者理應能獲得較高的信心分數 (Wang, 2018) 。

3.1.2 流暢度 (Fluency)

流暢度也是音韻的其一面向，關乎受試者的講話語速、遲疑程度等。我們在單字級別的流暢度分析，會收集字數、語速、不流利度(Disfluency)、重複字數等資訊。根據(Loukina and Yoon, 2019)的研究，英文程度好的第二外語受試者，往往能在相同時間內講出更多字詞。至於不流利度的衡量，我們會透過 ASR 轉錄之文字，以計算「um」、「uh」、和「hmm」 這些遲疑文字的個數。而在停頓 (Silence) 和較長停頓 (Long Silence) 的特徵的細節上，我們使用美國教育測驗服務社(Educational Testing Service, ETS)的方式來認定，當停頓超過 0.145 秒時，會做計算，而超過 0.495 秒時，會當作較長停頓。

3.1.3 聲學特徵 (Acoustic Features)

理論上探討超音段級別 (Suprasegmental level) 資訊，是要獲得與韻律相關的特徵，我們需要透過聲音訊號計算持續時間 (Duration)、能量 (Energy)及基本頻率(Fundamental Frequency, F0)。但在本次任務中，持續時間作為探討流暢度面向的特徵之一，而非韻律面向考量之範疇。

持續時間 (Duration)： 持續時間就是一個音素或單詞發聲的長度。根據 (Neumeyer et al., 2000) 的論文，音素的相對持續時間和專家評分的分數高度相關。因為通常英語學習者在說英語時，需要邊思考邊說，此行為會干擾講話的速率使其不流暢。而英語學習者也易於產生前段敘述所提到的三種發音錯誤 (替代、增加、 刪除)，而導致其說英語時，會產生持續時間的差異，進而影響流暢度。

在計算持續時間時，我們統計在一次回答的過程中，音素及單詞層級發聲持續時間長度的平均值(Mean)、最大值(Max)、最小值(Min)、標準差(Standard Deviation, STD)、中位數(Median)、平均差(Mean Absolute Deviation, MAD)、總和(Summation, SUM)，作為兩個 7 維的特徵向量輸入 (Chao et al., 2022)

基本頻率(Fundamental Frequency, F0)： 基本頻率為語者聲帶振動的頻率，而反映在聽者的感知上，就會是音高。F0 的高低與重音(Stress)以及語調有關。然而，根據 Sluijter and van Heuven (1996) 針對荷蘭與美國英語上重音與口音的研究，發現 F0 與重音之間沒有可靠的相關性。但是對於如母語為華語的英語學習者而言，使用 F0 來探討英語發音音高還是有其必要性，因為華語是聲調語言，音高的變化會影響到語意的不同(Tepperman and Narayanan, 2005)，而在英語上，音高可能只是傳達不同語氣。在此次任務上，我們評測的對象為母語為華語的台灣大學生，因此 F0 仍作為韻律面向的評斷特徵。如前述之持續時間特徵，我們也使用相同統計量來表示 F0 以及標準化 F0。

能量 (Energy)： 能量能最直接的反映語者的音量大小，而能量的分佈與語調 (Intonation) 有關。 在我們的研究中，並沒有使用能量絕對值這個直覺的算法，因為其他研究顯示發音的品質和能量的絕對值沒有高度的相關性(Dong et al., 2004)。 相反地，我們使用均方根能量 (Root Mean Squared Energy, RMSE) 來計算每個音段的統計量作為韻律特徵 (Chao et al., 2022)，而我們使用與持續時間相同的統計向量來表示能量特徵。

3.2 特徵選擇 (Feature Selection)

在本論文中，我們使用極限樹分類器 (Extra Trees Classifier) 作為特徵選擇的方法。極限樹是隨機森林 (Leo, 2021) 的架構，其演算法在分割隨機樹的節點時，會隨機選擇切點；並且使用所有學習樣本來產生決策樹；在本節，我們使用極限樹分類器計算不純度 (Impurity) 作為特徵重要性，挑選適用之特徵。

3.3 分級模型(Grader)

自動化英文分級系統的優勢，在於透過統一標準來客觀地評論學生的 CEFR 分級，其公式可定義如下：

$$B_i = M(P_i, F_i, D_i, F0_i, En_i) \tag{2}$$

其中為面向，本論文實驗中表示音韻，根據i面向所選取的特徵分別為：發音特徵P_i、流暢度特徵F_i、持續時間特徵D_i、基頻特徵$F0_i$與能量特徵En_i。M代表分級模型，B_i為最終之 CEFR 分級。經過特徵選取的機制，我們將這些特徵向量作為輸入值，經由迴歸與分類模型的訓練，評測出受試者的英文程度並對應到 CEFR 的級數。

本研究中的迴歸模型，分別有簡單線性迴歸 (Simple Linear Regression, SLR) 、多變項線

性迴歸 (Multivariance Linear Regression, MLR) (Friedman et al., 2010; Kim et al., 2007) 、隨機森林迴歸 (Random Forest Regression, RFR) (Breiman, 2001; Geurts, 2006) 、支持向量迴歸 (Support Vector Regression, SVR) (Chang and Lin, 2001; Platt, 2000) 、梯度提升迴歸 (Gradient Boosting Regressor, GBR) (Friedaman, 2001; Hestie, 2009) 模型。根據多個特徵向量，我們使用迴歸模型分析這些向量間的關係來預測精熟度分數的連續數值，並在測試階段將迴歸模型預測的數值做分級，獲得 1 至 3 分的受試者分為 B1 以下; 獲得 4 分為 B1，獲得 5 分則為 B2。

而在分類模型，我們使用邏輯迴歸(Logistic Regression, LR)、隨機森林分類器(Random Forest Classifier, RFC) (Breiman, 2001)、支持向量機(Support Vector Machine, SVM) (Chang and Lin, 2001; Platt, 2000)、梯度提升分類器 (Gradient Boosting Classifier, GBC) (Friedman, 2001; Hestie, 2009)、線性分類感知器 (Perceptron) (Freund and Schapire, 1999)。在分類模型中，我們將特徵作為向量輸入，精熟度分數則作為獨立的預測標籤。分類模型在訓練過程中會擬和兩者之間關係，並在測試階段做 CEFR 分級。

4 實驗評估與分析 (Performance Evaluation and Analysis)

4.1 語料 (Data)

口說分級模型若要有好的表現，多半需要有大量的人工標記語料，但目前公開的英語語料集多半是母語語者，僅有少量母語為華語語者的資料集。為了能準確分析學生之音韻表現，本研究收集大學生英語口說測驗語料來測試分級系統的有效性。本論文所使用的語料為英語教學專家設計的口說測驗，測驗內容為三部分：朗讀短文、回答問題與看圖敘述：朗讀短文不限制回答時間。回答問題共 10 題，分為 15 秒簡答與 30 秒詳答。看圖敘述則限制為 90 秒。共 103 位受試者，詳細的統計資料可參考表 2。語料標注流程如下：首先，我們會透過 ASR 自動轉寫語音內容，再透過人工做二階段的校閱。接著，該語料

	朗讀短文	回答問題	看圖敘述
時數 (小時)	2.6	6.4	2.6
音檔數	103	103	103
最長回答 (詞數)	-	87	205
最短回答 (詞數)	-	1	6
平均回答 (詞數)	-	29	107

表 2. 實驗語料之統計資訊

會交由兩位教學經驗豐富的英文專家根據內容、音韻及詞語三面向分別給予 1 到 5 分的精熟度分數，該分數可對應 CEFR 等級，在 CEFR 的框架中，將受試者的程度分成 ABC 三個層級，其中又再細分為 A1/A2 (基礎使用者) 、B1/B2(獨立使用者)、C1/C2 (精熟使用者)[4]。我們的系統分級方式同樣採用劍橋的分級概念：獲得 1 到 3 分表示語者的精熟度未達 B1；得到 4 分表示有 B1 程度；超過 4 分，都視為 B2 程度。本研究是採用第三部分的看圖敘述，測試語料只使用音韻面向的評分。總長為 2.6 小時，學生的平均回答單詞數量為 107 個 (見表 2) ；在看圖敘述的任務中，學生的音韻精熟度分佈如圖 2 所示。

在此次任務中，人工標記的專家之間在看圖敘述部分，其綜合內容、音韻及詞語之關聯性係數 Cohen's Kappa 值為 0.45，而屬於音韻面向的相關係數 0.47，在 0.4 到 0.6 之間的

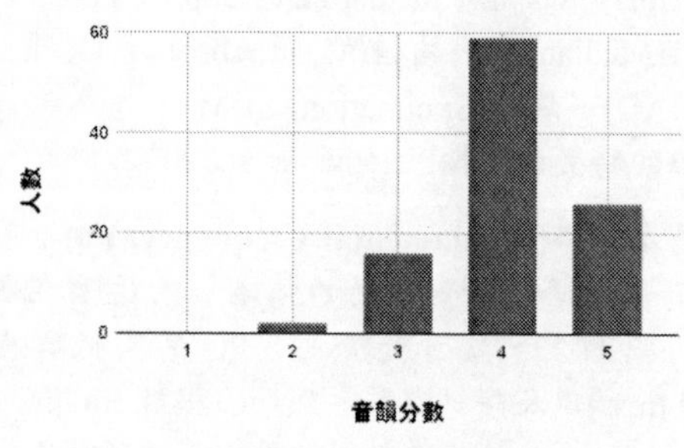

圖 2. 實驗語料之統計資訊

[4] 歐盟 CEFR 語言分級：https://reurl.cc/1mXRlG

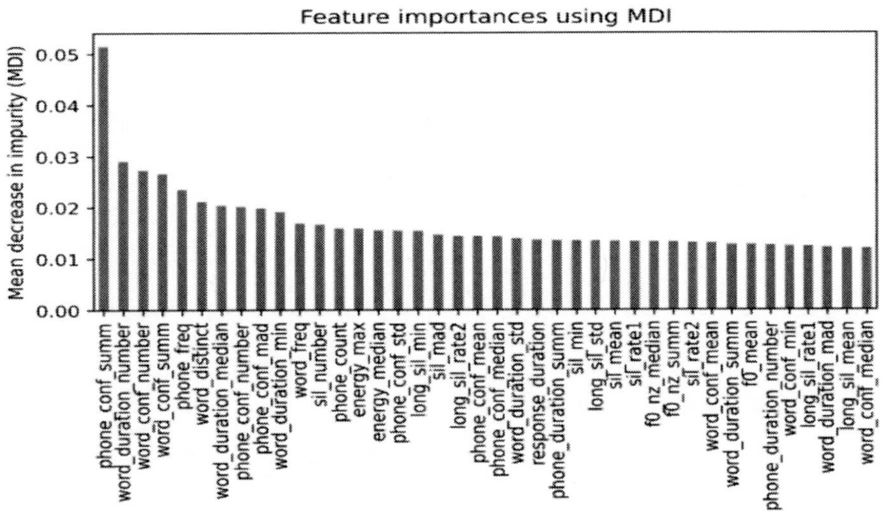

圖 3. 特徵重要性

範圍都只屬於一般信度(Moderate)。若兩位專家給予的評分相差一等級，則會請第三位專家給予實際等級。而這也相當程度反應人工標記語料之困難，因人類標記較易受個人所側重之觀點所影響，傾向於給印象分數而非實際表現分數。部分語料之語者，若是在音韻上表現較佳，而內容及詞語使用表現較一般，會產生評分結果不一致的情形。這種情況凸顯機器評測的重要性，因為機器能夠依照所設定之客觀標準分析語者口說程度。

4.2 實驗設定 (Settings)

本論文中，考量語音資料在不同情境下收音，需要克服噪音以利後續辨識，我們使用經多條件訓練 (Multi-condition Training, MCT) 的 ASR 模型，而聲學模型是使用改良的時間延類神經網路 (Time-Delay Neural Network, TDNN) (Povey et al., 2018)，是在深度神經網路 (Deep Neural Network, DNN) 的架構下，包含多層卷積網路和多層分解過的時間延類神經網路，簡稱為 TDNNF。語言模型則是使用 3-gram 語言模型。

在聲學模型的訓練語料上，我們使用有聲書讀物的英文公開語料 LibriSpeech (Panayotov et al., 2015) ，而語言模型則是使用 TED-LIUM 3 (Hernandez et al., 2018) 語料做訓練。在自動化英語分級這個任務上，我們的 ASR 詞錯誤率 (Word Error Rate. WER) 為 30.08%。

在我們的實驗中，流暢度與發音面向底下的特徵是由 ASR 所產生，而韻律面向所需要的聲學特徵是使用 Python 的 Librosa (McFee et al., 2015) 模組所抽取。另外，我們使用 k-fold 交叉驗證 (Cross-Validation)，k 值為 5；所有的實驗採用的特徵一致。

4.3 效能評估 (Evaluation)

我們使用精確率 (Precision)、召回率 (Recall)、F1-score 及正確率 (Accuracy) 來做效能評估。精確率指的是正確被辨識的項目，占所有被辨識項目的比例，召回率則是指正確辨識的項目占需要被辨識項目的比例。F1-score 則為精確率與召回率的調和平均數，而正確率則是正確辨識的項目佔總項目的比例。四項數值皆是越高越好。

4.4 實驗結果 (Results)

4.4.1 特徵重要性 (Feature Importance)

為探究我們所使用特徵選取的效果，在此節我們探討使用的特徵在此任務之重要性，在不同的交叉驗證過程中，其特徵選取所產生的特徵大致相同，我們以圖 3 為例。由圖 3 可

Regression Model	Precision	Recall	F1	Accuracy
SLR	0.67	0.65	0.63	0.65
MLR	0.71	**0.67**	**0.64**	**0.67**
RFR	0.55	0.59	0.56	0.59
SVR	**0.73**	**0.67**	0.63	**0.67**
GBR	0.62	**0.67**	0.63	**0.67**

表 3. 迴歸模型表現

Classification Model	Precision	Recall	F1	Accuracy
LR	0.71	0.70	0.69	0.70
RFC	**0.74**	**0.73**	**0.71**	**0.73**
SVM	0.50	0.45	0.40	0.45
GBC	0.67	0.67	0.65	0.67
Perceptron	0.44	0.50	0.43	0.50

表 4. 分類模型表現

Recall		RFC 預測結果		
		未達 B1	B1	B2
專家分級	未達 B1	0.52	0.43	0.05
	B1	0.02	0.84	0.14
	B2	0.00	0.36	0.64

表 5. 召回率混淆矩陣

Precision		RFC 預測結果		
		未達 B1	B1	B2
專家分級	未達 B1	0.92	0.14	0.04
	B1	0.08	0.73	0.32
	B2	0.00	0.14	0.64

表 6. 精確率混淆矩陣

以發現，最重要的特徵是音素層級的信心分數總和，為口說清晰度的指標，符合本研究發音面向所需的特徵。我們也發現，此表前半部分重要特徵，包含持續時間、信心分數、停頓數目等，則反映了我們流暢度面向的特徵。而後半部分的重要特徵有包含 F0 以及能量，能相當程度的考量語者的韻律特徵。總體來看，而對於機器而言，清晰度以及流暢度面向是重要指標，再來則是韻律面向。機器在特徵重要性的選擇上也符合我們從音韻角度思考並且設計特徵的趨勢，而多樣特徵的好處能夠使英語使用者不會因為單就音素發音錯誤，而被否定其流暢度以及韻律面向的表現，因為流暢度以及韻律這些超音段的特徵，也會影響到聽者的理解能力(Chen et al., 2016)。

4.4.2 分級模型表現 (Grader Performance)

於此節我們分別將方法歸類為迴歸模型及分類模型來探討實驗結果，如表3與表4所示。其中的精確率、召回率、 F1-score 是根據類別(未達 B1, B1, B2)的加權平均，再由五次交叉驗證取得平均而得到。

整體來看，大部分模型皆取得差異不大的精確率、召回率及 F1。在這個任務中，整體表現最好的模型是隨機森林分類器(RFC)，正確率為 73%、精確率為 71%，然而相比之下，隨機森林在迴歸模型的表現較差，我們推論是因為此迴歸模型無法在超出訓練集的範圍做有效預測，而這可能會導致在不同的交叉驗證訓練時，因使用不同特徵與資料子集(Subset)進行訓練，使此迴歸模型出現過度擬合的現象。在我們實驗中，的確有一次交叉驗證使用與其他驗證稍微不同的特徵，造成此迴歸模型獲得異常高的準確率。

從迴歸模型來看，簡單的迴歸模型(SLR)就能有 65%的表現，除了隨機森林迴歸模型(RFR)之外，支持向量迴歸(SVR)、多變項線性迴歸(MLR)與梯度提升迴歸(GBR)的準確率都為 67%，而 SVR 的表現又較突出。雖然此迴歸模型皆沒辦法勝過最好的分類模型，但總體表現比分類模型穩定。在分類模型上表現較差的支持向量機(SVM)和線性分類感知器(Perception)，我們推測原因是易受到資料量不足或標記信度不夠的極端資料之影響。

4.4.3 系統表現 (Performance Overview)

我們使用混淆矩陣來比較隨機森林分類器在預測結果跟人工分級上的分佈。在103份資料中，根據專家實際分級的結果：未達 B1 實際人數為 21 人；達 B1 者有 57 人；而 B2 程度者為 25 人。以召回率 (表 5)來看，所有為 B1 程度的學生中分級模型預測的召回率能達到 84%，大多可被模型歸類為 B1 等級，但從精確率 (表 6) 的角度來看，B1 的 73%精確率則稍差於未達 B1 的 92%精確率。

綜合兩張表格，我們發現機器若是沒有正確預測實際的分級，大部分的誤差也能落在一個級距以內。而這也反應和實際專家分級情境，在實際處理資料的過程中，評分專家也會有落差一個級距的情形。

因此，相比人工標記，專家之間音韻面向的相關係數只屬於一般信度(Moderate)，而機器的準確率都有六、七成，反應機器的表現相較於人為判斷可以相對客觀穩定。

5 結論 (Conclusion)

本論文是第一篇針對臺灣大學生發音之研究。使用語音學的觀點切入，探討如何為英語學習者的口說音韻精熟度分級，並且應用機器學習的模型，達到自動化分級英語精熟度的目的。從實驗結果發現，傳統的迴歸模型做法就能有良好的成效，若使用隨機森林分類器則能再提高準確率。未來我們將把持續時間加入至韻律面向，也加入不同的特徵，如：內容及文法特徵，至本英語精熟度評測系統，以期達到更全面的英語能力自動化分析，並給予英語學習者更清楚的回饋，進而幫助學習者提升整體的英語能力。此外，本次實驗因受限於少量資料，未能使用深度學習架構，未來除了會擴增相關語料外，也會探討少資源語料的訓練方向。

6 致謝 (Acknowledgements)

本研究特別感謝高教深耕計畫辦公室的支持。

參考文獻 (References)

Zhou Yu, Vikram Ramanarayanan, David Suendermann-Oeft, Xinhao Wang, Klaus Zechner, Lei Chen, Jidong Tao, and Yao Qian. 2015. Using bidirectional lstm recurrent neural networks to learn high-level abstractions of sequential features for automated scoring of non-native spontaneous speech. In *Proceedings of IEEE Workshop on Automatic Speech Recognition and Understanding (ASRU)*, pp. 338-345.

Eesung Kim, Jae-Jin Jeon, Hyeji Seo, and Hoon Kim. 2022. Automatic Pronunciation Assessment using Self-Supervised Speech Representation Learning. In *Proceedings of Interspeech*.

Nancy F. Chen and Haizhou Li. 2016. Computer-assisted pronunciation training: From pronunciation scoring towards spoken language learning. In *Proceedings of Asia-Pacific Signal and Information Processing Association Annual Summit and Conference (APSIPA ASC)*, pp. 1-7.

Yu Wang, Mark Gales, Katherine M. Knill, Kostas J. Kyriakopoulos, Andrey Malinin, Rogier van Dalen, and M. Rashid. 2018. Towards automatic assessment of spontaneous spoken English. *Speech Communication,* 104, 47-56.

Anastassia Loukina and Su-Youn Yoon. 2019. Scoring and filtering models for automated speech scoring. In Klaus Z. and Keelan E. (Eds), *Automated Speaking Assessment*. pp.75-97.

Fu-An Chao, Tien-Hong Lo, Tzu-I Wu, Yao-Ting Sung, and Berlin Chen. 2022. 3M: An Effective Multi-view, Multi-granularity, and Multi-aspect Modeling Approach to English Pronunciation Assessment, *arXiv preprint arXiv:2208.09110*.

Bin Dong, Qingwei Zhao, Jianping Zhang, and Yonghong Yan. 2004. Automatic assessment of pronunciation quality, in *Proceedings of ISCSLP*, pp. 137–140.

Silke Maren Witt and Steve Young. 2000. Phone-level pronunciation scoring and assessment for interactive language learning," *Speech Communication*.

Daniel Povey, Gaofeng Cheng, Yiming Wang, Ke Li, Hainan Xu, Mahsa Yarmohamadi, and Sanjeev Khudanpur. 2018. Semi-orthogonal low-rank matrix factorization for deep neural networks. In *Proceedings of Interspeech*, pp. 3743-3747.

Vassil Panayotov, Guoguo Chen, Daniel Povey, and Sanjeev Khudanpur. 2015. Librispeech: an asr corpus based on public domain audio books. In *Proceedings of IEEE international conference on acoustics, speech and signal processing (ICASSP)*, pp. 5206-5210.

François Hernandez, Vincent Nguyen, Sahar Ghannay, Natalia Tomashenko, and Yannick Estève. 2018. TED-LIUM 3: Twice as much data and corpus repartition for experiments on speaker adaptation. In *Proceedings of SPECOM*, pp. 198–208.

Leo Breiman. 2001. Random forests. *Machine learning*, 45(1), 5-32.

Brian McFee, Colin Raffel ,Dawen Liang, Daniel P.W. Ellis, Matt McVicar, Eric Battenbergk, and Oriol Nieto. 2015. Librosa: Audio and music signal analysis in python. In *Proceedings of the 14th python in science conference*, vol. 8, pp. 18-25.

Leonardo Neumeyer, Horacio Franco, Vassilios Digalakis, and Mitchel Weintraub. 2000. Automatic scoring of pronunciation quality. *Speech communication*, 30(2-3), 83-93.

Pavel Trofimovich and Wendy Baker. 2006. Learning Second language suprasegmentals: Effect of L2 Experience on Prosody and Fluency Characteristics of L2 Speech. *Studies in Second Language Acquisition*, 28(1), 1-30. doi:10.1017/S0272263106060013

Klaus Zechner, Xiaoming Xi, and Lei Chen. 2011. Evaluating prosodic features for automated scoring of non-native read speech. In *Proceedings of 2011 IEEE Workshop on Automatic Speech Recognition & Understanding (ASRU)*, pp. 461-466. *DOI:10.1109/ASRU.2011.6163975*

K. Knill, M. Gales, K. Kyriakopoulos, A. Malinin, A. Ragni, Y. Wang, and A. Caines. 2018. Impact of ASR performance on free speaking language assessment. In *Proceedings of the Annual Conference of the International Speech Communication Association (ISCA)*.

Hannah Craighead, Andrew Caines, Paula Buttery, and Helen Yannakoudakis. 2020. Investigating the effect of auxiliary objectives for the automated grading of learner English speech transcriptions. In *Proceedings of the 58th Annual Meeting of the Association for Computational Linguistics,* pp. 2258–2269, Online. Association for Computational Linguistics.

Diane Litman, Helmer Strik, and Gad S. Lim. 2018. Speech Technologies and the Assessment of Second Language Speaking: Approaches, Challenges, and Opportunities, in *Language Assessment Quarterly*. Vol. *15*, pp. 294–309, *Routledge*.

Mao Saeki, Yoichi Matsuyama, Satoshi Kobashikawa, Tetsuji Ogawa and Tetsunori Kobayashi. 2021. Analysis of Multimodal Features for Speaking Proficiency Scoring in an Interview Dialogue. In *Proceedings of IEEE Spoken Language Technology Workshop (SLT)*, pp. 629-635.

Jerome Friedman, Trevor Hastie, and Rob Tibshirani. 2010. Regularization Paths for Generalized Linear Models via Coordinate Descent. *Journal of statistical software*, 33(1), 1–22.

Seung-Jean Kim, K. Koh, M. Lustig, Stephen Boyd, and Dimitry Gorinevsky. 2007. An Interior-Point Method for Large-Scale L1-Regularized Least Squares. *In IEEE Journal of Selected Topics in Signal Processing, 2007.*

Pierre Geurts, Damien Ernst., and Louis Wehenkel. 2006. Extremely randomized trees. *Machine Learning, 63(1), 3-42.*

Chih-Chung Chang and Chih-Jen Lin. 2001. LIBSVM: a library for support vector machines (Software available at \url{http://www.csie.ntu.edu.tw/~cjlin/libsvm}

John Platt. 2000. Probabilistic Outputs for Support Vector Machines and Comparisons to Regularized Likelihood Methods. *Advances in Large Margin Classifiers.*

Jerome Friedman. 2001. Greedy Function Approximation: A Gradient Boosting Machine. *The Annals of Statistics, Vol. 29, No. 5*

Jerome H. Friedman. 2002. Stochastic Gradient Boosting In *proceedings of Computational Statistics & Data Analysis* 38(4):367-378

Trevor Hastie, Robert Tibshirani, and Jerome Friedman. 2009. Elements of Statistical Learning Ed. *2, Springer*

Yoav Freund and Robert Schapire. 1999. Large margin classification using the perceptron algorithm. *Machine Learning. 37 (3): 277–296. doi:10.1023/A:1007662407062. S2CID 58856 17*

Agaath Sluijter and Vincent Van Heuven. 1996. Acoustic correlates of linguistic stress and accent in Dutch and American English. *ICSLP 96. Proceedings of the Fourth International Conference on Spoken Language Processing ICSLP96, vol.2,* pp. 630 - 633. DOI:10.1109/ICSLP.1996.607440.

Joseph Tepperman and Shrikanth Narayanan. 2005. Automatic syllable stress detection using prosodic features for pronunciation evaluation of language learners. in *Proceedings of IEEE International Conference on Acoustics, Speech, and Signal Processing (ICASSP)*, pp. I/937-I/940 Vol. 1, doi: 10.1109/ICASSP.2005.1415269.

The 34th Conference on Computational Linguistics and Speech Processing (ROCLING 2022)
Taipei, Taiwan, November 21-22, 2022. The Association for Computational Linguistics and Chinese Language Processing

以民事訴訟之爭點分群為基礎的類似案件搜尋系統
Clustering Issues in Civil Judgments for Recommending Similar Cases

劉一凡 **Yi-Fan Liu** **劉昭麟** **Chao-Lin Liu** **楊婕** **Chieh Yang**

國立政治大學資訊科學系
Department of Computer Science, National Chengchi University
{108753213, chaolin}@g.nccu.edu.tw, 05141343@gm.scu.edu.tw

摘要

類似案件搜尋是法律實務中十分重要的任務，從中能獲取珍貴的法律見解。而爭點是民事訴訟中兩造互為對立的主張，代表審理案件時要考慮的核心事項。許多研究以不同角度計算判決書間相似度；而我們提出以爭點的分群編碼判決書的方法，來建構一個類似案件搜尋系統。我們以具有法律背景的人工評分來驗證系統的有效性，同時比較數種前處理程序和分群方法不同組合所達成的效果。

Abstract

Similar judgments search is an important task in legal practice, from which valuable legal insights can be obtained. Issues are disputes between both parties in civil litigation, which represents the core topics to be considered in the trials. Many studies calculate the similarity between judgments from different perspectives and methods. We first cluster the issues in the judgments, and then encode the judgments with vectors for whether or not the judgments contain issues in the corresponding clusters. The similarity between the judgments are evaluated based on the encoded messages. We verify the effectiveness of the system with a human scoring process by a legal background assistant, while comparing the effects of several combinations of preprocessing steps and selections of clustering strategies.

關鍵字：分群、資訊檢索、語意搜尋、法資訊學、類似案件

Keywords: clustering, information retrieval, semantic search, legal informatics, similar legal cases

1 緒論

判決書中富含法院對於法律問題的見解，而所謂「類似案件」是其中兩者在某個面向上類似且能提供有用資訊的判決書。法官在撰寫判決書、訴訟當事人及律師在準備攻防時，需要查找其他類似案件作為參考；法律實證研究者則需要蒐集類似案件以研究法律對於社會的影響及執行成效；民眾則可透過閱讀類似案件了解某些司法實務。如何有效地查找類似案件是基礎且重要的工作。

爭點，是兩造矛盾或互為對立的主張，包含事實上及法律上的爭議事項，一個案件中常含有數項不同爭點；法院會對這些爭點做出判斷，最終作出判決。爭點在法院的準備程序被統整並記載於筆錄，並不會公開；然而法官書寫判決書時經常將其作為論述的核心，記載於判決書中。爭點作為案件的審查要點，我們認為十分適合作為一種類似案件的面向。

一般的判決書檢索系統只能以使用者提供的關鍵字在全文或段落中搜尋。若使用者對一篇案件產生興趣，想要查看其他類似的案件，僅能依照自己的既有知識重新提供關鍵字搜尋，既不方便更無法獲得來自系統的額外資訊。

在這份研究中，我們提出以不同案件中爭點的分群 (clustering) 來編碼判決書，並以編碼後的匹配程度作為案件相似度的類似案件搜尋系統，其功能可以為一般判決書檢索系統推薦類似案例，希望能解決上述困境。

我們選擇三個系統元件當作研究變項，實驗並探討兩種資料萃取、三種文本向量化 (text vectorization)、兩種分群方法對於系統的影響。評估方面，一位法律系畢業的專任研

究助理為系統提供的數據做三種等級的標記，我們以此比較不同方法實作系統元件的效果。

2 相關研究

法律結合科技一向是熱門研究主題，近期國內法界學者開始進行人工智慧引入民事程序的可行性研究 (Ho, 2021)，越來越多機會正在產生。而法律資訊檢索的研究對象包含各式法律文獻間的搜尋，始終圍繞相似性這個主題。而 Bhattacharya et al. (2019) 對於研究法律案件相似性的方法提出總結，方法主要一是以引用為基礎 (citation-based) 計算；二是以文本為基礎 (text-based) 計算，包含使用全部文件、段落連結 (paragraph links)、主要論題相似性 (thematic similarity)、摘要等方法。

我們能以這樣的架構回顧更早期的研究。Kumar et al. (2011) 的研究表明使用法律詞彙相較於全部詞彙計算相似度對於尋找類似案件有更好效果。另外法律文書的書目耦合能加強共被引方法的效果；Raghav et al. (2016) 利用分群技術找出段落連結，結合案件引用的資訊計算案件的相似度。

然而，相對於採取判例法 (case law) 的海洋法系國家，我國法院裁判書並沒有這些引用判例的資訊。因此我們可以著重在如何更好地提取出文本的法律特徵。Ma et al. (2018) 利用法律知識圖譜將中文判決書提取為法律概念並學習相似度； Hong et al. (2020) 對中國判決書結構和類似案件匹配任務的挑戰進行分析，並提出結合法律特徵向量及預訓練語言模型。

許多學者對國內法資訊學的發展做出貢獻，這些不同任務的研究往往也聚焦在更好地提取及利用法律文本資訊，也可供我們效法。其中 Lin et al. (2012) 嘗試自動擷取 21 種針對強盜罪與恐嚇取財罪定義之標籤並利用於案件分類和量刑預測； Liu and Chen (2019) 提出能自動萃取出裁判書要旨句的模型，實驗多種類神經網路模型架構及特徵選擇的效果。除此之外，歷年來國內許多實作裁判書檢索系統的碩博士學位論文也能提供借鏡。Lan (2009) 提出將關鍵詞檢索結果以階層式分群法輸出，及共現詞彙建立索引的檢索系統；Lu (2021) 提出以空間向量模型合併 TF-IDF 詞權重調整之檢索系統；Tsao (2021) 以預訓練語言模型建立判決書的情境表示式，並提出案由分群亂度當作實驗指標。

3 問題定義與假設

$\boldsymbol{D}$ 表示包含 D 的所有判決書的集合。我們的目標是建立一個系統 f，能夠找出 D 的一些類似案件 $\boldsymbol{S}$。

$$D \in \boldsymbol{D} \tag{1}$$

$$f(D) \to \boldsymbol{S} \tag{2}$$

我們假定判決書 D 中的爭點具有足以代表該判決書的核心資訊，且具有越多相似爭點的判決書則越相似。因此，我們設計以下流程和定義：判決書首先以萃取出爭點的方法 e 取得爭點列表，隨後對其進行前處理 p；接著使用文本向量化的方法 v 將其轉換為數字向量；之後，我們使用分群方法 c 對所有判決書中的爭點進行分群；最後把每一個群 (clusters)以自然數編號後，將每一篇判決書中的爭點代換為其所屬之群的號碼，此過程稱為代換 r；這一組數字稱為群代碼 C。

至此，我們能將原始判決書的文本 D，經過一系列方法轉換為群代碼 C。我們將經過 $e, \mathrm{p}, v, c, \mathrm{r}$ 的過程合稱為分群編碼 t。

$$t\colon \quad D \xrightarrow[e,\mathrm{p},v,c,\mathrm{r}]{} C \tag{3}$$

類似案件定義為：C_1, C_2 為 S_1, S_2 的群代碼，若且為若 C_1, C_2 的交集數大於等於閥值 θ，則 S_1 與 S_2 互為類似案件。一群互為類似案件的集合則表示為 $\boldsymbol{S}$。

$$C_1 = t(S_1),\ C_2 = t(S_2) \tag{4}$$

$$S_1 \sim S_2 \ \Leftrightarrow\ |C_1 \cap C_2| \geq \theta \tag{5}$$

$$\boldsymbol{S} = \{S_1, S_2, \cdots\} \tag{6}$$

基於上述，我們將此類似案件的搜尋系統以分群編碼 t 實踐，記為 f_t。

我們想知道，具法律背景人士如何評價系統所找出的類似案件，並測試、比較系統中的一些不同方法產生之效果，以找出未來改進系統的方向。為此，我們以 2 種e、3 種v、2 種c 組合成的 $t_1, t_2, \cdots, t_{12}$（搭配固定的 p、r)，構建出總共 12 個系統 $f_{t_1}, f_{t_2}, \cdots, f_{t_{12}}$ 。評估方法於 9.2 節說明。

4 資料來源與篩選

司法院資料開放平臺[1]提供民國 85 年起至今超過千萬筆的判決書，每月持續更新。我們下載並篩選出案號字別[2]為「勞訴」，代表第一審勞動訴訟事件（以下簡稱勞訴）的判決書，時間分布自民國88年至110年為止，共15267篇。這些資料並沒有註明彼此的關係，每一篇僅提供法院、年分、日期、案號字別、案由及判決書文本；而民事訴訟法第 226 條[3]僅規定判決書必須出現的一些事項，其餘事項與格式則由法官依習慣及自由決定。因此判決書寫作上雖然存在一些常見的規律，但並沒有普遍適用的格式，可以視為富含資訊的非結構化的文本。為了簡化研究，我們不會使用全部的勞訴，而是以下面兩個步驟進一步篩選出具有共同性的研究資料。

4.1 步驟一：爭點段落

目前並沒有能普遍適用的方法可以定位出判決爭點，所以我們先聚焦在找出含有「爭點段落」的勞訴，定義及流程如下：首先以資料集內固定的數種章節編號（一、, 甲 ...等）和出現於行首的條件分段，將分段所得的語料稱為「章節分行」；進一步觀察發現，爭點段落的標題常具有固定模式，通常會包含「爭點」、「爭執(之)(事項|要旨|重點)」屬於正面的關鍵詞，不包含「不爭執」、「其餘」屬於反面的關鍵詞；爭點段落的下一段則會回到和開頭同一種章節編號的下一個編號，可以此定位爭點段落的結尾。我們以正規表示法[4] (regular expressions) 比對這些模式，定位出爭點段落的開頭與結尾，找出明確含有爭點段落的判決書共 5060 篇。然而，爭點段落的內容依不同法官風格而定，並不是含有爭點段落的判決書都適合拿來利用；我們將搭配下一個步驟進一步篩選語料。

反問	發問
含有關鍵詞：為什麼|還要|怎可能|孰能|違論|難道|如何能|又如何|何需|何須|何必|豈|否則|明知|何來|試問|焉|何以。	含有關鍵詞：問|說|證稱|你|我|們|嗎|所以|對不對|啊|...|那是|然後|那。 搭配前後的引號。

表 1. 反問及發問的模式

4.2 步驟二：爭點問句

不同判決書的爭點段落仍有各式不同寫法，可能包含當事人主張、法院見解、不同格式的爭點。為了找出具有普遍性、能提供充分語意的語料，我們選擇篩選出在爭點段落內具有符合「爭點問句」定義的判決書作為語料，共 3837 篇。

所謂爭點問句，定義為：以句號做為結尾且以正規表示法，排除模式上明顯為寫作上的反問語氣及言詞辯論程序記錄的發問。表 1 紀錄上述兩者的模式。設計爭點問句的後半部定義，其目的為雜訊抑制 (noise reduction)，即使不能完善也對提升語料品質有所助益。且上述須排除的反問及發問並不常見於爭點段落內；因此，即使不能保證全部排除，仍可確保語料擁有較高的品質。

5 資料萃取

原始判決書以 4.1 節所述分段方法切割為數個章節分行後，進一步觀察章節分行內的結構，能發現法院在列舉爭點時，時常將相關的爭點問句以群組的形式記錄在同一章節分行，例如：「一、被告對原告為解雇處分之事由為何？該解雇處分是否適法？有無逾越勞基法及被告聘雇人員工作規則所定除斥期間？」、「二、原告得否向被告請求退休金？得請求之金額為若干？」；有時也會發生爭點問句與論述夾雜的情況，若不對章節分行切割則無

[1] https://opendata.judicial.gov.tw/

[2] https://law.judicial.gov.tw/GetFile.ashx?pfid=0000309583

[3] 民事訴訟法第 226 條：「1 判決，應作判決書，記載下列各款事項：一、當事人姓名及住所或居所；當事人為法人、其他團體或機關者，其名稱及公務所、事務所或營業所。二、有法定代理人、訴訟代理人者，其姓名、住所或居所。三、訴訟事件；判決經言詞辯論者，其言詞辯論終結日期。四、主文。五、事實。六、理由。七、年、月、日。八、法院。2 事實項下，應記載言詞辯論時當事人之聲明，並表明其聲明為正當之攻擊或防禦方法要領。3 理由項下，應記載關於攻擊或防禦方法之意見及法律上之意見。4 一造辯論判決及基於當事人就事實之全部自認所為之判決，其事實及理由得簡略記載之。」。

[4] https://pypi.org/project/regex/

法萃取出資料。這讓我們必須考量在「拆開個別子句」和「保持原子句群組」兩種做法間，有取得更單純語意和保持語料相關性及完整性之取捨；因此我們設計兩種萃取爭點問句的方法，在具有爭點問句的判決書 3837 篇中，以方法一 NS 處理後每篇平均有 3.3 句爭點問句，每句平均有 46.8 字；以方法二 EX 處理後每篇平均有 4.8 句爭點問句，每句平均有 32.7 字。

5.1 方法一：NS

第一型保留法院原始的爭點問句群組，只篩選該章節分行是否為爭點問句，定義於 4.2 節。其優點如上所述能保持相關性及完整性；缺點則為擁有更複雜的語意，且少數情況下可能夾帶法院見解或是當事人主張。我們將此種資料萃取方式稱為 NS，代表 Non-Split 之意思。

5.2 方法二：EX

第二型考量為有利取得更單純語意之句向量，以及盡可能找出被包覆在其他無關資訊中的爭點問句，先將章節分行做「分句」處理，再進行爭點問句篩選。分句主要以章節編號和三種具有置於完整語意句末的標點「。！？」來切割章節分行。此種方法會將一個原先群組化的爭點問句拆分成數個子句，缺點是可能分句出語意太狹隘子句，例如「有無理由？」、「金額若干？」。我們將此種資料萃取方式為 EX，代表 Extracted 之意思。

5.3 抽樣及分析

以上兩種萃取爭點問句的方法各有其優劣處，為了進一步了解它們所帶來的誤差，我們簡單隨機抽樣 3837 篇中的 383 篇，以人工檢驗試圖了解萃取方法的效果。抽樣的結果中 NS 方法有 56 篇 (16.4%)、EX 方法有 27 篇 (7%) 有未能完全萃取出所有爭點問句或萃取錯誤的情形，其誤差範圍大多數在二句之內。

進一步分析這些錯誤樣本，發現造成的理由大致可分為四類：1. 寫作風格（法官將理由與爭點書寫於同一段而重複提及該爭點問句導致冗餘；部分爭點不以問句的方式呈現；爭點問句被夾在長句子當中等）、2. 分段誤差

原始	變換後
⑶教師法第十四條第一項第六款行為不檢有損師道…	教師法第 14 條第 1 項第 6 款行為不檢有損師道...
㈠原告係 79 年 7 月 13 日或 84 年 4 月 28 日起受被告僱用？	原告係自某時或某時起受被告僱用？
(一)世新視訊股份有限公司與被告公司是否具有實體同一性？	某團體與被告公司是否具有實體同一性？
（一）王淑芬之死亡是否屬職業災害？	某人之死亡是否屬職業災害？

表 2. 原始及變換後之爭點問句

（涵蓋到額外的段落）、3. 錯誤切割子句（同一個句子中使用到章節編號時被意外切割為二句）、4. 錯誤排除（反問語氣及言詞辯論程序記錄的發問）。四類理由中法官寫作風格差異為最大宗，分別佔 83.9% (NS) 與 66.6% (EX)。

6 資料前處理

6.1 法規條文正規化

爭點問句中記載的法規條文，常因不同的書寫習慣或簡稱而導致缺乏一致的形式，例如「勞資爭議處理法第一條」和「勞資法第 1 條」具有相同意義。若是不對其正規化會導致機器將其視為不同單元而造成錯誤分群。

為此，我們將其中文數字代換為阿拉伯數字，以及利用從全國法規資料庫[5]蒐集的法規條文和自行建立的字典將簡稱代換為原本的名稱。

6.2 細節模糊化

排除掉上述法規條文，爭點問句常常有過多私人性質的訊息，如人名、地址、數字細節等。為了使其更具一般性，我們希望將這些訊息模糊化，意即將它們轉為文字代號。

首先是關於數字細節。章節編號、金額、時間、算式等能以正規表示法找出的數字細節被替換成統一的文字代號，如某金額、某時等。再來是運用命名實體辨識 (named-entity recognition) 技術替換細節的方法。除了數字細節，人名、地址、某團體等不易以規則辨識的命名實體也需要模糊化。我們選用中研院開源的 CKIP Transformers[6]套件之 bert-base-chinese-ner 模型進行命名實體辨識，將辨識所得替換成某人、某地、某團體等文字代號。經過上述程序變換後的一些例子如表 2。

[5] https://law.moj.gov.tw/

[6] https://github.com/ckiplab/ckip-transformers

6.3 斷詞

詞彙是文本中語意的最小單位。詞袋模型 (bag-of-words model) 將文本表達為一群詞彙的組合，不考慮文法及順序，並可以詞彙出現的頻率或其他方式做為特徵。然而中文在書寫上不像英文以空白區分出詞彙；為了使用詞袋模型來表達文本，必須先將其斷詞 (word segmentation)。我們使用 CKIP Transformers[7]套件中的 bert-base-chinese-ws 模型，並搭配上述兩個小節調整斷詞結果，使得法規條文和文字代號不被斷開。

7 文本向量化

為了讓機器能識別文本中所蘊含的文意，需要將文本轉化為數字形式，且能表現出該文本語意上、語言學上的特徵，稱為文本向量化 (text vectorization)。我們選用兩種常見的文本向量化方式來轉化語料以便進行分群。一是基於深度學習的句嵌入 (sentence embedding) 技術；二是基於詞袋模型擴展出的 n-gram 模型搭配資訊檢索領域中常用的 tf-idf 加權技術 (term frequency-inverse document frequency weighting)。這些技術在接下來的小節提供介紹。

7.1 Sentence-BERT(SBERT)

Reimers et al. (2020) 以孿生類神經網路（Siamese neural network）及三連體類神經網路（Triplet neural network）架構修改預訓練 BERT 語言模型 (Devlin, 2018)，以得到具有語意、能以 cosine similarity[8] 比較相似度的的句嵌入技術。

孿生類神經網路是以兩個共享權值 (weights) 的子類神經網路所建構而成 (Bromley, 1993)。將兩筆資料輸入進兩個類神經網路進行特徵轉換 (feature transformation)、特徵提取 (feature extraction) 後，以 loss function 計算兩者的相似度。而三連體類神經網路則是以前者改進，改為三個輸入與子類神經網路，藉由正樣本與負樣本的組合來計算。

SBERT 將標記好相似性的句子對做為訓練資料，將 transformers 類的網路結合上述類神經網路，比較多種目標函數及整合特徵向量的效果，產生出一批預訓練語言模型，能夠將一定長度內的句子輸出成固定維度的句向量。他們發現與 BERT 相比，在一大群句子（約一萬筆）中尋找最相似句子對的任務上能大幅度節省時間（65 小時縮減至 5 秒鐘），並且在諸多語意相似度 (semantic textual similarity) 任務上成為最先進的 (state of art) 模型。由於上述特性，SBERT 更適合我們的分群任務上。實作上，使用 sentence-transformers[9]套件，並選用較為貼近實驗設計的 paraphrase-multilingual-mpnet-base-v2 模型。由於缺乏成對的相似句組能作為訓練資料，我們沒有進行 fine-tune。

7.2 TFIDF-RAW

tf-idf 由統計得來的詞頻（term frequency, tf）及逆向文件頻率（inverse document frequency, idf）組成，兩者相乘可以表示詞彙的重要程度。一般來說，某詞彙在特定文件中的詞頻計算方式為在該文件中該詞彙出現的次數，除以該文件中所有詞彙出現次數之合；某詞彙的逆向文件頻率計算方式則為總文件數目除以包含該詞彙之文件的數目，再取以 10 為底的對數 (Jones, 1972)。

將句子以詞袋模型表示，搭配 tf-idf 加權技術，可得到固定維度的句向量。我們以 TF-IDF-RAW 表示這種向量化方法。

實作方面，我們使用 scikit-learn 套件中的 TfidfVectorizer[10]。設定其所提供的一些參數：norm='l2', use_idf=True, smooth_idf=True, sublin ear_tf=False，這會讓 idf 的計算方式成為：

$$\mathrm{idf(t)} = \log\frac{n+1}{\mathrm{df(t)}+1} + 1 \tag{7}$$

n 代表總文件數，df(t) 代表包含詞彙 t 的文件數。為了避免除數為零錯誤 (zero division error) 及平滑化 (smoothing)，分子及分母都加上數字 1。最後會對計算出的 tf-idf 向量做 l2 正規化 (normalization)：

$$v_{norm} = \frac{v}{\sqrt{v_1^2+v_2^2+\cdots+v_n^2}} \tag{8}$$

[7] https://github.com/ckiplab/ckip-transformers

[8] cosine similarity: $c(a, b) = \frac{a \cdot b}{|a||b|}$

[9] https://www.sbert.net/

[10] https://scikit-learn.org/stable/modules/generated/sklearn.feature_extraction.text.TfidfVectorizer.html

另外值得一提的是，設定中 analyzer='word'，使得輸入的字串根據空白切割出詞彙（為此要準備詞彙間以空白隔開的句子）。設定 token_pattern=r"(?u)\b\w+\b" 使其能以空白分割出詞彙且不會過濾掉長度為 1 的中文詞彙。我們沒有使用停用詞 (stop words)。

7.3 TFIDF-NGRAM

n-gram 模型可以視為詞袋模型的擴展，它將 n 個連續詞彙組合成新的詞彙，以此捕捉連續詞彙之間的關係，再將文本表達為一堆詞彙的集合。我們以 TFIDF-NGRAM 表示使用 tf-idf 技術同時搭配 unigram+bigram+trigram (分別代表 n=1,2,3) 為特徵的向量化方法。實作工具及設定與上一段基本相同，額外設定 ngram_range=(1,3) 以使用 n-gram 模型。

8 分群與搜尋機制

我們設計的類似案件搜尋系統需要利用分群結果，並以其對文本（爭點問句）進行「分群編碼」。這一節將會先介紹我們所使用的兩種分群演算法，再說明使用分群結果得到群代碼及以群代碼搜尋出類似案件。

8.1 Affinity Propagation (AP)

AP 是基於資料點間相互資訊傳遞求得群集中心，再以此得出不同群的分群演算法 (FREY, 2007)。步驟是初始化各資料點間的責任值（Responsibility）、可用值（Availability），計算任兩資料點間的上述數值，重複迭代直到各資料點收斂。s(i,k)代表 i,k 兩點的相似度，則對資料點 i, k 來說，責任值 r 的更新公式為：

$$r(i,k) \leftarrow s(i,k) - \max[a(i,k') + s(i,k')\forall k' \neq k] \quad (9)$$

可用值 a 的更新公式為：

$$a(i,k) \leftarrow \min[0, r(k,k) + \textstyle\sum_{i' s.t. i' \notin \{i,k\}} r(i',k)] \quad (10)$$

透過給定參考度（Preference）而不指定分成幾群，得到基於資料特性的分群結果，我們將其設定為所有輸入向量彼此相似度之平均。為了優化結果，我們進行 grid search 後決定以下的 hyper-parameters: convergence_iter=15, max_iter=1000, damping=0.9, random_state=0。

affintiy 則根據向量化方法，TFIDF-RAW, TFIDF-NGRAM 為"euclidean [11] "，SBERT 為 "precomputed"，事先計算其 Cosine Similarity。

8.2 Hierarchical Clustering (HC)

HC 是一種分群演算法的類型，以資料點之間的距離計算出不同的群。主要分成 1. 首先所有資料視為一群，再依距離一一分出不同群。2. 把每筆資料視為一群，自下而上聚合，得到樹狀結構的分群結果。若不設定停止條件，最終根節點是聚合所有樣本的單一群，所有葉節點則是只含有一個樣本的群。我們使用自下而上的聚合方法 (agglomerative)。為了優化結果，以 grid search 決定 hyper-parameters：TFIDF_RAW, TFIDF_NGRAM 二者同被設定為 affinity='euclidean',linkage='ward',distance_threshold=1.9; SBERT 則被設定為 affinity='cosine', linkage='complete', distance_threshold=0.3。

8.3 分群編碼與類似案件搜尋

當我們以上述兩種方法得到分群結果後，把每一個群以自然數編號，將判決書中的爭點問句代換為其所屬的群代碼。至此，我們完成從原始判決書到群代碼的轉換，而這一系列的流程稱為分群編碼。

我們可以選定其中一篇為查詢 (query)，計算它與其他文件的群編碼交集數，以交集數由大到小排序，作為返回的搜尋結果，這稱為類似案件搜尋。

9 實驗設計

9.1 研究限制

由於我們研究的是真實世界資料以及嶄新的類似案件定義，並不事先存在這樣的標記可以使用，且基於人力、經費等限制，我們無法事先準備類似案件、分群的標準答案以進行監督式學習。因此，實驗設計以標記者對系統提供的答案進行評估，得到兩兩案件間相似度的標記資料後，衡量不同實驗變項之系統的成效差異。在未來，我們能以這些標記資料訓練模型以改善類似案件搜尋系統。

[11] Euclidean distance: $d(p,q) = \sqrt{(q_1 - p_1)^2 + \cdots + (q_n - p_n)^2}$

9.2 實驗變項

我們共選擇三個實驗變項，其中欲比較的方法說明理由如下：

資料萃取方面，比較第5節所述的兩種方法：NS與EX。兩者的關鍵差別在於爭點問句群組化與否，導致語意複雜程度、語料相關性及完整性的差距。我們想知道對系統而言的影響程度及選擇何者。

文本向量化方面，比較第7節所述的三種方法：SBERT, TFIDF_RAW, TFIDF_NGRAM。我們想知道近期的句嵌入技術與傳統詞袋模型及統計為基礎的方法，在系統中的效果以及改善方法為何。

分群演算法方面，使用第8節所述的兩種演算法：AP與HC。我們希望盡可能地以資料特性決定分群結果，因此這兩種選用的分群演算法都不是直接決定群的數量，而是藉由設定能決定資料點間是否為一群的標準。這個標準在AP裡是參考度，設定為所有資料點的相似度平均 (SBERT以cosine similarity計算，TFIDF-RAW, TFIDF-NGRAM 則以 Euclidean distance 計算)；在 HC 裡則是相似度 (SBERT 以 cosine similarity=0.3，TFIDF-RAW, TFIDF-NGRAM則以Euclidean distance=1.9計算)。由於語料經過不同實驗變項組合的處理，以上述的標準分群後會產生出不同的分群結果。我們將這些分群結果之群的數量紀錄在表3。

9.3 評估方法

將上述實驗變項組合，得到 12 種不同分群編碼的系統。以相同流程評估這些系統，如下：

第一步，將資料集內每一篇判決書作為查詢進行類似案件搜尋，會得到 3837 個（資料集大小）搜尋結果。第二步，提取出每組最高分的搜尋結果，經過「篩選」後得到數組「提問與推薦」的組合，稱為推薦案件組，接著經過資料庫的比對，以避免重複評分。篩選的辦法希望排除 1.個別法院內對於爭點整理的固有習慣。2.類似程度不高的判決書。因此設計過濾規則：1.來自相同法院 2.分群交集數小於3的推薦案件組。這裡的3即為第3節中的閾值θ。第三步，請一位法學系畢業的專任助理（簡稱為標記者），以其中各自爭點問句的類似程度，對推薦案件組作三種等級的評分，分別是：比較類似、勉強類似、不類似，隨後將標記過的推薦案件組評分記錄到資料庫中。以上三項步驟產生出不同方法組合的評分統計結果於表4。

方法組合	群數
EX + AP + SBERT	883
EX + AP + TFIDF-NGRAM	2421
EX + AP + TFIDF-RAW	1603
EX + HC + SBERT	1390
EX + HC + TFIDF-NGRAM	1446
EX + HC + TFIDF-RAW	1374
NS + HC + SBERT	807
NS + HC + TFIDF-NGRAM	813
NS + HC + TFIDF-RAW	877
NS + AP + SBERT	630
NS + AP + TFIDF-NGRAM	1559
NS + AP + TFIDF-RAW	1094

表 3. 不同實驗變項之群的數量

接下來我們可以就評分統計中不同評分所占的比例來對不同面向做討論，做為評估方法。兩個方法組合相比，有較高比例的比較類似與較低比例的不類似者，我們定義其為較佳的表現，反之則為較差的表現。

10 實驗數據與討論

首先觀察表3群數和表4不同方法合計的案件數的關係：可以看出若群數越少則合計的案件數越多。這是由於在篩選推薦案件組的過程會根據8.3節所計算的交集數，而較少的分群數則更容易產生群代碼的交集。

接下來，我們將分別以資料萃取、向量化、分群方法的三個面向來比較其在系統中的表現，以及探討所造成的原因。

首先，比較不同資料萃取方法：大致上 NS 比起 EX 有著稍微較佳的表現。我們認為這顯示 NS 保留法院所提供群組化的爭點問句，其句向量的語意更為豐富，因此分群的結果更為細緻，從而後續步驟所得的推薦案件組較能得到標記者的青睞。

再來，比較三種向量化方法： TFIDF-RAW 比起 TFIDF-NGRAM 皆得到較高比例的比較類似、較低比例的不類似。我們認為這是由於 TFIDF-NGRAM 雖然更能考慮詞彙的相鄰性，但其較大的維度反而不利相似度計算；而 SBERT 和另外兩向量化方法相比，能提供較多推薦案件組及更穩定的表現。我們認為這要歸功於其將不同詞彙但意思相近之句子

評分等級 / 方法組合	比較類似		勉強類似		不類似		所有標記
	數量	比例	數量	比例	數量	比例	數量
EX + AP + SBERT	181	55.7%	70	21.5%	74	22.8%	325
EX + AP + TFIDF-NGRAM	51	56.0%	15	16.5%	25	27.5%	91
EX + AP + TFIDF-RAW	103	59.5%	41	23.7%	29	16.8%	173
EX + HC + SBERT	449	54.9%	176	21.5%	193	23.6%	818
EX + HC + TFIDF-NGRAM	178	36.4%	77	15.7%	234	47.9%	489
EX + HC + TFIDF-RAW	121	52.6%	44	19.1%	65	28.3%	230
NS + HC + SBERT	204	55.4%	82	22.3%	82	22.3%	368
NS + HC + TFIDF-NGRAM	75	27.0%	28	10.1%	175	**62.9%**	278
NS + HC + TFIDF-RAW	45	63.4%	10	14.1%	16	22.5%	71
NS + AP + SBERT	60	60.6%	25	25.3%	14	14.1%	99
NS + AP + TFIDF-NGRAM	18	60.0%	4	13.3%	8	26.7%	30
NS + AP + TFIDF-RAW	38	**67.9%**	11	19.6%	7	12.5%	56
平均	126.9	50.3%	48.6	19.3%	76.8	30.4%	252.3

表 4. 評分統計表

嵌入為相似向量的能力，以及它較小的特徵維度。

最後，關於兩種分群演算法：我們注意到 AP 相較於 HC 得到較好且較穩定的結果；然而不能排除這是受到分群演算法相關參數的影響所導致，因此不能以此宣稱 AP 是適合本任務的分群演算法；我們仍可以得到不同分群演算法及其設定對於類似案件搜尋結果有較大影響的結論。

值得注意的是，EX + HC + TFIDF-NGRAM 與 NS + HC +TFIDF-NGRAM 分別得到使用 EX 和 NS 的所有方法組合中最差的表現，且與其他方法組合的表現差距甚大。我們認為造成此現象的原因為， TIDF-NGRAM 有較高的為度，而 HC 在高維度時計算 Euclidean distance 所得的相似性效果較差，SBERT 則計算 cosine similarity 而受到影響較少。

整體而言，12 個不同變項組合的系統所取得的類似案件組平均有 50.3% 的比較類似、30.4% 的不類似；而我們實驗組中的最好結果則有 67.9% 的比較類似、12.5% 的不類似。考量判決書中爭點本身的多樣性、相似性及重複率尚屬未知，我們認為這樣的類似案件系統具備有效性，且能夠提供往後研究者一個基準以及研究方向。

11 結論

在這份研究中，我們設計了一套以民事訴訟之爭點分群為基礎的類似案件搜尋系統，並且嘗試比較 12 組不同資料萃取、向量化、分群方法對系統的影響。以具有法律背景的人工評分結果顯示，我們表現最好的系統，所找到的類似案例組中 67.9% 被評為比較類似(最高等級的評分)，僅有 12.5% 被評為不相似；而 12 組系統平均有 50.3% 的被評為比較類似、30.4% 的不類似，顯示我們的方法具備一定的有效性，足以作為後續研究的基準。而這些實驗所得的標記資料，能開啟未來監督式學習的研究路徑。

致謝

本研究承國科會研究計畫 107-2221-E-004-009 -MY3 與 110-2221-E-004-008-MY3 與國立政治大學高教深耕校內補助計畫 111H124D-13 之部分補助，謹此致謝。

References

Paheli Bhattacharya, Kripabandhu Ghosh, Arindam Pal, Saptarshi Ghosh. 2019. Methods for Computing Legal Document Similarity: A Comparative Study. *LDA 2019 workshop.* the Fundation for Legal Knowledge Based System. https://doi.org/10.48550/arXiv.2004.12307

Jane Bromley, Isabelle Guyon, Yann LeCun, Eduard Sickinger and Roopak Shah. 1993. Signature Verification using a "Siamese" Time Delay Neural Network. *Advances in Neural Information Processing Systems 6*, pages 737-744. Neural Information Processing Systems foundation https://doi.org/10.1142/S0218001493000339

Jacob Devlin, Ming-Wei Chang, Kenton Lee, Kristina Toutanova. 2018. BERT: Pre-training of Deep Bidirectional Transformers for Language Understanding. *Computing Research Repository,* arXiv.1810.04805

Brendan J. Frey , Delbert Dueck. 2007. Clustering by Passing Messages Between Data Points. *SCIENCE, 315*(5814)972-976. https://doi.org/10.1126/science.1136800

Jim-How Ho. 2021. AI 引入民事程序可行性之研究 (The Feasibility Research on Introducing Artificial Intelligence into Civil Procedures) [In Chinese] Doctoral Dissertation, Department of Information Management, National Taiwan University of Science and Technology. https:/hdl.handle.net/11296/pkvh27

Zhilong Hong, Qifei Zhou, Rong Zhang, Weiping Li, Tong Mo. 2020. Legal Feature Enhanced Semantic Matching Network for Similar Case Matching. *2020 International Joint Conference on Neural Networks* pages 1-8. the Institute of Electrical and Electronics Engineers.https://doi.org/10.1109/IJCNN48605.2020.9207528

Karen Spark Jones. 1972. A statistical interpretation of term specificity and its application in retrieval. *Journal of documentation, 28*(1), pages 11-21. https://doi.org/10.1108/eb026526

Sushanta Kumar, P. Krishna Reddy, V. Balakista Reddy, Aditya Singh. 2011. Similarity analysis of legal judgments. *COMPUTE '11: Proceedings of the Fourth Annual ACM Bangalore Conference* pages 1-4. Association for Computing Machinery. https:doi.org/10.1145/1980422.1980439

Chia-Lian Lan. 2009. 中文訴訟文書檢索系統雛形實作 (A Prototype of Information Services for Chinese Judicial Documents)[In Chinese]. Master's Thesis, Department of Computer Science, National Chengchi University. https://hdl.handle.net/11296/hgfrwt

Chao-Lin Liu, Kuan-Chun Chen. 2019. Extracting the Gist of Chinese Judgments of the Supreme Court. *ICAIL '19: Proceedings of the Seventeenth International Conference on Artificial Intelligence and Law* pages 73–82. Association for Computing Machinery. https://doi.org/10.1145/3322640.3326715

Wan-Chen Lin, Tsung-Ting Kuo, Tung-Jia Chang, Chueh-An Yen, Chao-Ju Chen, and Shou-de Lin. 2012. 利用機器學習於中文法律文件之標記、案件分類及量刑預測 (Exploiting Machine Learning Models for Chinese Legal Documents Labeling, Case Classification, and Sentencing Prediction) [In Chinese]. *December 2012-Special Issue on Selected Papers from ROCLING XXIV. 17.* International Journal of Computational Linguistics & Chinese Language Processing. https://aclanthology.org/O12-5004

Kai-Yu Lu. 2021. 基於向量空間模型之智慧型文件搜尋系統開發-以台灣醫療糾紛判決書為例 (Development an Intelligent Document Search System Based on Vector Space Model - A Case Study of Taiwan Medical Malpractice Claim Judgment) [In Chinese]. Master's Thesis, Department of Medical Informatics, Chung Shan Medical University. https://hdl.handle.net/11296/ceu267

Yinglong Ma, Peng Zhang, Jiangang Ma. 2018. An Efficient Approach to Learning Chinese Judgment Document Similarity Based on Knowledge Summarization. *Computing Research Repository,*. arXiv.1808.01843

K. Raghav, Pailla Balakrishna Reddy, V. Balakista Reddy, Polepalli Krishna Reddy. 2016. Text and Citations Based Cluster Analysis of Legal Judgments. *Mining Intelligence and Knowledge Exploration. 9468*, pages 449–459. International Conference on Mining Intelligence and Knowledge Exploration. https://doi.org/10.1007/978-3-319-26832-3_42

Nils Reimers and Iryna Gurevych. 2020. Making Monolingual Sentence Embeddings Multilingual using Knowledge Distillation. *Proceedings of the 2020 Conference on Empirical Methods in Natural Language Processing.* Association for Computational Linguistics. https://arxiv.org/abs/2004.09813

Hsi-Chang Tsao. 2021. 基於深度學習模型之判決書情境相似檢索技術之研究(Research on Similar Situation Retrieval Technique for Court's Judgment Based on Deep Learning Model) [In Chinese]. Master's Thesis, Department of Computer Science and Engineering, National Chung Hsing University. https://hdl.handle.net/11296/gjs6z4

The 34th Conference on Computational Linguistics and Speech Processing (ROCLING 2022)
Taipei, Taiwan, November 21-22, 2022. The Association for Computational Linguistics and Chinese Language Processing

正體中文斷詞系統應用於大型語料庫之多方評估研究
Multifaceted Assessments of Traditional Chinese Word Segmentation Tool on Large Corpora

Wen-Chao Yeh
Institute of Information Systems and Applications
National Tsing Hua University
Taiwan
wyeh@m109.nthu.edu.tw

Yu-Lun Hsieh
Graduate Institute of Data Science
Taipei Medical University
Taiwan
morpheus.h@gmail.com

[1] **Yung-Chun Chang**
Graduate Institute of Data Science
Taipei Medical University
Taiwan
changyc@tmu.edu.tw

Wen-Lian Hsu
Department of Computer Science and Information Engineering
Asia University
Taiwan
Pervasive AI Research Labs
Ministry of Science and Technology
Taiwan
hsu@iis.sinica.edu.tw

摘要

本研究之目的在於運用多種數值指標及實驗資料來評估 CKIP、Jieba、MONPA 等三種廣泛應用於臺灣自然語言處理產學界的正體中文斷詞器。我們特別針對運算效能、資源需求等等面向，檢驗其應用於大型語言文字資料集時，處理斷詞、詞性標註及命名實體辨識等工作之成效。實驗結果顯示，MONPA 利用圖形運算加速器（GPU）進行批次處理斷詞時，可以大幅度縮減巨量中文資料的運算時間，且其斷詞、詞性標註、命名實體辨識等多功能標籤均達到令人滿意的品質，且其產出之標註結果可有效輔助提升中文自然語言處理的後續相關任務成效。

Abstract

This study aims to evaluate three most popular word segmentation tool for a large Traditional Chinese corpus in terms of their efficiency, resource consumption, and cost. Specifically, we compare the performances of Jieba, CKIP, and MONPA on word segmentation, part-of-speech tagging and named entity recognition through extensive experiments. Experimental results show that MONPA using GPU for batch segmentation can greatly reduce the processing time of massive datasets. In addition, its features such as word segmentation, part-of-speech tagging, and named entity recognition are beneficial to downstream applications.

關鍵字：自然語言處理，中文斷詞，詞性標註，命名實體辨識

Keywords: NLP, Chinese Word Segmentation, POS, NER

1 緒論

近幾年來人工智慧應用發展可說是突飛猛進，但據我們觀察，可以處理正體中文的人工智慧模型仍存在進步空間，主要肇因於中文自然語言處理（NLP）的基礎設施仍未到

[1] Corresponding author

位。其中，特別是斷詞（Word Segmentation）這個自然語言處理流程中一個重要步驟，因有別於英文書寫上可用空白（white space）為線索來找到詞彙的邊界，中文書寫系統中的空白並不帶有任何詞語邊界的意義。正因為中文可以將單字或多字視為一個詞彙，要使用計算機來分析、擷取中文的資訊，就需要先以特殊工具完成斷詞處理。綜觀現今國內外產學界在中文自然語言處理，我們歸納出最常用來處理正體中文斷詞的工具為MONPA[2]、CKIP[3]、Jieba[4] 等三種。

一般認為 Jieba 斷詞系統速度較快，但正確率較低；CKIP 最新版本增加開發了 python 套件，保持其長久以來優良的成效，且更方便使用。 MONPA 對正體中文的支援度與 CKIP 處於伯仲之間。然而，至今尚未有嚴謹的學術研究針對這三種工具作完整的評測實驗。故本文將以上述三種斷詞工具對正體中文的斷詞、詞性標註、命名實體辨識等功能做多樣化的性能分析研究。更詳細來說，我們將實驗並紀錄三種工具的套件載入及斷詞運行時間，再分別以 SIGHAN 歷年來多筆 Share Task 的公開資料集，與專業人工標註的新聞語料等資料進行正確率驗證。最後，從網際網路以爬蟲技術搜集大量資料集供做文本分類任務使用，以驗證不同斷詞工具的斷詞結果是否影響機器學習的分類表現。

綜合實驗結果顯示，MONPA 利用 GPU 施行批次斷詞處理，可以大幅度縮減巨量中文資料的斷詞時間，且其斷詞、詞性標註、命名實體辨識等成果亦具有相當可靠的品質，有益於後續應用機器學習作中文自然語言處理的相關任務。

2 研究方法

Jieba 是基於簡體中文語料，透過 HMM 模型 (Baum et al., 1970) 所訓練出來的工具。就原始版本而言，對正體中文的支援度不佳，但可透過手動載入正體字詞字典檔來改善斷詞效果。CKIP 為歷史悠久的斷詞工具，經中研院 CKIP Lab 以較新穎的 BiLSTM 架構訓練模型 (Li et al., 2020)，並以 Python 套件釋出。MONPA (Hsieh et al., 2017) 最初為基於遞歸神經網路 (Recurrent Neural Network, RNN) 所建立的模型，並包含雙向 (bidirectional) 結構以便學習更廣泛的語境知識，同時也引入注意力 (attention) 機制，達到更佳的斷詞、標註等效果。

除了所採用的模型及理論基礎不同以外，這三種斷詞工具在工程層面亦有所差異，因此運行的環境也不盡相同。除 Jieba 採用自行開發的程式框架，CKIP 利用了 Tensorflow 這個深度學習工具庫為基礎架構，MONPA 則是採用 Pytorch 架構開發。為了盡可能的降低環境變因，所以，本研究的實驗環境將基於同一硬體設備，以 conda 建構 python 運行環境。我們的硬體設置如下：

- CPU: 4 * AMD EPYC 7252 8-Core Processor
- GPU: 7 * NVIDIA GeForce RTX 3090 (24GB memory)
- Memory: 8 * 32 GB (DDR4 3200 MT/s)
- OS: Ubuntu 20.4 LTS

2.1 斷詞工具版本

- Jieba：安裝 0.42.1 版本[5]，並另外下載約 4 MB 大小的正體中文詞典。實驗時將分別測試：(1) 預設版本，後稱 Jieba； (2) 匯入正體中文字典檔版本，後稱 JiebaD。
- CKIP：安裝 0.2.1 版本[6]，並另外下載約 1.8 GB 大小的模型檔，運行於 Tensorflow 2.6.0 架構。後稱 CKIP。
- MONPA：安裝 0.3.3 版本[7]（內含 8.9 MB 大小的模型檔），運行於 Pytorch 1.11.0 架構。實驗時將分別測試：(1) MONPA 預設的單句斷詞方法，後稱 MONPA；(2) 應用 GPU 效能的批次斷詞方法，後稱 MONPA Batch。

2.2 評測項目

本研究將實驗上述三種斷詞工具對正體中文的斷詞、詞性標註、命名實體辨識等功能的成果及效率。首先，我們紀錄三種工具的套件載入及斷詞運行時間，再分別以 SIGHAN (AFNLP, 2003; AFNLP, 2005; Ng & Kwong, 2006; AFNLP, 2008) 歷年來多筆 Share Task 的公開資料集，及經過專業人工標註的新聞語料等資料集驗證。另外，我們也從網際網路

[2] https://github.com/monpa-team/monpa/
[3] https://github.com/ckiplab/ckiptagger
[4] https://github.com/fxsjy/jieba
[5] https://pypi.org/project/jieba/
[6] https://pypi.org/project/ckiptagger/
[7] https://pypi.org/project/monpa/

以爬蟲搜集三種文本分類任務的資料集，以檢驗不同斷詞工具的斷詞結果，是否會影響機器學習的分類表現。

2.2.1 斷詞執行效率

此實驗分三階段測試斷詞工具的執行效率，依序為：載入套件時間、一千句內的小資料集斷詞時間、5,000 句至 40,000 句的大資料集斷詞時間。運行時間以 python 基本套件 time 執行紀錄，每筆測資皆運行 10 次取平均值。

- 載入套件時間：三種斷詞工具皆是 python 套件，因此本次實驗將先紀錄斷詞工具的套件載入需要費時多久。
- 小資料集斷詞時間：每一句皆是由 200 個字元長度組成，實驗從一句到 990 句的斷詞執行時間各需多久。
- 大資料集斷詞時間：每一句皆是由 200 個字元長度組成，分別測試對 5,000 句、10,000 句、15,000 句、20,000 句、25,000 句、30,000 句、35,000 句、 40,000 句的斷詞執行時間各需多久。

2.2.2 斷詞、詞性標註、命名實體辨識的檢測

雖然本次實驗所包含的工具在各自相關論文中均有提到斷詞成效，但在經過數年的科技發展和資料更替後，我們認為仍需再次驗證其最新結果。所以，本研究將使用以下資料集進行實驗：

- SIGHAN 2003 ~ 2008 年競賽的公開資料集，用以驗證三種工具的斷詞成效。
- SIGHAN 2006 競賽的公開資料集，用以驗證 CKIP 及 MONPA 的命名實體辨識成效。
- 從網路搜集的新聞語料隨機抽出 30 筆文本，經語言專家以人工標註出詞性標註、命名實體辨識等資料，用以驗證詞性標註及命名實體等多工成效。

以往斷詞、詞性標註、命名實體辨識的檢測皆以 Perl 寫成的 conlleval[8] 評分，本研究採用以 python 改寫的 seqeval[9] 套件 (Nakayama, 2018)，並經測試驗證評分標準及結果同 conlleval。

2.2.3 不同斷詞文本對機器學習方法的影響

這部份的實驗資料，是利用爬蟲從網際網路公開網頁搜集約四萬筆新聞文本、四萬筆旅館正負評文本，及 5,500 筆電影正負評文本等三種內容各異的資料。特別注意的是，新聞文本將作為文件分類的資料使用，其中包含六個新聞類型。我們將分別以三種工具對上述正體中文語料進行斷詞，並將結果作為機器學習方法的訓練及測試文本，以藉此實驗輸入不同的斷詞資料是否會影響機器學習分類方法的預測效果。四種機器學習皆是引用 scikit-learn[10] 套件 (Pedregosa et al., 2011) 中內建的方法，包含：

- Naïve Bayes: 使用 ComplementNB() 方法，參數均為預設值。
- Decision Tree: 使用 DecisionTreeClassifier() 函數，參數均為預設值。
- KNN: 使用 KneighborsClassifier()，參數 n_neighbors 設定為 500，其餘皆為預設值。
- SVM: 使用 svm.SVC()，參數 kernel 設定為 linear，gamma 設定為 0.8，C = 1.2，其餘皆為預設值。

3 斷詞效率之實驗結果與討論

3.1 載入套件時間

本實驗在 Jupyter Lab 重啟核心後載入單一套件（標示為 0），隨後以 reload() 重新載入套件兩次（標示為 1 及 2），經紀錄時間後繪製為圖 1。Jieba 及 JiebaD 為單純 python 套件，並無需先載入其他運行架構，可以從三次測試時間皆相仿得知。但因 JiebaD 要進一步匯入約 4 MB 大小的字典檔，所以在載入套件花費最多時間。CKIP 需要基於 Tensorflow 架構來運作，所以在初次啟動時要先載入 Tensorflow 架構和本身的程式部件等，因此需要花費較多時間。隨後，在 reload 動作進行時，因 Tensorflow 已在運行環境中而僅需載入其自有程式部分，我們推測所需時間主要是花費在載入近 1.8 GB 大小的模型檔上。

[8] CoNLL-2000 shared task, https://www.clips.uantwerpen.be/conll2002/

[9] https://github.com/chakki-works/seqeval

[10] https://scikit-learn.org/

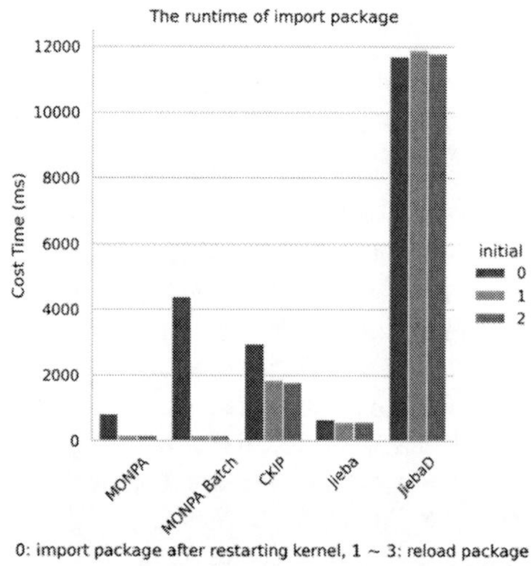

圖 1. 載入斷詞套件所需時間

MONPA 及 MONPA Batch 需要基於 Pytorch 架構來運作，所以同樣在初次執行時要先載入 Pytorch 架構，與自有的套件程式等，因此需要花費較多時間。隨後 reload 動作亦因 Pytorch 已在環境中而僅需重新載入自身套件，所需時間主要是處理近 8.9 MB 大小的模型檔。另外值得注意的是，MONPA Batch 因為需使用 GPU 資源做批次斷詞，所以初次啟動要比 MONPA 預設單線程版本花費更多時間在將模型的參數搬移到 GPU 記憶體中。由此可見，不管是採用深度學習架構或是其他統計式演算法，都需要花費時間載入模型檔或是字典檔。正因如此，模型或資料檔案大小與該斷詞工具的啟動時間高度相關。

3.2 小資料集斷詞時間

準備單句不超過 200 字元長度的正體中文文本，並複製為 1 句到 990 句的不同文本。實驗紀錄各工具處理一篇 1 句到一篇 990 句的文本斷詞，每次執行需要多久時間，不包含載入套件等啟動時間。將時間紀錄繪製成圖 2 。Jieba 及 JiebaD 對 990 句（每句<200 字元）做文本斷詞的花費時間不會比斷一句的時間多出太多，幾乎呈現水平延伸，表現出快速斷詞的效率。CKIP 對資料多寡的斷詞時間呈現正線性，但增長斜率不大，啟動後預設以多線程執行斷詞任務，表現出穩定的斷詞效率。

MONPA 預設單線程斷詞方法花費時間最多，990 句就要多於 60 秒的執行時間。所以，MONPA Batch 的批次斷詞功能就是改善預設單句斷詞較緩慢的缺點，幾乎貼近 Jieba 的快速效率表現。

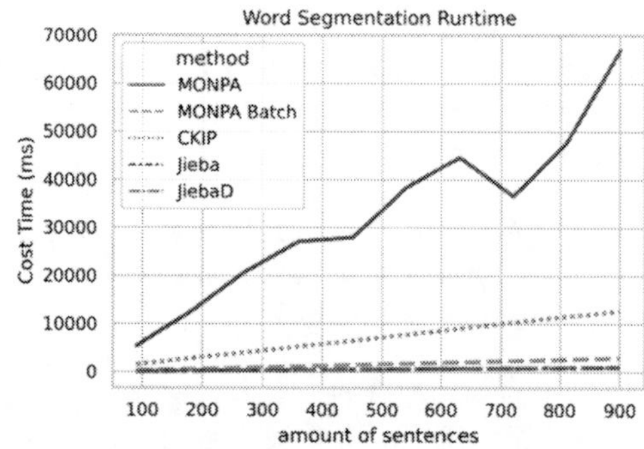

圖 2. 小資料集斷詞耗費時間

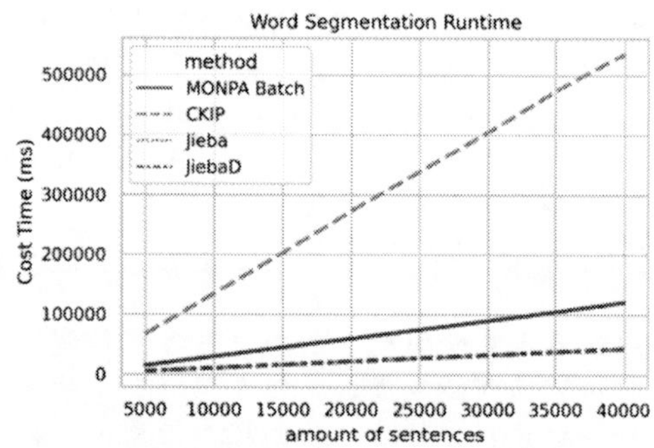

圖 3. 大資料集斷詞耗費時間

3.3 大資料集斷詞時間

本部分實驗將每篇文本包含的句子數增加到 5,000 ~ 40,000 的規模，之後紀錄各工具處理各篇的文本斷詞所需執行時間，同樣的也不包含載入套件等啟動時間。另外，基於前述實驗結果，本部分將排除速度最慢的 MONPA 單線程法。實驗時間紀錄可見圖 3 。Jieba 及 JiebaD 依然是具有最高效率的斷詞工具，CKIP 仍呈現線性增長，但在這個數量規模下，其所花費的時間將明顯高於其他工具。最後，MONPA Batch 的批次斷詞效率表現良好，與 Jieba 的差距不大。整體來說，我們可以得到以下結論：無論小資料或大資料集，在不考慮斷詞正確與否的前提下，Jieba 確實是最快速的斷詞工具。另外，若有 GPU 設備，MONPA 工具可得到大幅度的速度提升。

4 斷詞效能之實驗結果與討論

此部分的實驗針對三種系統的斷詞、詞性標註、命名實體辨識進行檢測，除了考量速度以外，斷詞工具的正確率更是值得關注的指標。因三種工具皆已釋出多年，亦經多次改版，效能應該有所不同。在以下各節中，我們將重新驗證各工具於常用資料集之表現，並討論與分析其結果。

4.1 斷詞驗證：SIGHAN 競賽公開資料集

本部分實驗應用了 SIGHAN 2003 ～ 2008 年的競賽資料集。在三種工具的預設安裝狀態，並且未使用上述搜集的訓練資料集重新訓練的條件下，實驗已載入正體中文字典檔的 JiebaD、CKIP 及 MONPA 對資料集之斷詞成果。我們採用 Precision (P)、 Recall (R) 以及 F1-score (F) 等指標來評估，也就是一個 token 左右兩方的詞界 (boundary) 與標準答案一樣時，視為斷詞正確。

從表 1 可以看出，使用簡體中文語料與 HMM 模型所訓練出來的 Jieba 套件，雖匯入正體中文字典檔，其斷詞效果依然沒有太大提升。而以 Chinese Gigaword 5 (Central News Agency, CNA 部分)、Wikipedia (2019-05-20 pages-articles dump，中文部分)、中央研究院漢語平衡語料庫 (ASBC 4.0) 及 OntoNotes 5.0 (中文部分) 等超過兩千兩百萬句正體中文語句當作訓練語料[11]所開發出的 CKIP，確實能在 SIGHAN 資料集取得非常好的成績。另一方面，MONPA 雖僅以約十萬句正體中文新聞語料訓練出的套件，應用於 SIGHAN 的資料也有不錯的表現。這也顯示出，使用深度學習方法，搭配足夠大量的資料，能夠獲得令人滿意的訓練結果。因此，建構一個大量且同時含有中文斷詞、詞性標註、以及命名實體資訊的語料庫，是現今中文自然語言處理工具不可或缺的資源，同時也是產學界必須面臨的挑戰。

4.2 命名實體辨識驗證：SIGHAN 2006 競賽公開資料集

命名實體辨識實驗是採用 SIGHAN 2006 年競賽的測試資料集，且斷詞後的命名實體辨識結果，需要同時具備詞界與專有名詞的類型都正確，才會視為辨識成功。Jieba 預設套件沒有命名實體辨識功能，故無法包含於此實驗中。本部分實驗的結果可見表 2。綜合來說，此實驗所包含的兩個工具均有很大的進步空間，我們認為這可能與訓練語料中的命名實體定義標準有關，故進行了接下來的實驗。

	System	F1-Score (%)			
		2003	*2005*	*2006*	*2008*
AS	Monpa	94.24	92.33	92.40	93.14
AS	CKIP	**98.22**	**97.68**	**98.06**	**97.90**
AS	JiebaD	76.52	73.87	74.32	74.97
City U	Monpa	89.10	88.85	89.72	-
City U	CKIP	**91.50**	**90.59**	**91.61**	-
City U	JiebaD	72.85	74.06	75.43	-

表 1. 各工具於 Academia Sinica (AS) 與 City University (City U) 資料集之斷詞效能結果

System	F1-Score (%)			
	LOC	*ORG*	*PER*	*Overall*
MONPA	**74.04**	35.34	79.80	66.94
CKIP	69.75	**37.13**	**88.60**	**67.02**

表 2. 各工具於 SIGHAN 2006 資料集的命名實體辨識效能

System	F1-Score (%)			
	LOC	*ORG*	*PER*	*Overall*
MONPA	**83.73**	**70.14**	**95.53**	**88.28**
CKIP	79.37	63.38	92.93	79.38

表 3. 各工具於隨機抽選新聞文本的命名實體辨識效能

4.3 綜合驗證：隨機抽選新聞文本

鑑於 CKIP 及 MONPA 對 SIGHAN 2006 資料集的命名實體辨識驗證結果不甚完美，我們另外從網路搜集了 30 則公開的臺灣新聞語料，並請具備語言學背景的專家進行詞性和命名實體標註後，做為本次實驗的驗證測試資料。表 3 的結果支持前述的推論，也就是 CKIP 和 MONPA 在 SIGHAN 2006 效果差強人意，可能與訓練語料的標註標準差異有關。當使用這兩個工具對正體中文的文本斷詞及進行命名實體辨識時，若是採用台灣用語為

[11] https://github.com/ckiplab/ckiptagger/wiki/Corpora

Corpus/System		P/R/F_1			
		Naïve Bayes	**Decision Tree**	**KNN**	**SVM**
News (#Train: 30,000, #Test: 10,000)	**Monpa**	78.43/82.83/**79.22**	63.13/64.20/59.40	77.12/81.40/**77.87**	76.69/79.42/**75.12**
	CKIP	78.16/82.62/78.94	63.08/64.30/59.45	76.43/80.49/76.71	76.58/79.28/74.93
	Jieba	77.72/82.09/78.50	63.84/65.09/60.67	76.26/79.63/76.50	75.97/78.79/74.52
	JiebaD	77.74/82.07/78.50	64.45/65.29/**60.94**	76.3079.65/76.53	75.92/78.72/74.45
Hotel Review (#Train: 30,000, #Test: 10,000)	**Monpa**	87.16/85.12/85.78	83.14/83.05/**83.09**	85.98/80.60/**81.60**	88.69/88.73/88.71
	CKIP	87.38/85.15/85.84	82.52/82.30/82.40	85.75/79.80/80.81	89.08/89.13/**89.10**
	Jieba	88.00/85.70/**86.42**	81.36/81.32/81.34	85.77/79.98/80.98	88.91/88.95/88.93
	JiebaD	88.00/85.70/**86.42**	81.25/81.16/81.20	85.85/80.05/81.06	88.91/88.95/88.93
Movie Review (#Train: 5000, #Test: 500)	**Monpa**	82.90/82.83/**82.70**	67.40/67.42/67.39	78.90/78.84/**78.86**	89.19/89.23/**89.20**
	CKIP	82.24/82.21/82.10	69.13/69.14/**69.10**	78.15/78.00/78.03	88.78/88.81/88.79
	Jieba	78.36/78.09/77.87	66.27/66.28/66.28	73.21/73.24/73.20	80.98/80.98/80.98
	JiebaD	78.44/78.19/77.97	63.29/63.30/63.29	73.01/73.04/73.00	81.18/81.17/81.18

表 4. 各工具於三種資料集之斷詞結果用在機器學習分類任務之效能評估結果，粗體字代表在各資料集中表現最佳的方法之 F1 分數。

標準來進行評估，成效將會大幅提升，同時也增進了實用性。

4.4 不同斷詞對機器學習方法的影響

雖然斷詞結果可由標準答案來驗證其成效優劣，但另一方面來看，將斷詞結果當作機器學習分類任務的訓練文本時，不同的斷詞結果可能會影響預測效果。一個好的斷詞工具，應該要能夠產出優良的標註來輔助後續機器學習的任務。因此，我們從網際網路公開網頁搜集共四萬筆，含六種新聞類別的文本資料 (News)，與四萬筆旅店正負評文本資料 (Hotel Review)，及 5,500 筆電影正負評文本資料 (Movie Review)。將這些實驗語料分別以三種工具斷詞，並篩選出詞性標註為動詞、名詞、副詞、形容詞、命名實體 (LOC, ORG, PER) 的詞彙組合作為機器學習模型的訓練文本及測試文本，採用前述機器學習的參數進行實驗，結果如表 4 所示。其中可發現，對正體中文斷詞成效較優的 CKIP 與 MONPA 工具，於三種資料集之斷詞結果，同樣也對機器學習分類任務的表現有所助益。

5 結論與未來展望

本研究透過多方面的實驗，評估 Jieba、CKIP、MONPA 等三種在正體中文自然語言研究社群常用的斷詞器，以期找出最適用於大型資料集的斷詞、詞性標註及命名實體辨識的多功能研究工具。在實驗過程中，我們觀察到 MONPA 在 0.3 版本以後，採用 Huggingface[12] 工具所提供的預訓練模型資料庫中的 ALBERT[13] (Lan et al., 2020) 模型，替換了初版的 Bi-LSTM 網路後，對比前版在 SIGHAN 的斷詞成效雖略低 0.002 左右，但模型檔案大小也從 55.1 MB 大幅縮減到 8.9 MB，達到以 pip 直接安裝，不須再額外下載模型檔或是字典檔的便利性。為了改善預設單線程斷詞的速率表現，支援利用 GPU 施行批次斷詞，從而大幅縮減巨量中文資料的斷詞時間；而斷詞、詞性標註、命名實體辨識

[12] https://github.com/huggingface/transformers

[13] https://huggingface.co/albert-base-v1

等功能皆可有效輔助中文自然語言處理的後續相關任務提升其表現。

未來，我們期待 MONPA 能進一步加大訓練語料，例如將原先的 10 萬句新聞語料擴展至其他語境的中文語料，甚至是維基百科正體中文版全部資料等，並以此更新其語言模型。基於這樣的巨量資料，可訓練出最貼近語文使用現況的斷詞模型；另外，亦可對主程式作進一步的最佳化，如改善單線程斷詞運行效能或者應用最新深度學習工具進行模型加速等。我們相信，所有正體中文自然語言處理領域的專家、學者、工作者們，都能夠受益於此項研究成果。

致謝

本研究承蒙國家科學及技術委員會計畫 MOST111-2221-E-038-025 之補助，並感謝臺北醫學大學大數據科技及管理研究所研究生陳彥銘及林亨優協助開發爬蟲搜集旅館評論語料及電影評論語料。

References

AFNLP. (2003, July). *Proceedings of the Second SIGHAN Workshop on Chinese Language Processing*. https://aclanthology.org/W03-1700

AFNLP. (2005). *Proceedings of the Fourth SIGHAN Workshop on Chinese Language Processing*. https://aclanthology.org/I05-3000

AFNLP. (2008). *Proceedings of the Sixth SIGHAN Workshop on Chinese Language Processing*. https://aclanthology.org/I08-4000

Baum, L. E., Petrie, T., Soules, G. W., & Weiss, N. (1970). A Maximization Technique Occurring in the Statistical Analysis of Probabilistic Functions of Markov Chains. *Annals of Mathematical Statistics*, *41*, 164–171.

Hsieh, Y.-L., Chang, Y.-C., Huang, Y.-J., Yeh, S.-H., Chen, C.-H., & Hsu, W.-L. (2017). MONPA: Multi-objective Named-entity and Part-of-speech Annotator for Chinese using Recurrent Neural Network. *IJCNLP*.

Lan, Z., Chen, M., Goodman, S., Gimpel, K., Sharma, P., & Soricut, R. (2020). ALBERT: A Lite BERT for Self-supervised Learning of Language Representations. *ArXiv:1909.11942 [Cs]*. http://arxiv.org/abs/1909.11942

Li, P.-H., Fu, T.-J., & Ma, W.-Y. (2020). *Why Attention? Analyze BiLSTM Deficiency and Its Remedies in the Case of NER* (arXiv:1908.11046). arXiv. http://arxiv.org/abs/1908.11046

Nakayama, H. (2018). *seqeval: A Python framework for sequence labeling evaluation*. https://github.com/chakki-works/seqeval

Ng, H. T., & Kwong, O. O. (2006). Proceedings of the Fifth SIGHAN Workshop on Chinese Language Processing. *Proceedings of the Fifth SIGHAN Workshop on Chinese Language Processing*.

Pedregosa, F., Varoquaux, G., Gramfort, A., Michel, V., Thirion, B., Grisel, O., Blondel, M., Prettenhofer, P., Weiss, R., Dubourg, V., Vanderplas, J., Passos, A., Cournapeau, D., Brucher, M., Perrot, M., & Duchesnay, E. (2011). Scikit-learn: Machine Learning in Python. *Journal of Machine Learning Research*, *12*, 2825–2830.

The 34th Conference on Computational Linguistics and Speech Processing (ROCLING 2022)
Taipei, Taiwan, November 21-22, 2022. The Association for Computational Linguistics and Chinese Language Processing

針對特定領域之中英語碼語音辨識系統
Mandarin-English Code-Switching Speech Recognition System for Specific Domain

邱川溥 Chung-Pu Chiou, 林厚安 Hou-An Lin, 陳嘉平 Chia-Ping Chen
國立中山大學資訊工程學系
National Sun Yat-sen University
Department of Computer Science and Engineering
m103040061@nsysu.edu.tw, m093040066@nsysu.edu.tw, cpchen@cse.nsysu.edu.tw

摘要

本文將介紹利用自動語音辨識 (Automatic Speech Recognition, ASR) 技術處理帶有特定領域的語音內容。我們將以 Conformer 端到端模型做爲系統架構，並利用純中文資料進行初步訓練，再以遷移式學習（Transfer learning）技術對系統以中英語碼轉換 (Mandarin-English Code Switching) 資料進行一次微調，最後利用帶有特定領域的中英語碼轉換資料對模型進行最終微調，使其在特定領域的語音辨識上達到一定的效果。我們以不同微調方式進行實驗，最終錯誤率從 82.0% 降到 34.8%。

Abstract

This paper will introduce the use of Automatic Speech Recognition (ASR) technology to process speech content with specific domain. We will use the Conformer end-to-end model as the system architecture, and use pure Chinese data for initial training. Next, use the transfer learning technology to fine-tune the system with Mandarin-English code-switching data. Finally, use the Mandarin-English code-switching data with a specific domain makes the final fine-tuning of the model so that it can achieve a certain effect on speech recognition in a specific domain. Experiments with different fine-tuning methods reduce the final error rate from 82.0% to 34.8%.

關鍵字：語音辨識、語碼轉換、語音識別、語言模型、遷移式學習

Keywords: Speech Recognition、Code switching、Language model、Transfer learning

1 緒論

近幾年在全球疫情的影響下，許多會議以及課程等事項都逐漸以遠距的方式來執行。而在課程方面，有些老師或機構都紛紛成立自己的 Youtube 頻道，並將原先實體授課的內容紀錄下來再上傳到 Youtube 中，此做法能夠避免在疫情嚴重的情況下造成群聚的風險，學生也能夠更方便的學習知識。

雖然將課程放上 Youtube 能夠方便學生學習，但影片的錄製方式也會直接影響到播放的聲音品質。當影片錄製是直接在課堂上進行收音時，整段影片音訊會充滿各種環境噪音，學生也因此不容易聽清楚老師所講授的內容。對於以上問題可以利用人工添加字幕的方式來解決，不過此方法非常耗時耗力。我們希望利用語音辨識（Automatic Speech Recognition, ASR）系統來提昇上字幕的效率，但課程中難免會受到課程領域而有不同中文和英文專有名詞的影響，因此本論文提出針對特定領域的中英語碼轉換語音辨識（Mandrin-English Code-Switching Speech Recognition System For Specific Domain）系統。

本文基於 (Lin and Chen, 2021) 的實驗方法，但在基礎架構上採用 Conformer (Gulati et al., 2020b) 端到端（End-to-End, E2E）架構來進行實驗。

在實驗中，首先以中文資料集先對 ASR 模型進行訓練，當作具有中文能力的基礎語音辨識系統。另外，我們從 Youtube 擷取一些教育相關內容的語音資料，並分成 Education 資料集與 Course 資料集。接著使用由 (Wang and Zheng, 2015) 所提出的遷移式學習（Transfer Learning）對中文 ASR 模型以帶有中英語碼轉換的 Education 資料集進行一次微調，使其能學習處理中英夾雜的語音，另外也使用帶有領域資訊的 Course 資料集進行一次微調，來與前者進行比較。最後利用以 Education 資料集微調後再以 Course 資料集微調的二次微調與上述兩者比較，藉此使我們的 ASR 模型達到能夠處理特定領域中專有名詞的能力。

在接下來的章節中，第二章會詳細介紹我們的實驗架方法，第三章爲使用的資料集與實驗設置，第四章將呈現我們的實驗結果和結果分析，第五章爲我們本次實驗的結論與見解。

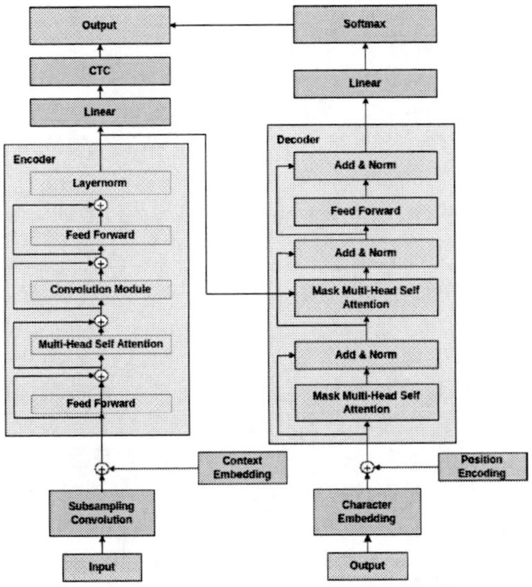

圖 1. Conformer 架構，連續時序分類器 (Connectionist Temporal Classification, CTC) 和 Transformer 解碼器將接收到 Conformer 編碼器的輸出。

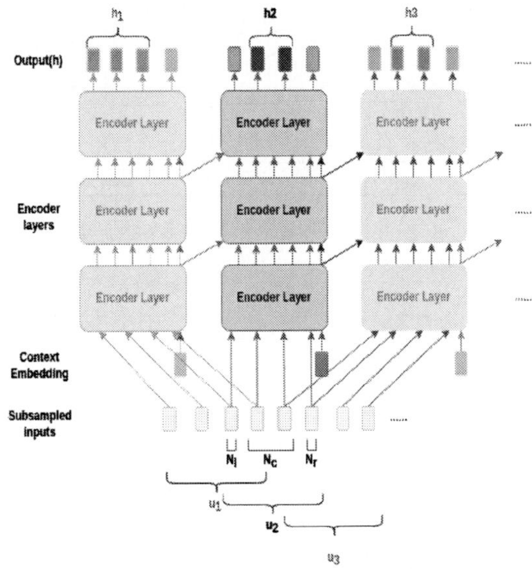

圖 2. Contextual Block Processing 示意圖。其中 u_i 爲 block，並包含著數個 frames，這些 frames 將被標記成過去、目前、未來 $\{N_l, N_c, N_r\}$ 三個部份。在訓練過程中，較後面的 block 將繼承前面 block 的訊息。

2 實驗方法

我們使用 Conformer 端到端架構聯合訓練連續時序分類器 (Connectionist Temporal Classification, CTC) (Graves et al., 2006) 當作 ASR 模型，而在編碼器與解碼器上結合 (Lin and Chen, 2021) 所利用到的 Contextual Block Processing (Tsunoo et al., 2019) 和 Blockwise Synchronous Beam Search (Tsunoo et al., 2020) 使 ASR 模型擁有 Streaming 的效果，其中 Contextual Block Processing 如圖 2 所示。實際訓練過程中以中文資料集來訓練一個中文語音辨識系統，再利用遷移式學習以 Education 資料集進行一次微調當作基準，並以 Course 資料集做二次微調後來與基準做比較，另外也單獨以 Course 資料集行一次微調加入比較。以下將介紹我們使用的模型架構以及訓練方法。

2.1 端到端模型

本篇論文我們所使用的 Conformer 端到端 ASR 模型架構如圖 1 所示，其利用 Conformer 區塊取代了 Transformer (Vaswani et al., 2017) 編碼器的部分。Conformer 架構如圖 1 所示。

2.2 編碼器

輸入的 80 維梅爾頻譜圖（mel-spectrogram）資料首先會經過由兩層捲積神經網路（Convolutional neaural network）和 ReLU 激活函數所組成的降採樣模塊（Subsampling Convolution），kernel 大小爲 3 及 stride 爲 2，channel 數爲 256，其中 channel 爲自注意力機制（Self-attention）特徵的維度。經過降採樣後的音訊序列資料會輸入到數個 Conformer 區塊 (Gulati et al., 2020a) 中，其結合自注意力機制和卷積，前者學習交流 global 等級的資訊，而後者捕捉 local 等級的資訊。Conformer 區塊之架構如圖 1 左側所示，輸入 a_i 進到第 i 個 Conformer 區塊產生輸出 x_i 之數學表示式爲:

$$\tilde{a} = a_i + \frac{1}{2}\mathrm{FFN}(a_i)$$
$$a_i' = \tilde{a}_i + \mathrm{MHSA}(\tilde{a}_i)$$
$$a_i'' = a_i' + \mathrm{Conv}(a_i')$$
$$x_i = \mathrm{Layernorm}(a_i'' + \frac{1}{2}\mathrm{FFN}(a_i''))$$

FFN 指的是 Feed Forward 模組，MHSA 指的是 Multi-Head Self-Attention 模組，Conv 指的是 Convolution 模組。最後編碼器輸出爲 X_e 。

2.3 解碼器

Transformer 解碼器將接收到 Conformer 編碼器的輸出 X_e 和序列的 token IDs Y[1:u] = Y[1],...,Y[u]，此 token IDs Y[1:u] 及編碼器輸出 X_e 將被用來計算序列的後驗機率（poste-

資料集	音檔數	總時長（小時）
NER-Trs-Vol1	21,089	126.65
AISHELL-1	20,000	24.82
AISHELL-2	20,000	19.87
科技大擂台	24,102	50.50
total	85191	221.84

表 1. 中文資料集的音檔數以及總音檔時長

資料集	音檔數	總時長（小時）
訓練集	2301	9.36
驗證集	254	1.05
測試集	1047	2.55
total	3602	12.96

表 2. Education 資料集的音檔數以及總音檔時長

rior probabilities):

$$[p_{\mathrm{s2s}}(Y[2]|Y[1],X_e),...,p_{\mathrm{s2s}}(Y[u+1]|Y[1:u],X_e)] = \mathrm{softmax}(Z_d W_{\mathrm{att}} + b_{\mathrm{att}})$$

$$p_{\mathrm{s2s}}(Y|X_e) = \prod_u p_{\mathrm{s2s}}(Y[u+1]|Y[1:u],X_e)$$

Z_d 爲編碼器的輸出，$W_{\mathrm{att}} \in \mathbb{R}^{d_{\mathrm{att}} \times d_{\mathrm{char}}}, b_{\mathrm{att}} \in \mathbb{R}^{d_{\mathrm{char}}}$ 爲可學習之參數，d_{char} 爲字元數量。Transformer 解碼器如圖 1 右側所示。

2.4 訓練方法

我們採用聯合訓練 CTC 的方式。連續時序分類器 (Connectionist Temporal Classification, CTC) 會將每個語音特徵與輸出字元做對齊，聯合訓練 CTC 能使學習速度提昇，並且使模型更快速的收斂 (Kim et al., 2017)。在訓練階段損失函數結合解碼器和 CTC 的負對數機率 (Kim et al., 2017; Nakatani, 2019)，如下所示：

$$L_{\mathrm{mtl}} = -\alpha \log p_{\mathrm{s2s}}(Y|X_e) - (1-\alpha)\log p_{\mathrm{ctc}}(Y|X_e)$$

p_{ctc} 爲 CTC 的後驗機率，α 爲超參數，能夠用來調整 CTC 與模型之間的比例。

2.5 遷移式學習

遷移式學習 (Wang and Zheng, 2015) 是將之前訓練好的模型當做基礎，稱爲其爲預訓練模型，接下來的訓練將繼承預訓練模型已訓練好的參數再進一步使用新資料去進行微調（Fine-tune），因此遷移式學習能在資料量小的情況下，依然使模型具有其他領域能力的效用。

資料集	音檔數	總時長（小時）
訓練集	17145	15.18
驗證集	2143	1.86
測試集	2144	2.80
total	21432	19.84

表 3. Course 資料集的音檔數以及總音檔時長

3 實驗設置與資料集

在本篇論文使用的資料集分爲三種，其中包含中文資料集和兩個教育資料集，而兩個教育資料集皆包含中英語碼轉換的內容，另外教育資料集大部份是直接在教室進行錄製，因此也包含著各種環境噪音。另外，我們使用 ESPnet2 (End-to-End Speech Processing tookit) (Watanabe et al., 2018) 這套端到端語音處理工具包來進行 ASR 相關實驗。

3.1 中文資料集

中文資料集總共由四個部份所組成，此資料集的資訊以表 1 表示。

(1) NER-Trs-Vol: 由國立教育廣播電台所提供，資料內容爲談話性節目及新聞報導的朗讀式語音，總時長爲 126.8 小時，共 21,089 筆資料。

(2) AISHELL-1：由 AISHELL 公司所提供 (Bu et al., 2017)，內容紀錄著 400 位來自中國不同地區的人的語音，而其語音內容包含 11 個不同領域，像是智慧家庭、無人駕駛等。我們將其文本從簡體字轉爲繁體字並隨機抽出 20000 筆來當作訓練資料。

(3) AISHELL-2：由 AISHELL 公司所提供 (Du et al., 2018)，內容紀錄著 1991 位來自中國不同地區的人的語音，而其語音內容包含 12 個不同領域，像是智慧家庭、無人駕駛等。我們將其文本從簡體字轉爲繁體字並隨機抽出 20000 筆來當作訓練資料。

(4) 科技大擂台（Formosa Grand Challenge）：由國研院科技政策研究與資訊中心提供，其語音內容爲華語能力測驗，並且分成文章、題目和選項。此資料集總時長爲約 400 小時，我們利用其中的部份問題及選項加入到訓練集中，總時長爲 50.5 小時，共 24,102 筆資料。

3.2 教育資料集

首先是 Education 資料集，此資料集是在 Youtube 上的一些教育相關內容且其語音包含中英語碼轉換。部份資料集語音是在安靜的環境下錄製，其他則是直接在教室裡面錄製，因此較爲吵雜，Education 資料集詳細資料以表 2 表示。

另外，Course 資料集爲同一位教授現場講授資料結構課程的語音，因此資料中有各種環境雜音，內容也包含中英語碼轉換。我們將原先在 Youtube 上的課程的影片音訊與經校正過的字幕檔做讀取，再將音訊從原先的 48,000 採樣率轉爲 16,000 採樣率以便訓練，最後利用字幕檔的時間標籤將完整音訊依照對應文本切割爲多個片段音訊，其中取得 2144 筆當作最終測試集，Course 資料集詳細資料以表 3 表示。

3.3 資料增強

我們在資料前處理上使用了兩種資料增強的方法，分別爲速度擾動（Speed Perturbation）(Ko et al., 2015) 以及 SpecAugment (Park et al., 2019) 來解決我們資料量過少的問題。速度擾動能將原始音訊資料經過三個不同倍率來產生不同速度的新資料，而我們採用的倍率爲 0.9、1.0、1.1，此方法能有效的增加資料量。SpecAugment 則是對梅爾頻譜圖分別進行時間扭曲（Time Warping），也就是在時間軸上對頻譜圖的特定區塊進行平移，以及在時間（Time）與頻率（Frequency）軸上對頻譜圖進行遮罩的動作。

3.4 端到端模型設置

我們所採用的端到端架構爲 Conformer ，其中包含 12 層的 Conformer 編碼器以及 6 層的 Transformer 解碼器，Conformer 中深度卷積的 kernel 大小爲 15，另外使用了 (Tsunoo et al., 2019, 2020) 的方式使所有輸入的 frames 重疊一半，且在 block 中的過去、目前、未來三個部份以 $\{N_l, N_c, N_r\}$ 表示，我們的設置爲 $\{8, 16, 16\}$。在 (Tsunoo et al., 2019) 提到的 Contextual Embedding Vector 中，我們採用了將 block 中的 frames 取平均的方式來當作初始值，並利用 Position Encoding 區分不同 block 的序列。此外，我們在多任務學習方法（multitask learning）的超參數 α 設爲 0.3，解碼階段的超參數 λ 與 γ 分別設爲 0.5 和 0.3。採用 Adam Optimizer (Kingma and Ba, 2017) 當作優化器。

模型	CER(%)
Conformer-FT-Education	82.0
Conformer-FT-Course	35.4
Conformer-FT-Education-Course	34.8

表 4. 利用 Course 測試集比較在 Conformer 模型上利用不同資料集做微調的表現，其中 FT 爲 Fine-Tune 簡稱。

```
REF：接下來是space<space>complexity
微調 1：Education 資料集
HYP：接下來的speate<space>co**nesi*s
Eval：       S   I  S           DDS  S DS
微調 2：Course 資料集
HYP：接下來***splace<space>complacity
Eval：       D   I                    SS
微調 3：Education 資料集、Course 資料集
HYP：接下來***space<space>complacity
Eval：       D                       SS
```

圖 3. REF、HYP、Eval 分別爲 Reference、Hypothesis、Evaluation。另外，D 代表刪字錯誤，S 代表換字錯誤，I 代表插字錯誤，<space> 爲空格。

4 實驗結果

我們以 Course 測試集來對兩個模型進行評分，並使用字元錯誤率（CER）當做評斷標準，實驗結果以表 4 表示。首先可以看到在單純使用有中英語碼轉換的 Education 資料集進行微調後，模型在字元錯誤率表現爲 82.0%，使用 Course 資料集微調後錯誤率降到 35.4%，而經過 Education 資料集與 Course 資料集的二次微調後，字元錯誤率來到了 34.8%。另外，由圖 3 的微調 2 與微調 3 可以觀察到有加入 Education 資料集的微調方式仍然在英文能力上有幫助。

4.1 領域影響

圖 3 爲我們分別從三種不同的微調方式取出對同一筆資料的預測結果，由圖中可以觀察到只有經 Education 資料集微調過後的模型在 Hypothesis 中，英文專有名詞部份的辨識率非常差，此原因爲 Education 資料集並無包含資料結構領域的內容，因此常出現在資料結構領域的英文專有名詞要被辨識出來是比較困難的。而有經過 Course 資料集微調後的模型在 Hypothesis 中，英文專有名詞有更大的機率辨識出正確結果。

4.2 資料品質影響

由於教育資料集大部份音訊是以現場授課的形式呈現，因此裡面包含著學生的說話聲、環境音等，再加上收音裝置與錄音軟體對音訊品質的影響，以上各種因素也直接影響了模型效能，因此在錯誤率方面仍然有進步空間。

5 結論

由本次實驗能發現在特定領域中時常出現專有名詞的狀況，例如在課程上可能會有至少一半的句字出現專有名詞，若 ASR 模型在訓練過程中未學習過此領域的資訊，此因素將會使效能銳減。另外，在實際情況下專有名詞也常會以英文的形式出現，因此我們使用遷移式學習的方式先使模型在資料缺乏的情況下，能夠擁有語碼轉換與特定領域的能力，而在我們的實驗結果上有顯著的改善。

另外，由於教育資料集大部份帶有環境雜音的關係，因此錯誤率仍然還有很大的進步空間，其中我們也嘗試過使用語言模型輔助，但也許是語言模型訓練資料的問題造成實驗上錯誤率不減反增，因此我們仍然會對語言模型部份持續實驗，並嘗試加入語言分類器來增加中英語碼轉換的效能。

References

Hui Bu, Jiayu Du, Xingyu Na, Bengu Wu, and Hao Zheng. 2017. Aishell-1: An open-source mandarin speech corpus and a speech recognition baseline. In *2017 20th conference of the oriental chapter of the international coordinating committee on speech databases and speech I/O systems and assessment (O-COCOSDA)*, pages 1–5. IEEE.

Jiayu Du, Xingyu Na, Xuechen Liu, and Hui Bu. 2018. Aishell-2: Transforming mandarin asr research into industrial scale. *arXiv preprint arXiv:1808.10583*.

Alex Graves, Santiago Fernández, Faustino Gomez, and Jürgen Schmidhuber. 2006. Connectionist temporal classification: labelling unsegmented sequence data with recurrent neural networks. In *Proceedings of the 23rd international conference on Machine learning*, pages 369–376.

Anmol Gulati, James Qin, Chung-Cheng Chiu, Niki Parmar, Yu Zhang, Jiahui Yu, Wei Han, Shibo Wang, Zhengdong Zhang, Yonghui Wu, and Ruoming Pang. 2020a. Conformer: Convolution-augmented transformer for speech recognition.

Anmol Gulati, James Qin, Chung-Cheng Chiu, Niki Parmar, Yu Zhang, Jiahui Yu, Wei Han, Shibo Wang, Zhengdong Zhang, Yonghui Wu, et al. 2020b. Conformer: Convolution-augmented transformer for speech recognition. *arXiv preprint arXiv:2005.08100*.

Suyoun Kim, Takaaki Hori, and Shinji Watanabe. 2017. Joint ctc-attention based end-to-end speech recognition using multi-task learning. In *2017 IEEE international conference on acoustics, speech and signal processing (ICASSP)*, pages 4835–4839. IEEE.

DP Kingma and J Ba. 2017. Adam: A method for stochastic. *optimization*.

Tom Ko, Vijayaditya Peddinti, Daniel Povey, and Sanjeev Khudanpur. 2015. Audio augmentation for speech recognition. In *Sixteenth annual conference of the international speech communication association*.

Hou-An Lin and Chia-Ping Chen. 2021. Exploiting low-resource code-switching data to mandarin-english speech recognition systems. In *Proceedings of the 33rd Conference on Computational Linguistics and Speech Processing (ROCLING 2021)*, pages 81–86.

Tomohiro Nakatani. 2019. Improving transformer-based end-to-end speech recognition with connectionist temporal classification and language model integration. In *Proc. Interspeech*.

Daniel S Park, William Chan, Yu Zhang, Chung-Cheng Chiu, Barret Zoph, Ekin D Cubuk, and Quoc V Le. 2019. Specaugment: A simple data augmentation method for automatic speech recognition. *arXiv preprint arXiv:1904.08779*.

Emiru Tsunoo, Yosuke Kashiwagi, Toshiyuki Kumakura, and Shinji Watanabe. 2019. Transformer asr with contextual block processing. In *2019 IEEE Automatic Speech Recognition and Understanding Workshop (ASRU)*, pages 427–433. IEEE.

Emiru Tsunoo, Yosuke Kashiwagi, and Shinji Watanabe. 2020. Streaming transformer asr with blockwise synchronous beam search.

Ashish Vaswani, Noam Shazeer, Niki Parmar, Jakob Uszkoreit, Llion Jones, Aidan N Gomez, Łukasz Kaiser, and Illia Polosukhin. 2017. Attention is all you need. *Advances in neural information processing systems*, 30.

Dong Wang and Thomas Fang Zheng. 2015. Transfer learning for speech and language processing.

Shinji Watanabe, Takaaki Hori, Shigeki Karita, Tomoki Hayashi, Jiro Nishitoba, Yuya Unno, Nelson Enrique Yalta Soplin, Jahn Heymann, Matthew Wiesner, Nanxin Chen, et al. 2018. Espnet: End-to-end speech processing toolkit. *arXiv preprint arXiv:1804.00015*.

The 34th Conference on Computational Linguistics and Speech Processing (ROCLING 2022)
Taipei, Taiwan, November 21-22, 2022. The Association for Computational Linguistics and Chinese Language Processing

Legal Case Winning Party Prediction With Domain Specific Auxiliary Models

Sahan Jayasinghe, Lakith Rambukkanage, Ashan Silva, Nisansa de Silva, Amal Shehan Perera

Department of Computer Science & Engineering, University of Moratuwa, Sri Lanka
{sahanjayasinghe.17, rambukkanage.17, ashansilva.17, nisansaDds, shehan}@cse.mrt.ac.lk

Abstract

Sifting through hundreds of old case documents to obtain information pertinent to the case in hand has been a major part of the legal profession for centuries. However, with the expansion of court systems and the compounding nature of case law, this task has become more and more intractable with time and resource constraints. Thus automation by Natural Language Processing presents itself as a viable solution. In this paper, we discuss a novel approach for predicting the winning party of a current court case by training an analytical model on a corpus of prior court cases which is then run on the prepared text on the current court case. This will allow legal professionals to efficiently and precisely prepare their cases to maximize the chance of victory. The model is built with and experimented using legal domain specific sub-models to provide more visibility to the final model, along with other variations. We show that our model with critical sentence annotation with a transformer encoder using RoBERTa based sentence embedding is able to obtain an accuracy of 75.75%, outperforming other models.

Keywords: Natural Language Processing, Legal Domain, Case Law, Transformer Encoders

1 Introduction

Natural Language Processing (NLP) is undergoing rapid development and has proven to be practically useful across many text rich domains. With the proper utilization of tools and technologies, effective methodologies can be derived to tackle various problems that are repetitive, cognitively demanding and time consuming otherwise. Legal domain is such a text rich domain with a growing need for task automation. Legal domain corpora consists of statutes, regulations, constitutions and case law documents among many others which have to be repeatedly and constantly sifted through by legal professionals to obtain information pertinent to their current case. This research is primarily carried on Case Law documents where a model is train on a corpus of existing case law documents so that a prediction of the winning party in a current case law document can be obtained.

1.1 Case Law

In the legal domain, when confronted with a new case, where statues, regulations and constitutions cannot be used to straightforwardly arrive at a case decision, the courts refer to Case Law. Case Law is the practice of using the information and verdicts of previous cases as arguments for the case in hand where the older cases bear some semblance in one aspect or another to the contemporary case. (Cornell Law School, 2020a).

Since case law documents have a predictive, or rather a prescriptive value, in the domain itself, they are valuable resources for predictive tasks in both research and practical applications. As time goes on and more and more cases are closed, cases available to refer grow in abundance on a daily basis. For human legal professionals, this is a negative as it makes their task of remembering and referring to these cases increasingly hard. But on the perspective of deep learning models, this growth is a blessing rather than a hindrance as more and more data is gathered, the reliability and accuracy of the models increase. In this study, we have used case law documents to train our models.

1.2 Legal Party

In all legal cases two main parties are present (Cornell Law School, 2020b). One party corresponds to the party filing the case who is referred to as *petitioner* or *plaintiff*. In criminal cases they may also be referred to as the *prosecutor* which is a government entity. On the other hand, we have the party responding to the case which is referred to as the *defendant* or *respondent*. In criminal cases, this party may also be referred to as the *accused*. These parties may consist of individuals, groups of people, or organizations. Also there may be third parties in a case who are unaffected by the case decision. It is important to note that, in the case of an appeal, the party appealed will become the petitioner in the new case (Cornell Law School, 2020c). For the benefit of readability, for the rest of this paper, we will refer to the two parties as *petitioner* and *defendant*.

1.3 NLP in the Legal Domain

Recently many researchers have conducted legal domain specific researches. Among these, researches on legal domain specific embedding (Sugathadasa et al., 2017, 2018; Jayawardana et al., 2017a), legal ontology (Jayawardana et al., 2017a,c,b), sentiment analysis (Gamage et al., 2018; Ratnayaka et al., 2020), and discourse analysis (Ratnayaka et al., 2018, 2019b,a) can be observed. Also, granular objectives such as party identification (Samarawickrama et al., 2020; de Almeida et al., 2020; Samarawickrama et al., 2021), Party Based Sentiment Analysis (Rajapaksha et al., 2020; Mudalige et al., 2020; Rajapaksha et al., 2021), and critical sentence identification (Jayasinghe et al., 2021) have been explored among these researches. However, there is still the need and opportunity for these models to be used for higher level derivations that are more human readable or practically useful.

1.4 Winning Party Prediction

Legal professionals, among other preparations, go through case law documents in order to prepare for ongoing court cases. The use of case law documents during preparation and during the court case, gives the intuition that these documents contain a prescriptive values and can be used as a data source for predictions of court case decisions. Also in United States courts, all the facts that are to be brought up in the case is known in advance by both parties. With this, legal professional can prepare a document with arguments they are going to use and arguments their opposing party may use which is similar to a case law document. If this document can be given a benchmark, that is to predict if the case can be won by the given arguments and facts, it would be a valuable insight for legal professionals. They can revise their facts and arguments with inclusions, exclusions and introductions of new facts to increase their likelihood winning the case. Dorf (1994) observes by pointing to Holmes (1920) that this practice of trying to predict the outcome of a court case at hand predates any attempt at automation.

In this research we discuss a novel approach to predict the winning party of a court case using case law documents from the United States Supreme Court. The past work that have been carried out is discussed in Section 2. The formulation of our methodology is discussed in Section 3 and the experiments carried out and the achieved results are discussed in Section 4.

2 Related Work

In the work by Shaikha et al. (2020), they have categorized the past approaches to predict the outcome of a legal case into three categories. Three approaches are distinguished by the use of 1) political or social science based, 2) linguistics based or 3) legal domain based features as the descriptors for the machine learning algorithms they use. 19 features have been formalized with respect to the legal domain, that has the potential to impact the decision of a criminal court case. It is important to note that feature extraction is manually done by going through court cases, and therefore it requires experts to identify the features. After feature extraction and preprocessing, researchers have conducted classification under 8 different algorithms such as Regression Trees, Bagging and Random Forests, Support Vector Machines and K-nearest neighbours. Classification and Regression Trees have been found to be the best performing.

In the research by Waltl et al. (2017), they have conducted their research fundamentally on German tax law cases. The research is conducted on features extracted using mostly regular expressions and manual annotations. A Naive Bayes classifier have been chosen as the best performing machine learning model. They have achieved 0.57 precision, 0.58 F1 score and 0.60 recall for positive outcomes.

Research done by Aletras et al. (2016) on predicting the decision of the European court of human rights, is identified as the first systematic approach to predicting winning parties by using NLP, as per the authors. They have modeled the problem as a binary classification problem, while using Support Vector Machines and N-grams and topics as features for the model.

Liu and Chen (2017) also proposes a classification approach for identifying the winning party of a court case. The process consists of two phases. In the 1st phase, an Article Classification model extracts top k articles that are cited in the case document. In the 2nd phase, the Judgement Classification model tries to predict the judgement of the court case. They have considered domain specific aspects such as punishment, cited statutes and features derived using NLP such as sentiment, as features for their model.

A tree based approach which uses new feature engineering techniques is proposed in the research conducted by Katz et al. (2014). The dataset used in this research consist of cases from the United States Supreme Court. Researchers have considered the impact from political biases for the decisions as well. They have used data ranging over multiple presidential terms to generalize the model more. Features already present with there chosen dataset have been used and some has been introduced by them. With the 7700 cases used, they have succeeded in getting 69.7% accuracy and individual judge votes with 70.9% accuracy.

Lage-Freitas et al. (2019) have proposed a machine learning approach to develop a system that predicts Brazilian court decisions. Researchers have suggested for it to be used as a supporting tool or a benchmark for legal professionals. The approach to calculate both the decision class and the unanimity of decisions have been designed. They have achieved good accuracy for some of the many model variations.

3 Methodology

In this section, the approach used for dataset preparation and the methodology for deriving the architecture used in this research are be discussed.

3.1 Dataset Preparation

As observed by Kreutzer et al. (2022), the quality of the data sets used often play a vital role in research. This research was conducted on a dataset extracted from the case law website[1] ranging from the year 2000 to year 2010 and belonging to the criminal category. The extracted cases were pre-processed by removing paragraphs at the beginning and the end. These paragraphs include the introductory paragraphs where the background of the case is summarized and the last paragraphs where the decision is stated. Afterwards several preprocessing steps were applied to the remaining paragraphs to remove citations and other notations, as they do not add any semantic meaning to the case. In our data pair, these cleaned and remaining paragraphs constitute the input. Since the decision of each case was found in the aforementioned removed paragraphs with a retrievable convention in almost all the cases, the decision of the court cases were extracted automatically. In our data pair, this extracted verdict constitutes the expected output.

Stanza NLP Library (Qi et al., 2020) was used to split a court case document into a list of sentences as for the representation purposes discussed in Section 3.2. Since Stanza is a general purpose NLP library (not specifically trained on legal context), there could be sentences divided by the periods in between abbreviations (some of which are specific jargon of the legal domain) and the periods within brackets. So, further pre-processing steps were needed to be taken to make the sentence splitting process accurate.

- Removed text within rounded brackets.

[1] `https://caselaw.findlaw.com/`

- Replaced abbreviations specific to legal domain with their long form. As shown in the following examples:
  - Fed.R.Crim.P.→ Federal Rule of Criminal Procedure
  - Fed.R.Evid.→ Federal Rule of Evidence
- Removed square brackets around letters or words. (Ex: [T]he, Extend[ed], [petitioner])
- Removed numbering from topic sentences (Ex: II., A., 3.)

A case document in US Supreme Court is generally structured as follows:

- Background information of the Case (represented Jury, Date of Hearing)
- A description of the case scenario
  1. Involved parties and their members (petitioners and defendants)
  2. How the case is formed (cause for filing the case)
  3. Available Evidence
  4. Lower court decision (Where the case was initially called)
- Supreme Court hearing
  1. Charges against the petitioner (he/she is the defendant in the first hearing by lower court)
  2. Opinions of Jury
  3. Arguments brought forward by each party
- Footnotes

After case documents were labeled with the decision, notion of *winning* was defined with respect to the petitioner party. *Affirmation*, *dismissal* or *rejection* of a case by US Supreme Court results in petitioner losing the case. *Reversal* of the lower court decision results in the petitioner winning the case.

3.2 Model Architecture

The approach taken to predict the winning party of is discussed in this section. Each case document is represented as a sequence of sentences. The model takes the corresponding sentence vector sequences as input.

Dimensions containing additional information about a case sentence, such as the criticality of a sentence towards a party, can be annotated using *Critical Sentence Identification model* which is derived in the work by Jayasinghe et al. (2021). Given a case sentence, their system outputs probabilities for four classes which defines the criticality of the sentence within that court case.

1. Has a negative impact towards petitioner in a case where petitioner loses
2. Has a positive impact towards petitioner in a case where petitioner loses
3. Has a negative impact towards petitioner in a case where petitioner wins
4. Has a positive impact towards petitioner in a case where petitioner wins

A sentence is considered to be critical if it has a negative impact towards petitioner party in a case where petitioner loses. Also, a sentence which has a positive impact towards the petitioner party is considered critical in a case where petitioner wins. Sentences predicted with a high probability for other classes considered to be non-critical.

Probabilities for the four criticality classes provided by the *Critical Sentence Identification model* are appended to sentence vectors there by increasing the dimension. The impact of the addition is discussed in Experiments and Results section 4

The sentence vector sequence representing a court case document is then passed on to Document Encoder model which is configured by using Recurrent Neural Networks (RNN) or Transformer Encoder layers. The output of the Document Encoder model is used to obtain petitioner party winning probability via the classifier component. This classifier component is configured by using a Linear Neural Network. Linear neural network ends with a single-node layer which outputs the probability of petitioner party winning the case. The discussed overall workflow of the process is depicted in Fig. 1.

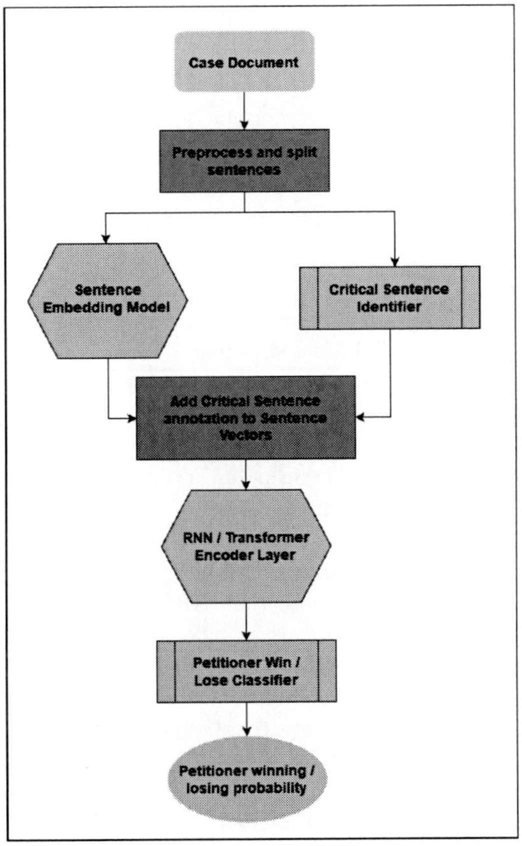

Figure 1: Winning Party Prediction Workflow

When the nature of a legal case is considered, often times the case is that the probability of Defendant party winning the case is equal to the probability of Petitioner party losing the case. There maybe cases for which it is not necessarily true, but we have followed that convention in this research.

The internal architecture for RNN based Wining Party Prediction model is displayed in Fig. 2 and for transformer encoder is displayed in Fig. 3.

In the RNN based model architecture (Fig. 2), Document Encoder consists of a single layer of either GRU (Chung et al., 2014) or LSTM (Hochreiter and Schmidhuber, 1997) where the final state vector is passed on to the classifier as the input. Classifier is built using a series of Dense Layers gradually down sized

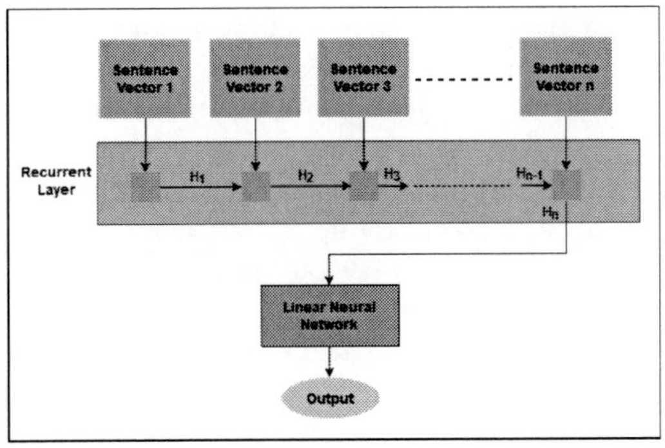

Figure 2: RNN based Model

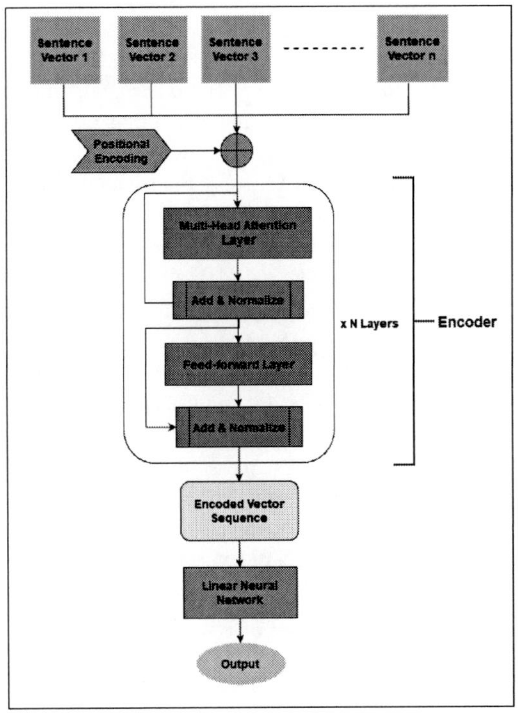

Figure 3: Transformer Encoder based Model

to a single node which is trained to predict the probability of winning of the petitioner party.

Transformer Encoder based model architecture (Fig. 3) is built using the encoder component of the original Transformer implementation (Vaswani et al., 2017). Document Encoder takes the sequence of sentence vectors as the input and adds the positional encoding to it. Positional encoding vector is calculated using the dimension of the input sentence vectors. Then the processed vector sequence is passed through a series of internal encoder layers. These encoder layers are duplicates of the same configuration and are built up of multi-head attention and position-wise feed forward layers. As per the definition of the Transformer Encoder by Vaswani et al. (2017), Multi-head attention layer is performing scaled-dot product on the input sequence. A normalization layer is used after multi-head attention layer and point-wise feed forward network to normalize the output vector of each layer. Global average pooling is used to reduce the 3-D output vector of the final encoder to a 2-D vector which is passed as input to the Classifier.

4 Experiments and Results

Experiments are performed by varying the Document Encoder model configurations and application of additional details to case sentences using the Critical Sentence Identification model (Jayasinghe et al., 2021). Document Encoder is experimented using different RNN configurations and Transformer Encoder configurations. To identify the number of layers best suitable for the transformer encoder, it was experimented with layers 6,3,2, and 1. As seen in the Fig 4, the best number of layers for the transformer encoder was found to be 1 in this case. RNN and Transformer Encoder components are used to encode the case documents. RNN models are experimented with both GRU and LSTM variations. Pre-trained *Sentence-BERT* by Reimers and Gurevych (2019), based on BERT (Devlin et al., 2018) and *DistilBERT* by Sanh et al. (2019),a distilled version of the RoBERTa-base (Liu et al., 2019), models are used for sentence embedding. Model building, training and evaluation are done using Tensorflow v2.8.

The following configurations were used for the Transformer Encoder:

- Number of Encoder layers = 1
- Number of Attention Heads = 8
- Vector Dimension = 768

Classifier model, which predicts the probability of petitioner winning takes the output from document encoder as the input and it is configured using a sequence of Dense Layers starting from 128 nodes.

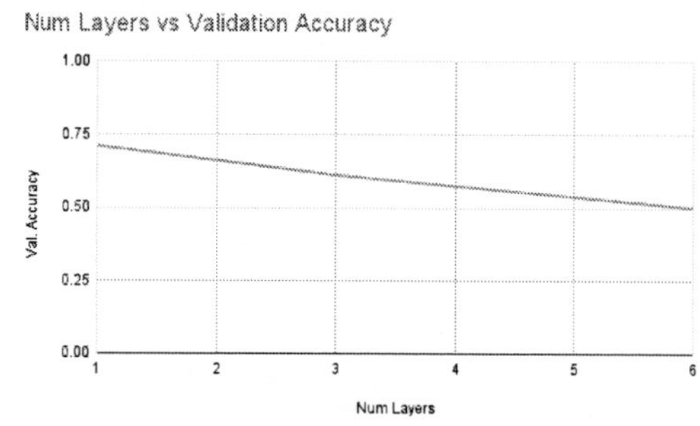

Figure 4: Number of Layers vs Validation Accuracy

Due to its suitability to handle datasets with imbalanced classes, Binary Focal Loss (Lin et al., 2017) is used to calculate the loss at each train step. At each training step, Focal Loss down-weights the loss for examples classified with higher accuracy of the dominant class and up-weights the loss for incorrectly classified examples of the minority class.

We summarize out findings in Table 1. It is curious to note that GRU with *Sentence-BERT* edges out the random baseline of 50% by only a narrow margin. This is an testament to the fact that the problem of *Winning Party Prediction* is non-trivial. The additional details provided by the critical sentence identification model (Jayasinghe et al., 2021), proved to be effective in predicting the winning party as per the results depicted in Table 1. This improvement is better visible in the case of GRUs than in the case of Transformers. Nevertheless, even with transformers, the improvement is relatively significant. *DistilBERT* (Sanh et al., 2019) embeddings have clearly outperformed pure *Sentence-BERT* (Reimers and Gurevych, 2019) configurations. The best performing configuration therefore is to use transformer encoders with *DistilBERT* sentence embeddings and the critical sentence annotation.

5 Conclusion and Future Work

Legal domain corpora carries its own complexities due to the domain nature. Therefore applying NLP in the legal domain requires domain specific approaches. In this study, we showed that our model with critical sentence annotation with a transformer encoder using RoBERTa based sentence embedding is able to

Model	Sentence Embedding	Critical Sentence Annotation	Accuracy	Macro F1
GRU	*Sentence-BERT*	N	56.32	53.14
	DistilBERT	N	65.71	57.14
	DistilBERT	Y	73.05	63.27
LSTM	*DistilBERT*	Y	72.04	65.52
GRU - Bidirectional	*DistilBERT*	Y	75.46	63.88
Transformer Encoder	*Sentence-BERT*	N	69.26	60.85
	DistilBERT	N	74.88	64.96
	DistilBERT	Y	**75.75**	**66.54**

Table 1: Winning Party Prediction Metrics

obtain an accuracy of 75.75%, outperforming other models. The need for domain-specific models can also be seen by the increase in accuracy when the critical sentence annotation is used. This system can be horizontally extended by adding more sub models to provide features to the final model. While the results obtained by *DistilBERT* (Sanh et al., 2019) sentence embeddings are impressive, extending the conclusions drawn by Sugathadasa et al. (2017) for word embeddings, it can be postulated that legal-domain specific sentence embeddings would potentially reap better results. Also as future work, the impact of having models trained with supervised approaches and unsupervised approaches should be experimented, as legal domain has a deficit of labeled data compared to its large corpora.

References

Nikolaos Aletras, Dimitrios Tsarapatsanis, Daniel Preoţiuc-Pietro, and Vasileios Lampos. 2016. Predicting judicial decisions of the european court of human rights: a natural language processing perspective. *PeerJ Computer Science*, 2:e93.

Melonie de Almeida, Chamodi Samarawickrama, Nisansa de Silva, Gathika Ratnayaka, and Amal Shehan Perera. 2020. Legal Party Extraction from Legal Opinion Text with Sequence to Sequence Learning. In *2020 20th International Conference on Advances in ICT for Emerging Regions (ICTer)*, pages 143–148. IEEE.

Junyoung Chung, Caglar Gulcehre, KyungHyun Cho, and Yoshua Bengio. 2014. Empirical evaluation of gated recurrent neural networks on sequence modeling. *arXiv preprint arXiv:1412.3555*.

Cornell Law School. 2020a. Case law. `https://www.law.cornell.edu/wex/case_law`. Accessed: 2022-08-18.

Cornell Law School. 2020b. Legal party. `https://www.law.cornell.edu/wex/party`. Accessed: 2022-08-18.

Cornell Law School. 2020c. Petitioner. `https://www.law.cornell.edu/wex/petitioner`. Accessed: 2022-08-18.

Jacob Devlin, Ming-Wei Chang, Kenton Lee, and Kristina Toutanova. 2018. Bert: Pre-training of deep bidirectional transformers for language understanding. *arXiv preprint arXiv:1810.04805*.

Michael C Dorf. 1994. Prediction and the rule of law. *UCLA L. Rev.*, 42:651.

Viraj Gamage, Menuka Warushavithana, Nisansa de Silva, Amal Shehan Perera, Gathika Ratnayaka, and Thejan Rupasinghe. 2018. Fast Approach to Build an Automatic Sentiment Annotator for Legal Domain using Transfer Learning. In *Proceedings of the 9th Workshop on Computational Approaches to Subjectivity, Sentiment and Social Media Analysis*, pages 260–265.

Sepp Hochreiter and Jürgen Schmidhuber. 1997. Long short-term memory. *Neural computation*, 9(8):1735–1780.

Oliver Wendell Holmes. 1920. The path of the law. *Collected Legal Papers*, pages 167–173.

Sahan Jayasinghe, Lakith Rambukkanage, Ashan Silva, Nisansa de Silva, and Amal Shehan Perera. 2021. Critical sentence identification in legal cases using multi-class classification. In *2021*

IEEE 16th International Conference on Industrial and Information Systems (ICIIS), pages 146–151. IEEE.

V. Jayawardana, D. Lakmal, Nisansa de Silva, A. S. Perera, K. Sugathadasa, B. Ayesha, and M. Perera. 2017a. Word Vector Embeddings and Domain Specific Semantic based Semi-Supervised Ontology Instance Population. *International Journal on Advances in ICT for Emerging Regions*, 10(1):1.

Vindula Jayawardana, Dimuthu Lakmal, Nisansa de Silva, Amal Shehan Perera, Keet Sugathadasa, and Buddhi Ayesha. 2017b. Deriving a Representative Vector for Ontology Classes with Instance Word Vector Embeddings. In *2017 Seventh International Conference on Innovative Computing Technology (INTECH)*, pages 79–84. IEEE.

Vindula Jayawardana, Dimuthu Lakmal, Nisansa de Silva, Amal Shehan Perera, Keet Sugathadasa, Buddhi Ayesha, and Madhavi Perera. 2017c. Semi-Supervised Instance Population of an Ontology using Word Vector Embedding. In *Advances in ICT for Emerging Regions (ICTer), 2017 Seventeenth International Conference on*, pages 1–7. IEEE.

Daniel Martin Katz, Michael J Bommarito II, and Josh Blackman. 2014. Predicting the behavior of the supreme court of the united states: A general approach. *arXiv preprint arXiv:1407.6333*.

Julia Kreutzer, Isaac Caswell, Lisa Wang, Ahsan Wahab, Daan van Esch, Nasanbayar Ulzii-Orshikh, Allahsera Tapo, Nishant Subramani, Artem Sokolov, Claytone Sikasote, et al. 2022. Quality at a Glance: An Audit of Web-Crawled Multilingual Datasets. *Transactions of the Association for Computational Linguistics*, 10:50–72.

André Lage-Freitas, Héctor Allende-Cid, Orivaldo Santana, and Lívia de Oliveira-Lage. 2019. Predicting brazilian court decisions. *arXiv preprint arXiv:1905.10348*.

Tsung-Yi Lin, Priya Goyal, Ross Girshick, Kaiming He, and Piotr Dollár. 2017. Focal loss for dense object detection. In *Proceedings of the IEEE international conference on computer vision*, pages 2980–2988.

Yihung Liu and Yen-Liang Chen. 2017. A two-phase sentiment analysis approach for judgement prediction. *Journal of Information Science*, 44.

Yinhan Liu, Myle Ott, Naman Goyal, Jingfei Du, Mandar Joshi, Danqi Chen, Omer Levy, Mike Lewis, Luke Zettlemoyer, and Veselin Stoyanov. 2019. Roberta: A robustly optimized bert pretraining approach. *arXiv preprint arXiv:1907.11692*.

Chanika Ruchini Mudalige, Dilini Karunarathna, Isanka Rajapaksha, Nisansa de Silva, Gathika Ratnayaka, Amal Shehan Perera, and Ramesh Pathirana. 2020. Sigmalaw-absa: Dataset for aspect-based sentiment analysis in legal opinion texts. *arXiv preprint arXiv:2011.06326*.

Peng Qi, Yuhao Zhang, Yuhui Zhang, Jason Bolton, and Christopher D Manning. 2020. Stanza: A python natural language processing toolkit for many human languages. *arXiv preprint arXiv:2003.07082*.

Isanka Rajapaksha, Chanika Ruchini Mudalige, Dilini Karunarathna, Nisansa de Silva, Gathika Rathnayaka, and Amal Shehan Perera. 2020. Rule-based approach for party-based sentiment analysis in legal opinion texts. *arXiv preprint arXiv:2011.05675*.

Isanka Rajapaksha, Chanika Ruchini Mudalige, Dilini Karunarathna, Nisansa de Silva, Amal Shehan Perera, and Gathika Ratnayaka. 2021. Sigmalaw PBSA-A Deep Learning Model for Aspect-Based Sentiment Analysis for the Legal Domain. In *International Conference on Database and Expert Systems Applications*, pages 125–137. Springer.

G. Ratnayaka, T. Rupasinghe, Nisansa de Silva, M. Warushavithana, V. Gamage, M. Perera, and A. S. Perera. 2019a. Classifying Sentences in Court Case Transcripts using Discourse and Argumentative Properties. *ICTer*, 12(1).

Gathika Ratnayaka, Thejan Rupasinghe, Nisansa de Silva, Viraj Gamage, Menuka Warushavithana, and Amal Shehan Perera. 2019b. Shift-of-Perspective Identification Within Legal Cases. In *Proceedings of the 3rd Workshop on Automated Detection, Extraction and Analysis of Semantic Information in Legal Texts*.

Gathika Ratnayaka, Thejan Rupasinghe, Nisansa de Silva, Menuka Warushavithana, Viraj Gamage, and Amal Shehan Perera. 2018. Identifying Relationships Among Sentences in Court Case Transcripts Using Discourse Relations. In *2018 18th International Conference on Advances in ICT for Emerging Regions (ICTer)*, pages 13–20. IEEE.

Gathika Ratnayaka, Nisansa de Silva, Amal Shehan Perera, and Ramesh Pathirana. 2020. Effective approach to develop a sentiment annotator for legal domain in a low resource setting. *arXiv preprint arXiv:2011.00318*.

Nils Reimers and Iryna Gurevych. 2019. Sentence-BERT: Sentence Embeddings using Siamese BERT-Networks. In *Proceedings of the 2019 Conference on Empirical Methods in Natural Language Processing*. Association for Computational Linguistics.

Chamodi Samarawickrama, Melonie de Almeida, Amal Shehan Perera, Nisansa de Silva, and Gathika Ratnayaka. 2021. Identifying legal party members from legal opinion texts using natural language processing. Technical report, EasyChair.

Chamodi Samarawickrama, Melonie de Almeida, Nisansa de Silva, Gathika Ratnayaka, and Amal Shehan Perera. 2020. Party Identification of Legal Documents using Co-reference Resolution and Named Entity Recognition. In *2020 IEEE 15th International Conference on Industrial and Information Systems (ICIIS)*, pages 494–499. IEEE.

Victor Sanh, Lysandre Debut, Julien Chaumond, and Thomas Wolf. 2019. DistilBERT, a distilled version of BERT: smaller, faster, cheaper and lighter. *ArXiv*, abs/1910.01108.

Rafe Athar Shaikha, Tirath Prasad Sahua, and Veena Anand. 2020. Predicting Outcomes of Legal Cases based on Legal Factors using Classifiers. *Procedia Computer Science 167 (2020) 2393—2402*.

Keet Sugathadasa, Buddhi Ayesha, Nisansa de Silva, Amal Shehan Perera, Vindula Jayawardana, Dimuthu Lakmal, and Madhavi Perera. 2017. Synergistic Union of Word2Vec and Lexicon for Domain Specific Semantic Similarity. *IEEE International Conference on Industrial and Information Systems (ICIIS)*, pages 1–6.

Keet Sugathadasa, Buddhi Ayesha, Nisansa de Silva, Amal Shehan Perera, Vindula Jayawardana, Dimuthu Lakmal, and Madhavi Perera. 2018. Legal Document Retrieval using Document Vector Embeddings and Deep Learning. In *Science and Information Conference*, pages 160–175. Springer.

Ashish Vaswani, Noam Shazeer, Niki Parmar, Jakob Uszkoreit, Llion Jones, Aidan N Gomez, Łukasz Kaiser, and Illia Polosukhin. 2017. Attention is all you need. *Advances in neural information processing systems*, 30.

Bernhard Waltl, Georg Bonczek, Elena Scepankova, Jörg Landthaler, and Florian Matthes. 2017. Predicting the outcome of appeal decisions in germany's tax law. In *Electronic Participation*, pages 89–99, Cham. Springer International Publishing.

The 34th Conference on Computational Linguistics and Speech Processing (ROCLING 2022)
Taipei, Taiwan, November 21-22, 2022. The Association for Computational Linguistics and Chinese Language Processing

Early Speech Production in Infants and Toddlers Later Diagnosed with Cerebral Palsy: A Retrospective Study

Chien Ju Chan
National Kaohsiung Normal University
gina861120@gmail.com

Li-Mei Chen
National Cheng Kung University
leemay@mail.ncku.edu.tw

Li-Wen Chen
National Cheng Kung University Hospital
muffychen@gmail.com

Abstract

In this retrospective study, we compared the early speech development between infants with cerebral palsy (CP) and typically developing (TD) infants. The recordings of utterances were collected from two CP infants and two typically-developing (TD) infants at approximately 8 and 24 months old. The data was analyzed by volubility, consonant emergence, canonical babbling ratio (CBR), mean babbling level (MBL). The major findings show that comparing with TD group, CP group has the characteristics of: 1) lower volubility 2) CBR^{utter} below 0.15 at 2 years old 3) MBL score below 2 at the age of 2 with a feature of above 95% in level 1 4) using consonants mainly at two oral places (bilabials and velars) and three manners of articulation (nasal, fricative, and stop) at 2 years old.

Keywords: volubility, consonant emergence, canonical babbling ratio (CBR), mean babbling level (MBL)

1 Introduction

Cerebral palsy (CP) is a non-progressive and permanent motor disorder, caused by the impairment of neurodevelopment in the fetal or infant brain (Rosenbaum et al., 2007). More than 60% of children with CP has communication problems stemming from the language or/and speech impairments, including delayed language development, voice disorders, and speech disorder (Sadowska et al., 2020).These abnormality in speech may adversely affect the following ability in terms of communication, intelligibility, phonological awareness and literacy (Peeters et al., 2009). For children with CP, these difficulties may eventually result in the poor performance in academy, problems in relationship, and also less career opportunities. As a result, many researches have suggested early intervention not only aim to diminish the negative impact of the limited motor functions but also provide mental health support for the caregivers(Novak et al., 2017).

Previous studies have widely documented similar transition in developing stages for infants' vocalization in the first and second year of life and showed the strong relation to the future language ability(D'Odorico et al., 2011). However, rare speech development related studies included data with CP infants under 2 years old.

Studying early infants' vocalization has helped enriched our knowledge about disorders, such as hearing impairment, down syndrome, fragile X syndrome (Belardi et al., 2017), autism (Patten et al., 2014), and CAS (M. Overby & Caspari, 2015; M. S. Overby et al., 2019), reducing the severity and providing evident-based support for clinical decision. Volubility, consonant inventory, and the development of canonical babbling are three widely studied domain in early infant speech production, and many has shown to be a precursor to later language ability (Smith & Stoel-Gammon, 1996).

Hustad et al. (2014) measured the speech and language development of 27 children at the age between 24 and 30 months, finding that three groups of children with CP with different level of language ability (i.e., not talking, emerging talking, and established talking) can be identified at the age of 2. Speech and/or language delay was found in two groups of children (nearly 85% of the children in this study) and also suggested speech and language assessment and intervention before 2 years old.

Since obvious differences appeared at the age of 2, more data is required to clarify the details of the progression in speech development. Therefore, the goal of this study is to investigate the speech development of 2 CP and 2 TD infants and try to answer the following questions:

- What are the differences in the volubility, the diversity of consonant emergence, CBR and MBL of CP group and TD group at 1 and 2 years old?
- What are the changes in speech development of CP group and TD group at 1 and 2 years old?

2 Method

2.1 Participants and equipment

Speech data of two TD infants and two CP at approximately 8 and 24 months were collected (Table 1).

participants	TD1	TD2	CP1	CP2
Gender	F	F	F	F
Type	-	-	Spastic hemiplegia	Unidentified
GMFCS	-	-	IV	-
Recording Age 1 (month, day)	12,09	12,18	10,19	08,22
Length (minute: second)	53:48	54:02	35:16	41:27
Recording Age 2 (month, day)	24,00	24,11	21,19	23,16
Length (minute: second)	43:41	53:05	44:10	44:38
Total utterances	369	646	137	234

Table1. Data recordings

All recordings were taken at either hospital or home under the natural interaction with caregivers and/or an experimenter. For each infant, one recording is included by the age around 1 year and 2 years old. Each recording session lasted for around 35 to 60 minutes. A SHURE wireless mini microphone was clipped to the cloth near infants' mouth and connected to a TASCAM recorder.

2.2 Coding process

The coder was trained by another experienced coder first, and a completed coding recording is checked by the experienced coder before formally conducting the rest of the recordings. For inter-judge reliability, another coder randomly checked 10% of the coding results. Infant's utterance boundaries are roughly marked by Elan and the utterances was coded with Worldbet (Hieronymus et al., 1993) conducted in Praat (Lab & 2013, n.d.). Eventually, the data extracted from coded recording is analyzed by a script to obtain results including, volubility, consonant inventory, MBL, and CBR.

2.3 Deciding an utterance

One distinctive utterance is defined as the voluntary vocal sound made by the child, produced by the egressive airstream in a breath group. The boundaries of the utterance are required to be established by at least one second silence, others' voice, or any other sound which meet the exclusion standard.

2.4 Inclusion and exclusion standard of utterances for coding

The standard of the inclusion and exclusion of utterances are extracted from Stoel-Gammon (1989), and was added with several modifications. The included utterances are considered as speech-like by coder's subjective judgement, and must contain at least one vocal element featured with voicing. Other non-speech like sound (i.e., cry, laugh, scream, cough, and vegetative sound), singing, and sounds overlapped with other background sound or others' voice are excluded from coding. In addition, if the quality of the recording is poor and thus can't be transcribed by the coder under four trials, the utterance was not acceptable for coding. All the meaningful utterances identified as non-Mandarin were also excluded.

2.5 CBR

Three ways of counting CBR were widely used in different studies as an index for the onset of CB (Kimbrough & Eilers, 1988; Kimbrough Oller et al., 1994; Nyman & Lohmander, 2018). However, CBR^{utter} was reported to have strong correlation with the other two ways. Meanwhile, it was less time-consuming in calculation, and the categorization of the utterances can also be done instantly (Nyman & Lohmander, 2018; Willadsen et al., 2022). Therefore, the result of CBR^{utter} was collected for analysis. The formula of CBR^{utter} is listed below:

$$CBR = \frac{\text{number of utterances with conanical syllables}}{\text{total number of utterances}}$$

2.6 Scoring of MBL

MBL level was created by Stoel-Gammon (1989) and sorted by Morris in 2010. Level 1includes the utterances with only one, sequencing or the combination of vowel and consonant of glide or glottal. Level 2 and level 3 includes the combination of true consonants, and respectively meet the definition of Oller's canonical babbling stage and variegated babbling stage. Total number of utterances in each level is multiple with different numbers: Level 1 multiple with 1, level 2 multiple with 2, and level 3 multiple with 3. The mean babbling level is calculated by dividing the sum of each weighted level with the total numbers of utterances. The formula of MBL is described below:

$$MBL = \frac{\text{level } 1 \times 1 + \text{level } 2 \times 2 + \text{level } 3 \times 3}{\text{total number of utterances}}$$

3 Result and discussion

In this study, we investigate volubility, consonant emergence, canonical babbling in order to enrich the knowledge about early speech production in CP infants. The results are also considered as several possible warning signs for CP infants who may have language and/or speech problems in the future.

3.1 Volubility

A total of 1386 utterances were collected and analyzed across all children. The volubility, calculated as utterances per minutes in each recording, was found higher in TD group than in CP group regardless of age (TD mean = 5.40, CP mean = 3.97 at around 1 year old; TD mean = 4.68, CP mean = 1.59 at around 2 years old). However, a reduction of volubility with age was found in both TD and CP group (Figure1).

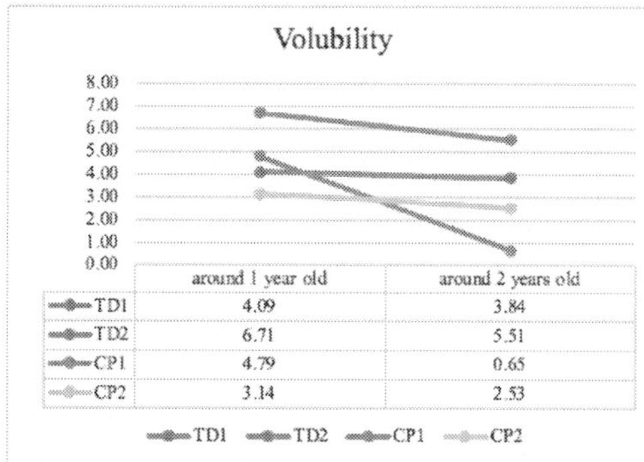

Figure 1. Volubility at 1 and 2 years old

Previous studies indicated that volubility in typically developing infants would increase with age (Stark et al., 1993). However, in recent studies, with a different criterion of annotating the boundaries of utterances, the volubility reduced with age (Iyer et al., 2016). In this study, the volubility in TD and CP also reduced with age, but either at around 1 year old or 2 years old, all CP children tended to vocalized fewer than TD children. The low volubility compared with the roughly same age of peers may be a warning sign for development in speech sound.

3.2 Consonant emergence

Consonants of infants' vocalizations are analyzed based on the feature of place (bilabial, labiodental, alveolar, retroflex, palatal, and velar) and manner (stop, fricative, affricate, liquid and nasal). At around 1 year old, TD group used massively alveolars (mean = 37.92%), bilabials (mean = 25.15%), and velars (mean = 32.68%), which was similar in CP1 (alveolar = 31.24%, bilabial = 40.62, velars = 28.12%). However, CP2 developed almost exclusively bilabials (92%) with little velar /h/ (8%). TD group had developed consonants at almost all different oral places, but CP group developed consonants on limited oral places (mainly bilabial and velar). At around 2 years old, TD group still mainly used consonants at the places of alveolar and velar, but the proportion of other places, such as retroflex and palatal, increased. As to CP group, only consonants at bilabial (mean = 68.34%) and velar (mean = 31.66%) places were used in vocalizations. The diversity of the consonants with the feature of places were seemingly decreased with age in CP group.

In terms of the feature of manner, TD children used excessively stops (mean = 64.64%) and nasals (mean = 16.93%) at 1 around 1 year old, and similar consonant division was also found in CP at the same age, but with a reverse proportion (stop = 22.06%, nasal = 59.88%). While at around 2 years old, TD children used most stops (45.85%) and affricates (22.98%) in utterances, but CP children used merely nasal /m/ (63.34%) and fricatives (31.66%) with little stops (5%) in speech. CP children vocalized with very limited manners in consonants compare with TD children.

In summary, CP group only developed consonants at two oral places (bilabials and velars) and three manners of articulation (nasal, fricative, and stop). The restricted consonants found in CP group could be another warning sign.

3.3 CBR and MBL

At around 1 year old, CBR of all children were > 0.15, showing a success on the onset of canonical babbling, though the figures were relatively higher in TD children (Table 2).

	TD1	TD2	CP1	CP2
Age (month, day)	12,09	12,18	10,19	08,22
CBR^{utter}	0.33	0.31	0.17	0.16
Age (month, day)	24,0	24,11	21,19	23,16
CBR^{utter}	0.93	0.91	0.04	0.04

Table 2. CBR

The differences were found in two groups around age 2. CBR^{utter} in CP children greatly declined and fell below the CB onset standard, while the TD children steadily increased.

CBR has been used widely for the purpose of understanding the speech development in typically-developing infants from 10 to 12 months old and also in neurodevelopmental disordered population (Lohmander et al., 2017; Nyman & Lohmander, 2018). Different formulas and standard for onset CB were studied recently. Nyman et al. (2021) pointed out the use of 0.14 may be more sensitive to detect the BC onset in 10-month-old infants, but further research is required to reach the agreement of the criterion. Similar results were found in this study and in (Levin, 1999). that some CP infants were able to enter CB stage, though using a different formula to obtain the result of CBR. However, with the trend of decreasing after 1 year old, none CP infants remained at the CB stage or move further to the next stage, showing that CP infants' development of speech sound did not improve with age. Therefore, the third possible warning sign may be the score of CBR^{utter} failing to reach above 0.15 at 2 years old.

Some researchers suggested that the sole judgment of CBR for describing the developmental status of speech was not enough (Lang et al., 2019). In this study, MBL score provides additional information for children's maturity of syllable structure. For example, a score of 1.4 may indicates infant's speech characterized with various vowels and some true consonants (Morris, 2010). Overall, the score of MBL in TD group is higher than the CP group at around 1 year old and 2 years old (TD mean = 1.36, CP mean = 1.18 at around 1 year old; TD mean = 2.60, CP mean = 1.04 at around 2 years old). Two groups had a seemingly start of the MBL score, but end differently with the TD continuously increasing and CP gradually going down around age 2 (Figure 2).

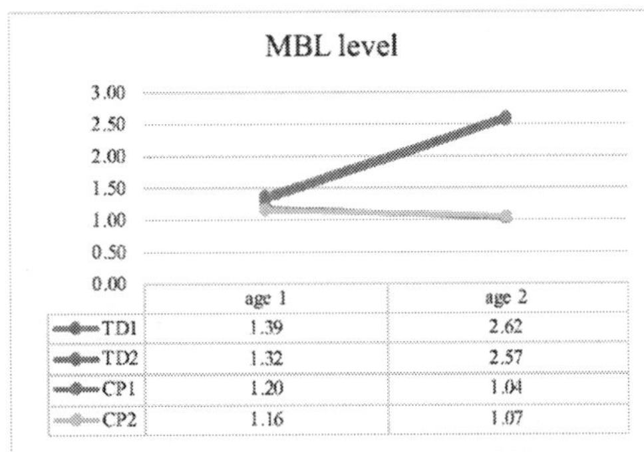

Figure 2. MBL at 1 and 2 years old

The frequency of occurrence in three MBL levels were similar in all children at 1 year old, presenting a ratio tendency: level 1, level 2, and level 3 (from high to low). However, the utterances of TD were twice more concentrated in Level 2, showing a sign of developing more consonants compared with CP at the same age. The situation was a lot different at age 2. The proportion of utterances in TD children were presented in a reverse order: level 3, level 2, level 1 (from high to low). Above 65% of the utterances were variegated babbling. On comparison, the division of utterances in CP subjects at around age 2 remained approximately the same, but the division became even more concentrated on level 1. An obvious decline at level 2 and level 3 were observed (Figure 3).

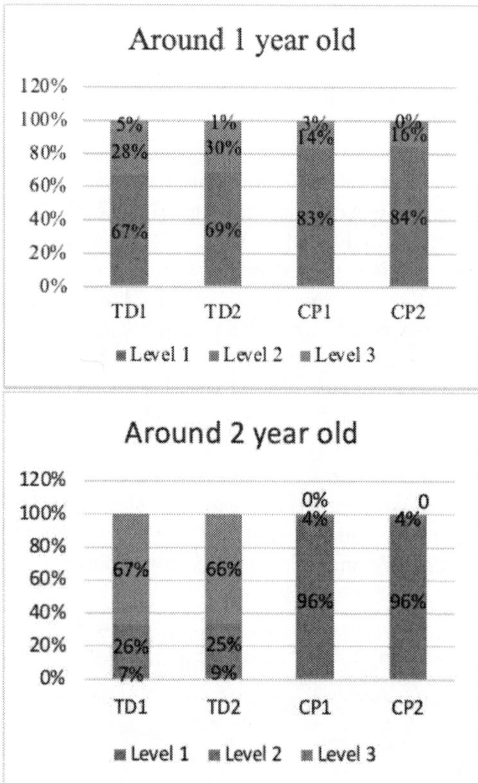

Figure 3. MBL in TD and CP

In summary, the division of the three levels were similar at 1 year old, but obvious differences between 2 groups were also showed at around 2 years old. Therefore, the last possible warning sign may be the MBL score below 2 at age 2 with a feature of above 95% in level 1.

4 Conclusion

Findings in this investigation imply the speech development differences between TD infants and CP infants at the age between 8 to 24 months old. Although it is a preliminary study, the below possible warning sign might be clinical warning sign that could help the identification of infants and toddlers at risk for later diagnosis of speech and language problem in children with CP: (1) low volubility (2) $CBR^{utter} < 0.15$ at 2 years old (3) MBL score < 2 at the age of 2 with a feature of above 95% in level 1 (4) use consonants only at two oral places (bilabials and velars) and three manners of articulation (nasal, fricative, and stop) at most at 2 years old. More data and studies are required for clarifying the changing course between 1 and 2 years old. More amounts of subjects are also suggested to be included in future studies.

Acknowledgement

This research was supported through funds from National Science and Technology Council in Taiwan (MOST 106-2410-H-006-048) to Li-Mei Chen. A special thank you is extended to the families of the children in this longitudinal study for their support of this project.

References

Belardi, K., Watson, L. R., Faldowski, R. A., Hazlett, H., Crais, E., Baranek, G. T., McComish, C., Patten, E., & Oller, D. K. (2017). A Retrospective Video Analysis of Canonical Babbling and Volubility in Infants with Fragile X Syndrome at 9–12 Months of Age. *Journal of Autism and Developmental Disorders*, *47*(4), 1193–1206. https://doi.org/10.1007/s10803-017-3033-4

D'Odorico, L., Majorano, M., Fasolo, M., Salerni, N., & Suttora, C. (2011). Characteristics of phonological development as a risk factor for language development in Italian-speaking pre-term children: A longitudinal study. *Clinical Linguistics and Phonetics*, *25*(1), 53–65. https://doi.org/10.3109/02699206.2010.511759

Hieronymus, J. L., Bell Laboratories, Lucent Technologies, & Murray Hill. (1993). ASCII Phonetic Symbols for the World's Languages: Worldbet. *Ournal of the International Phonetic Association, Ournal of the International Phonetic Association*, *23*(72).

Hustad, K. C., Allison, K., McFadd, E., & Riehle, K. (2014). Speech and language development in 2-year-old children with cerebral palsy. Developmental Neurorehabilitation, 17(3), 167–175.

https://doi.org/10.3109/17518423.2012.747009

Iyer, S. N., Denson, H., Lazar, N., & Oller, D. K. (2016). Volubility of the human infant: Effects of parental interaction (or lack of it). *Clinical Linguistics and Phonetics*, *30*(6), 470–488. https://doi.org/10.3109/02699206.2016.1147082

Karen Levin. (1999). Babbling in infants with cerebral palsy. In *clinical linguistics & phonetics* (Vol. 13, Issue 4). http://www.tandf.co.uk

Kimbrough, D., & Eilers, R. E. (1988). The Role of Audition in Infant Babbling. In *Source: Child Development* (Vol. 59, Issue 2). http://www.jstor.org/page/info/about/policies/terms.jsp.http://www.jstor.org

Kimbrough Oller, D., Eilers, R. E., Steffens, M. L., Lynch, M. P., & Urbano, R. (1994). Speech-like vocalizations in infancy: an evaluation of potential risk factors. *Cambridge.Org*, *21*, 33–58. https://www.cambridge.org/core/journals/journal-of-child-language/article/speechlike-vocalizations-in-infancy-an-evaluation-of-potential-risk-factors/27178384F58472C43867CA69B7239324

Lab, W. S.-U. of C. at B. P., & 2013, undefined. (n.d.). Using Praat for linguistic research. *Cs.Columbia.Edu*. Retrieved April 16, 2022, from http://www.cs.columbia.edu/~julia/courses/CS6998-20/UsingPraatforLinguisticResearchLatest.pdf

Lang, S., Bartl-Pokorny, K. D., Pokorny, F. B., Garrido, D., Mani, N., Fox-Boyer, A. v., Zhang, D., & Marschik, P. B. (2019). Canonical Babbling: A Marker for Earlier Identification of Late Detected Developmental Disorders? *Current Developmental Disorders Reports 2019 6:3*, *6*(3), 111–118. https://doi.org/10.1007/S40474-019-00166-W

Lohmander, A., Holm, K., Eriksson, S., & Lieberman, M. (2017). Observation method identifies that a lack of canonical babbling can indicate future speech and language problems. *Acta Paediatrica, International Journal of Paediatrics*, *106*(6), 935–943. https://doi.org/10.1111/apa.13816

Morris, S. R. (2010). Clinical application of the mean babbling level and syllable structure level. *Language, Speech, and Hearing Services in Schools*, *41*(2), 223–230. https://doi.org/10.1044/0161-1461(2009/08-0076)

Novak, I., Morgan, C., Adde, L., Blackman, J., Boyd, R. N., Brunstrom-Hernandez, J., Cioni, G., Damiano, D., Darrah, J., Eliasson, A. C., de Vries, L. S., Einspieler, C., Fahey, M., Fehlings, D., Ferriero, D. M., Fetters, L., Fiori, S., Forssberg, H., Gordon, A. M., … Badawi, N. (2017). Early, accurate diagnosis and early intervention in cerebral palsy: Advances in diagnosis and treatment. In *JAMA Pediatrics* (Vol. 171, Issue 9, pp. 897–907). American Medical Association. https://doi.org/10.1001/jamapediatrics.2017.1689

Nyman, A., & Lohmander, A. (2018). Babbling in children with neurodevelopmental disability and validity of a simplified way of measuring canonical babbling ratio. *Clinical Linguistics & Phonetics*, *32*(2), 114–127. https://doi.org/10.1080/02699206.2017.1320588

Nyman, A., Strömbergsson, S., & Lohmander, A. (2021). Canonical babbling ratio – Concurrent and predictive evaluation of the 0.15 criterion. *Journal of Communication Disorders*, *94*, 106164. https://doi.org/10.1016/J.JCOMDIS.2021.106164

Overby, M., & Caspari, S. S. (2015). Volubility, consonant, and syllable characteristics in infants and toddlers later diagnosed with childhood apraxia of speech: A pilot study. *Journal of Communication Disorders*, *55*, 44–62. https://doi.org/10.1016/J.JCOMDIS.2015.04.001

Overby, M. S., Caspari, S. S., & Schreiber, J. (2019). *Volubility, Consonant Emergence, and Syllabic Structure in Infants and Toddlers Later Diagnosed With Childhood Apraxia of Speech, Speech Sound Disorder, and Typical Development: A Retrospective Video Analysis*. https://doi.org/10.23641/asha

Patten, E., Belardi, K., Baranek, G. T., Watson, L. R., Labban, J. D., & Oller, D. K. (2014). Vocal patterns in infants with autism spectrum disorder: Canonical babbling status and vocalization frequency. *Journal of Autism and Developmental Disorders*, *44*(10), 2413–2428. https://doi.org/10.1007/s10803-014-2047-4

Peeters, M., Verhoeven, L., de Moor, J., & van Balkom, H. (2009). Importance of speech production for phonological awareness and word decoding: The case of children with cerebral palsy. *Research in Developmental Disabilities*, *30*(4), 712–726. https://doi.org/10.1016/J.RIDD.2008.10.002

Rosenbaum, P., Paneth, N., Leviton, A., Goldstein, M., & Bax, M. (2007). A report: the definition and classification of cerebral palsy April 2006. *Developmental Medicine and Child Neurology. Supplement*, *109*(SUPPL. 2), 8–14. https://doi.org/10.1111/j.1469-8749.2007.tb12610.x

Sadowska, M., Sarecka-Hujar, B., & Kopyta, I. (2020). *Cerebral Palsy: Current Opinions on Definition, Epidemiology, Risk Factors, Classification and Treatment Options*. https://doi.org/10.2147/NDT.S235165

Smith, B. L., & Stoel-Gammon, C. (1996). A quantitative analysis of reduplicated and variegated babbling in vocalizations by Down syndrome infants. *Clinical Linguistics and Phonetics*, *10*(2), 119–129. https://doi.org/10.3109/02699209608985166

Stoel-Gammon, C. (1989). Prespeech and early speech development of two late talkers. First Language, 9(6), 207–223. https://doi.org/10.1177/014272378900900607

Stark, R. E., Bernstein, L. E., & Demorest, M. E. (1993). Vocal communication in the first 18 months of life. *Journal of Speech and Hearing Research*, *36*(3), 548–558. https://doi.org/10.1044/jshr.3603.548

Willadsen, E., Cooper, R., Conroy, E. B., Gamble, C., Albery, L., Andersen, H., Appelqvist, M., Bodling, P., Bowden, M., Brunnegard, K., Enfalt, J., van Eeden, S., Goncalves, C., Fukushiro, A., Jørgensen, L., Lemvik, J., Leturgie, L., Liljerehn, E., Lodge, N., … Persson, C. (2022). Inter-rater reliability in classification of canonical babbling status based on canonical babbling ratio in infants with isolated cleft palate randomised to Timing of Primary Surgery for Cleft Palate (TOPS). *Clinical Linguistics & Phonetics*. https://doi.org/10.1080/02699206.2021.2012259

The 34th Conference on Computational Linguistics and Speech Processing (ROCLING 2022)
Taipei, Taiwan, November 21-22, 2022. The Association for Computational Linguistics and Chinese Language Processing

Automatic Generation of Abstracts for Research Papers

Dushan Kumarasinghe
Department of Computer Science and Engineering
University of Moratuwa
dushan.21@cse.mrt.ac.lk

Nisansa de Silva
Department of Computer Science and Engineering
University of Moratuwa
nisansadds@cse.mrt.ac.lk

Abstract

Summarizing has always been an important utility for reading long documents. Research papers are unique in this regard, as they have a compulsory summary in the form of the *abstract* in the beginning of the document which gives the gist of the entire study often within a set upper limit for the word count. Writing the abstract to be sufficiently succinct while being descriptive enough is a hard task even for native English speakers. This study is the first step in generating abstracts for research papers in the computational linguistics domain automatically using the domain-specific abstractive summarization power of the GPT-Neo model.

Keywords: NLP, Summarization, GPT-Neo

1 Introduction

The *abstract* of a research paper provides a quick summery of the entire paper: from the problem to the proposed solution to the result. Thus by definition, this section is expected to be concise and informative (de Silva et al., 2017). Text summarization is one of the main domains in Natural Language Processing (NLP) which has numerous use cases. There are two broad categories for this: *extraction* and *abstraction*. In *extractive* methods it uses existing words, phrases or sentences to form a summary. In contrast, *abstractive* methods follow a more complex mechanisms. First, a semanatic representation of the content is built. Then natural language generation mechanisms are used to create the summary using the aforementioned representation. This research proposes a hybrid mechanism of text summarization to generate the abstract scientific papers with evaluating several paths for the proposed solution.

The objective of this research is to reduce the burden on researchers by automatically generating the abstract section by using the sections of the paper that follows it. The researchers then may do minor adjustments to the generated section and publish.

Considering existing summarization techniques, abstractive solutions have domain specific limitations. On the other hand, domain specific implementations perform better in the perspective of precise representation of the subject matter. Abstractive solutions gain domain specificity from the process of models being built upon and information extracted from the training documents. Despite the loss of generalization, this improves the accuracy of the solution within the selected domain. Thus, we propose to build and test our solution for research paper abstract generation with the scope limited to the domain of *Computational Linguistics*. As future work, it may then be extended to other research domains.

2 Related Work

El-Kassas et al. (2021) emphasize the importance of developing abstractive automatic text summarization methods. The paper describes the different approaches, methods, building blocks, techniques, datasets, evaluation methods, and future research directions of summarization methods. Referring Dutta et al. (2019), El-Kassas et al. (2021) claim that different algorithms produce different summaries from the same input texts and it is very promising to combine outputs from multiple summarization algorithms to produce better summaries. Also the recommendation of Mahajani et al. (2019) to benefit from the advantages of both extractive and abstractive approaches by proposing hybrid automatic text summarization systems, has motivated the authors to create a comprehensive survey for researchers to enhance summary generation by combining different approaches and/or methods.

Extractive text summarization methods have

The 34th Conference on Computational Linguistics and Speech Processing (ROCLING 2022)
Taipei, Taiwan, November 21-22, 2022. The Association for Computational Linguistics and Chinese Language Processing

Technique	ROUGE-2
Ranking-based MMR (Yang et al., 2014)	0.1262
MCMR (B&B) (Alguliev et al., 2011)	0.1221
SpOpt-comp (Yao et al., 2015a,b)	0.1245
MCMR (PSO) (Alguliev et al., 2011)	0.1165
AdaSum (Zhang et al., 2008)	0.1172
Uni + Max (Ouyang et al., 2011)	0.1133
Sum_Sparse (Li et al., 2015a,b)	0.0920
PNR[2] (Li et al., 2008)	0.0895
MDS-Sparse-div (Liu et al., 2015)	0.0645

Table 1: ROUGE score of the text summarization methods on DUC 2007 dataset in Gambhir and Gupta (2017)

been developed more often since they are less complex than abstractive methods. Gambhir and Gupta (2017) presents a comprehensive survey of recent text summarization extractive approaches developed in the last decade. A few number of abstractive and multilingual text summarization approaches also have been discussed in the paper. Their needs, advantages and disadvantages are identified and states the useful future directions. Moreover the authors have compared the summarization techniques against DUC 2007[1] dataset and calculated the ROUGE-2 (Lin, 2004) scores extracted from Gambhir and Gupta (2017) are shown in Table 1.

Moratanch and Chitrakala (2016) have done a survey on abstractive text summarization techniques, their challenges and the state of the art datasets. They claim that abstractive summarization is an efficient form if summarization compared to extractive summarization and it generates a summary that will be in more coherent form, easily readable and grammatically correct.

Abstractive summarization can be categorized into two main types as Structure based approach and semantic based approach. Moratanch and Chitrakala (2016) note that major issue of abstractive summarization is there is no generalized framework, parsing and alignment of parse trees is difficult. Extracting important sentences, sentence ordering as in original source and information diffusion are open issues according to Moratanch and Chitrakala (2016)

Bidirectional Encoder Representations from Transformers (BERT), proposed by Devlin et al. (2018), has become a mainstay in various NLP applications and have proved to produce state of the art results for numerous tasks (Ratnayaka et al., 2022). Liu and Lapata (2019) show how BERT can be applied in text summarization and propose a general framework for both extractive and abstractive summarization models. They propose a novel document level encoder based on BERT that can encode a document into representations for its sentences. Their extractive model is built in top if this encoder by stacking several intersentense transformer layers to capture document level features for extracting sentences. Their abstractive model uses an encoder-decoder architecture, combining the same pretrained BERT encoder with a randomly-initialized transformer decoder Vaswani et al. (2017).

Abstractive text summarization can be naturally cast as mapping and input sequence if words in a source document to a target of words called summary according to Nallapati et al. (2016). These deep learning based models are called sequence to sequence models. Nallapati et al. (2016) model abstractive text summariation using attentional encoder-decoder RNN and show that they achieve state of the art performance on Gigaword corpus (decribed in Rush et al. (2015)) and DUC corpus [2]. These sequence to sequence modes have been successful is many problems such as machine translation Bahdanau et al. (2014), speech recognition Bahdanau et al. (2016) and video captioning Venugopalan et al. (2015). Comparing machine translation authors highlight the challenges in summarization is unlike in translation, summarization needs to compress the original document in a lossy manner such that key concepts in the original document are preserved. But in machine translation it is expected to be loss-less and almost one-to-one word level alignment.

Nallapati et al. (2016) use an attentional encoder-decoder RNN model similar to Bahdanau et al. (2014) and show that it perform well for the metioned two corpus. They have presented a new corpus by modifying Hermann et al. (2015), named CNN/Daily Mail corpus (See, 2021) which has become a standard benchmark dataset used for evaluating the performance of different summarization models .

Cohan et al. (2018) proposed a discourse aware model for abstractive summarizing of single longer form documents such as research papers. In their encoder, they first encode each discourse section and with them then encode the document. Most of the other approaches (Liu and Lapata, 2019) and

[1]https://www-nlpir.nist.gov/projects/duc/data/2007_data.html

[2]https://duc.nist.gov/data.html/

data sets in literature such as CNN, Daily Mail (See, 2021) and New York Times (Sandhaus, 2008) articles are news paper articles which are smaller in size compared to research papers. One advantage in attempting to summarize scientific papers is that they follow a standard discourse structure and come with ground truth summaries. Thus, Cohan et al. (2018) have made two datasets collected from scientific repositories: arXiv.org[3] and PubMed.com[4].

3 Methodology

In this section, we discuss the data set generation as well as the methods used for comparative analysis.

3.1 Dataset Generation

Since we are focusing on *computational linguistics* as our domain for the abstract generation, a specific dataset was generated by collecting publicly available research papers in this domain from arXiv.org. More than 7000 research papers were downloaded in the form of LaTeX sources.

3.2 Data Preparation

Papers downloaded as LaTeX sources were then processed to *json* files by separating the sections in the paper so that abstracts can be separated in the training and testing steps. Regular expression based implementations were mainly used for the section separation task. Cleaning the LaTeX text was also done to remove unwanted latex command that won't contribute to the meaning of the text. But citations were kept remained in the cleaned text.

One constraint we had to satisfy in the model training was the max chunk size. 2048 is the maximum size we can use. Limiting number of words to this max chunk size was another problem we had to solve since research papers are comparatively long documents. This limited 2048 token size is divided into abstract, text and tags as shown in Fig 1

This size portion calculation requires a decision on the number of tokens N, to be declared as the token size of the abstract section. Instead of defining it in an arbitrary manner, we generated the Fig 2 which shows the token size distribution of the abstract sections in our data set. Thus, by looking at the 3rd quartile boundary, we selected 185 as the number of desired tokens in abstracts, N, for the

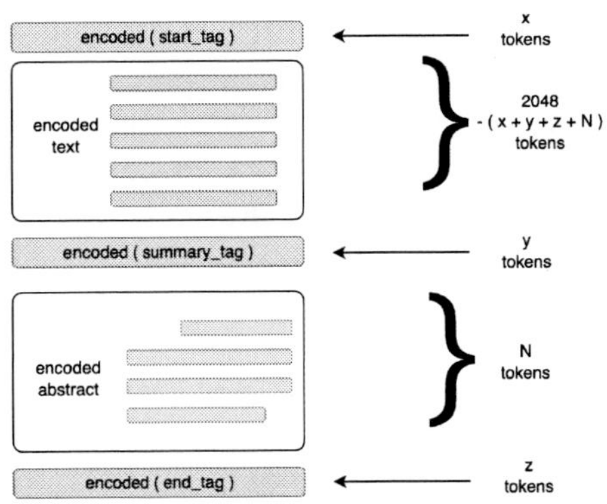

Figure 1: Token size portions for GPT-Neo model feeding

process of generating formatted text for feeding the model for training and prediction.

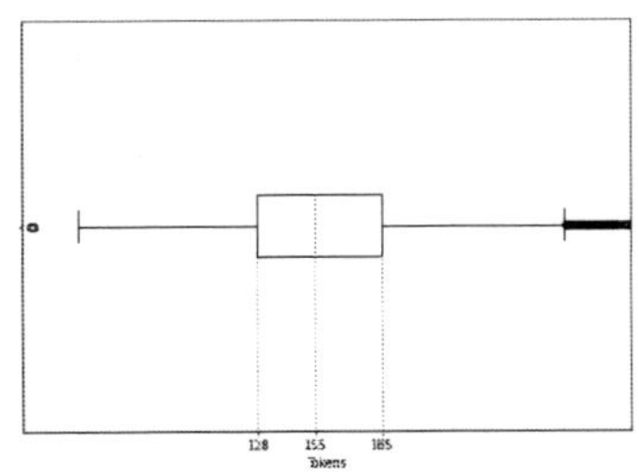

Figure 2: Token size distribution of abstract sections

After determining this N value we calculated the text body size within the constraint of 2048 total tokens. This constraint is imposed by model trained chunk size of GPT-Neo. Thus, the first N tokens are reserved for the abstract. Then. x,y and z number of tokens are put aside to carry the *start*, *summary* and *end* tags. Thus, the body text size is calculated to be $2048 - (x + y + z + N)$ number of tokens. However, as we discussed above, research papers are long documents and thus, the above calculated **Body Size** let alone even the full length of 2048 is not enough to cover the entirety of a research paper.

For this we used the pre-summarization to limit the body text into the window of **Body Size**.

3.3 Pre-Summarization

For this pre-summarization, two main mechanisms were tested.

1. Vector average method

[3]https://arxiv.org/

[4]https://pubmed.ncbi.nlm.nih.gov/

2. Extractive method

These two approach of converting long text into a trainable or predictable vector is shown in Fig 3. After the text is decreased, it will be encoded and formatted with predefined tags.

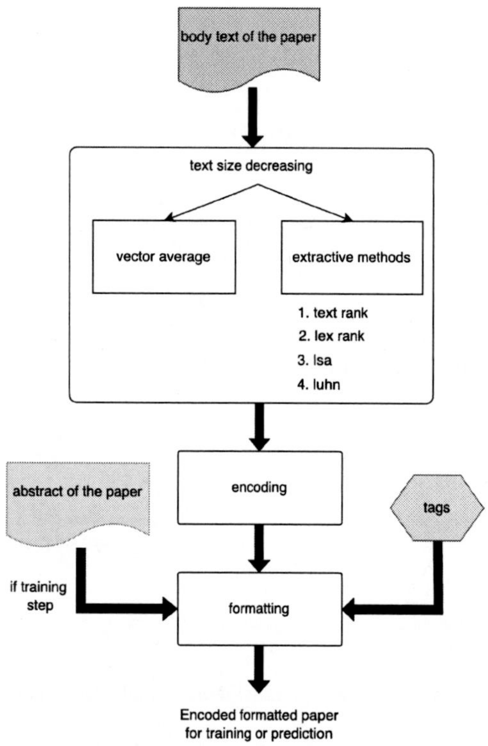

Figure 3: Data preparation overview

In **Vector average method** we divided the research paper text sans the abstract into chunks of **Body Size** and converted them using GPT-2 Tokenizer (Radford et al., 2019), which were then sent through an average pooling operation. With this, we obtain a vector of token size 2048 where the first N tokens represent the abstract with no information loss, the three flag tokens, and finally the average pooled context of the rest of the research paper like shown in the Fig 4

Extractive method simply chooses max number of sentences that can be fit inside the given token limit and it is shown in the Fig 5. But the algorithm has to select those limited sentences with preserving the original meaning of the full text. For that we have used 4 algorithms separately and evaluated the results for each method.

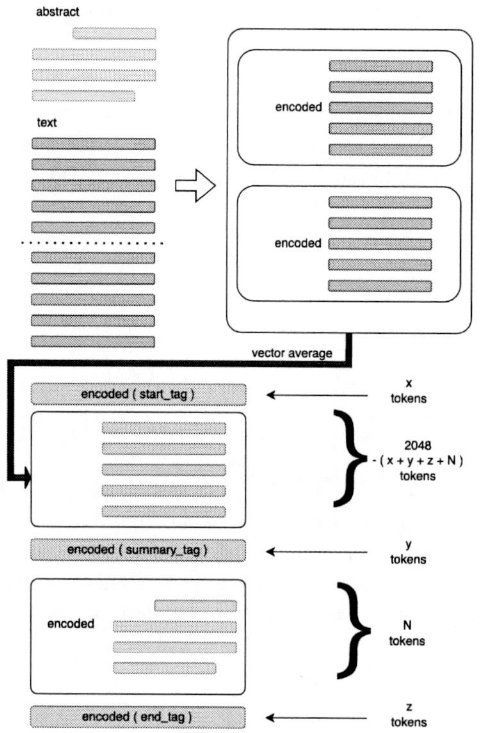

Figure 4: Tokenization strategy of vector average method

1. Lex Rank Erkan and Radev (2004) which is a stochastic graph-based method

2. Text Rank Mihalcea and Tarau (2004) which is a graph based ranking model

3. Latent Semantic Analysis(LSA) Landauer et al. (1998) which is a semantic based algorthm

4. Luhn (Luhn, 1958) which is a significance based algorithm

After these text is limited to to the given **Body Size** by any of the method describe above, they were then converted to *tfrecords* which supports distributed datasets and leverages parallel I/O. Generation of these *tfrecords* were done by encoding the LaTeX source of each paper. A predefined *start tag*, *summary tag*, and *end tag* were applied in this encoded vector so that the model can be guided on what type of text to predict in the respective subsections of the predicted text.

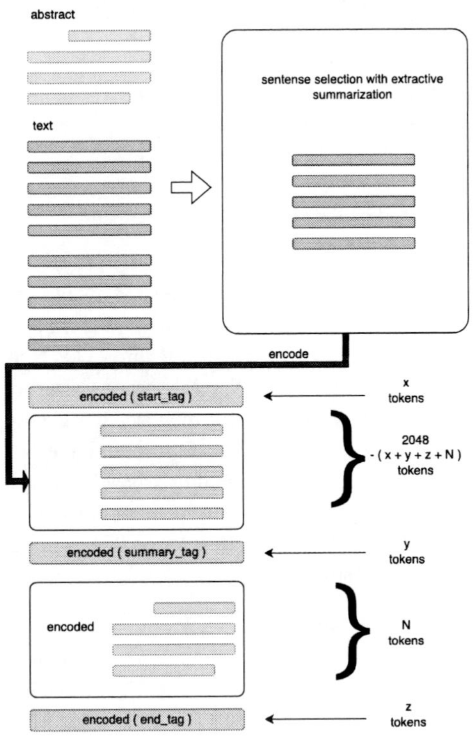

Figure 5: Tokenization strategy of extractive methods

3.4 Model Tuning

GPT-Neo (Black et al., 2021) model was fine tuned with the dataset after text size reduction as described in Fig 3.2 and tokenized with GPT-2 tokenizer. Fine tuining was done using Google Colab[5] with the TPUs. Since using TPUs dataset and pretrained model were stored in the google cloud[6] and then processed with colab with the power of TPUs[7]. Fine tuning text format is shown in the Fig 6 GPT-Neo model was fine-tuned with batch size of 8, mesh shape of x:4,y:2, train steps of 1000 and steps per checkpoint of 500.

3.5 Prediction

Fine tuned GPT-Neo (Black et al., 2021) models were used with encoded text of the papers by related pre-summarization methods. Prediting was also done using Google Colab with the power of TPUs. Prediction text format is shown in Fig 7. As shown in Fig 7, abstract tag is provided so that GPT-Neo can predict the text from that point until

[5]`https://colab.research.google.com/`
[6]`https://cloud.google.com/storage`
[7]`https://cloud.google.com/tpu`

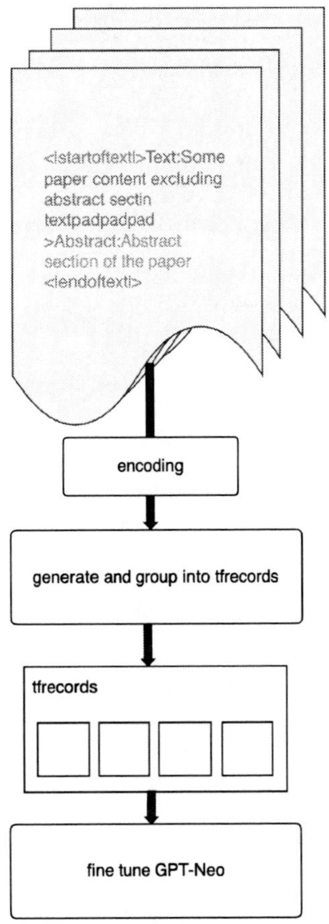

Figure 6: Fine tuning GPT-Neo

it predict the end of text tag.

For the prediction, GPT-Neo model was utilized with batch size of 1, mesh shape of x:4,y:2, train steps of 1000 and steps per checkpoint of 500. This effectively mirrors our training configuration discussed in Section 3.4.

4 Results

Separately fine tuned GPT-Neo models were evaluated for each pre-summerizer as shown in Table 4; where it can be observed that Latent Semantic Analysis and Luhn based pre-summarizations have obtained the best results for the tested *ROUGE* scores.

It was then decided to analyse the configurations given in Table even further by considering the Precision and Recall measures as there are different research domains that give priority to one over the other. For example, de Silva (2020) discussed how in the case of medical domain NLP, recall takes precedence over precision. Same is discussed for

Pre-Summarization Method	ROUGE-1	ROUGE-2	ROUGE-L
Vector Average	0.1843	0.0204	0.1698
Lex Rank	0.2612	0.0478	0.2359
Text Rank	0.2548	0.0441	0.2304
LSA	**0.2629**	0.0472	**0.2382**
Luhn	0.2602	**0.0483**	0.2343

Table 2: ROUGE Scores comparison of the models based on the pre-summarization method

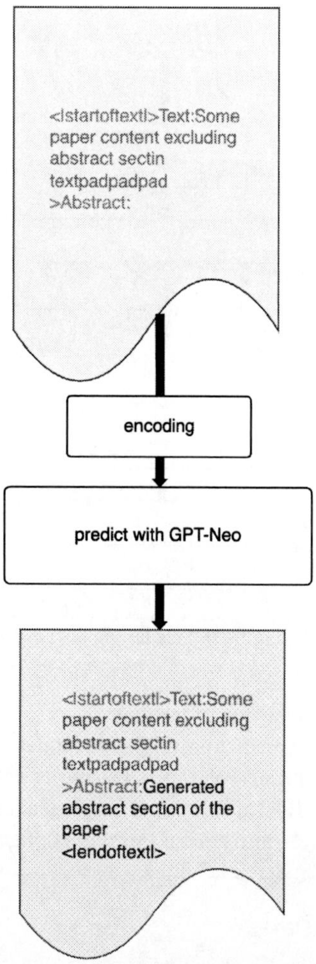

Figure 7: Predicting summary with GPT-Neo

the legal domain by Samarawickrama et al. (2020). Even though there is no definitive meta-study on the content in the research papers of the computational linguistics domain to conclude such a bias towards precision or recall, it was deemed prudent to report these values. For the ease of reading and comparison, the F1 values of Table are also brought forward.

Average vector method takes the average of encoded vectors of the chunks divided from the text of the paper before passing it into GTP-Neo for training or predicting. While average vector model seems to be too trivial for this task at a glance, recent prior work in the NLP domain have proved its usefulness at establishing a baseline for even complex tasks such as sentiment analysis (Jayawickrama et al., 2021). Results of this method are shown in Table 3.

ROUGE	F	P	R
1	0.1843	0.2157	0.1684
2	0.0204	0.0242	0.0187
L	0.1698	0.1987	0.1551

Table 3: ROUGE Scores of average vector based pre-summarizing.

Lex rank (Erkan and Radev, 2004) is a stochastic graph-based method for computing relative importance of textual units. It is based on the concept of eigenvector centrality in a graph representation of sentences. Similar, but mathematically simpler methods have shown promise in NLP applications in the Legal domain (Jayawardana et al., 2017). Model we trained with Lex rank has given the results shown in Table 4.

ROUGE	F	P	R
1	0.2612	0.3032	0.2384
2	0.0478	0.0568	0.0435
L	0.2359	0.2742	0.2152

Table 4: ROUGE Scores of Lex rank based pre-summarizing.

Since the advent of *PageRank* algorithm (Page, 1997; Page et al., 1999), using graph-based methods to rank text documents has been a popular solution for document level analysis (Karannagoda et al., 2013). *TextRank* (Mihalcea and Tarau, 2004) is also a graph based sentence extraction method which creates a graph for each sentence and rank them based on the similarity. In their legal document retrieval system, Sugathadasa et al. (2018) showed how *TextRank* can be utilized in representing documents in a semantically consistent manner. Pre-summarization based on this method has scored as shown in the Table 5.

ROUGE	F	P	R
1	0.2548	0.2916	0.2342
2	0.0441	0.0514	0.0403
L	0.2304	0.2637	0.2117

Table 5: ROUGE Scores of Text rank based pre-summarizing.

LSA (Latent Semantic Analysis) (Landauer et al., 1998) method is extracting and representing the contextual-usage meaning of words by statistical computations applied to the text. We have calculated the ROUGE scores of this method as a pre-summarizer with GPT-Neo and the results are shown in Table 6.

ROUGE	F	P	R
1	0.2629	0.302	0.2421
2	0.0472	0.0547	0.0435
L	0.2382	0.2737	0.2194

Table 6: ROUGE Scores of LSA based pre-summarizing.

Luhn algorithm (Luhn, 1958) calculates the significance of a sentence by considering frequency of word occurrence in the text and the relative position within a sentence. GPT-Neo Model trained Luhn algorithm as a pre-summarizer gave the results shown in Table 7.

ROUGE	F	P	R
1	0.2602	0.2954	0.2406
2	0.0483	0.0551	0.0448
L	0.2343	0.2663	0.2164

Table 7: ROUGE Scores of Luhn based pre-summarizing.

LSA based pre-summarization method has been scored the highest on ROUGE-1 and ROUGE-L while Luhn based pre-summarization method is scoring higher on ROUGE-2. All extractive pre-summarizations has been scored more than the twice of the score of the baseline, vector average method, in ROUGE-2.

5 Conclusion

We have used transfer learning with GPT-Neo for generating abstracts of research papers automatically. GPT-Neo model provides a language model that can be utilized for many tasks but we have to face the token limitation. We managed this limited token size with two main approaches which are, an average-pooling of the body context vectors and an extractive summarization. Observations have shown that extractive pre-summarization with GPT-Neo has better results compared to average pooling. We intend to extend the findings to generate the introduction as well.

References

Rasim M Alguliev, Ramiz M Aliguliyev, Makrufa S Hajirahimova, and Chingiz A Mehdiyev. 2011. Mcmr: Maximum coverage and minimum redundant text summarization model. *Expert Systems with Applications*, 38(12):14514–14522.

Dzmitry Bahdanau, Kyunghyun Cho, and Yoshua Bengio. 2014. Neural machine translation by jointly learning to align and translate. *arXiv preprint arXiv:1409.0473*.

Dzmitry Bahdanau, Jan Chorowski, Dmitriy Serdyuk, Philemon Brakel, and Yoshua Bengio. 2016. End-to-end attention-based large vocabulary speech recognition. In *2016 IEEE international conference on acoustics, speech and signal processing (ICASSP)*, pages 4945–4949. IEEE.

Sid Black, Leo Gao, Phil Wang, Connor Leahy, and Stella Biderman. 2021. GPT-Neo: Large Scale Autoregressive Language Modeling with Mesh-Tensorflow. If you use this software, please cite it using these metadata.

Arman Cohan, Franck Dernoncourt, Doo Soon Kim, Trung Bui, Seokhwan Kim, Walter Chang, and Nazli Goharian. 2018. A discourse-aware attention model for abstractive summarization of long documents. *arXiv preprint arXiv:1804.05685*.

Jacob Devlin, Ming-Wei Chang, Kenton Lee, and Kristina Toutanova. 2018. Bert: Pre-training of deep bidirectional transformers for language understanding. *arXiv preprint arXiv:1810.04805*.

Soumi Dutta, Vibhash Chandra, Kanav Mehra, Sujata Ghatak, Asit Das, and Saptarshi Ghosh. 2019. *Summarizing Microblogs During Emergency Events: A Comparison of Extractive Summarization Algorithms: Proceedings of IEMIS 2018, Volume 2*, pages 859–872.

Wafaa S. El-Kassas, Cherif R. Salama, Ahmed A. Rafea, and Hoda K. Mohamed. 2021. Automatic text summarization: A comprehensive survey. *Expert Systems with Applications*, 165:113679.

Günes Erkan and Dragomir R Radev. 2004. Lexrank: Graph-based lexical centrality as salience in text summarization. *Journal of artificial intelligence research*, 22:457–479.

Mahak Gambhir and Vishal Gupta. 2017. Recent automatic text summarization techniques: a survey. *Artificial Intelligence Review*, 47.

Karl Moritz Hermann, Tomás Kociský, Edward Grefenstette, Lasse Espeholt, Will Kay, Mustafa Suleyman, and Phil Blunsom. 2015. Teaching machines to read and comprehend. *CoRR*, abs/1506.03340.

Vindula Jayawardana, Dimuthu Lakmal, Nisansa de Silva, Amal Shehan Perera, Keet Sugathadasa, and Buddhi Ayesha. 2017. Deriving a Representative Vector for Ontology Classes with Instance Word Vector Embeddings. In *2017 Seventh International Conference on Innovative Computing Technology (INTECH)*, pages 79–84. IEEE.

Vihanga Jayawickrama, Gihan Weeraprameshwara, Nisansa de Silva, and Yudhanjaya Wijeratne. 2021. Seeking sinhala sentiment: Predicting facebook reactions of sinhala posts. *arXiv preprint arXiv:2112.00468*.

E. L. Karannagoda, H. M. T. C. Herath, K. N. J. Fernando, M. W. I. D. Karunarathne, N. H. N. D. de Silva, and A. S. Perera. 2013. Document Analysis Based Automatic Concept Map Generation for Enterprises. In *Advances in ICT for Emerging Regions (ICTer), 2013 International Conference on*, pages 154–159. IEEE.

Thomas K Landauer, Peter W Foltz, and Darrell Laham. 1998. An introduction to latent semantic analysis. *Discourse processes*, 25(2-3):259–284.

Chen Li, Yang Liu, and Lin Zhao. 2015a. Using external resources and joint learning for bigram weighting in ilp-based multi-document summarization. In *Proceedings of the 2015 Conference of the North American Chapter of the Association for Computational Linguistics: Human Language Technologies*, pages 778–787.

Piji Li, Lidong Bing, Wai Lam, Hang Li, and Yi Liao. 2015b. Reader-aware multi-document summarization via sparse coding. In *Twenty-Fourth International Joint Conference on Artificial Intelligence*.

Wenjie Li, Furu Wei, Qin Lu, and Yanxiang He. 2008. Pnr2: Ranking sentences with positive and negative reinforcement for query-oriented update summarization. In *Proceedings of the 22nd international conference on computational linguistics (Coling 2008)*, pages 489–496.

Chin-Yew Lin. 2004. ROUGE: A package for automatic evaluation of summaries. In *Text Summarization Branches Out*, pages 74–81, Barcelona, Spain. Association for Computational Linguistics.

He Liu, Hongliang Yu, and Zhi-Hong Deng. 2015. Multi-document summarization based on two-level sparse representation model. In *Twenty-ninth AAAI conference on artificial intelligence*.

Yang Liu and Mirella Lapata. 2019. Text summarization with pretrained encoders. *arXiv preprint arXiv:1908.08345*.

Hans Peter Luhn. 1958. The automatic creation of literature abstracts. *IBM Journal of research and development*, 2(2):159–165.

Abhishek Mahajani, Vinay Pandya, Isaac Maria, and Deepak Sharma. 2019. A comprehensive survey on extractive and abstractive techniques for text summarization. *Ambient Communications and Computer Systems*, pages 339–351.

Rada Mihalcea and Paul Tarau. 2004. Textrank: Bringing order into text. In *Proceedings of the 2004 conference on empirical methods in natural language processing*, pages 404–411.

N Moratanch and S Chitrakala. 2016. A survey on abstractive text summarization. In *2016 International Conference on Circuit, power and computing technologies (ICCPCT)*, pages 1–7. IEEE.

Ramesh Nallapati, Bowen Zhou, Caglar Gulcehre, Bing Xiang, et al. 2016. Abstractive text summarization using sequence-to-sequence rnns and beyond. *arXiv preprint arXiv:1602.06023*.

You Ouyang, Wenjie Li, Sujian Li, and Qin Lu. 2011. Applying regression models to query-focused multi-document summarization. *Information Processing & Management*, 47(2):227–237.

Lawrence Page. 1997. Method for node ranking in a linked database. *USA Patent*, 6.

Lawrence Page, Sergey Brin, Rajeev Motwani, and Terry Winograd. 1999. The pagerank citation ranking: Bringing order to the web. Technical report, Stanford InfoLab.

Alec Radford, Jeffrey Wu, Rewon Child, David Luan, Dario Amodei, Ilya Sutskever, et al. 2019. Language models are unsupervised multitask learners. *OpenAI blog*, 1(8):9.

Gathika Ratnayaka, Nisansa de Silva, Amal Shehan Perera, Gayan Kavirathne, Thirasara Ariyarathna, and Anjana Wijesinghe. 2022. Context sensitive verb similarity dataset for legal information extraction. *Data*, 7(7).

Alexander M. Rush, Sumit Chopra, and Jason Weston. 2015. A neural attention model for abstractive sentence summarization. *CoRR*, abs/1509.00685.

Chamodi Samarawickrama, Melonie de Almeida, Nisansa de Silva, Gathika Ratnayaka, and Amal Shehan Perera. 2020. Party identification of legal documents using co-reference resolution and named entity recognition. In *2020 IEEE 15th International Conference on Industrial and Information Systems (ICIIS)*, pages 494–499. IEEE.

Evan Sandhaus. 2008. The new york times annotated corpus.

Abigail See. 2021. Github - abisee/cnn-dailymail: Code to obtain the cnn / daily mail dataset (non-anonymized) for summarization.

Naida Hewa Nisansa Dilushan de Silva. 2020. *Semantic Oppositeness for Inconsistency and Disagreement Detection in Natural Language*. Ph.D. thesis, University of Oregon.

Nisansa de Silva, Dejing Dou, and Jingshan Huang. 2017. Discovering Inconsistencies in PubMed Abstracts Through Ontology-Based Information Extraction. In *Proceedings of the 8th ACM International Conference on Bioinformatics, Computational Biology, and Health Informatics*, ACM-BCB '17, pages 362–371, New York, NY, USA. ACM.

Keet Sugathadasa, Buddhi Ayesha, Nisansa de Silva, Amal Shehan Perera, Vindula Jayawardana, Dimuthu Lakmal, and Madhavi Perera. 2018. Legal Document Retrieval using Document Vector Embeddings and Deep Learning. In *Science and information conference*, pages 160–175. Springer.

Ashish Vaswani, Noam Shazeer, Niki Parmar, Jakob Uszkoreit, Llion Jones, Aidan N Gomez, Łukasz Kaiser, and Illia Polosukhin. 2017. Attention is all you need. In *Advances in neural information processing systems*, pages 5998–6008.

Subhashini Venugopalan, Marcus Rohrbach, Jeffrey Donahue, Raymond Mooney, Trevor Darrell, and Kate Saenko. 2015. Sequence to sequence-video to text. In *Proceedings of the IEEE international conference on computer vision*, pages 4534–4542.

Libin Yang, Xiaoyan Cai, Yang Zhang, and Peng Shi. 2014. Enhancing sentence-level clustering with ranking-based clustering framework for theme-based summarization. *Information sciences*, 260:37–50.

Jin-ge Yao, Xiaojun Wan, and Jianguo Xiao. 2015a. Compressive document summarization via sparse optimization. In *Twenty-Fourth International Joint Conference on Artificial Intelligence*.

Jin-ge Yao, Xiaojun Wan, and Jianguo Xiao. 2015b. Phrase-based compressive cross-language summarization. In *Proceedings of the 2015 conference on empirical methods in natural language processing*, pages 118–127.

Jin Zhang, Xueqi Cheng, Gaowei Wu, and Hongbo Xu. 2008. Adasum: an adaptive model for summarization. In *Proceedings of the 17th ACM conference on Information and knowledge management*, pages 901–910.

The 34th Conference on Computational Linguistics and Speech Processing (ROCLING 2022)
Taipei, Taiwan, November 21-22, 2022. The Association for Computational Linguistics and Chinese Language Processing

Speech Timing in Typically Developing Mandarin-Speaking Children From Ages 3 To 4

Jeng Man Lew
National Kaohsiung Normal University
jengmanss@gmail.com

Li-Mei Chen
National Cheng Kung University
leemay@mail.ncku.edu.tw

Yu Ching Lin
National Cheng Kung University Hospital
yuchinglin2011@gmail.com

Abstract

This study aims to develop a better understanding of the speech timing development in Mandarin-speaking children from 3 to 4 years of age. Data were selected from two typically developing children. Four 50-min recordings were collected during 3 and 4 years old based on natural conversation among the observers, participants, and the parents, and the picture-naming task. Speech timing were measured by Praat, including speaking rate, articulation rate, mean length of utterance (MLUs), mean utterance duration, mean word duration, pause ratio, and volubility. Major findings of the current study are: 1) Five measurements (speaking rate, mean length of utterance (MLUs), mean utterance length, mean word duration and volubility) decreased with age in both children; 2) Articulation rate of both children increased with age; 3) Comparing with the findings from previous studies, pause ratio of both slightly increased with age. These findings not only contribute to a more comprehensive data for assessment, it also can be a reference in speech intervention.

Keywords: speaking rate, mean length of utterance (MLUs), mean utterance length, mean word duration, volubility

1 Introduction

Speech timing, also known as speaking rates, is a product of several factors, including biological factors (e.g., anatomic growth, neurologic and neuromuscular maturation), sensorimotor and language processes (e.g., motor learning, and semantic, lexical, and phonologic access, and motor programming and planning) (Kent, 2004; Nip and Green, 2013; Redford, 2015). Speaking rates could be a crucial indicator of typical speech development and speech disorders, for example, stuttering, cluttering, specific language impairment, apraxias, and dysarthrias. (Hall et al., 1999; Smith et al., 2011; Flipsen, 2002). Speaking rate not only serves as a metric, it can also be a common target in speech intervention to improve speech production in individuals with speech motor involvement.

2 Purpose of Study and Research Questions

Due to limited longitudinal studies and lack of data on Mandarin-speaking children, our knowledge of speech rate development in Mandarin-speakers remains inadequate. Hence, this study was to develop a better understanding of the speech rate development in Mandarin-speaking children from 3 to 4 years of age.

Research questions include: 1) Are there any differences in speaking rate, articulation rate and pause ratio between 3 and 4 years old? 2) Are there any gender differences in speaking rate, articulation rate and pause ratio in Taiwanese Mandarin-speaking children?

3 Literature Review

3.1 Speech Rate

Speech rate reflects a speaker's global aspects of speech production (e.g. language formation, speed of articulator movement, cognitive, linguistic, and motor workloads). Speech rate is measured from the onset to the offset of the spoken words or sentences including articulation rate, pauses, disfluencies and repetitions. To be more specific, it is calculated by dividing the number of syllables produced by sentence duration, in the unit of words per minute (WPM) or word per second (WPS) and/or syllables per minute (syl/m) or syllables per second (syl/s). In Mandarin Chinese, each word contains only one syllable, which means the number of words is equivalent to the number of syllables, thus, words per minute (WPM) or word per second (WPS) can be used as calculation unit.

3.2 Articulation Rate and Pauses

Articulation rate indicates our speech and /or exactness of articulatory movement, and reflects the time used for speech motor control during speech. It calculates only the total number of perceptual fluently syllables or words in a particular amount of time. Perceptual fluently utterance excludes any disfluencies, hesitations, or pauses greater than 250ms (Yaruss, 1997). Walker et al. (1992) indicated that articulation rates in both syllables per second and phones per second were significantly faster in the 5-year-olds than in the 3-year olds.

Pauses is dividing pause duration by total speech duration and may serve as different functions: physiological functions (breathing, swallowing), linguistic functions (syntactic or semantic), super-ordinated, higher-level functions (language formation), pragmatic function (indicating a change of topic or speaker) (Schelten-Cornish, 2007). Pausing will decrease over the remainder of childhood (Tendera et al., 2019).

3.3 Different Variables of Speech Timing

3.3.1 *Ages*

Several age-related studies suggest speaking rates are gradually increase from the one-word stage in toddlerhood until it reaches a stable level in adolescence or early adulthood (Nip and Green, 2013; Tingley and Allen, 1975). As cited in Tendera et al., (2019), Amster (1984) suggested children between ages 2;6 and 3;5 show a slight increase from 2.78 to 2.91 syllables per. However, possible absence of change in speech rate between ages 4;0 and 6;0 (Amir and Grinfield, 2011; Hall et al., 1999; Pindzola et al., 1989), and 7;0 and 9;0 (Sturm and Seery, 2007) suggests that speaking rate development is not in a smooth developmental trajectory.

3.3.2 *Cognitive-linguistics load and Contextual Differences*

Other studies suggest that both articulation rate and pause time vary with cognitive–linguistic load and contextual differences (Logan et al., 2012; Nip and Green, 2013; Walker and Archibald, 2006; Walker et al., 1992). Darling-White and Banks (2021) suggested that sentence length differentially impacts the component parts of speech rate, articulation rate and pause time. By around age 3, pausing will become more frequent due to children attempting to produce more complex linguistic structures (Rispoli and Hadley, 2001). Hence, increases in sentence length led to increases in speech rate, primarily due to increases in articulation rate.

For the context differences, as cited in Tremblay and Deschamps (2017), according to Duchin and Mysak (1987, p.256), "Speech rate differs significantly, in decreasing order for oral reading, conversation, and picture description", which means narrative contexts may result in slower rates than rate in conversation speech, because narrative contexts require more language formulation than do conversational speech contexts.

4 Methodology

4.1 Participants

Two typically developing children (one male and one female) are involved in current research. For inclusion in the study, participants were native speakers of Mandarin Chinese with no significant defects in the structure or function of the speech and hearing mechanisms, no significant cognitive deficits or psychosocial dysfunction. The data is part of a database with about 30 children conducted through grants from National Science and Technology Council. In this ongoing longitudinal study, the data have been recorded once every 3 months and annotated for future research purposes. In current research, data were selected at two ages of two children (3;0 and 4;0). All recordings were taken at home under the natural interaction with caregivers and an experimenter. A total of 4 recordings were selected; each session lasted for around 50 minutes. The SHURE mini microphone connected to TASCAM recorder were used to collect speech sounds. To ensure children speech were recorded properly, the mini microphone was stapled on children's clothes.

Subject	Sex	1st Recording *(year; month, day)*	2nd Recording *(year; month, day).*
Child A	F	3;0,11	4;0,10
Child B	M	3;3,01	4;0,07

Note. F=female; M=male.

Table 1. Ages of the two children in each recording.

4.2 Coding and Data Analysis

The child's speech was divided into utterances. Utterances were defined as follows: "it is a string of words that communicate an idea, is bounded by a simple intonational contour, and/or grammatically complete" (Golinkoff and Ames 1979). For 3-17 years old individuals, if two clauses were produced on a single breath, they were coded as one utterance. Utterances could not be clearly heard because of interfering toy noise or adult speech were excluded from analysis. Phrases were also excluded if (a) they were frank imitations of the examiner, (b) they were produced during obviously excited states, (c) utterances with any pause of 250ms or greater.

Each utterance was displayed in Praat (Boersma and Weenink, 2022) and an associated textgrid was generated. There were three tier added in Praat: the first tier was the total count of child's utterances, the second tier was the brief transcription of child's spontaneous speech, and the last tier was the number of syllables counted. Segmentation on onset and offset of each child's speech turn was done by using auditory judgment and visual cues. Onsets are at the first evidence of speech-related spectral energy evidenced on both the spectrogram and the waveform enhanced display; while offsets are at the last evidence of speech-related spectral energy within the displayed utterance.

5 Findings

Major findings of the current study are: 1) Except for the articulation rate and pause ratio, other five measurements (speaking rate, mean length of utterance (MLU), mean utterance length, mean word duration and volubility) decreased with age in both children; 2) Articulation rate of both children increased with age; 3) Comparing with the findings from previous studies, pause ratio of both slightly increased with age. The measures of each recording from the two participants were presented in Table 2 and 3.

	Child A	
Age of Recordings (year; month, day)	3;0,11	4;0,10
Total words	1441	1076
Speaking rate (w/sec)	0.464	0.354
Articulation rate (w/sec)	3.432	3.463
Mean utterance duration (syll/utt)	1.900	1.726
Mean word duration (syll/w)	0.291	0.289
Pause ratio (%)	86.48%	89.77%
Mean Length of Utterance, MLU (w/utt)	6.520	5.978
Volubility (utt/min)	4.270	3.555

Note. w=word; sec=second; syll=syllables; utt=utterance; min=minute.

Table 2. Age of recordings, total words and seven speech rate measurements of Child A.

	Child B	
Age of Recordings (year; month, day)	3;3,01	4;0,07
Total words	1386	877
Speaking rate (w/sec)	0.463	0.287
Articulation rate (w/sec)	3.273	4.196
Mean utterance duration (syll/utt)	1.546	1.187
Mean word duration (syll/w)	0.306	0.238
Pause ratio (%)	85.86%	93.16%
Mean Length of Utterance, MLU (w/utt)	5.058	4.983
Volubility (utt/min)	5.487	3.457

Note. w=word; sec=second; syll=syllables; utt=utterance; min=minute.

Table 3. Age of recordings, total words and seven speech rate measurements of Child B.

Figure 1 and Figure 2 describe the distribution of speech rate of two participants in 3 and 4 years old. In both participants, the speaking rate, mean length of utterance (MLU), mean utterance length, mean word duration and volubility decreased with age, while the articulation rate and pause ratio increased with age in both children. In 4 years old, the articulation rate and pause ratio of Child A are less than those in Child B (Figures 3 and 4).

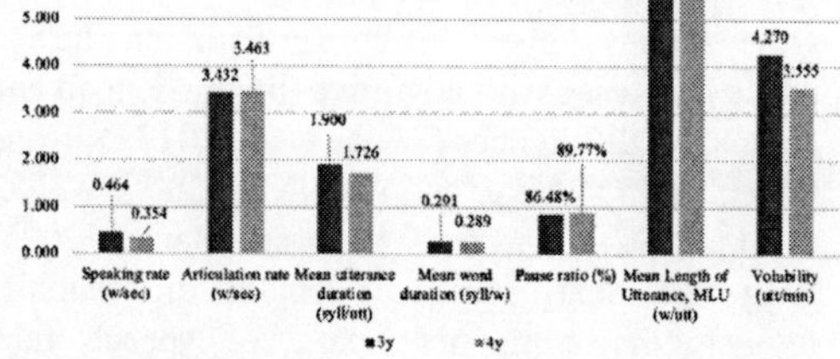

Figure 1. The distribution of speech rate of Child A in 3 and 4 years old.

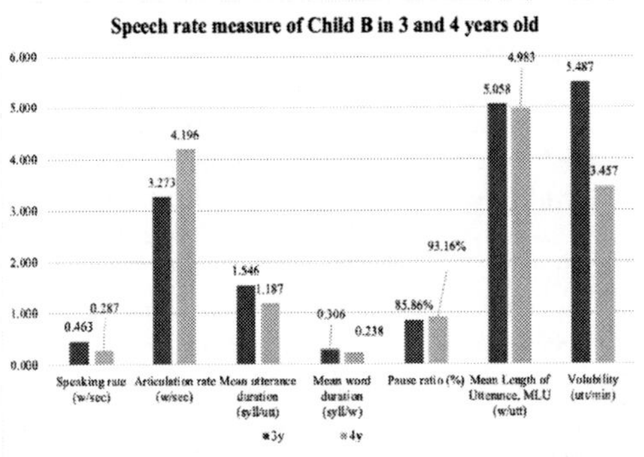

Figure 2. The distribution of speech rate of Child B in 3 and 4 years old.

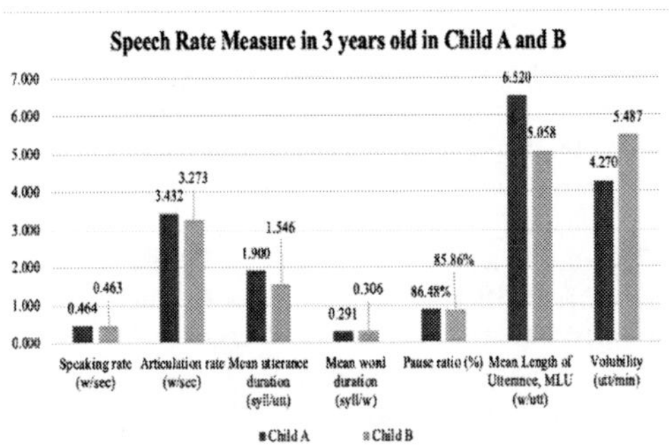

Figure 3. The distribution of speech rate in 3 years old of Child A and Child B.

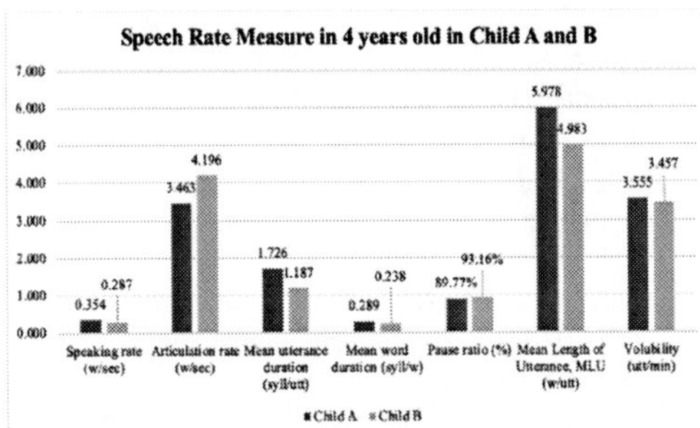

Figure 4. The distribution of speech rate in 4 years old of Child A and Child B.

6 Discussions

6.1 Comparision of speech rates with previous studies

In general expectation, speaking rate will increase gradually with age (Nip and Green, 2013; Tingley and Allen, 1975), while the pausing ratio will decrease with age. Results of this study show, contrary to expectations, that a developmental increase in speaking rate did not occur. The findings of the present study, together with those of Pindzola et al. (1989), Hall et al. (1999), Amir and Grinfeld (2011) and Walker and Archibald (2006) suggest that speaking rate may not increase with age in the preschool years. However, it is possible that speech rate development are nonlinear. In Amir and Grinfeld (2011), for example, the articulation rates of Hebrew-speaking participants (n=20) at age 3 and 5 were decreased (3;0=137.70 word per minute (WPM); 5;0=132.95 WPM; however increased at age 7 and 9 (7;0=162.13 WPM; 9;0=174.64 WPM). The increasing of pausing ratio suggest that children attempt to use more complex linguistic structures, especially by around age 3 (Rispoli and Hadley, 2001). Moreover, the correlation between speech rate and pause ratio is observed from the data, which is as the pause ratio increases, the speech rate decreases.

Only a few studies have reported sex differences in speech rate (Ryan, 2000; Walker and Archibald, 2006). In this study, the girl (Child A) speaks faster than the boy (Child B), but further statistical analysis is needed to prove if there are any significantly differences. In contrast, the boy produced significantly shorter utterances at age 3;0 (girl's MLU= 6.520; boy's MLU= 5.058) and 4;0 (girl's MLU= 5.978; boy's MLU= 4.983). Comparing with previous studies, these findings are controversial because most studies that reported sex comparisons did not find differences (e.g., Sturm and Seery, 2007; Walker and Archibald, 2006) or showed the opposite pattern in which preschool girls spoke slower than preschool boys (Tendera et al., 2019).

6.2 Limitations of the Study and Suggestions for Future Studies

Due to the limitations of time and data sources, the speech samples in this study only included two 3 to 4 years old children (only one male and one female). The findings, however, show that examining two age groups is insufficient to accurately represent the variations in rate that occur throughout time in the course of development in young children. Additional longitudinal studies with wider age groups and a larger number of children are needed to provide more definitive information on the nature of this development.

Overall speaking, for future research, speech samples could be collected through random sampling and include more participants with different age, gender and context (e.g. oral reading, conversation, and picture description) in order to develop a better understanding of the speech rate development in Mandarin-speaking children.

7 Acknowledgement

This research was supported through funds from National Science and Technology Council in Taiwan (NSC 99-2410-H-006 -102-MY2) to Li-Mei Chen. A special thank you is extended to the families of the children in this longitudinal study for their support of this project.

References

Amir, O., & Grinfeld, D. (2011). Articulation rate in childhood and adolescence: Hebrew speakers. *Language and speech*, *54*(Pt 2), 225–240. https://doi.org/10.1177/0023830910397496

Binos, Paris, and Elena Loizou (2019). Vocalization frequency as a prognostic marker of language development following early cochlear implantation. *Audiology research, 9*(1), 217. https://doi.org/10.4081/audiores.2019.217

Boersma, Paul and Weenink, David (2022). Praat: doing phonetics by computer [Computer program]. Version 6.2.12, retrieved 17 April 2022 from http://www.praat.org/

Darling-White, M., & Banks, S. W. (2021). Speech Rate Varies with Sentence Length in Typically Developing Children. *Journal of speech, language, and hearing research: JSLHR*, *64*(6S), 2385–2391. https://doi.org/10.1044/2020_JSLHR-20-00276

Duchin, S. W., and Mysak, E. D. (1987). Disfluency and rate characteristics of young adult, middle-aged, and older males. *Journal of Communication Disorders, 20*(3), 245–257. https://doi.org/10.1016/0021-9924(87)90022-0

Flipsen, P., Jr (2002). Longitudinal changes in articulation rate and phonetic phrase length in children with speech delay. *Journal of speech, language, and hearing research: JSLHR*, *45*(1), 100–110. https://doi.org/10.1044/1092-4388(2002/008)

Golinkoff, R. M., & Ames, G. J. (1979). A Comparison of Fathers' and Mothers' Speech with Their Young Children. *Child Development*, *50*(1), 28–32. https://doi.org/10.2307/1129037

Hall, K. D., Amir, O., and Yairi, E. (1999). A longitudinal investigation of speaking rate in preschool children who stutter. *Journal of speech, language, and hearing research: JSLHR, 42*(6), 1367–1377. https://doi.org/10.1044/jslhr.4206.1367

Kent, R. D. (2004). The uniqueness of speech among motor systems. *Clinical linguistics & phonetics*, *18*(6-8), 495–505. https://doi.org/10.1080/02699200410001703600

Logan, S. W., Robinson, L. E., Wilson, A. E., and Lucas, W. A. (2012). Getting the fundamentals of movement: a meta-analysis of the effectiveness of motor skill interventions in children. *Child: care, health and development, 38*(3), 305–315. https://doi.org/10.1111/j.1365-2214.2011.01307.x

Nip, Ignatius S B, and Jordan R Green. (2013). Increases in cognitive and linguistic processing primarily account for increases in speaking rate with age. *Child development*, *84*(4), 1324–1337. https://doi.org/10.1111/cdev.12052

Pindzola, R. H., Jenkins, M. M., and Lokken, K. J. (1989). Speaking rates of young children. *Language, Speech, and Hearing Services in the Schools, 20*, 133–138. https://doi.org/10.1044/0161-1461.2002.133

Redford, M. A. (2015). The perceived clarity of children's speech varies as a function of their default articulation rate. *The Journal of the Acoustical Society of America, 135*(5), 2952–2963. https://doi.org/10.1121/1.4869820

Rispoli, M., and Hadley, P. (2001). The leading-edge: The significance of sentence disruptions in the development of grammar. *Journal of Speech, Language, and Hearing Research, 44*(5), 1131–1143. https://doi.org/10.1044/1092-4388(2001/089)

Ryan, B. P. (2000). Speaking rate, conversational speech acts, interruption, and linguistic complexity of 20 pre-school stuttering and non-stuttering children and their mothers. *Clinical linguistics & phonetics*, *14*(1), 25–51. https://doi.org/10.1080/026992000298931

Schelten-Cornish, S. (2007). The Significance of Speaking Rate in Speech Treatment, *Die Sprachheilarbeit, 4*, 136 - 145.

Smith, A. B., Hall, N. E., Tan, X., and Farrell, K. (2011). Speech timing and pausing in children with specific language impairment. *Clinical linguistics and phonetics, 25*(2), 145–154. https://doi.org/10.3109/02699206.2010.514969

Smith, A. B., Roberts, J., Lambrecht Smith, S., Locke, J. L., and Bennett, J. (2006). Reduced speaking rate as an early predictor of reading disability. *American journal of speech-language pathology, 15*(3), 289–297. https://doi.org/10.1044/1058-0360(2006/027)

Sturm, J. A., and Seery, C. H. (2007). Speech and articulatory rates of school-age children in conversation and narrative contexts. *Language, speech, and hearing services in schools, 38*(1), 47–59. https://doi.org/10.1044/0161-1461(2007/005)

Tendera, Anna., Rispoli, Matthew., Ambikaipakan Senthilselvan, Torrey M Loucks. (2019). Early speech rate development: A longitudinal study.

Journal of Speech, Language, and Hearing Research, 62(12), 4370-4381. https://doi.org/10.1044/2019_JSLHR-19-00145

Tingley, Beth. M., and Allen, George. D. (1975). Development of speech timing control in children. *Child Development, 46*(1), 186–194. https://doi.org/10.2307/1128847

Tremblay, P., Sato, M., & Deschamps, I. (2017). Age differences in the motor control of speech: An fMRI study of healthy aging. *Human brain mapping, 38*(5), 2751–2771. https://doi.org/10.1002/hbm.23558

Walker, J. F., and Archibald, L. M. (2006). Articulation rate in preschool children: a 3-year longitudinal study. *International journal of language and communication disorders, 41*(5), 541–565. https://doi.org/10.1080/10428190500343043

Walker, J. F., Archibald,L.M.D., Cherniak,S.R., and Fish,V.G. (1992). Articulation rate in 3- and 5-year-old children. *Journal of Speech and Hearing Research, 35*, 4–13. https://doi.org/10.1044/jshr.3501.04

Yairi, E., Ambrose, N. G., Paden, E. P., and Throneburg, R. N. (1996). Predictive factors of persistence and recovery: Pathways of childhood stuttering. *Journal of Communication Disorders, 29*(1), 51–77. https://doi.org/10.1016/0021-9924(95)00051-8

Yaruss, J. Scott. (1997). *Clinical Measurement of Stuttering Behaviors.*

The 34th Conference on Computational Linguistics and Speech Processing (ROCLING 2022)
Taipei, Taiwan, November 21-22, 2022. The Association for Computational Linguistics and Chinese Language Processing

Right-Dominant Tones in Zhangzhou: On and Through Phonetic Surface

Yishan Huang
Linguistics Department
The University of Sydney
yishan.huang@sydney.edu.au

Abstract

This study conducts a systematic acoustic exploration into the phonetic nature of rightmost tones in a right-dominant tone sandhi system based on empirical data from 21 native speakers of Zhangzhou Southern Min, which presents eight tonal contrasts at the underlying level. The results reveal that, (a) the F0 contour shape realisation of rightmost tones in Zhangzhou appears not to be categorically affected by their preceding tones. (b) Seven out of eight rightmost tones have two statistically significantly different variants in their F0 onset realisation, indicating their regressive sensitivity to the offset phonetics of preceding tones. (c) The forms of rightmost tones are not straightforward related to their counterparts in citation. Instead, two versions of the F0 system can be identified, with the unmarked forms resembling their citation values and the marked forms occurring as a consequence of the phonetic impact of their preceding tones and the F0-declining effect of utterance-final position. (d) The phonetic variation of rightmost tones reflects the across-linguistic tendency of tonal articulation in connected speech but contradicts the default principle for identifying the right dominance of tone sandhi in Sinitic languages.

Keywords: Right-dominant tones, Zhangzhou

1 Introduction

The realisations of tones can be alternated when they come into contact with one other in connected speech. The process of contextually triggered tonal alternation is referred to as tone sandhi in the linguistic literature (Benedict, 1948; Pike, 1948; Leiste, 1976; Gandour, 1978; Ballard, 1988; Chen, 2002; Zhang, 2007; Ratliff, 2015). Amongst those languages where tone sandhi is prevalent, they vary considerably in the way that tones change, what has motivated tones to change, and under what domain tones are supposed to change, resulting in a dynamic and diverse profile of tone sandhi as a language phenomenon particularly. This can be straightforward illustrated by the classification of the tone sandhi system in Sinitic languages, which is conventionally categorised into either right-dominant or left-dominant, depending on the position where syllables are supposed to retain the forms of their corresponding citation tones and keep the range of tonal contrasts. For example, Shanghainese and many Wu dialects are often reported to exhibit a left-dominant sandhi system, in which the initial syllables preserve their citation forms and syntagmatically extend the realisations rightwards over the entire sandhi domain (Ballard, 1998; Chen, 2000; Duanmu, 2005; Zhang, 2007). In contrast, other Sinitic languages like Southern Wu and most Min are classified as having a right-dominant sandhi system because the final (rightmost) syllables are assumed to remain the tonal contrasts and values of citation forms, while those of non-final tones are replaced by their corresponding sandhi forms (Wright, 1983; Shih, 1986; Ballard, 1988; Chen, 2000; Zhang, 2007; Rose, 2016).

Thus, the preservation of citation forms has been regarded as a default principle to classify the dominancy of a tone sandhi system. However, are the citation forms intactly preserved without any change? Are the forms not affected by the surrounding contexts, even at the phonetic level? Does not the continuous motion of vocal apparatus in connected speech production cause any effect on the realisation of tones at the dominant/prominent position? These have been open questions to be addressed because there is still a lack of systematic investigations to clarify such concerns in the literature. It is thus still far from the satisfaction that an insightful picture can be provided to shape and deepen our understanding in this regard.

Driven by these intriguing questions, this study is designed to explore to what extent the citation forms are preserved for those tones at the rightmost position of multisyllabic constructions. It is built upon a relatively large scale of empirical data from 21 native speakers of Zhangzhou Southern Min that presents a typical right-dominant tone sandhi with eight tonal contrasts at the underlying level. Acoustic normalisations on tonal F0 and duration are applied to abstract away variable indexical content from invariable linguistic content in speech signals, while the statistical technique of pairwise t-test is conducted to examine whether the F0 realisation of rightmost tones is affected by their preceding tones; if so, to what extent they are affected, and what conditions the variation?

Incorporating field linguistics, phonetics, phonology, and statistical testing gives this study a strong foundation of generalisable samples, objective instruments, and scientific patterns while helping this study achieve a higher level of generalisation and explanation. It directly fills in the research gap in the tonal study of this dialect. It also sheds important light on those Asian languages that exhibit tone sandhi as an important phenomenon in their sound systems.

2 Zhangzhou and Speech

Zhangzhou 漳州, romanised differently as Chiang Chiu or Changchow, is a prefecture-level city situated in the Southern Fujian province of Mainland China, with the latitude and longitude coordinates at 24.5130° N, 117.6471° E. It faces the Taiwan Strait to its east; borders the Fujian cities of Xiamen, Quanzhou, and Longyan on its east, northwest, and west, respectively, while its southwest region borders the Chaozhou city of Guangzhou province. Zhangzhou covers an area of approximately 12,600 square kilometres, with a registered population of about 5.6 million in the 2020 census. The language spoken by native people is predominantly Southern Min (known as Hokkien), which is mutually intelligible with Southern Min varieties of Quanzhou, Xiamen and Taiwan; it has a certain degree of mutual intelligibility with Teochew and Leizhou Southern Min but is unintelligible with other Chinese dialects (e.g., Mandarin, Hakka, Cantonese, Wu, Xiang, and Gan). Mandarin, as the official language of China, is commonly used on public occasions. Hakka dialect is also found but only spoken by a relatively small population living in western mountainous areas, like Hua'an, Nanjing, Pinghe, and Zhao'an counties which border a major Hakka-speaking city of Longyan (FCCEC, 1998; Guo, 2014).

As a consequence of long-standing maritime trade, the speech of Zhangzhou, along with other Southern Min dialects (e.g., Xiamen and Quanzhou), has been spread to many regions in Asia since the early 12th century and historically served as a lingua franca among Chinese communities, such as Singapore, Malaysia, and Indonesia (Ma, 1994). Therefore, the locality must be clarified when conducting a rigorous linguistic study of Zhangzhou's speech. The research area being concerned in this study is Longwen and Xiangcheng, the inner districts of Zhangzhou city in Fujian province. Restricting research area in specific urban regions help in minimising the effects of regional variations while specifying the research aim to examine how tonal realisations in the citation and dominant contexts are related from a scientific and statistical point of view.

3 Research Material and Design

3.1 Stimulus

The data being addressed were obtained by the author in 2015 in the urban districts of Xiangcheng and Longwen of Zhangzhou city from 21 native speakers (9 males and 12 females). They were selected based on a set of criteria that included age, intellectual curiosity, physical condition, birthplace, language environment, occupation, education, and competence in another language (s), with an average age of 56.5 for males and 50 for females. The corpus incorporated about 588 disyllabic phrases for investigating tone sandhi behaviour across 64 (=8 tones * 8 tones) disyllabic tonal combinations and about 160 monosyllabic morphemes for the citation tone investigation. Tokens were chosen across syllable types and contained comparable numbers of onsets with different manners and places of articulation and vowels of varying height and backness to maximally balance the intrinsic perturbation effects on tonal F0 from tautosyllabic segments. They were recorded from individual speakers in an acoustically absorbent room of Zhangzhou Hotel via a professional cardioid condenser microphone at a sampling frequency of 44100 Hz.

3.2 Acoustic Processing

The obtained field data were acoustically processed in Praat, with the tonally relevant duration identified as incorporating all elements except syllable onsets. The durational onset was set at the glottal pulse, where the amplitude of air pressure fluctuation began to increase; the periodicity of speech wave vibration appeared regular, and the formant patterns in the spectrogram were stable and identifiable. The offset was set at the point where periodicity and formant patterns ceased to be visible. Figure 1 illustrates how tonally relevant duration was identified in this study. Based on the labelled duration, F0 and duration values were extracted using a script at 10 equidistant sampling points.

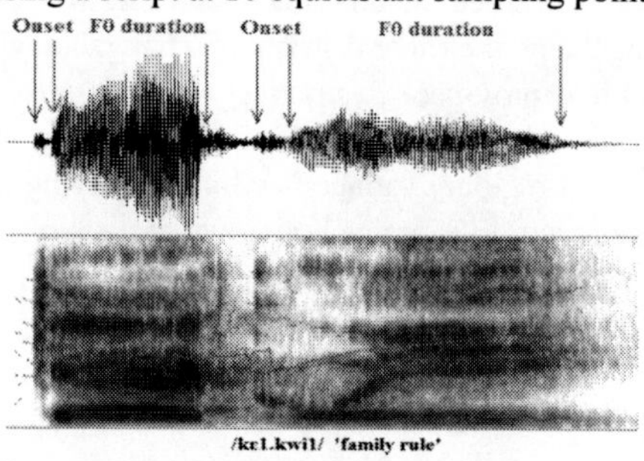

Figure 1: Praat labelled disyllabic example /kɛ1.kwi1/ 'family rule' (WYF, male).

Because acoustic signals are easily affected by extralinguistic information, such as speakers' sociocultural background, pragmatic intent, vocal tract anatomy, and physiology (Anderson, 1978; Ladefoged, 1999; Harrington, 2010; Rose, 1987, 2016), processes of normalisation were applied to abstract away the variable indexical context from the invariable linguistic content in this study. These included the z-score approach for F0 normalisation as in formula (1) and the absolute approach for duration normalisation as in (2) (Huang et al., 2016; Huang 2018; 2020).

$$Z_i=(X_i-m)/s \quad (1)$$

$$D_{norm}=(D/D_{mean})*100 \quad (2)$$

In (1), m and s, separately, stand for the raw mean F0 value and the standard deviation estimated from all sampling F0 values for all tokens of all tones in a specific context from a given speaker. X_i is an observed F0 value at a given sampling point, while Z_i is its corresponding normalised value derived as the distance from the mean F0 value, corresponding to the speakers' neutral pitch. In (2), D_{mean} represents the mean raw duration estimated from the average duration of all tokens in all tones from individual speakers. D is the duration observed for a given tone, while D_{norm} is its corresponding normalised value expressed as a percentage of the average duration of all tones from the speaker being considered.

3.3 Statistical Testing

This study applied the statistical technique of pairwise t-test by effect sizes to determine (a) whether the F0 realisations of tones at the right-dominant position are statistically significantly affected by their preceding tones. (b) If yes, to what extent are they affected, and what conditions the variations? The application of this testing requested all possible pairwise comparisons of the values derived from acoustic quantification and normalisation. For example, each tone would have 28 (8*7/2) paired normalised F0 differences at the 10% sampling point to be tested and examined whether its onset realisation was significantly affected by the offset of preceding tones. The Bonferroni correction was performed to control for the Type I Error and achieve significance (Levshina, 2015; Huang 2018). The corrected alpha was calculated by dividing the critical P value by the number of comparisons being considered. The testing result was visualised using the hierarchical clustering algorithm, and the threshold at one was consistently selected to determine the distance for significance.

4 Zhangzhou Citation Tones

Numerous works have documented Zhangzhou citation tones. However, the majority of studies are impressionistic and describe a seven-way tonal contrast (Dong, 1959; Lin, 1992; Ma, 1994; FJG, 1998; ZJG, 1999; Gao, 1999; Zhou, 2006; Chen, 2007; Yang, 2008; Guo, 2014; Huang et al., 2016). Huang (2018; 2020)'s studies were principally acoustic and advocated an eight-tonal system based on the assertion that, (a) relying on one single context of citation, and a single parameter of F0/pitch is not sufficient to figure out the totality of tonal contrasts, because tonal neutralisation occurs across linguistic contexts, including the citation position; and tones that have similar F0 contour can differ significantly in other parameter.

As an extension to explore the nature of Zhangzhou tones in synchronic speech, this study adopts the eight-tone proposal. The pitch system of the eight tones in the citation is summarised in Table 1 with examples of (semi-) minimal pairs and their corresponding Middle Chinese (MC) tonal categories, making them diachronically traceable

The 34th Conference on Computational Linguistics and Speech Processing (ROCLING 2022)
Taipei, Taiwan, November 21-22, 2022. The Association for Computational Linguistics and Chinese Language Processing

and synchronically comparable with other Sinitic dialects. Figure 2 visualises the F0 pattern of the eight citation tones in Zhangzhou derived from quantifying 21 speakers' monosyllabic utterances.

Tone		Pitch/F0	Example
1	Yinping	mid rising [35]	/kɔ/ 'mushroom'
2	Yangping	mid-low level [22]	/kɔ/ 'glue'
3	Shang	high falling [51]	/kɔ/ 'drum'
4	Yinqu	mid-high falling [41]	/kɔ/ 'look after'
5	Yangqu	mid level [33]	/hɔ/ 'rain'
6	Yinru	stopped mid-high falling [41]	/kɔk/ 'country'
7	Yangru	stopped mid-low level [221]	/tɔk/ 'poison'
8	Yangru	mid-low level [22]	/kɔ̃/ 'snore'

Table 1. Pitch system of Zhangzhou citation tones.

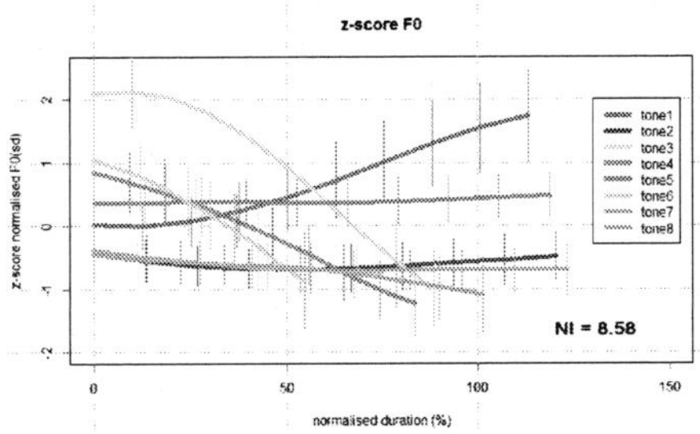

Figure 2: F0 pattern of Zhangzhou citation tones.

As indicated, Zhangzhou citation tones vary considerably in pitch/F0. Three contour shapes—rising (tone 1), level (tones 2, 5, and 8), and falling (tones 3, 4, 6, and 7)— and four contour heights—mid-low (tones 2, 7, and 8), mid (tones 1, and 5), mid-high (tones4, and 6), and high (tone 3)—can be identified in the F0 inventory. Tones 4 and 6 appear to have a similar mid-high falling contour [41] in the citation context, but the duration of tone 6 is shorter. Tones 2 and 8 share a similar low-level contour [22] in the citation. Still, they are observed behaving differently in the sandhi (non-rightmost) environment, with tone 2 being realised as a mid-level [33] and tone 8 as a mid-falling [32] (Huang 2018; 2020). In other words, tones with a similar F0/pitch contour can differ considerably in other phonetic parameters and linguistic contexts. The description serves as a reference to investigate to what extent the citation forms are preserved in the rightmost position of disyllabic constructions and to what extent the realisations of rightmost tones are affected by their preceding tones.

5 Right Dominance of Zhangzhou Tone Sandhi

Zhangzhou presents a typical right-dominant tone sandhi system. This can be justified from three major aspects. The first significant aspect is that the realisations of those non-rightmost tones are changed to forms entirely different from their citation forms at both phonological and phonetic levels. This can be seen from Table 2 about the pitch realisation of eight individual tones before tone 2, patterned in X+2 where X refers to tone number. For example, the pitch of tone 3 is changed to a mid-rising [25] from a high-falling contour [51] in the citation. In addition, neutralisation processes occur in this non-rightmost context: tones 1 and 2 are neutralised to a mid-level [33]; while tones 5, 7 and 8 neutralise their pitches to a mid-falling [32] before tone 2. These two characteristics in the non-rightmost position can be demonstrated by the acoustic pattern in Figure 3, which is derived from normalising 21 speakers' disyllabic utterances.

X+2	Non-right	Citation	Example
1+2	[33]	[35]	/tsʰɛ̃1.tɛ2/ 'raw tea'
2+2	[33]	[22]	/ʔɐŋ2.tɛ2/ 'black tea'
3+2	[25]	[51]	/tsɐ3.tɛ2/ 'morning tea'
4+2	[63]	[41]	/swɐ̃4.tɛ2/ 'unpacked tea'
5+2	[32]	[33]	/ʔjɔŋ5.tɛ2/ 'have tea'
6+2	[65]	[41]	/sip6.tɛ2/ 'moisten tea'
7+2	[32]	[221]	/sik7.tɛ2/ 'colorful tea'
8+2	[32]	[22]	/pɛ8.tɛ2/ 'Bai tea'

Table 2. Examples of X+2 sandhi pattern.

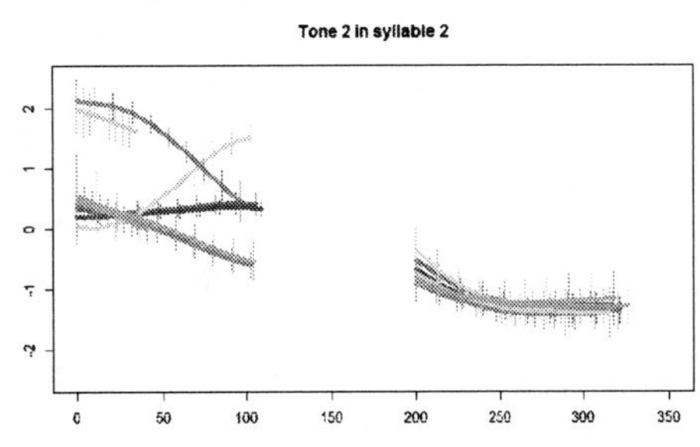

Figure 3: F0 contours of X+2 pattern in Zhangzhou.

This third significant aspect is that the pitch contours of the rightmost tones are observed to be categorically similar to their corresponding citation forms. This can be seen from Table 3 about the pitches of eight individual tones after tone 2. For example, tone 5 is realised as a mid-level [33] in the 2+5 pattern as in the citation. However, the realisations are not always straightforwardly the same because the contour onsets of rightmost tones are observed as being phonetically sensitive to surrounding contexts and present variations. For example, tones 2 and 8 are realised as [211] in the rightmost position but as [22] in the citation. Such a slight phonetic difference can be ascribed to be affected by the effect of final-position declination. The two characteristics of rightmost tones (contour shape preservation and contour onset variation) can be demonstrated in Figure 4, which plots the normalised F0 contours of the 2+X pattern.

2+X	Right	Citation	Example
2+**1**	[34]	[35]	/tɛ2.hwɐ1/ 'camellia'
2+**2**	[211]	[22]	/tɛ2.dɐw2/ 'tea house'
2+**3**	[52]	[51]	/tɛ2.ɓi3/ 'dried tea'
2+**4**	[41]	[41]	/tɛ2.tjɐm4/ 'tea store'
2+**5**	[33]	[33]	/tɛ2.tsʰju5/ 'tea tree'
2+**6**	[41]	[41]	/tɛ2.sik6/ 'tea colour'
2+**7**	[211]	[221]	/tɛ2.sit7/ 'tea dessert'
2+**8**	[211]	[22]	/tɛ2.ɦjɵ8/ 'tea leaf'

Table 3. Examples of 2+X sandhi pattern.

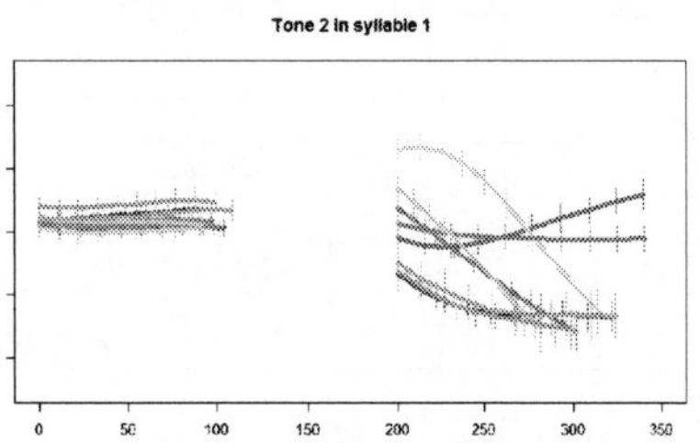

Figure 4: F0 contours of 2+X pattern in Zhangzhou.

As seen, the contour shape preservation of citation forms in the rightmost context justifies the existence of a right dominant tone sandhi system in Zhangzhou. However, the observed contour onset variations conflict with the general assumption that the rightmost tones are straightforwardly related to the citation tones, with the citation-tone pitch values preserved and unchanged. It thus appears to be a crucial issue to investigate to what extent the citation forms are preserved, and to what extent the rightmost tones are affected by surrounding phonetics, and how such effects can be justified and generalised using scientific methods and modern linguistic theories. These are about to be discussed in the next section in the hope of superseding our understanding of the right dominancy in tonal languages.

6 Phonetics of Rightmost Tones

This section discusses the acoustic property of individual rightmost tones as a function of their preceding tones in disyllabic phrases of Zhangzhou speech. Figure 5 plots the acoustic patterns and the clustering results of pairwise t-tests derived from empirical data from 21 native speakers, representing the central tendency of Zhangzhou speech as an independent variety.

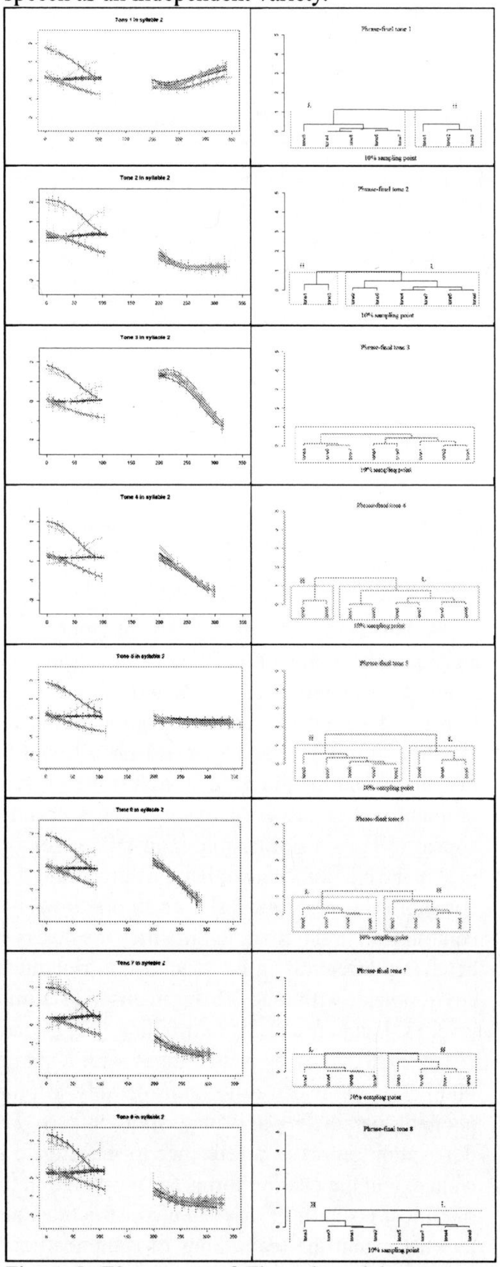

Figure 5: F0 patterns of Zhangzhou rightmost tones from 21 native speakers.

Tone 1-Yinping: all normalised F0 contours of rightmost tone 1 are rising as a function of eight preceding tones but have variation at the onset that can be justified by the pairwise t-test comparison by effect sizes. As shown on the right panel of Figure 5, the normalised F0 values representing different X+1 patterns are clustered into two groups at the 10% sampling point, with the value significantly higher after tones 1, 2, and 3 than it is after other tones. The common feature of tones 1, 2 and 3 at the non-right position is [-falling]. Thus, it can be generalised that if a preceding tone has the feature of [-falling], the onset value of tone 1 is statistically significantly higher.

Tone 2-Yangping: all normalised F0 contours of tone 2 are falling with a low-level plateau during the second half across different combinations. The pairwise t-tests reveal statistically significant but marginal differences in the F0 onset, with the values higher after tone 3 than after any other tones at the 10% sampling point. The conditioning factor appears to be contour-relevant because the phrase-initial tone 3 presents a rising trend. Thus, it can be generalised that if the preceding tone has a [-falling; -level] feature, the onset value of tone 2 turns out to be statistically significantly higher.

Tone 3-Shang: the F0 contours of rightmost tone 3 consistently show a high-falling tendency across X+3 patterns. Statistically, the pairwise *t*-test comparisons reveal no significant difference among the normalised F0 values of this tone at the 10% sampling point. This can be seen in Figure 5. The eight tonal combinations are clustered into one single net. Thus, the F0 realisation of this rightmost tone 3 is unaffected by its preceding tones. This may be ascribed to its high onset value, which is high enough that made it not easy to be affected.

Tone 4-Yinqu: the F0 contours of this tone are consistently falling across different combinations but with slight differences in the onset values. The statistical testing result reveals that its F0 values are significantly higher after tones 3 and 6 than after other tones. This can be seen from the figure that tones 3 and 6 are clustered together at the 10% sampling point. Thus, the F0 onset realisation of the phrase-final tone 4 is also sensitive to the F0 offset of preceding tones. If the preceding tone possesses a feature of [+high offset] (shared by tones 3 and 6), its onset is supposed to be statistically significantly higher.

Tone 5-Yangqu: this tone consistently presents a level contour around the midpoint across all tonal combinations. The pairwise t-testing result reveals that its onset values are significantly affected by the offset of preceding tones; as shown in Figure 5, the eight terminal nodes are clustered into two groups at the 10% sampling point. The values tested are significantly lower after tones 4, 5, and 8, which share a falling trend with a low offset. Thus, the conditioning factor for its onset variation can be generalised as [falling; low offset]. If the preceding tone has a downward contour [+falling] with an offset lower than the midpoint [+low offset], the onset of this tone 5 is supposed to be statistically significantly lower, and vice versa.

Tone 6-Yinru: all normalised F0 contours of this tone are falling as a function of the non-rightmost tones but with variation in the onset height. As shown in the figure, the terminal nodes on the right panel have been clustered into two groups at the 10% sampling point, with the values being significantly higher after tones 1, 2, 3, and 6 have an offset at or above the midpoint. Thus, similar to the variation in tone 5, if preceded by a tone that has a [+high offset] at or above the midpoint, the onset of this tone is supposed to be statistically significantly higher, and vice versa.

Tone 7-Yangru: the F0 contours of this tone all present a falling tendency with a low-level plateau across X+7 patterns but also have considerable variation in onset values. As visualised in Figure 5, the eight tones on the right panel, signifying the eight combinations that the tone is assigned with, are clustered into two groups at the 10% sampling point, with the values after tones 1, 2, 3, and 6 being significantly higher than the values in another group. Therefore, the F0 onset realisations of tone 7 are also sensitive to preceding tones. The conditioning factor can also be generalised as [low offset] and [falling]. If the preceding tone has a non-falling contour with an offset at or above the midpoint, featured as [-low offset] and [-falling], the onset of this tone 7 should be statistically significantly higher, and vice versa.

Tone 8-Yangru (New tone): similar to tones 2 and 7, the normalised F0 contours of this tone are all falling in the first half but tend to be level in the second across X+8 combinations, as seen in Figure 5. The onset realisation is also regressively sensitive to the phonetics of preceding tones, with the values significantly higher after tones 1, 2, 3, and 6 than after other tones at the 10% sampling point; however, the effect appears to be marginal. Similarly, the conditioning environment for the onset variations of tone 8 can also be generalised as [low offset] and [falling]. If the preceding tone is featured of [-low offset] and [-falling], the onset of this tone is supposed to be statistically significantly higher, and vice versa.

7 Onset Variations of Rightmost Tones

As described above, the contour shapes of rightmost tones are generally not affected by preceding tones because regardless of whether preceded by a rising, falling or levelling contour, each rightmost tone is seen having its contour shape consistently the same. However, the contour height of most rightmost tones is phonetically sensitive to the contour offset of preceding tones, causing them to have dynamic variations in F0 onset values that are tested to be statistically significantly different. This section summarises how the F0 onsets of rightmost tones are affected by the non-right ones and how their forms are related to corresponding citation values.

(1) The F0 realisation of right-most tones does not always resemble their citation forms, although they are very similar in contour shape. This can be seen in Table 4, which showcases the F0 values of the eight rightmost tones across 64 tonal combinations. The top row shows the eight tones concerned with their corresponding citation F0 values for comparison. In contrast, the leftmost column shows the non-rightmost tones with their sandhi F0 values to examine how they affect their following tones. The divergence between the rightmost forms and citation forms can be ascribed to two significant factors. One is their phonetic sensitivity to the F0 offset of preceding tones, causing them to have dynamic and diverse outputs at the surface level, as discussed above. The other factor may be ascribed to the pitch/F0 declination effect in the utterance-final position (Lieberman, 1967; Pierrehumbert, 1987; Maeda, 1976; Cohen et al., 1982; Ladd, 1984; Yuan & Liberman, 2010; Rose, 2014). They appear to have a lower F0 height than their citation forms. For example, tones 2, 7, and 8 are realised as either [211] or [311] in the phrase-final context, with a low-level plateau about one degree lower than that in citation [22]. Apart from the F0-declining effect, the F0 range of the rightmost tones appears lower than that of the non-rightmost tones. This can be seen from the F0 contour distributions in Figure 5, in which the normalised F0 range is between -0.84 and 2.33 for the non-rightmost tones but between -1.7 and 1.64 for the rightmost tones. Such a lowering F0 range may also be considered a declining effect of the utterance-final position.

Tone	T1 [31]	T2 [22]	T3 [51]	T4 [41]	T5 [33]	T6 [41]	T7 [221]	T8 [22]
T1[33]	35	211	52	41	33	41	211	211
T2[33]	35	211	52	41	33	41	211	211
T3[25]	34	311	52	51	33	51	311	311
T4[63]	34	211	52	41	33	41	211	211
T5[32]	35	211	52	41	33	41	211	211
T6[65]	34	311	52	51	33	51	311	311
T7[32]	35	211	52	41	33	41	211	211
T8[32]	35	211	52	41	33	41	211	211

Table 4. F0 inventory of rightmost tones across 64 tonal combinations.

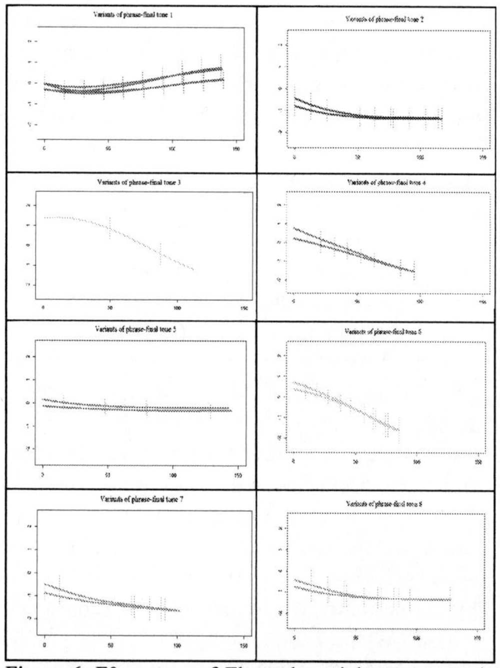

Figure 6: F0 system of Zhangzhou rightmost tones in disyllabic tonal combinations from 21 native speakers.

(2) The F0 contour shapes of rightmost tones tend not to be categorically affected by the tones that precede them. Regardless of whether the preceding tone has a rising, level, or falling F0 contour, the individual rightmost tones present a consistent tendency in their contour shape across different combinations. In other words, the change of contour shape of their preceding tones does not cause any categorical change in their contour realisation. For example, as plotted in Figure 5, tone 1 consistently presents a rising contour, while tone 3 shows a falling contour in any tonal combination. In addition, the contour shape of individual rightmost tones remains categorically

the same as their corresponding citation form. For example, tone 1 presents a rising contour in both the phrase-final (rightmost) position and the citation. This property to a great degree justifies the right-dominancy of the tone sandhi system in this dialect because no paradigmatic substitution occurs for the tones in this position, though they are connected with other tones within the same constructions.

(3) The rightmost tones do not always have an identical F0 realisation as a function of their preceding tones. All tones except tone 3 have two statistically significantly different variants in their onset height because of their phonetic sensitivity to the F0 offset of the tones that precede them. This can be seen in Figure 6, which plots all F0 variants that can be identified based on the acoustic quantification and pairwise t-testing results. In general, the F0 contours tend to have a statistically significantly higher onset after tones ending in a [-low offset] and [-falling] but have a lower onset if the preceding tone is characteristic of [+falling] and [+low offset]. The two different versions of onset realisation, although predictable, raise a theoretical issue as to which onset form, the raised F0 or the lowered F0, should be considered as the unmarked form for the underlying representation and which one should be treated as the derived form that occurs in a marked context.

8 Discussion

As discussed, most rightmost tones have two statistically significantly different F0 onsets. Incorporating the auditory observation, acoustic distribution, position-induced depressing effect, and the correlation with citation form, it is appropriate to consider the lowered F0 onset as the unmarked form while the raised one as the marked form whose occurrence is motivated by the F0 offset of preceding tone. Thus, a linguistically phonetic F0 system of the rightmost tones can be derived and represented using numerical notation, with 5 indicating the highest F0 level and 1 the lowest, as summarised in Table 5, along with the citation values for comparison purposes.

Tone	Rightmost		Citation
	Unmark	**Marked**	
1	[34]	[35]	[35]
2	[211]	[311]	[22]
3	[52]	[52]	[51]
4	[41]	[51]	[41]
5	[33]	[43]	[33]
6	[41]	[51]	[41]
7	[211]	[311]	[221]
8	[211]	[311]	[22]

Table 5. A linguistically phonetic F0 system of Zhangzhou's rightmost tones in disyllabic construction.

The unmarked forms of the rightmost tones generally resemble their corresponding citation forms. Tones 2, 7, and 8 have a lower levelling trend that can reasonably be considered a consequence of the pitch/F0 declining effect of utterance-final position. The marked forms of most tones have one degree higher than their unmarked and citation forms, which is predicted to occur as regressive assimilation to preceding tones that are featured [-low offset] and [-falling].

The phonetic sensitivity, on the one hand, reflects the across-linguistic phenomenon of tonal coarticulation, particularly concerning the carryover effect (i.e., the influence of the preceding tones on phrase-final tones) (e.g., Scholz & Chen 2014; Xu 1994; Zhang & Liu 2011). Such a dynamic tonal behaviour is not arbitrary. Still, it reflects a continuous motion of the vocal apparatus of human beings in speech production, which can cause considerable overlapping in articulatory gestures while giving rise to diverse outputs that can be perceived and generalised in real-world data. However, on the other hand, this linguistic finding of Zhangzhou right-most tones contradicts and challenges the default principle for the identification of the right-dominance of tone sandhi in Sinitic languages, which considers that the right-dominant tones are straightforwardly related to their corresponding citation tones, with the citation values preserved and unchanged (e.g., Wright 1983; Shih 1986; Ballard 1988; Chen 2000; Zhang 2007). As discussed above, a set of marked forms are statistically justified as utterly different from the citation forms. Thus, tones behave far more dynamically than expected, but the behaviours are generally predictable following an intrinsic set of grammar that can be generalized and justified using scientific patterns.

References

Stephen R Anderson. 1978. Tone features. In Victoria Fromkin (Ed.), *Tone: A linguistic survey* (pp. 133-175). New York, NY: Academic Press.

William Ballard. 1988. The history and development of tonal systems and tone alternations in South China (Vol. 22). *Study of Languages and Cultures of Asia and Africa*: Monograph Series 22.

Paul K Benedict. 1948. Tonal systems in Southeast Asia. *Journal of the American Oriental Society*, 68, 184-191.

Matthew Y Chen. 2000. *Tone sandhi*. Cambridge, England: Cambridge University Press.

Zhengtong Chen. 2007. *Southern Min dictionary of Zhangzhou variety*. Beijing, China: Zhonghua Shuju.

Antonie Cohen, Rene Collier and Johan 't Hart. 1982. Declination: Construct or intrinsic feature of speech pitch? *Phonetica*, 39, 254-273.

Tonghe Dong. 1959. *Four Southern Min varieties*. Taipei: Zhongyang Yanjiuyuan.

San Duanmu. 2005. The tone-syntax interface in Chinese: Some recent controversies. *Proceedings of the Symposium Cross-Linguistic Studies of Tonal Phenomena, Historical Development, Tone-Syntax Interface, and Descriptive Studies*, (pp. 16-17).

FCCEC. 1998. *Fujian Province Gazette-Dialect Volume*. Beijing, China: Fangzhi Chubanshe.

Jackson T Gandour. 1978. The perception of tone. In Victoria Alexandra Fromkin (Ed.), *Tone: A linguistic survey* (pp. 41-76). New York, NY: Academic Press.

Ran Gao. 1999. Introduction to the sound system of Zhangzhou. In *Minnan dialect-studies of Zhangzhou variety* (pp. 109-116). Beijing, China: Zhongguo Wenlian Chubanshe.

Jinfu Guo. 2014. *Zhangzhou Southern Min*. Zhangzhou, China: Zhangzhou Library.

Jonathan Harrington. 2010. Acoustic phonetics. In William. J. Hardcastle, John Laver and Fiona E Gibbon (Eds.), *The handbook of phonetic sciences* (2nd ed., pp. 81-129). Hoboken, NJ: Wiley-Blackwell.

Yishan Huang, Mark Donohue, Paul Sidwell and Phil Rose. 2016. Normalization of Zhangzhou citation tones. In C. Carignan, & M. Tyler (Eds.), *Proceedings 16th Australasian International Conference on Speech Science & Technology*, (pp. 217-220). Sydney, Australia: The Australian Speech Science & Technology Association.

D Robert Ladd. 1984. Declination: A review and some hypotheses. *Phonology* 1, 53-74.

Peter Ladefoged. 1999. Instrumental techniques for linguistic phonetic fieldwork. In William Hardcastle, John Laver, and Fiona Gibbon (Eds.), *The Handbook of Phonetic Sciences*. Blackwell Reference Online. Retrieved from http://www.blackwellreference.com/subscriber/tocnode.html?id=g9780631214786_chunk_g97806312147865

Natalia Levshina. 2015. *How to do Linguistics with R: data exploration and statistical analysis*. Amsterdam, Netherlands: John Benjamins Publishing Company.

Philip Lieberman. 1967. *Intonation, perception and language*. Cambridge, MA: MIT Press.

Baoqin Lin. 1992. Zhangzhou vocabularies. *Fangyan*, 1-3.

Chongqi Ma. 1994. *Studies of Zhangzhou dialect*. Hongkong: Zongheng Chubanshe.

Shinji Maeda. 1976. *A characterisation of American English intonation*. Cambridge, MA: MIT Press.

Janet Pierrehumbert 1989. *A preliminary study of consequences of intonation for the voice source*. Stockholm, Sweden: Royal Institute of Technology, Speech Transmission Laboratory.

Kenneth L Pike. 1948. *Tone languages. A technique for determining the number and type of pitch contrasts in language, with studies in tonemic substitution and fusion*. Ann Arbor: University of Michigan Press.

Martha Ratliff. 2015. Tonoexodus, tonogenesis, and tone change. In Patrick Honeybone and Joseph Salmons (Eds.), *The Oxford handbook of historical phonology* (pp. 245-261). Oxford, England: Oxford University Press.

Phil Rose. 1987. Considerations in the normalisation of the fundamental frequency of the linguistic tone. *Speech Communication*, 6 (4), 343-352.

Phil Rose. 2016. Comparing normalisation strategies for citation tone F0 in three Chinese dialects. In C. Carignan & M. D. Tyler (Eds.), *Proceedings of the 16th Australasian International Conference on Speech Science and Technology*, (pp. 221-224). Sydney: Australian Speech Science and Technology Association.

Franziska Scholz and Yiya Chen. 2014. The independent effects of prosodic structure and information status on tonal coarticulation: Evidence from Wenzhou Chinese. In Johanneke Caspers, Yiya Chen., Willemijn Heeren, Jos Pacilly, Niels Schiller and Ellen van Zanten (Eds). *Above and Beyond the Segments: Experimental Linguistics and*

Phonetics (pp. 275-287). Amsterdam, Netherland: John Benjamins Publishing Company.

Chilin Shih. 1986. *The prosodic domain of tone sandhi in Chinese* (Doctoral dissertation, University of California at San Diego). Retrieved from https://www.researchgate.net/publication/36071823_The_Prosodic_Domain_of_Tone_Sandhi_in_Chinese

Martha Susan Wright. 1983. *A metrical approach to tone sandhi in Chinese dialects* (Doctoral dissertation, University of Massachusetts Amherst). Retrieved from http://scholarworks.umass.edu/dissertations/AAI8310348

Yi Xu. 1994. Production and perception of coarticulated tones. *The Journal of the Acoustical Society of America*, 95(4), 2240-2253.

Xiuming Yang. 2008. *Studies of tones and regional cultures of Zhangzhou dialect*. Beijing, China: Zhongguo Shehui Kexue Chubanshe.

Jiahong Yuan and Mark Liberman 2010. F0 declination in *English and Mandarin broadcast news speech*. Eleventh Annual Conference of the International Speech Communication Association.

ZCCEC. 1999. *Zhangzhou City Gazette-Dialect Volume (Vol. 49)*. Beijing, China: Zhongguo Shehui Kexue Chubanshe.

Jie Zhang. 2007. A directional asymmetry in Chinese tone sandhi systems. *Journal of East Asian Linguistics*, 16, 259-302.

Jie Zhang, and Jiang Liu 2011. Tone sandhi and tonal coarticulation in Tianjin Chinese. *Phonetic*a, 68(3), 161-191.

Changyi Zhou. 2006. *The great Southern Min dictionary*. Fuzhou, China: Fujian Renmin Chubanshe.

The 34th Conference on Computational Linguistics and Speech Processing (ROCLING 2022)
Taipei, Taiwan, November 21-22, 2022. The Association for Computational Linguistics and Chinese Language Processing

支援訓練語句分析與擴增之 Web API 對話機器人生成機制
Web-API-Based Chatbot Generation with Analysis and Expansion for Training Sentences

王聖凱 (Sheng-Kai Wang)
國立臺灣海洋大學 /
202 基隆市中正區北寧路 2 號
nssh94879487@gmail.com

游婉琳 (Wan-Lin You)
國立臺灣海洋大學 /
202 基隆市中正區北寧路 2 號
gn01868184@gmail.com

馬尚彬 (Shang-Pin Ma)
國立臺灣海洋大學 /
202 基隆市中正區北寧路 2 號
albert@ntou.edu.tw

摘要

對話機器人 (Chatbot) 是近年來受到廣泛歡迎的新穎技術，在 Web API 技術日趨成熟的趨勢下，如何結合 Web API 與 Chatbot 技術也開始成為備受關注的議題。本研究規劃建立一個可基於 Web API 生成 Chatbot 之半自動化方法 BOTEN 及其實作平台，透過此方法，可協助應用程式開發者快速建置出指定 Web API 的 Chatbot 介面。為了確保 Chatbot 具備足夠的自然語言理解 (Natural Language Understanding, NLU) 能力，本研究透過 TF-IDF、WordNet 與 SpaCy 技術評估開發者撰寫的訓練語句，對品質不佳的訓練語句提出警訊，以提供訓練語句修改之建議；此外，本研究亦提出一個自動擴增訓練語句數量之方法，以進一步提升 Chatbot 的意圖辨識能力。

Abstract

With Web API technology becoming increasingly mature, how to integrate Web API and Chatbot technology has become an issue of great interest. This study plans to build a semi-automatic method and tool, BOTEN. This method allows application developers to build Chatbot interfaces with specified Web APIs quickly. To ensure that the Chatbot has sufficient natural language understanding (NLU) capability, this research evaluates the training sentences written by the developer through TF-IDF, WordNet, and SpaCy techniques, and suggests the developer modify the training sentences with poor quality. This technique can also be used to automatically increase the number of training sentences to improve the capability of Intent recognition.

關鍵字：對話機器人、Web API、Rasa、WordNet、SpaCy

Keywords: Chatbot, Web API, Rasa, WordNet, SpaCy

1 緒論

對話機器人 (Chatbot) 利用電腦程式模擬真人來與使用者互動，並透過通訊平台等介面讓使用者可以用文字或語音與其進行交談，也會搭配自然語言處理來幫助對話機器人判斷使用者意圖、實體，其應用包括電子商務、客戶服務、內容宣傳、推播通知、個人助理等 (Brandtzaeg & Følstad, 2017)。目前許多企業都開始使用對話機器人於實際的營運上，典型案例包含協助處理飯店客戶問題的機器人 (Michaud, 2018)、可協助團隊管理的機器人 (Toxtli, Monroy-Hernández, & Cranshaw, 2018)、以及作為特定領域之推薦專家的機器人 (Cerezo, Kubelka, Robbes, & Bergel, 2019) 等，在應用上相當多元。

另一方面，在 Web API 技術日趨成熟的趨勢下，越來越多的公司將自身服務包裝為 Web API，以提供給第三方開發者進行應用開發及服務整合，而延續此技術趨勢，如何結合 Web API 與 Chatbot 技術也開始成為備受關注的議題。根據 Stackoverflow 的研究調查 (Abdellatif, Costa, Badran, Abdalkareem, & Shihab, 2020)，開發者對於 Integration 類型的問題最為重視，特別是 Chatbot 與 Web API 之整合。在先前相關的研究上，Vaziri 等學者開發了 SwaggerBot (Vaziri, Mandel, Shinnar, Siméon, & Hirzel, 2017)，欲試圖解決上述之議題，SwaggerBot 是一個利用 OpenAPI 規範加入擴充規範後，透過編譯器生成的 Chatbot，Web API 之開發者只要能提供具備完整規範的

Swagger (亦稱為 OAS: OpenAPI Specification ("OpenAPI Specification," 2021)) 文件，便能編譯出一個能存取 REST API 的 Chatbot。然而，SwaggerBot 以每個 API 端點的名稱作為唯一的訓練語句，故產生的 Chatbot 自然語言理解能力較不理想，需透過 Power User 為既有功能的存取創造捷徑以及捷徑的同義詞，補強其 NLU 能力。其次，各端點之間的呼叫缺乏一個完整的故事流程規劃，所以無法提供終端使用者一個友善的使用者體驗。

我們再進一步分析 Web API 與 Chatbot 之整合工作，從開發者角度有三個較困難的環節：(1) 開發者需具備 Chatbot 開發框架的詳盡知識，需要熟悉對話流程所需的文件設定與操作步驟；(2) 需能撰寫 Chatbot 與 Web API 之轉接元件(Adapter)，除了要能透過程式將 Chatbot 之組成元素 (如 Intent、Entity、Slot 等) 與 Web API 之服務功能銜接起來，還要能妥善處理服務回應結果 (Service Response) 之呈現；(3) 需要撰寫足夠品質與數量的訓練語句，以訓練出具備足夠 NLU 能力的 Chatbot，正確判斷終端使用者的意圖(Intent)，並做出適當的回覆。因此，為能降低 Chatbot 開發之複雜度，我們採取的策略是基於模型驅動工程(Model-Driven Engineering) (Schmidt, 2006) 的概念，希望能讓開發者聚焦於 Web API 與 Chatbot 之概念整合方式，而非底層框架細節與轉接元件之開發。由於 Swagger 是目前最被廣泛運用的 Web API 之描述語言，許多 Web API 之開發者均已提供 Swagger 描述文件，以供客戶端與其他開發者運用，本研究首先遵循 Swagger 之標準擴充機制，以在 Swagger 文件中加入 Chatbot 之相關元素，再建立一個可剖析與生成 Chatbot 之執行引擎： BOTEN，來輔助開發者以半自動化的方式建構指定 Web API 之 Chatbot。

在另一方面，一般常見的 Chatbot NLU 模型都會對使用者輸入的語句辨識其背後的意圖 (Intent)，以此作為後續動作的執行依據。NLU 模型還可計算置信度 (Confidence)，代表對辨識結果的信心程度，Confidence 過低可能造成辨識錯誤。因此，為了提昇 Confidence、增強 Chatbot 的 NLU 能力，我們提供訓練語句的填寫機制，讓開發者可以填入多種不同句型的訓練語句，並對其進行評估，若是有不同意圖的訓練語句意思過於相近，會透過 BOTEN 介面對開發者提出警訊，建議開發者進行修改。建構完 Chatbot 後，亦可以讓開發者選擇是否要透過 WordNet 技術自動生成更多的訓練語句，以增強 Chatbot 的 NLU 能力。

預期的運作模式是由 Chatbot 開發者在 Web API 之 Swagger 文件上補充 Chabot 相關設定，填入訓練語句，接著將文件送至 BOTEN 系統後，即可自動生成可執行的 Chatbot，還可以進一步自動增加訓練語句，後續終端使用者即可使用此 Chatbot 系統，以對話的方式去使用 Web API 之功能，並能直接查看彙整過的服務回應結果，降低整合 Web API 與 Chatbot 的複雜度與開發成本。

2 背景知識與相關研究

2.1 Rasa

Rasa (Bocklisch, Faulkner, Pawlowski, & Nichol, 2017) 是開源的機器學習框架，可以用來創建有上下文功能的對話機器人。Rasa 框架具有 Rasa NLU、Rasa core sdk 兩個主要功能，Rasa NLU 負責自然語言的斷句、訓練 model，而 Rasa core sdk 負責之後的關鍵字抓取。在構建對話機器人時，意圖 (Intent)、動作 (Action) 和關鍵字 (Entity) 三者扮演了重要角色。意圖是指使用者語句的目的，由開發者所設定，在每個意圖當中都可以抓取關鍵字。

在 Rasa 的資料設定內也可以設定記憶變數 (Slot)。在多階段對話中記憶變數扮演了階段間溝通的角色，例如在第二階段時若需要第一階段的關鍵字，就可以使用記憶變數來進行儲存。本研究採用 Rasa 作為對話機器人之自然語言理解核心引擎。

2.2 凝聚力(Cohesion) 與耦合力(Coupling)

在軟體工程領域，凝聚力(Cohesion) 係指程式模組內部功能或資料的相依程度，耦合力 (Coupling) 則是程式模組之間的獨立程度 (Josikakar, 2021)。一般而言，開發者會希望提高 Cohesion 使程式較易維護並且適合再利用，降低 Coupling 以提高模組間的獨立程度，減少系統溝通錯誤的可能性，以達成 "High Cohesion, Low Coupling"之目標。

在撰寫 Swagger 時，我們同樣希望開發者能夠注意訓練語句之間的 Coupling，降低不同 Intent 之間訓練語句的相似度，避免因為不同 Intent 的訓練語句意思過於相近，導致訓練出的 NLU 模型發生不同 Intent 間的辨識錯誤，此外還能提高模型辨識的置信度 (Confidence)，讓訓練出的模型更加準確。至於同一意圖之下訓練語句的相似度 (Cohesion)，為了避免訓練出的 Chatbot 模型發生過度擬合 (Overfitting)，開發者應盡量撰寫多樣化的訓練語句句型，因此本研究未將 Cohesion 之改善列為研究目標。

2.3 TF-IDF、WordNet 與 SpaCy

為了提高 Chatbot 模型的自然語言理解能力，在 Swagger 文件前處理的階段，我們會利用 TF-IDF、WordNet 與 SpaCy 技術計算訓練語句之間的相似度，對不同 Intent 間意思過於相近的語句提出警訊，建議開發者修改。之後可以選擇是否要進一步利用 WordNet 將使用者輸入的訓練語句進行擴增，然後又使用 SpaCy 把擴增出的語句過濾掉與原句意思相差較大的句子，進而訓練出品質更好的模型。

TF-IDF (riturajsaha, 2022) 是一種用於資訊檢索與文字探勘的常用加權技術，為一種統計方法，用來評估單詞對於文件的集合或詞庫中一份文件的重要程度。其包含兩個部分：詞頻 (term frequency，TF) 跟逆向文件頻率 (inverse document frequency，IDF)，TF 係指某一個給定的詞語在某文件中出現的次數，IDF 則是將該詞語總共出現在幾篇文件的文件數取倒數，透過將 TF 與 IDF 相乘，即可計算給定詞語在某文件中所佔的權重。

WordNet ("What is WordNet?,") 是一個由普林斯頓大學認知科學實驗室心理學教授 George A. Miller 的指導下建立和維護的英語字典。WordNet 根據 word 的意義將它們分組，每一組具有相同意義的 word 稱為一個 synset（同義詞集合），這些集合之間也由各種關係連接。透過查詢 WordNet ，系統可以找出訓練語句中，每個 word 的同義詞，然後再排列組合出原句的多個同義句。

SpaCy ("Word vectors and semantic similarity,") 是用於自然語言處理的開源程式庫，主要開發者為 Matthew Honnibal 和 Ines Montani，其透過其語料庫中的預訓練模型來生成 word 向量，便可以用向量間的 cosine 相似度直接比較兩句的相似度。

2.4 相關研究

Telang (Telang, Kalia, Vukovic, Pandita, & Singh, 2018) 等學者為對話機器人提出了一個概念框架 (Conceptual Framework)，該概念框架由五個相關職責組成： Dialog Manager (管理自然語言對話)；Inference Engine (提取使用者意圖)；Knowledge Base (進行推理和規劃)；Planner (產生執行計畫)；External Services (結合外部功能以能實際執行對話互動)，與現有的 IFTTT (If this, then that) 框架相比，複雜的對話機器人可以透過較靈活的方式開發。

Soler (Pérez-Soler, Guerra, & Lara, 2020) 等學者提出了一種用於對話機器人開發的模型驅動工程方法，設計了 Chabot 之 meta model 和領域特定語言 (DSL: Domain Specific Language): Conga，可搭配多個 Chatbot 平台如 (Dialogflow 或 Rasa) 的程式碼解析器 (Parser) 與程式碼生成器 (Generator)，以生成 Chatbot。此方法亦提供一個平台推薦器，可根據 DSL 建議合適的目標 Chatbot 平台。

Pietro (Chittò, Baez, Daniel, & Benatallah, 2020) 等學者提出一個對話機器人生成方法，其透過網頁 HTML 之標註 (annotation) 去生成對話機器人，可設定意圖、對話語句、關鍵字、類別。此方法希望達成對話式網站瀏覽，即基於自然語言對話，讓使用者可以透過「與網站交談」來查詢所需之內容和功能，不透過鍵盤和滑鼠來操作圖形 UI，而是運用 Selenium 去自動化操作瀏覽器。

Daniel (Daniel, Cabot, Deruelle, & Derras, 2020) 等學者提出了開源的 Xatkit 平台，設計了兩種領域特定語言 (DSL)，來建構對話機器人：(1) Intent Package 使用訓練語句、上下文訊息和匹配條件來描述使用者意圖；(2) Execution Package 串聯使用者意圖與回應動作，以作為對話機器人行為定義的一部分，在執行部分通常涉及對後端服務之呼叫，則再藉由 Platform Package 之定義來實現。Xatkit 除了提供領域特定語言以定義對話機器人外，亦提供一個模組化的執行引擎，可自動部署對話機器人應用程式，並在所選平台上管理定義的對話邏輯。

3 系統設計與方法

3.1 操作概念

底下透過兩個應用情境來分析本系統之操作流程與運作模式，第一部分為開發者部署階段，第二部分為使用者操作對話機器人之情境，整體使用情境如圖 1 所示。

在此操作概念腳本中，開發者希望開發一個整合推薦景點 API 的對話機器人，為了達到這個目的，開發者需要撰寫擴充之 Swagger 文件 (BotSwagger)，並使用 BOTEN 來獲取建置 Chatbot 的設定檔。開發者輸入 BotSwagger 文件後會經過格式驗證與訓練語句品質檢查，此時可以對內容再做修改，接著便會轉換為 Rasa 的設定檔，並 Push 到 GitHub 進行版本控制。這時開發者可以決定是否要自動擴增 Rasa 的訓練語句，不論有無進行擴充，開發者都可以接著部署對話機器人。

於操作階段中，終端使用者能透過開發者建置好的對話機器人來使用 API，使用者僅需要向對話機器人下達指令，並遵循對話機器人的指示便能使用 API，獲得以表格呈現之 API 執行結果。

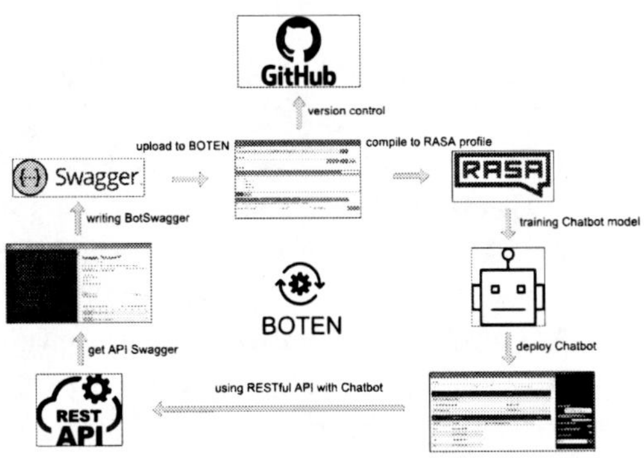

圖 1. BOTEN 使用情境圖

3.2 系統架構圖

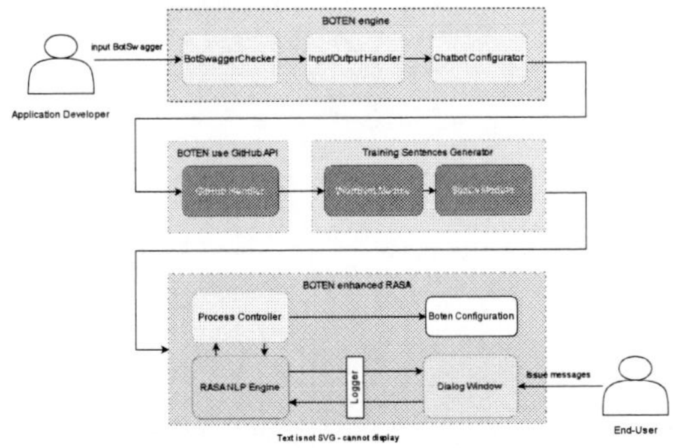

圖 2. 系統架構圖

本研究提出的 BOTEN 系統架構分為四個部分，分別為轉換階段、版本控制階段、擴增語句階段與執行階段，如圖 2 所示。(1) 轉換階段是以管線 (Pipeline) 的方式將 BotSwagger 依照順序轉換為對話機器人之設定；(2) 在版本控制階段，開發者可將 BOTEN 產生的 Rasa 設定檔推送至 GitHub Repository 進行版本控制；(3) 在擴充語句階段，BOTEN 會將生成的 Rasa 設定檔作進一步分析與處理，以提升意圖辨識能力；(4) 在執行階段中，開發者可建置與部署 Chatbot，建置好的 Chatbot 是以 Rasa 框架為底層的對話應用程式，可搭配前端 Web 介面讓終端使用者與 Chatbot 交談。

3.3 BotSwagger 訓練語句品質分析

開發者輸入 BotSwagger 時，BOTEN 會進行分析，其中訓練語句會利用 TF-IDF 技術，以所有的語句文本為基礎，先將所有文字轉成小寫，去除不具備重要意義的停用詞 (Stop Words)， 對剩餘的詞語做詞形還原 (lemmatization)，接著計算所有詞語在個別語句中所佔的權重，建立語料庫索引 (corpus index) 。將每個訓練語句的組成詞語用權重值來表示，即可將句子轉成一維向量，計算句子向量間的餘弦相似度 (Cosine Similarity)，即可得到兩個句子的相似度值。

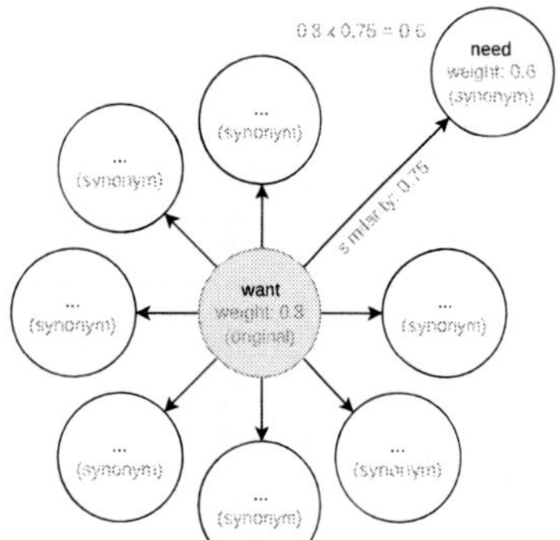

圖 3. WordNet 擴增同義詞的權重計算方式

由於 Chatbot 的訓練語句長度通常較短，有可能發生兩句雖然意思相近，但卻因為剛好沒有出現相同的詞語，導致計算出的餘弦相似度仍然偏低的情況，為此本研究提出兩種改善方法：(1) 透過 WordNet 技術以查字典的方式，找出所有訓練語句所用詞語的同義詞，並將這些同義詞也加到語料庫索引中，利用 SpaCy 技術計算同義詞與原始詞語間的相似度，以原始詞語的權重值乘上同義詞與原始詞語間的相似度，作為該同義詞在語料庫索引中的權重值，如圖 3 所示。我們將這些同義詞也視作原始詞語所屬句子的詞語，重新計算所有訓練語句間的相似度。(2) 除了透過 TF-IDF 得到的權重值計算句子間的餘弦相似度，同時也利用 SpaCy 計算句子間的相似度，由於兩種計算方式的語料庫 (Corpus) 不同，故計算出的相似度也會不同，因此便得到了兩句間的兩種不同的相似度數值，再將這兩個數值以特定比率加權計算，作為兩句間的加權相似度。

透過同時使用上述兩種相似度計算方式，目前本系統已經能準確評估訓練語句間的相似度 (Coupling)，並對相似度過高但卻屬於不同 Intent 的句子提出警訊。BOTEN 對於高相似度的判斷方式如圖 4 所示，所有的句子輪流當作基準句 (圖 4 以句子 2-1 作為基準句)，讓自己以及其他句子與基準句比較並計算相似度，基準句自身與自身的相似度則為 1.0；取得所有相似度數值後，將相同 Intent 的句子相似度相加，並比較這些相加後的數值，若有 Intent 相似度相加後的數值大於基準句所屬 Intent 的數值，則將該 Intent 相加前最大的相似度數值，所屬的語句視為相似度過高的句子。透過此方法既能保留相同 Intent 之下語句的自由度，又能找出相似度過高的句子，不論相同 Intent 之下的語句如何變化，只要其相似度的總和不要大於基準句 Intent 的相似度總和即可。關於 WordNet 尋找同義詞的標準，兩種句子相似度計算方式的權重比率，以及此方法有效性的驗證，會在後續實驗章節中說明。

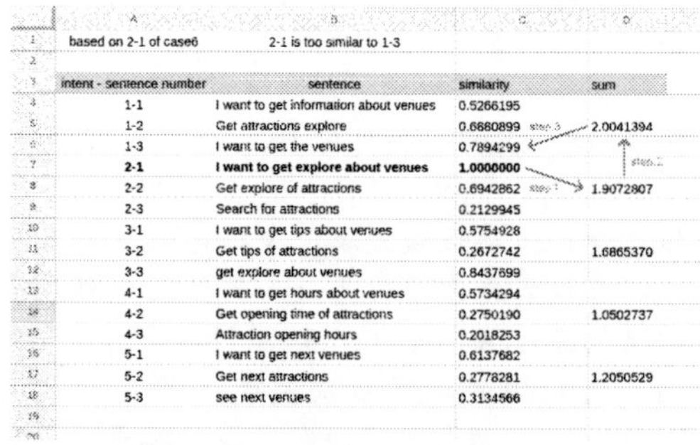

based on 2-1 of case6   2-1 is too similar to 1-3

intent - sentence number	sentence	similarity	sum
1-1	I want to get information about venues	0.5266195	
1-2	Get attractions explore	0.6680899	2.0041394
1-3	I want to get the venues	0.7894299	
2-1	**I want to get explore about venues**	**1.0000000**	
2-2	Get explore of attractions	0.6942862	1.9072807
2-3	Search for attractions	0.2129945	
3-1	I want to get tips about venues	0.5754928	
3-2	Get tips of attractions	0.2672742	1.6865370
3-3	get explore about venues	0.8437699	
4-1	I want to get hours about venues	0.5734294	
4-2	Get opening time of attractions	0.2750190	1.0502737
4-3	Attraction opening hours	0.2018253	
5-1	I want to get next venues	0.6137682	
5-2	Get next attractions	0.2778281	1.2050529
5-3	see next venues	0.3134566	

圖 4. 語句相似度過高之判斷方式

3.4 訓練語句擴充機制

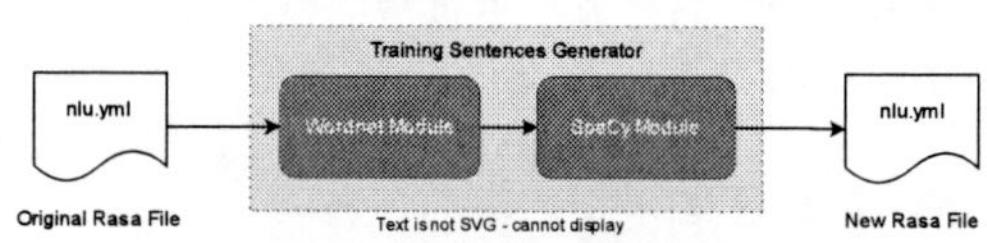

圖 5. 訓練語句擴充機制

除了 BOTEN 核心功能之外，我們亦提出了一個專門用於生成 Rasa 訓練語句的服務，透過 BOTEN 串接此服務，開發者能做到 Rasa 訓練語句的擴充，其內部機制可分為 WordNet Module 與 SpaCy Module 兩部份，如圖 5 所示。

為了將訓練語句中比較有意義的詞彙進行擴充，我們使用 WordNet 的 wup_similarity (Gupta_OMG, 2022) 相似度演算法進行擴充後新的句子與原句的比較，其全名為 Wu-Palmer Similarity，它根據同義詞在上位詞樹中相對於彼此的位置來計算相似度，LCS (Least Common Subsumer) ("Sample usage for wordnet,") 為分類樹中最深的共同祖先，depth 則是指在分類樹中的深度，其計算公式如下：

$$Wup_{similarity}(w1, w2) = 2 * \frac{depth(lcs(w1,w2))}{(depth(w1)+depth(w2))} \quad (1)$$

語句擴增的處理流程分為以下步驟：(1) 首先我們將所有的訓練語句進行斷詞，把一個句子切成一個個 Token；(2) 接著我們把每個 Token 詞型還原成 Lemma；(3) 剔除掉不重要的 Stop Word 後，完成擴充前的準備；(4) 利用

WordNet 查詢每個有意義 Token 的同義詞；(5) 透過 wup_similarity 演算法評估查詢到的同義詞與原始的 Token 的相似度，利用笛卡爾乘積交叉比較兩組同義詞的相似度，並計算平均值；(6) 只要平均值高於 0.3 則視為該 Token 的同義詞 (平均值參數取 0.3 的理由會在後續實驗章節說明)；(7) 將這些同義詞與先前剃除掉的 Stop Word 依它們在原始句中的相對位置，將 Stop Word 以外的字詞輪流替換成新生成的同義詞，組合出多句與原句相同意思的同義句。

WordNet 擴充後新生成的眾多語句中會存在與原句意思相差過大的句子，這可能會導致 Rasa 訓練出不準確的模型，因此我們透過 SpaCy 進一步對新生成的句子進行過濾，這會使用到 SpaCy 的相似度演算法 ，其計算機制如下：(1) 將每個句子斷詞後建立多個 Token 的集合；(2) 透過 Word Embedding 的演算法，由語料庫中的預訓練模型來生成 Word 向量；(3) 計算該句所有詞向量的內積作為其句向量；(4) 比較句子向量間的 Cosine 相似度，其計算公式如下：

$$SpaCy_{similarity}(s1, s2) = \frac{\vec{s1} \cdot \vec{s2}}{\|s1\| \times \|s2\|} \tag{2}$$

在使用上可分為以下步驟：(1) 把所有新生成的句子與原句逐一比較相似度，(2) 最後保留相似度大於 0.7 的句子寫回 nlu.yml 當作訓練語句，完成擴充 (相似度參數取 0.7 的理由，將在後續實驗章節說明)。

4 案例與實驗

4.1 實驗說明

本實驗所使用的 Web API 主要來源是 APIs.guru ，此為開源的 OAS 儲存庫，目前已經發佈了大量的 Swagger 文件(Web API 描述文件)。實驗準備期間我們基於現有的 Swagger 文件將其擴增為 BotSwagger，接著我們會將撰寫好的 BotSwagger 文件上傳至 BOTEN，以進行後續實驗。

4.2 實驗目標

本實驗分為三個部份：

- **BOTEN 可行性分析**：為能評估 BOTEN 核心功能是否實際可行與有效，我們進行了 11 個案例實驗，在此我們以其中 2 個最具代表性的案例進行說明。
- **語句 Coupling 分析之參數設定實驗**：為能於 BotSwagger 訓練語句品質之 Coupling 評估時，能找出最適合的評估方法及指標，我們進行了 BotSwagger Preprocessing 相關實驗。
- **語句擴充方法參數設定與有效度實驗**：擴充 Rasa 訓練語句時，為了找出最適合的相似度參數，我們進行了一系列實驗，以評估擴充語句後 Rasa 訓練模型與真人的 Intent 分類判斷是否一致。

4.3 BOTEN 可行性分析

- **實驗案例 E1 – Foursquare:** 實驗 E1 使用 Foursquare 的景點推薦服務，使用者能透過評論定位地點來獲取獎勵。此實驗使用了所有 BOTEN 提供之擴充功能，包括設定故事性的流程，搜尋推薦景點後查詢此景點的開放時間和介紹等、提供預設參數和自動取得地理位置功能，使用者也可直接使用開發者所提供的 Client ID 來使用服務，並根據 Html5 Geolocation API 自動取得經緯度，將經緯度直接填入參數，此實驗測試了完整的 BOTEN 功能。
- **實驗案例 E2 – The Movie Database:** 實驗 E2 使用 The Movie Database 的電影推薦服務，The Movie Database 為一個電影相關資料庫，其包含電影、演員、電視節目等。此實驗設定了一個故事的流程，在搜尋熱門電影後查詢電影的詳細資訊，且使用預設參數，使用者無需申請 API key 即可使用此對話機器人。

表 1 為所有實驗運用到的 BOTEN 功能與其結果，顯示「Yes」的部分為開發者有運用到的 BOTEN 功能，顯示「N/A」的部分則是沒有運用到的 BOTEN 功能，目前分析項目不包含版本控制等通用功能。本研究的實驗案例皆成功整合了 Web API 與 Chatbot，能更便利地建置以提供 API 服務為目標之對話機器人，使用者也能方便地使用 API 服務。

驗證之功能特性	**實驗 E1**	**實驗 E2**
多個服務串接	Yes	Yes
自動取得地理位置	Yes	N/A
使用預設參數	Yes	Yes
使用 Regex	Yes	Yes
使用 JSON Path 呈現表格	Yes	Yes

表 1. 案例實驗結果分析

4.4 語句 Coupling 分析之參數設定實驗

本階段實驗以前階段之實驗案例作為參考案例，並為他們各自撰寫了一份品質良好的 BotSwagger。在 BotSwagger 轉換階段，會對開發者輸入的 BotSwagger 進行一系列驗證，評估 Chatbot 訓練語句的品質。若出現不同意圖之下的訓練語句意思過於相近，會回傳警訊訊息，一則訊息就代表一對過於相近的句子，本研究透過計算警告訊息的數量來評估實驗結果，期望品質良好的 BotSwagger 能夠完全不出現警告訊息，若出現警告訊息則視為假警報 (False Negative)。

由於 Chatbot 的訓練語句通常長度較短，單純使用 TF-IDF 效果不佳，所以本研究提出兩種改善方法，其一是透過 WordNet 對原始的語句擴充，增加彼此出現相同詞語的機會，其二是同時使用 SpaCy 計算句子相似度，而後再與先前計算的句子相似度加權計算。為使用這兩種方法，我們透過以下實驗找出以下參數：(1) WordNet 生成同義詞的判斷標準，以及 (2) TF-IDF 相似度與 SpaCy 相似度的加權比率。

- **實驗 P1 - WordNet 同義詞:** 本實驗的目的為 WordNet 生成同義詞的階段，試圖找出相似度演算法參數的最佳解。使用 WordNet 生成訓練語句詞語的同義詞時，為了生成與原始詞語意思足夠相近的同義詞，可以使用 wup_similarity 演算法或是 SpaCy 演算法計算原始詞語與同義詞的相似度，並得到介於 0 到 1 之間的相似度數值，我們以 0.1 為單位，將 0.0 至 1.0 的每個刻度作為參數，當相似度數值大於參數時，就把該同義詞視作原始句子的詞語，加入語料庫索引計算權重。

- **實驗 P2 - TF-IDF 與 SpaCy 加權比率:**本實驗的目的為找出 TF-IDF 與 SpaCy 兩種句子相似度演算法，能得到最佳結果的加權比率。我們以 TF-IDF 比 SpaCy 比率為 1：1、2：1、1：2 三種比率分別測試，將能得到最少假警報的比率作為實驗結果。

實驗 P1 的結果發現，不論相似度參數為何，SpaCy 演算法的假警報數量普遍少於 wup_similarity 演算法，且計算時間較短，故本研究以 SpaCy 作為 BotSwagger 轉換階段，WordNet 生成同義詞的判別依據。另外還從結果觀察到，在相似度參數大於 0.6 之後，便不再出現假警報。

實驗 P2 的結果如表 2 所示，案例 E1 在相似度參數為 0.8 時，能得到最好的結果，不論 TF-IDF 與 SpaCy 的加權比率為何，皆不會產生假警報，故我們取 0.8 作為相似度參數。接著，在案例 E2 則可以發現將相似度參數設為 0.8 時，TF-IDF 比 SpaCy 比率 2：1 的實驗結果最好，只有出現一則假警報，故我們取 2：1 作為加權比率。

	案例 E1			**案例 E2**		
Similarity	1：1	1：2	2：1	1：1	1：2	2：1
0.0	11	9	11	5	4	4
0.1	10	11	13	5	4	4
0.2	9	9	12	2	1	2
0.3	7	5	10	4	3	4
0.4	3	3	5	1	1	1
0.5	1	1	2	2	2	2
0.6	0	0	1	3	3	2
0.7	0	0	1	3	3	3
0.8	0	0	0	3	3	1
0.9	0	0	1	2	3	1
1.0	0	0	1	2	3	1

表 2. TF-IDF 與 SpaCy 加權比率實驗假警報數

4.5 語句擴充方法參數設定與有效度實驗

本階段實驗比較擴充訓練語句後所獲得的訓練模型之 Confidence，試圖找出各項變因的最佳組合(可得到最高的 Confidence)。同時我們請三位平常有 Chatbot 使用經驗的使用者協助實驗，請他們決定訓練語句對應的正確 Intent 為何，並以多數決作為正確答案，評估 Rasa 模型的判斷是否正確。接著將此案例得到的各項變因組合，套用到實驗 E2 案例中，驗證是否同樣能提昇自然語言理解能力。最後我們結合前階段 BotSwagger Preprocessing 實驗，整合所有的實驗結果，驗證是否能訓練出具備良好 NLU 能力的 Chatbot。

- **實驗 C1 - WordNet:** 本實驗目的為測試擴充語句的 WordNet 階段，試圖找出相似度演算法參數的最佳解。作法同實驗 P1，最後以能得到最佳 Confidence 的參數為實驗結果。

- **實驗 C2 - Stop Words and Lemmatisation:** 本實驗目的為測試擴充語句的前處理階段，去除原始句子的 Stop Words ，並將 Token 進行詞型還原，判斷是否能提昇模型訓練結果的 Confidence，並根據結果對最佳相似度參數進行調整。

- **實驗 C3 - SpaCy:** 本實驗目的為測試擴充語句的 SpaCy 階段，試圖找出相似度演算法參數的最佳解。將前兩次實驗的結果作為參數代入本次實驗，生成新的句子後，將原句與新生成的句子逐一比較其相似度，過濾掉部份意思相差過遠的句子。作法同實驗 P1，將能得到最佳 Confidence 的參數作為實驗結果。

- **實驗 C4 -案例 E2 擴充語句:** 將前三次實驗的結果代入本實驗，測試在不同的案例中，同樣的相似度參數是否也能提昇 Confidence，並以真人判斷當作答案，比較 Rasa 模型的判斷與真人是否相同。

本階段實驗結果如表 3、表 4 及表 5 所示，參數 0.1、0.2 及顯示為「N/A」的實驗，係因為擴充語句或著訓練模型時間過長而無法完成的實驗，其餘部份「c」(correct) 代表 Intent 判斷正確且 Confidence 高於 0.9，「a」(acceptable) 代表 Intent 雖然判斷正確，但是 Confidence 低於 0.9，至於 Intent 判斷錯誤的情況，以「i」(incorrect) 表示，最後我們將表格中最佳的結果用粗體表示。

實驗	**Original**	**0.3**	**0.4**	**0.5**	**0.6**	**0.7**	**0.8**	**0.9**
實驗 C1	4c 1a 5i	N/A	**6c 1a 3i**	5c 1a 4i	4c 0a 6i	5c 0a 5i	4c 2a 4i	4c 1a 5i
實驗 C2	4c 1a 5i	**9c 0a 1i**	7c 1a 2i	7c 1a 2i	7c 1a 2i	3c 4a 3i	6c 2a 2i	5c 3a 2i
實驗 C3	4c 1a 5i	8c 0a 2i	8c 0a 2i	8c 0a 2i	7c 2a 1i	**10c 0a 0i**	7c 1a 2i	9c 0a 1i

表 3. Confidence 參數比較

實驗	**結果**
實驗 C4 - 擴充前	1c 5a 4i
實驗 C4 - 擴充後	**10c 0a 0i**

表 4. 案例 E2 擴充語句前後比較

根據實驗 C1 的結果，我們發現 WordNet 的 wup_similarity 演算法在相似度設為 0.4 時結果最好，所以將這個結果與實驗 C2 比較，此時卻發現在移除 Stop Word 與詞型還原的情況下，相似度若設為 0.3，Confidence 能有更好的表現，於是我們將這個結果代入下一次實驗。接著到了實驗 C3 ，若 SpaCy 相似度參數設為 0.7 ，則 Confidence 能有最好的表現，所有 Intent 皆判斷正確，由此得知 WordNet wup_similarity 參數設為 0.3，SpaCy 參數設為 0.7 ，為本階段實驗的最佳解。

透過實驗 C4，我們發現在其他案例，擴充語句同樣能夠有效提升 Confidence 表現，避免 Intent 判斷錯誤。

4.6 語句 Coupling 分析與擴充語句機制整合實驗

最後，我們對已整合語句 Coupling 分析與擴充語句機制之 Chatbot 進行整合驗證，對於三個案例 (E1, E2, 以及另一個案例 E3: Graph Hopper Direction API) 執行完整的 Chatbot 生成流程，以驗證是否真的能生成具備良好 NLU 能力的 Chatbot。

- **實驗案例 E3 – Graph Hopper Direction API:** 實驗案例 E3 為一路線規畫服務，此外還能判斷使用者的所在地以及給定時間內能到達的地方。本研究替以上三種不同服務的呼叫端點，各自撰寫訓練語句，並透過語句 Coupling 分析的建議，改善訓練語句的內容，接著進一步透過 WordNet 擴充語句，實驗是否能增加 Chatbot 的 NLU 能力。

此實驗的結果如表 5 所示。從三個案例的實驗結果可得知，透過語句 Coupling 分析進而改善之語句 (改善語句相似度過高問題) 皆能有效提高問答正確率，而透過案例 E2 及 E3 則可發現，透過 WordNet 擴充語句，能夠更進一步提高問答準確率，建立出 NLU 能力更佳的 Chatbot。

案例	**原始之語句、未擴充**	**原始之語句、有擴充**	**改善之語句、未擴充**	**改善之語句、有擴充**
案例 E1	2c 0a 3i	2c 0a 3i	4c 1a 0i	4c 1a 0i
案例 E2	0c 3a 2i	3c 0a 2i	4c 0a 1i	**5c 0a 0i**
案例 E3	2c 0a 2i	3c 0a 1i	3c 0a 1i	**4c 0a 0i**

表 5. 整合實驗結果

5 結論與未來研究方向

本研究提出了一個基於 Web API 之半自動化對話機器人生成機制：BOTEN，可協助應用程式開發者快速建置出指定 Web API 的 Chatbot 介面。實驗展示了 BOTEN 核心系統功能均有成功實現、自然語言理解能力亦有有效的提升。

未來我們規劃進行兩個改善方向：(1) 優化 API Chatbot 之使用流程，讓使用者可以詢問先前填入了哪些參數，以提升使用便利性。此機制將由系統以自動化的方式提供，無需開發者特別撰寫此意圖的訓練語句。(2) 規劃更豐富的 API 回應資料之呈現方式，除了現有的表格形式，規劃提供包含超連結、圖片、影片等豐富資料之回覆結果。

參考文獻

Abdellatif, A., Costa, D., Badran, K., Abdalkareem, R., & Shihab, E. (2020). *Challenges in chatbot development: A study of stack overflow posts.* Paper presented at the Proceedings of the 17th international conference on mining software repositories.

Bocklisch, T., Faulkner, J., Pawlowski, N., & Nichol, A. J. a. p. a. (2017). Rasa: Open source language understanding and dialogue management.

Brandtzaeg, P. B., & Følstad, A. (2017). *Why people use chatbots.* Paper presented at the International conference on internet science.

Cerezo, J., Kubelka, J., Robbes, R., & Bergel, A. (2019). *Building an expert recommender chatbot.* Paper presented at the 2019 IEEE/ACM 1st International Workshop on Bots in Software Engineering (BotSE).

Chittò, P., Baez, M., Daniel, F., & Benatallah, B. (2020). *Automatic generation of chatbots for conversational web browsing.* Paper presented at the International Conference on Conceptual Modeling.

Daniel, G., Cabot, J., Deruelle, L., & Derras, M. J. I. A. (2020). Xatkit: a multimodal low-code chatbot development framework. *8*, 15332-15346.

Gupta_OMG, M. (2022). NLP | WuPalmer – WordNet Similarity. Retrieved from https://www.geeksforgeeks.org/nlp-wupalmer-wordnet-similarity/

Josikakar. (2021). Software Engineering | Coupling and Cohesion. Retrieved from https://www.geeksforgeeks.org/software-engineering-coupling-and-cohesion/

Michaud, L. N. J. I. P. (2018). Observations of a new chatbot: drawing conclusions from early interactions with users. *20*(5), 40-47.

OpenAPI Specification. (2021). Retrieved from https://github.com/OAI/OpenAPI-Specification/blob/main/versions/3.1.0.md

Pérez-Soler, S., Guerra, E., & Lara, J. d. (2020). *Model-driven chatbot development.* Paper presented at the International Conference on Conceptual Modeling.

riturajsaha. (2022). Understanding TF-IDF (Term Frequency-Inverse Document Frequency). Retrieved from https://www.geeksforgeeks.org/understanding-tf-idf-term-frequency-inverse-document-frequency/

Sample usage for wordnet. Retrieved from https://www.nltk.org/howto/wordnet.html

Schmidt, D. C. J. C.-I. C. S.-. (2006). Model-driven engineering. *39*(2), 25.

Telang, P. R., Kalia, A. K., Vukovic, M., Pandita, R., & Singh, M. P. J. I. I. C. (2018). A conceptual framework for engineering chatbots. *22*(6), 54-59.

Toxtli, C., Monroy-Hernández, A., & Cranshaw, J. (2018). *Understanding chatbot-mediated task management.* Paper presented at the Proceedings of the 2018 CHI conference on human factors in computing systems.

Vaziri, M., Mandel, L., Shinnar, A., Siméon, J., & Hirzel, M. (2017). *Generating chat bots from web API specifications.* Paper presented at the Proceedings of the 2017 ACM SIGPLAN international symposium on new ideas, new paradigms, and reflections on programming and software.

What is WordNet? Retrieved from https://wordnet.princeton.edu/

Word vectors and semantic similarity. Retrieved from https://spacy.io/usage/linguistic-features#vectors-similarity

The 34th Conference on Computational Linguistics and Speech Processing (ROCLING 2022)
Taipei, Taiwan, November 21-22, 2022. The Association for Computational Linguistics and Chinese Language Processing

漢字難度分析暨回饋系統之建置與發展
The Design and Development of a System for Chinese Character Difficulty and Features

Jung-En Haung[1], Hou-Chiang Tseng[1], Li-Yun Chang[2], Hsueh-Chih Chen[3], Yao-Ting Sung[3]

[1] Graduate Institute of Digital Learning and Education, National Taiwan University of Science and Technology
[2] Department of Chinese as a Second Language/Chinese Language and Technology Center, National Taiwan Normal University
[3] Department of Educational Psychology and Counseling, National Taiwan Normal University
samuel8781@gmail.com, tsenghc@mail.ntust.edu.tw, { liyunchang , chcjyh , sungtc }@ntnu.edu.tw

摘要

漢字特徵分析（如：部件頻次、功能及結構組合等）在字本位教學中具有關鍵作用，但目前缺少部件結合難度的文本分析系統，本研究根據中文部件組字與形構資料庫以及學習者難度分級，建置漢字特徵與難度分析系統，功能包含：分析文本的漢字難度、提供文本漢字部件解構以及文本部件衍生字資訊，給予使用者深入且直觀的文本分析結果。本系統之預期效益能在教學面裨益教學者編排識字教材與出題，在研究面應用漢字特徵於中文自然語言處理之任務。

Abstract

Feature analysis of Chinese characters plays a prominent role in "character-based" education. However, there is an urgent need for a text analysis system for processing the difficulty of composing components for characters, primarily based on Chinese learners' performance. To meet this need, the purpose of this research was to provide such a system by adapting a data-driven approach. Based on Chen et al.'s (2011) Chinese Orthography Database, this research has designed and developed an system: Character Difficulty – Research on Multi-features (CD-ROM). This system provides three functions: (1) analyzing a text and providing its difficulty regarding Chinese characters; (2) decomposing characters into components and calculating the frequency of components based on the analyzed text; and (3) affording component-deriving characters based on the analyzed text and downloadable images as teaching materials. With these functions highlighting multi-level features of characters, this system has the potential to benefit the fields of Chinese character instruction, Chinese orthographic learning, and Chinese natural language processing.

關鍵字：漢字難度、漢字特徵、字本位教學 、漢字教學系統

Keywords: character difficulty, character features, character-based education, instructional system for Chinese character education

1 緒論

1.1 研究背景

隨著全球各地的華語使用者人數不斷上升，華語教育成為近年來重要的研究方向。特別在近期中國孔子學院式微後，臺灣致力擴展華語師資、教材與資源之輸出，如國家教育研究院自 2013 年執行華語文教育八年計畫，以推動華語組織，並整合華語文資源之系統資源為目標（教育部，2013）。其中「建置應用語料庫及標準體系」從漢字、詞語、語法點各面向提供教學、教材設計與測驗評量的參考標準（國家教育研究院，2020），凸顯了難度建置與分級之於因材施教的重要性。

漢字作為組成文本的基礎單位，從形音義來看皆具有多層次的特徵。如：一字多音、一字多義，特別是漢字的數量與複雜的字形組成，常是華語學習者的難點（葉德明，2000）；為將漢字特徵進行整理能應用於華語教育，陳學志等人（2011)針對 6097 個正體中文字從筆畫、部件、偏旁、結構位置關係到整字，進行竭盡式的探究。該研究發展之中文部件組字與形構資料庫包含成字部件 246 個、非成字部件 193 個，並找出 11 種結構關係：

單獨存在、垂直組合、水平組合、封閉包圍、上方三面包圍、下方三面包圍、左方三面包圍、左上包圍、右上包圍、左下包圍、左右夾擊等結構與部件組合的關係；上述漢字字形特徵之分析，搭配字音、字義面的語言學特徵，有助於對漢字教學提出以證據為基礎之建議，並且此類漢字特徵亦有別於目前自然語言處理中的語言模型，如 BERT（Devlin, 2019）。未來可望進一步探討是否有助於中文自然語言處理的任務。例如，在文本可讀性模型加入漢字部件來作為訓練模型的特徵，期望可以有效提升模型之效能。

在漢字教學中，「字本位」的教學導向在語境和詞本位的教學常態下經常被探討，原因在於詞本位教學容易使漢字配合課文語境或詞語的功能出現，而忽略了漢字本身的特性和學習規律，以致在漢字的教學上成效不彰（呂必松，2005；張金蘭，2016）。為提升漢字學習成效，「字本位」教學導向的核心觀念是以漢字為教學的基本單位，藉由形音義的特性設計學習進度。其中，字形特性的教學，又以分析漢字部件對識字教學助益最大(黃沛榮，2001) 。學習者透過掌握部件與結構位置的組合規律，更高效率地建立識字的辨認系統，例如：當學生在遇到「馬」這個部件，教師可運用部件衍生字的概念，引導學生留意當「馬」部件出現在左右結構的左側位置，衍生的「騎」、「駐」、「馭」、「駛」、「駝」等字，多半表示對使用馬所做的衍生動作；出現在右側位置，例如: 「媽」、「嗎」、「瑪」、「碼」等，則多與「馬」部件的讀音相似。透過部件衍生字的教學，有助於學生發展組字覺識（orthographic awareness）且有助於促進識字量提升（王瓊珠，2005）。

若要具備基本讀寫能力，學生識字量至少須達 3000 字以上，且數量隨教育程度提高（王瓊珠等人，2008）教師若想要運用部件衍生字等教法輔助閱讀學習，勢必需要拆解漢字至部件或更小的單位；其過程費時費力，即便運用字典或知曉漢字資料庫，若是一筆一筆資料逐筆搜查，恐怕勞神費時。因此多半尋找漢字語料網站作為工具，讓教材製作或試題編寫更省時省力。

以下本研究列舉以華語作為第一語言或第二語言的教學領域中，常見的能提供檢索功能的漢字語料網站，選取依據為漢字資料、難度分析和部件衍生字分析等做整理（如表 1 所示）。

1.2 漢字部件與難度分析相關系統整理

平台名稱	漢字資料、難度、部件相關功能	教學效益
漢語多功能字庫(香港中文大學人文電算研究中心)	• 整理漢字演變，以及常見字的背景介紹 • 以古字部件樹的方式呈現字的組成結構 • 字的衍生成語 尚缺: • 文本分析功能 • 部件衍生字的整理系統 • 漢字的難度分析等級	• 古字部件輔助學習理解漢字的形成 • 部件古字和結構有益拆解漢字學習 可精進: - 文本整體分析和單一部件資料整理
國際電腦漢字及異體字知識庫(中央研究院)	• 漢字的讀音、部首和字卡 • 部件查詢可找尋包含部件的衍生字 尚缺: • 非成字部件之衍生字查詢 • 詞語和文本部件查詢 • 漢字難度分析	• 漢字資訊和教學字卡 • 部件查詢益於同部件衍生難字教學 可精進: -文本分析和非成字部件衍生字
ACCESS 全漢字檢索系統(國語中心)	• 漢字讀音、結構、部件、筆畫分解等資訊 • 將部件衍生分成四級的難度 • 文本分析並分解成部件，但排列方式只依照出現順序 尚缺: • 同部件在文本者中出現的整理	• 使用者文本部件分析 • 漢字資料的字卡作為教學用途 • 等級難度作為教學先後的參考 可精進 -部件衍生資訊為固

	• 更細分的學習者漢字難度分級	定內容，應該隨文本做變化
華語教學標準體系應用查詢系統-漢字分級標準檢索系統(國家教育研究院)	• 將漢字分為基礎、進階和精熟三個等別以及十一個級別 • 提供漢字在書面和口語每百萬出現字頻 尚缺: • 沒有部件相關漢字資料 • 無法進行文本的整體分析	•掌握漢字的難度以安排教學的順序 •透過字頻高低和類型安排學習情境可精進 - 查詢難度以文本會更便於使用者，搭配部件更有助於教學

表 1. 相關系統平台整理

漢字相關系統平台整理如表 1，可以發現許多平台側重於讓學習者或教學者去認識漢字的演變或背景故事，進而對部件為何而組成有印象，雖在資料的完整上有充足的呈現，對於許多漢字的特徵也有很詳盡的解釋，但也容易讓學生將每個字以獨立的個體來記憶和識別，無法像部件教學那樣以部件衍生出新的漢字；「全漢字檢索系統」落實了文本分析和按照部件分類，若教學者欲查詢文本及其中的漢字部件是十分方便且清楚呈現的，可惜的是系統目前只能按照文本中出現的部件順序(如圖 1 所示)，而且延伸學習的部件是按照學習者難易度做多寡呈現，作為教學補充尚且足夠，但教學者若是欲分析授課文本，會需知悉其他相同部件的生字，在此教學者需求此功能就較為不足。

在漢字難度面向，具有分析功能的系統為「華語教學標準體系應用查詢系統」和「全漢字檢索系統」，教學者可透過專家訂定之詞組和漢字難度，判別學習者掌握的難易，然而兩者在查詢上皆以單獨漢字對應查詢為主，教學者若要進行文本分析，要重複的鍵入生字進行查詢，操作上較為耗時費力。

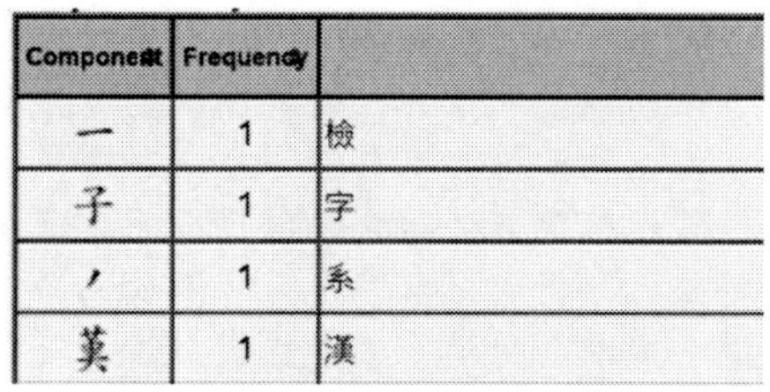

Component	Frequency	
一	1	檢
子	1	字
⺊	1	系
莫	1	漢

圖 1. 全漢字檢索系統部件順序

綜上所述，過往系統在漢字教學相當需要的難度分級以及特徵分析資訊兩面向，然而上述系統能提供的教學功能仍有突破的空間。再者，國家教育研究院的系統雖有難度分析功能，但由於其難度分級來自專家共識，未考量漢字各特徵的複雜度，亦未蒐集學習者於上千個漢字的學習表現，所以可能在客觀的漢字特徵指標計算以及難度的心理實質性上有待提升；為填補此研究缺口，Sung 等人進行實徵研究，以 675 位學習者為對象，蒐集每位學習者在 3,190 個漢字的作答反應，並以試題反應理論(item response theory, IRT; Drasgow & Hulin, 1990)分析學習者作答反應，估算每一個漢字的難度，改進了主觀認定的限制，為漢字難度提供更高的外部效度。本研究奠基於該 IRT 分析成果，彙整學習者表現之實徵資料以及中文部件組字與形構資料庫(陳學志等人，2011)，發展漢字難度分析暨回饋系統，整體目標在提供使用者信而有徵的漢字難度與特徵資訊，並且透過系統之建置，提供更便捷的使用管道，以下分述系統設計、方法與各項功能說明。

2 漢字特徵分析平台系統設計

2.1 系統設計理念與架構

本研究設計的漢字特徵分析系統，包含三項主要功能：文本分析、難度分級與部件分布。第一、以文本分析功能對輸入的文字進行難度分析，並提供所組成的部件、結構、生詞等資訊，將文本整體和段落難度進行顏色的視覺化，並提供點選詳細漢字資訊以下載字卡之功能。第二、難度分級則期望讓使用者用數據化的方式，掌握高字頻以及在文本中高頻率出現之漢字的難度。本研究所有的難度分級，皆依據學習者的作答反應分析研究，因此適合教學者判別學習者可能遇到瓶頸的漢字。教學者除可安排讓學習者從高頻漢字進行認讀，亦可依照文本漢字難度作為選擇教學文本的依據。第三、部件分布功能結合部件和結構，讓教學者能以部件切入，參照文本中相同部件的衍生字，按照難度進行教學，例如:以「魚」部件搭配字卡，教授文本中其他含有「魚」部件且較難的漢字如：「鯉」、「鯛」等字。

2.2 開發環境

本系統以微軟的網頁開發框架 Visual Studio ASP.NET 進行系統開發。此框架具有相容性高和編程穩定等特性，使系統架設更符合普遍使用者的規格需求。考量網頁系統美觀和使用者體驗的完善，系統前端程式引入 CSS 及 jQuery 等技術來進行前端程式之開發，讓使用者操作流暢兼具美觀。此外，本系統亦大量採用 Visual Studio.NET 內建的程式工具來進行開發。例如：將具有大量數據的漢字資料以 GridView 功能來進行表格的分類呈現，讓使用者可以一目瞭然系統分析的結果，並有條理的查閱漢字特徵資料。目前系統可以處理兩千字以內的文本分析，並過濾漢字以外字元。系統需對應使用者欲分析之文本難度、部件等資訊呈現，由於語料庫已經將 6097 個漢字以特徵和部件等相關資料整理成 Excel 表格，因此系統使用「C＃Dictionary」功能進行資料儲存和排序，再依據功能做查表和資訊呈現。針對語料庫外的漢字和其他字符，如：英文字母、標點符號等，系統設計有過濾和不計入分析結果的功能，使用者輸入文本時，不會因為語料庫外的字元影響分析結果。依據不同功能，系統設計有相應的漢字分析的演算法，以「渣」的部件拆解為例，語料庫中的部件資料為「|(氵, -(木, -(日, 一)))」，將資料依結構順序進行左右、上下拆解成「氵、木、日、一」四個部件，進而呈現字卡、文本高頻部件排序等功能。系統所使用的語料庫詳盡地歸納漢字資料，因此在各功能的呈現都能以簡潔快速的演算法做運算。目前此網站支援主流的瀏覽器，如 Google Chrome、Microsoft Edge 及 FireFox 等，以下針對本系統功能詳細描述與舉例。

3 漢字特徵分析系統各功能設計呈現

3.1 功能一：文字分析

- 使用步驟

(1) 在左框輸入文本

(2) 點選「分析」按鈕

(3) 在右框，點選想查看的字；可依需求，下載字卡

- 分析結果

首先，使用者輸入欲分析的文本，系統會顯示每個漢字的難度(見圖 2-1、圖 2-2)，再者點選漢字連結會呈現漢字字卡(見圖 3)，內容包含漢字、簡體寫法、筆劃、注音、六書、難度、漢語拼音、文字結構、部首和部件，最後使用者可下載成字卡圖片。特別值得注意的是本系統給予每個難度對應顏色，在文本分析時，能在視覺上做直觀辨別。

- 教學效益

教學者可透過此功能直觀檢視文本中的漢字難度分布，點選所需教學漢字獲取資訊，下載字卡圖片，在教學上彈性使用，例如：字卡上有【選擇呈現詞首、詞中、詞尾】的功能，教學者可選擇不呈現字的詞尾，引導學生自行發想衍生詞彙，或者進行形成性評量（以字造詞、造句；寫出課本中包含該字的詞…；亦可在完成難度分析或部件分析後，將欲教學的衍生字以字卡方式呈現給學習者。

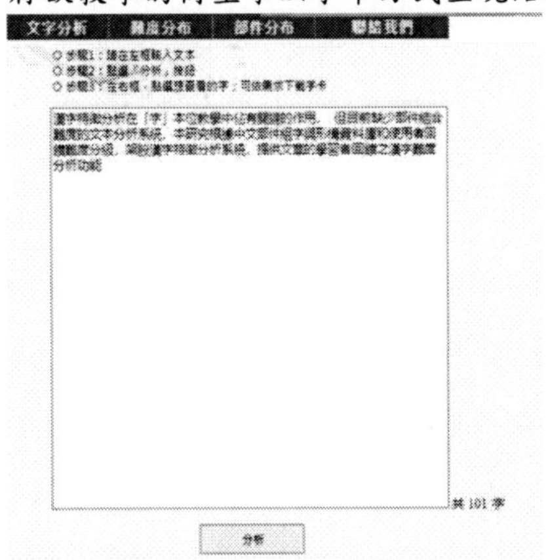

圖 2-1.漢字特徵分析輸入方格

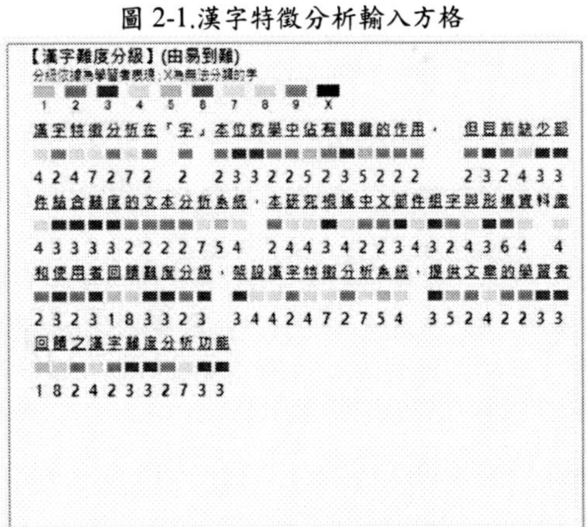

圖 2-2.文本漢字難度呈現

The 34th Conference on Computational Linguistics and Speech Processing (ROCLING 2022)
Taipei, Taiwan, November 21-22, 2022. The Association for Computational Linguistics and Chinese Language Processing

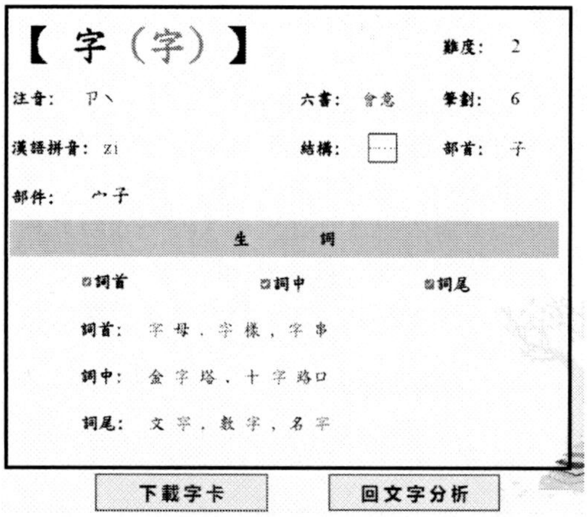

圖 3. 漢字字卡呈現

3.2 功能二：難度分布分析

- 使用步驟

(1) 在左框輸入文本

(2) 點選「分析」按鈕，系統自動呈現文本的漢字次數統計在右框

(3) 在右框，請依需求，選擇結果呈現方式:依照出現次數由高到低排列；依照難度排列分析結果

- 分析結果

難度分布功能的呈現方式有二：首先，依據漢字在文本的出現次數做排序(見圖 4)，讓使用者檢視文本中高頻率出現的漢字及其難度；再者，使用者亦可以按照難度做分級呈現(見圖 5)，檢視文本的平均漢字難度以及哪些難度出現較頻繁，透過上方難度按鈕，選取顯示特定難度。重要的是，當使用者以兩者交叉比較，能以數據看見最高頻率出現的字為何種難度，以及最常出現的是哪些難度的漢字。

- 教學效益

教學者可運用此功能，評估特定文本難度對學習者可能造成的學習負荷，例如學習者可能會在哪些較難的漢字遇到問題，進而在教學上做先備識字的輔助或閱讀文本後的加強，例如：文本中(見圖 5)「的」出現比例最高，該字之難度因為「難度低」(在 9 個等級中，排第 2 級)，因此可判斷為基礎且重要的漢字，在教學中值得優先介紹；或者選擇整篇文本中，難度較高的第 7 級漢字:「徵」、「析」、「率」等字，以部件拆分搭配字形結構的拆解，讓學生更細部了解較難的漢字，減輕識字學習上的負荷。

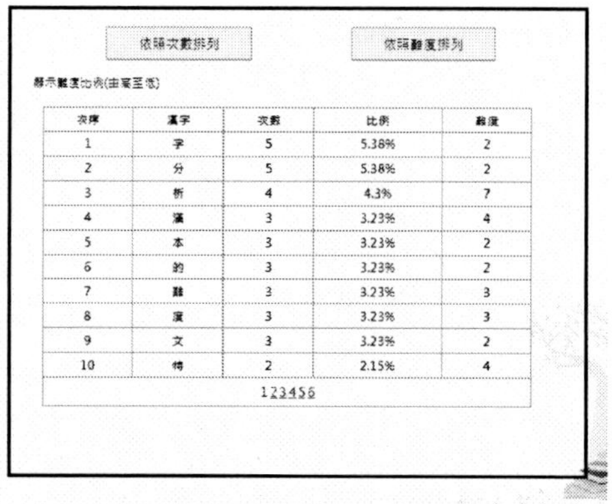

次序	漢字	次數	比例	難度
1	字	5	5.38%	2
2	分	5	5.38%	2
3	析	4	4.3%	7
4	漢	3	3.23%	4
5	本	3	3.23%	2
6	的	3	3.23%	2
7	難	3	3.23%	3
8	度	3	3.23%	3
9	文	3	3.23%	2
10	特	2	2.15%	4
123456				

圖 4. 漢字按出現頻率排序功能

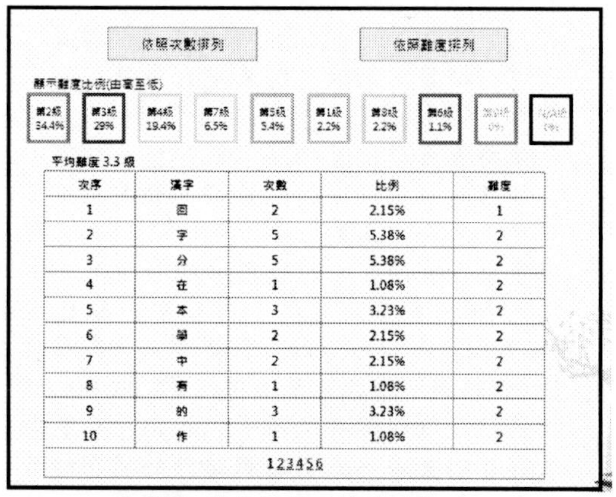

次序	漢字	次數	比例	難度
1	回	2	2.15%	1
2	字	5	5.38%	2
3	分	5	5.38%	2
4	在	1	1.08%	2
5	本	3	3.23%	2
6	學	2	2.15%	2
7	中	2	2.15%	2
8	有	1	1.08%	2
9	的	3	3.23%	2
10	作	1	1.08%	2
123456				

圖 5. 漢字按難度排序功能

3.3 功能三：部件分布分析

- 使用步驟

(1) 請在左框輸入文本

(2) 點選「分析」按鈕，系統自動拆解文本中漢字的部件組成

(3) 在右框，點選想查看的部件；可依需求，下載字卡

- 分析結果

首先，部件分布功能能讓使用者透過分析結果，檢視部件在文本中出現的頻率(見圖 6)，接著，使用者點入特定部件的連結後，會呈現該部件是否成字，以及文本中還有哪些漢字有此部件(見圖 7)，最後可下載字卡。值得注意的是，衍生字會顯示難度分級，使用者可以依據難度，進行部件的衍生字教學。

- 教學效益

教學者可搭配漢字難易度，針對同部件的衍生字，由難度低至高進行教學，讓學生學習較高難度級別的漢字前，能有循序漸進的鷹架（scaffolding），例如:「口」部件在文本中的出現頻次高，教學者可安排讓學生學習「口」這個基礎部件字後，再學習較進階的衍生字：在左右結構中，兩個部件的「和」，三個部件的「結」，一直到包含三個口部件的「讓」，學生透過慢慢疊加的部件數來學習，相對於直接學習生難字，預計更能漸進掌握生字。

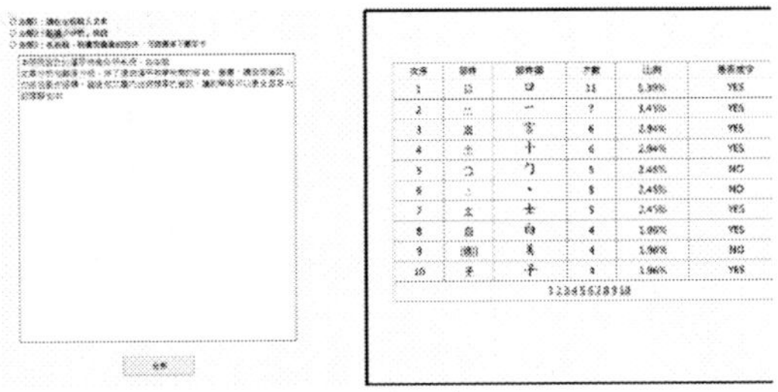

圖 6. 漢字部件分布功能

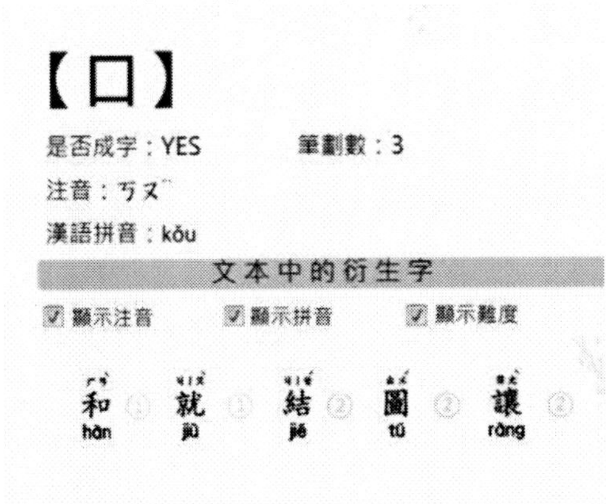

圖 7. 部件資料和衍生字字卡呈現

4 討論與未來發展

本研究所發展之「漢字難度分析暨回饋系統」提供使用者多面向地了解文本中漢字特徵的功能，包含：每個字的難度與特徵資訊（功能一：文字分析）、文本中漢字的難度分布與頻率分布（功能二、難度分布）、文本中的部件頻率與相關特徵（功能三：部件分布）。對使用者而言，如果能靈活搭配各功能，將快速掌握文本，進而編寫教材、發展教具或設計識字之評量題目，裨益教師、家長、出版社、教材開發者或任何對漢字難度與特徵感興趣之使用者。

為了有效地運用蒐集自學習者的難度資料，本系統未來將開發「建議學習內容」之功能，透過輸入文本的漢字難度，提供更豐富的訊息，讓使用者透過選單等方式，除了理解文本中的資料外，能查詢所需衍生學習的漢字資料，例如：搭配漢字難度（比現階段難度更低的漢字選項，或難度更高的漢字選項）與字形特徵（都是上下結構或左右結構的漢字、都具有特定部首的漢字）落實語言教學中的 i+1 教學觀點（Krashen, 1981），即透由此項「建議學習內容」，讓使用者更快速掌握鷹架，選擇下一階段所適合學習的漢字。

除此之外，本研究未來也將進行驗證並蒐集使用者意見，進而優化本系統。例如：邀請教師使用系統、蒐集教學者和網站設計專業人員之回饋，期能透過問卷分析和質性使用者體驗晤談等方式，對系統進行功能和介面上的修正以符應教學需求。本研究設計之漢字難度特徵分析系統目標能成為漢字教學的輔助系統，讓教學者透過分析文本後平台提供之漢字的難度分級、部件分布等資訊，更有規劃的進行教學設計，裨益於識字學習，未來也可能透過數據蒐集與分析，將本研究的漢字特徵納入自然語言處理的判斷依據，對中文文本的可讀性相關研究作出貢獻。

參考文獻

Devlin, J., Chang, M., Lee, K., & Toutanova, K. (2019). BERT: Pre-training of Deep Bidirectional Transformers for Language Understanding. *In Proceedings of the 2019 Conference of the North American Chapter of the Association for Computational Linguistics: HumanLanguage Technologies, Volume 1 (Long and ShortPapers) (pp. 4171–4186). Association for Computational Linguistics.*

Drasgow, F., & Hulin, C. L. (1990). Item response theory. In M. D. Dunnette & L. M. Hough (Eds.), *Handbook of industrial and organizational psychology*(pp.577–636). Consulting Psychologists Press.

Krashen, S. D. (1981). *Second Language Acquisition and Second Language Learning*. Pergamon Press Inc., Oxford

王瓊珠、洪儷瑜、張郁雯、陳秀芬 (2008)。一到九年級學生國字識字量發展。*教育心理學報，394*(4)，555-568。

王瓊珠 (2005)。高頻部首／部件識字教學對國小閱讀障礙學生讀寫能力之影響。*臺北市立師範學院學報*。*36*(1)，95-124。

教育部 (2013)。邁向華語文教育產業輸出大國八年計畫。中華民國教育部。

張金蘭 (2016)。*中國傳統識字教育給對外漢字教學帶來的啟示*。《第六屆「開創華語文教育與僑民教育之新視野」國際學術研討會》，未出版。

國家教育研究院 (2020)。*遣詞用「據」－臺灣華語文能力第一套標準*。國家教育研究院。

陳學志、張瓅勻、邱郁秀、宋曜廷、張國恩 (2011)。中文部件組字與形構資料庫之建立及其在識字教學的應用。*教育心理學報*，43(閱讀專刊)，269-290。

黃沛榮 (2001)。漢字教學的理論與實踐。樂學書局。

葉德明 (2000)。*外籍生漢字書寫策略探討*。第六屆世界華語文教學研討會論文集(三)，311-320。世界華語文教育學會。

The 34th Conference on Computational Linguistics and Speech Processing (ROCLING 2022)
Taipei, Taiwan, November 21-22, 2022. The Association for Computational Linguistics and Chinese Language Processing

Image Caption Generation for Low-Resource Assamese Language

Prachurya Nath[1], Prottay Kumar Adhikary[1], Pankaj Dadure[2], Partha Pakray[1], Riyanka Manna[3], Sivaji Bandyopadhyay[1]
[1]National Institute of Technology, Silchar, India
[2]University of Petroleum & Energy Studies, Dehradun, India
[3]ADAMAS University, Kolkata, India
{prachuryanath00, prottay71@gmail, krdadure, parthapakray, riyankamanna16, sivaji.ju.cse}@gmail.com

Abstract

Image captioning is a prominent Artificial Intelligence (AI) research area that deals with visual recognition and a linguistic description of the image. It is an interdisciplinary field concerning how computers can see and understand digital images & videos, and describe them in a language known to humans. Constructing a meaningful sentence needs both structural and semantic information of the language. This paper highlights the contribution of image caption generation for the Assamese language. The unavailability of an image caption generation system for the Assamese language is an open problem for AI-NLP researchers, and it's just an early stage of the research. To achieve our defined objective, we have used the encoder-decoder framework, which combines the Convolutional Neural Networks and the Recurrent Neural Networks. The experiment has been tested on Flickr30k and Coco Captions dataset, which have been originally present in the English language. We have translated these datasets into Assamese language using the state-of-the-art Machine Translation (MT) system for our designed work.

Keywords: Caption Generation, Low-resource Language, Attention, Assamese.

1 Introduction

Over 24 million native speakers speak the Assamese language in the north-eastern part of India. It is an eastern Indo-Aryan (Indic) language which is the official language of India's Assam state. Assamese is an indigenous Indo-Aryan language which has been influenced in vocabulary, phonetics, and structure by the region's close association with Tibeto-Burman dialects. Its grammar is notable for its highly inflected forms, different pronouns, plural noun markers, and honorific and non-honorific constructions. The Assamese script is very close to the Bengali script. Assamese, like English, is written from left to right.

The Assamese literary tradition can be traced back to the 13th century. In the 16th century, prose texts, most notably buranjis (historical works), began to appear. The Assamese alphabet (Assamese, Oxomiya bornomala) is shown in Fig. 1 which is the Bengali-Assamese script used in the Assamese language. Other north-eastern languages that are using the script include Bodo (now Devanagari), Khasi (now Roman), Mising (now Roman), Jaintia (now Roman), and others. The Kamarupi script was used to create it. Since Fifth century Umachal/Nagajari-Khanikargaon rock inscriptions written in an eastern variant of the Gupta script, the script has evolved continuously, with significant influences from the Siddha script in the 7th century (Saharia and Konwar, 2012). The current format is identical to the Bengali alphabet with the exception of two letters, (ro) and (vo); and the letter (khya) has progressed into an independent consonant with its own phonetic quality, however in the Bengali alphabet it is a conjunct of two letters.

Attempting to make computers mimic humans' ability to interpret the visual world is one of the long goal of artificial intelligence researchers. Even though significant advancement have been made in numerous computer vision tasks, for example, attribute classification (Lampert et al., 2009), object identification (Felzenszwalb et al., 2009), action classification (Maji et al., 2011), scene recognition (Zhou et al., 2014), and image classification (Krizhevsky et al., 2012), the field of Natural Language Processing have seen recent huge advances with the addition of transformer ar-

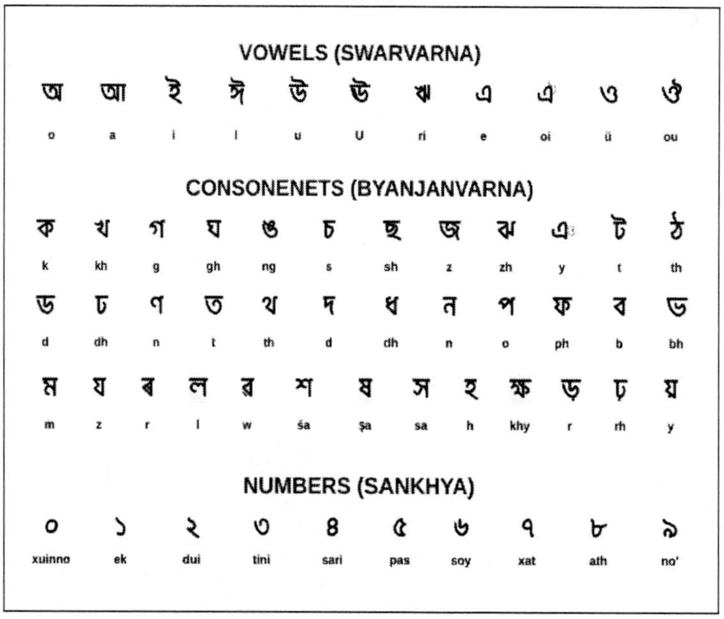

Figure 1: Assamese alphabets

chitectures. Moreover, allowing a computer to automatically describe an image in human language is a comparatively new task.

Image caption generation is the process of describing the visual information of an image based on the objects and actions depicted in the image using a machine's visual perception and a language model. The study of how computers can apprehend digital images and videos as well as describe them in a language that humans can understand is an interdisciplinary field.

Recent advancements in the field of Natural Language Generation (NLG) have helped the advancements of a plethora of fields like Machine Translation, Text Summarization, Answer Generation, and Image Captioning (Min et al., 2021). The inclusion of several pre-trained transformer-based language models such as BERT (Devlin et al., 2019) have taken the Natural Language Processing (NLP) to new heights. The interpretation of an image is highly dependent on acquired image features. In the prior studies, there are two approaches that have been taken into consideration to accomplish this task (Wang et al., 2020): one that uses a statistical probability language model to generate handcrafted features, and another one uses the neural network models based on encoder-decoder language model to extract the deep features.

In this paper, we propose an encoder-decoder framework for creating image captions in Assamese. The proposed model is based on a separate language model and a visual understanding machine. The rest of this paper has placed out as follows: Section 2 presents the works that has common factors with our work. The data used in our experiment has been discussed in 3 section. 4 section contains the procedures we used to prepare our system. The results, advantages and drawbacks have been discussed in 5 section. Finally, in Section 6, the paper is concluded with a discussion on future work.

2 Related Works

Most of the image caption generation systems comprised of rudimentary vision-based signifiers and language models which have been used during the early stage of the research. These systems mainly includes rule-based and hand-coded approaches. These systems only worked on a limited set of images. In recent time, the image captioning systems produced significantly improved results, following the same deep learning-based architecture as machine translation, as deep learning methods enhanced. These works was using the same encoder-decoder framework and framed image captioning as a text-to-image translation. CNN was used to encode images and RNN was used to decode the images into sentences in these systems.

Vinyals et al. (2015) (Vinyals et al., 2015) used CNN as an encoder to encode images and RNN-LSTM to decode image features into text, where image captioning is defined as predicting the probability of a sentence based on the input image feature. The most simple LSTM-based captioning architecture is based on a single-layer LSTM. During training, input words are taken from the ground-truth sentence, while during inference, input words are those generated at the previous step. Donahue et al. (2014) (Donahue et al., 2017) provide both image and text features to the sequential language model at each time step, rather than inputting image features to the system at the start. The encoder-decoder framework's next advanced version is an attention guided framework. Xu et al. (Xu et al., 2015) proposed the first attention mechanism in image caption generator. The encoder-decoder framework is more focused on the salient region of an image while generating an image description. It is a method that allows you to weight different areas of an image differently. It can, for example, add more weights to an image's important region. The attention model developed by them involved assigning weights to a random portion of an image. As a result, some critical aspect of an image was overlooked in order to generate a caption. To address this limitation, You et al. (You et al., 2016) developed a semantic attention model that focuses on linguistically significant objects or action in the image. In the preceding attention mechanism, the model forces visual attention to be active for every word, even those that do not explain visual information. Stop words such as 'the', 'of', and so on do not explain the image object. To address this issue, Lu et al. (Lu et al., 2018) developed an adaptive attention mechanism, which automatically determines whether to rely on the visual signal or the language model. Whenever the adaptive attention model starts paying attention to a visual signal, it will automatically decide which part of the image to focus on.

Vaswani et al (Vaswani et al., 2017) described the fully-attentive paradigm which has changed the way people think about language generation completely. The Transformer model was fully embraced as the defacto architecture for several language understanding tasks, as well as the groundwork for other advancements in NLP, such as BERT and GPT.

The Transformer architecture has been used for image captioning because it can be viewed as a sequence-to-sequence problem. A masked self-attention operation is applied to words in the standard Transformer decoder, followed by a cross-attention operation. Words serve as queries, and the final encoder layer's outputs serve as key / value, as well as an ultimate feed-forward network. Improvement of language generation and visual feature encoding have also been proposed.

The North-East of India is one of the country's most linguistically and culturally diverse regions. Every state has its own culture, language, and customs. Languages serve as a link between people and aid in the formation of bonds. The languages are mostly divided into three groups: Indo-Aryan, Sino-Tibetan, and Austro-Asiatic. Assamese, Bengali, English, Hindi, Manipuri, and Nepali are the most widely spoken languages in the Northeast. As a result, the Northeast is also known as India's multilingual and multicultural region. For natural languages, a large number of different NLP applications is being developed in India, as well as across the world. As Saiful Islam et al. (Devi and Purkayastha, 2018) described , there are only a few NLP applications for NE languages have been developed in India.

Natural Language Processing in Assamese is being worked on in a number of different ways. Assamese is a computationally underdeveloped language, and NLP study is still in its early stages. Works have mainly been carried out in the fields of Machine Translation as we can see in the work of English to Assamese using Statistical Machine Translation(SMT) (Singh et al., 2014). Laskar et al worked on multi-modal translation using both textual and visual features (Laskar et al.,

2019). Other works have been done in the field of Automatic Speech recognition by Agarwalla et al (Agarwalla and Sarma, 2016) and Supervised named entity recognition in Assamese language (Talukdar et al., 2014). In this piece of writing, we are suggesting an encoder-decoder framework for writing Assamese image captions. The suggested model is based on a unique language model and a machine that can understand visuals.

3 Dataset

A number of datasets are available for high-resource languages such as English, Hindi, etc., to carry out the experiments in image caption generation. For low-resource languages, the unavailability of sufficient data is the prime challenge faced by the researcher. In the low-resource Assamese language, there is no data available for the task of image caption generation. In this proposed work, we have generated the data using the Translator Cognitive Service provided by Microsoft Azure. Herein, we have used the Flickr30k and MS COCO Dataset (Lin et al., 2014) which are initially available in English. Moreover, we have used the machine translation systems (Translator Cognitive Service provided by Microsoft Azure) to translate the captions of these datasets into the Assamese language. The generated dataset is pictorially depicted in Fig. 2. The designed datasets differ in several ways, including the number of images, the number of captions per image, the format of the captions, and the size of the images.

3.1 Flickr30k

Flickr30K (Young et al., 2014) is one of the most popular datasets used for automatic image description and grounded language understanding. It includes 30000 Flickr images and 158000 human-annotated captions. Initially, it does not provide predefined image splits for training, testing, and validation. Herein, the researchers are free to select their own numbers for training, testing, and validation splits as per the requirements.

3.2 MS COCO Dataset

The Microsoft COCO (MS COCO) Dataset (Chen et al., 2015) is a popular massive dataset used for several tasks like image recognition, object segmentation, and captioning dataset. It contains multiple objects per class, with over 300,000 images, over 2 million instances, 80 object categories. In this dataset, 5 captions have been available for each input image.

Table 1: Dataset Description

Name of Dataset	Train	Test
Flickr30k	29783	2000
Coco17	118287	5003
Combined	148070	7003

In this work, we have used Flickr30k and MS Coco datasets. For more promising results, we have combined both datasets and analyzed the performance in terms of domain-independent perspective. Flickr30k consisting of 31,783 images and Microsoft Coco(MS-COCO) 2017 Captions dataset which has 118287 training images. Both Flickr30k/Coco Captions come with 5 human-annotated captions for each image. Table 1 shows the statistics of the used dataset.

4 Framework

The architecture of the proposed model is shown in Fig. 3 which primarily relies on the encoder-decoder mechanism. In the proposed model, image features are encoded using a convolutional neural network, and the image captions (word sequences) are encoded using a recurrent neural network. Later, the encoded image is passed to a text feature decoder which predicts the caption word by word. As it generated each word of the caption, the model used attention to focus on the most important part of the image.

4.1 Image Features Encoder

We use transfer learning to preprocess the raw files, using a CNN-based system which has already been trained. The images are fed into this process, which produces encoded image vectors that capture the image's essential features. For image feature extraction, we have used pre-trained VGG16 (Simonyan and Zisserman, 2015) and EfficientNetB3 (Tan and Le, 2020). It was trained using the ImageNet dataset. Historically, neural networks with

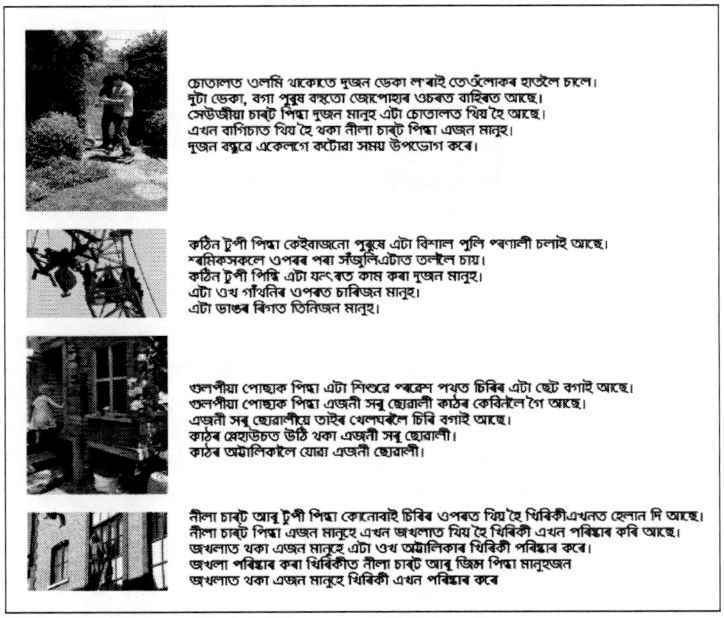

Figure 2: Overview of the source data

many layers have performed well in pattern recognition. Apart from this, these models are also suffer from the overfitting and difficult to optimise. Residual CNNs are comprised of many layers with interconnections between them. Identity mapping is decided to carry out by these connections. VGG16 has 16 layers and is simpler than EfficientNetB3. EfficientNetB3 are simple to optimise, and their performance improves as network depth increases. We used only the encoded image features produced by the hidden layers and discarded the pretrained models' final output layer because it contains the final output of classification.

4.2 Word Sequences Encoder

We tokenize our sentences with Tensorflow and extract the tokens from the top 25000 words. The tokens are then passed through an Embedding layer with embedding size=256 and an RNN based on Gated Reccurent Units (GRU). Kyunghyun Cho et al. (Cho et al., 2014) introduced GRU, which has been successfully used for machine translation and sequence generation.

The Generalized Recurrent Neural Network (GRU) is an improved version of the Recurrent Neural Network. The update gate and reset gate are used in standard RNN to solve the vanishing gradient problem. These two gates are in charge of the cell's behaviour. The memory cell at the heart of the GRU model stores information about each time step (what input has been observed up to this point). The update and reset gates are the vectors which determines the forwarding of the specific information to the output. The two gates have been developed to save input from earlier time steps without losing it and to eliminate data which is unrelated to the forecast.

The main distinction between Gated Reccurent Units (GRU) and Long Short Term Memory (LSTM) (Hochreiter and Schmidhuber, 1997) is that GRU's bag has two gates: reset and update, whereas LSTM's bag has three gates: input, output, and forget. Because GRU has fewer gates than LSTM, it is less complex. GRU is 29.29% faster than LSTM for same dataset in terms of model training speed; and in terms of results, GRU will outcompete LSTM in the case of long text and comparatively tiny data sources, but will fall well short in other instances.

4.3 Attention Mechanism

For our experiments, we have used Bahnadau Attention, as described in the research articles 'Neural Machine Translation by Jointly

The 34th Conference on Computational Linguistics and Speech Processing (ROCLING 2022)
Taipei, Taiwan, November 21-22, 2022. The Association for Computational Linguistics and Chinese Language Processing

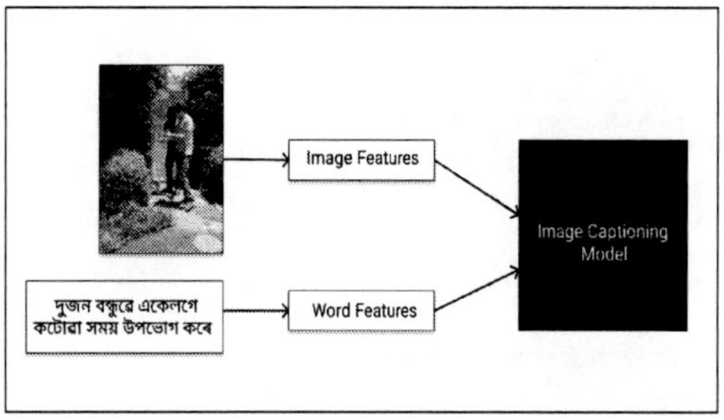

Figure 3: Model Overview

Learning to Align and Translate' (Bahdanau et al., 2016). The attention features shape for VGG16 is 49, while it is 100 for EfficientNetB3. The context vector generated by the pretrained model's last hidden layer is passed to attention layer. GRU obtains the context vector as an input and produces an image description. This architecture outperforms traditional CNN and RNN architectures that use Long Short Term Memory (LSTM) as a decoder.

At each keyframe, the Attention module receives the encoded image along with the previous timestep's hidden state from the Decoder. It generates an Attention Score, which gives each pixel in the encoded image a weight. The higher a pixel's weight, the more likely it is that the word will be output at the next timestep. For example, if the target output sequence is A boy is kicking the ball, the boy' s pixels in the photo are highlighted when generating the word boy, while the ball's pixels are highlighted for the word 'ball'.

Attention is the process of focusing on a distinct aspect of information whilst dismissing other apparent information. It's a way of telling the model where to focus in order to generate the corresponding word instead of the entire image. The decoder pays specific attention to some regions of the image at time t, on the basis of the hidden state, and by the use of spatial image features, it measures context vector.

4.4 Caption Generation

The caption generator is composed of a simple decoder with a Dense layer and Rectified Linear Unit (ReLU) activation. The dense layer, which also includes attention weights, receives the output of the picture feature encoder. The dense layer generates a softmax prediction of the next word in the sequence for each word in the vocabulary, then chooses the word with the highest probability. Instead of raw photos, we pass these encoded image attributes into our Image Caption algorithm. The target captions for each encoded image are also passed in. By decoding visual information, the model attempts to predict captions that compliment the intended caption. During the training phase, we use the Teacher forcing method to predict the next word where the target word is passed as the next input to the decoder. This procedure is repeated until a final token is generated.

5 Results

The results evaluation of the proposed approach for Assamese language is quantitatively and qualitatively challenging task. The system generated results values are remarkable and it set benchmark for other existing systems for the task of caption generation in Assamese language. There are a variety of evaluation metrics used in image captioning tasks that can be found in the literature. The BLEU score (Papineni et al., 2002) is the most commonly used metric. In addition to this, the Rouge score (Lin, 2004) is also one of the popular metric to computes the performance of the image caption generation system. These metrics works by comparing a system generated captions with a set of reference summaries.

The test sets of Flickr30k and COCO 2017 datasets contain 2000 and 5000 test images, to evaluate the proposed model's performance. For the test dataset, BLEU has been recorded. We also experimented with our combined dataset, which contains 150k images in the training set and 7000 test images in the test set. We keep track of both our BLEU and ROUGE and presented the scores in Table 2.

The majority of the images in this dataset, feature's human subjects with captions that are nearly identical. As a result of being trained on a large number of similar human subjects, the model during testing is unable to distinguish and describe non-human subjects. Machine translation of English captions to Assamese language has some limitation to translate compound sentences. The combined sys-

Table 2: Evaluation scores

Name of Dataset	Model	BLEU	Rouge
Flickr30k	VGG16	0.2833	0.1011
	EfficientNet	0.3084	0.1137
Coco17	VGG16	0.2694	0.1054
	EfficientNet	0.2677	0.1049
Combined	VGG16	0.2134	0.0778
	EfficientNet	0.2389	0.0889

tem was supposed to give a better accuracy in terms of BLEU and rouge score. But, they surprisingly gave a bit worse result as both the datasets contained different type of images so combining both the dataset was not good for our system. Although, it leaves us a space for future to work better how to get better results after the combination of two datasets.

As shown in the Table 3, we get a fairly close match to the reference captions. It lacks in areas where the word does not appear frequently, so applying one shot learning for objects that doesn't contain many samples. In our results, the distinction between source and predicted captions is that some sources contain a detailed definition of the image. Moreover, the designed system tries to give the overall details of the image. Another limitation of the proposed approach is that the caption mainly focuses on one main area, as simplified version of Bahnadau attention is use.

- The caption mentioned in Table 3 for the first image, the scissor is incorrectly referred to as sunglasses as the dataset contains a number of images of people with glasses.

- For second image, the proposed method analyses the different objects occurring in the image and attempts to predict the caption for the same. The generated caption is slightly confusing and semantically incorrect.

- Moreover, the source caption of the fourth image is overly detailed and the prediction is reasonable.

- In the third and fifth images, there is too much depth on the source caption.

Some drawbacks can be solved by the use of multi head attention which can help to solve this problem by focusing on more than one region. Also, transformers have a long way to go in the field of image captioning as the data is not always processed in the same order by transformers, and the attention mechanism provides context for any position in the input sequence.

6 Conclusions and Future Work

In this paper, we have proposed an encoder-decoder framework for creating image captions in Assamese. We looked at the Assamese alphabet and its presence in the Devanagari script, drawing parallels to the Bengali language. The current model is based on a separate language model and a visual understanding machine. Our primary focus was on translating English sentences, but in the long run, we are motivated to create a Gold Dataset for Assamese image captions. With the sudden rise in the use of Transformer-based frameworks in Machine Translation and other NLP tasks, image captioning using Attention-based Transformers could be a good experiment to investigate in the future.

Our main motivation was to create a benchmark model for Image Captioning in a low-resource language like Assamese for the first time. We hope that other machine learning researchers will work in this area to develop better models and improve the system's functionality and accuracy which may benefit many coming researchers. In the future, we'll explore the possibility of using a combination of different encoder and decoder architectures to enhance the result even further. We'll also experiment with different sampling techniques to see if we can eliminate the bias toward certain phrases. The gain of this experiment can be added to the research on Assamese image captioning and treated like a baseline model for further studies and future research.

Table 3: Caption Generated using Proposed Approach

Input Image	Captions
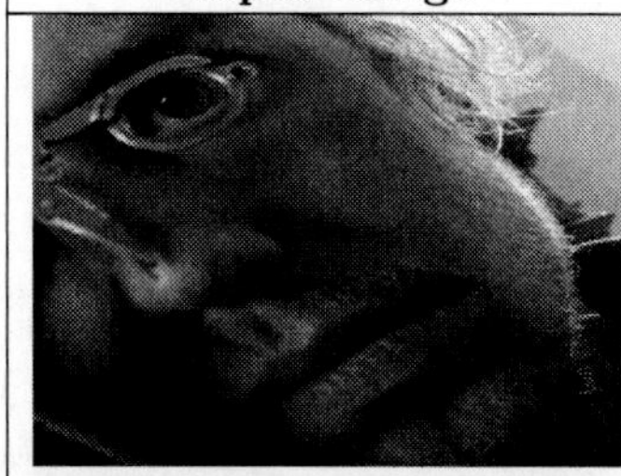	**Source** As: এজন মানুহে কিছুমান কেঁচিৰ হেণ্ডেলৰ মাজেৰে চাই আছে। En: A man is looking through the handle of a scissor. **Predicted** As: চানগ্লাছ পিন্ধা মানুহজনে সক্ৰিয়ভাৱে এক গুৰুতৰ দেখাইছে। En: The man in sunglasses actively looks serious.
	**Source** As: নিৰ্মাণ কৰ্মীসকলে বাহিৰত পাইপ সামগ্ৰী একত্ৰিত কৰে। En: Construction workers assemble pipe material outside. **Predicted** As: নিৰ্মাণ কৰ্মীসকলে চহৰৰ মাজভাগত বেৰ জাঁপ প্ৰদৰ্শন কৰে En: Construction workers demonstrate wall jumps in the heart of the city
	**Source** As: এজন মানুহে হ্ৰদৰ কাষৰ শিলৰ পথত এখন বাইক ৰৈ আছে। En: A man is waiting on a bike on a rock path near the lake. **Predicted** As: বাইক চলাই থকা হেলমেট পিন্ধা এজন ব্যকত। En: A person wearing helmet riding bike
	**Source** As: কিছুমান গছৰ সন্মুখত পোলকা ডট চাৰ্ট আৰু চশমা পিন্ধা এগৰাকী যুৱতী। En: A girl wearing a polka dot shirt and glasses in front of a tree. **Predicted** As: ফটো তুলিবলৈ পোজ দিয়া এগৰাকী মহিলা En: A woman posing for a photo
	**Source** As: ক'লা ৱেটচুট পিন্ধা এজন ব্যক্তিয়ে অকলে ঢৌত চাৰ্ফিং কৰে En: A person in a black wet suit is alone surfing in waves. **Predicted** As: এজন মানুহে সাগৰৰ পাৰৰ সৈতে ঢৌ চলাই আছে। En: A man is riding a wave along the beach

References

Swapna Agarwalla and Kandarpa Kumar Sarma. 2016. Machine learning based sample extraction for automatic speech recognition using dialectal assamese speech. *Neural Networks*, 78:97–111. Special Issue on "Neural Network Learning in Big Data".

Dzmitry Bahdanau, Kyunghyun Cho, and Yoshua Bengio. 2016. Neural machine translation by jointly learning to align and translate.

Xinlei Chen, Hao Fang, Tsung-Yi Lin, Ramakrishna Vedantam, Saurabh Gupta, Piotr Dollár, and C Lawrence Zitnick. 2015. Microsoft coco captions: Data collection and evaluation server. *arXiv preprint arXiv:1504.00325*.

Kyunghyun Cho, Bart van Merrienboer, Caglar Gulcehre, Dzmitry Bahdanau, Fethi Bougares, Holger Schwenk, and Yoshua Bengio. 2014. Learning phrase representations using rnn encoder-decoder for statistical machine translation.

Maibam Devi and Bipul Purkayastha. 2018. Advancements on nlp applications for manipuri language. *International Journal on Natural Language Computing*, 7:47–58.

Jacob Devlin, Ming-Wei Chang, Kenton Lee, and Kristina Toutanova. 2019. BERT: Pre-training of deep bidirectional transformers for language understanding. In *Proceedings of the 2019 Conference of the North American Chapter of the Association for Computational Linguistics: Human Language Technologies, Volume 1 (Long and Short Papers)*, pages 4171–4186, Minneapolis, Minnesota. Association for Computational Linguistics.

Jeff Donahue, Lisa Anne Hendricks, Marcus Rohrbach, Subhashini Venugopalan, Sergio Guadarrama, Kate Saenko, and Trevor Darrell. 2017. Long-term recurrent convolutional networks for visual recognition and description. *IEEE Transactions on Pattern Analysis and Machine Intelligence*, 39(4):677–691.

Pedro F Felzenszwalb, Ross B Girshick, David McAllester, and Deva Ramanan. 2009. Object detection with discriminatively trained part-based models. *IEEE transactions on pattern analysis and machine intelligence*, 32(9):1627–1645.

Sepp Hochreiter and Jürgen Schmidhuber. 1997. Long short-term memory. *Neural computation*, 9:1735–80.

Alex Krizhevsky, Ilya Sutskever, and Geoffrey E Hinton. 2012. Imagenet classification with deep convolutional neural networks. *Advances in neural information processing systems*, 25.

Christoph H Lampert, Hannes Nickisch, and Stefan Harmeling. 2009. Learning to detect unseen object classes by between-class attribute transfer. In *2009 IEEE conference on computer vision and pattern recognition*, pages 951–958. IEEE.

Sahinur Rahman Laskar, Rohit Pratap Singh, Partha Pakray, and Sivaji Bandyopadhyay. 2019. English to Hindi multi-modal neural machine translation and Hindi image captioning. In *Proceedings of the 6th Workshop on Asian Translation*, pages 62–67, Hong Kong, China. Association for Computational Linguistics.

Chin-Yew Lin. 2004. ROUGE: A package for automatic evaluation of summaries. In *Text Summarization Branches Out*, pages 74–81, Barcelona, Spain. Association for Computational Linguistics.

Tsung-Yi Lin, Michael Maire, Serge Belongie, James Hays, Pietro Perona, Deva Ramanan, Piotr Dollár, and C. Lawrence Zitnick. 2014. Microsoft coco: Common objects in context. In *Computer Vision – ECCV 2014*, pages 740–755, Cham. Springer International Publishing.

Di Lu, Spencer Whitehead, Lifu Huang, Heng Ji, and Shih-Fu Chang. 2018. Entity-aware image caption generation. In *Proceedings of the 2018 Conference on Empirical Methods in Natural Language Processing*, pages 4013–4023, Brussels, Belgium. Association for Computational Linguistics.

Subhransu Maji, Lubomir Bourdev, and Jitendra Malik. 2011. Action recognition from a distributed representation of pose and appearance. In *CVPR 2011*, pages 3177–3184. IEEE.

Bonan Min, Hayley Ross, Elior Sulem, Amir Pouran Ben Veyseh, Thien Huu Nguyen, Oscar Sainz, Eneko Agirre, Ilana Heintz, and Dan Roth. 2021. Recent advances in natural language processing via large pre-trained language models: A survey. *CoRR*, abs/2111.01243.

Kishore Papineni, Salim Roukos, Todd Ward, and Wei-Jing Zhu. 2002. Bleu: A method for automatic evaluation of machine translation. In *Proceedings of the 40th Annual Meeting on Association for Computational Linguistics*, ACL '02, page 311—318, USA. Association for Computational Linguistics.

Navanath Saharia and Kishori M Konwar. 2012. LuitPad: A fully Unicode compatible Assamese writing software. In *Proceedings of the Second Workshop on Advances in Text Input Methods*, pages 79–88, Mumbai, India. The COLING 2012 Organizing Committee.

Karen Simonyan and Andrew Zisserman. 2015. Very deep convolutional networks for large-scale image recognition.

Moirangthem Tiken Singh, Rajdeep Borgohain, and Sourav Gohain. 2014. An english-assamese machine translation system. *International Journal of Computer Applications*, 93:1–6.

Gitimoni Talukdar, Pranjal Protim Borah, and Arup Baruah. 2014. Supervised named entity recognition in assamese language. In *2014 International Conference on Contemporary Computing and Informatics (IC3I)*, pages 187–191.

Mingxing Tan and Quoc V. Le. 2020. Efficientnet: Rethinking model scaling for convolutional neural networks.

Ashish Vaswani, Noam Shazeer, Niki Parmar, Jakob Uszkoreit, Llion Jones, Aidan N. Gomez, Lukasz Kaiser, and Illia Polosukhin. 2017. Attention is all you need.

Oriol Vinyals, Alexander Toshev, Samy Bengio, and Dumitru Erhan. 2015. Show and tell: A neural image caption generator.

Haoran Wang, Yue Zhang, and Xiaosheng Yu. 2020. An overview of image caption generation methods. *Computational intelligence and neuroscience*, 2020.

Kelvin Xu, Jimmy Ba, Ryan Kiros, Kyunghyun Cho, Aaron Courville, Ruslan Salakhudinov, Rich Zemel, and Yoshua Bengio. 2015. Show, attend and tell: Neural image caption generation with visual attention. In *Proceedings of the 32nd International Conference on Machine Learning*, volume 37 of *Proceedings of Machine Learning Research*, pages 2048–2057, Lille, France. PMLR.

Q. You, H. Jin, Z. Wang, C. Fang, and J. Luo. 2016. Image captioning with semantic attention. In *2016 IEEE Conference on Computer Vision and Pattern Recognition (CVPR)*, pages 4651–4659, Los Alamitos, CA, USA. IEEE Computer Society.

Peter Young, Alice Lai, Micah Hodosh, and Julia Hockenmaier. 2014. From image descriptions to visual denotations: New similarity metrics for semantic inference over event descriptions. *Transactions of the Association for Computational Linguistics*, 2:67–78.

Bolei Zhou, Agata Lapedriza, Jianxiong Xiao, Antonio Torralba, and Aude Oliva. 2014. Learning deep features for scene recognition using places database. *Advances in neural information processing systems*, 27.

The 34th Conference on Computational Linguistics and Speech Processing (ROCLING 2022)
Taipei, Taiwan, November 21-22, 2022. The Association for Computational Linguistics and Chinese Language Processing

利用監督式對比學習來建構增強型的自迴歸文件檢索器
Building an Enhanced Autoregressive Document Retriever Leveraging Supervised Contrastive Learning

Yi-Cheng Wang[1], Tzu-Ting Yang[1], Hsin-Wei Wang[1], Yung-Chang Hsu[2], Berlin Chen[1]
[1]National Taiwan Normal University
[2]EZ-AI Inc.
[1]{yichengwang, tzutingyang, hsinweiwang, berlin}@ntnu.edu.tw
[2]mic@ez-ai.com.tw

摘要

資訊檢索系統的目標是從大量的文件中，找出與使用者查詢 (Query) 最相關的文件。在傳統的資訊檢索流程中，需要經過多次的比對許多文件才能找出最相關的文件。近期，有一種基於可微搜索索引 (Differentiable Search Index, DSI) 的新穎資訊檢索策略被提出，並展現相當優異的效能。DSI 透過單一個 Transformer 模型先將文件集中所有的資訊編碼在模型的參數中；在應用時，使用者可以將查詢輸入 Transformer，再由 Transformer 以自迴歸的方式直接地產生其相關文件的編號 (Document IDs)，因而能大幅地簡化與加速整個檢索過程。先前的研究指出，DSI 是以文件編號作爲橋梁來建立查詢與文件之間的關係，但在訓練資料中並不是每篇文件都會有相關的查詢，這將導致這些文件沒辦法被順利的建立起關係。有鑑於此，在模型訓練階段，我們提出先使用監督式對比學習來增強查詢與文件在潛在語意空間中的對應關係，並在模型推理階段時，透過最鄰近搜尋法來進一步的輔助模型產生文件編號。因此，我們提出的方法能有效增強 DSI 中文件與查詢薄弱的對應關係，在公開的語料集 Nature Question 上也驗證了它的成效。

Abstract

The goal of an information retrieval system is to retrieve documents that are most relevant to a given user query from a huge collection of documents, which usually requires time-consuming multiple comparisons between the query and candidate documents so as to find the most relevant ones. Recently, a novel retrieval modeling approach, dubbed Differentiable Search Index (DSI), has been proposed. DSI dramatically simplifies the whole retrieval process by encoding all information about the document collection into the parameter space of a single Transformer model, on top of which DSI can in turn generate the relevant document identities (IDs) in an autoregressive manner in response to a user query. Although DSI addresses the shortcomings of traditional retrieval systems, previous studies have pointed out that DSI might fail to retrieve relevant documents because DSI uses the document IDs as the pivotal mechanism to establish the relationship between queries and documents, whereas not every document in the document collection has its corresponding relevant and irrelevant queries for the training purpose. In view of this, we put forward to leveraging supervised contrastive learning to better render the relationship between queries and documents in the latent semantic space. Furthermore, an approximate nearest neighbor search strategy is employed at retrieval time to further assist the Transformer model in generating document IDs relevant to a posed query more efficiently. A series of experiments conducted on the Nature Question benchmark dataset confirm the effectiveness and practical feasibility of our approach in relation to some strong baseline systems.

關鍵字：資訊檢索、自迴歸檢索系統、對比學習

Keywords: Information Retrieval, Autoregressive Retrieval System, Contrastive Learning

1 緒論

爲了滿足使用者的資訊需求 (Information Needs)，資訊檢索 (Information Retrieval) 系統需要依據使用者的查詢，從大量的語料庫中找出相關的文件。文件檢索的方式分別是以詞匹配 (Term-matching) 與語意匹配 (Semantic-matching) 作爲基礎。TF-IDF 和 BM25 (Robertson et al., 2009) 爲詞匹配類中常見的作法，它們將使用者的查詢 (Query) 與文件 (Document) 用高維的稀疏向量來表徵，透過簡單的向量相似度計算，可以快速的匹配關鍵詞。雖然詞匹配的方法能簡單且快速的找出相關的文件，但它卻無法考慮到文字與

文字之間的順序和語意上的關聯。爲此，許多以語意匹配作爲基礎的檢索系統被紛紛提出，包含潛藏語意分析 (Latent Semantic Analysis, LSA) (Deerwester et al., 1990) 主題模型 (Topic Model) (Hofmann, 1999; Papadimitriou et al., 2000; Blei et al., 2003) 等。與詞匹配不同的是語意匹配用了密集向量來表徵，可以看做是將查詢與文件投影到潛在的語意空間 (Latent Semantic Space)，同義詞與一詞多義的關聯就能有效的在這個空間中被捕捉到。

隨著深度學習的蓬勃發展，近年來自監督 (Self-supervised Learning) 的預訓練語言模型 (Pre-trained Language Model) 在許多自然語言處理的任務上都有突破性的表現。其中 (Dense Passage Retriever, DPR) (Karpukhin et al., 2020) 爲一個著名的語意匹配檢索系統，它使用兩個不同的 BERT (Devlin et al., 2019) 預訓練語言模型，來將查詢及文件分別以密集的向量表徵，並使用簡單的向量相似度計算，來求得相關的文件。由於 DPR 有著 BERT 強大的語意表示能力及雙編碼器 (Dual Encoder) 的設計，讓它可以預先計算全部文件的向量表示，在效果及速度上都能超越被視爲標準的 BM25 檢索系統。最近，另外一種資訊檢索的方法被提出，如圖1所示，(Differentiable Search Index, DSI) (Tay et al., 2022) 有別於以往的檢索系統需要進行大量的向量比對，來找出相關的文件，這個方法利用序列到序列 (Sequence-to-sequence) 的預訓練語言模型，將所有的文件資訊編碼進一個 Transformer (Vaswani et al., 2017) 的參數中。DSI 在訓練時分爲兩個步驟，第一步驟爲索引 (Indexing Phase)，第二步驟爲檢索 (Retrieval Phase)。在索引的階段，模型學習如何將文件的內容 (Document Texts) 對應到文件的編號 (Document Identifiers)。在檢索的階段，模型學習如何將查詢 (Query) 對應到相關文件的編號。最後在模型推理 (Inference) 時，使用者只需要輸入查詢，這個檢索模型就會自迴歸 (Autoregressive) 的產生潛在相關的文件編號，大幅的簡化整個檢索過程。DSI 的作者也顯示當使用更大的預訓練語言模型時，檢索的效果也會跟著上升，在現今模型參數量快速成長的趨勢下，這類的方法展現了十足的潛力。

強大的檢索系統通常需表現出以下幾點能力 (Lewis et al., 2021)，從最簡單的記憶訓練時看過的查詢，到使用訓練時看過的答案來回答新的查詢表述，最後是使用完全新的答案表述來回答新的查詢表述。 (Lewis et al., 2021) 指出，將回答查詢所需的所有知識都儲存在模型參數中的閉卷模型 (Closed-book Model)，在遇到新的查詢表述時，容易傾向回答訓練時看過的答案，這個現象顯示出此類模型的泛化能力不足。而 DSI 同爲閉卷模型的一種，在 (Zhuang et al., 2022) 的研究中也指出它的泛化能力不足。 (Zhuang et al., 2022) 提到 DSI 模型在學習建立查詢與相關文件之間的關聯時，是透過索引與檢索的兩個階段來學習，但是在大部分的訓練資料中，並不是每篇文件都會有對應的查詢，所以若有文件編號未被任何查詢對應過，而導致模型無法爲該文件與相關的查詢建立關聯，模型在推理時就會傾向回答有被順利對應過的文件編號。(Differentiable Search Index With Query Generation, DSI-QG) (Zhuang et al., 2022) 提出了一個簡單直覺的解決方法，它使用另一個序列到序列的預訓練語言模型，先將所有的文件產生出對應的查詢，確保每篇文件都有對應的查詢後，再進行 DSI 模型的訓練，經過這個方法訓練後，模型在泛化能力上的表現大幅提升。

然而，我們認爲原本的 DSI 模型只使用文件編號來在建立查詢與文件之間的關聯太爲薄弱，爲了增強這之間的對應關係，本研究提出使用 (Supervised Contrastive Learning, SCL) (Khosla et al., 2020) 將查詢與文件先在語意空間中建立關聯。實驗在公開語料集 Nature Question (Kwiatkowski et al., 2019) 上，我們提出的 (Building an Enhanced Autoregressive **D**ocument **R**etriever Leveraging **S**upervised **C**ontrastive **L**earning, DR-SCL) 能進一步的改善模型的泛化能力，在與 DSI-QG 結合後，我們的模型能超越強大的 DPR 檢索模型，讓此類模型向實際應用又邁進了一步。

2 相關研究

2.1 Dense Retriever

隨著深度學習在自然語言處理上的突破，預訓練語言模型 BERT (Devlin et al., 2019)、RoBERTa (Liu et al., 2019) 帶來了強大的語意表示能力，在過去幾年中各式各樣的深度檢索模型也相繼被提出。依據不同查詢與文件的表徵方式及不同計算相似度的方式， (Zhu et al., 2021) 將深度檢索模型分成了三類:Representation-based, Interaction-based, Representation-interaction Retriever。

Representation-based Retriever 也稱做雙編碼器 (Dual Encoder) 檢索模型，這類模型使用兩個不同的編碼器來將查詢與文件以密集向量的方式表徵，透過向量相似度計算來評估查詢與文件的相關程度。其中，

The 34th Conference on Computational Linguistics and Speech Processing (ROCLING 2022)
Taipei, Taiwan, November 21-22, 2022. The Association for Computational Linguistics and Chinese Language Processing

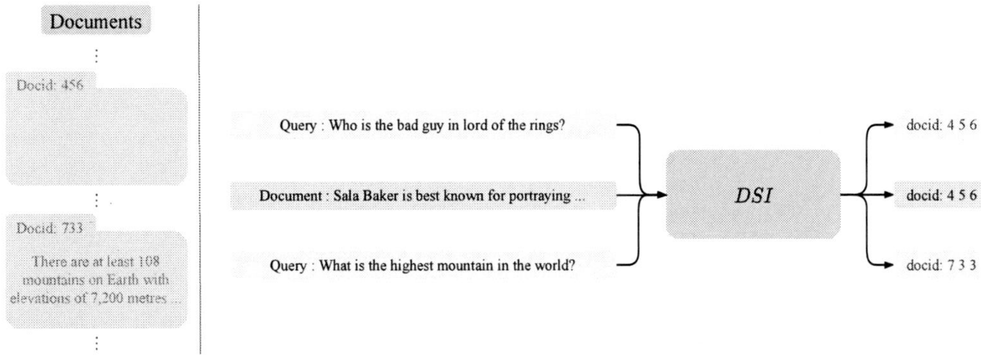

圖 1. (左) 爲許多文件所組成的語料庫。(右) 爲 DSI 的模型架構圖。在 DSI 訓練時，模型透過索引階段 (Indexing Phase) 學習如何將文件對應到它的文件編號，並再透過檢索階段 (Retrieval Phase) 學習如何將查詢對應到與它相關的文件的文件編號。在使用者出入一個查詢後，DSI 會自迴歸的產生相關的文件編號。如果需要，可以使用束搜索來產生潛在相關文件編號的排序列表。另外，爲了幫助模型分辨查詢與文件，在文字輸入進模型前，會先在前面加上任務提示 (Task Prompt)，例如文件會加上 *Document:* 、查詢會加上 *Query:* 。

DPR (Karpukhin et al., 2020) 爲這類模型的著名的方法，它使用了兩個參數不共享的 BERT 編碼器來分別將查詢及文件表徵。在訓練階時，使用對比學習 (Contrastive Learning) 讓目前的查詢在語意空間中和相關的文件拉近，並同時推遠不相關的文件。此類模型有著優良的檢索速度，因爲所有文件的向量表示都能事先被計算好並儲存在記憶體中，當模型進行推理時，只需要計算查詢的向量表示，並將它與儲存在記憶體中的文件向量計算相似度，就能快速的找到相關的文件。但也因爲查詢與文件的表示是獨立獲得，透過簡單的向量相似度計算，兩者之間只有淺層的互動，導致模型犧牲掉不少檢索的效果。

Interaction-based Retriever 也稱做跨編碼器 (Cross Encoder)，這類模型將查詢與文件同時輸入進一個編碼器中，通過它們之間的字符層級 (Token-level) 互動，模型能捕捉查詢與文件間的豐富資訊。 (Nie et al., 2019; Nogueira and Cho, 2019) 使用了 BERT 做爲跨編碼器，它們將 Dense Retrieval 視爲二元分類的問題，若查詢與文件相關爲 1，反之則爲 0。因爲查詢與文件能有深度的互動，所以此類方法有著非常良好的檢索效果，但因查詢與文件必須同時計算，所以在檢索的效率上有很大的限制。

Representation-interaction Retriever 爲了在速度與準確度上取得平衡，這類模型結合了 representation-based 與 interaction-based 兩者的特點。ColBERT (Khattab and Zaharia, 2020) 是此類模型中著名的方法，它延伸了雙編碼器的做法，先使用不同的編碼器分別取得查詢與文件的向量表示，再由字符層級的相似度計算方法來求得兩者之間的關聯程度。值得注意的是，雙編碼器是用一個向量來表徵整個查詢或文件，而此類方法是使用多個字符層級的向量來表示，雖然能取得更好的檢索效果，但在儲存文件向量表示時會需要更大的空間。

2.2 Autoregressive Retriever

另一種檢索系統設計的方式是使用序列到序列 (Sequence-to-sequence) 的自迴歸 (Autoregressive) 模型。此類模型利用預訓練語言模型 T5 (Raffel et al., 2020)、BART (Lewis et al., 2020) 對語意理解的強大能力，將所有回答查詢所需的知識都儲存在模型的參數中，並使用自迴歸的解碼器 (Decoder) 來產生答案。在此小節中，我們預計介紹三個使用自迴歸的檢索系統，分別爲 Autoregressive Entity Retrieval (Cao et al., 2021), DSI (Tay et al., 2022), DSI-QG (Zhuang et al., 2022)

Autoregressive Entity Retrieval 是一個使用序列到序列的預訓練語言模型 BART 來預測實體連結 (Entity Linking) 的系統。使用者將句子輸入到模型後，如果句子中可能存在有實體，模型就會將其對應到語料庫中預設的同義實體，並透過自迴歸的方式輸出。在此研究中，作者使用 Wikipedia 作爲語料庫，而每篇維基百科中的文章的標題則當作是實體名稱。此方法可以看作是特殊類別的檢索系統。

Differentiable Search Index 使用了一個序列到序列的預訓練語言模型 T5 來進行文件檢索，如圖1所示。它先將所有文件資訊編碼進模型的參數中，並在使用者輸入查詢後，自迴歸的產生相對應的文件編號。如果需要，可以使用束搜索 (Beam Search) 來產生潛在相關

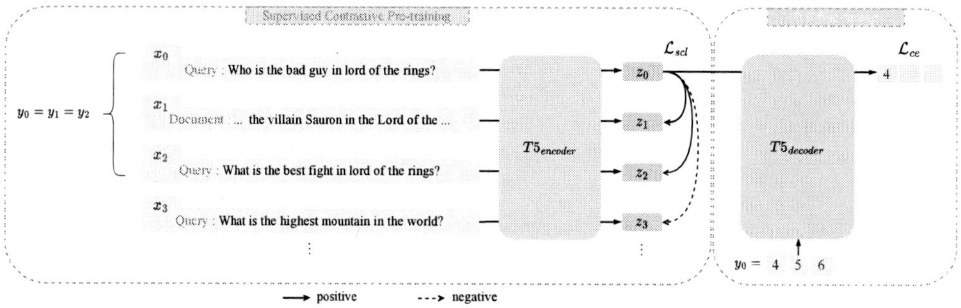

圖 2. 爲本研究提出的 DR-SCL 模型架構。DR-SCL 的模型架構是由一個 T5 預訓練語言模型組成。在訓練階段時，模型爲了將查詢與相關的文件在語意空間中拉近，反之則推遠，首先使用監督式對比學習來預訓練編碼器。在預訓練好模型的編碼器後，我們使用與 DSI 相同的訓練方式來微調模型的解碼器。

文件編號的排序列表。在訓練模型時分爲兩個步驟，第一步驟爲索引 (Indexing Phase)，第二步驟爲檢索 (Retrieval Phase)。在索引的階段，模型學習如何將語料庫中的每一篇文件 $x_d \in X_d$ 對應到它的文件編號 $y_d \in Y_d$。模型將文件內容當作輸入而文件編號當爲輸出，與一般序列到序列的模型訓練方式相同，損失函數爲交叉熵 (Cross Entropy)。以下爲索引階段模型使用的損失計算公式：

$$\mathcal{L}_{indexing} = -\sum_{x_d \in X_d} \log p(y_d | T5(x_d)). \quad (1)$$

如果只有第一階段的訓練，模型只學會文件與文件編號的對應，並不知道如何將查詢對應到它相關的文件內容。所以在第二階段時，模型利用訓練資料中的每一個查詢 $x_q \in X_q$ 與人工標記的相關文件的文件編號 $y_q \in Y_q$ 來建立對應關係。下面爲檢索階段模型使用的總損失計算公式：

$$\mathcal{L}_{retrieval} = -\sum_{x_q \in X_q} \log p(y_q | T5(x_q)). \quad (2)$$

(Tay et al., 2022) 提到如果先訓練索引階段再訓練檢索階段，模型會產生災難性遺忘 (Catastrophic Forgetting) 的現象。爲此，作者改用與 T5 預訓練方式相同的多任務訓練 (Multi-task Learning) 來同時訓練這兩個階段。此外，爲了讓模型能區分查詢及文件的表示，在輸入到模型之前，查詢與文件會分別在開頭加上任務提示 (Task Prompt) 的字串。以下爲 DSI 模型使用的總損失計算公式：

$$\mathcal{L}_{DSI} = -\sum_{x \in X} \log p(y | T5(x)), \quad (3)$$

其中 $x \in X = \{X_d \cup X_q\}, y \in Y = \{Y_d \cup Y_q\}$。

在模型推理 (Inference) 的階段中，輸入一個查詢 x 後，模型會自迴歸的產生對應的文件編號 y。給定查詢 x 模型產生文件編號 y 的機率，可以使用下面的公式來描述：

$$p(y|x) = \prod_{m=1}^{M} p(y_m | T5(x, y_{1:m-1})). \quad (4)$$

作者提到了非常多種產生文件編號 y 的方式，從簡單的流水號 (Atomic Docid) 到使用隨機字符組成的字串編號 (String Docid)，最後是有語意結構的字串編號 (Semantically Structured Docid) 也是其中效果最好的表示方法。爲了產生有語意結構的文件編號，如圖3所示，需先經由一個 BERT 編碼器將所有的文件投影到語意空間中，再使用階層式群集 (Hierarchical Clustering) 演算法，將語意相近的文件歸類到同個群，最後只需要搜尋產生出的樹狀結構，即可指派每篇文件的文件編號。

Differentiable Search Index With Query Generation 提到 DSI 模型是使用索引階段時文件對應到文件編號的訓練，及檢索階段時查詢對應到文件編號的訓練，來建立查詢與相關文件之間的關聯，但在訓練資料中並不是每一篇文件都會有對應到的查詢，所以 X_q 可能爲很小的集合甚至是空集合。爲了解決上述的問題，DSI-QG 使用了一個簡單直覺的解決方式，它先利用了另一個序列到序列的語言模型 T5，學習如何在給定一篇文件後產生其對應的查詢內容。使用此查詢生成模型幫助所有文件產生完對應的查詢後，再使用這些資料與原訓練資料來訓練 DSI 模型。此方法能有效的改善模型無法順利對應到文件的問題。

3 研究方法

3.1 Overview

本篇研究專注於如何增強在 DSI 模型中，查詢與文件之間的對應關係。爲此，我們提出了一個新穎的方法，先使用對比學習 (Contrastive Learning) 來預訓練模型的編碼器，再來進行原本的 DSI 模型訓練。我們使用的模型架構與 DSI 相同，是一個由編碼器與解碼器組成的 T5 (Raffel et al., 2020) 預訓練語言模型。

其中，查詢與文件在輸入模型前會先加上個別的任務提示 (Task Prompt)，如圖2所示。輸入文字序列 x_ℓ 後，模型的編碼器會產生一串序列的向量表示，依據 (Ni et al., 2022) 的做法我們使用平均池化來取得表示整個序列的向量 z_ℓ ，以下面的公式表示：

$$z_\ell = MeanPooling(T5_{encoder}(x_\ell)). \quad (5)$$

3.2 Contrastive Pre-training

爲了增強模型在查詢與文件之間的對應關係，我們先使用對比學習來將查詢與相關的文件在語意空間中拉近，並推遠不相關的文件。由此一來，在新的查詢表述進來時，這個查詢在語意空間中的表示就會更容易的與它相關的文件表示相近，因此也會對後續的自迴歸文件編號生成有所幫助。爲了設計適合的對比學習方法來增強 DSI 模型中查詢與文件的對應關係，我們嘗試了使用與 DPR 模型相同的對比學習方法。給定一個包含 N 筆資料的訓練集 $B_{cl} = \{(x_{q,v}, x_{d,v})\}_{v=1..N}$，其中 $x_{d,v} \in X_d$ 爲查詢 $x_{q,v} \in X_q$ 相關的一篇文件。

訓練資料中的查詢與文件在經過第 (5) 式後，得到向量表示 $\{(z_{q,v}, z_{d,v})\}_{v=1..N}$。令 $i \in I = \{1, .., N\}$ 爲訓練資料的索引。接著，DPR 所用的對比學習可以使用以下的式子來描述：

$$\mathcal{L}_{cl} = -\sum_{i\in I} \log \frac{\exp(z_{q,i} \cdot z_{d,i})}{\sum_{a\in I} \exp(z_{q,i} \cdot z_{d,a})}, \quad (6)$$

其中 $\cdot$ 表示使用內積運算，而文件 $z_{d,i}$ 爲查詢 $z_{q,i}$ 的正樣本，在訓練資料中除了 $z_{d,i}$ 以外的 $N-1$ 筆文件則當作是 $z_{q,i}$ 查詢的負樣本。

考量到後續的自迴歸文件編號生成任務，類似於序列分類的問題，如果我們能將同一類 (有著相同的文件編號) 的查詢或文件拉近，並將不同類別的推遠，那對於序列的分類必定會有更大的幫助。監督式對比學習 (Khosla et al., 2020) 將同類別的資料都視爲正樣本，不同類別的資料視爲負樣本，由此一來如果我們使用監督式對比學習就可以比 (6) 式有著更多的正樣本。在訓練時也不會侷限於只能以查詢作爲錨點 (Anchor) 來拉近與推遠文件，而是能任意讓查詢或文件來當作錨點拉近相同類別與推遠不相同的類別。給定一個包含 N 筆資料的訓練集 $B_{drscl} = \{(x_u, y_u)\}_{u=1..N}$，其中 $x_u \in X, y_u \in Y$。在訓練資料中的 x_u 經過 (5) 式後，得到向量表示 $\{(z_v, y_v)\}_{u=1..N}$。

令 $A(i) = I \setminus \{i\}$ 爲索引 I 扣除掉 i 後的集合，$S(i) = \{s \in A(i) : y_s = y_i\}$ 爲索引 i 的所有正樣本的索引。監督式對比學習可以使用下面的公式來描述：

$$\mathcal{L}_{scl} = -\sum_{i\in I} \frac{1}{|S(i)|} \sum_{s\in S(i)} \log \frac{\exp(z_i \cdot z_s)}{\sum_{a\in A(i)} \exp(z_i \cdot z_a)}, \quad (7)$$

其中 $|S(i)|$ 爲集合 $S(i)$ 的大小。

3.3 DSI Fine-tuning

爲了不讓建立好的語意空間受到後續訓練序列分類的影響，在預訓練完模型的編碼器後，我

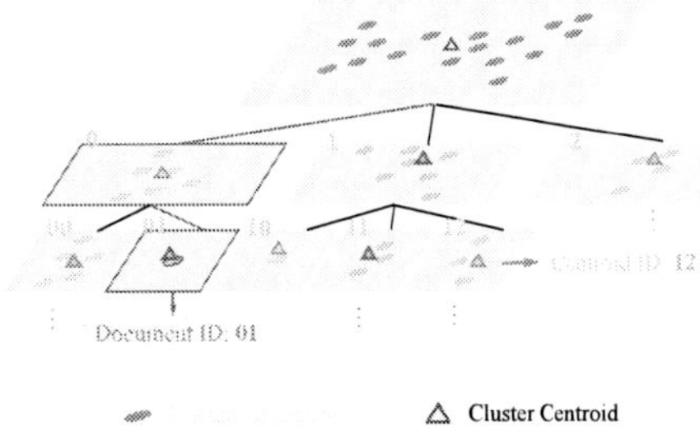

圖 3. 爲產生有語意結構的文件編號時用的階層式分群的示意圖。

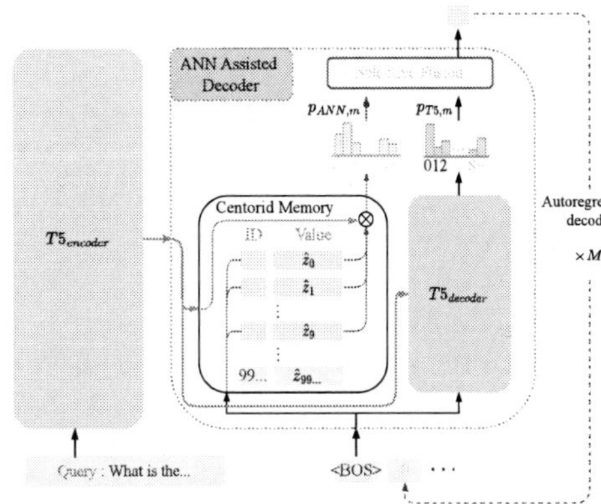

圖 4. 爲 DR-SCL 在模型推理時的架構圖。模型會使用最鄰近搜尋法 ANN 來輔助模型解碼器自迴歸的生成文件編號。

們的作法與 (Khosla et al., 2020) 相同，先將模型編碼器的參數凍結住，之後再進行模型解碼器的微調 (Fine-tune)。在微調模型的解碼器時，訓練方式與 DSI 相同，使用多任務學習來同時訓練文件對應到文件編號的索引階段 (Indexing Phase)，與查詢對應到文件編號的檢索階段 (Retrieval Phase)。給定訓練資料 B_{drscl}，模型的損失函數爲：

$$\mathcal{L}_{ce} = -\sum_{i \in I} \log p(y_i | T5(x_i)). \tag{8}$$

3.4 Document IDs

有鑑於在 DSI 中使用結構化語意 (Semantically Structured) 的文件編號模型會有最好的表現，所以我們也使用語意結構化的方法來表示文件編號。在 DSI 中，作者使用 BERT 預訓練語言模型來抽取出所有文件的語意向量，在取完所有文件向量後，DSI 使用階層式的 k-means 分群法將相近的文件分在一起 (在這裡 $k = 10$)，經過階層式分群後會產生一個十元樹 (Decimal Tree)，從樹根走訪到文件所在的葉節點的過程中，經過的節點編號所組成的字串就爲文件的編號，如圖3 所示。與 DSI 不同的是，我們使用已經預訓練好的模型編碼器，並經過第 (5) 式來產生所有文件的語意向量，如此一來也不需要有額外的模型加入。

3.5 Inference

經過了預訓練後的編碼器，本身就具備著文件檢索的能力。我們利用這項優勢，將 DR-SCL 的編碼器透過最鄰近搜尋法 (Approximate Nearest Neighbor Search, ANN) 來輔助模型解碼器的自迴歸文件編號生成。在模型進行推理前我們先使用在 3.4 小節中，產生好的文件向量與十元樹，來計算樹上每一群的中心點的向量，計算完的中心點向量以 $\hat{z}_c \in \hat{Z}$ 表示，而群中心點的編號 c 則以樹根走訪到 $\hat{z}_c$ 所在的節點，當中經過的節點編號所組成的字串來表示，如圖3所示。在模型推理時，ANN Assisted Decoder 同時參考模型編碼器得到的 ANN 分數與模型解碼器得到的分數，來決定下一個時間點要產生的文件編號字符。

T5 Decoder 在第 m 個時間點文件編號字符 $y_{i,m}$ 產生的機率可以由下面的式子來描述：

$$P_{T5,m} = p(y_{i,m} | T5(x_i, y_{i,1:m-1})), \tag{9}$$

ANN Search 在第 m 個時間點文件編號字符 $y_{i,m}$ 產生的機率可以由下面的式子來描述：

Dataset	$\|D\|$	Train Pairs	Test Pairs
NQ10k	10k	8k	2k
NQ100k	100k	80k	20k

表 1. 爲我們實驗中使用的 Nature Question Dataset 的語料集統計資訊。$|D|$ 表示語料集中，文件的總數。

Dataset	Document Overlap
NQ10k	20.65%
NQ100k	60.89%

表 2. 爲 Test-train 語料集中的重疊比例。Document Overlap 是計算有多少爲答案的文件同時出現在測試資料與訓練資料中。

$$\begin{aligned} P_{ANN,m} &= p(y_{i,m} | ANN(x_i, y_{i,1:m-1})) \\ &= \frac{\exp(z_i \cdot \hat{z}_{y_{i,1:m}})}{\sum_{c \in Child(y_{i,1:m-1})} \exp(z_i \cdot \hat{z}_c)}, \end{aligned} \tag{10}$$

其中 z_i 爲 x_i 經過第 (5) 式後得到的向量表示，$C = Child(c)$，C 是由中心點編號 c 的所有子節點的中心點編號所組成的集合。

Selective Fusion 我們使用另外兩個超參數 α, β 來控制 $P_{T5,m}$ 與 $P_{ANN,m}$ 的結合：

$$P_{Fusion,m} = \exp(\alpha \log P_{T5,m} + (1-\alpha) \log P_{ANN,m}). \tag{11}$$

$$p(y_i | x_i) = \prod_{m=1}^{M} \left(\begin{cases} P_{Fusion,m} & m \leq \beta \\ P_{T5,m} & m > \beta \end{cases} \right). \tag{12}$$

其中 α 控制在產生第 m 個時間點的文件編號字符機率時，$P_{ANN,m}$ 所佔的權重。β 則是控制計算時要往下參考 $P_{ANN,m}$ 幾個時間點，如果 $\beta = 0$，模型的輸出就是正常的 T5 模型的輸出，若 $\beta = \infty$ 則代表使用 ANN 輔助整個文件編號的生成。最後模型在推理階段看到查詢 x_i 後，產生文件編號 y_i 的機率，可以由第 (12) 式來描述。值得注意的是，使用 ANN 能有效減少搜尋的次數，生成一筆完整的文件編號所需的最大搜尋次數爲 $10 \times M$。

4 實驗與討論

4.1 語料集

本研究使用的語料集爲 (Nature-Question, NQ) (Kwiatkowski et al., 2019)，NQ 是專爲端到端 (End-to-end) 的開域問答系統 (Open-domain Question Answering System) 所設計

	NQ10k						NQ100k					
	Total		Overlap		No Overlap		Total		Overlap		No Overlap	
Model	**Hit@1**	**Hit@10**	**Hit@1**	**Hit@10**	**Hit@1**	**Hit@10**	**Hit@1**	**Hit@10**	**Hit@1**	**Hit@10**	**Hit@1**	**Hit@10**
BM25	51.60	73.70	49.39	73.84	52.17	73.66	35.31	59.99	32.03	59.48	40.41	60.77
DPR	61.25	**83.80**	62.71	**88.13**	**60.86**	**82.67**	**53.84**	**79.18**	53.78	81.00	**53.94**	**76.33**
DSI	13.10	30.10	44.06	67.79	5.04	20.28	33.09	50.71	52.11	72.55	3.47	16.69
DSI+QG	56.35	73.90	63.92	82.08	54.37	71.77	51.62	72.13	59.42	80.33	39.48	59.36
DR-SCL (β=0)	25.80	52.20	56.17	77.23	17.89	45.68	37.58	57.47	56.06	75.93	8.79	28.71
DR-SCL+QG (β=0)	56.75	75.40	62.95	86.19	55.13	72.58	52.14	73.34	**60.00**	81.29	39.90	60.96
DR-SCL+QG (α=0.7, $\beta=\infty$)	**61.70**	79.80	**65.85**	87.89	59.16	77.63	53.40	77.12	58.78	**83.31**	45.00	67.48

表 3. 爲基準模型與我們提出的方法，在 NQ10k 與 NQ100k 的測試語料集上的結果。Overlap 指的是有多少爲答案的文件同時出現在測試資料與訓練資料中。

的語料集，其中總共有 307k 筆的訓練資料，每一筆訓練資料中含有一個眞實 Google 搜尋的查詢及一篇人工標記爲相關的 Wikipedia 文件。給定一個查詢，檢索系統必須找出一篇與這個查詢相關的 Wikipedia 文件。我們將 NQ 語料集切成兩個大小 NQ10K 與 NQ100k，來觀測模型對於不同大小語料集的表現，相關的統計資訊如表1所示。

爲了檢視我們提出來的模型是否能改善在遇到新的查詢表述後，模型傾向於回答在訓練過程中看過的答案文件的查詢。我們依據 (Lewis et al., 2021) 將測試語料集再細分成重疊 (Overlap) 與沒有重疊 (No Overlap)，其中重疊代表在測試語料集爲答案的文件，也出現在訓練資料中，而沒有重疊就是沒有在訓練資料出現過，表2爲文件在訓練語料集中重疊的統計資訊。

4.2 實驗設置

我們的模型使用 Huggingface (Wolf et al., 2019) 開源的 T5-base 模型，在進行模型編碼器的預訓練前，我們先使用有著較好語意表示能力的 Sentence-T5 (Ni et al., 2022) 來初始化模型編碼器的參數。在我們提出的 DR-SCL 中，輸入查詢的長度最長爲 32 個字符，而文件的長度我們則是依照 DSI (Tay et al., 2022) 的做法，只保留文件前 32 個字符，並在最前面並接上文件的標題。模型訓練時的批次大小 N 設定爲 64，並訓練 50 代。

4.3 評估指標與基準模型

我們使用 Hit@k 作爲評估模型的指標，其中 $k \in \{1, 5, 10\}$，這個指標與 Top-k Accuracy 相同，它計算前 k 個模型找回的文件中，有出現正確相關文件的比例。

基準模型包含了經典的詞匹配模型 BM25 (Robertson et al., 2009) 與語意匹配的 DPR (Karpukhin et al., 2020) 模型，而在自迴歸的檢索模型上，還有 DSI 與使用額外的查詢生成 (Query Generation) 模型來加強的 DSI-QG 模型 (Zhuang et al., 2022)。其中，我們使用 Sentence-T5 來當作 DPR 中編碼器所使用的模型。在 DSI-QG 中，我們將每篇文件生成對應的五個查詢，再使用這些新生成的查詢與原訓練資料結合來訓練模型。

4.4 實驗結果

我們首先討論基準模型與我們提出的 DR-SCL 模型在整體 NQ10k 和 NQ100k 上的表現，結果如表 (3) 所示。使用語意匹配爲基礎的 DPR 模型在兩個語料集時，皆領先使用詞匹配爲基礎的 BM25 模型，代表著預訓練語言模型的加入，大幅的改善無法只使用詞語匹配來找到答案的問題。致使 DSI 模型在整體 NQ10k 與 NQ100k 的表現相較於 BM25 都來的差，可以發現 DSI 模型只要在遇到查詢的答案文件沒有在訓練時的檢索階段 (Retrieval Phase) 被訓練過 (No Overlap) 的情況下，表現都會非常差，這個現象也印證 DSI 模型在泛用能力上的低落，而若是遇到查詢的答案文件有在訓練時的檢索階段被訓練過 (Overlap)，DSI 模型就能領先 BM25，至於模型在 NQ10k 上檢索效果低於 BM25，我們推測是因爲相較於 NQ100k，NQ10k 有大部分的文件能用詞匹配的方式來達成，所以 DSI 的效果會略輸於 BM25。另外，DSI 在 NQ100k 的表現優於 NQ10k，是因爲在 NQ100k 的測試資料中有較多爲答案的文件也有出現在訓練資料中，如表2所示。我們提出的方法 DR-SCL($\beta = 0$) 在 NQ10k No Overlap 上，相較 DSI 進步了 12%，在 NQ100k No Overlap 上也進步了 5%，驗證了使用對比學習來增強原本 DSI 模型中查詢與文件之間的薄弱關係的有效性。再來是 DSI-QG 模型，它使用額外的查詢生成模型來產生更多與文件相關的查詢，這個方法簡單的解決了 DSI 在訓練檢索階段 (Retrieval Phase) 文件沒有被對應過的查詢，在 No Overlap 的表現上都有大幅的進步。DR-SCL+QG($\beta = 0$) 爲我們的方法加上一個額外的查詢生成模型，額外使用生成的模型再搭配使用對比學習方法加強查詢與文件的關係後，能比 DSI+QG 的方法效果再好一些。最後，當我們的方法 DR-

Encoder	Additional Pre-trained	Hit@1	Hit@10
T5	-	13.10	30.10
Sentence-T5	-	16.90	40.75
Sentence-T5	DPR Loss (6)	22.95	46.00
Sentence-T5	SCL Loss (7)	**24.00**	**48.30**

表 4. 爲使用不同的預訓練方法來訓練編碼器，對整體表現的影響。

Encoder	Additional Pre-trained	Hit@1	Hit@10
Sentence-T5	-	24.00	48.30
Sentence-T5	SCL Loss (7)	**25.80**	**52.20**

表 5. 爲使用不同模型編碼器來產生有語意結構的文件編號對整體表現的影響。

SCL+QG($\alpha = 0.7, \beta = \infty$) 在模型解碼文件編號時，如果犧牲一點運算速度參考模型編碼器提供的 ANN 分數，我們的提出的方法在 NQ10k Hit@1 時就能超越強大的 DPR 模型，讓自迴歸的檢索模型向實際應用又更邁進了一步。

4.5 消融研究 (Ablation Study)

4.5.1 Contrastive Pre-training

在這個小節中，我們將分析何種模型編碼器的預訓練方法對我們提出的模型會有最好的效果，結果如表4所示。直接使用沒有額外預訓練的 T5 模型，是其中效果最差的，因爲 T5 語言模型在設計時不像 BERT 一樣專注在語意特徵的的學習上，這導致了 T5 模型的編碼器沒辦法產生最佳的語意表示。我們嘗試使用額外以句子相似度訓練的 Sentence-T5 來直接初始化模型的編碼器，可以發現有著更強的語意表示對於自迴歸文件檢索模型是有幫助的。對比用與 DPR 相同的對比學習方式 (6)，使用監督式對比學習 (7) 來預訓練模型的編碼器可以取得最好的效果，這是因爲監督式對比學習有更多的正樣本與查詢和文件間有更豐富的互動。

4.5.2 Document IDs

在這個小節中，我們將探討使用哪一種編碼器來產生有語意結構的文件編號，會對我們的模型有最好的效果，結果如表5所示。可以發現有經過監督式對比學習訓練過的編碼器，在產生文件的語意向量時能有最好的效果，這是因爲經過訓練資料訓練過的編碼器能將不相關的文件推遠，相比直接使用沒看過訓練資料的 Sentence-T5 來的更好。

4.5.3 Alpha & Beta

在這個小節中，我們想了解模型在推理階段時超參數 α, β 的設置，結果如圖5所示。α 負責在產生第 m 個文件編號的字符時，控制 ANN

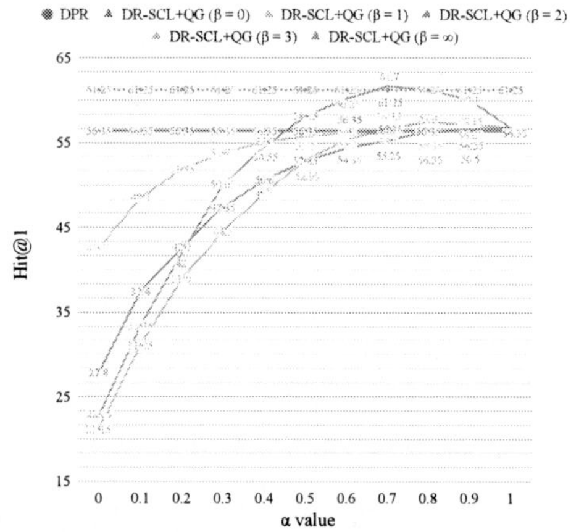

圖 5. 爲使用不同超參數 α, β 設定時，對整體表現的影響。

分數的比重，α 越小表示 ANN 分數所佔的比重越高。β 控制要使用 ANN 輔助產生幾個文件編號的字符，β 越大表示使用 ANN 輔助產生越多文件編號的字符。當 $\beta = 0$ 時，模型完全不使用 ANN 來輔助輸出; 而在 $\alpha = 0, \beta = \infty$ 時，模型的輸出即是 ANN 的輸出。最後在 $\alpha = 0.7, \beta = \infty$ 模型解碼器參考些許 ANN 的分數來預測文件編號時，模型會有最好的表現。

5 結論

在本研究中，我們提出了將監督式對比學習應用在自迴歸的檢索模型 DSI 上，來改善 DSI 在遇到新的查詢表述時，泛化能力不足的問題。並且，我們也提出了一個使用最近鄰居搜尋法 (ANN) 來輔助模型產生文件編號，讓模型可以在推理時，透過超參數的控制來平衡模型的精準度與速度。在公開的 Nature Question 語料集上，我們提出的方法與 DSI-QG 結合後，在 Hit@1 能超越強大的 DPR 模型，讓自迴歸的檢索模型向實際應用又邁進了一步。在未來的研究裡，我們希望不靠額外的查詢生成模型來輔助 DR-SCL，就能找到一個好的方式讓模型記憶文件資訊，且在查詢進入到模型後能順利的檢索出相關的文件，這將會是我們主要研究的方向。除此之外，因爲自迴歸的檢索模型可以完全端到端的訓練，它可以當作是一個大模型中具備檢索能力的元件，這是非常有潛力的。

References

David M Blei, Andrew Y Ng, and Michael I Jordan. 2003. Latent dirichlet allocation. *Journal of machine Learning research*, 3(Jan):993–1022.

Nicola De Cao, Gautier Izacard, Sebastian Riedel, and Fabio Petroni. 2021. Autoregressive entity retrieval. In *9th International Conference on Learning Representations, ICLR 2021, Virtual Event, Austria, May 3-7, 2021*. OpenReview.net.

Scott Deerwester, Susan T Dumais, George W Furnas, Thomas K Landauer, and Richard Harshman. 1990. Indexing by latent semantic analysis. *Journal of the American society for information science*, 41(6):391–407.

Jacob Devlin, Ming-Wei Chang, Kenton Lee, and Kristina Toutanova. 2019. BERT: pre-training of deep bidirectional transformers for language understanding. In *Proceedings of the 2019 Conference of the North American Chapter of the Association for Computational Linguistics: Human Language Technologies, NAACL-HLT 2019, Minneapolis, MN, USA, June 2-7, 2019, Volume 1 (Long and Short Papers)*, pages 4171–4186. Association for Computational Linguistics.

Thomas Hofmann. 1999. Probabilistic latent semantic indexing. In *Proceedings of the 22nd annual international ACM SIGIR conference on Research and development in information retrieval*, pages 50–57.

Vladimir Karpukhin, Barlas Oguz, Sewon Min, Patrick S. H. Lewis, Ledell Wu, Sergey Edunov, Danqi Chen, and Wen-tau Yih. 2020. Dense passage retrieval for open-domain question answering. In *Proceedings of the 2020 Conference on Empirical Methods in Natural Language Processing, EMNLP 2020, Online, November 16-20, 2020*, pages 6769–6781. Association for Computational Linguistics.

Omar Khattab and Matei Zaharia. 2020. Colbert: Efficient and effective passage search via contextualized late interaction over BERT. In *Proceedings of the 43rd International ACM SIGIR conference on research and development in Information Retrieval, SIGIR 2020, Virtual Event, China, July 25-30, 2020*, pages 39–48. ACM.

Prannay Khosla, Piotr Teterwak, Chen Wang, Aaron Sarna, Yonglong Tian, Phillip Isola, Aaron Maschinot, Ce Liu, and Dilip Krishnan. 2020. Supervised contrastive learning. *Advances in Neural Information Processing Systems*, 33:18661–18673.

Tom Kwiatkowski, Jennimaria Palomaki, Olivia Redfield, Michael Collins, Ankur Parikh, Chris Alberti, Danielle Epstein, Illia Polosukhin, Matthew Kelcey, Jacob Devlin, Kenton Lee, Kristina N. Toutanova, Llion Jones, Ming-Wei Chang, Andrew Dai, Jakob Uszkoreit, Quoc Le, and Slav Petrov. 2019. Natural questions: a benchmark for question answering research. *Transactions of the Association of Computational Linguistics*.

Mike Lewis, Yinhan Liu, Naman Goyal, Marjan Ghazvininejad, Abdelrahman Mohamed, Omer Levy, Veselin Stoyanov, and Luke Zettlemoyer. 2020. BART: denoising sequence-to-sequence pre-training for natural language generation, translation, and comprehension. In *Proceedings of the 58th Annual Meeting of the Association for Computational Linguistics, ACL 2020, Online, July 5-10, 2020*, pages 7871–7880. Association for Computational Linguistics.

Patrick S. H. Lewis, Pontus Stenetorp, and Sebastian Riedel. 2021. Question and answer test-train overlap in open-domain question answering datasets. In *Proceedings of the 16th Conference of the European Chapter of the Association for Computational Linguistics: Main Volume, EACL 2021, Online, April 19 - 23, 2021*, pages 1000–1008. Association for Computational Linguistics.

Yinhan Liu, Myle Ott, Naman Goyal, Jingfei Du, Mandar Joshi, Danqi Chen, Omer Levy, Mike Lewis, Luke Zettlemoyer, and Veselin Stoyanov. 2019. Roberta: A robustly optimized bert pretraining approach. *arXiv preprint arXiv:1907.11692*.

Jianmo Ni, Gustavo Hernandez Ábrego, Noah Constant, Ji Ma, Keith B. Hall, Daniel Cer, and Yinfei Yang. 2022. Sentence-t5: Scalable sentence encoders from pre-trained text-to-text models. In *Findings of the Association for Computational Linguistics: ACL 2022, Dublin, Ireland, May 22-27, 2022*, pages 1864–1874. Association for Computational Linguistics.

Yixin Nie, Songhe Wang, and Mohit Bansal. 2019. Revealing the importance of semantic retrieval for machine reading at scale. In *Proceedings of the 2019 Conference on Empirical Methods in Natural Language Processing and the 9th International Joint Conference on Natural Language Processing, EMNLP-IJCNLP 2019, Hong Kong, China, November 3-7, 2019*, pages 2553–2566. Association for Computational Linguistics.

Rodrigo Nogueira and Kyunghyun Cho. 2019. Passage re-ranking with bert. *arXiv preprint arXiv:1901.04085*.

Christos H Papadimitriou, Prabhakar Raghavan, Hisao Tamaki, and Santosh Vempala. 2000. Latent semantic indexing: A probabilistic analysis. *Journal of Computer and System Sciences*, 61(2):217–235.

Colin Raffel, Noam Shazeer, Adam Roberts, Katherine Lee, Sharan Narang, Michael Matena,

Yanqi Zhou, Wei Li, and Peter J. Liu. 2020. Exploring the limits of transfer learning with a unified text-to-text transformer. *J. Mach. Learn. Res.*, 21:140:1–140:67.

Stephen Robertson, Hugo Zaragoza, et al. 2009. The probabilistic relevance framework: Bm25 and beyond. *Foundations and Trends® in Information Retrieval*, 3(4):333–389.

Yi Tay, Vinh Q Tran, Mostafa Dehghani, Jianmo Ni, Dara Bahri, Harsh Mehta, Zhen Qin, Kai Hui, Zhe Zhao, Jai Gupta, et al. 2022. Transformer memory as a differentiable search index. *arXiv preprint arXiv:2202.06991*.

Ashish Vaswani, Noam Shazeer, Niki Parmar, Jakob Uszkoreit, Llion Jones, Aidan N. Gomez, Lukasz Kaiser, and Illia Polosukhin. 2017. Attention is all you need. In *Advances in Neural Information Processing Systems 30: Annual Conference on Neural Information Processing Systems 2017, December 4-9, 2017, Long Beach, CA, USA*, pages 5998–6008.

Thomas Wolf, Lysandre Debut, Victor Sanh, Julien Chaumond, Clement Delangue, Anthony Moi, Pierric Cistac, Tim Rault, Rémi Louf, Morgan Funtowicz, et al. 2019. Huggingface's transformers: State-of-the-art natural language processing. *arXiv preprint arXiv:1910.03771*.

Fengbin Zhu, Wenqiang Lei, Chao Wang, Jianming Zheng, Soujanya Poria, and Tat-Seng Chua. 2021. Retrieving and reading: A comprehensive survey on open-domain question answering. *arXiv preprint arXiv:2101.00774*.

Shengyao Zhuang, Houxing Ren, Linjun Shou, Jian Pei, Ming Gong, Guido Zuccon, and Daxin Jiang. 2022. Bridging the gap between indexing and retrieval for differentiable search index with query generation. *arXiv preprint arXiv:2206.10128*.

The 34th Conference on Computational Linguistics and Speech Processing (ROCLING 2022)
Taipei, Taiwan, November 21-22, 2022. The Association for Computational Linguistics and Chinese Language Processing

A Quantitative Analysis of Comparison of Emoji Sentiment: Taiwan Mandarin Users and English Users

Fang-Yu Chang
Graduate Institute of Linguistics,
National Taiwan University
R07142005@ntu.edu.tw

Abstract

Emojis have become essential components in our digital communication. Emojis, especially smiley face emojis and heart emojis, are considered the ones conveying more emotions. In this paper, two functions of emoji usages are discussed across two languages, Taiwanese Mandarin and English. The first function discussed here is sentiment enhancement and the other is sentiment modification. Multilingual language model is adopted for seeing the probability distribution of the text sentiment, and relative entropy is used to quantify the degree of changes. The results support the previous research that emojis are more frequently-used in positive contexts, smileys tend to be used for expressing emotions and prove the language-independent nature of emojis.

Keywords: emoji, sentiment enhancement, sentiment modification

1 Introduction

With the considerable growth of social media, emojis have become increasingly popular and widely used across the world. During the last few years, emojis change the way we communicate online. They allow us to interact with each other more clearly when we struggle to express our emotions through pure texts. It is an explicit acknowledgment that emojis are now part of how we express our emotions, intents and feelings.

Aside from emotion expression, emojis are believed to enhance and modify the sentiment of a text. A sentence may convey an emotion, but its emotion would be strengthened after the addition of emojis, which is called sentiment enhancement.

On the other hand, if the emotion of the sentence is weakened or altered to the opposite emotion, that is called sentiment modification. Moreover, research shows that emojis used to convey emotions are mostly smileys and hearts, which belong to the Smiley & Emotion group in the Unicode emoji categories.

However, though emojis' non-verbal nature suggests that they are universal across cultures, their usages may change from language to language and culture to culture. Over the past few years, great concern has arisen in the research of cross-cultural or cross-language emoji usage. Some of them discuss which kinds of emoji patterns are the same or different across cultures. Some studies build the emoji sentiment lexicon with the data from different languages. But little was done on the degree of how each emoji can enhance or modify the text across languages.

This paper aims to compare the degree of sentiment enhancement and sentiment modification of emojis which are used by Taiwanese Mandarin users and English users with the help of a multilingual language model. Recently, large pre-trained neural models such as BERT have achieved great success in NLP, motivating more and more research to investigate what aspects of language they are able to learn from unlabeled data.

2 Background and Related Work

Many people believe emojis are like the older emoticons, which provide a visual representation using punctuation marks. Emojis and emoticons function as the non-verbal cues (paralanguages) in face-to-face communication, which are believed to convey emotions more effectively and efficiently than the words themselves are saying. In fact, the reason punctuation marks came into existence was to complement emotional engagement in written texts. (Evans, 2017) Moreover, Guibon et al. (2016)

propose that emojis not only add an emotion to a sentence, but also enhance and modify the emotion of a sentence. They also state that emojis are ambiguous and unreliable without context and emojis are often placed at the end of sentences to express emotions.

Further works are done to support that emojis and emoticons result in higher sentiment and have higher contribution in overall sentiment score. Davidov (2010) uses KNN-like strategy to show that punctuations, words and pattern features (including emoticon tags) can improve the quality of sentiment classification tasks. Agarwal (2011) suggest that specific features like emoticons and hashtags also add marginal value to the sentiment classifier. Hogenboom (2013) puts forward that sentiment classifiers are more accurate when they train on emoticons. Ayvaz and Shiha (2017) collects positive and negative data to analyze the influence of emojis in sentiment analysis, they find that emojis not only increase sentiment score in both polarities, but more frequently used to show positive opinions. Tian's study on Facebook data across four different countries (2017) proves that emojis and texts can update the meaning of each other, suggesting there is a correlation between emojis and linguistic contexts, the author also states that sarcasm, irony and politeness can be interpreted by analyzing emojis.

However, previous works mainly take emojis as features to better the performance on sentiment analysis. This approach would not take the impact of emojis on the texts into account, since an emoji has different influences on different contexts. We can know a smiley has a positive impact on texts, but it might be difficult to obtain how much degree of the impact of a smiley on two unrelated texts. Along with the development of the attention network, Lou et al. (2020) first use attention mechanisms to train emoji and text embeddings simultaneously on a Bi-LSTM model. Conneau et al. (2020) present a transformer-based multilingual pre-trained on texts in 100 languages.

The most widely used genre among emoji is facial expressions, Gao (2020) states that they are keys to convey emotions. When people look at a smiley face online, the same parts of the brain are activated like they look at a real human face. However, facial expressions are not universal signals. The interpretation of emotions and attitude is strongly influenced by different cultural backgrounds. (Jack et al., 2009) According to the study, overt emotional demonstration is the norm in Western cultures, while subtle emotional demonstration is the norm in Eastern cultures. Researchers also suggests that these differences extend to the use of emojis. (Gao and VanderLaan, 2020)

From another perspective, there are researches exploring the meanings and usages across cultures and languages. Barbieri et al. (2016) adopt various experiments to compare the usage of emojis across four Western languages. They observe that the frequently used emojis share similar semantic usages across these four languages, supporting that emojis are language independent. On the other hand, they find that the usages of particular emojis differ due to the cultural influences.

3 Methods

Data collection: Taiwanese Mandarin users data is from Dcard and Instagram, since they are both popular among young people in Taiwan. Dcard is the largest anonymous social media platform in Taiwan with over eighteen million unique visitors per month, and there have been over ten million Taiwanese Instagram users until 2022. On the other hand, English users' data is from Twitter and Instagram. According to the statistics[1], both are on the list of the top five social media platforms in the US (Instagram and Twitter are more closely related to microblog/social media platforms on the list). Dcard data were collected from the public Dcard API, Instagram data were crawled from the Instagram-scraper, and Twitter data were collected from the Twitter API using tweepy [2] Python package2. All data were randomly collected from October 2021 to July 2022 with no repeat. The texts in Dcard articles, Instagram posts and tweets were splitted into sentences, and only sentences with one emoji remained. Since the number of Taiwanese Mandarin sentences (23646 sentences) exceeds the number of English ones (17876 sentences), the Taiwanese Mandarin data were randomly selected from the original data in order to make the two dataset have equal amounts.

[1] https://www.oberlo.com/statistics/most-popular-socialmedia-in-the-us

[2] https://docs.tweepy.org/en/stable/api.html

Therefore, both dataset contain 17876 sentences respectively, with one emoji in each sentence.

Data pre-processing: To clean the data, irrelevant and redundant information like hashtags (#happy), URLs, user tags(@username) and spams were deleted. A sentence is made to a sentence pair, one with the emoji and one without emojis.

Multilingual language model: The language model adopted here is XLM-T, which is trained on XLM-R (Conneau et al., 2020), and then finetuned for various monolingual and multilingual applications. Emoji plays an important role in this model, which is applicable to explore the impact of the emojis on texts. XLM-T and associated data is released at https://github.com/cardiffnlp/xlm-t. I use the NLP pipeline in huggingface[3]. The output of each sentence contains 3 labels (positive, neutral, negative) with three scores being probability distribution.

Measuring frequency: The quantity of each emoji is divided by the sum of total quantities of emojis for two languages.

Measuring frequency of Unicode categories: The quantity of each emoji is divided by the sum of total quantities of emojis in each Unicode emoji category for two languages.

Measuring the degree of sentiment enhancement and sentiment modification: Relative entropy or Kullback-Leibler Divergence (Kullback and Leibler, 1951) is a method of comparing probability distributions over the same variables. Higher values of the divergence mean less similarity between the distributions. It can be used to quantify the change between sentence pairs. To measure the degree of sentiment enhancement and sentiment modification, all sentence pairs in two languages are grouped into four categories. For positive sentiment enhancement, both sentences in the same pair must be labeled with "positive", while both sentences must be labeled with "negative" in the negative sentiment enhancement category. On the other hand, for positive sentiment modification, the sentence without emoji in a pair is labeled with "negative", and the sentence with the emoji is labeled with "positive". For negative sentiment modification, the sentence without emoji in a pair is labeled with "positive", and the sentence with the emoji is labeled with "negative". Applied to the comparison of sentence pairs in four categories, KLD gives us an indication of the degree of sentiment difference between two languages as well as the features that are primarily associated with a difference. In addition, the Spearman correlation coefficient (SCC) of the emojis' degree (those appearing in both languages) in four categories are measured. The SCC is abbreviated as "r s".

Rank:	1	2	3	4	5	6	7	8	9	10	11	12	13	14	15
Taiwan	[illegible]	[illegible]	♥	[illegible]	[illegible]	[illegible]	[illegible]	[illegible]	[illegible]	[illegible]	[illegible]	[illegible]	[illegible]	[illegible]	[illegible]
Ratio	6.33	3.94	3.6	2.35	2.32	2.2	2.11	2.1	1.64	1.56	1.44	1.27	1.24	0.97	0.9
US	[illegible]	♥	[illegible]	[illegible]	[illegible]	[illegible]	[illegible]	[illegible]	[illegible]	[illegible]	[illegible]	[illegible]	[illegible]	[illegible]	[illegible]
Ratio	6.76	5.03	3.8	3.49	2.59	2.01	1.94	1.44	1.25	1.21	1.05	0.98	0.92	0.92	0.83

Figure 1: Top 15 frequent emoji in Taiwanese Mandarin and English, their rank order correlation is 0.767.

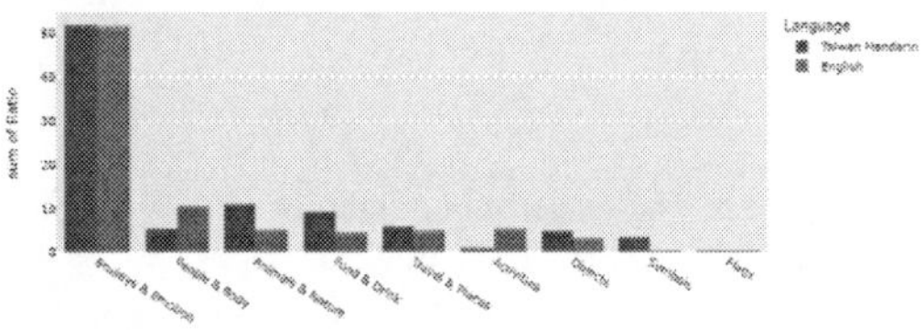

Figure 2: Frequency of emojis grouped by Unicode categories.

Category	Spearman Correlation Coefficient
Smileys & Emotions	0.64
People & Body	0.73
Animals & Nature	0.42
Foods & Drink	0.61
Travel & Place	0.46
Activity	0.76
Objects	0.38
Symbols	0.63
Flags	0.32

Figure 3: The correlation of the frequency of emoji usage in each category across Taiwanese Mandarin and English.

4 Results and Discussion

Frequency of emoji usages: Figure 1 shows 20 most frequently seen in both languages. Across two languages, Spearman correlation coefficient (SCC) is 0.767, indicating that two groups of different language users favor similar types of emoji. "Face with tears of joy" emoji has high ranks in two languages. Figure 2 and Figure 3 show the

[3] https://huggingface.co/cardiffnlp/twitter-xlm-roberta-basesentiment

frequency of emoji categories and their SCC values. The values range from 0.32 to 0.74, depending upon categories. Not surprisingly, the frequency of emojis in "Smiley and Emotions" exceeds other categories greatly in both languages. There are relatively low correspondences in "Animal & Nature", "Travel & Place", "Objects" and "Flags". To drill down the details, the data shows that Taiwanese Mandarin users use more animals while English users use more plants. In the "Activity", the highly frequent emojis are related to birthday or celebration, which is quite different from the previous research (Guntuku et al., 2019). The correlation of emojis in "Activity" category in their research across the east and the west users is low.

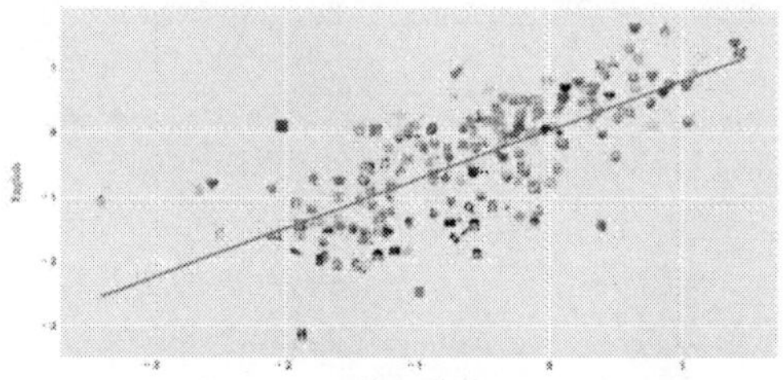

Figure 4: The scatter plot of emojis used by Taiwanese Mandarin users and English users in positive enhancement. ($r_s = 0.604$)

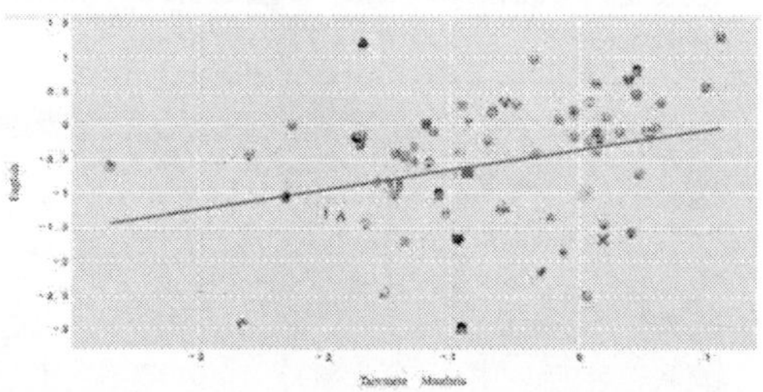

Figure 5: The scatter plot of emojis used by Taiwanese Mandarin users and English users in negative enhancement. ($r_s = 0.547$)

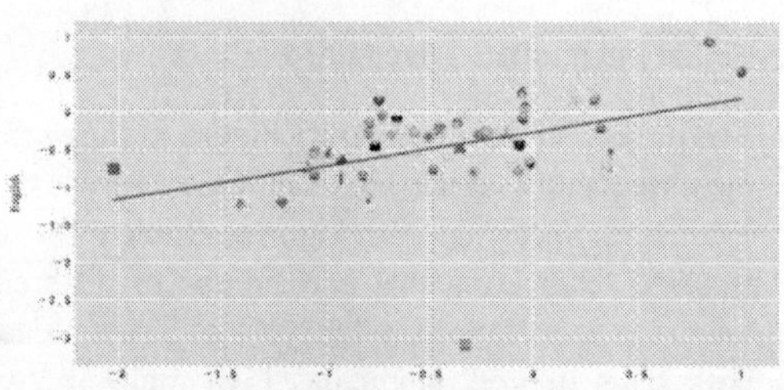

Figure 6: The scatter plot of emojis used by Taiwanese Mandarin users and English users in positive modification. ($r_s = 0.751$)

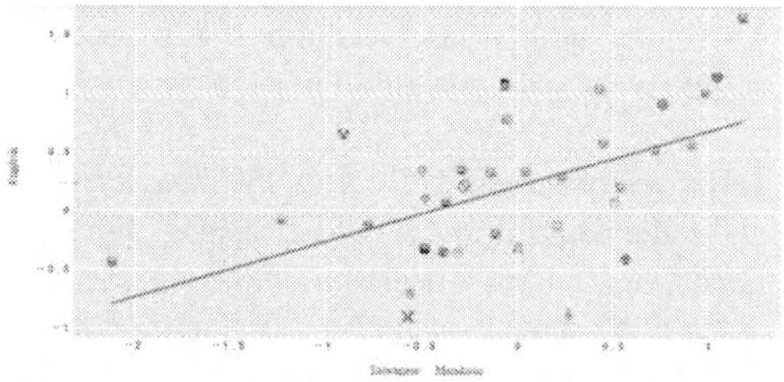

Figure 7: The scatter plot of emojis used by Taiwanese Mandarin users and English users in negative modification. ($r_s = 0.771$)

Sentiment Enhancement: Figure 4 and Figure 5 show the scatter plots of emojis for sentiment enhancement in both languages. In Figure 4, 192 types of emojis are used for positive enhancement, the amount is more than emojis used for negative enhancement (only 74 types). Moreover, smileys and hearts highly increase positive feelings in both languages, whereas emojis in other categories also enhance the positive sentiment. Therefore, emojis are frequently used in positive feelings and convey positive feelings in general. In Figure 5, most of the emojis for negative enhancement are classified into negative emojis (sad faces and angry faces), which are considered to increase negative feelings. And most of the emoji types for negative enhancement belong to the "Smiley and Emotion". The percentage of emoji types in "Smiley & Emotion" category is 22.3% for positive enhancement and 72.3% for negative enhancement. And the total number of smileys in positive enhancement and negative enhancement across two languages are over 99%.

Sentiment Modification: Figure 6 and Figure 7 show the scatter plots of sentiment modification in both languages, the usages for this purpose across two languages have relatively high correlation, implying that the effects of emojis might surpass the texts in both languages. Compared with sentiment enhancement, the emoji types for sentiment modification are relatively low with 42 types for positive modification and 34 types for negative modification. The percentage of emoji in the "Smiley & Emotion" category is 47.6% for positive modification and 79.4% for negative modification. Similar to negative sentiment enhancement, the percentage of smileys faces and hearts emojis are higher than the positive ones. The total number of smileys in positive modification and negative modification across two languages are over 99%.

5 Conclusion

In this research the sentiment degree of emojis used by Taiwanese Mandarin users and English users is compared. For the similar part, the usages of smileys and hearts support the agreement that emojis can be used universally. While there is no significance in the difference in two languages due to data amount. These are only preliminary results, more extensive analyses of the function of emojis are planned to run further.

References

Apoorv Agarwal, Boyi Xie, Ilia Vovsha, Owen Rambow, and Rebecca Passonneau. 2011. Sentiment analysis of Twitter data. In *Proceedings of the Workshop on Languages in Social Media (LSM '11)*. Association for Computational Linguistics, USA, pages 30–37.

Subashini Annamalai and Sobihatun Abdul Salam. 2017. Undergraduates' Interpretation on WhatsApp Smiley Emoji. *Jurnal Komunikasi, Malaysian Journal of Communication.* 33(4):79-103. https://doi.org/https://doi.org/10.17576/JKMJC-2017-3304-06.

Serkan Ayvaz and Mohammed O. Shiha. 2017. The Effects of Emoji in Sentiment Analysis. *International Journal of Computer and Electrical Engineering.* 9. 360-369. https://doi.org/10.17706/IJCEE.2017.9.1.360-369.

Francesco Barbieri, Luis Espinosa Anke and Jose Camacho-Collados. 2022. XLM-T: Multilingual Language Models in Twitter for Sentiment Analysis and Beyond. LREC 2022. https://doi.org/10.47550/arXiv.2104.12250.

Francesco Barbieri, Francesco Ronzano, and Horacio Saggion. 2016. What does this Emoji Mean? A Vector Space Skip-Gram Model for Twitter Emojis. Language Resources and Evaluation conference, LREC, Portoroz, Slovenia, May 2016.

Francesco Barbieri, German Kruszewski, Francesco Ronzano, and Horacio Saggion. 2016. How Cosmopolitan Are Emojis?: Exploring Emojis Usage and Meaning over Different Languages with Distributional Semantics. *MM '16: Proceedings of the 24th ACM International Conference on Multimedia*, Oct 2016, pages 531–535. https://doi.org/https://doi.org/10.1145/2964274.2967277.

Owen Churches, Mike Nicholls, Myra Thiessen, Mark Kohler, and Hannah Keage. 2014. Emoticons in mind: an event-related potential study. *Social neuroscience*, 9(2), pages 196–202. https://doi.org/10.1070/17470919.2013.773737.

Alexis Conneau, Kartikay Khandelwal, Naman Goyal, Vishrav Chaudhary, Guillaume Wenzek, Francisco Guzmán, Edouard Grave, Myle Ott, Luke Zettlemoyer and Veselin Stoyanov. 2020. Unsupervised cross-lingual representation learning at scale. In *Proceedings of the 58th Annual Meeting of the Association for Computational Linguistics*, pages 7440–7451. https://doi.org/10.47550/arXiv.1911.02116.

Dmitry Davidov, Oren Tsur, and Ari Rappoport. 2010. Enhanced Sentiment Learning Using Twitter Hashtags and Smileys. In *Coling 2010: Posters*, pages 241–249, Beijing, China. Coling 2010 Organizing Committee.

Vyvyan Evans. 2017. The Emoji Code: The Linguistics Behind Smiley Faces and Scaredy Cats. Picador.

Boting Gao and Doug P VanderLaan. 2020. Cultural Influences on Perceptions of Emotions Depicted in Emojis. *Cyberpsychology, Behavior, and Social Networking*, 23(7):567-570. https://doi.org/10.1079/cyber.2020.0024.

Gaël Guibon, Magalie Ochs, and Patrice Bellot. From Emojis to Sentiment Analysis. 2016. *WACAI 2016, Lab-STICC; ENIB; LITIS*, Jun 2016, Brest, France.

Sharath C. Guntuku, Mingyang Li, Louise Tay, and Lyle H. Ungar. 2019. Studying Cultural Differences in Emoji Usage across the East and the West. *Proceeding of the Thirteenth International AAAI Conference on Web and Social Media (ICWSM 2019)*.

Alexander Hogenboom, Daniella Bal, Flavius Frasincar, Malissa Bal, Franciska de Jong, and Uzay Kaymak. 2013. Exploiting emoticons in sentiment analysis. In *Proceedings of the 28th Annual ACM Symposium on Applied Computing (SAC '13)*. Association for Computing Machinery, New York, NY, USA, 703–710. https://doi.org/10.1145/2470362.2470497.

Rachael E. Jack, Caroline Blais, Christoph Scheepers, Philippe G. Schyns, and Roberto Caldara. 2009. Cultural Confusions Show that Facial Expressions are not Universal. *Current Biology*, Sep 2009, 19:1543-1547. https://doi.org/10.1016/j.cub.2009.07.051

Solomon Kullback and Richard A. Leibler. 1951. On Information and Sufficiency. *The Annals of Mathematical Statistics*, 22(1):79–76.

Lou Yinxia, Yue Zhang, Fei Li, Tao Qian and Donghong Ji. 2020. Emoji-Based Sentiment Analysis Using Attention Networks. *ACM Transactions on Asian and Low-Resource Language Information Processing*. 19, pages 1-13. https://doi.org/10.1145/3379035.

Ye Tian, Thiago Galery, Giulio Dulcinati, Emilia Molimpakis, and Chao Sun. 2017. Facebook sentiment: Reactions and Emojis. *Proceedings of the Fifth International Workshop on Natural Language Processing for Social Media*, pages 11-16, Valencia, Spain. Association for Computational Linguistics.

The 34th Conference on Computational Linguistics and Speech Processing (ROCLING 2022)
Taipei, Taiwan, November 21-22, 2022. The Association for Computational Linguistics and Chinese Language Processing

應用自動資訊擷取於故事書問答生成之研究
Applying Information Extraction to Storybook Question and Answer Generation

高愷言 Kai-Yen Kao
中央大學資訊工程學系
kykao@g.ncu.edu.tw

張嘉惠 Chia-Hui Chang
中央大學資訊工程學系
chia@csie.ncu.edu.tw

摘要

從故事文本中產生高品質且通順的問題—答案配對是一件耗時且耗力的事情，問題的生成目的不是要讓學生回答不出來，而是幫助學生了解故事所要傳達的訊息，因此需要經過巧妙的設計將文本中的重要資訊當成答案，並且生成與之相對應的問題。在本文中，我們通過將問題類型及其類型定義結合到輸入中來改進 FairyTaleQA 問題生成方法，以微調 BART (Lewis et al., 2020) 模型改進問題生成效能。此外，我們進一步利用 (Zhong and Chen, 2021) 中的實體和關係提取作爲基於模板的問題生成的元素。使用 pipeline 的方法 (Zhong and Chen, 2021)，最後將擷取出來的關係作爲模板式生成的要素。

Abstract

For educators, how to generate high quality question-answer pairs from story text is a time-consuming and labor-intensive task. The purpose is not to make students unable to answer, but to ensure that students understand the story text through the generated question-answer pairs. In this paper, we improve the FairyTaleQA question generation method by incorporating question type and its definition to the input for fine-tuning the BART (Lewis et al., 2020) model. Furthermore, we make use of the entity and relation extraction from (Zhong and Chen, 2021) as an element of template-based question generation.

關鍵字：問題-答案配對生成、問題回答、資訊擷取

Keywords: Question-Answer Pairs Generation, Question Answering, Information Extraction

1 簡介

大量閱讀是語文教育相當重要的一環，可以讓學生在學習中保持新鮮感與熱情。若能搭配互動式教學，與學生進行故事書討論，藉由提出故事書中的問題，讓學生思考並且回答，可以評估學生對於故事書的理解，同時增進學生口語表達能力。本篇研究的目標是幫助老師自動生成與故事相關的問題—答案配對，讓學生能根據問題去思考閱讀過的故事書，培養閱讀以及統整資訊的能力。

Xu 等人 (Xu et al., 2022) 將故事書的提問方式分爲 7 類，包括角色 (Character)、場景 (Setting)、發生事件 (Action)、人物感受 (Feeling)、因果關係 (Causal Relationship)、產生結果 (Outcome resolution)、以及未來預測 (Prediction)，透過這七種面向來設計問題—答案，涵蓋故事文本中大部分的內容。

問題生成的方式主要有兩種，模板式產生以及使用序列模型進行生成，傳統的模板式生成大多是以人工產生的規則進行問題的產生，本研究利用實體與關係擷取技術，可以將文本中重要的資訊擷取出來，取代人工撰寫模板的複雜成本，使得模板式生成也可以產生出具有品質的問題—答案配對。生成式的模型，可以取決於是否先提供答案進行生成，本研究使用先提供答案 (answer-aware) 的方式來生成問題，擷取答案的方法可以使用 Heuristic-based 的方式，故只要使用一個模型就可以生成問題—答案配對。

在本篇論文中，我們對於問題生成使用了兩種方法，在生成式的方法中，我們加入了問題類別與其定義，在 FairyTaleQA(Xu et al., 2022) 的資料集中與 baseline 模型相比可以在 $ROUGE-L$(Recall-Oriented Understudy for Gisting Evaluation) 上提升 0.034，接著我們在生命教育故事進行人工評估，加入問題類別與其定義的問題皆獲得比較高的分數，藉由自動評估與人工評估，皆顯示加入問題類別與定義可以獲得更好的成果。我們也透過了問題回答的任務來對於問題—答案配對進行評估，其結果與人工評估之間的相關性是比使用 ranking model 的相關性略高，也說明了我們使用這種評估方法也可以很好的對於問題—答

案配對進行篩選。在模板式生成問題方面，我們使用了自動資訊擷取的技術，將故事中文本的資訊擷取出來，應用在模板式問題生成，可以對於問題生成有另一種角度的產生。

2 相關研究

2.1 問題生成 (Question Generation)

問題生成 (Question Generation,QG) 是給定一段文本或句子，生成具有可讀性以及與文本相關的流暢問句。傳統的問題生成作法是屬於規則式的產生 (Das et al., 2016)，藉由人工設計的規則、模板、句法分析將文本中的句子轉變爲疑問句的形式，以此來獲得問題，但是這樣的作法會因爲文本的豐富度大量耗費人力，擴展性也不佳，後續較少使用。

問題生成也可以用是否給定「答案」來做區分。有答案 (answer-aware) 的問題生成 (Zhou et al., 2017) 是會先根據文本內容產生特定答案，這個答案可以是文本中的詞語、句子或是人工產生的，在生成問題時，答案可以提供模型在生成問題時有更多的資訊，也可以將問題限制在答案下生成。無答案 (answer-unaware) 的問題生成顧名思義在生成時沒有給定答案 (Du et al., 2017)，模型可以對文本中的任意位置進行問題的產生，沒有答案的資訊以及約束，其產生的問題會較分散且參差不齊，這方面的研究相對 answer-aware 少很多。

Zhou 等人 (Zhou et al., 2017) 在 seq2seq(Sequence to sequence) 架構下，增加了答案 (answer-aware) 進行生成，後續對於問題生成的任務多採用 seq2seq 的架構來實做，而預訓練模型的出現也使得這個任務又有更好的成效，故現在的研究幾乎都使用預訓練模型：而使用 BERT(Dai et al., 2019)、BART(Lewis et al., 2020)、T5(Raffel et al., 2020) 等。

Xu 等人在 2022 年提出的 FairyTaleQA(Xu et al., 2022) 的資料集是以故事爲目標所建立的問答生成資料集，其故事來源是來自古騰堡計畫 (Project Gutenberg) 所收集的書籍，並且以"Fairytale" 爲關鍵字所蒐集的故事書共 278 本。本研究參考 Paris(Paris and Paris, 2003) 所提出的 7 種類型問題，邀請教育專家根據故事文本中的內容、以及 7 種類別，進行問題—答案配對的生成。

2.2 資訊擷取 (Information Extraction)

資訊擷取 (Information Extraction)，是從自然語言文本 (非結構性資料) 中，抽取結構化資料的一個過程，是自然語言理解的基本任務。主要可以分爲三個子任務：實體擷取 (Entity Extraction)、關係擷取 (Relation Extraction)、事件擷取 (Event Extraction)。

2.2.1 實體擷取 (Entity Extraction)

實體擷取 (Entity Extraction, EE) 是一種從文本中，將命名實 lewis-etal-2020-bart 體識別、擷取爲預定義類別的任務，包括：人物 (PER)、地點 (LOC)、組織 (ORG)、時間 (TIME) 等，將原本非結構性的文本，進行序列標記，擷取出特定實體。

實體擷取的主流方法大概可以分爲兩種，較爲傳統的作法爲透過建立辭典 (Wu et al., 2020)，再用其來比對文本中的詞語，另一種是透過機器學習訓練模型進行序列標記的任務來擷取出實體。

在進行實體擷取時，常常會結合 CRF(Conditional Random Field)，將 CRF 當作模型的輸出層。而雙向長短期記憶模型 (Bidirectional Long Short-Term Memory，BiLSTM)，BiLSTM-CRF(Huang et al., 2015) 的架構可以利用記憶功能來保留較長距離的上下文資訊，以此來提升序列標記的準確度。而使用 Bidirectional Encoder Representations from Transformers (BERT)(Dai et al., 2019) 對於實體擷取的任務又能更上一層樓，將 BERT 的預訓練模型當作 embedding 層，除了可以更好的保留上下文關係，更可以有效提升小樣本資料的擷取準確度。

2.2.2 關係擷取 (Relation Extraction)

關係擷取 (Relation Extraction, RE) 是資訊擷取 (Information Extraction, IE) 中很重要的子任務，其可以將文本中一對實體之間的語義關係所擷取出來，大多數的關係擷取都是以二元關係爲主，關係可以定義爲 (e_i, r, e_j)，e_i 與 e_j 分別代表兩個實體，r 代表兩個實體之間的關係，可以把原本非結構性的文本內容整理成結構化且具有意義的資訊。

關係擷取通常會搭配實體擷取任務一起進行，目前主流的方法有兩種 (Zhong and Chen, 2021)，第一種是 Pipeline 的方式，將兩者視爲獨立的任務，兩個任務的模型訓練不會互相影響，另一種方法是將兩個任務進行聯合學習 (Joint Learning)，其優點是兩個子任務之間的資訊可以共同被使用，用來協助另一個子任務進行預測，缺點則是整體模型的架構龐大且複雜。

Pipeline 的方法裡，Zhong 等人 (Zhong and Chen, 2021) 在進行實體與關係擷取時採用了 pipeline 的架構，這個模型是本篇論文在做實體與關係擷取所使用的模型。

在聯合學習的方法中，Shang 等人 (Shang

et al., 2022) 提出了一種將關係擷取視爲分類任務的方法，而這篇論文所提出的標記方法也可以有效的降低在標記時所浪費的空間以及時間成本。

2.2.3 事件擷取 (Event Extraction)

事件擷取 (Event Extraction, EE) 是一種從非結構化的文本中，擷取出與目標相關的事件與相關資訊，識別特定類型的事件後，並將事件中的要素標示出來。根據任務的需求，事先訂定事件的類別，擷取的資訊大致可以分爲以下幾種：事件類別 (event type)、觸發詞 (trigger word)、事件要素 (event arguments)。

事件擷取的流程大致可以分爲以下幾個部分：事件觸發詞偵測、事件觸發詞分類、事件要素偵測、事件要素分類，早期的研究可以分爲 Pipeline 與聯合學習兩種，前者的缺點是會有錯誤傳遞的問題，可以利用聯合學習的方式來改善，而不管是哪種方法，都需要大量的標記資料，也需要設計各個子任務的最佳組合，因此 End2End 生成式的事件擷取漸漸被提出來作爲選項之一。

因此 Lu 等人 (Lu et al., 2021) 提出 Text2Event 模型，是一種 Sequence-to-Structure 的事件擷取方法，採用 End2End 的方式直接從文本中擷取事件。

3 Generative 問題生成方法

生成式 (Generative based) 的問題產生 (Question Generation) 一般採用 pipeline 的架構，並使用 answer-aware 的方式，以先擷取的答案來當作生成問題的參考，最後透過 Ranking model 與問題回答 (Question Answering) 來進行評估。這個任務是基於預訓練模型 BART(Lewis et al., 2020) 進行實作，以下依序介紹問題定義、模型架構、資料集、實驗。

3.1 問題定義

在問題產生任務中，會先將文本分成多個句子：$S_1, S_2, ...S_N$，根據句子 X_i 產生跟語句相關的問題 $q_i^1, q_i^2, ...q_i^n$ 與答案 $a_i^1, a_i^2, ...a_i^n$，形成問題—答案配對 (q_i^j, a_i^j)，這個任務的輸出就是多組的 $(q_i^j, a_i^j), 1 < i < N$，最後並爲每個問題—答案配對產生分數。

3.2 模型架構

我們參考 Yao 等人 (Yao et al., 2022) 提出的架構，採用 pipeline 的方式進行問題生成，如圖1所示，架構包含三個 module，第一個爲答案產生模組，第二個爲問題產生模組，第三個爲問題—答案配對排序模組。由於這個架構是在 answer-aware 的情況下產生問題，可以得到與答案相對應的問題，也可以根據答案的種類，生成不同種類的問題，讓整體的問題—答案配對品質更好，故先利用 heuristics-based 的答案產生模組，先產生答案來當作問題生成的指引。

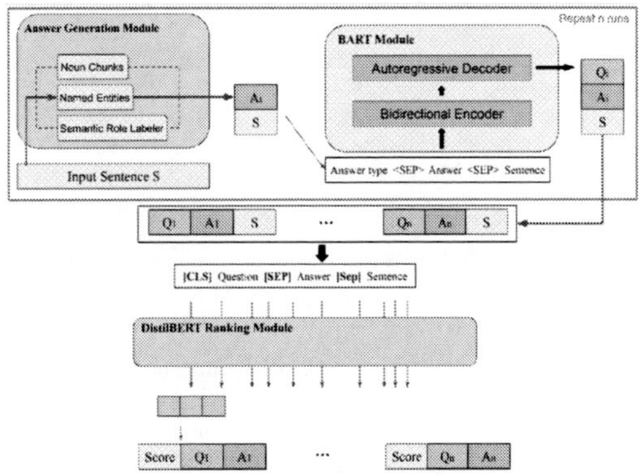

Figure 1: 問題生成模型

Yao 等人對於答案產生模組的做法是透過 Spacy(Honnibal and Montani, 2017) 的套件來擷取出命名實體與名詞片語，並利用 AllenNLP(Gardner et al., 2018) 的 bert-base srl 來進行語義角色標註 (Semantic Role Labeling)，將句子以動詞進行切分，可以將與動詞相關的主詞、受詞解析出來，最後組成主詞、動詞、受詞來當成候選的答案。

第二個模組是問題產生的核心，由於 BART 在預訓練時就是使用 sequence-to-sequence 的方法進行訓練，所以很適合用來進行序列產生的下游任務 fine-tuned。不同於 Yao 等人的做法，我們除了使用答案以及句子外，還加入了答案的類別以及此類別（角色、場景、感受、動作、因果、結果、預測）的定義 (如表1) 進行訓練，讓問題可以根據類別生成更適合的問題。由於 BART 本身具有 Autoregressive Decoder，所以可以直接對於生成任務進行微調，將 source：問題類別、答案、句子中間分別以 <SEP> token 連接起來輸入 Encoder，再將 target：根據答案與句子生成的問題輸入 Decoder，即可進行訓練。在進行問題生成時，輸入問題類別、答案、句子，模型即可生成出相對應的問題，來完成得到問題—答案配對的任務。

第三個模組是使用 DistilBERT(Sanh et al., 2019) 來對於經過前面兩個模組產生的問題—答案配對進行排序，可以將排序的任務視爲模型產生的問題—答案配對與訓練資料標記的問題—答案配對的分類任務，透過 DistilBERT 進行下游任務：序列分類 (Sequence Classification) 的微調，在進行分類任務時，需要再

The 34th Conference on Computational Linguistics and Speech Processing (ROCLING 2022)
Taipei, Taiwan, November 21-22, 2022. The Association for Computational Linguistics and Chinese Language Processing

Question-Answer Type	Definition
Character	Ask test takers to identify the character of the story or describe characteristics of characters.
Setting	Ask about a place or time where/when story events take place and typically start with "Where" or "When."
Feeling	Ask about the character' s emotional status or reaction to certain events and are typically worded as "How did/does/do . . . feel"
Action	Ask characters' behaviors or additional information about that behavior
Casual Relationship	Focus on two events that are causally related where the prior events have to causally lead to the latter event in the question. This type of question usually begins with "Why" or "What made/makes."
Outcome Resolution	Ask for identifying outcome events that are causally led to by the prior event in the question. This type of question is usually worded as "What happened/happens/has happened. . . after..."
Prediction	Ask for the unknown outcome of a focal event. This outcome is predictable based on the existing information in the text

Table 1: FairytaleQA 7 種問題—答案類別 (Xu et al., 2022)

輸入句子的最前端加入特殊 token [CLS] 來代表模型是要進行分類任務，最後根據模型產生的標籤機率，轉換爲分數後，即可得到問題—答案配對的分數。

3.3 實驗

我們採用將 FairytaleQA(Xu et al., 2022) 資料集做爲我們實驗的資料集。其故事書共 278 本，訓練資料集包括 232 本書、8548 個 QA-pairs；驗證資料集包括 23 本書、1025 個 QA-pairs；測試資料集包括 23 本書、1007 個 QA-apirs。這些問題—答案配對的比例如圖2，大體上 7 個類別在訓練、驗證、測試集的比例皆算一致。

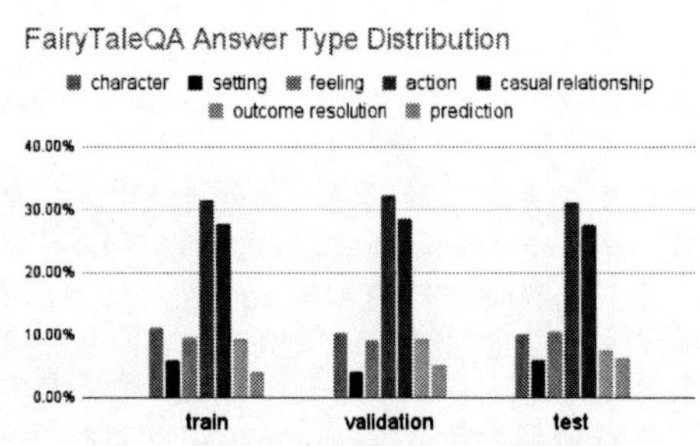

Figure 2: FairyTaleQA 答案類型分佈

3.3.1 評估方法

模型生成出來的問題可以使用 *ROUGE-L* 指標來和標記資料進行評估，其中 L 代表最長公共子序列 (Longest Common Subsequence, LCS)，其中 X 爲 golden sequence，Y 爲生成的句子，見公式1。

$$ROUGE\text{-}L = \frac{LCS(X,Y)}{len(X)} \quad (1)$$

3.3.2 Testing on Given Answers

我們首先忽略答案產生模組的影響，利用測試資料中給定的問題答案配對中的答案做爲輸入，探討使用不同輸入 fine-tuned 的模型在 FairytaleQA 測試資料上面的效能，以及加入問題種類對於整個模型生成問題的效果有所提升。由於每一個 QA 配對均有問題類型，我們在訓練時可以加入問題類型以及定義來進行訓練。測試時，我們再將 QA 配對中的答案當成模型的輸入，再將產生的問題與 QA 配對中的問題進行 $ROUGE-L$ 評估，在 $ROUGE-L$ 約提升 0.2，若是更進一步加入問題答案類別的定義，模型可以在效能上再取得 0.16 的進步，在生成時可以更加根據問題類別來產生相對應的問題。

經過排序模組後，我們取評估分數爲正的問題做平均，以及計算評估分數爲正的問題—答案配對數量。見表2，加入問題種類進行 fine-funed 的模型，可以產生更多數量 (676 –> 690) 的問題、以及更高的分數 (6.30–>6.36)。

3.3.3 Testing on Heuristic Answers

確認使用問題種類可以生成更好的問題後，接著進行由答案產生模組輸出的答案做爲問題生成的輸入，答案產生方法分爲 Entity、Noun Chunk、Semantic Role Labeling (SRL)3 類，其中 entity 的平均長度爲 1.66、chunk 的平均長度爲 2.46、SRL 的平均長度爲 9.46。

以下比較不同答案產生方式在生成問題上的效能比較。見表3，我們選擇 ranking score 爲正的分數進行比較，並且計算其數量。entity 的平均分數是小幅領先 srl，與 chunk 之間

	ROUGE-L	Mean Positive Score	Count
Baseline(Yao et al., 2022)	0.506	6.30	676
+ question type	0.524	6.36	690
+ question type and definition	**0.540**	**6.37**	**692**

Table 2: 生成式問題於 fine-tuned 模型的效能

有著 0.65 的差距，與給定的答案進行實驗時一樣，在加入問題類別與其定義後，可以在 ranking score 取得較好的表現。

3.3.4 Testing on 24 Life Educational Story Books

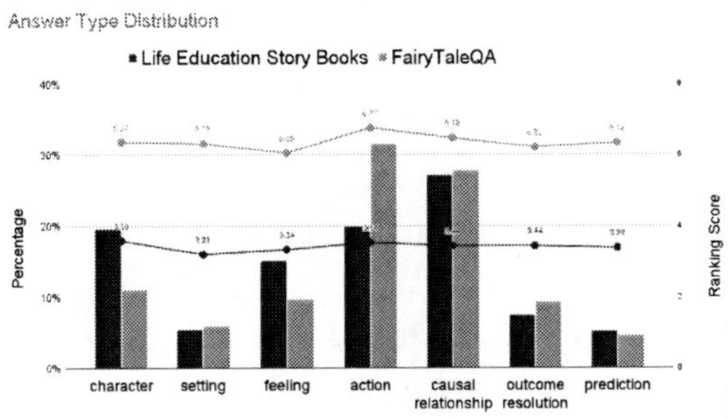

Figure 3: FairyTaleQA 與生命教育故事問題類別分布

最後在 24 本生命教育故事書來測試模型，先採用 Heuristic-based 的方法擷取出故事文本的答案，在透過 3 種不同的輸入方式來產生問題—答案配對，結果如上表4，由結果可以看到，在不同的答案上，有加上問題種類與其定義來進行生成在自動評估上是可以得到比較好的結果。而利用實體擷取模型擷取出來的 Entity 也可以在 ranking score 上面幫助模型生成問題，不管是在數量與 Ranking Score 皆獲得比較好的表現，見表5。

接著比較 FairytaleQA 測試集 (人工標記問答) 與生命教育故事的問題類別分布，見圖3，左邊的 Y 軸是表示不同問題類別的百分比，可以看到兩者的比例是相當接近的，也就是在生命教育故事來進行後續的實驗是相當洽當的。右邊的 Y 軸則是表示各個類別的 Ranking Score，上方的折線分別表示兩個資料集在 7 種問題類別的 ranking score。

這邊探討 7 種不同的問題類別分數的分布，如圖4，可以看到在不同類別的分數主要集中在中間，呈現一個類似於常態分布的狀態。

3.3.5 使用問題回答進行評估

問題回答的模型架構基本上與 BART-Based 的問題生成相同，都是 sequence-to-sequence 的架構，差別只在於輸入與輸出的差異，對

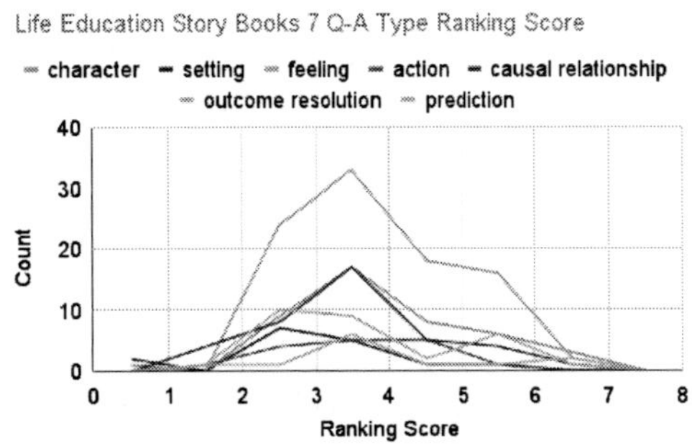

Figure 4: 生命教育故事問題類別分數分布

於問題回答任務，其輸入是以問題、文本中間加 <SEP> token 做爲 Encoder 輸入，透過 Decoder 輸出答案進行訓練，在生成時模型即可以根據問題與文本找出相對應的答案。

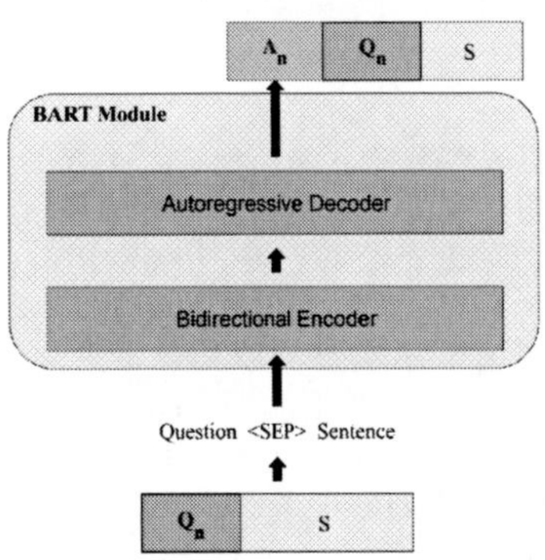

Figure 5: BART-Based 問題回答模型

我們使用 FairyTaleQA 以及 SQuAD 兩個資料集進行訓練，而測試的資料集則選擇兩個，第一個是 FairyTaleQA 的測試資料集中的人工標記問答以及 Heuristic Answer，第二個是 24 本生命教育故事書經過問題生成後的問題—答案配對進行評估。透過 Rouge-L 來計算生成的答案與標記答案之間的相似度。如表6，可以看到使用 SQuAD 進行訓練比 FairyTaleQA 的效果還要好，其因是 SQuAD 的資料數量是 FairyTaleQA 的將近 10 倍，故有更好的效能。

透過問題回答這個任務，我們可以用來評估問題—答案配對生成的品質，提供除了排序

Mean Positive Score	Entity	Noun Chunk	SRL	Avg.	Count
Baseline (Yao et al., 2022)	4.27	3.84	4.08	4.06	40
+ question type	4.47	4.00	4.35	4.27	56
+ question type and definition	**4.66**	**4.01**	**4.65**	**4.44**	**70**

Table 3: Heuristic Answer 於 fine-tuned 模型的效能：Mean Positive Score 和 Count

Models	Mean Positive Score		Count	
	Chunk	SRL	Chunk	SRL
Baseline (Yao et al., 2022)	2.83	4.03	5	17
+ question type	3.10	3.92	6	29
+ question type and definition	**3.23**	**3.98**	**10**	**29**

Table 4: 24 本生命故事於 fine-tuned 模型的效能 (Chunk, SRL)：Mean Positive Score 和 Count

Models	Mean Positive Score		Count	
	Entity	ACE Entity	Entity	ACE Entity
Baseline (Yao et al., 2022)	3.43	3.22	41	107
+ question type	3.45	3.51	58	131
+ question type and definition	**3.69**	**3.75**	49	116

Table 5: 24 本生命故事於 fine-tuned 模型的效能 (Entity, ACE Entity)：Mean Positive Score 和 Count

Rouge-L	FairyTaleQA	SQuAD
FairyTaleQA (Gold Answer)	0.491	**0.502**
FairyTaleQA (Heuristic Answer)	0.445	**0.484**
Life Education Story Books	0.474	**0.675**

Table 6: 問題回答效能比較: ROUGE-L

模組第二個評估方法。換言之，我們會計算問題—答案配對中的答案與問題回答所生成的回答之間的最長公共子序列，以 Rouge-L 做爲評估的指標。圖6是利用問題回答來對 24 本生命教育故事書產生的問題答案配對進行評估，可以看到在 feeling、causal relationship 以及 outcome resolution 的地方，srl 是可以比 entity 與 chunk 得到更好的結果，因爲其擷取出來的答案是具有動詞以及相關資訊，較可以用來提供這方面的問題。

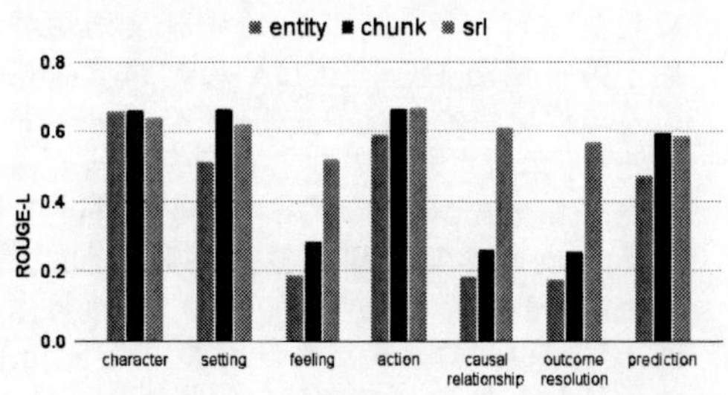

Figure 6: 使用問題回答對 24 本生命教育故事進行評估 (Rouge-L)

圖7是使用散佈圖來觀察使用問題回答以及 ranking model 兩種不同方式評估之間的相關性，可以看到兩者之間的分布較散，有些 Rouge-L 分數爲 0 的問答句的分數也相當高，顯然並不合理。因此我們進一步採用人工評估對生成的問答配對進行評估。

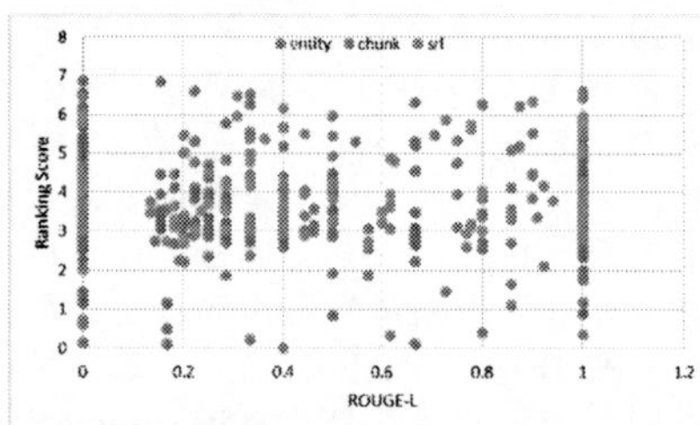

Figure 7: 使用問題回答對 24 本生命教育故事進行評估散佈圖

3.4 人工評估

由於在做序列生成任務時，除了上述自動評估的方法可以當成效能的指標，問題的通順程度以及問題—答案配對之間的相關性是較難衡量的，這時候就需要人工評估來協助判斷，這邊以 3 個指標來對於問題—答案配對進行評估。第一個指標是問題的通順程度 (Question Readability)，這個指標可以用來檢視所生成的問題是否通順，符合閱讀的直覺，第二個指標是問題與文本之間的相關程度 (Question-Text Relevancy)，用來判斷問題是否有問到文本中的內容，第三個指標是答案的相關性

(Question-Answer Relevancy)，用來說明問題—答案配對之間的相關程度，用來判斷所產生的問題與答案之間是否能有很好的匹配性。每個指標的分數區間爲 0 到 5，進行人工評估的標註者爲 3 人，最後以三人平均分數呈現。

首先使用 24 本生命故事書，每個問題類別各隨機挑選一個問答配對（不排除負值的排序分數），由三位研究生進行人工評估。結果如圖8所示，可以看到各個類別在不同評估指標下的分數差異。

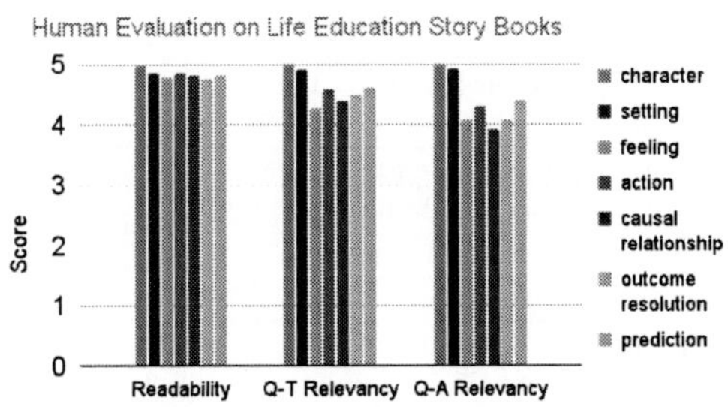

Figure 8: 人工評估結果：7 種問題類別

從人工評估與排序分數散佈圖 (圖9) 可以看到 Ranking module 在分數上分布的較不均勻，分數從高到低皆有，相關係數僅爲 0.121。而人工評估與 Rouge-L 的散佈圖 (圖10) 可以看到右上角分布的較有一致趨勢，相關係數爲 0.245，顯示透過問題回答來進行問題—答案配對的評估比較有意義。

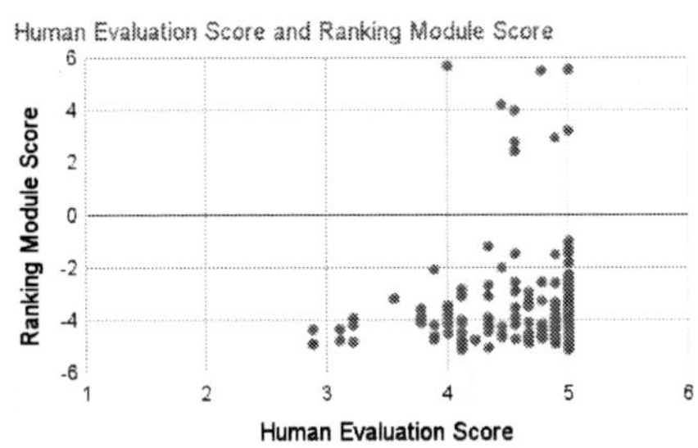

Figure 9: 人工評估結果與 Ranking Score 散佈圖

接著使用 24 本生命故事來進行人工評估的資料，在當中選取 10 本故事書，每本故事書取 3 組問題—答案配對來進行，分別比較不同的模型輸入的影響，共產生 90 組 QA pairs ，結果見表7前三列。由人工評估的結果來看，與自動評估相同，不管是在語句的通順程度抑或是問題—答案配對之間的相關性，加上問題種類與其定義確實能夠在問題生成上得到更好的結果。

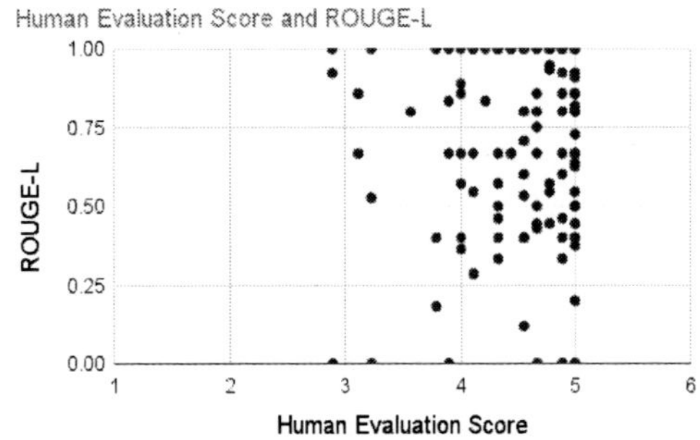

Figure 10: 人工評估結果與問題回答評估分數散佈圖

3.5 Case Study

在給定相同的故事內容以及答案的情況下，加入問題類別以及定義的問題生成可以產生具有更多資訊的語句，如表8、9，在生成問題時，原本的 baseline 模型生成的問句較爲粗略，問得比較是大範圍的問題，而加入問題類別以及定義的生成問句，則是可以看出來有提到文章中的更多資訊，描述的也比較精準。

4 Extraction Enhanced 問題生成

在這個章節，會介紹如何使用資訊擷取任務來幫助模板式的問題生成，其中分爲兩個部分：關係 (Relation) 與事件 (Event)，最後在對模板式的問題生成進行人工評估。

4.1 模板式問題生成方法：Relation

故事文本經過關係模型擷取 (Zhong and Chen, 2021) 後，會得到兩個實體之間的關係。透過這種結構，可以設計模板式的問題產生，使用關係類別來當作答案的部分，而問題產生可以是詢問「兩個實體之間是什麼關係?」，以此得到問題—答案配對。抑或是與 7 種答案類別進行配對，以此生成多樣性的問題。關係擷取的部分，共有 6 種類別以及 18 種子類別，如表10：

Type	Subtype
ART	User-Owner-Inventor-Manufacturer
GEN-AFF	Citizen-Resident-Religion-Ethnicity, Org-Location
ORG-AFF	Employment, Founder, Ownership, Student-Alum, Sports-Affiliation, Investor-Shareholder, Membership
PART-WHOLE	Artifact, Geographical, Subsidiary
PER-SOC	Business, Family, Lasting-Personal
PHYS	Located, Near

Table 10: ACE2005: Relation Types (Walker et al., 2006)

	Question Readability	Q-T Relevancy	Q-A Relevancy
Baseline (Yao et al., 2022)	4.60	3.87	4.06
+ question type	4.52	4.07	4.27
+ question type and definition	**4.84**	**4.64**	**4.61**
Template-based	**4.96**	4.60	3.96

Table 7: 人工評估結果

Story Text	All the notes in her music books and all the things related to music were all gone.
Answer	all the things related to music
Baseline (Yao et al., 2022)	what were all gone from the house?
+ question type	what was missing from the girl's books?
+ question type and definition	what was missing from the notes in her music books?

Table 8: 24 本生命故事：Question Generation Example 1

Story Text	"Yes dear. That's because Sophie is very special. She has Down Syndrome," her mom explained.
Answer	Down Syndrome
Baseline (Yao et al., 2022)	what was special about Sophie ?
+ question type	what was special about Sophie ?
+ question type and definition	what kind of special condition does Sophie have ?

Table 9: 24 本生命故事：Question Generation Example 2

4.2 模板式問題生成方法：Event

使用 text2event(Lu et al., 2021) 的 API 可以從故事文本中擷取出事件，其中包含三個部分，第一部分爲 *Role*：代表這個事件中的人、事、時、地、物，第二部分 *Type*：代表事件的類別，如攻擊、結婚、運輸... 等，第三部分爲 *Trigger*：代表句子中被判斷爲事件的關鍵字。

對於事件的模板式問題生成，可以一樣分爲三個部份去詢問，從 *Role*、*Type*、*Trigger* 的角度來產生問題，以這幾種模板式的方式可以增加問題—答案配對的豐富性。同樣的可以用 7 種答案類別來生成模板性的問題。事件擷取的部分，共有 8 種類別以及 33 種子類別，如表11：

Type	Subtype
Life	Be-Born, Marry, Divorce, Injure, Die
Movement	Transport
Transaction	Transfer-Ownership, Transfer-Money
Business	Start-Org, Merge-Org, Declare-Bankruptcy End-Org
Conflict	Attack, Demonstrate
Contact	Meet, Phone-Write
Personnel	Start-Position, End-Position, Nominate, Elect
Justice	Arrest-Jail, Release-Parole, Trial-Hearing Charge-Indict, Sue, Convict, Sentence, Fine Execute, Extradite, Acquit, Appeal, Pardon

Table 11: ACE2005: Event Types (Walker et al., 2006)

4.3 評估

在人工評估的部分，模板式的問題在問題的可讀性上取得了很高的分數，見表7的最後一列，因爲是透過模板來產生問題，所以可以取得通順的問題，而在問題—答案之間的關聯性，則是因爲擷取出來的資訊是固定模板的，故在整體關聯性上會較低，此時就可以透過生成式的問題—答案配對來補足。

5 結論

本研究主要在探討如何從故事書中產生高品質且具有多樣性的問題，在生成式模型的部分，採用先擷取出答案，再根據答案來產生與之相對應的問題，這種方法可以有效的將問題與答案之間的相關性提高。透過加入問題類別與定義，提升問題—答案配對的生成。在模板式問題生成的部分，我們採用了實體與關係擷取的結果，應用於樣板式問答生成，搭配 7 種問題類別來產生不同面向的問題。

最後我們使用問題回答的方式來對於問題—答案配對進行 Rouge-L 評估，相較於排序模型，Rouge-L 與人工評估的相關性更高。透過排序模型及問題回答這兩種評估方法，更有效的篩選生成的問題—答案配對。

References

Zhenjin Dai, Xutao Wang, Pin Ni, Yuming Li, Gangmin Li, and Xuming Bai. 2019. Named entity recognition using bert bilstm crf for chinese electronic health records. In *2019 12th International Congress on Image and Signal Processing, BioMedical Engineering and Informatics (CISP-BMEI)*, pages 1–5.

Rubel Das, Antariksha Ray, Souvik Mondal, and Dipankar Das. 2016. A rule based question generation framework to deal with simple and complex sentences. In *2016 International Conference on Advances in Computing, Communications and Informatics (ICACCI)*, pages 542–548. IEEE.

Xinya Du, Junru Shao, and Claire Cardie. 2017. Learning to ask: Neural question generation for reading comprehension. In *Proceedings of the 55th Annual Meeting of the Association for Computational Linguistics (Volume 1: Long Papers)*, pages 1342–1352, Vancouver, Canada. Association for Computational Linguistics.

Matt Gardner, Joel Grus, Mark Neumann, Oyvind Tafjord, Pradeep Dasigi, Nelson F. Liu, Matthew Peters, Michael Schmitz, and Luke Zettlemoyer. 2018. AllenNLP: A deep semantic natural language processing platform. In *Proceedings of Workshop for NLP Open Source Software (NLP-OSS)*, pages 1–6, Melbourne, Australia. Association for Computational Linguistics.

Matthew Honnibal and Ines Montani. 2017. spaCy 2: Natural language understanding with Bloom embeddings, convolutional neural networks and incremental parsing. To appear.

Zhiheng Huang, Wei Xu, and Kai Yu. 2015. Bidirectional lstm-crf models for sequence tagging. *CoRR*, abs/1508.01991.

Mike Lewis, Yinhan Liu, Naman Goyal, Marjan Ghazvininejad, Abdelrahman Mohamed, Omer Levy, Veselin Stoyanov, and Luke Zettlemoyer. 2020. BART: Denoising sequence-to-sequence pre-training for natural language generation, translation, and comprehension. In *Proceedings of the 58th Annual Meeting of the Association for Computational Linguistics*, pages 7871–7880, Online. Association for Computational Linguistics.

Yaojie Lu, Hongyu Lin, Jin Xu, Xianpei Han, Jialong Tang, Annan Li, Le Sun, Meng Liao, and Shaoyi Chen. 2021. Text2Event: Controllable sequence-to-structure generation for end-to-end event extraction. In *Proceedings of the 59th Annual Meeting of the Association for Computational Linguistics and the 11th International Joint Conference on Natural Language Processing (Volume 1: Long Papers)*, pages 2795–2806, Online. Association for Computational Linguistics.

Alison H Paris and Scott G Paris. 2003. Assessing narrative comprehension in young children. *Reading Research Quarterly*, 38(1):36–76.

Colin Raffel, Noam Shazeer, Adam Roberts, Katherine Lee, Sharan Narang, Michael Matena, Yanqi Zhou, Wei Li, Peter J Liu, et al. 2020. Exploring the limits of transfer learning with a unified text-to-text transformer. *J. Mach. Learn. Res.*, 21(140):1–67.

Victor Sanh, Lysandre Debut, Julien Chaumond, and Thomas Wolf. 2019. Distilbert, a distilled version of bert: smaller, faster, cheaper and lighter. *arXiv preprint arXiv:1910.01108*.

Yu-Ming Shang, Heyan Huang, and Xianling Mao. 2022. Onerel: Joint entity and relation extraction with one module in one step. In *Proceedings of the AAAI Conference on Artificial Intelligence*, volume 36, pages 11285–11293.

Christopher Walker, Stephanie Strassel, Julie Medero, and Kazuaki Maeda. 2006. Ace 2005 multilingual training corpus. *Linguistic Data Consortium, Philadelphia*, 57:45.

Chuhan Wu, Fangzhao Wu, Tao Qi, and Yongfeng Huang. 2020. Named entity recognition with context-aware dictionary knowledge. In *Proceedings of the 19th Chinese National Conference on Computational Linguistics*, pages 915–926, Haikou, China. Chinese Information Processing Society of China.

Ying Xu, Dakuo Wang, Mo Yu, Daniel Ritchie, Bingsheng Yao, Tongshuang Wu, Zheng Zhang, Toby Li, Nora Bradford, Branda Sun, Tran Hoang, Yisi Sang, Yufang Hou, Xiaojuan Ma, Diyi Yang, Nanyun Peng, Zhou Yu, and Mark Warschauer. 2022. Fantastic questions and where to find them: FairytaleQA – an authentic dataset for narrative comprehension. In *Proceedings of the 60th Annual Meeting of the Association for Computational Linguistics (Volume 1: Long Papers)*, pages 447–460, Dublin, Ireland. Association for Computational Linguistics.

Bingsheng Yao, Dakuo Wang, Tongshuang Wu, Zheng Zhang, Toby Li, Mo Yu, and Ying Xu. 2022. It is AI's turn to ask humans a question: Question-answer pair generation for children's story books. In *Proceedings of the 60th Annual Meeting of the Association for Computational Linguistics (Volume 1: Long Papers)*, pages 731–744, Dublin, Ireland. Association for Computational Linguistics.

Zexuan Zhong and Danqi Chen. 2021. A frustratingly easy approach for entity and relation extraction. In *North American Association for Computational Linguistics (NAACL)*.

Qingyu Zhou, Nan Yang, Furu Wei, Chuanqi Tan, Hangbo Bao, and Ming Zhou. 2017. Neural question generation from text: A preliminary study. In *National CCF Conference on Natural Language Processing and Chinese Computing*, pages 662–671. Springer.

The 34th Conference on Computational Linguistics and Speech Processing (ROCLING 2022)
Taipei, Taiwan, November 21-22, 2022. The Association for Computational Linguistics and Chinese Language Processing

基於常識知識的移情對話回覆生成
Improving Response Diversity through Commonsense-Aware Empathetic Response Generation

黃紫嫺 Tzu-Hsien Huang
中央大學資訊工程學系
christy514@g.ncu.edu.tw

張嘉惠 Chia-Hui Chang
中央大學資訊工程學系
chia@csie.ncu.edu.tw

摘要

本篇論文著重在移情對話生成任務上。先前研究關於移情對話生成的方法 (Majumder et al., 2020b; Lin et al., 2019) 主要集中在檢測和利用用户的情緒來產生移情反應。本研究將使用額外的常識知識圖譜做爲機器人對常識性的背景知識。我們針對非預訓練和預訓練模型各使用不同的方式增強多樣性，在非預訓練模型上我們將 AdaLabel(Wang et al., 2021) 應用在 CEM 模型 (Sabour et al., 2022) 上，而對於預訓練模型我們使用 BART 模型結合多種常識知識讓模型能生成更有資訊的移情回應。研究結果顯示所提出的模型在 EMPATHETICDIALOGUES 和 DailyDialog 資料集上都優於基線模型，並且在個案研究中可以看到模型產生更多信息和同理心的回應。

Abstract

Due to the lack of conversation practice, the main challenge for the second-language learners is speaking. Our goal is to develop a chatbot to encourage individuals to reflect, describe, analyse and communicate what they read as well as improve students' English expression skills. In this paper, we exploit COMMET, an inferential commonsense knowledge generator, as the background knowledge to improve the generation diversity. We consider two approaches to increase the diversity of empathetic response generation. For non-pretrained models, We apply AdaLabel (Wang et al., 2021) to Commonsense-aware Empathetic model (Sabour et al., 2022) and improve Distinct-2 score from 2.99 to 4.08 on EMPATHETIC DIALOGUES (ED). Furthermore, we augment the pretrained BART model with various commonsense knowledge to generate more informative empathetic responses. Not only has the automatic evaluation of distinct-2 scores improved from 9.11 to 11.21, but the manual case study also shows that CE-BART significantly outperform CEM-AdaLabel.

關鍵字：移情對話回應生成、知識感知回應生成、回應多樣性

Keywords: Empathetic response generation, Commonsense aware response generation, response diversity

1 緒論

提升學生英語口說能力的方法之一是透過大量的對話練習，因此建構一個聊故事機器人，讓同學們透過有主題的故事和機器人進行聊天，是教育型對話機器人的一個重要研究方向 (Liu et al., 2022)。我們的目標是開發一個聊故事機器人，在英文閱讀活動中讓機器人扮演陪伴與支持的角色，藉由和學生一同談論英文故事書、分享心得，促進其英文閱讀之興趣發展。

聊故事機器人雖然可以由機器人主導對話的進行，但是當學習者回答之後，如何接續使用者的回應是一個相當大的挑戰。爲了產生合理的回應，近年的對話系統研究試圖應用知識圖譜來豐富對話回應內容，例如 KEMP(Li et al., 2022) 及 MIME(Majumder et al., 2020b) 引用 ConceptNet 於 Empathetic Dialogues (ED) 資料集上的對話回應生成，彌補機器人背景知識的不足，讓對話系統可以生成包含同理心的回應，合理地回應他人的情況和感受，避免對話過於單調和死板。

雖然 ConceptNet 包含多語言的詞彙知識、以及不同詞彙之間的關係 (例如：UsedFor, RelatedTo, Antonym)、也有物理常識知識 (例如：HasA, PartOf)，然而 ConceptNet 對於事件描述涵蓋有限，僅 800 萬的節點中不到百分之一的節點屬於事件，而 2,100 萬鏈結中僅有不及千分之六的鏈結是關於事件。因此著重於在"If-Then" 推論知識的 ATOMIC(Sap et al., 2019) 的推出送到相當大的關注。同時通過微調預訓練語言模型 (GPT-2(Radford et al., 2018)、BART(Lewis et al., 2020))，Bosselut 等人更提出 COMET(Bosselut et al., 2019) 常識推論模型，可以生成更多不存在於原始知識庫的常識知識。

Sabour et al.即應用 COMET 生成的常識，有效增加 ED 對話集回應的新穎單字 (Dist-1) 及雙字 (Dist-2) 多樣性到 0.66% 及 2.99%。本篇論文著重在結合常識知識於移情對話生成，並提高模型生成多樣性，針對非預訓練模型和預訓練模型兩種模型使用不同增強生成多樣性的方法。本篇論文貢獻有以下幾點：

- 我們成功將一個可以自適應估計目標標籤分布的方法 AdaLabel 應用在 CEM 模型上面，自動評估結果表明，與 CEM 模型的方法相比，CEM-AdaLabel 可以分別提升 Dist-1 及 Dist-2 至 0.79% 及 4.08%。
- 我們提出 CE-BART 透過預訓練的 BART 模型和 5 種類型的常識來增強同理心反應生成的方法，同時提升 Dist-1 及 Dist-2 至 2.35% 及 11.21%。
- CE-BART 在自動評估和人工評估上都取得很高的效能，並且在個案研究（Case Study）結果表明 CE-BART 可以產生更多信息和同理心的反應。

2 相關研究

2.1 常識知識圖與知識擷取生成

現有常識知識包括 WordNet, ConceptNet, FrameNet, Atomic, 等常識知識庫。ConceptNet(Liu and Singh, 2004) 是一個多語言的知識庫，主要表示單詞或短語之間的常識關係。此知識庫是以起始節點、關係標籤和結束節點的三元組形式表示一段關係 (例: A *net* is used for *catching fish*，可以表示成 (*net*, UsedFor, *catching fish*))。在 ConceptNet (v5.7)(Speer et al., 2017) 中資料來源爲透過眾包收集並與 Wikitionary、WordNet、OpenCyc 和 DBPedia 等現有知識庫合併，總共包含 2100 萬個邊、800 萬個以上的節點和 36 個關係 (relation)，主要關注在詞彙知識 (例如：UsedFor, RelatedTo, Antonym) 和物理常識知識 (例如：HasA, PartOf)，所以 ConceptNet 偏向詞與詞之間的關係，對於事件描述涵蓋有限。

ATOMIC (An atlas of machine commonsense)(Sap et al., 2019) 則是著重在"If-Then" 的推論知識，收集了約 88 萬個以上的推理知識實例。"If-Then" 關係可以分成三大類：(1) 事件導致心理狀態 (If-Event-Then-Mental-State)，(2) 事件導致事件 (If-Event-Then-Event)，(3) 事件導致表像人格 (If-Event-Then-Persona)，共提供九種關係類別: oEffect、oReact、oWant、xAttr、xIntent、xNeed、xEffect、xReact 和 xWant，"x" 代表事件和原因是發生在人身上，而"o" 則是發生在其他人身上。不同於其他知識庫，ATOMIC 中的節點形式爲 free-text 的方式，所以可以在日常常識方面更具表現力。

因開放式對話中所包含的常識是無限的，可能會有事件無法對應到現有知識庫的狀況，所以 Bosselut 等人 (Bosselut et al., 2019) 提出 COMET 模型，通過在現有常識知識庫上微調預訓練語言模型 (GPT-2(Radford et al., 2018)、BART(Lewis et al., 2020))，此模型可以生成更多不存在於原始知識庫的常識知識。

COMET 模型可以爲任何事件或短語按照需要的關係生成常識知識，這種靈活性使他可以快速的應用在許多任務中，近年常被用於對話回覆任務像是基於角色的對話 (Majumder et al., 2020a) 和移情對話 (Ghosal et al., 2020; Sabour et al., 2022; Zhu et al., 2021)。

2.2 移情對話回應生成

同理心是人類日常對話中重要的技巧，它使人可以感知、理解和適當地回應他人的情況和感受。早期移情對話系統的研究 (Wang and Wan, 2018; Zhou et al., 2018) 比較集中在特定情緒下產生反應，但在近期研究中認爲移情更重要的是去理解對話中說話者的情感並產生包含同理心的回覆，偵測說話者的情感對於生成移情回應是必須的 (Rashkin et al., 2019)。Lin 等人 (Lin et al., 2019) 提出 MoEL 模型爲每種情緒設計單獨的解碼器，並"*softly combine*" 解碼器的輸出，這樣的設計可以明確地學習如何根據對上下文情感的理解來選擇適當的反應; Majumder 等人 (Majumder et al., 2020b) 認爲移情反應需要模仿說話者的情緒，回應的情緒除了會與說話者一致外，有時也會是包含正負面的情緒，所以作者將情緒分成消極和積極兩組，在訓練過程中適當地組合來平衡用户情感的模仿，相較於 MoEL，此模型因包含多樣情緒所以可以生成更多樣的回覆。

爲了讓對話系統的回覆能更具同理心和人性化，近期研究更是將理性與情感結合，使得生成的回覆除了包含信息外還能有適當的情緒，讓用户得到更滿意的回覆。Zhong 等人 (Li et al., 2021) 提出 CARE 模型並建構了一個基於情感的常識知識圖譜 (EA-CKG)，使用與 ConceptNet 的 n-gram 匹配來從 message 和 response 中提取 concept，情感三元組被定義爲 {message concept, emotion, response concept}，除了用匹配提取的方式，此論文在 EA-CKG 上訓練一個知識

The 34th Conference on Computational Linguistics and Speech Processing (ROCLING 2022)
Taipei, Taiwan, November 21-22, 2022. The Association for Computational Linguistics and Chinese Language Processing

Dialogue History

Speaker: I feel like a terrible sibling right now .
Listener: What did you do to feel that way ?
Speaker: My sister , who lives out of state and I do not see often , was recently in town visiting our dad . I did not visit with them .

Response

I am sorry to hear that , you could make it up to them by going to visit ?

Figure 1: Empathetic Dilogues (ED) 資料集對話範例。

嵌入模型 TransE(Bordes et al., 2013) 來學習全局概念和關係的嵌入，並透過關聯性的計算來擷取任意數量的新的相關概念，最後將 EA-CKG 構建的常識和情感合併到基於 Transformer(Vaswani et al., 2017) 的回覆生成模型中，與 ConceptFlow(Zhang et al., 2020) 不同的是，CARE 不受常識庫的範圍限制，它可以產生新的常識來生成回覆。Li 等人 (Li et al., 2022) 也在同年提出 KEMP 模型，利用歷史對話、ConceptNet 和情感辭典 NRC_VAD(Mohammad, 2018) 來構建情緒知識圖，相較於 CARE 是預先將所有對話構建成一個基於情感的常識知識圖譜，KEMP 是針對每個對話提取對應到 ConceptNet 中更高情感強度值的 concept 來構成圖譜，並使用 multi-head graph attention 來更新 node，故可以增強移情對話生成模型的情感感知。

3 回應生成任務描述

我們首先定義回應生成任務，接著介紹 COMET 常識知識生成方法。

3.1 回應生成任務定義

此任務需要一個對話模型來扮演聽眾的角色並產生同理心的反應。輸入一個包含 N 個話語的對話歷史 $D = [u_1, u_2, u_3, ..., u_N]$，其中第 i 個話語 $u_i = [w_1^i, w_2^i, w_3^i, ..., w_{n_i}^i]$ 是由 n_i 個詞組成。我們的目標是產生一個與上下文一致、具有適當情感和信息豐富的回應 $Y = [y_1, y_2, y_3, ..., y_M]$。如圖1 所示，此爲所使用資料集中的對話資料，我們將 Dialogue History 的部分當作模型輸入，並希望模型經過訓練以後生成移情回覆。

3.2 常識知識獲取

考量到對話中會包含情緒以及信息，而 ConceptNet 較缺乏包含情緒的關係類別，ATOMIC 則在 xReact 這個關係類別中有較多的情緒字，故我們將使用 ATOMIC 作爲此兩個模型的常識知識庫。所提出的模型都是要以聽眾的角色來回覆說話者，所以在常識知識方面比較在意的是以說話者本人推斷的關係，在 ATOMIC 中對於事件和原因發生在參與事件的人身上總共有六種常識關係：事件對人的影響（xEffect）、人對事件的反應（xReact）、人在事件之前的意圖（xIntent）、爲了使事件發生人需要什麼（xNeed）、事件發生後人想要什麼（xWant），以及人的特徵屬性（xAttr）。由於 xAttr 這個類別是其他人推斷一個人的特徵，並不包含在移情反應中，因此我們使用的是剩餘的其他五個關係 (xEffect、xReact、xIntent、xNeed、xWant)。爲了達成給定事件生成常識推理，我們採用在 ATOMIC-2020 數據集上進行訓練的 COMET 模型去預測接下來回應中會含有的 Commonsense。

對於輸入歷史對話序列 D，分別將五個特殊 token ([xReact]、[xEffect]、[xWant]、[xNeed]、[xIntent]) 加在對話歷史中最後一個話語後面，並使用 COMET 針對每個關係生成五個常識知識，將生成的常識知識連接以獲得其常識序列 $K_r = k_1^r \oplus k_2^r \oplus ... \oplus k_5^r$，$r \in xReact$。

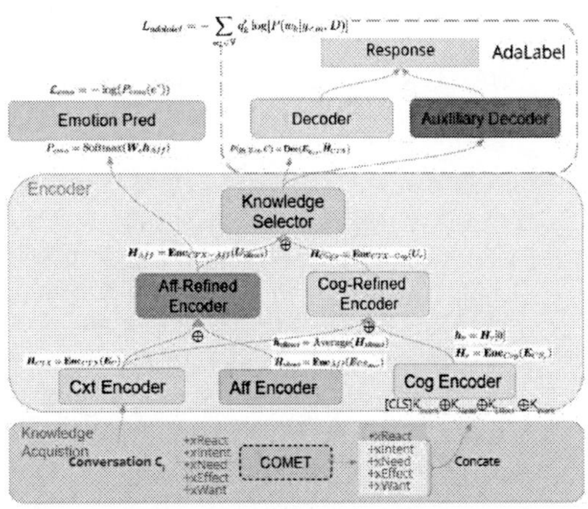

Figure 2: CEM-adalabel 架構圖

The 34th Conference on Computational Linguistics and Speech Processing (ROCLING 2022)
Taipei, Taiwan, November 21-22, 2022. The Association for Computational Linguistics and Chinese Language Processing

4 常識感知的移情回應生成模型

我們提出兩個增強生成多樣性的常識移情對話回應生成模型架構，分別是 CEM-AdaLabel 和 CE-BART。

4.1 CEM-AdaLabel

此模型基於 Transformer(Vaswani et al., 2017)，上下文及常識知識編碼器解碼器實現 CEM(Sabour et al., 2022)，而多樣性損失的部分實現 Adaptive Label Smoothing(AdaLabel)(Wang et al., 2021)，模型架構如圖2。由於論文空間限制，CEM-AdaLabel 方法請參考 (Huang, 2022)。

4.2 CE-BART

本論文則著重在介紹 Commonsense-aware Empathetic BART（簡稱 CE-BART)。此模型基於預訓練 BART 模型 (Lewis et al., 2020)，並結合在 ATOMIC-2020 數據集上進行訓練的 COMET 模型，模型架構如圖3，包含三個部分：常識知識獲取 (Knowledge Acquisition)、情感識別 (Auxiliary Emotion Recognition) 和回應生成 (Response generation)。

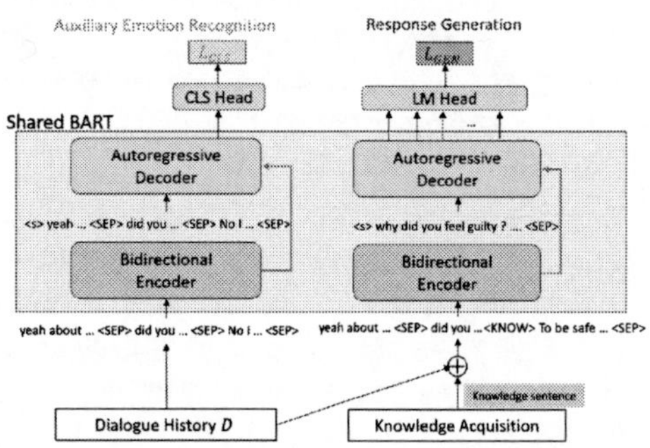

Figure 3: CE-BART 模型架構

BART 是一個基於 Transformer 架構的模型，有雙向編碼器 (Bidirectional encoder) 和自回歸解碼器 (Autoregressive decoder)，他的訓練方式是用任意噪聲函數破壞文本和學習模型來重建原始文本。與 BERT 不同的是，BERT 只使用 [MASK] token 去替換文本中的字，但 BART 爲了防止模型依賴像是序列長度的相關序列結構資訊，採用了多種 noise 函數去破壞掉這些資訊，所以它比 BERT 更適合自然語言生成的任務，且因爲包含雙向編碼器所以也比 GPT2 多了雙向上下文的信息。微調 BART 模型就可以快速地應用在其他任務上 (例如: 序列分類任務、序列生成任務、token 分類任務和機器翻譯)。而我們透過多任務學習 (Multi-task learning) 來學習回應生成和情感識別。

4.2.1 回應生成

將回應生成視爲序列生成任務，BART 模型本身有一個自回歸解碼器，所以它可以直接對序列生成任務進行微調。把對話歷史中的話語連接起來並在話語之間加上一個特殊 token <SEP>，而常識知識的部分是將章節3.2得到的 5 個常識知識序列連接並在前面添加特殊 token $[Know]$，目的是爲了讓模型知道這些是常識知識，最後將常識知識序列連接在對話歷史序列後面形成序列 $K = [K_{xReact} \oplus K_{xIntent} \oplus K_{xNeed} \oplus K_{xEffect} \oplus K_{xWant}]$，將此序列輸入到 BART 的共享嵌入層，來得到話語中每個 token 的隱藏狀態，然後將其送到 BART 的編碼器和解碼器，在訓練過程中解碼器的輸入會是右移 (right-shifted) 的回覆如圖3。目標回覆 $Y = [y_1, y_2, y_3, ..., y_M]$ 長度爲 M，生成回應損失 L_{GEN} 爲計算負對數似然損失 (Negative log-likelihood loss)。

$$L_{GEN} = -\sum_{j=1}^{M} \log P(y_j | D \oplus [Know] \oplus K, y_{<j}) \tag{1}$$

4.2.2 情感識別

情感識別可以被視爲序列分類任務，相同的輸入被送到 BART 編碼器和解碼器，然後取解碼器最後一個 token 對應的最終隱藏狀態作爲 label，輸入給一個線性多分類器 (multi-class linear classifier)。如果對話歷史 D 的正確情緒標籤是 e，則模型從 D 推斷出 e。一樣用負對數似然損失 (Negative log-likelihood loss) 計算分類損失 L_{CLS}。

$$L_{CLS} = -\log P(e|D) \tag{2}$$

4.2.3 Loss Weighting

模型訓練的損失 L 由兩部分組成：生成回應損失 L_{GEN} 和分類損失 L_{CLS}。L 是以上兩部分的加權和，它們的權重之和等於 1，α 是生成回應損失的權重。

$$L = (1 - \alpha) L_{CLS} + \alpha L_{GEN} \tag{3}$$

5 實驗

5.1 資料集

爲了驗證本篇論文所提出常識移情對話回應生成模型有加強生成多樣性的效能，在資料集上使用 ED (Rashkin et al., 2019) 來評估及比較現有的方法。ED 是在 Amazon Mechanical Turk 上收集的大規模多輪移情對話資料集，包含約 25k 的一對一開放域對話，被廣泛使用於移情對話回應生成的基準資料集。收集方式是將兩個標記者配對：一個當作說話者、一個當作聆聽者。說話者被要求談個人的情感感受，聆聽者則是透過說話者所說的話推斷出潛在的情感，並做出善解人意的回應。該數據集提供了 32 個均勻分佈的情緒標籤。我們將對話歷史視爲模型輸入，將聆聽者的回應視爲目標輸出，整理後在訓練集中獲得 40,201 個對話，在驗證集中獲得 5,359 個對話，在測試集中獲得 4,836 個對話。

5.2 自動評估

我們採用 Perplexity (PPL) 和 Distinct-n (Dist-n) 作爲我們的主要自動評估指標。PPL 代表模型對其候選回應集的置信度，根據每個詞來估計一句話出現的概率，並用句子長度做正規化，如公式5 M 是句子長度，$p(w_i)$ 是第 i 個詞的概率。置信度越高，PPL 越低，可以用來評估生成回應的總體品質。

$$PPL = P(w_1 w_2 \dots w_M)^{-\frac{1}{M}} \tag{4}$$

$$= \sqrt[M]{\prod_{i=1}^{M} \frac{1}{P(w_i|w_1 w_2 \dots w_{i-1})}} \tag{5}$$

Distinct-n 測量生成的回應中不同 n-gram 的比例，公式6中，$Count(unique \quad n-gram)$ 表示回應中不重複的 n-gram 數量, $Count(word)$ 表示回應中 n-gram 詞語的總數量，Distinct-n 越大表示生成的多樣性越高，通常用於評估生成多樣性。此外，由於我們提出的模型將情感分類作爲訓練過程的一部分，因此也會評估情緒預測的準確度（Acc）如公式7，公式中 TP 是正確分類的正例數量，TN 是正確分類的負例數量，FP 是錯誤分類的負例數，FN 是被錯誤分類的正例數量。

$$Distinct\text{-}n = \frac{Count(unique \quad n\text{-}gram)}{Count(word)} \tag{6}$$

$$Accuracy = \frac{(TP + TN)}{(TP + FP + FN + TN)} \tag{7}$$

自動評估結果如表1，其中基線系統包括 MIME, KEMP, CEM 以及結合 CEM 與 AdaLable 的 CEM-AdaLabel (Huang, 2022)。我們提出的 CE-BART 上在所有自動評估指標方面都大大優於以上四種基線模型，CE-BART 在 PPL、Dist-1 和 Dist-2 上比沒有使用 COMET 生成常識知識資訊的 CE-BART 有更好的結果，代表增加外部知識有助於提高生成質量，儘管在情感準確性上有一點損失。實驗顯示 BART 模型因爲已經有在大規模的資料集訓練過，所以只要微調 BART 模型後，雖然在訓練上需要花得比較久，但得到的結果與沒有使用預訓練模型的方法在效能上有很大的差異。

5.3 Case Study

表2 列出了從基線 KEMP、CEM、BART 和我們提出的方法 CEM-AdaLabel 、CE-BART 生成的回應。在第一種範例中基線模型中，KEMP 將這句話語誤認爲是個好主意，而 CEM 生成的比較通用的話語去詢問說話者發生甚麼事了，CEM-AdaLabel 則是用偵測到說話者隱含的情緒 (scared) 所以知道有不好的事情發生，但還是缺少認知的常識知識。CE-BART 很好的偵測到說話者被嚇到並且因爲有人闖入他的家所以可能需要打電話給警察，相較於其他 Baseline 他生成包含情感 (oh no!) 和認知 (Did you call the police ?) 的回應。由此可知將預訓練模型與常識知識結合可以生成出更好的移情回覆。

第二個案例顯示了在多輪對話表達情感和認知的能力，KEMP、CEM 和 CEM-AdaLabel 忽略了說話者提到的"Thet've helped a a lot"，這句意味著他們的父母很好幫助了他們，所以 CE-BART 擷取到並認爲他們是很慷慨的很好的家人。

5.4 人工評估

在先前生成回應任務研究中，人工評估可以分成兩種方式進行。第一種是要求標註人員根據流暢性、相關性和同理心等方面對生成的回應進行 1 到 5 的評分；第二種是要求在同一對話歷史下的兩個模型之間選擇更好的回應。但是，給出 1 到 5 分的標準很可能在不同人之間有所不同，這導致標註者之間的一致性較低，所以此指標不適合評估模型性能。此外，要求標註者在沒有任何標準的情況下選擇更好的答案，僅依靠個人的喜好也不是可靠的指標，因爲每個人在做出選擇時可能會考慮不同的方面。

因此，我們參考 Sabour 等人 (Sabour et al., 2022) 的人工評估方法，對於給定的對話歷史，將 CEM-AdaLabel 和 CE-BART 的回應兩兩配對，並要求標註者根據對話歷史和以下三個標準選擇更好的回應：

The 34th Conference on Computational Linguistics and Speech Processing (ROCLING 2022)
Taipei, Taiwan, November 21-22, 2022. The Association for Computational Linguistics and Chinese Language Processing

Model	PPL	Dist-1	Dist-2	Acc(%)
MIME(Majumder et al., 2020b)	37.09	0.47	1.9	31.36
KEMP(Li et al., 2022)	36.89	0.55	2.29	**39.31**
CEM(Sabour et al., 2022)	36.11	0.66	2.99	39.11
CEM-AdaLabel	36.3	**0.79**	**4.08**	38.1
BART	12.87	1.9	9.11	**52.33**
CE-BART	**12.59**	**2.35**	**11.21**	51.29
Gold Response	-	5.98	36.84	-

Table 1: 自動評估的結果

Emotion Dialog History	lonely **Speaker:** I there, don't know what to do, just broke up with my girlfriend, we were 8 years together.
Knowledge	**sad**, to be alone, to break up with his girlfriend, **to find a new girlfriend**, gets depressed
KEMP CEM BART	That is a good idea. I hope you have a great time! Oh no! What happened? Oh no, that is terrible. Did you find out who did it?
CE-BART	Oh no , **i am sorry to hear that** . i hope you can **find a new girlfriend** soon .
Gold	Sorry to hear! Do you have any idea about the break up? Did you think about it?
Emotion Dialog History	grateful **Speaker:** When my wife and I had to move for her to go to school, we had a lot of trouble finding a place to live until my parents were nice enough to cosign on a loan. **Listener:** You must be so thankful ! **Speaker:** We are. They've helped a lot during my life, but this might have been the biggest one.
Knowledge	**happy**, **good**, to be grateful to them, **to be helpful**
KEMP CEM BART	That is great to hear! I hope you have a great time. That is great news! That is a great credit! I am glad you had a good support system.
CE-BART	That is so **generous** of them! You are so lucky to have such a **great family**.
Gold	They are really wonderful. Do you have plans to show how thankful you are?

Table 2: 本論文提出模型和 baseline 模型生成回應的案例研究

1. 同理心（Emp.）：哪個回應有很好的理解說話者的情況，且呈現出更貼切的情緒。

2. 連貫性（Coh.）：哪個回應更連貫並與對話歷史相關。

3. 信息量（Inf.）：哪個回應傳達了有關對話歷史的更多信息。

我們隨機從測試集抽取了 100 對回應，並分配了兩個人員來標註每一對。標記允許平手，但鼓勵標註者盡量選擇其中一個回應，並使用 Cohen's kappa 係數 (κ) 來分析兩個標註者之間的一致性，其中 $0.4 < \kappa < 0.6$ 表示中等一致性。

如表3 所示，CE-BART 在三個方面都優於 CEM-AdaLabel ，所以使用預訓練模型後能夠產生更連貫、包含同理心和更多信息的回應。在連貫性的部分 CEM-AdaLabel 相較於其他兩個部分比例稍高的原因，是因爲我們觀察到 CE-BART 會生成較長的回應 (13.23 個單詞/回應)，而 CEM-AdaLabel 會生成較短的回應 (10.24 個單詞/回應)。造成標註者認爲 CE-BART 生成的回復可能只有前半部分是與對話歷史相關，而 CEM-AdaLabel 較短但整句是與對話歷史有關的。

6 結論

現有教育型對話機器人並未結合移情對話生成模組，使得機器人只有講故事或問問題的功能。我們引用了「動態回顧循環」（Active

Comparisons	Aspects	Win	Loss	κ
	Emp.	86%	5.5%	0.61
CE-BART vs.	Coh.	85.5%	9%	0.73
CEM-AdaLabel	Inf.	94%	2.5%	0.56

Table 3: 人工評估的結果

Reviewing Cycle）提問法，透過 4F 解說技巧一事實（Facts）、感受（Feelings）、發現（Findings）及未來（Future），引導學生從不同角度反思時故事內容、個人感受、成長經驗、以及未來的發展方向，而透過 Feeling 和 Future 講到個人日常經驗的內容時，尤其需要結合常識知識圖譜來增強機器人的回應多樣性。我們提出利用預訓練的 BART 模型結合 COMET 生成的常識知識來生成移情對話，雖然在訓練時間上需要 3 個小時多，但在自動評估、案例研究和人工評估都表明，我們提出的 CE-BART 都優於 MIME, KEMP, CEM, 及 CEM-AdaLabel 等基線模型，並證明了移情對話的生成受益於預訓練模型和外部知識。

References

Antoine Bordes, Nicolas Usunier, Alberto Garcia-Durán, Jason Weston, and Oksana Yakhnenko. 2013. Translating embeddings for modeling multi-relational data. In *Proceedings of the 26th International Conference on Neural Information Processing Systems - Volume 2*, NIPS'13, page 2787—2795, Red Hook, NY, USA. Curran Associates Inc.

Antoine Bosselut, Hannah Rashkin, Maarten Sap, Chaitanya Malaviya, Asli Celikyilmaz, and Yejin Choi. 2019. COMET: Commonsense transformers for automatic knowledge graph construction. In *Proceedings of the 57th Annual Meeting of the Association for Computational Linguistics*, pages 4762–4779, Florence, Italy. Association for Computational Linguistics.

Deepanway Ghosal, Navonil Majumder, Alexander Gelbukh, Rada Mihalcea, and Soujanya Poria. 2020. COSMIC: COmmonSense knowledge for eMotion identification in conversations. In *Findings of the Association for Computational Linguistics: EMNLP 2020*, pages 2470–2481, Online. Association for Computational Linguistics.

Tzu-Hsien Huang. 2022. Two simple ways to improve commonsense-aware empathetic response generation. Master's thesis, National Central University.

Mike Lewis, Yinhan Liu, Naman Goyal, Marjan Ghazvininejad, Abdelrahman Mohamed, Omer Levy, Veselin Stoyanov, and Luke Zettlemoyer. 2020. BART: Denoising sequence-to-sequence pre-training for natural language generation, translation, and comprehension. In *Proceedings of the 58th Annual Meeting of the Association for Computational Linguistics*, pages 7871–7880, Online. Association for Computational Linguistics.

Pengfei Li, Peixiang Zhong, Kezhi Mao, Dongzhe Wang, Xuefeng Yang, Yunfeng Liu, Jianxiong Yin, and Simon See. 2021. ACT: an attentive convolutional transformer for efficient text classification. In *Thirty-Fifth AAAI Conference on Artificial Intelligence, AAAI 2021, Thirty-Third Conference on Innovative Applications of Artificial Intelligence, IAAI 2021, The Eleventh Symposium on Educational Advances in Artificial Intelligence, EAAI 2021, Virtual Event, February 2-9, 2021*, pages 13261–13269. AAAI Press.

Qintong Li, Piji Li, Zhaochun Ren, Pengjie Ren, and Zhumin Chen. 2022. Knowledge bridging for empathetic dialogue generation. *AAAI*.

Zhaojiang Lin, Andrea Madotto, Jamin Shin, Peng Xu, and Pascale Fung. 2019. MoEL: Mixture of empathetic listeners. In *Proceedings of the 2019 Conference on Empirical Methods in Natural Language Processing and the 9th International Joint Conference on Natural Language Processing (EMNLP-IJCNLP)*, pages 121–132, Hong Kong, China. Association for Computational Linguistics.

Chen-Chung Liu, Mo-Gang Liao, Chia-Hui Chang, and Hung-Ming Lin. 2022. An analysis of children' interaction with an ai chatbot and its impact on their interest in reading. *Computers & Education*, 189:104576.

H. Liu and P. Singh. 2004. Conceptnet — a practical commonsense reasoning tool-kit. *BT Technology Journal*, 22(4):211–226.

Bodhisattwa Prasad Majumder, Harsh Jhamtani, Taylor Berg-Kirkpatrick, and Julian McAuley. 2020a. Like hiking? you probably enjoy nature: Persona-grounded dialog with commonsense expansions. In *Proceedings of the 2020 Conference on Empirical Methods in Natural Language Processing (EMNLP)*, pages 9194–9206, Online. Association for Computational Linguistics.

Navonil Majumder, Pengfei Hong, Shanshan Peng, Jiankun Lu, Deepanway Ghosal, Alexander Gelbukh, Rada Mihalcea, and Soujanya Poria. 2020b. Mime: Mimicking emotions for empathetic response generation. In *EMNLP*, pages 8968–8979.

Saif Mohammad. 2018. Obtaining reliable human ratings of valence, arousal, and dominance for 20,000 English words. In *Proceedings of the 56th Annual Meeting of the Association for Computational Linguistics (Volume 1: Long Papers)*, pages 174–184, Melbourne, Australia. Association for Computational Linguistics.

Alec Radford, Karthik Narasimhan, Tim Salimans, Ilya Sutskever, et al. 2018. Improving language understanding by generative pre-training. *OpenAI.*

Hannah Rashkin, Eric Michael Smith, Margaret Li, and Y-Lan Boureau. 2019. Towards empathetic open-domain conversation models: a new benchmark and dataset. In *ACL*.

Sahand Sabour, Chujie Zheng, and Minlie Huang. 2022. Cem: Commonsense-aware empathetic response generation. *Proceedings of the AAAI Conference on Artificial Intelligence*, 36(10):11229–11237.

Maarten Sap, Ronan Le Bras, Emily Allaway, Chandra Bhagavatula, Nicholas Lourie, Hannah Rashkin, Brendan Roof, Noah A. Smith, and Yejin Choi. 2019. ATOMIC: an atlas of machine commonsense for if-then reasoning. In *The Thirty-Third AAAI Conference on Artificial Intelligence, AAAI 2019, The Thirty-First Innovative Applications of Artificial Intelligence Conference, IAAI 2019, The Ninth AAAI Symposium on Educational Advances in Artificial Intelligence, EAAI 2019, Honolulu, Hawaii, USA, January 27 - February 1, 2019*, pages 3027–3035. AAAI Press.

Robyn Speer, Joshua Chin, and Catherine Havasi. 2017. Conceptnet 5.5: An open multilingual graph of general knowledge. In *Proceedings of the Thirty-First AAAI Conference on Artificial Intelligence*, AAAI'17, page 4444—4451. AAAI Press.

Ashish Vaswani, Noam Shazeer, Niki Parmar, Jakob Uszkoreit, Llion Jones, Aidan N Gomez, Łukasz Kaiser, and Illia Polosukhin. 2017. Attention is all you need. *Advances in neural information processing systems*, 30.

Ke Wang and Xiaojun Wan. 2018. Sentigan: Generating sentimental texts via mixture adversarial networks. In *IJCAI*, pages 4446–4452.

Yida Wang, Yinhe Zheng, Yong Jiang, and Minlie Huang. 2021. Diversifying dialog generation via adaptive label smoothing. In *Proceedings of the 59th Annual Meeting of the Association for Computational Linguistics.*

Houyu Zhang, Zhenghao Liu, Chenyan Xiong, and Zhiyuan Liu. 2020. Grounded conversation generation as guided traverses in commonsense knowledge graphs. In *Proceedings of the 58th Annual Meeting of the Association for Computational Linguistics*, pages 2031–2043, Online. Association for Computational Linguistics.

Hao Zhou, Minlie Huang, Tianyang Zhang, Xiaoyan Zhu, and Bing Liu. 2018. Emotional chatting machine: Emotional conversation generation with internal and external memory. In *Proceedings of the AAAI Conference on Artificial Intelligence*, volume 32.

Lixing Zhu, Gabriele Pergola, Lin Gui, Deyu Zhou, and Yulan He. 2021. Topic-driven and knowledge-aware transformer for dialogue emotion detection. In *Proceedings of the 59th Annual Meeting of the Association for Computational Linguistics and the 11th International Joint Conference on Natural Language Processing (Volume 1: Long Papers)*, pages 1571–1582, Online. Association for Computational Linguistics.

The 34th Conference on Computational Linguistics and Speech Processing (ROCLING 2022)
Taipei, Taiwan, November 21-22, 2022. The Association for Computational Linguistics and Chinese Language Processing

運用少量語料於漢字轉客文字之類神經機器翻譯系統初步探討
A Preliminary Study on Mandarin-Hakka neural machine translation using small-sized data

洪翌翔 Yi-Hsiang Hung, 黃奕欽 Yi-Chin Huang
國立屏東大學電腦科學與人工智慧學系
Department of Computer Science and Artificial Intelligence
National Pingtung University
gbaian10@gmail.com, ychuangnptu@mail.nptu.edu.tw

摘要

在本研究中，我們利用注意力機制 (Attention) 與卷積 (Convolution) 模型的架構來實作一套中文轉四縣腔客文的機器翻譯系統。其中，爲了解決南北四縣腔的常用詞差異問題，我們透過語料的統計整理與詞典的定義方式，將兩種腔調的差異用法獨立出來，並分別訓練翻譯模型。

此外，爲了解決客語語料數量稀少而導致翻譯時遇到未知詞的狀況，在我們的模型中，透過實驗的驗證尋找適當的閥值以拒絕掉不適合的翻譯結果，並透過中文詞的替換以及客文常用詞的強制斷詞方式，讓最終的翻譯句獲得更佳的結果。最終，本研究所開發的系統可在少量語料下達到不錯的翻譯結果，並可應用於在地化的客語教學以及作爲中客文夾雜之語音合成系統的前端部分。

Abstract

In this study, we implemented a machine translation system using the Convolutional Neural Network with Attention mechanism for translating Mandarin to Sixan-accent Hakka. Specifically, to cope with the different idioms or terms used between Northern and Southern Sixan-accent, we analyzed the corpus differences and lexicon definition, and then separated the various word usages for training exclusive models for each accent.

Besides, since the collected Hakka corpora are relatively limited, the unseen words frequently occurred during real-world translation. In our system, we selected suitable thresholds for each model based on the model verification to reject non-suitable translated words. Then, by applying the proposed algorithm, which adopted the forced Hakka idioms/terms segmentation and the common Mandarin word substitution, the resultant translation sentences become more intelligible. Therefore, the proposed system achieved promising results using small-sized data. This system could be used for Hakka language teaching and also the front-end of Mandarin and Hakka code-switching speech synthesis systems.

關鍵字：神經機器翻譯、中文翻譯客文、南北四縣腔

Keywords: Neural Machine Translation, Mandarin to Hakka translation, Northern/Southern Sixian-accent

1 緒論

一個語言的傳承與推廣可以經由聽、說、讀、寫四個部份，而類似客家語、閩南語這種地方方言很容易出現會聽會說但卻不會讀文字或拼音和完全不會寫的窘境，而這樣就容易導致一個語言最後容易只能口耳相傳，導致自學不易。所以如何把一句想說的話從中文轉成客文並能唸出就是一個問題。本文主要在研究將中文翻譯成四縣腔客語的方法，並在細分成南四縣腔與北四縣腔。

客家語是台灣地方方言中使用量第二多的語言，僅次於閩南語。而台灣客家語又可分成各種腔調，依照使用比例由高至低分別爲四縣腔、海陸腔、大埔腔、饒平腔、詔安腔 (WillPete, 2022)，其中四縣腔是台灣所有客家語腔調中使用率最高的，且例如大眾運輸中的廣播系統使用的客語腔調正是四縣腔，故母語非客語者通常會選擇四縣腔做第一個選擇。四縣腔又因各地區不同並隨著時間的發展差異，又可分爲北四縣腔與南四縣腔。北四縣腔的使用人口主要分佈在苗栗多數鄉鎮，以及新竹和桃園的部份鄉鎮；南四縣腔的使用人口主要分佈在高雄和屏東的六堆地區 (臺灣教育部, 2018)。

雖然南北四縣兩腔調存在在部份使用的詞彙不同，或者音韻上差異，但基本上兩腔調同屬四縣腔，所以日常中大致上是可以直接進行溝通不會有太大問題。此處將舉兩個簡單的句子當作範例參考兩腔調的用詞差異，如表1。

The 34th Conference on Computational Linguistics and Speech Processing (ROCLING 2022)
Taipei, Taiwan, November 21-22, 2022. The Association for Computational Linguistics and Chinese Language Processing

中文句子	外面很涼	冬至吃湯圓
北四縣翻譯	外背當涼	冬節食雪圓仔
南四縣翻譯	外背蓋涼	冬至食圓粄仔

Table 1: 南北四縣翻譯差

從表1也可看出南北四縣腔整體句子架構高度相似，只有部份用詞上有差別，例如上述例子中的「湯圓」，北四縣翻譯成「雪圓仔」，南四縣翻譯成「圓粄仔」。除了句子架構相似之外，南北四縣腔所使用的拼音系統也相同 [1]，所以多數語料都是可直接共用，但如果要做出兩者差異，則必須將兩者不同之處的透過分析與設計語料，並經由訓練機器翻譯模型使其產生不同腔調的翻譯。

近年來由於機器學習竄紅，而在機器翻譯領域中應用這類的方法稱爲神經機器翻譯 (Neural Machine Translation，NMT)，本論文將利用神經機器翻譯來處理中文文字轉換爲客文文字的問題。

本篇論文的架構如下：第一章爲緒論，描述研究背景，其中包含南北四縣腔的差異，以及將使用深度學習方法來解此翻譯問題。第二章爲相關研究，說明在機器翻譯上別人有使用哪些方法，各有什優缺點。第三章爲語料庫，詳細描述使用了哪些語料庫，各有多少資料量，並對這些資料分別做了哪些處理以符合自身研究的要求。第四章爲研究方法，說明以使用 Fairseq-CNN 作爲基礎，並用何種方法解決在資料量稀疏的情況下處理未知詞的問題。第五章爲實驗結果分析。第六章爲本文的結論。

2 相關研究

機器翻譯是用電腦將文字從一種語言翻譯成另一種語言的過程，而無需額外的人力。機器翻譯從過去需要語言學家來制定各種規則來逐字翻譯，到後來開始使用大量資料來做統計翻譯，最後演變到現在的神經機器翻譯不再是簡單的逐字翻譯，機器會分析所有文字元素並識別字詞間的相互影響方式，並將原始語言透過神經網路轉換成目標語言。

神經網路機器翻譯通常是基於序列到序列 (sequence-to-sequence，seq2seq) 做處理，seq2seq 主要就是分成編碼器 (encoder) 和解碼器 (decoder) 兩部份，編碼器負責將來源語言編碼成一個具有表示原本句子意義的隱含向量做訓練，最後在經由解碼器解碼成目標語言的文字。

[1]南北四縣腔的聲調都使用去聲 55、陰平 24、陽平 11、上聲 31、陰入 2、陽入 5，其他腔調例如海陸腔則不同

2.1 機器翻譯

較早期的機器翻譯方法有以下幾種，第一種方法是基於規則的字對字機器翻譯 (Rule-based Machine Translation，RBMT) (Forcada et al., 2011)，這種方法主要預先準備雙語字典、一些單字的規則 (例如-er、-est 等等字尾含意)，這種翻譯通常蛤需要該語言的專業語言學家制定各種詳細的規則，但一些語法結構上的問題依然很容易無法處理很多狀況。例如：臺灣大學陳信希 (Lin and Chen, 1999) 等老師的中文到台語翻譯、聯合大學黃豐隆教授 (Lin et al., 2014) 等老師的中文到客語、Charoenpornsawat 等人的英文到泰文 (Charoenpornsawat et al., 2002) 都使用此類方法。

第二種方法是基於例子的機器翻譯 (Example-Based Machine Translation，EBMT) (Somers, 1999), (Chunyu et al., 2002)，這種方法主要預先準備好大量已經翻譯好的句子來提供比對，例如句子「我今天在學校吃中餐」，如果現在要翻譯的句子成「我今天在學校吃晚餐」，經過比對後發現與前面中餐的句子最爲相近，只有一個詞有差異，則將不一樣的詞替換掉後就翻譯完成了。這種方法的優點在於只要準備好大量已經翻譯好的句子就能夠更容易翻譯出好的結果，而不用像 RBMT 一樣設計了多個規則，但還是有無法處理的狀況，然而此方法若要處理不存在資料庫中的句子時，依然會出現不合理的翻譯結果。例如：Ayu (Ayu and Mantoro, 2011) 等人使用 EBMT 將印尼語翻譯成英語。

第三種方法就是統計機器翻譯 (Statistical Machine Translation，SMT) (Koehn, 2009)，相較於前兩種方式是透過語言學的知識設計或定義相關的規則，而產生翻譯的結果，統計式機器翻譯是採用大量語料庫來進行機器學習，這種方法只要有大量資料就可進行機器翻譯，這種翻譯可統計詞的用量和基於前後文字來做的各種不同翻譯，例如 bank 是銀行還是河岸，可通過前後文來做個推測。而有不少的統計機器翻譯都是使用基於短語的機器翻譯 (Zens et al., 2002)，例如：Google 在 2006 年 4 月時候的宣佈未來 Google 翻譯將改使用 SMT 的翻譯系統 [2]。基於短語 (Phrase-Based) 的翻譯結果相較於較早期的基於規則 (Rule-Based) 的方法已經進步許多，然而因爲是以短語爲單位在做翻譯，這些短語拼湊出來的句子翻譯依然不夠自然。

近年來開始出現神經機器翻譯 (Neural Machine Translation，NMT) (Bahdanau et al.,

[2]https://ai.googleblog.com/2006/04/statistical-machine-translation-live.html

2014)，相較於 RBMT 和 EMBT 等兩種傳統方法，NMT 不需要太多該語言領域的相關知識，也不需要額外準備如雙語字典、大量例句來幫助翻譯，因爲若這些資料量不足會大大影響翻譯結果的好壞，NMT 是僅靠大量平行語料來做訓練，在資料取得上會容易許多。而對比 SMT，NMT 是一次翻譯整個句子而不是切成較短語來做翻譯，這樣在翻譯上更容易考慮句子的前後關係，進而翻譯出更順暢的句子。NMT 也幫助各語言之間更容易直接互相翻譯，以前 Google 翻譯會先將源語言翻譯成英文，然後將英文翻譯成目標語言，而不是直接從一種語言翻譯成另一種語言。例如:Google 機器翻譯系統 (Wu et al., 2016) 於 2016 年開始逐步將多個語言慢慢從 SMT 改成使用 NMT，並通過應用基於實例的 (EBMT) 機器翻譯來改善結果。

2.2 Seq2Seq

近年來在處理文字翻譯這種具有時間順序關係上的資料時候經常使用 seq2seq 架構 (Sutskever et al., 2014)。不只在機器翻譯上，近年來 seq2seq 在自然語言處理 (Natural Language Processing，NLP) 領域中如：語音識別 (Chorowski et al., 2015)、文本摘要 (Rush et al., 2015; Nallapati et al., 2016) 等都取得了良好的結果。

seq2seq 主要由編碼器和解碼器所組成，當一串文字丟入編碼器經過編碼轉換成一個固定長度的隱含內文向量 (context vector)，最後這個向量在經由解碼器轉換回人類所看的語言。而一般編碼器和解碼器內部通常由循環神經網路 (Recurrent Neural Network，RNN)、長短期記憶 (Long Short-Term Memory，LSTM) (Hochreiter and Schmidhuber, 1997)、門控循環單元 (Gated Recurrent Unit，GRU) (Cho et al., 2014) 等這類以 RNN 爲基礎的循環神經網路做處理。然而上述的編碼器解碼器架構有個致命的問題，就是他不管任何長度的原始內容壓縮成一個固定大小向量時，越長的文字就越容易損失訊息，也因此除非在較簡單的問題，否則現在通常還會加入注意力機制 (Vaswani et al., 2017) 來解決此問題。

綜上所述，我們最後決定使用一個基於 seq2seq 並帶有 attention 機制的神經機器翻譯系統，來幫助一些非客語領域專精的人也能做出的翻譯系統。

3 語料庫

本研究中會需要中文到客文的翻譯平行語料，並且由於後續 Fairseq-CNN 模型將會需要斷詞資訊，然而像漢語此類的語系不像英文語系本身就有空格來當作斷詞的效果，中文客文的斷詞因爲目前所使用的語料庫本身多半都沒有附人工處理好的斷詞資訊，所以斷詞這部份得另外處理，斷詞處理將會在下一章節 4.2說明。

在北四縣模型訓練中我們將會使用北四縣腔調的語料：北四縣哈客、萌典；在南四縣模型訓練中我們將會使用：南四縣哈客、美濃客家寶典、萌典 (南四縣)。

3.1 北四縣語料

3.1.1 北四縣哈客

北四縣客語語料來源其中一個是來自客委會的四縣腔初級、中高級客語認證教材 (客家委員會, 2021)。其中分爲初級 1284 個、中級 1767 個、中高級 2146 個，共 5197 個客語單詞，每個單詞除了對應的中文、客文拼音、使用該詞的範例句 (至少一句) 以及與該句子其相對應的中文翻譯。由於每個單詞可能不只一個客文例子，最後經整理將初、中、中高三個級別的每個單詞所有的客文句子整理合併後共有 5801 個句子。透過標點符號進行切分後共有 9488 個小句子。

另外如果該詞有南北四縣對相同意思的中文在使用單詞上有差異時候則會有括號附註南四縣的用法如表2，總共包含 834 個。

3.1.2 萌典

另一個北四縣語料是以來自教育部的《臺灣客家語常用詞辭典》爲原始資料所編制成的萌典 (唐鳳, 2013)，萌典共有 14713 個客語單詞，同樣擁有中文、客文拼音以及該詞的零到多個客文句及該句中文翻譯句。北四現在萌典中使用了全部的資料，最後經整理且經過標點符號切分後共有 21302 個小句子。

3.2 南四縣語料

3.2.1 南四縣哈客

南四縣語料的其中一個原始資料來源也是客委會的客語認證教材，並經由本校人員人工處理過，與北四縣哈客的不同之處在於南四縣哈客只使用了部份的資料，並且全部都換成南四縣的用詞，另外有些客語句子的中文翻譯有些許不同。最後總共有 4196 個句子。經過標點符號切分後共 7350 個小句子。

類號	級	類	號	客語標音	客家語
17-29	A	17	29	ted 【hed】	忒【核】
18-13	A	18	13	dag bai 【mi bai】	逐擺【每擺】
18-20	A	18	20	dong 【goi】	當【蓋】

Table 2: 強制斷詞差異

3.2.2 美濃客家寶典

南四縣哈客的另一個資料來源是由本校的劉明宗老師著作的《美濃客家語寶典》(劉明宗, 2016)，同樣經由本校人員人工處理過，只有客文句子和中文翻譯，共有 3345 句，標點符號切分後共 8547 個小句子。

3.3 重疊語料處理

3.3.1 哈客網

由於北四縣哈客與南四線哈客的原始資料來源同樣取自客委會哈客網資料，所以部份句子在使用詞上無差異時候，這些資料會與北四縣哈客完全重疊，這樣的句子共有 4044 個句子。有些則因爲中文翻譯與北四縣不同但客文原句是相同的，這樣的例子我們將同時把兩邊的中文翻譯句子都用在南北四縣語料中，這樣的例子有 304 個句子。其餘資料則是客文句子本身就與北四縣不同，這也是主要哈客語料需要分開的原因，也是後續模型需要學習的差異處。除了句子相似但用詞不同之外的例子之外，北四縣還包含一些南四縣未用的句子，上述兩種情況加起來，在北四縣中有 5139 個句子，在南四縣中有 3002 個句子。

因南四縣哈客語料由母語爲客語之專業人員進行標音處理後的例句中並未包含全部客委會所提供的例子，所以自行整理剩下未用上且沒有用詞上差異的句子加入南四縣語料中，以幫助擴增南四縣語料，總共有 1670 句。

3.3.2 萌典

由於萌典是以上所有語料庫中資料最多的語料，然而萌典的例句皆以北四縣用詞優先，但若未幫南四縣擴增萌典的語料，會使南四縣有大量的未知詞，爲此必須整理萌典語料並且盡可能避開有包含南北四縣使用詞上有差異的句子。

利用前面哈客網中所整理好的 834 個南北差異用詞，用這 834 個詞中的北四縣用詞在萌典的 21302 句子中過濾，只要含有這些差異用詞的句子則全部剔除，剩下總共有 15160 個句子，這些句子的中文與客文翻譯與北四縣完全相同。

	哈客網	萌典	美濃寶典	總和
北四縣	9488	21302	0	30790
南四縣	9020	15160	8547	32727

Table 3: 南北語料庫句數總和

4 研究方法

本章節說明使用 Fairseq-CNN 架構來實做客家語的翻譯、中文客文斷詞對訓練結果的影響、使用不同語料訓練出南北四縣腔的翻譯差異、當在資料稀疏下如何處理未知詞的問題。

4.1 Fairseq-CNN

2017 年 Facebook 提出以卷積神經網路 (Convolutional Neural Network，CNN) 爲基礎來處理 seq2seq 的問題 (Gehring et al., 2017)，文中主要提出三點使用 CNN 來處理這類問題對比 RNN 的優勢。

1. CNN 可以進行並行運算，而 RNN 是鏈式處理，必須等前一幀的結果出來才能處理下一個，故 CNN 在訓練速度上會快非常多。

2. CNN 網路可透過卷積的疊加，讓較低層處理輸入序列中鄰近字的交互關係，而讓較高層處理較遠字的交互關係。與 RNN 的結構相比，CNN 可用更短的路徑得到遠處的資訊。

3. 對於輸入的一組輸入而言，在 CNN 網路中，所有單詞經過的卷積核 (kernel) 和非線性計算的數量都是固定的，但在 RNN 網路中，第一個單詞要經過 n 次單元和非線性計算，但是最後一個單詞只經過一次，CNN 中同一組輸入中的每個詞有相同的計算將有助於訓練。

Fairseq-CNN 的整體模型架構如圖1

4.1.1 Position Embeddings

由於使用了 CNN 結構相比 RNN 來說少了位置訊息，所以必須加入個能表示輸入序列中的某詞在該序列位置的資訊 Position Embeddings。公式如下：

$$e = (w_1 + p_1, +...+, w_m + p_m) \quad (1)$$

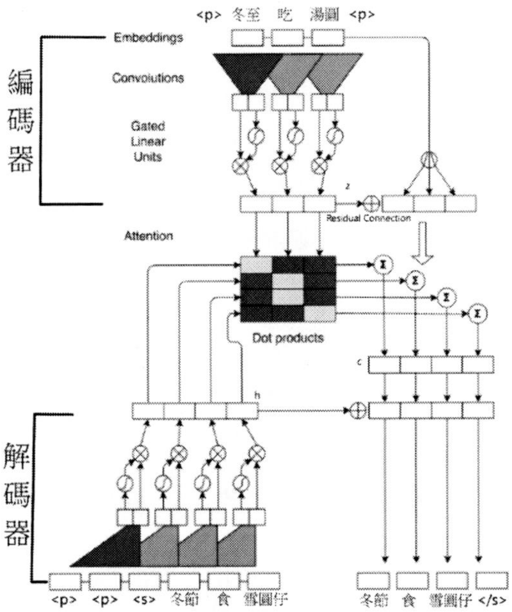

Figure 1: Fairseq-CNN 模型架構。正上爲 encoder 部分，左下爲 decoder 部分，中間爲 attention 部分。

w 表示詞向量 (word embedding)，p 表示位置向量 (position embeddings)，兩者相加可得到輸入元素 e，將作爲下一個卷積結構的輸入。

4.1.2 Convolutional Block Structure

編碼器與解碼器使用同一種卷積結構 (Convolutional Block Structure)，這種結構包含一個一維卷積和一個非線性單元 (Gated Linear Units，GLU) (Dauphin et al., 2017)。

輸入元素 e 經過參數爲 $W \in \mathbb{R}^{2d \times kd}$ 的一維卷積，其中 k 是卷積核寬度，代表一次段幾個詞做卷積處理，d 是詞向量的長度，最後被輸出爲兩倍維度的 $Y \in \mathbb{R}^{2d}$。

$Y = [A\ B] \in \mathbb{R}^{2d}$ 繼續被輸入到 GLU 中，GLU 公式如下：

$$v([A\ B]) = A \otimes \sigma B \tag{2}$$

其中 $A, B \in \mathbb{R}^d$，$\sigma(B)$ 負責控制與輸入上下文中哪些與 A 相關，A 與 $\sigma(B)$ 互相做點乘後得到輸出 $v([A\ B]) \in \mathbb{R}^d$。最後在加上殘差連接 (residual connections) (He et al., 2016)。

4.1.3 Multi-step Attention

每個解碼器層都有個單獨的注意力機制，爲了計算注意力權重 a，當前的解碼器狀態 h_j^l 與前一個目標元素 g_i 的 embedding 做結合，其公式如下式 3，W 爲權重，b 爲偏差 (bias)。

對於解碼器層 l 的注意力 a_{ij}^l (對第 i 時刻第 j 個來源元素的注意力權重)，解碼器狀態總和 d_i^l 與編碼器的最後輸出 z_j^u 做內積 (Dot Product)，其公式如下式 4。

最後利用注意力權重 a 對編碼器輸出 z 加上輸入向量 e 做加權，最後得到 c 最爲下一層卷積層的輸入，其公式如下式 5。

$$d_i^l = W_d^l h_i^l + b_d^l + g_i \tag{3}$$

$$a_{ij}^l = \frac{\exp(d_i^l \cdot z_j^u)}{\sum_{t=1}^{m} \exp(d_i^l \cdot z_t^u)} \tag{4}$$

$$c_i^l = \sum_{j=1}^{m} a_{ij}^l (z_j^u + e_j) \tag{5}$$

4.2 斷詞

由於 Fairseq 在訓練與翻譯之前都需要先將句子斷詞，而我們原始語料的句子都是沒有斷詞的，所以必須在訓練之前需先將中文和客文都先做斷詞。中文斷詞部份我們使用中研院的 CkipTagger (Peng-Hsuan Li, 2019) 系統，客文斷詞部份我們使用網路上的基於結巴的客文斷詞系統 (ldkrsi, 2018)，該客語斷詞系統的訓練資料來自苗栗、東勢、新屋、楊梅、龍潭、花蓮客語故事集、客家笑科、徐老師講古。

由於客文某些專用詞在資料不足的情況下不容易直接翻出，所以某些中文詞在斷詞時候直接將斷詞強制斷成客文詞對應的句子會比較容易成功翻譯出想要的特定客語用詞。例如：客家話的【食夜】，中文意思是【吃晚飯】，食夜在客語中是一個詞，但在中文吃晚飯會被斷詞層一個動詞 + 名詞的【吃晚飯】。在資料不足的情況下，若輸入【吃晚飯】很容易被翻譯成【食晚飯】而不是【食夜】，雖說該翻譯在語意表達上並沒有錯誤，但缺乏了客語與中文之間的用詞差異性。故我們提出在訓練模型之前就將中文的斷詞系統加入強制斷詞，讓專有的客語詞彙有著對應的中文斷詞結果，例如上述的【吃晚飯】將被斷成一個新的單詞。爲此我們從萌典整理出約 10600 個華客對應的詞典加入中客斷詞系統中。

4.3 未知詞處理

機器翻譯在翻譯時候一定會有未知詞的問題，一般狀況下在翻譯輸出每個詞時會選擇機率最高的翻譯詞作爲結果，但是模型預測出來的詞，可能因訓練語料中不存在合適的詞作爲翻譯的結果，導致其機率偏低。當這種狀況發生時，可以藉由設定一個閾值來調整是否相信模型預測的結果，在此使用未知詞懲罰值

(unknown word penalty，縮寫成 unkpen) 來達成。由於很多單詞的預測機率數字過低時，若以原本數字呈現不佳，故通常在呈現機率時候以對數的方式呈現，而機率是個介於 0 與 1 之間的數字，這區間的數字在 log 函數下都是負數，且原本機率越接近 0 時候，其 log 值會趨近於負無限大，爲了最佳化模型輸出的預測結果，我們可以經由調整 unkpen 的大小來調整。實際上的做法是透過將 unkpen 的 log 機率減掉一個介於-12 到 0 之間的值，調整其機率大小。若調整後 unkpen 的機率大於原始模型所預測的詞機率，則以 <unk> 取代原始預測的詞。

由於客語所收集到的語料較少，將會導致模型判斷不佳的可能性偏高。不過由於中文和客文在句型上跟用詞有時候是互通的，很多時候直接沿用中文就可以達到不錯的理解度。所以在客文翻譯結果中，當前述的未知詞取代的狀況發生時，有可能是中文跟客文的詞相似，所以沒有列入客語詞典中，或者剛好訓練資料未出現過。此時我們只要透過尋找模型中輸出的翻譯詞的來源注意力值往回尋找該詞的來源輸入是誰，就可以將該未知輸出替換成原本的輸入詞到結果中。

而造成輸出結果未知的可能大致可分爲兩種。一是訓練資料本身就未見過此新詞，在這種情況下大部分所有候選單詞輸出機率幾乎都會非常低，這時候 <unk> 本身的機率就不會比其他候選詞低多少，配上懲罰值就能輕易讓 <unk> 成爲最高機率候選詞並取代其他所有不理想的結果，如表4上半部，然後在利用前面所述的經過後處裡將未知詞的從來源中文直接當成答案，在多數情況下就會是個可接受的結果。

二是資料不足或者前後文判斷條件不夠多，導致推測答案的時候的不確定性因素過多，有多個相近機率的候選詞可選擇，此時可能有多個輸出的機率相近且明顯比多數不好的候選詞機率高非常多，如表4下半部中的候選詞 1 到 3 的機率特別高，但不代表最高的一定是正確的，有可能次高的才是相對較貼切的翻譯。爲此到底要選擇原本最高的機率當預測答案，或者挑個合適的懲罰值來讓答案變未知，並在用前述方法直接套用中文結果，便需要實驗來做測試。

5 實驗結果

本章節主要說明訓練模型的超參數設定、測試語料的來源與數量、用何種方法評估實驗結果的好壞、以及最後結果討論。

5.1 實驗設置

我們的 Fairseq 模型使用 CNN 架構，在原始論文中使用所有編碼器和解碼器使用 512 個隱藏單元，embedding 層和線性層皆使用 512 維，由於我們的語料庫大小以及所使用的詞彙量相較於原始論文的大數據來說都明顯少很多，所以我們將所有編碼器和解碼器中改使用 256 個隱藏單元，embedding 層和最後線性層的維度也改爲 256 維，kernel-size=3，dropout=0.2，學習率調整方式使用 inverse sqrt，損失函數使用 label smoothed cross entropy，優化器使用 adam。

南北四縣腔訓練語料將表3中各自的所有語料全用上，包含北四縣 30790 句、南四縣 32727 句，這些資料在各自以訓練集 90%、驗證集 5%、測試集 5% 做切分。

5.2 測試語料

測試語料是來自哈客網的“客語口說故事”中的其中十篇童話故事，其中包含，裡面含有相同中文並翻譯成南四縣和北四縣的人工翻譯結果，經過標點符號進行切分後共 1221 個小句子，這些測試語句並沒有包含在訓練語料中。

5.3 評估方法

我們使用萊文斯坦距離 (Levenshtein Distance) 來測試翻譯的結果與給定的答案的最短編輯距離，在萊文斯坦距離中，可以新增、刪除、取代字串中的任何一個字元，最後把所有 10 篇童話故事的所有句子的全部編輯距離做相加，數字越小代表越好。

5.4 實驗結果

我們的 baseline 系統是原句子做斷詞後的每個中文詞直接拿去查華客對應詞典，如果該中文詞在詞典中有對應的客文詞，則直接用對應的客文詞取代原有的中文詞，如果沒有對應的客文詞則沿用中文詞。此 baseline 系統在測試語料中的編輯距離爲 5078。

我們測試北四縣的測試語料結果如表5上半部所示，N 代表北四縣模型、N2 代表北四縣模型加入強制斷詞、S 代表南四縣模型、S2 代表南四縣模型加入強制斷詞，其中可見強制斷詞後的效果較佳，且效果比 redbaseline 系統和南四縣模型更好，並且未知詞懲罰值設定爲-8 時，可以得到最好的結果。

南四縣測試集結果如表5下半部所示，也可見強制斷詞後的效果較佳，且效果比 redbaseline 系統和北四縣模型更好，並且懲罰值一樣設定在-8 時可得到最好的結果。

南北四縣腔翻譯差異例子可參考表6。可見確實有將【湯圓】翻譯成對應腔調的文字。

	候選詞 1	候選詞 2	候選詞 3	候選詞 4	…	…	<unk>
原始機率	1.10E-15	8.54E-14	2.32E-12	9.15E-13	…	…	7.65E-13
log 機率	-14.9586	-13.0685	-11.6354	-12.0384	…	…	-12.1161

	候選詞 1	候選詞 2	候選詞 3	候選詞 4	…	…	<unk>
原始機率	0.45	0.33	0.23	9.15E-16	…	…	7.65E-09
log 機率	-0.3468	-0.4815	-0.6364	-15.0384	…	…	-8.1161

Table 4: 未知詞懲罰值範例。上半部爲所有候選詞機率皆非常低，下半部爲少數幾個特別高

北四縣資料	-10	-9	-8	-7	-6	-5	-4	-3	-2
N	6318	5775	5417	5282	5267	5278	5300	5307	5307
N2	4295	3954	3908	4060	4161	4250	4303	4311	4311
S	4321	4159	4151	4309	4482	4572	4645	4648	4651
S2	4317	4090	4050	4163	4291	4349	4362	4368	4368
南四縣資料	-10	-9	-8	-7	-6	-5	-4	-3	-2
S	4999	4778	4662	4802	4912	5006	5075	5079	5082
S2	4970	4679	4593	4691	4784	4839	4853	4858	4858
N	7012	6497	6143	5987	5954	5960	5983	5992	5992
N2	5261	4926	4827	4953	5044	5105	5143	5150	5150

Table 5: 童話故事測試集-南北四縣測試集的萊文斯坦距離總和

強制斷詞差異例子可參考表7，因爲【肚子餓】在原始斷詞下被斷成【肚子】跟【餓】，而原本【肚子餓】可翻譯成【肚飢】，若照原本斷詞則可能翻譯成肚屎 (肚子的客文) 跟枵 (餓的客文)。

另外我們發現使用原始斷詞方法 (N 模型) 的最佳懲罰值爲-6，而強制斷詞方法 (N2 模型) 的最佳懲罰值爲-8，懲罰值越接近 0 代表模型越相信它原本的判斷是正確的。

我們猜測是強制斷詞導致中文斷詞後的文法結構不穩定，例如前述的【肚子餓】，主詞會被強制連著動詞，但其餘沒有列入強制斷詞詞典中的主詞與動詞不會連在一起，這導致模型缺乏了一般性。在資料稀疏的狀況下此種強制斷詞方法雖然能夠幫助翻譯結果更容易出先客語專有詞，但當有巨量資料情況下則不需要藉此方法，模型可自己從資料中學習到之間的關係。而又因爲訓練資料有一半是來自萌典，而萌典原始資料是使用北四縣用詞，雖然有經過篩選句子，但句子本身應該依然更貼近北四縣腔，這使得訓練資料中的中客翻譯在北四縣腔上更加匹配，故北四縣模型 (N 模型懲罰值-6) 比起南四縣模型 (S 模型懲罰值-8) 更容易相信模型自身的判斷是正確的。

6 結論

我們使用神經網路機器翻譯 Fairseq-CNN 來處理中客翻譯問題，並使用不同語料針對不同腔調做訓練，可做出翻譯對應腔調的客文翻譯。並提出使用強制斷詞方法來提高翻譯出特定客語詞彙的機率，並使用最短編輯距離的方法測出一個最佳的未知詞懲罰值來當未知詞的一種閥值設定，並利用中文與客文的高相似性關係，直接使用來源中文詞取代客文的未知詞來當翻譯結果。

由於訓練資料的不足，導致翻譯系統有時會出現不佳的翻譯結果，如果有更多的訓練資料則可翻譯出更好的結果。當有良好的翻譯結果後，後續可將客語句子經過語音合成系統合出該句子的語音檔，最終完成一個由輸入中文文字轉成客語音檔的目標，將有利於客語學習。

中文	今晚吃湯圓	你又要買很貴的東西了
北四縣翻譯	暗晡夜食雪圓仔	你又愛買已貴个東西了
南四縣翻譯	暗晡夜食圓粄仔	你又愛買恁貴个東西咧

Table 6: 強制斷詞差異

S2	中文	客文
未斷詞	肚子餓的時候就不要挑食	
原始斷詞	肚子 餓 的 時候 就 不要 挑食	肚屎 枵 个 時節 就 莫 揀食
強制斷詞	肚子餓 的 時候 就 不要 挑食	肚飢 个 時節 就 毋好 揀食

Table 7: 南北四縣翻譯差異

References

Media A Ayu and Teddy Mantoro. 2011. An example-based machine translation approach for bahasa indonesia to english: An experiment using moses. In *2011 IEEE Symposium on Industrial Electronics and Applications*, pages 570–573. IEEE.

Dzmitry Bahdanau, Kyunghyun Cho, and Yoshua Bengio. 2014. Neural machine translation by jointly learning to align and translate. *arXiv preprint arXiv:1409.0473*.

Paisarn Charoenpornsawat, Virach Sornlertlamvanich, and Thatsanee Charoenporn. 2002. Improving translation quality of rule-based machine translation. In *COLING-02: machine translation in Asia*.

Kyunghyun Cho, Bart Van Merriënboer, Caglar Gulcehre, Dzmitry Bahdanau, Fethi Bougares, Holger Schwenk, and Yoshua Bengio. 2014. Learning phrase representations using rnn encoder-decoder for statistical machine translation. *arXiv preprint arXiv:1406.1078*.

Jan K Chorowski, Dzmitry Bahdanau, Dmitriy Serdyuk, Kyunghyun Cho, and Yoshua Bengio. 2015. Attention-based models for speech recognition. *Advances in neural information processing systems*, 28.

Kit Chunyu, Pan Haihua, and Jonathan J Webster. 2002. Example-based machine translation: A new paradigm. *Translation and information technology*, 57.

Yann N Dauphin, Angela Fan, Michael Auli, and David Grangier. 2017. Language modeling with gated convolutional networks. In *International conference on machine learning*, pages 933–941. PMLR.

Mikel L Forcada, Mireia Ginestí-Rosell, Jacob Nordfalk, Jim O' Regan, Sergio Ortiz-Rojas, Juan Antonio Pérez-Ortiz, Felipe Sánchez-Martínez, Gema Ramírez-Sánchez, and Francis M Tyers. 2011. Apertium: a free/open-source platform for rule-based machine translation. *Machine translation*, 25(2):127–144.

Jonas Gehring, Michael Auli, David Grangier, Denis Yarats, and Yann N Dauphin. 2017. Convolutional sequence to sequence learning. In *International conference on machine learning*, pages 1243–1252. PMLR.

Kaiming He, Xiangyu Zhang, Shaoqing Ren, and Jian Sun. 2016. Deep residual learning for image recognition. In *Proceedings of the IEEE conference on computer vision and pattern recognition*, pages 770–778.

Sepp Hochreiter and Jürgen Schmidhuber. 1997. Long short-term memory. *Neural computation*, 9(8):1735–1780.

Philipp Koehn. 2009. *Statistical machine translation*. Cambridge University Press.

ldkrsi. 2018. jieba-hakka. `https://github.com/ldkrsi/jieba-Hakka`.

Chuan-Jie Lin and Hsin-Hsi Chen. 1999. A mandarin to taiwanese min nan machine translation system with speech synthesis of taiwanese min nan. In *International Journal of Computational Linguistics & Chinese Language Processing, Volume 4, Number 1, February 1999*, pages 59–84.

Hsin-Wei Lin, Feng-Long Huang, Ming-Shing Yu, and Yih-Jeng Lin. 2014. 中文轉客文文轉音系統中的客語斷詞處理之研究 (research on hakka word segmentation processes in chinese-to-hakka text-to-speech system)[in chinese]. In *Proceedings of the 26th Conference on Computational Linguistics and Speech Processing (ROCLING 2014)*, pages 58–77.

Ramesh Nallapati, Bowen Zhou, Caglar Gulcehre, Bing Xiang, et al. 2016. Abstractive text summarization using sequence-to-sequence rnns and beyond. *arXiv preprint arXiv:1602.06023*.

Wei-Yun Ma Peng-Hsuan Li. 2019. Ckiptagger. `https://github.com/ckiplab/ckiptagger`.

Alexander M Rush, Sumit Chopra, and Jason Weston. 2015. A neural attention model for abstractive sentence summarization. *arXiv preprint arXiv:1509.00685*.

Harold Somers. 1999. Example-based machine translation. *Machine translation*, 14(2):113–157.

Ilya Sutskever, Oriol Vinyals, and Quoc V Le. 2014. Sequence to sequence learning with neural networks. *Advances in neural information processing systems*, 27.

Ashish Vaswani, Noam Shazeer, Niki Parmar, Jakob Uszkoreit, Llion Jones, Aidan N Gomez,

Łukasz Kaiser, and Illia Polosukhin. 2017. Attention is all you need. *Advances in neural information processing systems*, 30.

WillPete. 2022. 北四縣和南四縣有什麼不同？臺灣客家語四縣話難北部腔調的差異分析與比較整理. https://www.wpchen.net/zh/posts/hakka-taiwan-sixian-northern-southern-difference.

Yonghui Wu, Mike Schuster, Zhifeng Chen, Quoc V Le, Mohammad Norouzi, Wolfgang Macherey, Maxim Krikun, Yuan Cao, Qin Gao, Klaus Macherey, et al. 2016. Google's neural machine translation system: Bridging the gap between human and machine translation. *arXiv preprint arXiv:1609.08144*.

Richard Zens, Franz Josef Och, and Hermann Ney. 2002. Phrase-based statistical machine translation. In *Annual Conference on Artificial Intelligence*, pages 18–32. Springer.

邱國源劉明宗. 2016. 美濃客家語寶典, volume 1. 五南.

唐鳳. 2013. 萌典. https://www.moedict.tw/about.html.

客家委員會. 2021. 哈客網路學院-中級暨中高級教材及試題下載. https://elearning.hakka.gov.tw/hakka/download-files?c=3.

臺灣教育部. 2018. 【客語】臺灣客家語有哪幾種常見的腔調？. https://mhi.moe.edu.tw/faqList.jsp?ID=0&ID2=11.

The 34th Conference on Computational Linguistics and Speech Processing (ROCLING 2022)
Taipei, Taiwan, November 21-22, 2022. The Association for Computational Linguistics and Chinese Language Processing

NCU1415 at ROCLING 2022 Shared Task: A light-weight transformer-based approach for Biomedical Name Entity Recognition
基於 Transformer 的生醫輕量化命名實體識別系統

馮智詮 Zhi-Quan Feng, 陳柏凱 Po-Kai Chen, and 王家慶 Jia-Ching Wang
Dept. of Science and Information Engineering,
National Central University
No.300, Zhongda Rd., Zhongli Dist., Taoyuan City 32001, Taiwan

Abstract

NER (Name Entity Recognition)是傳統 NLP 任務中非常重要也是非常基礎的一項。在生醫領域，各廠商發展的各種技術中，NER 任務都有被廣泛地運用。其中包括句子語義分析 parsing、問答、對話系統中的關鍵訊息提取和替換以及知識圖譜的實際運用等等。在不同的領域，包括生物醫學、通訊、電商平台等，都需要 NER 技術來識別其中的藥物、疾病、商品等物件。本實作主要對於 ROCLING 2022 SHARED TASK(Lee et al. 2022)的生醫領域 NER 任務，基於語言模型做出了一定程度的調整和實驗。

Name Entity Recognition (NER) is a very important and basic task in traditional NLP tasks. In the biomedical field, NER tasks have been widely used in various products developed by various manufacturers. These include parsing, QA system, key information extraction or replacement in dialogue systems, and the practical application of knowledge parsing. In different fields, including bio-medicine, communication technology, e-commerce etc., NER technology is needed to identify drugs, diseases, commodities and other objects. This implementation focuses on the CLING 2022 SHARED TASK's(Lee et al. 2022) NER TASK in biomedical field, with a bit of tuning and experimentation based on the language models.

關鍵字：命名實體識別，生物醫學，ROCLING 2022 Shared Task
Keywords: Name Entity Recognition, Biomedical Science, ROCLING 2022 Shared Task

1 Introduction & Related work

隨著 NLP 領域技術的發展，不少廠商、研究機構均著力於發展更高效率和精度的自然語言處理模型和演算法。在許多不同的領域中，NER (Name Entity Recognition) 都是非常重要的任務。目前，NER 的任務主要通過一些經典的語言模型(Language Model)進行。

在自然語言處理任務中，最早從 RNN 開始，逐漸發展出基於 LSTM(Long Short-Term Memory)、GRU(Gated Recurrent Unit)的時序神經網路模型。而後在 2017 年，Transformer (Vaswani et al. 2017)的問世再一次改變了自然語言模型的主流。

1.1 NER implementations based on LSTM or GRU layers

基於 LSTM 和 GRU 的模型在 Transformer (Vaswani et al. 2017)沒有提出時是研究自然語言處理的主要方法，而在 Transformer 模型在 2017 年被提出後，雖然其數量有大量減少，但仍然有不少實作的論文利用其時序建模以及輕量化的特點來完成一些特定的任務。

ULMFiT(Howard et al. 2018)是於 2018 年推出的基於 LSTM 的系統，其預期設計也是基於分類任務和預訓練模型。在 ULMFiT 的系統中，為了讓不同的層學習不同的特徵，提出了兩個訓練方法，一是學習率分層區別化的微調(fine-tuning)方法，也就是越靠後學習率越大。二是從後向前，每訓練一個 epoch，就解凍一層的逐層解凍訓練方法。除此之外，論文中也採用了 warm-up 的機制，讓模型在沒有抓到特徵時有效獲取特徵。

在具體實作 NER 任務的方面，各廠商和研究機構也提出了不同的系統來解決此問題，例如 2016 年提出的 (Ma and Hovy, 2016) 通過 CNN 進行初步的特徵提取獲得 Char Representation，並用多層的 LSTM 層來進行後續的分類任務。以及 2016 年同年提出的 (Lample et al., 2016)基於多層的 LSTM 以及特徵的前向傳遞，來達到最終的分類目的。

1.2 Transformer-Based Implementations

Transformer 模型最早推出於 2017 年，是一個有深遠影響力的序列資料處理模型架構，其在 word embedding 的部分不僅僅是 token embedding，同時也加入了 position embedding、segment embedding 作為字元的更加精確化的表達。之後的多層 encoder 和 decoder 中，主要用 attention 的機制，提取和篩選序列資料中的特徵。

之後基於 Transformer 模型架構，發展的方向主要分為兩個，一是改進預訓練方法，二是改進模型結構。

在預訓練方法的改進上，比較具有代表性的是 BERT(Devlin et al., 2019)、BART(Lewis et al. 2020)、RoBERTa(Liu et al. 2019)等論文。BERT 提出於 2019 年，是 Transformer 模型提出以後的一次非常有代表性的預訓練結果，其中採用了 Mask Filling，NSP(Next Sentence Prediction)等任務，作為對於 Transformer 模型的一系列標準預訓練方法，該方法將 Transformer 模型的準確率進一步提高。

而 BART 在 BERT 的基礎上，增加了更多的預訓練操作，如打亂句子中部分字詞的順序、隨機替換等等。

RoBERTa 模型不僅在預訓練時去掉了 NSP 的流程，還加入了 Dynamic Masking 的動作，此外其採用了更大的 batch size，讓模型能夠更好地從每個 batch 中提取特徵。

在模型結構的改進方面，代表模型有增大層數規模的 GPT(Radford et al. 2018)、GPT2(Vashishth et al. 2019)等。隨著各種不同模型的陸續提出，人們為了提升模型的準確度，在不斷地增加模型的大小，資源的消耗也是水漲船高。

1.3 Our Approach

基於上述論文提啟發，也考慮到本實作的硬體規格限制，本實作採用 2019 年提出的經典模型 BERT 模型作為語言模型。此外，本實作也參考了 ULMFiT 的學習率分層和 warm-up 機制，再引入條件隨機場(Conditional Random Field，CRF)(Huang et al. 2015)的演算法作為輔助，來達到更好的 NER 識別效果。

2 Method

2.1 Data

本實作之資料來源於 Chinese HealthNER Corpus (Lee et al. 2021)，其公開資料之訓練(Train)、驗證(Val)資料集之資料量如表一，其

	Train	Val
Sentences	25345	2816
Average Length	49.36	50.12

表一：資料集單句數量與長度統計

Classes	Train B	Train I	Val B	Val I
O	1110186		123235	
EXAM	1957	4009	261	541
BODY	21022	26162	2218	2744
DISE	8287	18275	787	1723
SYMP	10279	12700	1144	1390
TREAT	2664	510	241	481
CHEM	5483	10369	607	1124
TIME	1451	2080	158	215
SUPP	1286	3264	117	288
INST	959	1914	88	156
DRUG	1925	4611	221	473

表二：資料集標籤數量統計

標籤數量分佈如表二所示。資料集中記錄了 Train 和 Val 資料集的句子數量和平均長度。其中，資料集中的資料均為生醫領域相關，所有標籤均為症狀、藥品、疾病等生醫相關內容，表二為各個種類標籤出現數量之統計結果。不難發現，訓練集和測試集資料量比例大致為 9:1，其中兩個資料集單句資料長度相當，個標籤所對應之 B(表示 name entity 的開始)與 I(表示 name entity 的內容)之比值也大致相同。

2.2 Model

本實作所用之模型如圖一所示，由 BERT 和分類器(classifier)組成，其中分類器包括兩層 Linear 函數，模型可獲得各個 token 的分類結果。其模型在最後的分數計算和損失函數(loss function)的部分採用的是 CRF 的機制。

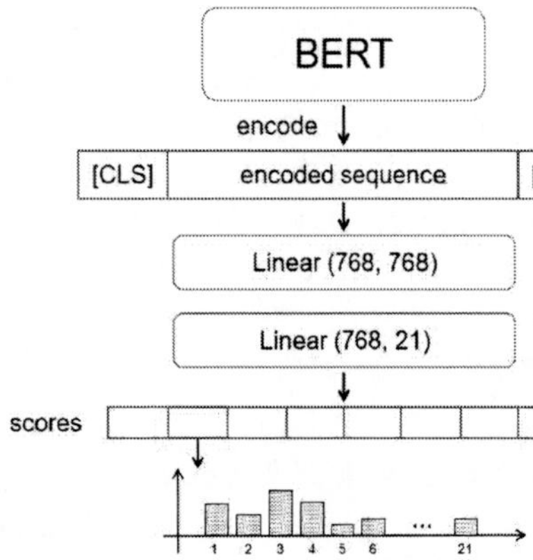

圖一：模型架構圖

2.2.1 Model Structure

本實作之模型架構主要先由 BERT 對輸入資料進行編碼，獲得模型輸出特徵(encoded sequence)，其中 BERT 模型參數源自(Devlin et al. 2019)這節省了大量模型預訓練時間。該輸出特徵再經過兩層 Linear 層的處理，輸入各類別的分數。

2.2.2 CRF

條件隨機場(Conditional Random Field，CRF)(Huang et al. 2015)是一種處理序列標註資料的演算法，其在 NER 問題中有非常廣泛的運用。其大致理念是通過中間矩陣(transitions)將不同字元的分類結果相互關聯，以提高 NER 任務的最終效果。其中間矩陣的維度為類別總數(tag_num)×類別總數，可以理解為相鄰分類標籤同時出現的幾率。如下公式所示：

$$transitions = \begin{pmatrix} t_{1,1} & \cdots & t_{1,tag\_num} \\ \cdots & \cdots & \cdots \\ t_{tag\_num,1} & \cdots & t_{tag\_num,tag\_num} \end{pmatrix} \quad (1)$$

我們假定模型的輸出分數為 x，標註值為 y，則 x 和 y 的序列如下所示：

$$x = (x_1, x_2, \ldots, x_n) \quad (2)$$

$$y = (y_1, y_2, \ldots, y_n) \quad (3)$$

其中標註值 y 也包含 y_0(START_TAG)以及 y_{n+1}(END_TAG)。基於此，其分數的計算式改寫為：

$$score\,(x, y) = \sum_{i=0}^{n} transition\ s_{y_{i+1}y_i} + \sum_{i=0}^{n} feats_{i,y_i} \quad (4)$$

其中 feats 為模型的輸出序列。由此，每一個輸出分數都和其他的分類結果相關聯，可以一定程度增加輸出結果的合理性。由此，由 x 生成 y 的過程可以表示為：

$$P(y\,|\,x) = \frac{\exp(score\,(x, y))}{\sum_{all\_possible\_\tilde{y}} \exp(score\,(x, \tilde{y}))} \quad (5)$$

由此可得損失函數表達式：

$$-\log P(y\,|\,x) = -\log \frac{\exp(score(x, y))}{\sum_{all\_possible\_\tilde{y}} \exp(score(x, \tilde{y}))} \quad (6)$$

$$= \log \sum_{all\_possible\_\tilde{y}} \exp(score(x, \tilde{y})) - score(x, y)$$

2.3 Fine-tuning

由於本實作基於預訓練模型，因此對預訓練模型進行微調(fine-tuning)是一項非常關鍵的任務。本實作在模型微調方面，不僅限於直接用測試資料，以低學習率直接微調，本實作也進行了一些特別的學習率處理。

2.3.1 Layered learning rate

本實作考慮到不同的層需要學習不同的特征，且不希望後續的微調(fine-tuning)過程對 BERT 預訓練的參數有過大的影響，所以採取了學習率分層衰減的方法。

本實作規定衰減率 k, BERT 模型的 embedding 部分、六層 encoder、六層 decoder、分類器分別定義為 14 個不同的區塊，每一個區塊採用不同的學習率。本實作規定分類器的學習率為 L_{base}, 從分類器往輸入方向，每向前一個區塊，學習率就在原來的基礎上乘以 k。由此，本實作分別研究了衰減率對模型輸出效果的影響。

本實作所採用之基礎學習率 L_{base} 和衰減率 k，根據多次實驗，確定其數值為 4e-5 和 1.2 作為最佳之數值。

	BERT+Cross Entropy			BERT+CRF		
k	Precision	Recall	F1	Precision	Recall	F1
1.0	**0.764**	0.667	0.705	0.709	0.715	0.702
1.1	0.751	0.682	0.709	0.726	**0.718**	0.718
1.2	0.754	**0.696**	**0.719**	0.767	0.697	**0.726**
1.3	0.748	0.669	0.702	**0.772**	0.676	0.717
1.4	0.741	0.650	0.693	0.766	0.679	0.716

表三：K與CRF的對比實驗結果

	BERT			RoBERTa			BART		
k	Precision	Recall	F1	Precision	Recall	F1	Precision	Recall	F1
1.1	0.726	0.718	**0.718**	0.710	0.712	0.706	**0.753**	0.677	0.709
1.2	**0.767**	0.697	**0.726**	0.760	**0.700**	0.723	0.742	0.698	0.714
1.3	**0.772**	0.676	**0.717**	0.770	0.672	0.714	0.746	0.705	0.716

表四：模型部分替換對比實驗結果

2.3.2 Warm-up and Decay

本實作考慮到，新加入的分類器處於未訓練狀態，因此如圖二所示，本實作考慮採用預熱(warm up)和逐漸下降的方法，先以低學習率讓模型能夠初步獲取特徵，在第二個 epoch 再調回預先設定的正常學習率，再往後，學習率逐漸下降，以對模型進行進一步細微調整。

本實作設計每當程式跑過預設的 step 數量，則重新更新一遍模型的優化器，重新為模型定義學習率。

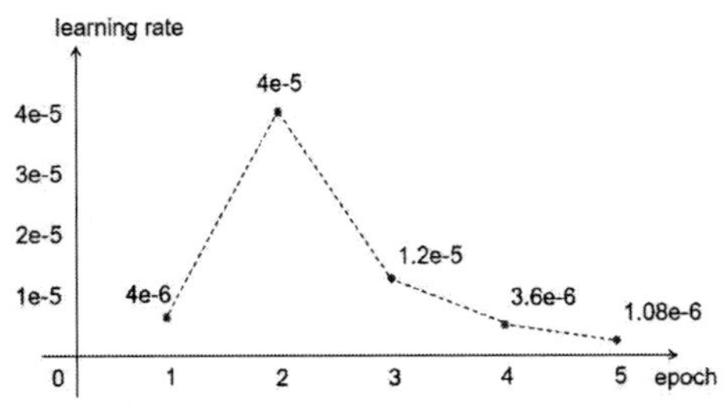

圖二：基礎學習率變化圖

2.3.3 Other details

本實作根據實驗結果，統一訓練三個 epoch(約 5k 個 step)，其中基礎學習率 L_{base} 為 4e−5, 因考慮到硬體設備條件限制，採用的批次大小為 16。

3 Electronically-available Resources

CPU: Intel(R) Xeon(R) CPU @ 2.20GHz
GPU: 1xTesla K80
CUDA cores: 2496
GPU RAM: 12.68GB
CPU cache size: 56320 KB

4 Experiments

4.1 About k and CRF

根據 Rocling2022 Shared Task(Lee et al. 2022) 的內部測試資料，本實作的準確度為 precision 74.56%，recall 72.81%，F1score 73.68

此外，基於本實作所述之實作方法，本實作進行了一些額外實驗，來驗證:學習率衰減率 k 對模型訓練成效的影響, CRF(Huang et al. 2015)和 cross-entropy 對於模型訓練成效的影響。

該實驗的三個模型均來自於已經過預訓練的預訓練模型。BERT 為(Devlin et al. 2019)，RoBERTa 為 (Conneau et al. 2020) ，BART 為 (Lewis et al. 2019)。同樣基礎學習率 L_{base} 為 4e-5，批次大小 16，訓練 5k 個 steps，所有數據均為分別訓練五次後的平均值。

本實作所設定之基本參數：基礎學習率 L_{base} 為 4e-5，批次大小 16，訓練 5k 個 steps(3 個 epoch)，其實驗結果如表三所示。

本實驗均訓練五次，記錄數據為五次之平均值。從實驗結果中不難看出，採用 CRF 作為 loss function 和計算分數的輔助，會有效提升模型訓練的 F1 分數。並且，在衰減率 k 為 1.2 左右時，測試結果的 F1 分數能夠達到最佳。

4.2 Replacing BERT to other models

除了對比人為設置的學習率參數以及損失函數，本實作還對採用的語言模型做了對比實驗。

本實作所對比之模型主要為目前主流之語言預訓練模型，RoBERTa(Liu et al. 2019)、BART(Lewis et al. 2020)。

實驗在 1.1、1.2、1.3 三個相對成果較好的學習率衰減率下以及 CRF 作為最後一層的設定下做了對比實驗，如表四所示。

其中不難看出，BERT-base 模型目前在該任務上能夠有更出色的效能，從 F1 分數上，能夠略強於其他兩種主流預訓練模型。也不難發現，從 F1 上看，BERT(Devlin et al., 2019)和 RoBERTa(Liu et al. 2019)的最佳衰減率都在 1.2 左右，而 BART 則在 1.3 左右。

5 Conclution

本實作為 ROCLING 2022 SHARED TASK (Lee et al. 2022)之生醫命名實體識別任務實作，參考了一些論文的實作方法，使用預訓練語言模型和一定程度的模型微調，來達到準確率局部最大化的目的。

通過對比實驗可知，CRF、學習率適當地逐層衰減以及 bert 預訓練模型在命名實體識別的任務上都能在一定程度上有所提升。

相比於模型微調的細節參數變化，系統效能與模型結構和預訓練方法對結果的影響可能更加具有決定作用，因此本實作若可能，之後預期在模型結構、預訓練等方面進行進一步細節上的處理，以提高效能。

6 Reference

Ashish Vaswani, Noam Shazeer, Niki Parmar, Jakob Uszkoreit, Llion Jones, Aidan N. Gomez, Łukasz Kaiser, “Attention Is All You Need” in NeurIPS 2017

Lung-Hao Lee, Chao-Yi Chen, Liang-Chih Yu, and Yuen-Hsien Tseng. 2022. Overview of the ROCLING 2022 shared task for Chinese healthcare named entity recognition. In Proceedings of the 34th Conference on Computational Linguistics and Speech Processing.

Lung-Hao Lee and Yi Lu, "Multiple Embeddings Enhanced Multi-Graph Neural Networks for Chinese Healthcare Named Entity Recognition," in IEEE Journal of Biomedical and Health Informatics, 2021, pp. 2801-2810

Jeremy Howard, Sebastian Ruder, “Universal Language Model Fine-tuning for Text Classification” in ACL 2018, pp. 328-339

Xuezhe Ma and Eduard Hovy, “End-to-end Sequence Labeling via Bi-directional LSTM-CNNs-CRF” in ACL 2016, pp. 1064–1074

Guillaume Lample, Miguel Ballesteros, Sandeep Subramanian, Kazuya Kawakami, Chris Dyer, “Neural Architectures for Named Entity Recognition” in NAACL 2016, pp. 260–270

Jacob Devlin, Ming-Wei Chang, Kenton Lee, Kristina Toutanova, “BERT: Pre-training of Deep Bidirectional Transformers for Language Understanding” in NAACL 2019, N19-1423, pp. 4171–4186

Mike Lewis, Yinhan Liu, Naman Goyal, Marjan Ghazvininejad, Abdel-rahman Mohamed, Omer Levy, Ves Stoyanov, Luke Zettlemoyer, “BART: Denoising Sequence-to-Sequence Pre-training for Natural Language Generation, Translation, and Comprehension” in 2020.acl-main.703, pp. 7871–7880

Yinhan Liu, Myle Ott, Naman Goyal, Jingfei Du, Mandar Joshi, Danqi Chen, Omer Levy, Mike Lewis, Luke Zettlemoyer, Veselin Stoyanov, 2019, “RoBERTa: A Robustly Optimized BERT Pretraining Approach”, arXiv:1907.11692

Sascha Rothe, Shashi Narayan, Aliaksei Severyn, TACL 2020, “Leveraging Pre-trained Checkpoints for Sequence Generation Tasks” in 2020.tacl-1.18, pp. 264–280

Zhiheng Huang, Wei Xu, Kai Yu, “Bidirectional LSTM-CRF Models For Sequence Tagging”, arXiv:1508.01991, 2015

Shikhar Vashishth, Shyam Upadhyay, Gaurav Singh Tomar, Manaal Faruqui, “Attention Interpretability Across NLP Tasks”, 2019, arXiv:1909.11218

Alec Radford, Karthik Narasimhan, Tim Salimans, Ilya Sutskever, “Improving Language Understanding by Generative Pre-Training” in OpenAI, 2018

Alexis Conneau, Kartikay Khandelwal, Naman Goyal, Vishrav Chaudhary, Guillaume Wenzek, Francisco Guzmán, Edouard Grave, Myle Ott, Luke Zettlemoyer, Veselin Stoyanov, “Unsupervised Cross-lingual Representation Learning at Scale” in ACL 2020, 2020.acl-main.747, pp. 8440–8451

The 34th Conference on Computational Linguistics and Speech Processing (ROCLING 2022)
Taipei, Taiwan, November 21-22, 2022. The Association for Computational Linguistics and Chinese Language Processing

命名實體識別：結合預訓練模型及對抗訓練的解決方案
CrowNER at Rocling 2022 Shared Task: NER using MacBERT and Adversarial Training

張秋霞 **Qiu-Xia Zhang***
國立臺灣大學資訊工程學系
Department of Computer Science and Information Engineering
National Taiwan University
r10922164@ntu.edu.tw

戚得郁 **Te-Yu Chi***
國立臺灣大學資訊工程學系
Department of Computer Science and Information Engineering
National Taiwan University
d09922009@ntu.edu.tw

楊德倫 **Te-Lun Yang***
國立政治大學資訊科學系
Department of Computer Science
National Chengchi University
111971029@nccu.edu.tw

張智星 **Jyh-Shing Roger Jang**
國立臺灣大學資訊工程學系
Department of Computer Science and Information Engineering
National Taiwan University
jang@mirlab.org

摘要

本研究使用「ROCLING 2022 中文健康照護命名實體辨識任務」(Lee et al., 2022) 中的訓練與驗證資料來進行建模。建模過程採用了資料擴增與資料後處理等技術，並使用 MacBERT 預訓練模型來建立一個專用中文醫療領域的 NER 辨識器。在微調過程中，我們也加入對抗式訓練的方法，如 FGM 和 PGD，最後調適所得的模型成效接近於任務評測最佳團隊。此外，藉由引入混合精度訓練，我們也大幅降低了訓練所需時間成本。

Abstract

This study uses training and validation data from the "ROCLING 2022 Chinese Health Care Named Entity Recognition Task" for modeling. The modeling process adopts technologies such as data augmentation and data post-processing, and uses the MacBERT pre-training model to build a dedicated Chinese medical field NER recognizer. During the fine-tuning process, we also added adversarial training methods, such as FGM and PGD, and the results of the final tuned model were close to the best team for task evaluation. In addition, by introducing mixed-precision training, we also greatly reduce the time cost of training.

關鍵字：MacBERT、條件隨機場域、命名實體辨識、對抗訓練

Keywords: MacBERT, Conditional Random Field, Name Entity Recognition, Adversarial Training

1 緒論

自然語言處理 (Natural Language Processing, NLP) 的持續發展，使機器逐漸能夠以人類大腦思考的方式來理解與解析語意，降低人類與

*These authors contributed equally to this work.

機器之間溝通的鴻溝，將人類常用的語言轉換成機器可以理解的格式，藉以進行文字上的分類、預測、推論等與自然語言理解 (Natural Language Understanding, NLU) 相關的任務。自然語言理解與語言學 (Linguistics) 有著密不可分的關係，它逐漸發展成包括人工智慧、計算機科學等領域的一門學科 (Bates, 1995)。近年來，隨著神經網路與機器學習技術的進步，以及網際網路上大量文字語料的取得，自然語言理解相關的理論與實務操作，得到了廣泛的應用。

機器在簡單閱讀理解任務上的表現，已經可以逐漸接近 (Rajpurkar et al., 2016) 甚至超越人類 (Yu et al., 2018)，然而在真實世界的應用上，卻還是有較大的效能差距 (Zheng et al., 2019)，會有這樣的差異，在於人類具有了解實際情況並且作出回應的能力，此能力易於將閱讀得到的文字資訊，自動地建立關聯，並賦予意義，雖然機器能夠將非結構性的文字透過斷詞技術 (word segmentation)，將不同的文句切割成字詞，但字詞之間並沒有辦法直接建立有意義的關聯，於是需要透過系統性的標註方式 (labelling)，讓機器理解上下文、段落、文句和字詞之類的關係，將重要的資訊提取出來，進而得到不同領域的知識，例如閱讀一則衛教 (Health Education) 文章，文章中會提及哪些人 (Who) 可能會得到什麼樣的疾病 (What)，通常這些疾病好發於什麼時間 (When) 如季節、月份等，以及爲什麼會得到這些疾病 (Why) 和如何治療 (How)，這些標註可以幫助機器更好地理解字詞之間的關係、順序和意義，掌握字詞的特徵，以便於了解文章整體的重點，這種資訊擷取 (Information Extraction) 的方法，稱之爲命名實體辨識 (Name Entity Recognition, NER)，是自然語言處理的基本任務之一。

本研究使用 ROCLING 2022 中文健康照護命名實體辨識 (Chinese Healthcare Named Entity Recognition) 任務 (Lee et al., 2022) 所提供的訓練與驗證資料，結合資料擴增 (Data Augmentation) 與資料後處理 (Post-Processing)，以 BERT 爲基礎的預訓練語言模型 MacBERT 進行微調訓練 (Fine-tune)，在評估語言模型的成效以後，計算出 F1-score 的結果爲 0.7796。而後，在既有的語言模型上加入了條件隨機場域 (Conditional Random Field, CRF) 等模型提升方法，計算出 F1-score 的結果爲 0.8076，提升了 2.8% 的效能，與任務評測最佳的系統，有著類似的成效與水平，並且藉由引入混合精度訓練，大幅減少訓練所需時間成本。

下一章將簡要地進行文獻回顧，第三章說明本研究所執行的步驟，包括採用的神經網路架構、資料處理的方式，第四章呈現系統展示的結果，並說明改善的方法。

2 相關研究

2.1 BERT

Bidirectional encoder representations from transformers (BERT) (Devlin et al., 2018) 是由 Google 於 2018 年提出的 NLP 預訓練模型，用以解決 NLP 在各種領域下游所遭遇的問題，例如：意圖分類問題、情緒分類問題、前後文預測問題等。

BERT 基於 Transformer (Vaswani et al., 2017) 的 Encoder 作爲其雙向訓練的架構；由於相同的詞 (word) 在上下文 (context) 中可能表示不同意義，BERT 將詞轉換爲 contextual word embedding，投射到一向量空間以表示其特徵並作爲 Transformer 的輸入；爲了讓文字的序列是有意義的，BERT 同時將 Position Encoding 作爲輸入傳入 Transformer 中。Transformer 的 Multi-head attention 則是在透過 self-attention 進行平行運算以獲得每個詞的上下關係。Transformer 的架構如圖 1。

BERT 訓練分爲兩個階段，分別爲預訓練 (Pre-training) 及微調 (Fine-tuning)。預訓練所使用的語料庫由 BooksCorpus (800M) 及英文維基百科 (2,500M) (僅取文字內容部分) 所擷取的詞所組成。預訓練共有兩個任務，分別爲 Masked LM (MLM) 及 Next Sentence Prediction (NSP)。MLM 任務藉由隨機遮蔽 15% 的詞 (替換爲 [MASK] 標籤) 並進行 Mask 的值預測；NSP 任務則是輸入兩個句子，藉由 [CLS] 標籤置於句首以識別進行分類，並在語句之間放置 [SEP] 表示斷句以進行上下文的預測。

MacBERT (Cui et al., 2021) 延伸自 BERT，主要優化的部分在於 BERT 在預訓練的 MLM 任務隨機將詞替換爲 [MASK]，然而實際上 [MASK] 並不出現於下游任務，MacBERT 將 MLM 任務更換爲 MLM as correction 任務，基於 word2vec 演算法計算詞的相似度，藉由相似詞取代 [MASK]，同時引入 Whole Word Mask (WWM) 及 N-Gram masking 技術，針對需要對 N-Gram 進行 Mask 時進行相似詞的查找替換，若無相似詞則使用隨機詞進行替換。另外 MacBERT 相較 BERT 有一大優勢即 MacBERT 的預訓練語料爲中文，可解決 BERT 無法應用於中文分類的缺陷。本研究最終使用 MacBERT 作爲主要的訓練模型。

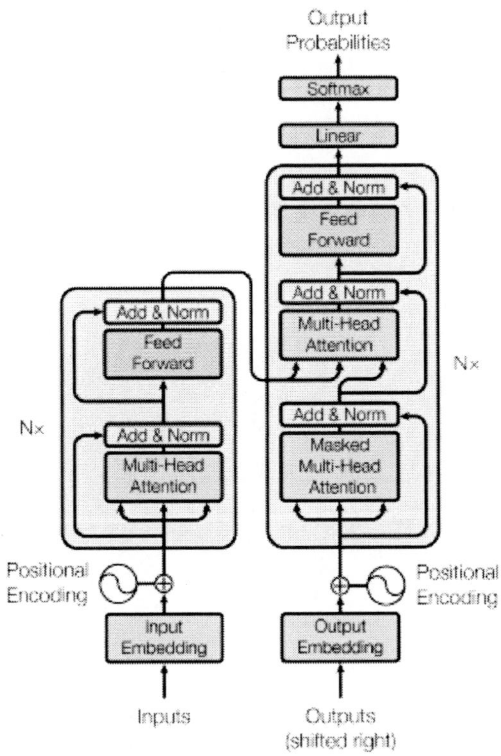

圖 1. Transformer 架構.

2.2 CRF

條件隨機場域 (Conditional Random Field, CRF) 是一種圖形結構的機率模型，用於分割與標註序列資料 (Lafferty et al., 2001)，成效優於傳統的隱形馬可夫模型 (Rabiner and Juang, 1986) 以及最大化熵馬可夫模型 (McCallum et al., 2000)。

隱形馬可夫模型 (Hidden Markov Model, HMM) 的觀察值 (Observation) 之間相互獨立，同時狀態 (State) 之間具有方向性，在狀態移轉的過程中，僅與前一個狀態有關，無法考慮序列之間的前後關係，限制其特徵選擇，實際上序列資料標註的品質，與了解字詞、文句、段落長度，以及上下文之間，有著很大的關係。如圖 2 所示，$\{y1, y2, ..., yn\}$ 爲狀態變數，即對應的序列標註，$\{x1, x2, ..., xn\}$ 爲觀察變數，即待標註的文本序列資料，在 $y1$ 移轉至 $y2$ 的過程中，$x1$ 的值僅依賴於當前的 $y1$，同時 $y2$ 值由 $y1$ 決定，不依賴其它變數，形成 $x1$ 到 xn 之間彼此獨立的現象。

最大化熵馬可夫模型 (Maximum-entropy Markov model, MEMM) 的狀態移轉過程同樣具有方向性，卻解決了 HMM 的觀察值獨

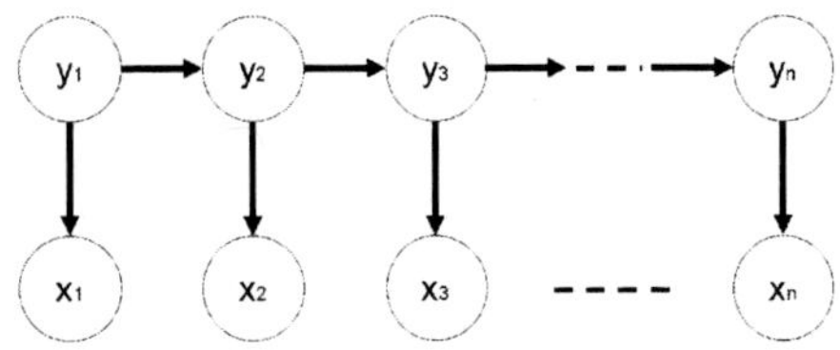

圖 2. Hidden Markov Model.

立問題，對相鄰狀態之間的依賴關係與整個觀察序列加以考量，可以任意選擇特徵，然而 MEMM 在狀態移轉的過程中，進行了局部歸一化，僅求出局部的最佳結果，傾向於選擇更少移轉的狀態，此種作法容易產生標註偏差的問題 (Label Bias Problem)，造成語料當中未曾或鮮少出現的字詞，容易被忽略。如圖3 所示，$y2$ 的值，是根據前一個狀態 $y1$ 與當前的觀察值 $x2$ 得出，每一個狀態移轉的過程，都要服從最大化熵的模型計算結果，形成局部歸一化，容易會有標註偏差問題的產生。

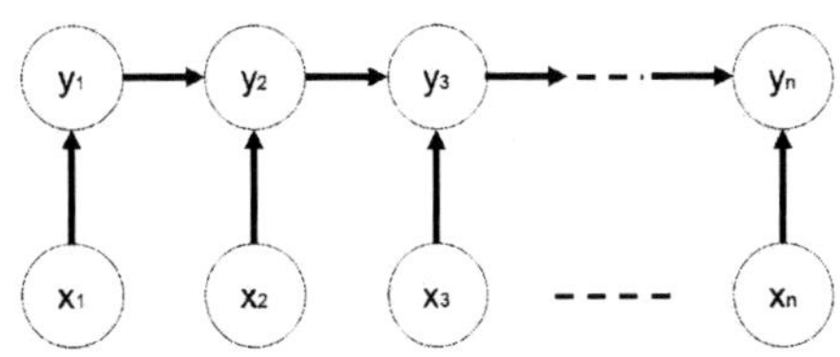

圖 3. Maximum-entropy Markov model.

CRF 能夠對所有觀察序列加以考量，且狀態移轉不具有方向性，代表不需要在每一個狀態移轉的情況下，各別進行局部歸一化，而是能夠將所有特徵進行全域性的了解，再進行歸一化，讓序列標註過程中的每一個狀態，都能與當前全部狀態有所關聯，也因此能夠得到最好的序列標註成效。如圖4所示，隨機輸入的 x 將會求出對應的 y，而 y 值的計算，是透過動態規劃 (Dynamic Programming) 的演算方式得知，試圖從鄰近的 y 預測出所有組合，找出最有可能的標註結果。本研究將使用標準

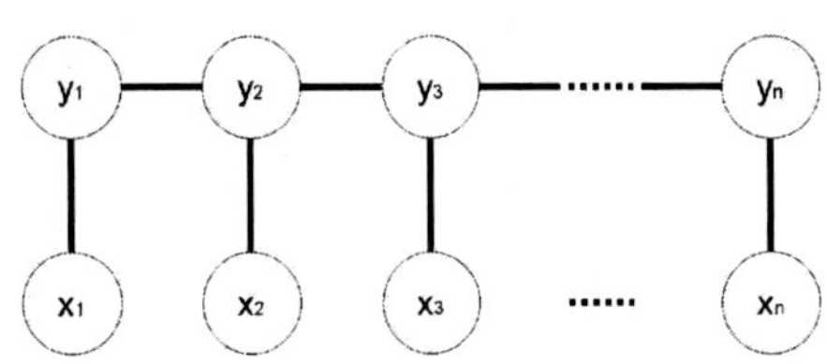

圖 4. Conditional Random Field.

的 CRF 模型。

2.3 對抗訓練

對抗訓練 (Adversarial Training) 由 Ian Goodfellow 等人於 2015 年提出 (Goodfellow et al., 2014)，該文設計一方法 FGSM (Fast Gradient Sign Method)，有效在高維的線性空間中將輸入資料上加入少量的擾動使得輸出結果預測錯誤 (圖5)；同時藉由所產生的資料作爲輸入樣本進行訓練以提高預測的準確率。公式如 (1)：

$$\eta = sign(\nabla x J(\theta, x, y)). \quad (1)$$

其中 θ 爲模型參數，x 爲輸入資料，y 爲輸出目標，$J(\theta, x, y)$ 則爲損失函數 (Cost function)。FGM (Fast Gradient Method) 同樣由

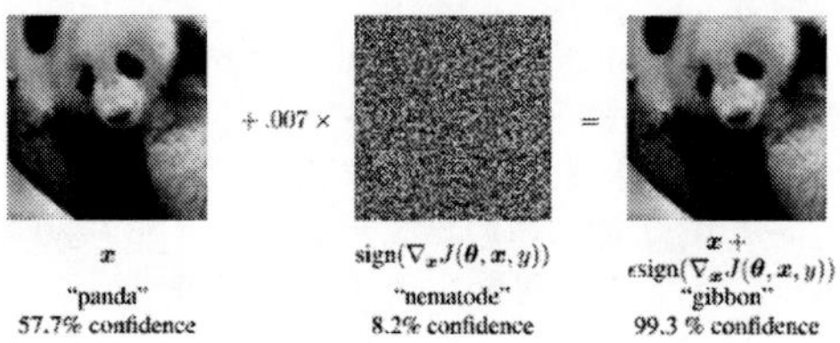

圖 5. FGSM 對抗樣本生成.

Ian Goodfellow 等人於 2017 年提出 (Miyato et al., 2016)，透過梯度的優化取代了 FGSM 中 Sign 的函式 (2) 以取得更好的對抗訓練樣本。

$$\begin{aligned} r_{adv} &= -\epsilon g/g||_2 \\ &\text{where } g = \nabla_x \log p(y|x:\hat{\theta}). \end{aligned} \quad (2)$$

PGD (Projected Gradient Descent) (Madry et al., 2017) 相較 FGM 透過 *epsilon* 參數進行一次性的擾動可能無法得到最佳解的可能，PGD (3) 透過迭代方式以確保擾動不會過大。

$$x^{t+1} = \prod_{x+S} (x^t + \alpha\ sgn(\nabla x L(\theta, x, y))). \quad (3)$$

本實驗將使用 FGM 及 PGD 作爲對抗訓練的模型用以強化訓練結果。

2.4 混合精度訓練

混合精度訓練 (Mixed Precision Training) (Micikevicius et al., 2017) 用意在於盡可能減少精度損失的前提下利用半浮點數 FP16 替代原 FP32 儲存權重及梯度，同時降低記憶體使用且能達到訓練時間成本降低的作用。雖然透過預訓練模型已大幅降低訓練時間，但對於模型的微調 (fine-tuning) 階段仍可能需要花費一定時間。透過混合精度訓練，在不影響預測精準度前提下有效節省訓練時間及記憶體使用。

混合精度訓練的最大挑戰是如何避免 FP16 半精度導致訊息損失。共有三種方式防止訊息丟失，分別是複製 FP32 的權重 (FP32 Master Copy of Weights)、Loss-scaling 以及高精度計算的改善 (ARITHMETIC PRECISION)。

2.4.1 複製 FP32 的權重

神經網路的正向傳播時，將權重由 FP32 轉成 FP16 並計算 Loss 及梯度，最終再轉回 FP32 進行更新。實際參考如圖6。

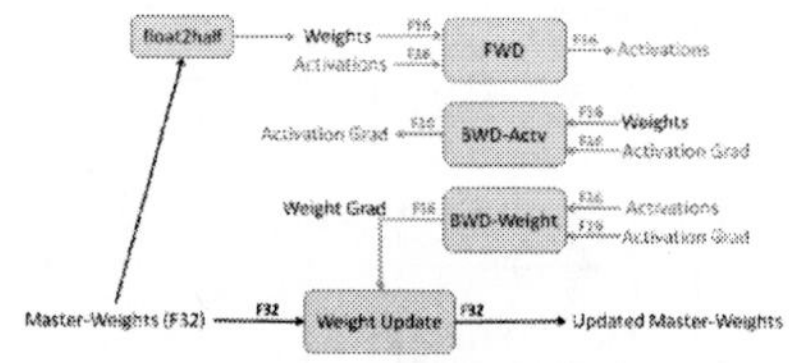

圖 6. 混合精度訓練迭代方式.

2.4.2 Loss-scaling

訓練過程中部分權重可能因轉換爲 FP16 梯度會變成 0(圖 7)，藉由 Loss-scaling 的方式進行 Loss 的縮放，通過 Loss 的放大在反向傳播時放大梯度，最後再更新 FP32 前再縮放還原。

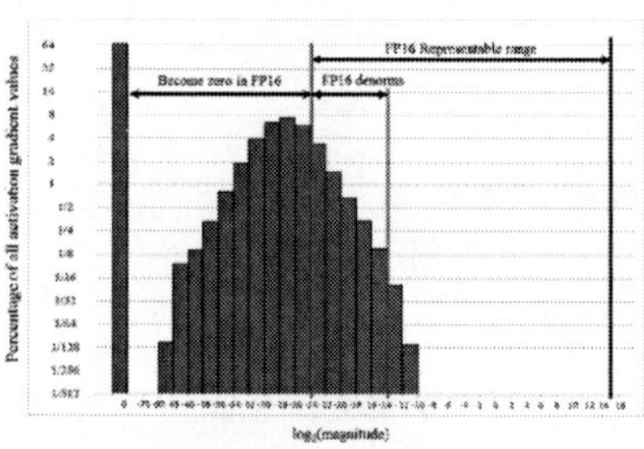

圖 7. Loss Scaling

2.4.3 高精度計算的改善

此研究發現重新優化其高精度的計算方式能夠有效減少訊息的損失。其計算方式爲將 FP16 的矩陣相乘後再與 FP32 的矩陣進行加法運算。

3 實驗

本實驗主要分爲幾個步驟，3.1 及 3.2 分別定義實驗的評估指標以及使用的資料集。3.3 嘗試藉由語料擴增提升預測精準度。3.4 說明本實驗所採用的預訓練模型及相關參數設定。3.5 嘗試藉由預測結果後處理提升預測精準度。最後，3.6 說明實驗結果。

3.1 評估標準

爲同時考慮實驗結果之精確率 (precision) 與召回率 (recall)，本研究中采用 F1-score 作爲實驗模型評估指標，F1-score 計算方式如 (4)，其中 TP、TN、FP、FN 分別代表 True Positive、True Negative、False Positive、False Negative：

$$
\begin{aligned}
Recall &= TP/(TP+FN) \\
Precision &= TP/(TP+FP) \\
F1-score &= 2*Precision*Recall \\
&\quad /(Precision+Recall).
\end{aligned}
\tag{4}
$$

3.2 資料集

本實驗使用 ROCLING-2022 Shared Task 所提供之資料，訓練集 Chinese Health NER Corpus(Lee and Lu, 2021) 包含 30,692 個句子，總計約 1,500,000 個字元或 91,700 個單詞；共有 68,460 個命名實體，涵蓋 10 種實體類型。測試集包含 3205 句中文句子。由於前期並未給出測試集，我們按照官方所提供之資料，將官方從訓練集切分出的 2,531 筆資料作爲實際測試集，其餘 28,161 筆資料作爲實際訓練集，並從實際訓練集中隨機地切分百分之十作爲訓練時的驗證集，即開發集。

3.3 資料擴增

爲使 NER 的分類能夠獲得更高的精準度，本實驗分別從康健網、醫聯網及 KingNet 國家網路醫藥三個醫療保健相關網站蒐集文章 (共計 2290 篇文章) 並進行人工標註作業。然而在實驗過程中，加入額外的訓練集並沒有在結果上帶來顯著的幫助，反而導致了 F1 降低的情況，推估原因可能在於人工標註仍存在著標註錯誤的可能，另一原因在於標註內容涵蓋範圍超出原訓練集的標註範圍，導致在識別命名時，多出原先無法識別 (標註爲 O) 的實體。文章標註參考如表1。

分類	標籤數量
Body (BODY)	22487
Symptom (SYMP)	17416
Instrument (INST)	706
Examination (EXAM)	1780
Chemical (CHEM)	6423
Disease (DISE)	21386
Drug (DRUG)	3851
Supplement (SUPP)	7037
Treatment (TREAT)	2444
Time (TIME)	952

表 1. 文章標注參考.

3.4 模型設計

實驗組別部分，我們使用 BiLSTM-CRF 模型作爲實驗的 Baseline，設置了五組實驗，其中前兩組分別用於選擇模型架構、提升訓練速度，後三組用於提升模型性能 (對抗訓練、Bert 選擇、資料增強及後置處理)。實驗程式部分，本實驗主要使用 pytorch、transformers、simple transformers 工具包，以 Bert 爲基礎的模型均來源於 huggingface (Wolf et al., 2020) 中的開源模型，分別用到'hfl/rbt6'、'hfl/chinese-bert-wwm'、'hfl/chinese-electra-base'、'hfl/chinese-macbert-base'。訓練參數部分，模型 learning rate 爲 3e-5，batch size 爲 32，training epoch 爲 50；爲了防止梯度爆炸，採取梯度裁剪 (gradient clipping) 的方式，最大 norm 值爲 5；使用 AdamW 優化器，weight decay 設定爲 0.01；爲了防止 overfitting，採用 early stopping 的方式，設定 patience 值爲 10，min delta 爲 2e-5，每次 F1-score 的值提升值大於 min delta 才算有改善。文字處理設定的部分，句子的最大長度爲當前批次中最長句子的長度，若當前批次所有句子的集合爲 B，則句子最大長度可表示爲 (5)：

$$
Lmax = arg\max_{s \in B}(\text{len(s)}). \tag{5}
$$

3.5 資料後處理

在實驗過程中，我們發現部分訓練集內的資料存在歧異性及標註錯誤的可能。嘗試藉由後處理進行模型輸出後的後處理，其處理方式如下：將訓練集的所有詞 (word) 整理成字典檔，並針對所有詞逐一進行結果的替換 (替換方式爲將相同詞進行命名實體的替換，如：維他命的 BIO 爲 [B-SUPP], [I-SUPP], [I-SUPP]；當輸出的句中包含維他命時即將其 BIO 進行替換)。替換後計算 F1-score 的結果；最後再篩選取得大於未進行後處理的測試集 F1 結果製作成字典檔作爲後處理的依據。惟此作法雖能在測試集獲得好的成績，但在最後的結果中並不如預期可有效提高準確率。

3.6 實驗結果

第一組實驗的目的是確定基礎的模型架構，我們以 BiLSTM-CRF 模型作爲 Baseline，選用 RoBERTa-wwm-ext 爲 BERT 系列模型代表，設置了 RoBERTa-softmax、RoBERTa-CRF、RoBERTa-BiLSTM-CRF 三種模型架構作爲對照實驗，實驗結果如表2。

model	dev_f1	test_f1
BiLSTM-CRF	0.7301	0.6919
RoBerta-Softmax	0.7541	0.7299
Roberta-CRF	0.7727	0.7453
Roberta-BiLSTM-CRF	0.7613	0.7496

表 2. 模型架構對比實驗結果.

相較 BiLSTM-CRF 模型，RoBERTa-softmax 直接使用具有雙向 Transformers 結構的 RoBERTa，即使未加入更複雜的 layer，亦能有明顯提升；加入 CRF 層的 RoBERTa-CRF 較 RoBERTa-softmax 效果更好；而相較 RoBERTa-CRF，RoBERTa-BiLSTM-CRF 的結構僅在測試集上有少許提升，我們猜測是由於 BERT 系列模型已經具有雙向 Transformers 結構，其效果與 BiLSTM 差不多，故沒有太明顯的提升。考慮到增加 BiLSTM 會增加了模型複雜度，我們將 RoBERTa-CRF 作爲基礎的模型架構，在後續實驗中以其作爲 Baseline。在實驗過程中，爲了提升訓練速度、減少記憶體空間，我們使用混合精度訓練的方式，第二組關於速度提升的實驗數據如表3。

平均一個 epoch 所需時間	平均一個 epoch 所需記憶體	dev_f1	test_f1
439s	10025MiB	0.7712	0.7514
296s	9445MiB	0.7728	0.7559

表 3. 混合精度訓練實驗結果.

使用混合精度訓練並未產生精度損失，並且訓練速度得到明顯提升，每個 epoch 所需時間較原來減少了 32.6%；同時，所需記憶體空間也有少許減少。第三組實驗用於增強模型的魯棒性 (Robustness)，我們通過在 embedding 層增加擾動 (perturbation) 的方式，分別實作了 FGM 和 PGD 兩種攻擊方式，並將其應用在對抗訓練中。對抗訓練具體實作方式分爲四個步驟：首先計算輸入樣本 x 的 loss function 和在 x 處的 gradient；接著使用 FGM 或是 PGD 方法進行攻擊，計算樣本 x 對應的擾動量 r_{adv}；得到對抗樣本 $x_{adv} = x + r_{adv}$ 後，再次輸入模型中，計算 x_{adv} 的 loss，並在正常的 gradient 上累積對抗訓練的 gradient；最後恢復 embedding 參數並進行下一個 batch。實驗中設置 FGM 的 ϵ 值爲 1.0，PGD 的 ϵ 值爲 1.0、α 值爲 0.3，迭代步數分別設置爲 1、3、5、7。實驗結果如表4。

model	train_f1	dev_f1	test_f1
RoBERTa-CRF	0.9893	0.7727	0.7453
RoBERTa-CRF-FGM	0.9766	0.7727	0.7568
RoBERTa-CRF-PGD,step=1	0.9887	0.7676	0.7487
RoBERTa-CRF-PGD,step=3	0.9767	0.7712	0.7514
RoBERTa-CRF-PGD,step=5	0.9787	0.7707	0.7585
RoBERTa-CRF-PGD,step=7	0.9920	0.7723	0.7461

表 4. 對抗訓練實驗結果.

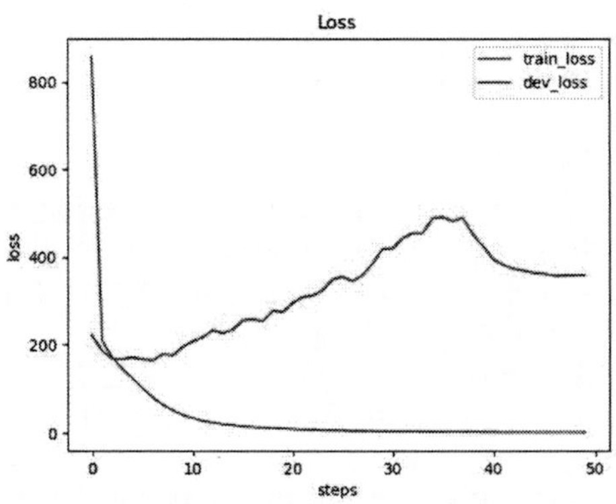

圖 8. The loss of RoBERTa-CRF.

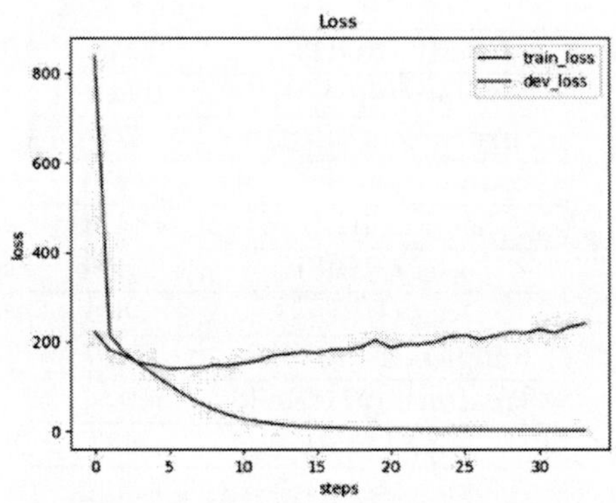

圖 9. The loss of RoBERTa-CRF-FGM.

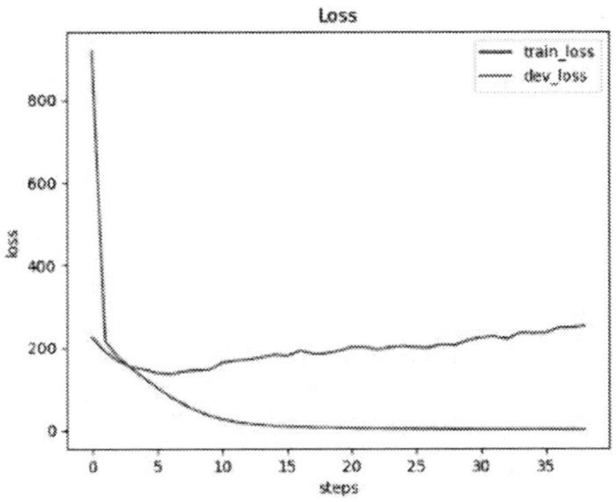

圖 10. The loss of RoBERTa-CRF-PGD,step=3.

使用對抗訓練後，模型在測試集上的 F1-score 分數更高，如圖8、9、10，使用對抗訓練後，能夠一定程度緩解模型過擬合的情況；對於使用 PGD 進行對抗訓練，步數爲 5 時效果最好，步數設定太多或太少模型效果均會變差；使用 FGM 和使用 PGD、步數爲 5 時效果差不多。

第四組實驗用於選擇合適的 BERT 模型，我們分別選用 BERT-wwm、RoBERTa-wwm-ext、ELECTRA、MacBERT-base，後接 CRF 層的模型架構，比較不同 BERT 系列模型的效果，表5爲實驗結果，我們最終選擇了效果最佳的模型 MacBERT-base。

model	train_f1	dev_f1	test_f1
ELECTRA	0.9923	0.6570	0.6067
BERT-wwm	0.9340	0.7608	0.7448
RoBERTa-wwm-ext	0.9893	0.7727	0.7453
MacBERT-base	0.9769	0.7669	0.7465

表 5. BERT 系列模型訓練結果.

最後一組實驗嘗試通過資料增強與資料後處理的方式提升模型的 F1-score 實驗結果如表6。

4 結論

本實驗最終提交了以 MacBERT-base 爲架構的三個模型作爲 ROCLING-2022 Shared Task 的比賽成績。其中 run1、run2 使用 ROCLING-2022 Shared Task 的所有訓練資料 (3205 筆) 作爲訓練集，run3 則加入了額外標注的 54946 筆資料；run2、run3 加入對資料的後處理；分別在官方測試集上取得了

model	dataset	dev_f1	test_f1
MacBERT-CRF+PGD 對抗訓練 + 混合精度訓練	原始資料集	0.7721	0.7599
MacBERT-CRF+PGD 對抗訓練 + 混合精度訓練	原始資料集 + 拓展資料	0.7338	0.7091
MacBERT-CRF+PGD 對抗訓練 + 混合精度訓練 + 後置處理	原始資料集		0.8004

表 6. 資料增强與後處理實驗結果.

0.7796、0.7512、0.6962 的 F1-score。

賽後我們持續優化模型，將 ROCLING-2022 Shared Task 的 3205 筆訓練資料作爲訓練集，並從訓練集中隨機切分百分之十作爲訓練時的驗證集進行訓練，使用官方提供之測試集作爲實驗測試集，在 MacBERT-base 的基礎上加入 CRF 層，使用混合精度訓練、對抗訓練，得到圖7結果，其中使用 MacBERT-CRF 模型，在使用 PGD 對抗訓練設置步數爲 5 時效果最佳 (表7)，F1-score 爲 0.8076，已趨近於官方公布的最佳成績。

基礎模型	模型改進方式	dev_f1	test_f1
MacBERT	無	0.7659	0.7786
MacBERT	CRF+ 混合精度訓練	0.7719	0.7987
MacBERT	CRF+ 混合精度訓練 +FGM 對抗訓練	0.7701	0.7983
MacBERT	CRF+ 混合精度訓練 +PGD 對抗訓練 (step=3)	0.7682	0.8011
MacBERT	CRF+ 混合精度訓練 +PGD 對抗訓練 (step=5)	0.7725	0.8056
MacBERT	BiLSTM+CRF+ 混合精度訓練 +PGD 對抗訓練 (step=5)	0.7687	0.8076

表 7. 綜合模型訓練結果.

藉由實驗證實混合精度訓練能夠有效提升模型訓練速度。CRF 對預測的精準度有一定程度的提升；PGD 對抗訓練能夠一定程度提升模型魯棒性，並少許提升模型的預測能力；BiLSTM 對模型精準度僅有輕微提升；使用外部資料進行資料擴充則沒有明顯的效果。資料後處理則依據不同的測試集效果不一。

本文的主要貢獻如下：(一) 以 BiLSTM + CRF 作爲實驗 Baseline，在 4 組實驗當中，得知預訓練模型 MacBERT-base + CRF 的成效明顯高於 Baseline 與其它實驗結果。(二) 在 MacBERT-base + CRF 的基礎之下，加入混合精度訓練和對抗訓練，大幅地降低模型訓練的時間，一定程度提升資料標註的效果，與任務評測最佳團隊的系統，有著類似的成效水準。

本研究所需要的運算資源，較過去實驗要多，隨著硬體與機器算力的進步，相信會得到解決。每當實驗次數的增加，便能不斷地提升模型的成效，希望未來能夠建立更完善的 NER 語言模型，以提供更多的應用案例。

參考文獻

Madeleine Bates. 1995. Models of natural language understanding. *Proceedings of the National Academy of Sciences*, 92(22):9977–9982.

Yiming Cui, Wanxiang Che, Ting Liu, Bing Qin, and Ziqing Yang. 2021. Pre-training with whole word masking for chinese bert.

Jacob Devlin, Ming-Wei Chang, Kenton Lee, and Kristina Toutanova. 2018. Bert: Pre-training of deep bidirectional transformers for language understanding. *arXiv preprint arXiv:1810.04805*.

Ian J Goodfellow, Jonathon Shlens, and Christian Szegedy. 2014. Explaining and harnessing adversarial examples. *arXiv preprint arXiv:1412.6572*.

John Lafferty, Andrew McCallum, and Fernando CN Pereira. 2001. Conditional random fields: Probabilistic models for segmenting and labeling sequence data.

Lung-Hao Lee, Chao-Yi Chen, Liang-Chih Yu, and Yuen-Hsien Tseng. 2022. Overview of the rocling 2022 shared task for chinese healthcare named entity recognition. in proceedings of the 34th conference on computational linguistics and speech processing.

Lung-Hao Lee and Yi Lu. 2021. Multiple embeddings enhanced multi-graph neural networks for chinese healthcare named entity recognition. *IEEE Journal of Biomedical and Health Informatics*, 25(7):2801–2810.

Aleksander Madry, Aleksandar Makelov, Ludwig Schmidt, Dimitris Tsipras, and Adrian Vladu. 2017. Towards deep learning models resistant to adversarial attacks. *arXiv preprint arXiv:1706.06083*.

Andrew McCallum, Dayne Freitag, and Fernando CN Pereira. 2000. Maximum entropy markov models for information extraction and segmentation. In *Icml*, volume 17, pages 591–598.

Paulius Micikevicius, Sharan Narang, Jonah Alben, Gregory Diamos, Erich Elsen, David Garcia, Boris Ginsburg, Michael Houston, Oleksii Kuchaiev, Ganesh Venkatesh, et al. 2017. Mixed precision training. *arXiv preprint arXiv:1710.03740*.

Takeru Miyato, Andrew M Dai, and Ian Goodfellow. 2016. Adversarial training methods for semi-supervised text classification. *arXiv preprint arXiv:1605.07725*.

Lawrence Rabiner and Biinghwang Juang. 1986. An introduction to hidden markov models. *ieee assp magazine*, 3(1):4–16.

Pranav Rajpurkar, Jian Zhang, Konstantin Lopyrev, and Percy Liang. 2016. Squad: 100,000+ questions for machine comprehension of text. *arXiv preprint arXiv:1606.05250*.

Ashish Vaswani, Noam Shazeer, Niki Parmar, Jakob Uszkoreit, Llion Jones, Aidan N Gomez, Łukasz Kaiser, and Illia Polosukhin. 2017. Attention is all you need. *Advances in neural information processing systems*, 30.

Adams Wei Yu, David Dohan, Minh-Thang Luong, Rui Zhao, Kai Chen, Mohammad Norouzi, and Quoc V Le. 2018. Qanet: Combining local convolution with global self-attention for reading comprehension. *arXiv preprint arXiv:1804.09541*.

Yukun Zheng, Jiaxin Mao, Yiqun Liu, Zixin Ye, Min Zhang, and Shaoping Ma. 2019. Human behavior inspired machine reading comprehension. In *Proceedings of the 42nd international ACM SIGIR conference on research and development in information retrieval*, pages 425–434.

The 34th Conference on Computational Linguistics and Speech Processing (ROCLING 2022)
Taipei, Taiwan, November 21-22, 2022. The Association for Computational Linguistics and Chinese Language Processing

SCU-MESCLab at ROCLING-2022 Shared Task: Named Entity Recognition Using BERT Classifier

Tsung-Hsien Yang
Chunghwa Telecom laboratories,
Taoyuan, Taiwan
yasamyang@cht.com.tw

Ruei-Cyuan Su, Tzu-En Su, Sing-Seong Chong and Ming-Hsiang Su
Department of Data Science, Soochow University, Taipei, Taiwan
{70613rex, 70614roy, chongzhishan123, huntfox.su}@ gmail.com

摘要

本研究構建了命名實體識別模型，並將其應用於醫療領域。資料是以BIO格式進行標記。例如"肌肉"會被標記成"B-BODY"和"I-BODY"，"咳嗽" 則是"B-SYMP"和"I-SYMP"。不屬於命名實體類別以外的字全標為"O"。訓練資料Chinese HealthNER Corpus 包含 30,692 句，其中的 2531 句切分為此次評測的驗證集(dev)，而最終大會提供另外的 3204 句的測試集(test)。我們分別使用 BLSTM_CRF、Roberta+BLSTM_CRF 與 BERT Classifier 三種方式提交三個預測結果。最後，提交為 RUN3 的 BERT Classifier 系統取得了最好的預測效能，其精準度為 80.18%、召回率為 78.3%，F1-score 為 79.23。

Abstract

In this study, named entity recognition is constructed and applied in the medical domain. Data is labeled in BIO format. For example, "muscle" would be labeled "B-BODY" and "I-BODY", and "cough" would be "B-SYMP" and "I-SYMP". All words outside the category are marked with "O". The Chinese HealthNER Corpus contains 30,692 sentences, of which 2531 sentences are divided into the validation set (dev) for this evaluation, and the conference finally provides another 3204 sentences for the test set (test). We use BLSTM_CRF, Roberta+BLSTM_CRF and BERT Classifier to submit three prediction results respectively. Finally, the BERT Classifier system submitted as RUN3 achieved the best prediction performance, with an accuracy of 80.18%, a recall rate of 78.3%, and an F1-score of 79.23.

關鍵字：命名實體識別、BERT 分類器、醫療

Keywords: Named Entity Recognition, BERT, Medical Domain

1 Introduction

醫療信息是指醫生或相關醫療學者傳達的語言訊息，這些醫療信息中包含具有人體及生物特定意義的實體，而醫生和患者溝通中的信息對於治療與健康影響扮演重要角色(Street and Richard, 2013)。在疫情的影響之下，醫生和患者的接觸大幅度的減少，醫療人員和患者之間的交流越來越多是通過遠端設備進行交流，由此可知電子訊息及健康系統普及化對醫療信息的擷取至關重要 (Weiner, 2012)。龐大醫療數據是可以運用深度學習協助醫生或研究人員進行相關研究，如醫學圖像分類(Azizi et al., 2021)，以及醫療保健對話(Konam and Rao, 2021)，有益於醫療進步。

本研究使用 2022 Rocling 會議之參賽資料進行醫療命名實體識別。此參賽資料是包含醫療相關信息之文字語料集，本研究提出一命名實體識別系統分辨醫療相關專有名稱。這些識別出之醫療相關專有名稱可以方便研究人員對醫療信息正確分析，以及有效協助病患提供醫療信息，或是避免醫療人員情急之下用藥錯誤等情況 (Patanwala et al., 2012)，如此對於醫學問題及協助上，有提供更好的幫助。

命名實體識別模型從傳統機器學習、隱藏式馬可夫模型 (hidden Markov model, HMM)，到深度學習的 BiLSTM、BERT 或 RoBERTa 方法搭配條件隨機場 (conditional random field, CRF) (Huang et al., 2015)，可以更有效提升我們效率以及精確度。因此在任務選擇上，分別採用三個方法來實施，第一個方法是單純

運用 BiLSTM+CRF，第二個的方法是運用 RoBERTa+BiLSTM+CRF，第三種方法是運用 BERT token classifier，分別訓練出各個模型。最後我們將各個預測資料採用標準精度、召回率和 F1 分數進行評估。

2 Dataset

本次研究當中，我們所使用的資料集名稱叫作 Chinese Healthcare Named Entity Recognition (HealthNER)，是由 NCUEE NLP 研究室人員收集與標記 (Lee et al., 2021)。資料是透過爬蟲的技術爬取相關新聞，醫療問答論壇和醫療保健信息。此資料集共有 30,692 句子總計約 150 萬個字。經過人工標注後，共有 68,460 個命名實體，涵蓋 10 種實體類型，根據其名稱分別為人體 (BODY)，症狀 (SYMP)，醫療器材 (INST)，檢驗 (EXAM)，化學物質 (CHEM)，疾病 (DISE)，藥品 (DRUG)，營養品 (SUPP)，治療 (TREAT)，時間 (TIME)。資料是以 BIO 格式去標記。例如"肌肉"會被標記成"B-BODY"和"I-BODY"，"咳嗽"則是"B-SYMP"和 "I-SYMP"，以此類推。類別以外的字全標為 "O"。而其中區分為訓練資料(train.json)擁有 28,161 句子和測試資料(test.json)有 2531 個句子和 7305 命名實體。由於大會最終是會提供另外的 3204 句當作最終的測試集(test)，故我們可以將 HealthNER 中的測試資料(test.json)當作我們模型的驗證資料集(dev)使用。

3 Proposed Method

3.1 Embedding method

Pytorch 的 embedding 轉換詞向量機制，為一個簡單的尋找表，其模型通常用於存儲詞向量並使用索引檢索它們。模型的輸入是索引列表，輸出是相應的詞嵌入。其模型的可學習權重，使用是初始化均值 (mean)為 0、方差 (variance) 為 1 的常態分佈 (normal distribution)。其輸入值是索引值的張量形式，輸出則是和輸入的張量相同形式維度形式。

得到詞向量後，使用自行定義好的特殊符號作為 mask 組成單元，有 [UNK] 表示 [未知詞]、[PAD] 表示 [填充]、[START] 表示 [文本開頭]、[END] 表示 [文本结束]，共 4 種特殊符號，將每一句子依照上方表示，轉換成每句完整的 mask，以提供標註作為所使用之 label，以此作為下一步驟要使用的輸入值。

3.2 BERT and RoBERTa

BERT (Bidirectional Encoder Representations from Transformer) 模型，是 Google 以無監督的方式利用大量無標記文本的模型。訓練資料來源于 Wikipedia 2.5B 語料集加上 BookCorpus 800M 語料集。批量大小為 1024 * 128 長度或 256 * 512 長度。BERT 分為 BERT-Base (12-layer, 768-Hidden, 12-head) 和 BERT-Large (24-layer, 1024hidden, 16-head) 兩種形式。BERT 無需標記好的資料或解釋即可進行分析。BERT 是 Transformer 的前半部分核心模組(encoder)，而注意力 (attention) 機制是 Transformer 的前段核心部分，主要是增強語義向量，在不同的字結合中，代表識別字所帶來的意思。因此在 BERT 中，注意力機制為 BERT 的主要構成之一。

RoBERTa 是 BERT 模型問世之後的優化模型之一，主要其優化為效能上的優化，用途為分類以及閱讀理解，而進而分別為中文上的預訓練模型以及英文上的模型，其中英文的 RoBERTa 主要訓練的數據集為維基百科及書籍語料庫，中文的 RoBERTa 主要是使用哈工大訊飛聯合實驗室發布的 RoBERTa-wwm-ext-large 模型(Cui et al., 2020)，該模型經過了第三方中文基準測試 CLUE 的驗證。CLUE 的基準測試包含了 6 個中文文本分類數據集和 3 個閱讀理解數據集，其中包括哈工大訊飛聯合實驗室發布的 CMRC 2018 閱讀理解數據集。在目前的基準測試中，哈工大訊飛聯合實驗室發布的 RoBERTa-wwm-ext-large 模型在分類和閱讀理解任務中都取得了當前最好的綜合效果 (Xu et al., 2020)。

3.3 LSTM

LSTM 是為了解決 RNN 的缺點，例如不能準確處理長期序列、時間的資料。LSTM 是由四個閘 (gate) 結構所組成，輸入閘 (Input Gate)，儲存細胞 (Memory Cell)，遺忘閘 (Forget Gate)，輸出閘 (Output Gate)。Input Gate 主要負責控制這個值輸入，Memory Cell 儲存值，下階段在使用，Output Gate 輸出結果，Forget Gate 是否保留或刪除 feature。LSTM 思路就是把輸入到類神經網路層處理產生出結果，過程當中，記住某些特征，然後會跟著這些經驗來判斷或學習。其中 (1) 至 (4) 分別為 Input Gate, Forget Gate 和 Output Gate 計算公式。其中 C_t 為 memory，h_{t-1}為 hidden state。

$$f_t = \sigma\left(W_f \cdot h_{t-1} + U_i \cdot X_t + b_f\right) \quad (1)$$
$$i_t = \sigma(W_i \cdot h_{t-1} + U_i \cdot X_t + b_i) \quad (2)$$
$$c_t = tanh(W_c \cdot h_{t-1} + U_c \cdot X_t + b_c) \quad (3)$$
$$C_t = f_t \times C_{t-1} + i_t \times c_t \quad (4)$$
$$o_t = \sigma(W_o \cdot h_{t-1} + U_o \cdot X_t + b_o) \quad (5)$$
$$h_t = o_t \times tanh(C_t) \quad (6)$$

Forget Gate，取決要忘記多少舊資料，Input Gate 則是取多少新資料從新 c_t (candidate memory) 取出，放入 C_t 成為下一次的 Memory，因此相互獨立，而 C_t 範圍超出正一到負一，需要 $tanh(C_t)$ 的 $tanh$ 進行標準化，最後相乘起來成為新的 hidden state，最後由各個参數 W 以及各個 U 決定 X_t 及 h_{t-1} 分別代表當前的輸入以及上一時間點的輸出，有了這些門的機制，LSTM 可以記住長期的資料訊息，也避免有梯度消失或爆炸的問題。而 BiLSTM 則使用在學習時間序列的關互關係，使此能夠有隱馬爾可夫模型類似的能力，為雙向循環神經網路 (Schuster & Paliwal, 1997)，通過訓練輸入閘、遺忘閘、輸出閘等權重來學習序列輸入中應該注意的權重信息，而在訓練時使用來自序列兩端的信息來估計輸出為雙向傳遞更新 (Graves & Schmidhuber, 2005)，也就是說，我們使用文字未來的字，以及過去文字的種種信息來進行預測。而我們任務中的並不是預測下一個字，而是整個句子的分析並且各個字之間帶有時間前後輸出信息向量，因此我們最佳選擇是使用 BiLSTM 完成此任務。

3.4 Conditional Random Field

條件隨機場 (conditional random field, CRF)，它經常使用於各種標籤的問題上，在此使用的是實體標籤，但不同於其他模型，其特點是狀態序列 (實體標籤序列: Y) 下觀測序列 (句子切割後序列: X) 的條件機率分布，使用 Hammersley-Clifford Theorem，損失函數為對數似然函數。基本條件隨機場的定義如下，設X與Y是隨機變數，$P(Y|X)$是在給定X的條件機率分布。如隨機變數Y構成一個由無向圖 $G = (V, E)$表示的馬爾可夫隨機場，則

$$P(Y_v|X, Y_W, w \neq v) = P(Y_v|X, Y_W, w{\sim}v) \quad (7)$$

對任意頂點 v 成立，稱條件概率分佈 $P(Y|X)$ 為條件隨機場，其中 $w{\sim}v$ 表示圖 $G = (V, E)$ 中與頂點 v 有邊連接的所有頂點 w，$w \neq v$ 表示頂點 v 以外的所有頂點，Y_v 與 Y_W 為頂點 v 與 w 對應的隨機變數。

實際應用上，是使用線性條件隨機場最為廣泛，一般設 X 和 Y 有相同的圖結構，定義如下，設 $X = (X_1, X_2, \dots X_n), Y = (Y_1, Y_2, \dots Y_n)$ 均為線性表示的隨機變數序列，若再給定隨機變數序列 X 的條件下，隨機變數序列 Y 的條件機率分布 $P(Y|X)$ 構成條件隨機場，即滿足馬爾可夫性。

$$P(Y_i|X, Y_1, \dots, Y_{i-1}, Y_{i+1}, \dots, Y_n) = P(Y_i|X, Y_{i-1}, Y_{i+1}) \quad (8)$$

而稱$P(Y|X)$是線性條件隨機場，其中 $i = 1,2, \dots, n$，在 $i = 1$ 和 n 時只考慮單邊。且將隨機變數 X 取值為 x 的條件下，隨機變數 Y 取值為 y 的條件機率具有以下形式。

$$P(y|x) = \frac{1}{Z(x)} \exp(\sum_{i,k} \lambda_k t_k(y_{i-1}, y_i, x, i) + \sum_{i,l} u_l s_l(y_i, x, i)) \quad (9)$$

上式表示輸入序列 x，對輸出序列 y 預測的條件概率，其中 $Z(x)$ 為為歸一化因子，t_k、s_l 是特徵函數，也是二值函數，函數值為 0 或者 1。

$$Z(x) = \sum_y \exp(\sum_{i,k} \lambda_k t_k(y_{i-1}, y_i, x, i) + \sum_{i,l} u_l s_l(y_i, x, i)) \quad (10)$$

換句話說，滿足特徵條件取值為 1，否則為 0，t_k 是定義在邊上的特徵函數，稱為轉移特徵，依賴於當前和前一個位置。

$$t_k(y_{i-1}, y_i, x, i) \begin{cases} 1, & condition \\ 0, & otherwise \end{cases} \quad (11)$$

另一個 s_l，是定義在節點的特徵函數，稱為狀態特徵，依賴於當前位置:

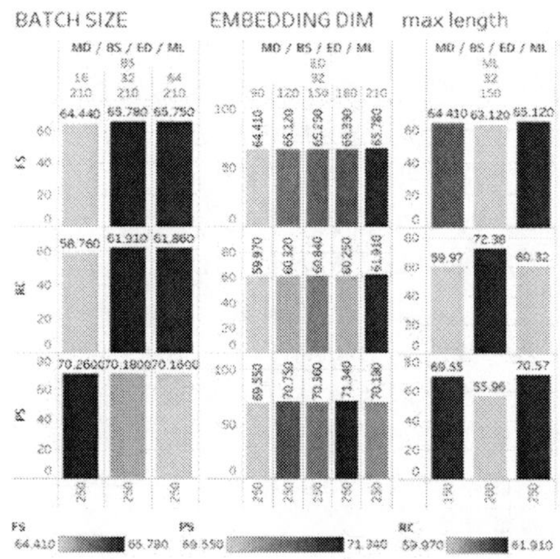

圖 1：批量大小、維度和長度對模型的評估

$$s_l(y_i, x, i)\begin{cases}1, & condition\\0, & otherwise\end{cases} \quad (12)$$

λ_k, u_l 為對應權重，接下來將轉移特徵和狀態特徵結合成，使用對數似然函數修正，用 Viterbi 學習算法取得最佳結果。

4 Experimental Result

此次競賽中，大會允許提交三個最佳的預測結果。我們在以下各小節分別說明三次提交(RUNS)採用的方法與相關參數設置。

4.1 BiLSTM+CRF (RUN 1)

RUN 1 採用目前在英語 NER 表現良好的 BiLSTM+CRF 網路模型。我們採用 Pytorch 的 embedding 轉換詞向量機制來對每個中文字進行向量編碼。參數設置上從圖 1 中，可以看到 batch size，在其他參數固定下，所設為 32 值的 F1 Score 以及 Recall 都比其餘兩者高，因此選擇 32 值作為 embedding dim 和 max length 的實驗固定參數。接著，看到 embedding dim，在 batch size 設為 32 值，max length 參數固定不變下，所設為 210 值的 F1 Score 以及 Recall 都比其餘四者高，因此選擇 210 值作為 max length 的實驗固定參數。最後，看到 max length，在 batch size 設為 32 值和 embedding dim 設為 210 值下，所設為 250 值的 F1 Score 以及 Precision 都比其餘兩者高，因此 max length 設為 250 值為最終實驗模型選擇參數值。所以要得到最優的模型，參數 max length 設為 250 值，batch size 設為 32 值 embedding dim 設為 210 值。實驗結果採用大會最終提供的測試集進行衡量如下表 1 中的 BiLSTM+CRF (RUN 1)所示，準確性(Accuracy) 82.23%、精確度(Precision) 55.96%、招回率(Recall) 72.38%與 F1 score 63.12%。

4.2 RoBERTa+BiLSTM + CRF (RUN 2)

RUN 2 採用 RoBERTa+BiLSTM + CRF 模型來進行實驗。我們分別選取句子長度以及批量大小來決定哪個模型可以訓練出較好的正確率，而句子長度分別使用長度為 150、200、250 個字，批量大小為 16、32、64 分別做為模型訓練。最後我們的模型使用 SGD 隨機梯度下降，學習率為 0.012，weight decay 為 1e-5，且利用 scheduler 每兩次 epoch 時學習率減少

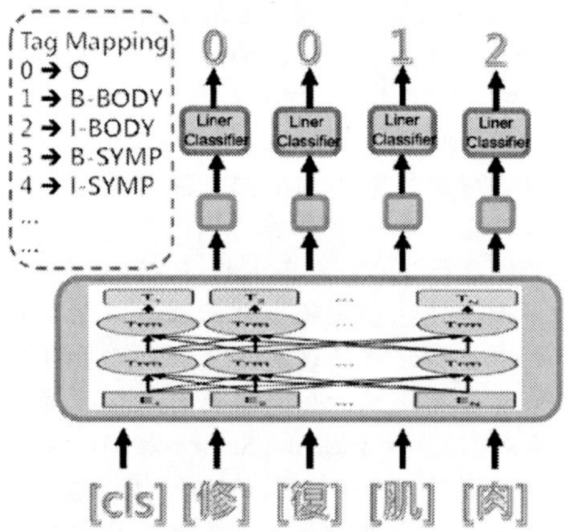

圖 2：BERT Token Classifier

0.9。實驗結果採用大會最終提供的測試集進行衡量如下表 1 中的 RoBERTa+BiLSTM + CRF (RUN 2)所示，準確性(Accuracy) 91.56%、精確度(Precision) 78.96%、招回率(Recall) 78.21%與 F1 score 78.58%。

4.3 BERT Token Classifier (RUN 3)

相對於文本分類的 BERT 和用於解決 NER 問題的 BERT，其做法上區別在於我們如何設置模型的輸出。如圖 2 所示，對於文本分類問題，我們僅使用來自特殊 [CLS] 標記的嵌入向量輸出。而 BERT 用於 NER 任務，我們需要使用所有標記的嵌入向量輸出。通過使用所有標記的嵌入向量輸出，我們可以對每個標記進行分類來預測每個標記的命名實體為何。

模型/效能	Accuracy	precision	recall	F1
BiLSTM+CRF (RUN 1)	82.23%	55.96%	72.38%	63.12%
RoBERTa+BiLSTM + CRF (RUN 2)	91.56%	78.96%	78.21%	78.58%
BERT_Based Token Classifier	91.75%	79.35%	76.24%	77.77%
BERT_Cont Token Classifier (RUN 3)	93.10%	80.18%	78.30%	79.23%

表 1: 實驗結果

RUN3 使用中研院中文計算語言研究小(Chinese Knowledge and Information Processing, CKIP) 所發布的 BERT 繁體中文預訓練模型(ckiplab/bert-base-chinese) (Yang and Ma, 2021)，對每句訓練語句的每個標記 token 產生 768 維的輸出向量。再將輸出向量接入一個線性分類器進行分類。然而在將這些文本輸入模型之前，我們需要先進行預處理。 也就是對這些輸入文字進行轉換為預訓練詞彙表中的相應 ID 並添加一些特殊的標記於句子前後([CLS] 和 [SEP])。再將每個句子填充(PAD)成同等長度的句子，我們設置訓練集中最大句子的長度 441 與 batch_size = 16 並以 adamw 為優化器進行訓練。 首先，我們以大會提供之訓練集 train.json 資料檔進行 BERT_Based 的模型訓練，並以驗證集 test.json 資料檔進行模型測試。發現到衡量指標 precision 只有 69.55%，推測應是 test.json 中包含 train.json 有未出現的新實體。借鏡吳恩達 (Andrew Ng) 近期提倡的以資料為中心的人工智慧 (Data-Centric AI)方式，持續提升資料品質能增進模型的預測能力。由於提升資料品質不是一次性能完成的任務，而是持續改進的循環過程。故我們先以 train.json 資料訓練一個基礎模型(BERT_Based) 再以預訓練模型的微調 (fine-tune) 方式加入 test.json 資料持續訓練一個模型(BERT_Cont)。最後以此模型預測大會的測試檔提交為 Run3。最後依據大會提供的標準答案(golden)所得到的實驗結果如表 1 所示。整體來說 BERT_Cont 模型表現較佳，其在準確性(Accuracy) 93.10%、精確度(Precision) 80.18%、招回率(Recall) 78.30%與 F1 score 79.23% 皆高於其它模型。

5 Conclusion and future work

在這項研究中，我們提交了三個命名實體識別的模型，並將其應用於醫療領域。根據其名稱分別為人體 (BODY)，症狀 (SYMP)，醫療器材 (INST)，檢驗 (EXAM)，化學物質(CHEM)，疾病 (DISE)，藥品 (DRUG)，營養品 (SUPP)，治療 (TREAT)，時間 (TIME)。資料是以 BIO 格式去標記。例如"肌肉"會被標記成"B-BODY"和"I-BODY"，"咳 嗽"是 "B-SYMP"和"I-SYMP"，以此類推。類別以外的字全標為"O"。最終我們使用 HealthNER 的所有資料30,692句子當訓練與驗證資料集而以大會提供的 3204 個句子為測試資料集分別對三種模型進行驗證。實驗結果表明，RUN1 使用的是 BiLSTM+CRF 網路模型其效能最差。RUN2 採用的是簡體中文模型的 RoBERTa+BiLSTM + CRF 就能取得不錯的實驗結果。而 RUN3 採用 CKIP 繁體中文的 BERT Classifier 系統取得了最好的系統效能，其準確性(Accuracy) 93.10%、精確度(Precision) 80.18%、招回率(Recall) 78.30%與 F1 score 79.23% 皆高於其它模型。由此可知，預訓練模型的方法在此實驗上有比過去表現良好的 BiLSTM+CRF 網路模型擁有較佳的效能表現。未來我們可再針對繁體中文的 BERT 模型再加上 CRF 來探討效能是否能再提升。

References

Street Jr, Richard L. 2013. How clinician–patient communication contributes to health improvement: modeling pathways from talk to outcome. *Patient education and counseling*. 92(3): 286-291. https://doi.org/10.1016/j.pec.2013.05.004.

Weiner, Jonathan P. 2012. Doctor-patient communication in the e-health era. *Israel journal of health policy research.* 1(33): 1-7. https://doi.org/10.1186/2045-4015-1-33.

Azizi, S., Mustafa, B., Ryan, F., Beaver, Z., Freyberg, J., Deaton, J., Loh A., Karthikesalingam A., Kornblith S., T. Chen, N. Vivek and Norouzi, M. 2021. Big self-supervised models advance medical image classification. *Proceedings of the IEEE/CVF International Conference on Computer Vision*, page 3478-3488.

Konam, S., and Rao S. 2021. Abridge: A Mission Driven Approach to Machine Learning for Healthcare Conversation. *Journal of Commercial Biotechnology*. 26(2): 62-66.

Patanwala, A. E., Sanders, A. B., Thomas, M. C., Acquisto, N. M., Weant, K. A., Baker, S. N., Merritt, E., and Erstad, B. L. 2012. A prospective, multicenter study of pharmacist activities resulting in medication error interception in the emergency department. *Annals of emergency medicine*. 59(5): 369-373. https://doi.org/10.1016/j.annemergmed.2011.11.013.

Huang, Z., Xu, W., and Yu, K. 2015. Bidirectional LSTM-CRF models for sequence tagging. *arXiv preprint* arXiv:1508.01991. https://doi.org/10.48550/arXiv.1508.01991

Lee, L. H., & Lu, Y. (2021). Multiple embeddings enhanced multi-graph neural networks for Chinese healthcare named entity recognition. IEEE Journal of Biomedical and Health Informatics, 25(7), 2801-2810. https://doi.org/10.1109/JBHI.2020.3048700.

Lee, L.-H., Chen, C.-Y., Yu, L.-C., and Tseng, Y.-H. 2022. Overview of the ROCLING 2022 shared task for Chinese healthcare named entity recognition. *Proceedings of the 34th Conference on Computational Linguistics and Speech Processing.*

Cui, Y., Che, W., Liu, T., Qin, B., Wang, S., & Hu, G. (2020). Revisiting pre-trained models for Chinese natural language processing. arXiv preprint arXiv:2004.13922.

Xu, L., Hu, H., Zhang, X., Li, L., Cao, C., Li, Y., Xu, Y., Sun, K., Yu, D., Yu, C., Tian, Y., Dong, Q., Liu, W., Shi, B., Cui, Y., Li, J., Zeng, J., Wang, R., Xie, W., Li, Y., Patterson, Y., Tian, Z., Zhang, Y., Zhou, H., Liu, S., Zhao, Z., Zhao, Q., Yue, C., Zhang, X., Yang, Z., Richardson, K., Zhenzhong Lan, Z. 2020. CLUE: A Chinese language understanding evaluation benchmark. *arXiv preprint* arXiv:2004.05986. https://doi.org/10.48550/arXiv.2004.05986.

Schuster, M., and Paliwal, K. K. 1997. Bidirectional recurrent neural networks. *IEEE transactions on Signal Processing.* 45(11): 2673-2681. https://doi.org/10.1109/78.650093.

Graves, A., and Schmidhuber, J. 2005. Framewise phoneme classification with bidirectional LSTM and other neural network architectures. *Neural networks.* 18(5-6): 602-610. https://doi.org/10.1016/j.neunet.2005.06.042.

Yang, Mu, and Ma, W.-Y. 2021. ckiplab/ckip-transformers. https://github.com/ckiplab/ckip-transformers

The 34th Conference on Computational Linguistics and Speech Processing (ROCLING 2022)
Taipei, Taiwan, November 21-22, 2022. The Association for Computational Linguistics and Chinese Language Processing

YNU-HPCC at ROCLING 2022 Shared Task: A Transformer-based Model with Focal Loss and Regularization Dropout for Chinese Healthcare Named Entity Recognition

Xiang Luo, Jin Wang and Xuejie Zhang
School of Information Science and Engineering
Yunnan University
Kunming, China
Contact: {wangjin,xjzhang}@ynu.edu.cn

Abstract

Named Entity Recognition (NER) is a fundamental task in information extraction that locates the mentions of named entities and classifies them in unstructured texts. Previous studies typically used hidden Markov model (HMM) and conditional random fields (CRF) for NER. To learn long-distance dependencies in text, recurrent neural networks, e.g., LSTM and GRU can extract the semantic features for each token with a sequential manner. Based on Transformers, this paper describes the contribution to ROCLING-2022 Share Task. This paper adopts a transformer-based model with focal Loss and regularization dropout. The focal loss is to overcome the uneven distribution of the label. The regularization dropout (r-drop) is to address the problem of vocabulary and descriptions that are too domain-specific. The ensemble learning is to improve the performance of the model. Comparative experiments were conducted on dev set to select the model with the best performance for submission. That is, BERT model with BiLSTM-CRF, focal loss and R-Drop has achieved the best F_1-score of 0.7768 and rank the 4th place.

Keywords: Chinese Healthcare Named Entity Recognition, Sequence Labeling, Information Extraction, Transformers, Conditional Random Fields

1 Introduction

Providing computer the ability to understand the abstract meaning of real world is a fundamental task. The shared task of ROCLING-2022 is Chinese healthcare named entity recognition task. Given a sentence about Chinese healthcare, the intelligent model is required to produce the entities in this sentence.

Table 1 provides a detailed description of all target labels. For example, the input is 膽汁長期滯留就會比較容易造成膽沙和膽結石了。, the intelligence model is expected to extract three entities, including 膽汁 as BODY, and both 膽沙 and 膽結石 as DISE. By using a sequence labeling approach, the corresponding labels for all tokens should be B-BODY, I-BODY, O, O, O, O, O, O, O, O, O, O, O, O, B-DISE, I-DISE, O, B-DISE, I-DISE, I-DISE, O, O. Here, the BIO schema is adopted, where B and I respectively means the begin and inside labels, while O indicates that a token belongs to other objects.

Previous studies used probabilistic model for named entity recognition on text, such as hidden Markov model (HMM) (Zhou and Su, 2002) and conditional random field (CRF) (Zheng et al., 2017). Recent advances in deep neural networks (DNN) (Krizhevsky et al., 2012) and representation learning (Bengio et al., 2013) have considerably improved the ability of NER models. It mainly consists of an encoder to learn hidden representation for each token, as well as a classifier to assign a label for the token. For encoders, traditional models are usually used recurrent neural networks (RNN), such as long short-term memory (LSTM) (Hochreiter and Schmidhuber, 1997) or gated recurrent units (GRU) to learn long-distance dependencies. Furthermore, attention mechanisms can be applied to improve the performance of RNN models to extract more task-specific features between tokens to provide meaningful information. Several effective approaches apply the pre-trained language models (PLM), such as BERT (Devlin et al., 2019), RoBERTa (Liu et al., 2019) and ALBERT (Lan et al., 2020), to provide powerful representation to boost the performance of

Entity Type	Description
Body(BODY)	The whole physical structure that forms a person or animal including biological cells, organizations, organs and systems.
Symptom(SYMP)	Any feeling of illness or physical or mental change that is caused by a particular disease.
Instrumenr(INST)	A tool or other device used for performing a particular medical task such as diagnosis and treatments.
Examination(EXAM)	The act of looking at or checking something carefully in order to discover possible diseases.
Chemical(CHEM)	Any basic chemical element typically found in the human body.
Disease(DISE)	An illness of people or animals caused by infection or a failure of health rather than by an accident.
Drug(DRUG)	Any natural or artificially made chemical used as a medicine
Supplement(SUPP)	Something added to something else to improve human health.
Treatment(TREAT)	A method of behavior used to treat diseases
Time(TIME)	Element of existence measured in minutes, days, years

Table 1: The detailed description of all target labels.

sequence labeling.

Furthermore, some studies have tried to transform the NER task as a machine reading comprehension (MRC) (Li et al., 2020) or a candidate span extraction (Ji et al., 2020). For the former, the multi-classification problem of named entity recognition is converted into a Q&A task. The model is asked each piece of data, and then answer it through the location information of the start and end position of the entity. For the latter, the candidate span extraction is divided into two parts, The first part is candidate extraction, and this part is similar in structure to most of the previous extractive question answering models, mainly responsible for extracting candidate answers from the passage. The second part is answer selection, which is mainly responsible for selecting the most reliable answer from all the candidate answers, and considering the relationship between all the candidate answers.

By using the sequence labeling manner, the task brings two difficulties may finally impact the performance of recent NER models. One of the biggest stumbling blocks is data distribution, which often appears in conventional sequence labeling tasks and corpora. Figure 1 provided other two examples of the shared tasks. Notably, most of the labels are O. The target tokens of Chinese healthcare entities in both examples only take respective ratios of 12.9% and 20.0%. The proportion of meaningless O label is dominate. By using a cross-entropy loss function, the model may tend to assign O label for all tokens thus the model can achieve the minimal cross-entropy. However, it will be useless for the task where these minority labels, e.g., BODY, CHEM and DISE, are more important than the majority labels. That is, false negatives can have higher importance, while false positives are of course

Input	專注於每個呼吸，透過鼻子的一吸一吐的換氣，促進舒緩與放鬆身心。
Output	B-BODY, I-BODY, O, O, O, O, O, O, O, O, O, O, O, O, B-DISE, I-DISE, O, B-DISE, I-DISE, I-DISE, O, O
Ratio	12.9%

Input	平時避免酒精、咖啡和茶等利尿食品，以防低血壓加重。
Output	O, O, O, O, B-CHEM, I-CHEM, O, O, O, O, O, O, O, O, O, O, O, O, O, B-DISE, I-DISE, I-DISE, O, O, O
Ratio	20.0%

Figure 1: The imbalanced examples in labeling of Chinese HealthNER Corpus.

undesirable. Another important issue is that the expression is healthy-related and domain-specific, thus may limit the learning ability of the encoders which are usually pretrained on domain-independent texts.

In this paper, we employed pretrained language models, including BERT, RoBERTa, ELECTRA (Clark et al., 2020) and ALBERT, for the Chinese healthcare named entity recognition task. To address the imbalance distribution of labels, we applied focal loss (Lin et al., 2020) on the CRF classifier. Further, a regularized dropout mechanism (Liang et al., 2021) was used to further enhance the performance of the base encoders. In addition, we tried to ensemble all base encoders as a more powerful model. Unfortunately, this did not bring any improvements on performance.

The rest of this paper is organized as follows. Section 2 describes all the models which are used in this task. Experimental results are summarized in Section 3. Conclusion is finally drawn in Section 4.

2 Model Description

This section will describe the architecture of the proposed model in details. There are several components in this section, including

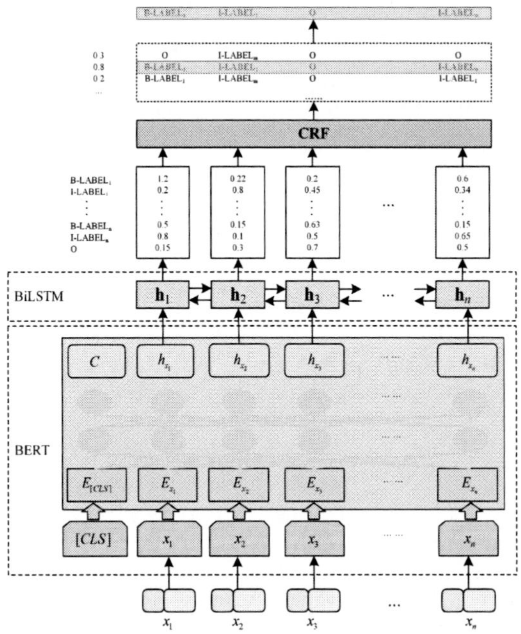

Figure 2: The overall architecture of the proposed method.

BERT, BiLSTM-CRF, focal loss, and R-Drop. The model architecture is shown in Figure 2.

2.1 Method

BERT. BERT was pretrained by two tasks, masked language model (MLM) and next sentence prediction (NSP), which is designed to pretrain deep bidirectional representations from unlabeled text by jointly conditioning on both left and right context in all layers. The checkpoint hfl/chinese-bert-wwm-ext (Cui et al., 2020) is used in the model, which uses 12-layer, 768-hidden, 12-heads and 110M parameters. For each layer, The attention takes its input in the form of three parameters, i.e., query, key and value. All three parameters are similar in structure, with each word in the sequence represented by a vector, denoted as,

$$Attention\,(Q, K, V) = softmax\left(\frac{QK^T}{\sqrt{d_k}}\right) V \quad (1)$$

The attention module splits its query, key, and value parameters N-ways and passes each split independently through a separate Head. All of these similar attention calculations are then combined together to produce a final attention score as follows,

$$\begin{array}{l} MutiHead\,(Q, K, V) = Concat\,(head_1, ..., head_h)\, W^O \\ where\ head_i = Attention\left(QW_i^Q, KW_i^K, VW_i^V\right) \end{array} \quad (2)$$

BiLSTM. The unidirectional LSTM model can only capture the information passed from head to tail. Conversely, the bidirectional LSTM can capture forward information and reverse information imultaneously, which makes the use of text information more comprehensive and the effect is better. And a linear layer is added after the final output layer of the BiLSTM network, which is used to project the output of the hidden layer generated by BiLSTM to an interval that expresses the meaning of the label features (Huang et al., 2015). The output of the BERT is used as the input of the BiLSTM as equation 3.

$$[H_1, H_2...H_N] = BiLSTM\,([h_1, h_2...h_N]) \quad (3)$$

CRF. Conditional random fields is a conditional probability distribution model for solving the output sequence given the input sequence. The CRF layer can add some constraints to ensure that the final prediction result is valid. The CRF layer can learn the constraints of the sentence. These constraints

MODEL	F_1-score	Submission
BERT+RoBERTa+ELECTRA+ALBERT	0.827	
RoBERTa+ELECTRA+ALBERT	0.826	
BERT+RoBERTa+ALBERT	0.830	
BERT+RoBERTa+ELECTRA	0.830	
BERT+ELECTRA+ALBERT	0.827	
ALBERT+ELECTRA	0.822	
RoBERTa+ALBERT	0.824	
RoBERTa+ELECTRA	0.830	
BERT+ALBERT	0.829	
BERT+ELECTRA	0.829	
BERT+RoBERTa	0.831	Submission3
RoBERTa	0.832	Submission2
ELECTRA	0.822	
ALBERT	0.790	
BERT	**0.833**	**Submission1**

Table 2: F_1-score of each ensemble model in dev data.

can be learned automatically by the CRF layer when training the data. The CRF loss function is as Eq. 4:

$$\begin{aligned}\mathcal{L}_{CRF} &= \log \frac{P_{\mathrm{Real}Path}}{P_1+P_2+\ldots+P_N} \\ &= -\log \frac{e^{S_{\mathrm{Real}Path}}}{e^{S_1}+e^{S_2}+\ldots e^{S_N}} \\ &= -\left(\log e^{S_{\mathrm{Real}Path}} - \log\left(e^{S_1}+e^{S_2}+\ldots+e^{S_N}\right)\right) \\ &= -\left(S_{\mathrm{Real}Path} - \log\left(e^{S_1}+e^{S_2}+\ldots+e^{S_N}\right)\right) \\ &= -\sum_{i=1}^{N} x_{iy_i} - \sum_{i=1}^{N-1} t_{y_i y_{i+1}} + \log\left(e^{S_1}+e^{S_2}+\ldots+e^{S_N}\right)\end{aligned} \tag{4}$$

where the e is a constant, S is the score of the path, $x_{i,j}$ is the score at which the i-th indexed word is labeled as j. $t_{i,j}$ is the score of label i to label j.

Focal Loss. Focal loss is a loss function that deals with the imbalance of sample classification. It focuses on adding weight to the loss corresponding to the sample according to the difficulty of distinguishing the sample, that is, adding a small weight to the easy-to-distinguish sample and adding a large weight to the difficult-to-distinguish sample. The expression of the focal loss is as follows.

$$\mathcal{L}_{Focal} = -\alpha_t(1-p_t)^{\gamma}\log(p_t) \tag{5}$$

where the α_t is a trainable parameter, the γ is a hyper-parameter and the p_t is the probability of class t.

R-Drop. Due to the existence of dropout, the same model with the same input will get two different distributions, where it can approximately be treated as two different model networks. Based on this, the different distributions produced by these two different models can be denoted as, $P_\theta(y|x)$ and $P'_\theta(y|x)$. The main contribution of R-Drop is to continuously lower the KL Divergence (KL divergence) between the two distributions during the training process. Due to the asymmetry of the KL divergence itself, the globally symmetric KL divergence is indirectly used by exchanging the positions of these two distributions, which is called bidirectional KL divergence. Additionally, the model is also trained on NLL loss terms for both distributions. The final loss is as follows:

$$\begin{aligned}\mathcal{L}_{R-drop} = &-\log P_\theta(y_i|x_i) - \log P'_\theta(y_i|x_i) \\ &+\alpha[D_{KL}\left(P_\theta(y_i|x_i)\,||P'_\theta(y_i|x_i)\right) \\ &+D_{KL}\left(P'_\theta(y_i|x_i)\,||P_\theta(y_i|x_i)\right)]\end{aligned} \tag{6}$$

The final objective of the used model is defined as follows:

$$\mathcal{L} = \mathcal{L}_{CRF} + \mathcal{L}_{Focal} + \mathcal{L}_{R-drop} \tag{7}$$

2.2 Ensemble Learning

In ensemble learning, multiple models are trained to solve the same problem and are combined to get better results. The most important assumption is that when weak models are combined correctly, the more accurate or robust models can be got. The stacking strategy are used as ensemble learning model. Stacking usually considers heterogeneous weak learners and stacking learning to combine base models with meta-model. Besides BERT, we tried some other models, such as RoBERTa, ELECTRA, ALBERT. The detail is as follows.

RoBERTa. RoBERTa is a robustly optimized BERT pretraining approach. It is an improved recipe for training BERT models, that can match or exceed the performance of all of the post-BERT methods. The modifications include (1) training the model longer, with bigger batches, over more data; (2) removing the next sentence prediction objective; (3) training on longer sequences; and (4) dynamically changing the masking pattern applied to the training data. The checkpoint **hfl/chinese-roberta-wwm-ext** is used in the model, which uses 12-layer, 768-hidden, 12-heads and 125M parameters.

ALBERT. ALBERT is a lite BERT for self-supervised learning of language representations which lead to models that scale much better compared to the original BERT and it uses a self-supervised loss that focuses on modeling inter-sentence coherence, and show it consistently helps downstream tasks with multi-sentence inputs. ALBERT base model with no dropout, additional training data and longer training. The checkpoint **clue/albert_chinese_tiny** is used in the model, which uses 4-layer, 312-hidden, 12-heads and 16M parameters.

ELECTRA. ELECTRA is a new method for self-supervised language representation learning. It can be used to pre-trained transformer networks using relatively little compute. ELECTRA models are trained to distinguish *real* input tokens vs. *fake* input tokens generated by another neural network, similar to the discriminator of a GAN. The checkpoint **hfl/chinese-electra-180g-small-discriminator** is used in the model, which uses 12-layer, 256-hidden, 4-heads and 12M parameters.

After comparing the meta-model, the random forest model (Breiman, 2001) are chosen to be the meta-model, and the BERT, RoBERTa, ELECTRA and ALBERT models are taken as the base models. After fine-tuning the parameters, the final result is shown in Table 2.

3 Experimental Results

In this section, comparative experiments were conducted to select the best model as the final submission. The details of the experiments are presented as follows.

3.1 Dataset

The train dataset (Lee and Lu, 2021) describes 10 entity types in total, and use the common BIO (Beginning, Inside, and Outside) format for NER tasks. The B-prefix before a tag indicates that the character is the beginning of a named entity and I-prefix before a tag indicates that the character is inside a named entity. An O tag indicates that a token belongs to no named entity.

In the raw dataset, there are some descriptions about the sentences, such as id, genre, word, word_label, character, character_label. Because the task focuses on the character level labeling, we choose the character and character_label as the input and output.

3.2 Evaluation Metrics

The performance is evaluated by examining the difference between machine-predicted labels and human-annotated labels. We adopt standard precision, recall, and F_1-score, which are the most typical evaluation metrics of NER systems at a character level. Precision is defined as the percentage of named entities found by the NER system that are correct. The definition of Precision is as follows:

$$P = \frac{TP}{TP + FP} \tag{8}$$

Recall is the percentage of named entities present in the test set found by the NER system. The definition of Recall is as follows:

$$R = \frac{TP}{TP + FN} \tag{9}$$

F_1-score is an indicator used in statistics to measure the accuracy of a binary (or multi-class) model, which takes into account the accuracy and recall of the classification model at the same time. The definition of F_1-score is as follows:

$$F_1 = \frac{2 \times P \times R}{P + R} \tag{10}$$

where TP is True Positive, FP is False Positive, FN is False Negative.

MODEL	LOSS	F_1-score
BERT+softmax	CrossEntropy	0.799
BERT+softmax	Focal	0.805
BERT+BiLSTM	Focal	0.812
BERT+BiLSTM+CRF	Focal	0.825
BERT+BiLSTM+CRF+R-Drop	**Focal**	**0.833**

Table 3: F_1-score of each strategy in dev data.

3.3 Implementation Details

The train data is split into train data and dev data. At first, we make pre-processing for the train data, which only obtain the characters and character labels. The tokenizer are used to convert token into vector, after that, we add the BiLSTM-CRF after the hidden output of the pre-trained model. And we find that the data is not evenly distributed in the dataset,so the focal loss is used to solve this kind of problems. It focuses on adding weight to the loss corresponding to the sample according to the difficulty of the sample discrimination.

Moreover, to strengthen the generalization of the model, the regularized dropout (R-Drop) is used. Due to the existence of dropout, the output of two models with the same parameters may also be different. In order to alleviate the inconsistency of this training process, we imposed restrictions on the output distribution, and the KL divergence loss of the data distribution metric is introduced, making the two data distributions generated by the same sample in the batch as close as possible.

Then we use dev data to select the best performing model and save it, where the evaluation metric is F_1-score. After that, the ensemble strategy is used to stack different models, and the random forest model is chosen to be the meta-model, which performs better than other classifier. There are many of combinations, we list the scores for each kind of model as well as the score for the base models in Table 2.

In addition, MRC is used in this task and MRC is quite used in NER task. When using MRC, the task is converted to a QA-type question. We need to allocate 10 queries to each sentence. Possibly due to the large amount of data, after the allocation, the whole amount of the data come to 230,000, or because the uneven distribution of the data, there are many "O" labels, which affect the model prediction. Besides, the questioning method of query is also an aspect that affects the prediction of the model. So the MRC approach doesn't perform well.

Label embedding (Akata et al., 2015) is also another trick to enhance the understanding of the text for the model. Label embedding is to add the label of each word to the hidden representation of each word. It helps the model better understand the literal meaning of the label. But it also doesn't perform well. We guess that the insertion position may be wrong, or the embedding generated during inference is not appropriate.

3.4 Parameters Tuning

In this part, we use warm up strategy, which is an approach to optimize the learning rate. Warm up is a learning rate warm-up method mentioned in the ResNet (He et al., 2016) paper, which chooses to use a smaller learning rate at the beginning of training, and trains some epochs, and then modify it to a preset learning rate for training. Since the weights of the model are randomly initialized at the beginning of training, if a larger learning rate is selected at this time, the model may become unstable. Using the warm up method can make the learning rate smaller in several epochs at the beginning of training. Under the preheated small learning rate, the model can gradually become stable. When the model is relatively stable, the preset learning rate is selected for training, which makes the model converge faster and works better. The parameter tuning process is shown in the following Figure 3 and Figure 4.

Moreover, the grid search is used to find the optimal parameters. Finally the learning rate is set to 1e-4, the epoch is set to 25, the weight decay is set to 1e-7, and the warm up ratio is

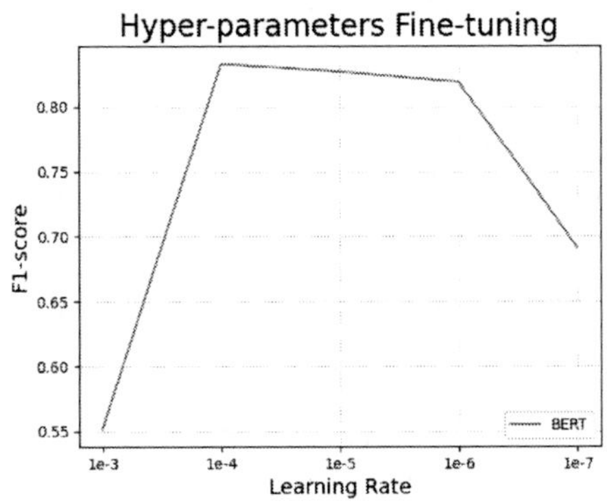

Figure 3: The performance of different learning rate on F_1-score.

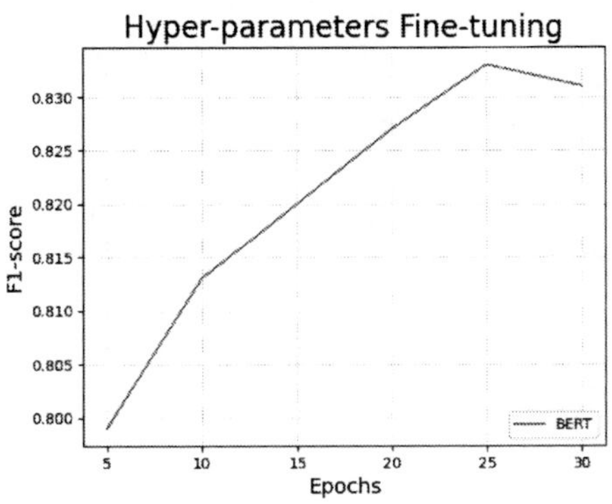

Figure 4: The performance of different epoch on F_1-score.

set to 0.1.

3.5 Comparative Results

The quantitative ablation experiments were conducted to select the best model. In the experiment, the BERT model get the highest F_1-score, which is 0.833, and the RoBERTa model get the second highest F_1-score, which is 0.832. The detailed F_1-score for each strategy is listed in the Table 3. For the final submission, we submitted three files. The results are predicted by RoBERTA, BERT+ELECTRA and BERT and their performance differences are shown in Table 2. BERT also achieved the best results in test dataset (Lee et al., 2022), which is 0.7768.

4 Conclusions

In this paper, we describe our entire experimental procedure, and finally achieve the best F_1-score of 0.7768 and rank the 4th place. For implementation, several different approaches were applied, such as MRC and label embedding. Unfortunately, they didn't perform well. We applied a BERT-BiLSTM-CRF architecture with warm up strategy and R-Drop, to get the best score.

Future works will attempt to explore more different span-based extraction methods for the Chinese healthcare NER task.

Acknowledgement

This work was supported by the National Natural Science Foundation of China (NSFC) under Grants Nos. 61966038 and 62266051. The authors would like to thank the anonymous reviewers for their constructive comments.

References

Zeynep Akata, Florent Perronnin, Zaid Harchaoui, and Cordelia Schmid. 2015. Label-embedding for image classification. *IEEE Transactions on Pattern Analysis and Machine Intelligence*, 38(7):1425–1438.

Yoshua Bengio, Aaron Courville, and Pascal Vincent. 2013. Representation learning: A review and new perspectives. *IEEE Transactions on Pattern Analysis and Machine Intelligence*, 35(8):1798–1828.

Leo Breiman. 2001. Random Forests. *Machine Learning*, 45(1):5–32.

Kevin Clark, Minh-Thang Luong, Quoc V. Le, and Christopher D. Manning. 2020. ELECTRA: pre-training text encoders as discriminators rather than generators. In *8th International Conference on Learning Representations, ICLR 2020, Addis Ababa, Ethiopia, April 26-30, 2020*. OpenReview.net.

Yiming Cui, Wanxiang Che, Ting Liu, Bing Qin, Shijin Wang, and Guoping Hu. 2020. Revisiting pre-trained models for Chinese natural language processing. In *Findings of the Association for Computational Linguistics: EMNLP 2020*, pages 657–668, Online. Association for Computational Linguistics.

Jacob Devlin, Ming-Wei Chang, Kenton Lee, and Kristina Toutanova. 2019. BERT: Pre-training of deep bidirectional transformers for language understanding. In *Proceedings of the 2019 Conference of the North American Chapter of the Association for Computational Linguistics: Human Language Technologies, Volume 1 (Long and Short Papers)*, pages 4171–4186, Minneapolis, Minnesota. Association for Computational Linguistics.

Kaiming He, Xiangyu Zhang, Shaoqing Ren, and Jian Sun. 2016. Deep Residual Learning for Image Recognition. In *2016 IEEE Conference on Computer Vision and Pattern Recognition (CVPR)*, pages 770–778, Las Vegas, NV, USA. IEEE.

Sepp Hochreiter and Jürgen Schmidhuber. 1997. Long short-term memory. *Neural computation*, 9(8):1735–1780.

Zhiheng Huang, Wei Xu, and Kai Yu. 2015. Bidirectional LSTM-CRF Models for Sequence Tagging. ArXiv:1508.01991 [cs].

Bin Ji, Jie Yu, Shasha Li, Jun Ma, Qingbo Wu, Yusong Tan, and Huijun Liu. 2020. Span-based joint entity and relation extraction with attention-based span-specific and contextual semantic representations. In *Proceedings of the 28th International Conference on Computational Linguistics*, pages 88–99.

Alex Krizhevsky, Ilya Sutskever, and Geoffrey E Hinton. 2012. Imagenet classification with deep convolutional neural networks. In *Advances in Neural Information Processing Systems*, volume 25. Curran Associates, Inc.

Zhenzhong Lan, Mingda Chen, Sebastian Goodman, Kevin Gimpel, Piyush Sharma, and Radu Soricut. 2020. Albert: A lite bert for self-supervised learning of language representations. In *International Conference on Learning Representations*.

Lung-Hao Lee, Chao-Yi Chen, Liang-Chih Yu, and Yuen-Hsien Tseng. 2022. Overview of the rocling 2022 shared task for chinese healthcare named entity recognition. In *Proceedings of the 34th Conference on Computational Linguistics and Speech Processing*.

Lung-Hao Lee and Yi Lu. 2021. Multiple embeddings enhanced multi-graph neural networks for chinese healthcare named entity recognition. *IEEE Journal of Biomedical and Health Informatics*, 25(7):2801–2810.

Xiaoya Li, Jingrong Feng, Yuxian Meng, Qinghong Han, Fei Wu, and Jiwei Li. 2020. A unified MRC framework for named entity recognition. In *Proceedings of the 58th Annual Meeting of the Association for Computational Linguistics*, pages 5849–5859, Online. Association for Computational Linguistics.

Xiaobo Liang, Lijun Wu, Juntao Li, Yue Wang, Qi Meng, Tao Qin, Wei Chen, Min Zhang, and Tie-Yan Liu. 2021. R-Drop: Regularized Dropout for Neural Networks. In *Advances in Neural Information Processing Systems*, volume 34, pages 10890–10905. Curran Associates, Inc.

T. Lin, P. Goyal, R. Girshick, K. He, and P. Dollar. 2020. Focal loss for dense object detection. *IEEE Transactions on Pattern Analysis amp; Machine Intelligence*, 42(02):318–327.

Yinhan Liu, Myle Ott, Naman Goyal, Jingfei Du, Mandar Joshi, Danqi Chen, Omer Levy, Mike Lewis, Luke Zettlemoyer, and Veselin Stoyanov. 2019. RoBERTa: A Robustly Optimized BERT Pretraining Approach. *arXiv:1907.11692 [cs]*. ArXiv: 1907.11692.

Suncong Zheng, Feng Wang, Hongyun Bao, Yuexing Hao, Peng Zhou, and Bo Xu. 2017. Joint Extraction of Entities and Relations Based on a Novel Tagging Scheme. In *Proceedings of the 55th Annual Meeting of the Association for Computational Linguistics (Volume 1: Long Papers)*, pages 1227–1236, Vancouver, Canada. Association for Computational Linguistics.

GuoDong Zhou and Jian Su. 2002. Named Entity Recognition using an HMM-based Chunk Tagger. In *Proceedings of the 40th Annual Meeting of the Association for Computational Linguistics*, pages 473–480, Philadelphia, Pennsylvania, USA. Association for Computational Linguistics.

The 34th Conference on Computational Linguistics and Speech Processing (ROCLING 2022)
Taipei, Taiwan, November 21-22, 2022. The Association for Computational Linguistics and Chinese Language Processing

基於語言模型與詞典方法的三種命名實體辨識模型架構之比較

NERVE at ROCLING 2022 Shared Task: A Comparison of Three Named Entity Recognition Frameworks Based on Language Model and Lexicon Approach

林柏劭 Bo-Shau Lin
國立高雄科技大學
資訊工程系
Department of Computer Science and Information Engineering National Kaohsiung University of Science and Technology
Kaohsiung, Taiwan, R.O.C

陳建和 Jian-He Chen
國立高雄科技大學
資訊工程系
Department of Computer Science and Information Engineering National Kaohsiung University of Science and Technology
Kaohsiung, Taiwan, R.O.C

張道行 Tao-Hsing Chang
國立高雄科技大學
資訊工程系
Department of Computer Science and Information Engineering National Kaohsiung University of Science and Technology
Kaohsiung, Taiwan, R.O.C

{c108151121, c107151129, changhth}@nkust.edu.tw

摘要

此次任務的目的是設計一個方法標記在句子中的醫療實體詞以及它們的類別。本研究提出三種模型。第一種是以 BERT 模型結合線性分類器；第二種是一個兩階段模型，兩階段都是 BERT 模型結合分類器的次模型，但一階段只判斷句子中是否有醫療實體詞、二階段才專注於實體類別分類。第三種是結合前兩種模型以及一個基於詞典的模型，整合三個模型的結果後預測。實驗顯示這些模型在驗證與測試集的表現差異不大，最佳的模型 Run 1 在 F1 的值為 0.7569。

Abstract

ROCLING 2022 shared task is to design a method that can tag medical entities in sentences and then classify them into categories through an algorithm. This paper proposes three models to deal with NER issues. The first is a BERT model combined with a classifier. The second is a two-stage model, where the first stage is to use a BERT model combined with a classifier for detecting whether medical entities exist in a sentence, and the second stage focuses on classifying the entities into categories. The third approach is to combine the first two models and a model based on the lexicon approach, integrating the outputs of the three models and making predictions. The prediction results of the three models for the validation and testing datasets show little difference in the performance of the three models, with the best performance on the F1 indicator being 0.7569 for the first model.

關鍵字: 中文命名實體辨別, BERT, 集成式學習
Keyword: Chinese NER, BERT, Ensemble Learning

1 緒論

命名實體(Named Entity, NE)是指一種真實存在的事物，例如人、地點、組織以及產品等等，通常以專有名稱命名，例如梅克爾、柏林、基督教民主聯盟等等。由於命名實體通常是文件中的重要訊息，因此如何辨識命名實體成為自然語言處理領域重要且持續研究的問題，也稱為命名實體辨識(Named Entity Recognition, NER)。在中文文本上這個問題又更加困難，因為中文句子中的詞彙間並無空白加以區隔，因此對中文句而言，不僅要判斷句子中是否有NE、也要判斷 NE 在句中的起始位置與結束位置。此外，NE 的類別辨識也相當重要，因為在

如	何	治	療	胃	食	道	逆	流	症
O	O	O	O	B-DISE	I-DISE	I-DISE	I-DISE	I-DISE	I-DISE

圖 1. 句子被標記後的標籤樣式

實際應用中，不同類別的NE有著不同的性質、功能或用途，若能正確分類對於實際應用上有很大的幫助。而由於不同專業領域的NE特徵也有不同，因此為了提高NER的正確率，會針對特定領域探討NER如何解決。

ROCLING 2022 Shard Task(以下簡稱此次任務)由Lee et al.(2022)提出，是一項針對中文醫療NER的任務，其難度除了包含中文可以同時以單字詞與多字詞表達語意的複雜性，還包含中文醫療命名實體的詞典資源稀少、而新產生的NE會不斷產生。因此，此次任務目標為：研究者須找出一個句子中是否有NE，並分辨該NE屬於10種實體類別(如表1所列)中的何者。

此次任務具體要求如下。研究者需要設計一個模型，針對一個句中每一個字元給予標籤。該標籤由兩部分資訊組成：該字元是否是NE的一部分，以及若是NE、其所屬類別。第一部分有三個標記：B表示該字元為一個NE的起始字元、I表示該字元為一個NE的非起始字元、O表示該字元不是任一NE的一部份。當一個字元被標記為B或I時，在第二部分需標記其所屬的類別，標籤種類如表1中所列。上方圖1為一個句子被標記後標籤樣式的範例。

實體類別	標籤	範例
人體	BODY	脊髓
症狀	SYMP	咳嗽
醫療器材	INST	達文西手臂
檢驗	EXAM	腦電波圖
化學物質	CHEM	糖化血色素
疾病	DISE	帕金森氏症
藥品	DRUG	青黴素
營養品	SUPP	益生菌
治療	TREAT	胃切除術
時間	TIME	青春期

表 1. 此次任務要辨識的10個實體類別

由於「如何治療」不是NE，所以四個字元都標記為「O」；「胃」是命名實體「胃食道逆流症」的第一個字，「食道逆流症」是非起始字，而胃食道逆流症是一種疾病，因此「胃」標記為「B-DISE」、其他字標記為「I-DISE」。綜上所述，此次任務是要將句子中的每個字元標記21個標籤之一。

此次任務訓練與驗證資料集是由Chinese HealthNER(Lee and Lu, 2021)所提供給研究者作為建立模型之用，資料集中各類別數量與比例如表2所示。本文針對此次任務設計了三種方法，在以下小節說明本文所提方法。本文第二節會回顧NER任務相關的研究；第三節介紹本文提出的三種模型；第四節會介紹本文所使用的實驗資料集以及評估指標。最後我們會從實驗結果探討本文所提方法的特性與限制，並提出未來工作的可能方向。

實體類別	訓練集(比例)	驗證集(比例)
人體	23,240(38.01%)	3,171(43.41%)
症狀	11,423(18.67%)	1,481(20.27%)
醫療器材	1,047 (1.71%)	42 (0.58%)
檢驗	2,218 (3.63%)	404 (5.53%)
化學物質	6,090 (9.96%)	744 (10.18%)
疾病	9,074 (14.84%)	1,005(13.76%)
藥品	2,146 (3.51%)	79 (1.08%)
營養品	1,403 (2.29%)	122 (1.67%)
治療	2,905 (4.75%)	203 (2.78%)
時間	1,609 (2.63%)	54 (0.74%)

表 2. 此次任務訓練與驗證資料集各類別數量及比例

2 相關工作

近年來NER研究多聚焦在深度學習神經網路模型。Luo et al. (2018)指出，在化學領域的NER任務上，普遍都是以傳統的機器學習的方法來解決，但這些傳統方法的效能取決於特徵工程。該研究提出了基於注意力機制的BiLSTM-

The 34th Conference on Computational Linguistics and Speech Processing (ROCLING 2022)
Taipei, Taiwan, November 21-22, 2022. The Association for Computational Linguistics and Chinese Language Processing

修	齊	指	甲	O	K	,	有	一	位	3	0	多	歲	男	性
O	O	B-BODY	I-BODY	O	O		O	O	O	O	O	O	O	O	O

圖 2. 特殊句標記範例

CRF 模型，透過注意力機制去學習一個標籤在不同前後文中都能被標記為同一個標籤。該研究指出此設計在 CHEMDNER 以及 CDR 的兩個資料集中，其 F1 分別達到 91.14 以及 92.57。

Liu et al. (2021)認為先前 NER 模型在使用由巨量的訓練語料庫預訓練後的模型直接進行 NER 通常表現不佳，可能原因為數據集中包含專業領域的資料量佔比極低，所以建立的語意空間與專業領域的語意空間有所差別，導致模型的性能受限。為此 Liu et al. 進行了 BERT 的訓練語料庫改良，此研究創建了一個質量較高的大量 NER 語料庫，用此語料庫進行 BERT 的訓練，得到的預訓練模型稱之為 NER-BERT。此研究指出此模型的效能比原來的 BERT 在 NER 的表現更佳。

Lu & Lee (2020)提出一個門控圖序列神經網路的模型架構，用於中文健康照護領域命名實體辨識。該架構整合了輸入句的詞嵌入資訊與字典中已知的詞彙，之後輸入給一個 BiLSTM-CRF 模型對句子進行序列標註。該研究以網路爬蟲的方式擷取資料後以人工標記，再以人工標記結果測試該模型。實驗結果顯示該模型架構能比單純的 BiLSTM-CRF 或是 ME-CNER 模型的表現來得更好。

也有研究專注在辨識效率的問題。Gui et al. (2019)則指出，雖然 BiLSTM 在 NER 任務上有相當好的效果，但運算相當耗時。該研究利用基於 CNN 的模型架構，此方法的特點在於可以平行處理構建句中每個字的語意向量與找出句中的 NE，此研究指出此架構的效率為原本 3.21 倍。

3 實驗方法

本文對此次任務主要是以 Bidirectional Encoder Representations from Transformers (BERT)為基礎設計模型。BERT (Devlin et al., 2019)是知名的語意向量模型，其主要運用注意力機制(self-attention)為基礎，可以輸出句子的句意向量以及句中每個字的語意向量。BERT 主要運作原理是透過注意力機制(self-attention)使得模型可以因為單字的前後文來產生語意向量，這意味著儘管是同樣的一個字，也會因為出現的位置和前後文不同，因而產生出不同的輸出。

本文設計了三個基於 BERT 的模型，分別稱為 Run1、Run2 與 Run3。這三個模型雖然都使用 BERT，但在策略與架構上有所不同，本文將在下列各小節分別介紹。近幾年，有越來越多的語意向量模型被提出，如 RoBERTa (Liu et al., 2019)、ELECTRA (Clark et al., 2020)等等。由於此次任務只能送出三個結果，而本文希望比較不同的策略和架構的效果，因此只使用 BERT 為產生語意向量的核心。

3.1 Run 1 模型

Run1 是以非常直觀的方法來使用 BERT 解決 NER 任務，也就是用 BERT 輸出每個字的語意向量直接進行分類。此方法的想法是經過微調訓練後的 BERT，同一標籤的不同字其語意向量應該彼此接近、不同標籤的字其語意向量應距離較遠。只要在使用一個分類器就能學習將彼此相近的字輸出同一個類別，進而完成任務。此方法實際設計是在 BERT 輸出一個字的 768 維度向量後輸入給一層線性層(linear layer)，線性層輸出一個 21 維度的向量，每個維度代表一個標籤，維度值代表對應標籤的機率值，機率值最高者為此方法標定該字元的標籤。此模型有採用 dropout 與 fine-tune 策略優化模型。

經過上述程序，句子中的每一個字都會得到一個分類。但由於 BERT 會將數字、英文單字及多字符符號(例如刪節號)合併視為一個字，與此次任務的標記規則不同，因此需要進行前處理。舉例來說，此次任務資料集中句子「修齊指甲 OK」與「有一位 30 多歲男性」應該被標記為如圖 2 所示。

由於 BERT 會將「OK」和「30」視為一個字，不符合此次任務的輸出規格，因此本文會先將 10 個阿拉伯數字替換成在訓練資料中未曾出現過的 10 個特殊符號、例如@、#等等。另外，本文將會發生上述問題之英文字母與多字符符號的 57 句從資料集中移除，移除後訓練資料集中有 28,106 個句子，驗證資料集中有

2,529 個句子。

此外，訓練資料集有資料不均衡的問題，其中數量最少的標籤「B-INST」僅有 1,040 個，數量最多的標籤「O」則有多達 1,229,263 個，是前者的 1,000 多倍。這樣的情況可能會導致模型傾向將所有的字元都預測為標籤「O」就能有不錯的效能。本文因此設計了 loss 函數如下：

$$loss = \sum_{i=1}^{n} w_i \times y_i \times \log \hat{y_i} \qquad (1)$$

其中n為標籤類別數，y為正確答案經過 one-hot encoding 後的結果，$\hat{y}$為模型輸出經過 softmax 轉為機率的結果，w為每項特徵的權重。此公式改良自 cross entropy 函數，差別在w參數。而類別i的w計算公式如下：

$$w_i = {}^{a_o}/_{a_i} \qquad (2)$$

其中a_i表示類別i在訓練集中出現的次數；a_O表示類別 O 在訓練集中出現的次數。此公式會使得出現次數越少的類別得到愈大的權重，使得模型會重視資料量少的類別的損失。

一個句子經本文所提方法標記後，可能會出現標記結果不合理的情形。例如連續的標籤「O」之後出現一個標籤「I-xxxx」(xxxx 表示 10 種實體類別之一)，由於任何一個 NE 的第一個字一定是「B-xxxx」而非「I-xxxx」，出現上述情況是明顯地不合理。本文所提方法會對模型輸出結果進行後處理程序，以修正輸出結果邏輯上不合理之處。後處理程序由以下兩條規則所組成：

(1) 若句中單獨出現標籤「I-xxxx」，且其前後字元為標籤「O」，則將其替換為標籤「O」。

(2) 若是連續出現標籤「I-xxxx」，但這些標籤之前沒有標籤「B-xxxx」，則將第一個標籤「I-xxxx」替換為標籤「B-xxxx」。

3.2 Run 2 模型

Run 2 模型是基於以下構想：BERT 分類器模型一開始不需要將字元直接分類成 21 種不同的標籤，而是僅需要分辨與醫療 NE 無關或有關的字。若判斷一串連續字元與醫療NE有關，則再經由一個模型判斷這個字串屬於哪個分類。圖 3 為此構想所設計出的 Run 2 模型架構。

圖 3 中第一階段模型與 Run 1 模型相似，差別在於線性層的輸出為 2 維度，分別代表該字元與 NE 有關或無關。若無關，則該字元被標記標籤「O」；若有關，則進入第二階段模型。在第一階段中被視為有關的連續字元會被視作一個句子，輸入給第二階段模型。第二階段模型也與 Run 1 模型相似，差別在於 BERT 輸出給線性層的向量不是單一字元的語意向量，而是整個連續字串的句向量。線性層將句意向量分類為 10 種實體類別。最後，此連續字串的第一個字元被標記為「B-xxxx」，其餘標記為「I-xxxx」。此方法不會發生 Run 1 模型標記不合邏輯的情況，因此不需要對輸出加上後處理。

此模型所需的訓練與驗證資料需要進行前處理。對於第一階段模型，其訓練集資料中標籤「O」以外的各種類別標記重新標記為類別 1，而標籤「O」則標記為類別 0。對於第二階段模型，其訓練集是從原訓練集中抽出非標籤「O」之詞彙，並照原標籤「B-xxxx」或「I-xxxx」都替換成標籤「xxxx」。因此第二階段的訓練集由 61,155 個詞組成，而驗證資料集由 7,305 個詞組成。由於這兩階段模型的訓練集都沒有太嚴重的資料不均衡問題，因此在損失函數上只使用一般的 Cross Entropy 函數運算。

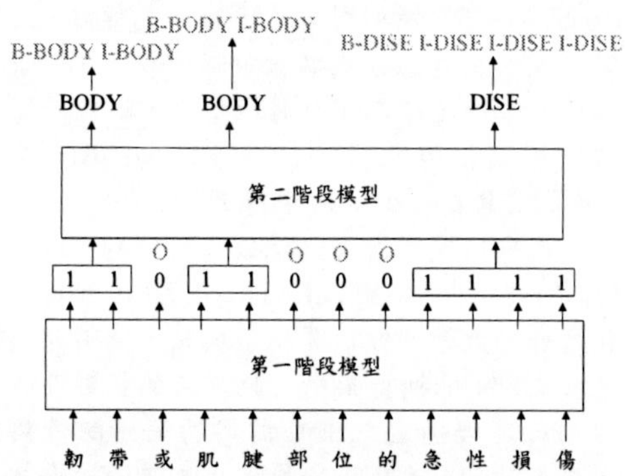

圖 3. Run 2 模型架構

3.3 Run 3 模型

Run 3 模型則是嘗試一種集成式 (ensemble) 架構。此架構由三個次模型組成，包括前兩小節提到的 Run 1 與 Run 2 兩個模型，以及一個詞典模型。詞典模型的核心是一個由訓練集中抽取曾出現過的 NE 所形成的詞典。例如在第一節提到的例子「如何治療胃食道逆流症」，由於訓練集中「胃食道逆流症」已被標記為 DISE，因此會被收錄至詞典並被記錄為 DISE。本文所提方法的詞典在收錄詞時會排除同時屬於多個類別的 NE。此外，由於單字詞 NE 很容易造成誤判，因此也被排除在詞典收錄之外。得到詞典後，本文所提方法會利用詞典對驗證集進行初步標記。標記方式為一個句子中如果有出現在詞典中的詞，則將該詞標記為該詞在詞典中紀錄的類別。由於只用此方式標記結果不完全準確，因此我們會蒐集驗證集中每個類別的預測精確率。以 DISE 類別為例，若是預測驗證集中有 1,000 個字元被預測為 DISE，其中人工標記 DISE 有 850 個、CHEM 有 100 個和 SYMP 有 50 個，本文所提方法就建立 DISE 的機率分布為 DISE 是 0.85、CHEM 是 0.10 和 SYMP 是 0.05。對於沒有出現的類別，會給予一個極小值避免機率為 0 的情形發生。

圖 4 中的詞典模型對於每一個字元都會視其所屬類別輸出一個 11 維的向量，這個向量就是前述的機率分布。例如當一個句子輸入詞典模型後，會先檢視句中是否有存在於詞典的 NE 並標記每個詞的類別。對於每個字元就輸出每個字元所屬類別在各類別的機率分布，也就是一個 11 維的向量。

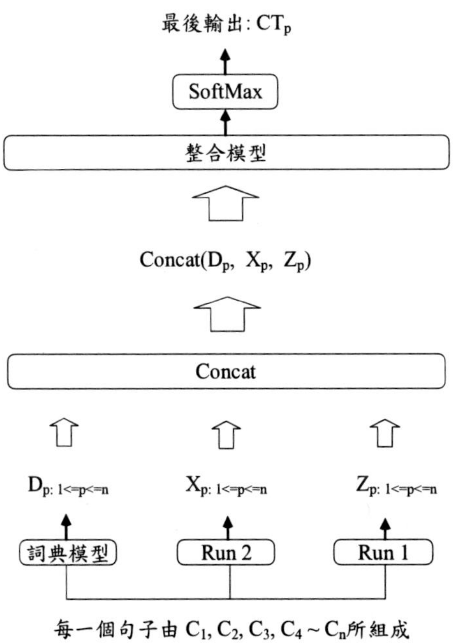

圖 4.　Run 3 模型架構

由於 Run 3 模型包含三個次模型，需要一個整合模型將三個次模型的輸出加以整合，輸出最後的預測結果。圖 4 為 Run 3 模型的架構圖。Run 3 模型輸入一個句子時，詞典模型和 Run 2 會分別對每個字輸出一個 11 維向量(也就是圖 4 的 D_p 與 X_p，p 為 1 到 n 的值)、Run 1 模型會對每個字輸出一個 21 維向量(也就是圖 4 的 Zp)。這三個向量會被串接成一個 43 維的向量輸入給整合模型。整合模型是一個三層全連接模型，各層神經元分別為 43、30 以及 21。輸出層的 21 個神經元分別輸出該字元屬於神經元對應類別的機率值。

最後經由 softmax 程序判定該字元類別為機率值最大的類別(也就是圖 4 的 CT_p)。此整合模型的參數設計都比照 Run 1 的分類器。

4 實驗

除了此次任務提供之資料集，以及由 Huggingface (Wolf et al., 2019)提供的已預訓練 BERT 模型外，本文各項模型沒有使用其他的外部資料。此次任務是以精確率(Precision)、召回率(Recall)以及 F1-score 作為評估指標，4.1 節將說明評估指標的算法。本文所提模型的評估結果於 4.2 節討論。

4.1 評估指標

此次任務會針對 21 個類別的每個類別分別計算其混淆矩陣的四個值。以表 3 的 I-BODY 標籤的預測結果為例，四個值為預測為 I-BODY 且真實值為 I-BODY 的真陽性(true positive, TP)、預測為 I-BODY 但實際值為其餘類別的偽陽性(false positive, FP) 、預測為其餘特徵但實際值為 I-BODY 的偽陰性(false negative, FN)以及預測為其餘特徵且實際值為其餘特徵的真陰性(true negative, TN)，如表 3 所示。

預測 / 人工	I-BODY	Others
I-BODY	TP	FN
Others	FP	TN

表 3. 單一類別之混淆矩陣示例

透過混淆矩陣得到的四個值，即可計算每個類別之精確率(Precision)以及召回率(Recall)，計算公式如下：

模型	NERVE Run 1		NERVE Run 2		NERVE Run 3	
	驗證集	測試集	驗證集	測試集	驗證集	測試集
Precision	0.7873	0.7959	0.6800	0.7165	0.7871	0.7573
Recall	0.6812	0.7309	0.7353	0.7895	0.7294	0.7358
F1-score	0.7304	0.7620	0.7056	0.7512	0.7571	0.7464

表 4. 本文所提模型之效能

$$Precision = \frac{TP}{TP+FP} \quad (3)$$

$$Recall = \frac{TP}{TP+FN} \quad (4)$$

$$F1-score = \frac{2 \times Precision \times Recall}{Precision+Recall} \quad (5)$$

在此次任務中，對於每一個模型，都會先計算該模型預測的每一個類別的精確率、召回率以及 F1，再將 21 個類別精確率加總平均後求得模型的預測精確率。模型的召回率以及 F1-score 亦復如是。

4.2 實驗結果

表 4 為 Run 1、Run 2 以及 Run 3 三個模型分別對此次任務所提供的驗證與測試資料集的預測結果。從表 4 可以發現，Run 1 和 Run 2 分別有較佳在精確率和召回率，而 Run 3 整合模型表現較預期為差。Run 3 對驗證集的結果是三種模型中最好的，不過對測試集的評估結果卻是最差的。我們猜測是由於加入了詞典模型導致的，因為訓練集和驗證集中有很多重複的 NE，因此詞典模型能夠正確指出詞的類別，使得評估數據較高；但測試資料中的 NE 卻是沒出現過的，使得詞典沒有收錄，就無法發揮其效能。

我們觀察資料發現 Run 1 與 Run 2 兩個模型對連續字元形成的較長字串會有不同的處理結果。Run 1 傾向將字串分割成多個不同類別的 NE，而 Run 2 則是傾向將字串視為單一類別的 NE。以圖 5 的句子為例，對於「中耳積水」這個詞，Run 1 會判斷「中耳」為 BODY 與「積水」為 SYMP，Run 2 則會判斷整個詞為 DISE。這是因為 Run 2 是將可能的 NE 交由第二階段判斷所屬類別，因此會將字串全部歸類於單一類別。

5 未來工作

在此次任務中，本文設計了三種不同的架構。其中最直觀的 Run 1 模型在整體表現是最好的，而另外兩個模型雖然有較細緻的設計，但測試資料集與驗證資料集的差異使得兩個模型雖然在部分指標或驗證資料集有較佳表現，但對測試資料集的整體表現不如直接而簡單的 Run 1 模型。由於另外兩個模型的設計理論上應該至少不遜於第一個模型，因此如何提高這兩個模型的強健性會是後續重要的研究方向。

此外，Run 3 模型表現較預期差的可能原因之一是詞典來源過於依賴訓練集。由於此次任務本文並未使用外部資源，因此未來可考慮使用外部資源、例如 wikipedia 或醫學書籍等，讓詞典模型能發揮應有功能。最後，已經有許多研究提出不同的語言模型，也有研究提出對特定領域修正後的預訓練語言模型，這些語言模型是否能提高本文所提方法的效能也值得嘗試。

誌謝

本研究由國家科學與技術委員會計畫編號 MOST 110-2511-H-992-003-MY3 提供部分補助，特此致謝。

文字	中	耳	積	水	的	定	義
NERVE Run1	B-BODY	I-BODY	B-SYMP	I-SYMP	O	O	O
NERVE Run2	B-DISE	I-DISE	I-DISE	I-DISE	O	O	O

圖 5. Run 1 以及 Run 2 輸出結果差異之說明範例

參考文獻

Lee, L. H., and Lu, Y., 2021. *Multiple embeddings enhanced multi-graph neural networks for Chinese healthcare named entity recognition*. IEEE Journal of Biomedical and Health Informatics, 25(7): 2801-2810.

Lee, L. L., Chen, C. Y., Yu, L. C., and Tseng, Y. H., 2022. *Overview of the ROCLING 2022 shared task for Chinese healthcare named entity recognition*. In Proceedings of the 34th Conference on Computational Linguistics and Speech Processing.

Liu, Z., Jiang, F., Hu, Y., Shi, C., & Fung, P. 2021. *NER-BERT: a pre-trained model for low-resource entity tagging*. arXiv preprint arXiv:2112.00405.

Lu, Yi., & Lee, L. L. 2020. *Chinese Healthcare Named Entity Recognition Based on Graph Neural Networks*. Computational Linguistics and Chinese Language Processing Vol. 25, No.2, December 2020, pp. 21-36

Luo, L., Yang, Z., Yang, P., Zhang, Y., Wang, L., Lin, H., & Wang, J. 2018. *An attention-based BiLSTM-CRF approach to document-level chemical named entity recognition. Bioinformatics*, *34*(8), 1381-1388.

Gui, T., Ma, R., Zhang, Q., Zhao, L., Jiang, Y. G., & Huang, X. 2019, August. *CNN-Based Chinese NER with Lexicon Rethinking*. In *IJCAI* (pp. 4982-4988).

Devlin, J., Chang, M. W., Lee, K., & Toutanova, K. 2018. *Bert: Pre-training of deep bidirectional transformers for language understanding*. arXiv preprint arXiv:1810.04805.

Liu, Y., Ott, M., Goyal, N., Du, J., Joshi, M., Chen, D., Levy, O., Lewis, M., Zettlemoyer, L., & Stoyanov, V. 2019. *Roberta: A robustly optimized bert pretraining approach*. arXiv preprint arXiv:1907.11692.

Clark, K., Luong, M. T., Le, Q. V., & Manning, C. D. 2020. *Electra: Pre-training text encoders as discriminators rather than generators. arXiv preprint arXiv:2003.10555*.

Wolf, T., Debut, L., Sanh, V., Chaumond, J., Delangue, C., Moi, A., Cistac, P., Rault, T., Louf, R., Funtowicz, M., Davison, J., Shlerifer, S.,von Platen, P., Ma, C., Jernite, Y., Plu, Julien., Xu, Canwen., Scao, L. T., Gugger, S., Drame, M., Lhoest, Q., Rush, M. A., Hugging Face & Brew, J. 2019. *HuggingFace's Transformers: State-of-the-art Natural Language Processing*. ArXiv, arXiv-1910.

The 34th Conference on Computational Linguistics and Speech Processing (ROCLING 2022)
Taipei, Taiwan, November 21-22, 2022. The Association for Computational Linguistics and Chinese Language Processing

生物醫學實體檢測模型之實驗與錯誤分析
SCU-NLP at ROCLING 2022 Shared Task: Experiment and Error Analysis of Biomedical Entity Detection Model

Sung-Ting Chiou
Soochow University
Dept. of Data Science
yuki1214888@gmail.com

Sheng-Wei Huang
Soochow University
Dept. of Data Science
kiwihwung11@gmail.com

Ying-Chun Lo
Soochow University
Dept. of Data Science
ginny880530@gmail.com

Yu-Hsuan Wu
Soochow University
Dept. of Data Science
Ikaroskasane28@gmail.com

Jheng-Long Wu
Soochow University
Dept. of Data Science
jlwu@gm.scu.edu.tw

摘要

生物醫學之命名實體辨識相較於一般命名實體辨識任務來得更加複雜。本次命名實體辨識任務以辨識醫療保健領域的十種命名實體類型為目的，預測句子的命名實體邊界和類別。我們探討了命名實體辨識的多種基礎方法，如隨機森林、隱馬爾可夫模型、條件隨機場和 BERT。提供未來在醫療領域的 NER 辨識中，能選擇最佳表現的基礎方法為基準進行改良。預測結果以 BERT 模型在 F-score 上較為顯著，取得了更好的結果。

Abstract

Named entity recognition generally refers to entities with specific meanings in unstructured text, including names of people, places, organizations, dates, times, quantities, proper nouns and other words. In the medical field, it may be drug names, Organ names, test items, nutritional supplements, etc. The purpose of named entity recognition in this study is to search for the above items from unstructured input text. In this study, taking healthcare as the research purpose, and predicting named entity boundaries and categories of sentences based on ten entity types, We explore multiple fundamental NER approaches to solve this task, Include: Hidden Markov Models 、 Conditional Random Fields、Random Forest Classifier and BERT. The prediction results are more significant in the F-score of the CRF model, and have achieved better results.

關鍵字：實體命名、隱馬爾可夫模型、條件隨機場、隨機森林

Keywords: Named entity recognition 、BERT、Random Forest Classifier 、 Hidden Markov 、 Conditional Random Field

1 緒論

命名實體辨識（Named entity recognition，NER）任務是自然語言處理的基本任務，同時也作為許多應用的基礎。例如：翻譯、文本摘要。因此進行 NER 任務能否使模型達到更好的辨識效果是許多研究所追求的。除此之外 NER 任務也根據領域的應用有所差異，且若採用監督學習也需另行標記實體的資料集。舉例而言 NER 常見的分類多為地點、時間、人名、組織等，然而應用上也能將此任務進行特定語句結構的實體辨識，例如激進言語、反諷等。本次的分享任務即是進行醫療領域的 NER 辨識。此類型的任務相當重要，NER 的效果將會影響後續任務的可靠性，因此探討如何提升醫療 NER 的辨識效果是本文的主軸。

本次的分享任務將進行醫療領域的中文 NER 辨識。中文 NER 相較於英文處理上較困難。如何正確的分辨實體的邊界也是難題之一。以此為基礎便延伸出基於字符的方法和基於單詞方法，本研究也將探討使用兩種詞

嵌入訓練的模型效果。現代在網路的資訊流通快速，用戶能夠通過網路搜尋醫療相關資訊，在進行就醫。因此網路上能產生很多醫療相關的文本，這也提供了建立醫療領域 NER 辨識的資料豐富度。自動識別醫療保健、生醫領域的實體能夠協助歸納或萃取醫療文本中的資訊。本次任務共需辨識 10 種實體類型，需預測每個給定句子的命名實體邊界和類別。使用的訓練與料庫為 Chinese HealthNER 語料庫(Lee and Lu, 2021)。包括 30,692 個句子，總計約 150 萬個字符或 91700 個單詞。經過人工註釋，有 68,460 個命名實體， 10 種實體類型分別是：身體、症狀、儀器、檢查、化學、疾病、藥物、補充劑、治療和時間。訓練資料集中包含了語句、字符、分詞的文本資料以及對應的 NER 分類(Lee et al., 2022)。

過往研究在 NER 的辨識任務上採取的策略都不同，然而在模型建構上的巧思可歸納為改良或組合多種模型，或是增加詞嵌入的資訊(如筆畫、部首等資訊)。本文旨在探討、比較基礎模型的效果以提供後續研究在改良模型時對基礎模型的選擇。本文針對機器學習方法、深度學習方法也進行了效果的比較。機器學習方法使用隨機森林，深度學習方法使用 Bidirectional Encoder representations from transformers (BERT)、隱馬爾可夫模型(Hidden Markov Model，HMM)、條件隨機場(conditional random field，CRF)等三種近年 NER 辨識任務中仍常用來改良或組合的基礎模型進行比較。

2 文獻回顧

Li 等人(Li, 2020) 對以往 NER 任務的解決方法進行深入探討，介紹了傳統 NER 方法建構，以及詳細介紹了近年使用深度學習取得的成果。傳統基於規則的 NER 辨識方法依賴於字典的建構，也由於此特性特定領域的規則和不完整的字典，從此類系統中經常觀察到高精度和低召回率，並且無法將系統轉移到其他領域。非監督學習方法也有研究證明了其效果的有效性和普遍性。監督方法進行 NER 依賴特徵工程，機器學習方法。常見的方法如 HMM、決策樹等等。其中 CRF 的 NER 已廣泛應用於各個領域的文本。包括生物醫學文本 、推文和化學文本 。基於這些傳統方法，對於 NER 的研究越來越多元，也釋出許多分享任務。Lee 等人 (2020) 針對臨床命名實體識別在未標記的臨床記錄上預訓練 BERT 模型。並使用長短期記憶（LSTM）和條件隨機場（CRF）提取文本特徵和解碼預測標籤，並提出一種將字典特徵整合到模型中的新策略。Segura Bedmar 等人 (2013) 提出了兩個子任務：1.藥物名稱的識別和分類 2.相互作用的提取和分類，作為 SemEval 2013 任務 9 的一部分，其研究結果顯示，在命名實體任務中，參與系統在識別已知實體方面表現良好。Alsehaimi 等人 (2022) 使用自然語言處理(natural language processing，NLP) 的 NER 技術在關於酒店的大量文本評論數據中找到主要實體的自動識別器。並在五種不同的分類模型如：Spacy, Naïve Bayes (NB), Stochastic Gradient Descent (SGD), Passive Aggressive,和 AdaBoost 之間進行比較，在 1000 多條記錄的真實數據集上進行實驗，結果顯示 NB 的準確率最高。

Kocaman 等人 (2021) 在 Apache Spark 之上重新實現 Bi-LSTM-CNN-Char 深度學習架構。Luo 等人 (2020) 通過標籤嵌入註意機制增強從獨立 BiLSTM 學習的句子表示。Mayhew 等人 (2020) 利用有噪聲的資料進行育訓練改善 BiLSTM-CRF 模型和 BERT 嵌入的效果。Han 等人 (2021)提出 MAF-CNER 模型，針對中文的多種特徵進行融合、訓練。Englmeier 和 Mothe (2020) 將 NER 應用於激進言語的偵測。Carbonell 等人 (2020) 使用圖神經網絡架構來解決半結構化文檔中的實體識別和關係提取問題。Wu 等人 (2021) 利用 Transformer 架構進行改良，將文字結構與字符資訊引入模型進行交叉注意力訓練。Wang 等人 (2021) 針對實體提及不連續的問題提出了解法，其模型成果優於最先進的結果， F1 上提高了 3.5 個百分點，並且實現了 5 倍的加速。Zhang 等人 (2020) 在中藥的 NER 辨識上提出了 Back-Labeling 的方法，分辨實體的跨度是否為連續，以此進行模型訓練提升效果。

Kumar 和 Starly (2021) 以 BiLSTM+CRF 的神經網絡模型建構了製造業的 NER 辨識模型，有利於製造業未來能有程序化查詢和檢索系統。Li 等人 (2021) 提出 MIN 模型，利用段級訊息和詞級依賴關係，結合一種交互機制來支持邊界檢測和類型預測之間的信息共享。Litake 等人 (2022) 針對各種BERT 的變體進行測試，並觀察多語言的預訓練模型與單語言的預訓練模型效果差異。此研究與本文的性質相似，本研究主旨在於將 NER 任務中常見的基礎神經模型進行效果差距的評估。Wang 等人 (2021) 認為實體檢測和關係提取模型設置兩個獨立的標籤空間可能會阻礙實體和關係之間的信息交互，因此將其融合。

綜上所述可知 NER 辨識不僅重要，且跨足多個領域都有需求。提升效果的方法更是多元，在標記階段改良、詞嵌入改良、模型組合改良皆有方法提出。近兩年的研究以神經網路進行 NER 辨識為主。因此本文旨在針對常見的神經模型 HMM、CRF 以及現今已被證實在多種 NLP 任務能提升整體任務效果的預訓練模型 BERT 之間的效果進行比較。鑒於機器學習方法進行 NER 辨識的研究仍持續精進，因此本研究也採取隨機森林(Random Forest Classifier，RFC)進行比較。

3 研究方法

本章節介紹本研究用於解決 NER 任務的四個模型，如 Random Forest Classifier 模型、HMM 模型和 CRF 模型和 BERT 模型。在將結果與分類器的預測輸出進行比較時，可能會出現不同的情況。例如，字符串匹配第二個類別，第三個預測不正確的類別。 模型檢測中缺少該類別，因此分別計算每個類別的 Precision、Recall 和 F1 分數。

3.1 Random Forest Classifier

隨機森林是一種基於決策樹的機器學習分類模型，可以根據標記的術語學習基本規則，由於具備準確性、簡單性、靈活性，使得 RFC 成為機器學習分類模型中流行的模型之一。

3.2 Hidden Markov Model

HMM 模型是一種觀察觀測值來估算狀態的模型，主要著重在觀測值的前後順序關係。也就是說，目標觀測值的前一個與後一個觀測值將會是影響估算目標狀態的主要因素。在 NLP 任務中，HMM 模型會藉由觀測目標字詞的前一個與後一個字詞，估算目標字詞之狀態。HMM 模型的優點在於能考慮字詞之間的前後關係，因為在句子當中字詞順序的確是重要的特徵之一。例如，給定一句話「她是一位女孩」，其中因為模型著重順序關係，因此「女孩」是會受到「她」影響的，這也與人們理解一般字詞之間的關係相符合。

3.3 Conditional Random Field

在前一節模型介紹的 HMM 模型主要考慮字詞順序性，然而並沒辦法呈現句子中最真實的狀態。舉例來說給定一句話「她是一位女孩」，雖然「女孩」一詞確實會受到「她」影響，但是 HMM 模型因為著重順序關係，因此模型中學習到影響「女孩」一詞最多的將會是「一位」而並非「她」，與事實有著些許不相符。而 CRF 模型相對於 HMM 模型，主要考慮的是字詞之間的相互關係，藉由計算整句句子中各字詞之間的條件機率，能學習到字詞之間最真實的關係。

3.4 BERT

BERT 是一種透過預訓練大量文本所得的文本表示模型，透過學習字與字之間的關係取得隱藏表示特徵。本研究使用 BERT 模型取得文本的隱藏表示特徵後，再經過預測分類層估算字與字之間的關係並取得最終分類結果。BERT 因為易於使用又能快速微調模型並串接各種不同任務，並且在各種自然語言處理任務中獲得良好的結果，可以說是目前 NLP 領域中最流行的模型。

4 實驗結果

本章節展示實驗資料在各個模型的實驗結果及比較，圖 1 為分別使用隨機森林與 BERT 以斷詞為輸入進行預測的結果，圖 2 為使用隨機森林、隱馬爾可夫模型(HMM)、條件隨機場(CRF)和 BERT 以字為輸入進行預測的結果，指標為 Precision、Recall 以及 F1-score。首先從表 1 中呈現了各個模型的實驗結果，本研究以分類任務中經常使用的 Precision、Recall 以及 F1-score 作為主要評估指標，並且分別列出針對 Word 及 Character 的分類結果。從表格中可以看出，不管是在 Word 還是 Character，BERT 在整體結果都能取得較好的效果，平均

Format	Model	Precision		Recall		F1-score	
		Mean	SD	Mean	SD	Mean	SD
Word	RandomForest Classifier	**0.82**	**0.14**	0.65	0.19	0.71	0.17
	BERT	0.79	0.13	**0.76**	**0.15**	**0.77**	**0.13**
Character	RandomForest Classifier	0.04	0.18	0.05	0.21	0.04	0.19
	HMM	0.59	0.18	0.65	0.14	0.61	0.15
	CRF	0.78	0.11	0.62	0.17	0.68	0.14
	BERT	**0.78**	**0.10**	**0.75**	**0.14**	**0.76**	**0.11**

表 1. 模型分數比較

F1-score 能取得 0.77 及 0.76 的成績。然而值得一提的是，以斷詞為輸入時，隨機森林的 Precision 效果較佳，推測以斷詞輸入時機器學習模型能較好的對照出正確答案，然而整體效果仍無法超越深度學習模型。這樣的結果也顯示，NER 任務使用機器學習的方式來解還是稍顯不足，透過深度學習的方式來學習字與字之間的隱藏關係能更有效的提升分類效果，讓模型達到精準分類的效果，此外預訓練也有助於效果得提升。

接續上述從圖 1 可以明顯看出若以斷詞為輸入進行命名實體預測時，深度學習模型相較於機器學習的效果在 F1-score 差距是明顯的。然而可以發現共通性是在醫療器具(INST)、藥物(DRUG)和治療(TREAT)的命名實體辨識上表現較差。這三種實體有較多專有名詞，可見需要特別處理，例如建立專有名詞的字典等等。

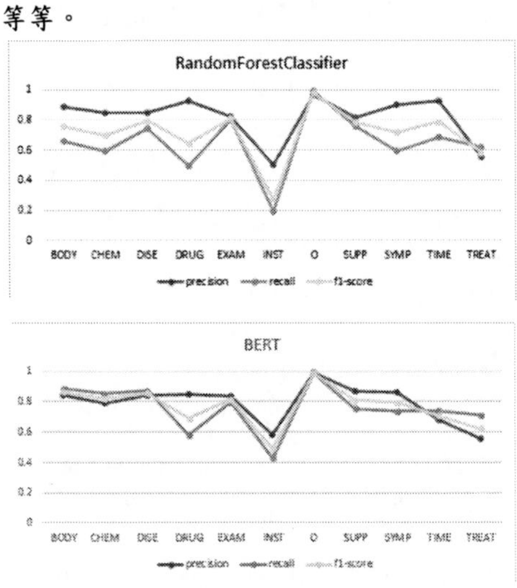

圖 1. 以斷詞為輸入隨機森林與 BERT 的結果

圖 2 可以看出隨機森林以斷字為輸入時無法進行學習，因此將所有分類都分為 O。隱馬爾可夫模型(HMM)、條件隨機場(CRF)和 BERT 三種模型在各實體的分類成效上有相似的趨勢。整體而言在所有實體分類的 F1-score 上 BERT 都優於 HMM 和 CRF。可知綜合性能上 BERT 相當出色。然而 Precision 則是 CRF 的優勢，CRF 模型的精準度得到與 BERT 相似的成果。值得一提的是 HMM 模型在治療(TREAT)和時間(TIME)的 Recall 取得與 BERT 相似的效果，推測為 HMM 訓練時考慮前後字的特性，因此在這兩種跨度較長的實體上表現較佳。

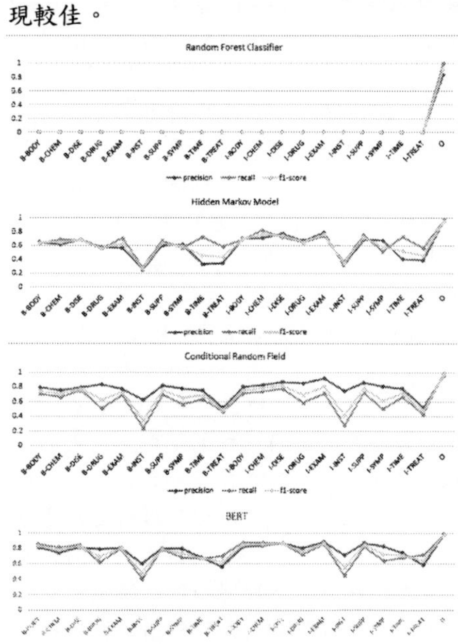

圖 2. 使用隨機森林、隱馬爾可夫模型、條件隨機場和 BERT 對斷字進行預測的 f1-score 結果

4.1 錯誤分析

針對 BERT 預測結果進行錯誤分析，本研究發覺，以詞為輸入比以字為輸入的預測效果佳。因此以下分析為，「以詞為輸入」時，特定詞的實體預測正確，然而「以字為輸入」時對應特定詞的個別字符實體預測錯誤的分析。舉例而言特定詞「尿糖」的正確分類為病徵(SYMP)，以詞為輸入的 BERT 模型預測也為病徵(SYMP)。然而以字為輸入的 BERT 模型預測會將「尿」預測為 B-BODY，「糖」預測為 I-BODY。簡言之以字為輸入的 BERT 模型將「尿糖」分類為身體(BODY)實體。類似的錯誤案例有共有 642 個詞實體預測正確，這些詞各自對應的字共 1030 個皆實體預測錯誤。推測此現象原因為，單一中文字提供的資訊較多的案例為身體器官，且實際案例中腎、肝、脾、胃...等等單一中文字就能構成器官，然而病徵、疾病、藥物...等其餘實體皆須整個詞才能構成完整的意義。

在字的實體預測中，將實體為 O 的字誤判的案例共有 314 個。其中誤判為 B 的案例共有 172 個，誤判為 I 的案例有 142 個。由於字級別能夠組合的資訊多樣而導致錯誤，這也是中文字的特性。舉例來說「細針」的實際實體為器材(INST)，然而模型的預測可能受到上下文影響將「細針穿刺」判斷為檢察(EXAM)，可見以字為輸入的模型在判斷組合上較為精細、彈性，表現出對上下文的適應，但實體的邊界可能較難掌握。類似的案例中，原文「也可以按摩血海穴來消除浮腫的身體」，其中「按摩」正確實體為 O 然而模型判斷「按」為 B-TREAT，「摩」為 I-TREAT。模型對於按摩多將其分類為治療(TREAT)，可見模型較難掌握特定名詞在何時屬於治療實體何時不屬於治療實體。

儘管以詞為輸入的模型表現較佳，本研究發現以字為輸入的模型效果差距並不大，推測以字為輸入的缺點在於邊界的資訊較難訓練。本研究在表 2 上呈現出各類別的跨度分類錯誤。篩選條件為，當以詞為輸入的模型預測正確的情況下，以字為輸入的模型預測的位置錯誤，在各類別上錯的個數。可以發現在 BODY 實體的錯誤較多，其中 I 的判斷錯誤較 B 多，原因可延續上述類別分類錯誤的問題，人的身體器官可能會混在病徵或是檢查內，因此可能在專有名詞中被錯誤的分類，或是造成位置的判斷錯誤。整體而言在 I 的位置錯誤上較多可以看出模型在跨度的判斷上表現較差，這也應證了目前 NER 任務最佳模型的方法都會混合字、詞的嵌入進行訓練的原因。

類別	B 位置錯誤	I 位置錯誤
BODY	57	78
SYMP	14	46
DISE	9	10
EXAM	3	4
CHEM	11	31
TREAT	2	0
TIME	0	0
INST	0	0
SUPP	2	0
DRUG	0	2

表 2.以字為輸入的模型跨度錯誤統計

5 結論與未來目標

總結本研究工作，本研究針對這次分享任務進行了目前 NER 任務中常用來改良或組合的基礎模型進行了表現的分析。其中以 BERT 的表現最佳，此結果的原因推測與 BERT 做的預訓練有關。BERT 預訓練中進行的遮罩訓練推測能提升模型針對跨度預測的表現，因此未來研究中能使用 BERT 作為基礎應用在字、詞嵌入或組合模型能有效提升效果。在字、詞嵌入的比較上，本研究發覺以字為輸入的模型在跨度上表現較以詞為輸入的模型稍差，差距體現在實體跨度的判斷上，然而以字為輸入的模型表現出了考慮上下文資訊的特性，能夠針對字詞的組合有彈性的判斷，因此本研究認為在判斷實體的研究中若要組合上下文的資訊進行判斷時採用以字為輸入應能提升模型效果。延續上述，本研究認為未來在 NER 任務的解法上，使用 BERT 為基礎改良，並且結合詞、字兩種嵌入作為輸入並考慮上下文的方法應能使整體效果更加提升。

References

ALSEHAIMI, Afnan Abdulrahman A., et al. A Smart Framework to Analyze Hotel Services after COVID-19. In: 2022 9th International Conference on Computing for Sustainable Global Development (INDIACom). IEEE, 2022. p. 415-419.

Baum, L. E.; Petrie, T. (1966). "Statistical Inference for Probabilistic Functions of Finite State Markov

Chains". The Annals of Mathematical Statistics. 37 (6): 1554–1563. doi:10.1214/aoms/1177699147

Carbonell, M., Riba, P., Villegas, M., Fornés, A., & Lladós, J. (2021, January). Named entity recognition and relation extraction with graph neural networks in semi structured documents. In *2020 25th International Conference on Pattern Recognition (ICPR)* (pp. 9622-9627). IEEE.

Englmeier, K., & Mothe, J. (2020, July). Application-oriented approach for detecting cyberaggression in social media. In *International Conference on Applied Human Factors and Ergonomics* (pp. 129-136). Springer, Cham.

Han, X., Zhou, F., Hao, Z., Liu, Q., Li, Y., & Qin, Q. (2021). MAF-CNER: A Chinese named entity recognition model based on multifeature adaptive fusion. *Complexity, 2021.*

J. Devlin, M. W. Chang, K. Lee, and K. Toutanova, "Bert: Pre-training of deep bidirectional transformers for language understanding." arXiv preprint arXiv:1810.04805. 2018

Kocaman, V., & Talby, D. (2021, January). Biomedical named entity recognition at scale. In *International Conference on Pattern Recognition* (pp. 635-646). Springer, Cham.

Kumar, A., & Starly, B. (2021). "FabNER": information extraction from manufacturing process science domain literature using named entity recognition. *Journal of Intelligent Manufacturing*, 1-15.

L. Breiman, "Random forests. Machine learning," 45(1),pp. 5-32. (2001)

Lafferty, J., McCallum, A., & Pereira, F. C. (2001). Conditional random fields: Probabilistic models for segmenting and labeling sequence data.

Li, F., Wang, Z., Hui, S. C., Liao, L., Song, D., Xu, J., ... & Jia, M. (2021, August). Modularized interaction network for named entity recognition. In *Proceedings of the 59th Annual Meeting of the Association for Computational Linguistics and the 11th International Joint Conference on Natural Language Processing (Volume 1: Long Papers)* (pp. 200-209).

Li, J., Sun, A., Han, J., & Li, C. (2020). A survey on deep learning for named entity recognition. *IEEE Transactions on Knowledge and Data Engineering*, *34*(1), 50-70.

Li, X., Zhang, H., & Zhou, X. H. (2020). Chinese clinical named entity recognition with variant neural structures based on BERT methods. *Journal of biomedical informatics*, *107*, 103422.

Litake, O., Sabane, M., Patil, P., Ranade, A., & Joshi, R. (2022). Mono vs multilingual BERT: A case study in hindi and marathi named entity recognition. *arXiv preprint arXiv:2203.12907*.

Lung-Hao Lee, and Yi Lu (2021). Multiple Embeddings Enhanced Multi-Graph Neural Networks for Chinese Healthcare Named Entity Recognition. IEEE Journal of Biomedical and Health Informatics, 25(7): 2801- 2810.

Lung-Hao Lee, Chao-Yi Chen, Liang-Chih Yu, and Yuen-Hsien Tseng. 2022. Overview of the ROCLING 2022 shared task for Chinese healthcare named entity recognition. In Proceedings of the 34th Conference on Computational Linguistics and Speech Processing.

Luo, Y., Xiao, F., & Zhao, H. (2020, April). Hierarchical contextualized representation for named entity recognition. In *Proceedings of the AAAI conference on artificial intelligence* (Vol. 34, No. 05, pp. 8441-8448).

Mayhew, S., Nitish, G., & Roth, D. (2020, April). Robust named entity recognition with truecasing pretraining. In *Proceedings of the AAAI Conference on Artificial Intelligence* (Vol. 34, No. 05, pp. 8480-8487).

SEGURA-BEDMAR, Isabel; MARTÍNEZ FERNÁNDEZ, Paloma; HERRERO ZAZO, María. Semeval-2013 task 9: Extraction of drug-drug interactions from biomedical texts (ddiextraction 2013).

Wang, Y., Sun, C., Wu, Y., Zhou, H., Li, L., & Yan, J. (2021). UniRE: A unified label space for entity relation extraction. *arXiv preprint arXiv:2107.04292.*

Wang, Y., Yu, B., Zhu, H., Liu, T., Yu, N., & Sun, L. (2021). Discontinuous named entity recognition as maximal clique discovery. *arXiv preprint arXiv:2106.00218.*

Wu, S., Song, X., & Feng, Z. (2021). Mect: Multi-metadata embedding based cross-transformer for chinese named entity recognition. *arXiv preprint arXiv:2107.05418.*

Zhang, D., Xia, C., Xu, C., Jia, Q., Yang, S., Luo, X., & Xie, Y. (2020). Improving distantly-supervised named entity recognition for traditional Chinese medicine text via a novel back-labeling approach. *IEEE Access*, *8*, 145413-145421.

The 34th Conference on Computational Linguistics and Speech Processing (ROCLING 2022)
Taipei, Taiwan, November 21-22, 2022. The Association for Computational Linguistics and Chinese Language Processing

中文醫療文件的命名實體辨識報告
MIGBaseline at ROCLING 2022 Shared Task: Report on Named Entity Recognition Using Chinese Healthcare Datasets

馬行遠 Hsing-Yuan Ma　**李韋杰** Wei-Jie Li　**劉昭麟** Chao-Lin Liu
Department of Computer Science
National Chengchi University
{110753132, 110753128, chaolin} @g.nccu.edu.tw

摘要

命名實體（Named Entity Recognition , NER）工具發展已久，但少有針對醫療專業領域的 NER 工具，因此建立一個適用於醫療文件的 NER 工具是至關重要的。本研究使用了在中英任務中表現出色的 W2NER 模型 ，藉由更改資料的輸入、選用不同的預訓練語言模型以及運用不同的訓練策略，建立一個適合於中文醫療資料集的 NER 模型。我們的最佳模型在該資料集獲得 81.93%的 F1 分數 ，並在 ROCLING 2022 NER 競賽(Lee et al., 2022)中排名第一。

Abstract

Named Entity Recognition（NER） tools have been in development for years, yet few have been aimed at medical documents. The increasing needs for analyzing medical data makes it crucial to build a sophisticated NER model for this missing area. In this paper, W2NER, the state-of-the-art NER model, which has excelled in English and Chinese tasks, is run through selected inputs, several pretrained language models, and training strategies. The objective was to build an NER model suitable for healthcare corpora in Chinese. The best model managed to achieve an F1 score at 81.93%, which ranked first in the ROCLING 2022 shared task.

關鍵字: 命名實體辨識、W2NER、醫療、中文
Keywords: NER, W2NER, Healthcare, Chinese

1 簡介

命名實體辨識（Named Entity Recognition, NER）在自然語言當中一直是非常重要的一個技術，該技術藉由標記資料來訓練模型，主要處理書籍、字典、新聞等一些非結構化文本，進行專有名詞的抽取與標記，主要針對一些重要的實體，通常包含人名、地名與專有名詞。抽取出來的詞組可以用來分析情意、關係擷取、事件追蹤…等功能。這技術還能讓斷詞（Word Segmentation, WS）的結果更加準確，因此大部分的斷詞工具都會使用這項技術。

現在通用的 NER 技術已經行之有年，技術也一直在進步，而各個專業領域隨著時間發展所創造的詞彙也越來越多，加上艱澀不成用的專業詞彙並不會在通用型 NER 中訓練，導致通用型 NER 在專業領域的標記結果不佳，也顯示基於專業領域資料所開發的 NER 模型的重要性。

至今許多領域的發展越來越離不開資訊與科技的協助，醫療產業也不例外。病人的醫療紀錄與問診都會產生出需要整理的資料，因此能處理醫療文字資料的 NER 已呈迫切的需求，因此我們希望藉由此研究提高相關主題的 NER 準確度滿足相關需求。

2 文獻探討

2.1 中文 NER 工具發展

NER 技術已經發展多年，實作方式也經過了多次的迭代，相關技術的演進可以分成三個階段(Lee & Lu, 2021)，1.傳統方法：rule-base、大量字典檔 2.機器學習方法：隱馬可夫模型（Hidden Markov Model, HMM）、最大熵馬可夫模型（Maximum Entropy Markov Model, MEMM）、條件隨機場（Conditional Random Field, CRF），University of Stanford 開發的 stanfordNLP 就是運用 CRF 技術完成的 3.深度學習方式 ：RNN-CRF、CNN-CRF、transformer、attention， 例如 CKIP-transformer(Li et al., 2020)

中文 NER 領域的發展也在近期取得了大量的進展，從只有三大套件，Jieba(Sun, 2020)、UnivJersity of Stanford 開發的 StanfordNLP(Manning et al., 2014)、中研院開發

的 CKIP(Ma & Chen, 2003)慢慢到現在有更先進與多功能的工具問世，像是最近有名的，中國中央師範大學學所開發的 NLP 工具 HanLP(He & Choi, 2021)以及 University of Stanford 開發的 Stanza(Qi et al., 2020)。

2.2 NER 模型與技術介紹

W2NER(Li et al., 2022)有別於常見的 NER 模型將 NER 任務分成四大類的做法，選擇將任務簡化為字與字之間的三種關係分類:

- None：表示兩個字之間沒有關係，且並不屬於同個實體。
- NNW：即 Next-Neighboring-Word，表示這兩個字是在同一個實體中相鄰
- THW-*：即 Tail-Head-Word-*，表示這兩個字是在同一實體中，且分別是開始與結尾。。

使其能夠統一解決扁平實體（flat)、重疊實體（overlapped）以及非連續實體（discontinuous）的 NER 任務。

一個簡單的範例可以參考圖 1 的（a)，裡面有兩個症狀實體"aching in legs"和"aching in shoulders"，分別當作 e1 和 e2，該模型會將此資料轉換成關係陣列（如圖 2)，並透過陣列釐清關係推導出圖 1 的（b）

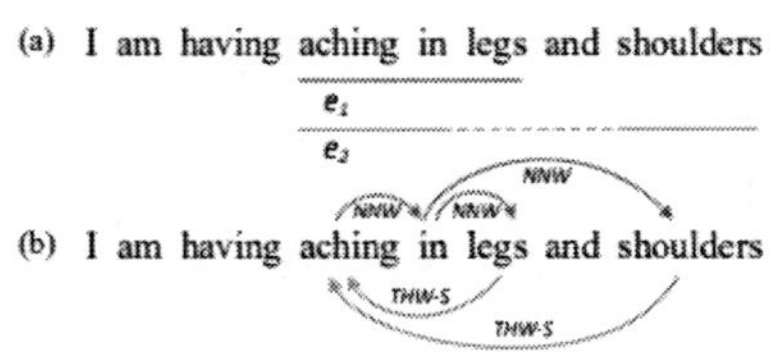

圖 1.NER 任務示意圖 [1]

W2NER 架構主要分成三層（如圖 3)，(1). Encoder layer (2). Convolution layer (3). Co-predictor layer，在 encoder layer 中，我們將文章經由 BERT 以及 BiLSTM 轉換，得到詞向量，接著輸入 convolution layer，經由 Conditional Layer Normalization 取得 distance、word、region embeddings，接著將這些 embeddings 經由 dilated convolution 處理，輸入至 Co-predictor layer，由 biaffine predictor 以及 multi-layer perceptron predictor 生成字與字的關係矩陣。

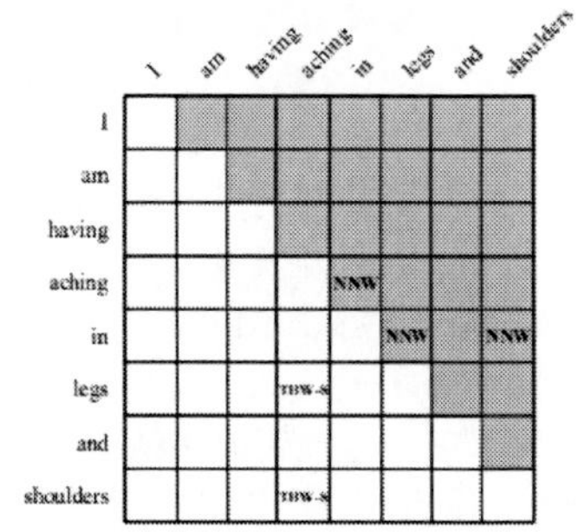

圖 2 .W2NER 生成矩陣 [1]

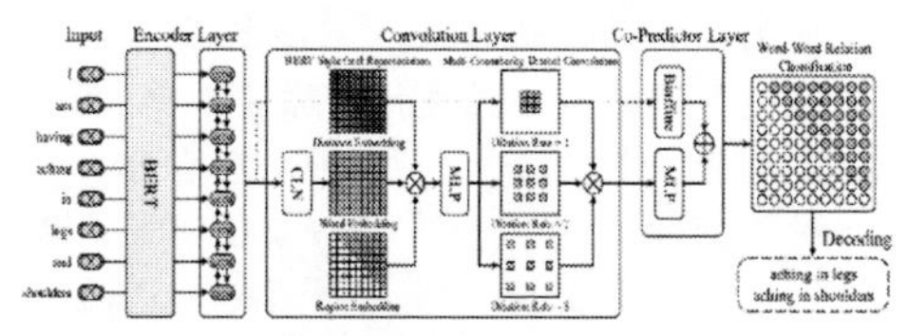

Figure 3: Overall NER architecture. CLN and MLP represent conditional layer normalization and multi-layer perceptron. ⊕ and ⊗ represent element-wise addition and concatenation operations.

圖 3.W2NER 架構圖 [1]

Google 於 2018 年發表了一個預訓練的 Transformer 模型 BERT（ Bidirectional Encoder Representations from Transformers）(Devlin et al., 2018)裡面的主要結構為 Transformer(Vaswani et al., 2017)的 encoding 層，訓練方式為使用英文維基百科與 BookCorpus 資料集配合遮罩預測與下句預測（Next sentence prediction, NSP）的訓練任務。這個模型如此成功的原因主要是因為其 Context-Based Embedding 的向量轉換方式，他能依上下文的關係給相同的字不同 vector 而不是傳統的 Context-free embedding 方式，像是 word2vec(Mikolov et al., 2013)，因此該模型成為了少數能考量前後文的語言模型，且因為該模型在做下層任務的時候還會改變他的變數，因此可以進行預訓練與微調，而這樣的訓練方法不但獲得比 Feature-based 模型還要多的資訊，還可以針對目標任務進行微調。

BERT 有許多變種的模型，本次實驗就選用了哈爾濱工業大學的 PERT(Cui et al., 2022)、

[1]引用來源 Jingye Li, Hao Fei, Jiang Liu, Shengqiong Wu, Meishan Zhanget al.Fei Li. (2022). Unified named entity recognition as word-word relation classification. Proceedings of the AAAI Conference on Artificial Intelligence,

MacBERT(Cui et al., 2020)和 Facebook 的 RoBERTa(Liu et al., 2019)與一同進行比較，這些模型與 BERT 的差別如下：

1. RoBERTa（A Robustly Optimized BERT）：此模型的目的就是要最佳化原本的 BERT 模型，因此該模型在 BERT-large 的基礎上加上了 CC-NEW、OPENWEBTEXT、STORIES 等 160GB 的資料集、更大 bacth size 與動態遮蔽字的訓練方式，動態遮罩方式主要是在資料及輸入的時候才動態產生，這樣就能夠在不同 epoch 相同資料有不同的遮罩，最後比較特別的地方是該模型移除了下一句預測的任務。
2. PERT（PRE-TRAINING BERT WITH PERMUTED LANGUAGE MODEL）：此模型是使用 BERT 原來的模型，僅更改遮罩預測任務的訓練方式，主要的差別在於他不使用遮罩的方式進行訓練（如圖 1），而是利用全詞遮罩（WWM）選定詞組並使用 Ngram 的方式將常見的前後字或是片語打亂掉，並去掉了下一句預測。這樣的好處在於不再使用 MASK 標記，能使訓練集更加接近測試集的樣子，準確度也跟著提高了不少。該中文模型的預訓練集為 EXT 數據集 [2]

	Input	Output
Original Text	研究表明这一句话的顺序并不影响阅读。	-
WordPiece	研 究 表 明 这 一 句 话 的 顺 序 并 不 影 响 阅 读 。	-
BERT	研 究 表 明 这 一 句 [M] 的 顺 [M] 并 不 [M] 响 阅 读 。	$Pos_7 \rightarrow$ 话 $Pos_{10} \rightarrow$ 序 $Pos_{13} \rightarrow$ 影
PERT	研 究 明 表 这 一 句 话 的 顺 序 并 不 响 影 阅 读 。	$Pos_2 \rightarrow Pos_3$ $Pos_3 \rightarrow Pos_2$ $Pos_{13} \rightarrow Pos_{14}$ $Pos_{14} \rightarrow Pos_{13}$

圖 1.PERT 與 BERT 差異 [3]

3. MacBERT：此模型是在 BERT 原本的基礎上修改了遮罩預測任務的訓練方式的遮罩方式，改用一種偵錯遮罩模型（MLM as correction，Mac）的方式。這種遮罩方式主要的差別在於它會在原有的遮罩基礎上去使用全詞遮罩（WWM）並使用 Ngram 的方式將常見的前後字或是片語直接遮蔽掉，再利用相近詞或是隨機詞去替換掉（如圖 2），這種遮罩方式可以提升詞之間的關聯度，相近詞的採用也使得模型獲得了更多預測的資訊，因此結果比原來有顯著提升。中文模型的預訓練集為 EXT 數據集 [2]

	Chinese
Original Sentence	使用语言模型来预测下一个词的概率。
+ CWS	使用 语言 模型 来 预测 下 一个 词 的 概率 。
+ BERT Tokenizer	使 用 语 言 模 型 来 预 测 下 一 个 词 的 概 率 。
Original Masking	使 用 语 言 [M] 型 来 [M] 测 下 一 个 词 的 概 率 。
+ WWM	使 用 语 言 [M] [M] 来 [M] [M] 下 一 个 词 的 概 率 。
++ N-gram Masking	使 用 [M] [M] [M] [M] 来 [M] [M] 下 一 个 词 的 概 率 。
+++ Mac Masking	使 用 语 法 建 模 来 预 见 下 一 个 词 的 几 率 。

圖 2.偵錯遮罩模型範例 [4]

2.3 NER 與醫療

NER 技術在醫學用途上一直都有需多應用，最近最大的挑戰就是完成病例分類與建檔，當中比較大的問題是分類項目的特殊性還有過多的專有名詞並不適合用通用性的 NER 來處理。因此華碩公司裡的 AICS 小組就開發 ALFER-BERT 模型來處理這件事情。

中國知識圖譜與語意計算大會（CCKS）也從 2017 年開始到 2020 年每年開放一份電子病歷的資料集給 NER 的開發者使用。以 2020 年的資料集為例，裡面包含了訓練集和測試集，其中訓練集包括 1050 個醫療記錄集，共有六大類項目（包括診斷和診斷、檢查、檢驗、原始數據、藥物、樣品測試）在當時有一組運用 BERT 模型對該份資料集做 NER 預測獲得了 91.54%的準確度(晏阳天 et al., 2020)，因此我們接下來打算去尋找類 BERT 的模型進行訓練。

3 實驗方法

3.1 實驗環境

本次實驗以 Ubuntu 20.04 的系統下運用 Nvidia GeForce RTX 3090 的 GPU 做為實驗環境，Python 與相關套件的本版如下:

[2] 由哈工大訊飛聯合實驗室中文維基百科，其他百科、新聞、問答等資料，數量多達 5.4B

[3] 引用來源 Yiming Cui, Ziqing Yang, and Ting Liu. (2022). PERT: Pre-training BERT with Permuted Language Model. *arXiv preprint arXiv:2203.06906.*

[4] 引用來源 Yiming Cui, Wanxiang Che, Ting Liu, Bing Qin, Shijin Wanget al.Guoping Hu. (2020). Revisiting Pre-Trained Models for Chinese Natural Language Processing.*Findings of the Association for Computational Linguistics: EMNLP 2020* Online.

- Python version: 3.8.10
- Torch version：1.8.0
- Cuda version： 11.1

3.2 資料處理

Chinese Healthcare NER Corpus 由中央大學電機系的自然語言實驗室（NCUEE NLP Lab）所製作(Lee & Lu, 2021)，內容為健康相關醫學新聞與醫學問答論壇的文章，裡面包含30,692 個句子、10 種實體類型共 68,460（如表 1）

實體類型	範例
身體	細胞核、神經組織
症狀	流鼻水、失眠
醫療器材	血壓計、達文西手臂
檢驗	聽力檢查、腦電波圖
化學物質	去氧核糖核酸
疾病	小兒麻痺症、帕金森氏症
藥物	阿斯匹靈、普拿疼
營養品	維他命、膠原蛋白
治療	藥物治療、胃切除術
時間	嬰兒期、幼兒時期

表 1.實體類型表格

3.2.1 資料格式

參數	意義	範例
Id	流水號	001
genre	類型	'SM'
sentence	句子	多種維生素
word	斷詞結果	[多種", "維生素]
word_label	每個詞的 NER 標記	["O", "SUPP",]
字符	切字	["多", "種", "維", "生", "素"]
character_label	每個字的 NER 標記	["O", "O", "B-SUPP", "I-SUPP", "I-SUPP"]

表 2.資料格式表格

3.2.2 資料前處理

我們首先分析標記內容是否有誤，將出現頻率低於 5 次的標記內容，用人工的方式檢查，並將我們認為明顯有誤的標記內容改正（如表 3）。

文字	原始標記	更正文字	更正標記
"上淋" "巴"	(BODY) (O)	"上" "淋巴"	(O) (BODY)
"人参"	(DISE)	"人参"	(DRUG)
"放、化療"	(TREAT)	"放化療"	(TREAT)
"腫漲"	(SYMP)	"腫脹"	(SYMP)

表 3.資料修改列表

3.3 Encoder 模型選擇

我們的實驗方法主要分成四個方向，第一個方向是嘗試更改 W2NER 輸入層使用的 Encoder 預訓練模型，找出最適合該資料集的 Encoder 預訓練模型。

- $BERT_{base}$：110M parameters
- $PERT_{base}$：110M parameters
- $RoBERTa_{large}$：355M parameters
- $MacBERT_{large}$：324M parameters
- $PERT_{large}$：330M parameters

3.4 統一格式實驗

第二個方向則是統一資料集的格式，鑒於 BERT、PERT、RoBERTa、MacBERT 處理 token 時全形半形會視為不同的 token，因此我們將英文數字、標點符號統一成全形或半形，藉此比較哪種格式會有較好的表現。

3.5 斷句實驗

第三個方向則是以句子還是以完整文本輸入的比較，我們考慮在 NER 任務中，標記的內容應該主要以句子為單位，即不需要看完整文本，只看句子也可以標記出實體位置。因此我們比較將文本經由段落標記（逗號、句號、問號與驚嘆號）切割以及保留完整內容的資料型態對於模型的結果是否有影響。

3.6 斷詞實驗

第四個方向則是比較有無斷詞資訊是否影響模型效果，基於 W2NER 預設以字元輸入模型，我們參考(Lee & Lu, 2021)中，將斷詞輸入模型，藉此得到更好的結果。我們認為加入斷詞資訊會影響模型效果，因為若 NER 標記皆為一個詞，使用 W2NER 生成字與字的關係矩陣，就可在 Co-predictor layer 把問題簡化，因此我們使用以下三種不同的斷詞法進一步將斷詞資訊輸入至模型中，並比較輸入字元以及輸入詞彙（如表 4）對於模型的結果是否有影響。

- CKIP transformer
- Finetuned CKIP transformer
- 資料集原始的斷詞資訊

Type	Input	Predict
Char	["雞","蛋","含","有","多","種","維","生","素","，","包","括","D","和","K"]	[Index:[6,7,8] Type: SUPP]
Word	["雞蛋","含有","多種","維生素","，","包括","D","和","K"]	[Index:[3] Type: SUPP]
Sentence	["雞","蛋","含","有","多","種","維","生","素"], ["包","括","D","和","K"]	[Index:[6,7,8] Type: SUPP], []

表 4. 不同資料型態對應預測標籤之比較

4 實驗結果

我們的實驗結果使用 Precision/Recall/F1-score（P/R/F1）評估指標，其中比較的訓練集、測試集以及其他參數除 cross-validation 有切割資料集外其餘皆為固定。

4.1 Encoder 模型結果

實驗結果（如表 5）顯示，PERT 的結果略為高於 BERT，而 Large 的模型皆優於 base 的模型，其中 PERT_{large} 有最佳的表現，因此以下的實驗皆會使用 PERT_{large} 作為 encoder 模型。

	P	R	F1
BERT_{base}	77.40	75.26	76.32
PERT_{base}	76.19	77.10	76.64
RoBERTa_{large}	76.82	76.66	76.74
MacBERT_{large}	**78.26**	76.15	77.19
PERT_{large}	76.46	**78.29**	**77.36**

表 5.模型實驗結果

4.2 統一格式差異

我們發現使用全形資料集訓練的模型，比用半形資料集的模型提高 F1 約 0.5%（如表 6），其原因可能為 PERT 預訓練時的資料集與統一全形的醫療資料集分布較類似，之後的實驗皆使用統一全形資料集。

	P	R	F1
統一半形	77.17	78.14	77.65
統一全形	**77.67**	**78.36**	**78.01**

表 6.統一規格比較實驗結果

4.3 斷句結果

實驗結果（如表 7）顯示，斷句不能加強模型的表現，其原因可能在於情境線索對於標記實體是重要的，可以看到缺少上下文訊息的模型雖然 Precision 有約 1.5%的提升，但 Recall 有接近 5%的下降。

	P	R	F1
Baseline	77.67	**78.36**	**78.01**
Sentence	**78.93**	73.48	75.93

表 7.斷句結果比較實驗結果

4.4 斷詞結果

我們發現在沒有任何預訓練的情況下，使用 CKIP-transformer 斷詞的模型表現比沒有斷詞的 baseline 還差，可見錯誤斷詞會造成模型的結果下降。在使用 finetuned 的 CKIP-transformer 斷詞後，訓練的模型結果有顯著提升，而使用原始斷詞訓練的模型甚至可以比 baseline 模型的 F1 還要高出將近 10%，可見斷詞資訊的好壞顯著影響模型結果（如表 8）。

	P	R	F1
Baseline	77.67	78.36	78.01
WS-CKIP	75.29	77.26	76.27
WS-Finetuned	79.89	82.46	81.15
WS-Original	**87.28**	**86.84**	**87.28**

表 8.斷詞結果比較實驗結果

4.5 最終結果

比賽最終的驗證資料集是由中央大學電機系的自然語言實驗室（NCUEE NLP Lab）所收集的醫療資料集(Lee et al., 2022)，但裡面並未提供斷詞資訊，且只能上傳三份預測結果，因此我們最終選擇了 Baseline 模型、WS-finetuned 模型以及 Baseline with 5 fold cross-validation 模型參加比賽(Lee et al., 2022)（如表 9），以 Baseline with 5 fold cross-validation 為最佳。

	P	R	F1
Baseline	78.55	79.46	79.00
WS-Finetuned	77.62	77.46	77.54
Baseline with 5 fold cross-validation	**81.99**	**81.88**	**81.93**

表 9.三個模型最終比賽結果

5 結論

本研究使用中文醫療 NER 資料集，探討從全形半形格式到文本的斷詞、斷句對於 W2NER 模型的影響。我們發現此次任務適合大的 Encoder 模型，其結果普遍比較小的模型要來得好，而資料集的全形與半形對模型的結果也是有影響的，斷句內容雖然提高了 NER 標記的 Precision，但是缺少上下文訊息使得 Recall 大幅下降。雖然斷詞與否在本次的比賽結果與訓練結果相反，但也表示斷詞的結果需要一定的準確度才能使 NER 結果有顯著增加，準確度不夠反而會降低模型的表現，我們可以從使用原始斷詞的模型看到有正確斷詞資料的結果有顯著的提升，但要做到更準確的斷詞是值得探討的難題。

若未來能增加更多資料集像是前面提到的中國知識圖譜與語意計算大會（CCKS）的電子病歷資料集並轉換成繁體，以及使用更多的資料去訓練一個專門處理醫學用的斷詞工具去配合這個 NER 模型，我們認為這樣會有更好的結果，也是未來發展的方向。

致謝

本研究承國科會研究計畫 110-2221-E-004-008-MY3 與國立政治大學高教深耕校內補助計畫 111H124D-13 之部分補助，謹此致謝。

References

Yiming Cui, Wanxiang Che, Ting Liu, Bing Qin, Shijin Wanget al.Guoping Hu. (2020). Revisiting Pre-Trained Models for Chinese Natural Language Processing.*Findings of the Association for Computational Linguistics: EMNLP 2020* Online.

Yiming Cui, Ziqing Yang, and Ting Liu. (2022). PERT: Pre-training BERT with Permuted Language Model. *arXiv preprint arXiv:2203.06906*.

Jacob Devlin, Ming-Wei Chang, Kenton Lee, and Kristina Toutanova. (2018). Bert: Pre-training of deep bidirectional transformers for language understanding. *arXiv preprint arXiv:1810.04805*.

Han He, and Jinho D. Choi. (2021). The stem cell hypothesis: Dilemma behind multi-task learning with transformer encoders. *arXiv preprint arXiv:2109.06939*.

Lung-Hao Lee, Chao-Yi Chen, Liang-Chih Yu, and Yuen-Hsien Tseng. (2022). *Overview of the ROCLING 2022 shared task for Chinese healthcare named entity recognition.* In Proceedings of the 34th Conference on Computational Linguistics and Speech Processing., Taipei.

Lung-Hao Lee, and Yi Lu. (2021). Multiple embeddings enhanced multi-graph neural networks for Chinese healthcare named entity recognition. *IEEE Journal of Biomedical and Health Informatics*, *25*(7), 2801-2810.

Jingye Li, Hao Fei, Jiang Liu, Shengqiong Wu, Meishan Zhanget al.Fei Li. (2022). Unified named entity recognition as word-word relation classification. Proceedings of the AAAI Conference on Artificial Intelligence,

Peng-Hsuan Li, Tsu-Jui Fu, and Wei-Yun Ma. (2020). Why attention? Analyze BiLSTM deficiency and its remedies in the case of NER. Proceedings of the AAAI Conference on Artificial Intelligence,

Yinhan Liu, Myle Ott, Naman Goyal, Jingfei Du, Mandar Joshiet al.Veselin Stoyanov. (2019). Roberta: A robustly optimized bert pretraining approach. *arXiv preprint arXiv:1907.11692*.

Wei-Yun Ma, and Keh-Jiann Chen. (2003). Introduction to CKIP Chinese word segmentation system for the first international Chinese word segmentation bakeoff. Proceedings of the second SIGHAN workshop on Chinese language processing,

Christopher D Manning, Mihai Surdeanu, John Bauer, Jenny Rose Finkel, Steven Bethardet al.David Mcclosky. (2014). The Stanford CoreNLP natural language processing toolkit. Proceedings of 52nd annual meeting of the association for computational linguistics: system demonstrations,

Tomas Mikolov, Kai Chen, Greg Corrado, and Jeffrey Dean. (2013). Efficient estimation of word representations in vector space. arXiv preprint arXiv:1301.3781.

Peng Qi, Yuhao Zhang, Yuhui Zhang, Jason Bolton, and Christopher D Manning. (2020). Stanza: A Python natural language processing toolkit for many human languages. arXiv preprint arXiv:2003.07082.

J Sun. (2020). 'Jieba'(Chinese for'to stutter') Chinese text segmentation: built to be the best Python Chinese word segmentation module.

Ashish Vaswani, Noam Shazeer, Niki Parmar, Jakob Uszkoreit, Llion Joneset al.Illia Polosukhin. (2017). Attention is all you need. Advances in neural information processing systems, 30.

晏阳天, 赵新宇, and 吴贤. (2020). 基于 BERT 与字形字音特征的医疗命名实体识别. Proceedings of the Evaluation Tasks at the China Conference on Knowledge Graph and Semantic Computing,

The 34th Conference on Computational Linguistics and Speech Processing (ROCLING 2022)
Taipei, Taiwan, November 21-22, 2022. The Association for Computational Linguistics and Chinese Language Processing

Overview of the ROCLING 2022 Shared Task for Chinese Healthcare Named Entity Recognition

Lung-Hao Lee, Chao-Yi Chen
Department of Electrical Engineering
National Central University
lhlee@ee.ncu.edu.tw, 110581007@cc.ncu.edu.tw

Liang-Chih Yu
Department of Information Management
Yuan Ze University
lcyu@saturn.yzu.edu.tw

Yuen-Hsien Tseng
Graduate Institute of Library and Information Studies
National Taiwan Normal University
samtseng@ntnu.edu.tw

Abstract

This paper describes the ROCLING-2022 shared task for Chinese healthcare named entity recognition, including task description, data preparation, performance metrics, and evaluation results. Among ten registered teams, seven participating teams submitted a total of 20 runs. This shared task reveals present NLP techniques for dealing with Chinese named entity recognition in the healthcare domain. All data sets with gold standards and evaluation scripts used in this shared task are publicly available for future research.

Keywords: named entity recognition, information extraction, health informatics, Chinese language processing

1 Introduction

Named Entity Recognition (NER) is a traditional and fundamental NLP task in the information extraction domain that locates and identifies mentions of named entities (e.g., person, organization, and location) in unstructured texts. The NER task is usually regarded as a sequence labeling problem, where entity boundaries and category labels are jointed predicted.

Chinese NER is correlated with word segmentation, since named entity boundaries are also word boundaries. Due to a lack of delimiters between characters and a lack of conventional features like capitalization, Chinese NER is more difficult to process than English NER. Incorrect word segmentation will cause error propagation in NER. For example, "思覺失調症" (schizophrenia) is a kind of mental disorder that affects the way a person thinks, feels, perceives reality, and relates to others. This named entity may be incorrectly segmented into three words: "思覺" (thinking and feeling), "失調" (disorder) and "症" (disease), resulting in fail to recognize it as a named entity belonging to disease type. Character-based methods have been found to outperform word-based approaches for breaking through this word segmentation limitation in Chinese NER (He and Wang, 2008; Li et al., 2014, Zhang and Yang, 2018).

Various methods have been proposed to tackle Chinese NER tasks. In addition to machine learning approaches, such as HMM (Hidden Markov Model) (Fu and Luke, 2005), Markov logistic network (Yu, 2007), and CRF (Conditional Random Field) (Chen et al., 2006), deep learning techniques have been widely used, with mostly promising results. A character-based LSTM (Long Short-Term Memory)-CRF model with radical-level features was proposed for Chinese NER (Dong et al., 2016). The BiLSTM (Bidirectional LSTM)-CRF model was trained based on character-word mixed embeddings to improve the recognition effectiveness of Chinese NER (E and Xiang., 2017). A BiLSTM-CRF model with a self-attention mechanism was proposed to integrate part-of-speech labeling information to capture the semantic features of input sequences for Chinese clinical NER (Wu et al., 2019). A residual dilated CNN (Convolution Neural Network) with CRF was also presented to enhance Chinese clinical

Entity Type (Tag)	Description	Examples
Body (BODY)	The whole physical structure that forms a person or animal including biological cells, organizations, organs and systems.	"細胞核" (nucleus), "神經組織" (nerve tissue), "左心房" (left atrium), "脊髓" (spinal cord), "呼吸系統" (respiratory system)
Symptom (SYMP)	Any feeling of illness or physical or mental change that is caused by a particular disease.	"流鼻水" (rhinorrhea), "咳嗽" (cough), "貧血" (anemia), "失眠" (insomnia), "心悸" (palpitation), "耳鳴" (tinnitus)
Instrument (INST)	A tool or other device used for performing a particular medical task such as diagnosis and treatments.	"血壓計" (blood pressure meter), "達文西手臂" (DaVinci Robots), "體脂肪計" (body fat monitor), "雷射手術刀" (laser scalpel)
Examination (EXAM)	The act of looking at or checking something carefully in order to discover possible diseases.	"聽力檢查" (hearing test), "腦電波圖" (electroencephalography; EEG), "核磁共振造影" (magnetic resonance imaging; MRI)
Chemical (CHEM)	Any basic chemical element typically found in the human body.	"去氧核糖核酸" (deoxyribonucleic acid; DNA), "糖化血色素" (glycated hemoglobin), "膽固醇" (cholesterol), "尿酸" (uric acid)
Disease (DISE)	An illness of people or animals caused by infection or a failure of health rather than by an accident.	"小兒麻痺症" (poliomyelitis; polio), "帕金森氏症" (Parkinson's disease), "青光眼" (glaucoma), "肺結核" (tuberculosis)
Drug (DRUG)	Any natural or artificially made chemical used as a medicine.	"阿斯匹靈" (aspirin), "普拿疼" (acetaminophen), "青黴素" (penicillin), "流感疫苗" (influenza vaccination)
Supplement (SUPP)	Something added to something else to improve human health.	"維他命" (vitamin), "膠原蛋白" (collagen), "益生菌" (probiotics), "葡萄糖胺" (glucosamine), "葉黃素" (lutein)
Treatment (TREAT)	A method of behavior used to treat diseases	"藥物治療" (pharmacotherapy), "胃切除術" (gastrectomy), "標靶治療" (targeted therapy), "外科手術" (surgery)
Time (TIME)	Element of existence measured in minutes, days, years	"嬰兒期" (infancy), "幼兒時期" (early childhood), "青春期" (adolescence), "生理期" (on one's period), "孕期" (pregnancy)

Table 1: Named entity types with descriptions and examples (Lee and Lu, 2021).

NER in terms of computational performance and training time (Qiu et al., 2019). A BERT-BiLSTM-CRF model was proposed to use BERT embedding for character representation and to train the BiLSTM-CRF model to recognize complex named entities (Lee et al., 2022).

Prior to scheduling a doctor's appointment for diagnosis and treatment of a perceived medical issues, people frequently seek healthcare-related information online from health-related news articles, digital health services, and medical question-answering forums. Domain-specific healthcare information usually includes many proper names. These often take the form of named entities such as "三酸甘油酯" (triglyceride), "電腦斷層掃描" (computer tomography, CT) and "靜脈免疫球蛋白注射" (intravenous immunoglobulin, IVIG), presenting language processing challenges for healthcare-related applications. Responding to this pronounced challenge in the healthcare domain, the ROCLING-2022 conference features a Chinese healthcare NER task, providing an evaluation platform for the development and implementation of Chinese healthcare NER system. Given a Chinese sentence, the NER system is expected to automatically recognize healthcare entities such as symptoms, chemicals, diseases, and treatments.

The rest of this article is organized as follows. Section 2 provides a description of the Chinese healthcare NER shared task. Section 3 introduces the constructed data sets. Section 4 describes the evaluation metrics. Section 5 compares evaluation results from the various participating teams. Finally, we conclude this paper with findings and offer future research directions in Section 6.

2 Task Description

The goal of this shared task is to develop and evaluate the capability of a Chinese healthcare NER recognizer. A sentence containing at least one named entity is given as the input. The recognizer should predict the named entity's boundaries and category for each given sentence. We use the common BIO (Beginning, Inside, and Outside) format for the NER task. The B-prefix before a tag indicates that the character is the beginning of a named entity and the I-prefix before a tag indicates that the character is inside a named entity. An O tag indicates that a character belongs to no named entity. We use the same entity types defined in the Chinese HealthNER Corpus (Lee and Lu, 2021). A total of 10 types are described for this Chinese healthcare NER task, and some examples are provided in Table 1.

The input is a sentence consisting of a sequence of character-based tokens including punctuation. The developed NER recognizer returns the corresponding BIO tags aligned to each token as the output. Example sentences are presented below. In Example 1, "肌肉" (muscle) and "骨骼" (skeleton) belong to the body entity type (denoted as BODY). "蛋白質" (protein) and "鈣質" (calcium) are chemicals (denoted as CHEM). In Example 2, we can find a disease "胃食道逆流症" (gastroesophageal reflux disease) (denoted as DISE).

Example 1

- *Input*: 修復肌肉與骨骼罪狀要的便是熱量、蛋白質與鈣質。
- *Output*: O, O, B-Body, I-Body, O, B-Body, I-Body, O, O, O, O, O, O, O, O, O, B-CHEM, I-CHEM, I-CHEM, O, B-CHEM, I-CHEM, O

Example 2

- *Input*: 如何治療胃食道逆流症？
- *Output*: O, O, O, O, B-DISE, I-DISE, I-DISE, I-DISE, I-DISE, O

3 Data Preparation

The Chinese HealthNER Corpus (Lee and Lu, 2021) was used as the training set. It includes 30,692 sentences with a total around 1.5 million characters or 91,700 words. The data was sourced from articles on websites that provide healthcare information, on-line health news and medical question/answer forums. After manual annotation, this corpus consists of 68460 named entities across 10 defined entity types.

We use the existing named entities in the Chinese HealthNER Corpus as the query terms and to find the corresponding articles in Chinese Wikipedia (zh_TW version). The first paragraph in the wiki articles was segmented into sentences for manual annotation. Three graduate students majoring in electrical engineering were trained in the named entity tagging task, producing a Fleiss' Kappa value of inter-annotator agreement of 89%. All annotators were asked to discuss differences and seek consensus. When agreement was reached, each annotator was then asked to process sentences individually. As a result, our constructed test set includes 3,205 sentences with a total of 118,116 characters and 13,369 named entities.

Entity Type	#Train (%)	#Test (%)
Body	26411 (38.58%)	5315 (39.76%)
Symptom	12904 (18.85%)	1944 (14.54%)
Instrument	1089 (1.59%)	250 (1.87%)
Examination	2622 (3.83%)	207 (1.55%)
Chemical	6834 (9.98%)	1718 (12.85%)
Disease	10079 (14.72%)	2609 (19.52%)
Drug	2225 (3.25%)	481 (3.60%)
Supplement	1525 (2.23%)	183 (1.37%)
Treatment	3108 (4.54%)	468 (3.50%)
Time	1663 (2.43%)	194 (1.44%)
Total	68460 (100%)	13,369 (100%)

Table 2: Detailed data statistics.

Table 2 shows detailed statistics of mutually exclusive training and test sets. The entity type distribution is similar in both the training and test sets. The most frequently occurring type was Body, followed by Symptom, Disease and Chemical, collectively accounting for about 83% of all named entity instances, with the remaining 6 types accounting for 17%.

In addition, sentences in the training set may contain named entities or not, each with an average of 49.31 characters and 2.23 named entities. However, all sentences in the test set contained at least one named entity, each with an average of 36.85 characters and 4.17 named entities. In summary, the average sentence length is short in the test set, but named entity density is relatively high.

4 Performance Metrics

Performance is evaluated by examining the difference between the machine-predicted and human-annotated BIO tags. Standard precision, recall and F1-score are the most typical evaluation metrics of NER systems at a character level, and are used here. If the predicted tag of a character in terms of BIO format was completely identical with the gold standard, the character in the testing instances was regarded as correctly recognized.

Rank	Team	Affiliation	Run#	Precision (%)	Recall (%)	F1
1	MIGBasline	National Chengchi University	Run 3	**81.99**	**81.88**	**81.93**
2	SCU-MESCLab	Soochow University	Run 3	80.18	78.3	79.23
3	crowNER	National Taiwan University	Run 1	77.82	78.1	77.96
4	YNU-HPCC	Yunnan University	Run 1	77.22	78.15	77.68
5	NERVE	National Kaohsiung University of Science and Technology	Run 1	79.59	73.09	76.2
6	NCU1415	National Central University	Run 2	74.56	72.81	73.68
7	SCU-NLP	Soochow University	Run 2	64.72	77.92	70.71

Table 3: Testing results of Chinese health named entity recognition task.

Precision is defined as the percentage of named entities found by the NER system that are correct. Recall is the percentage of named entities present in the test set found by the NER system. The F1-score is the harmonic mean of precision and recall.

5 Evaluation Results

The policy of this shared task is an open test. Participating systems are allowed to use other publicly available data for this shared task, but the usage should be specified in their system description paper. Each team was allowed to provide at most three submissions during the evaluation period. Among ten registered teams, seven submitted their testing results, providing a total of 20 submissions, from which the submission with the best F1-score of each team was kept in the leaderboard for performance ranking.

Table 3 summarizes the task testing results. NCU1415 team (Feng et al., 2022) uses BERT (Devlin et al., 2019) to encode sentences, followed by CRF for sequence labeling. SCU-MESCLab (Yang et al., 2022) represents sentences based on RoBERTa (Liu et al., 2019) embeddings, followed by BiLSTM-CRF to recognize named entities. NERVE (Lin et al., 2022) compares three NER frameworks based on BERT transformers and lexicons. SCU-NLP (Chiou et al., 2022) compares experimental results of well-known models, including random forest, HMM, CRF, and BERT and provides error analysis. The crowNER team (Chi et al., 2022) adopts adversarial learning and mixed precision training techniques to improve the performance achieved by MacBERT-CRF. YNU-HPCC (Luo et al. 2022) applies focal loss and regularized dropout mechanisms to enhance BERT-BiLSTM-CRF model performance. MIGBaseline team (Ma et al., 2022) uses PERT (Cui et al., 2022) as embedding representations to train the W2NER model (Li et al., 2022), achieving the best F1 score of 81.93 at this shared task evaluation.

In summary, the overall best results came from the MIGBaseline team (Ma et al., 2022), whose approach achieved the best scores across all the evaluation metrics, followed by SCU-MESCLab (Yang et al., 2022) and crowNER (Chi et al., 2022). The most frequently used neural architecture in this shared task is BiLSTM-CRF, which usually achieved promising results, matching findings from related studies for named entity recognition in the English language (Chiu and Nichols, 2016; Lample et al., 2016; Ma and Hovy, 2016; Liu et al., 2018).

6 Conclusions and Future Work

This paper provides an overview of the ROCLING-2022 shared task for Chinese healthcare named entity recognition, including task design, data preparation, performance metrics and evaluation results. We received a total of 20 testing submissions from seven participating teams. Regardless of actual performance, all submissions contribute to the development of an effective named entity recognition solution in the healthcare domain, and the individual system description papers for this shared task provide useful insights into Chinese language processing.

We hope the data sets collected and annotated for this shared task can facilitate and expedite future development of named entity recognizers. Therefore, in addition to publicly accessed Chinese HealthNER Corpus as the training set, the test set with gold standards and evaluation scripts are available from a public GitHub repository as follows

- Chinese HealthNER Corpus
https://github.com/NCUEE-NLPLab/Chinese-HealthNER-Corpus

- ROCLING-2022 Shared Task
https://github.com/NCUEE-NLPLab/ROCLING-2022-ST-CHNER

Future directions will focus on the development of Chinese healthcare entity-relationship extraction. We plan to build new language resources to develop techniques for the future enrichment of the research topic in open information extraction.

Acknowledgments

We thank all the participants for taking part in our shared task. We appreciate Tzu-Mi Lin, Man-Chen Hung, and Chien-Huan Lu for their efforts in data annotations. This work is partially supported by the National Science and Technology Council, Taiwan, under the grant MOST 111-2628-E-008-005-MY3, MOST 111-2628-E-155-001-MY2, and MOST 109-2410-H-003-123-MY3.

References

Aitao Chen, Fuchun Peng, Roy Shan, Gordon Sun. 2006. Chinese named entity recognition with conditional probabilistic models. In *Proceedings of the 5th SIGHAN Workshop on Chinese Language Processing*. Association for Computational Linguistics, pages 173-176.

Te-Yu Chi, Chiu-Hsia Chang, and Te-Lun Yang. 2022. crowNER at ROCLING 2022 shared task: NER using MacBERT and adversarial learning. In *Proceedings of the 34th Conference on Computational Linguistics and Speech Processing.*

Sung-Ting Chiou, Sheng-Wei Huang, Ying-Chun Lo, Yu-Hsuan Wu, and Jheng-Long Wu. 2022. SCU-NLP at ROCLING 2022 shared task: experiment and error analysis of biomedical entity detection model. In *Proceedings of the 34th Conference on Computational Linguistics and Speech Processing.*

Jason P. C. Chiu, and Eric Nichols. 2016. Named entity recognition with bidirectional LSTM-CNNs. *Transactions of the Association for Computational Linguistics*, 4: 357-370. http://dx.doi.org/10.1162/tacl_a_00104.

Yiming Cui, Ziqing Yang, and Ting Liu. 2022. PERT: pre-training BERT with permuted language model. *arXiv:2203.06906*. https://doi.org/10.48550/arXiv.2203.06906.

Jacob Devlin, Ming-Wei Chang, Kenton Lee, and Kristina Toutanova. 2019. BERT: pre-training of deep bidirectional transformers for language understanding. In *Proceedings of the 2019 Conference of the North American Chapter of the Association for Computational Linguistics: Human Language Technologies, Volume 1 (Long and Short Papers)*. Association for Computational Linguistics, pages 4171–4186. http://dx.doi.org/10.18653/v1/N19-1423.

Chuanhai Dong, Jiajun Zhang, Chengqing Zong, Masanori Hattori, and Hui Di. 2016. Character-based LSTM-CRF with radical-level features for Chinese named entity recognition. *Lecture Notes in Computer Science: Natural Language Understanding and Intelligent Applications*, 10102: 239-250. https://doi.org/10.1007/978-3-319-50496-4_20

Shijia E, and Yang Xiang. 2017. Chinese named entity recognition with character-word mixed embedding. In *Proceedings of the 26th ACM International Conference on Information and Knowledge Management*. Association for Computing Machinery, pages 2055-2058. https://doi.org/10.1145/3132847.3133088

Zhi-Quan Feng, Po-Kai Chen, and Jia-Ching Wang. 2022. NCU1415 at ROCLING 2022 shared task: a light-weight transformer-based approach for biomedical named entity recognition. In *Proceedings of the 34th Conference on Computational Linguistics and Speech Processing.*

Guohong Fu, and Kang-Kwong Luke. 2005. Chinese named entity recognition using lexicalized HMMs. *ACM SIGKDD Explorations Newsletter*, 7(1): 19-25. https://doi.org/10.1145/1089815.1089819.

Jingzhou He, and Houfeng Wang. 2008. Chinese named entity recognition and word segmentation based on character. In *Proceedings of the 6th SIGHAN Workshop on Chinese Language Processing*. Association for Computational Linguistics, pages 128–132.

Guillaume Lample, Miguel Ballesteros, Sandeep Subramanian, Kazuya Kawakami, and Chris Dyer.

2016. Neural architecture for named entity recognition. In *Proceedings of the 2016 Conference of the North American Chapter of the Association for Computational Linguistics: Human Language Technologies*. Association for Computational Linguistics, pages 260-270. http://dx.doi.org/10.18653/v1/N16-1030.

Lung-Hao Lee, and Yi Lu. 2021. Multiple embeddings enhanced multi-graph neural networks for Chinese healthcare named entity recognition. *IEEE Journal of Biomedical and Health Informatics*, 25(7): 2801-2810. https://doi.org/10.1109/JBHI.2020.3048700.

Lung-Hao Lee, Chien-Huan Lu, and Tzu-Mi Lin. 2022. NCUEE-NLP at SemEval-2022 task 11: Chinese named entity recognition using the BERT-BiLSTM-CRF model. In *Proceedings of the 16th International Workshop on Semantic Evaluation*. Association for Computational Linguistics, pages 1597-1602.

Haibo Li, Masato Hagiwara, Qi Li, and Heng Ji. 2014. Comparison of the impact of word segmentation on name tagging for Chinese and Japanese. In *Proceedings of the 9th International Conference on Language Resources and Evaluation*. European Language Resources Association, pages 2532-2536.

Jingye Li, Donghong Ji, Jiang Liu, Hao Fei, Meishan Zhang, Shengqiong Wu, Chong Teng, and Fei Li. 2022. Unified named entity recognition as word-word relation classification. In *Proceedings of the 36th AAAI Conference on Artificial Intelligence*.

Bo-Shau Lin, Jian-He Chen, and Tao-Hsing Chang. 2022. NERVE at ROCLING 2022 shared task: a comparison of three named entity recognition frameworks based on language model and lexicon approach. In *Proceedings of the 34th Conference on Computational Linguistics and Speech Processing*.

Yinhan Liu, Myle Ott, Naman Goyal, Jingfei Du, Mandar Joshi, Danqi Chen, Omer Levy, Mike Lewis, Luke Zettlemoyer, Veselin Stoyanov. 2019. RoBERTa: a robustly optimized BERT pretraining approach. *arXiv:1907.11692* https://doi.org/10.48550/arXiv.1907.11692

Liyuan Liu, Jingbo Shang, Xiang Ren, Frank F. Xu, Huan Gui, Jian Peng, Jiawei Han. 2018. Empower sequence labeling with task-aware neural language model. In P*roceeding of the 32nd AAAI Conference on Artificial Intelligence*. Association for Computing Machinery, pages 5253-5260.

Xiang Luo, Jin Wang, and Xuejie Zhang. 2022. YNU-HPCC at ROCLING 2022 shared task: a transformer-based model with focal loss and regularization dropout for Chinese healthcare named entity recognition. In *Proceedings of the 34th Conference on Computational Linguistics and Speech Processing*.

Xuezhe Ma, and Eduard Hovy. 2016. End-to-end sequence labeling via Bi-directional LSTM-CNNs-CRF. In *Proceedings of the 54th Annual Meeting of the Association for Computational Linguistics (Volume 1: Long Papers)*. Association for Computational Linguistics, pages 1064-1074. http://dx.doi.org/10.18653/v1/P16-1101.

Hsing-Yuan Ma, Wei-Jie Li, and Chao-Lin Liu. 2022. MIGBaseline at ROCLING 2022 shared task: reports on named entity recognition using Chinese healthcare datasets. In *Proceedings of the 34th Conference on Computational Linguistics and Speech Processing*.

Jiahui Qiu, Yangming Zhou, Qi Wang, Tong Ruan, and Ju Gao. 2019. Chinese clinical named entity recognition using residual dilated convolutional neural network with conditional random field. *IEEE Transactions on NanoBioscience*, 18(3): 306-315. https://doi.org/10.1109/TNB.2019.2908678.

Guohua Wu, Guangen Tang, Zhongru Wang, Zhen Zhang, and Zhen Wang. 2019. An attention-based BiLSTM-CRF model for Chinese clinic named entity recognition. *IEEE Access*, 7: 113942-113949. https://doi.org/10.1109/ACCESS.2019.2935223.

Tsung-Hsien Yang, Ruei-Cyuan Su, Tzu-En Su, Sing-Seong Chong, and Ming-Hsiang Su. 2022. SCU-MESCLab at ROCLING 2022 shared task: named entity recognition using BERT classifier. In *Proceedings of the 34th Conference on Computational Linguistics and Speech Processing*.

Xiaofeng Yu. 2007. Chinese named entity recognition with cascaded hybrid model. In *Proceedings of the Conference of the North American Chapter of the Association for Computational Linguistics, Companion Volume, Short Papers*. Association for Computational Linguistics, pages 197–200.

Yue Zhang, and Jie Yang. 2018. Chinese NER using lattice LSTM. In *Proceedings of the 56th Annual Meeting of the Association for Computational Linguistics (Volume 1: Long Papers)*. Association for Computational Linguistics, pages 1554–1564. http://dx.doi.org/10.18653/v1/P18-1144.

Association for Computational Linguistics
209 N. Eighth Street
Stroudsburg, Pennsylvania 18360

CURRAN ASSOCIATES INC.
proceedings.com

ISBN 978-1-7138-6764-7

9 781713 867647